Drug Abuse
SOURCEBOOK

Health Reference Series

First Edition

Drug Abuse
SOURCEBOOK

Basic Consumer Health Information about Illicit Substances of Abuse and the Diversion of Prescription Medications, Including Depressants, Hallucinogens, Inhalants, Marijuana, Narcotics, Stimulants, and Anabolic Steroids:

Along with Facts about Related Health Risks, Treatment Issues, and Substance Abuse Prevention Programs, a Glossary of Terms, Statistical Data, and Directories of Hotline Services, Self-Help Groups, and Organizations Able to Provide Further Information

Edited by
Karen Bellenir

Omnigraphics

615 Griswold Street • Detroit, MI 48226

Bibliographic Note

Because this page cannot legibly accommodate all the copyright notices, the Bibliographic Note portion of the Preface constitutes an extension of the copyright notice.

Each new volume of the *Health Reference Series* is individually titled and called a "First Edition." Subsequent updates will carry sequential edition numbers. To help avoid confusion and to provide maximum flexibility in our ability to respond to informational needs, the practice of consecutively numbering each volume will be discontinued.

Edited by Karen Bellenir

Health Reference Series

Karen Bellenir, *Series Editor*
Peter D. Dresser, *Managing Editor*
Joan Margeson, *Research Associate*
Dawn Matthews, *Verification Assistant*
Jenifer Swanson, *Research Associate*

EdIndex, Services for Publishers, *Indexers*

Omnigraphics, Inc.

Matthew P. Barbour, *Vice President, Operations*
Laurie Lanzen Harris, *Vice President, Editorial Director*
Kevin Hayes, *Production Coordinator*
Thomas J. Murphy, *Vice President, Finance and Comptroller*
Peter E. Ruffner, *Senior Vice President*
Jane J. Steele, *Marketing Consultant*

Frederick G. Ruffner, Jr., Publisher

© 2000, Omnigraphics, Inc.

Library of Congress Cataloging-in-Publication Data

Drug abuse sourcebook / edited by Karen Bellenir.--1st ed.
    p. cm. -- (Health reference series)
    Includes bibliographical references and index.
    ISBN 0-7808-0242-X
    1. Drug abuse--Prevention--Handbooks, manuals, etc. 2. Drug abuse--Treatment--Handbooks, manuals, etc. 3. Narcotic habit--Treatment--Handbooks, manuals, etc. I. Bellenir, Karen. II. Series

HV5801 .D724 2000
362.29--dc21
                                     00-055071

∞

This book is printed on acid-free paper meeting the ANSI Z39.48 Standard. The infinity symbol that appears above indicates that the paper in this book meets that standard.

Printed in the United States

Table of Contents

Preface ix

Part I: Drug Use and Abuse

Chapter 1—Let's Talk Facts about Substance Abuse 3
Chapter 2—Nationwide Trends in Drug Abuse 23
Chapter 3—Prescription Drug Abuse Trends 29
Chapter 4—Drug Use among American Teens 33
Chapter 5—Trends in Workplace Substance Abuse 39
Chapter 6—Pregnancy and Drug Use Trends 43
Chapter 7—The Controlled Substances Act 45
Chapter 8—Drugs and Crime Facts 59
Chapter 9—Emerging Drug Problems 69
Chapter 10—Does Marijuana Have a Place in
            Medicine? 79

Part II: The Nature of Addiction

Chapter 11—Addiction Is a Brain Disease 91
Chapter 12—The Addicted Brain: An Era of Scientific
            Breakthroughs 99
Chapter 13—Why do People Get Hooked? 103
Chapter 14—Studies Link Stress and Drug Addiction 113
Chapter 15—Pain Medications and Addiction 119

Part III: Drugs of Abuse

Chapter 16—Types of Drugs: An Overview 125
Chapter 17—Amphetamines 151
Chapter 18—Cocaine 155
Chapter 19—GHB (Gamma-Hydroxybutyrate) 165
Chapter 20—Heroin 167
Chapter 21—Inhalants 175
Chapter 22—Ketamine 179
Chapter 23—LSD (Lysergic Acid Diethylamide) 181
Chapter 24—Marijuana 185
Chapter 25—MDMA (Ecstasy) 193
Chapter 26—Methcathinone (Cat) 197
Chapter 27—Methamphetamine 201
Chapter 28—Methylphenidate (Ritalin) 211
Chapter 29—PCP (Phencyclidine) 213
Chapter 30—Rohypnol 217
Chapter 31—Steroids 219

Part IV: Drug-Related Health Risks: Recent Research

Chapter 32—Drug Use and HIV Transmission 225
Chapter 33—Cocaine before Birth 231
Chapter 34—Cocaine Abuse May Lead to Strokes
           and Mental Deficits 239
Chapter 35—Cocaine and Long-Lasting Impaired Function 245
Chapter 36—"Ecstasy" and Long-Term Brain Injury 247
Chapter 37—Effects of Marijuana on the Lung and It's
           Immune Defenses 249
Chapter 38—Depression and Substance Use Can Be a
           Lethal Combination for Teens 265
Chapter 39—Substance Abuse and Violent Death 269

Part V: Drug Abuse Treatment Issues

Chapter 40—Detoxification 275
Chapter 41—Legal and Ethical Issues for Detoxification
           Programs 289
Chapter 42—Treatment Methods and Medications 305
Chapter 43—Effective Medical Treatment for Opiate
           Addiction 311

Chapter 44—Higher Doses of Methadone Found to Be
Safe and Effective 327
Chapter 45—Buprenorphine Update 329
Chapter 46—Blood-Borne Medications Could Intercept
Drugs before They Reach the Brain 333
Chapter 47—Antistress Medications May Help Drug
Abuse Patients Avoid Relapse.......................... 339
Chapter 48—Serotonin Agonist Reduces Craving in
Cocaine Addicts 341
Chapter 49—Methylphenidate Reduces Drug Cravings
in Cocaine Users with Attention Deficit/
Hyperactivity Disorder 345
Chapter 50—The Changing Face of Addictions Treatment 349
Chapter 51—Clinician Adds Cultural Element to
Relapse Prevention Model 353
Chapter 52—Treatment Methods for Women 357
Chapter 53—Treatment Is Effective but Benefits May
Be Overstated.. 361

Part VI: Drug Abuse Prevention Issues

Chapter 54—Growing Up Drug Free: A Parent's Guide
to Prevention 373
Chapter 55—Preventing Inhalant Abuse 391
Chapter 56—How to Establish a Workplace Substance
Abuse Program.. 395
Chapter 57—Prevalence of Drug Testing in the Workplace ... 401
Chapter 58—A Review of the Evaluation of 47 Drug Abuse
Prevention Curricula Available Nationally........ 415
Chapter 59—Lessons from Prevention Research 433
Chapter 60—Ethnic Identification and Cultural Ties
May Help Prevent Drug Use 437
Chapter 61—Prevention Strategies for Specific
Populations 441

Part VII: Additional Help and Information

Chapter 62—Glossary of Substance Abuse Terms................. 457
Chapter 63—Dictionary of Street Terms 465
Chapter 64—Resource Guide for Parents............................ 515

Chapter 65—Mutual Self-Help Groups 539
Chapter 66—Federal Agencies 543
Chapter 67—Federal Drug Data Sources 553
Chapter 68—Drug Enforcement Administration Division
                       Offices 563
Chapter 69—State Resources 567

Index **585**

Preface

About This Book

According to statistics compiled by the U.S. Department of Labor, substance abuse has a significant impact in the workplace, with costs estimated at over $100 billion annually. In addition, a study conducted by the Institute for Health Policy, Brandeis University, found substance abuse to be the number one health problem in the country, resulting in more deaths, illnesses, and disabilities than any other preventable health condition.

This *Sourcebook* offers facts about specific drugs of abuse, including depressants, hallucinogens, inhalants, marijuana, narcotics, stimulants, and anabolic steroids. It explains the nature of addiction, describes related health risks, and provides information about various treatment strategies and drug abuse prevention issues. A glossary, a dictionary of street names for illicit drugs, and resource directories are also provided.

Readers seeking information about alcohol use and abuse, including alcohol's effects on the brain and other organs of the body, treatment for alcoholism, and alcohol abuse prevention programs, will find an in-depth presentation of these topics in *Alcoholism Sourcebook*, a separate volume in Omnigraphics' *Health Reference Series*.

How to Use This Book

This book is divided into parts and chapters. Parts focus on broad areas of interest. Chapters are devoted to single topics within a part.

Part I: Drug Use and Abuse provides background information and a statistical overview of drug abuse in the United States. The debate surrounding the medical use of marijuana is also addressed.

Part II: The Nature of Addiction describes the process by which people become addicted and some of the factors that place certain individuals at risk.

Part III: Drugs of Abuse provides summary information about some of the most commonly abused substances, including anabolic steroids, amphetamines, cocaine, heroin, inhalants, LSD, marijuana, and PCP.

Part IV: Drug-Related Health Risks: Recent Research presents updated findings about how some drugs can affect the mind and body.

Part V: Drug Abuse Treatment Issues offers information about detoxification and the maintenance of a drug-free lifestyle. It also includes information about medications and other aids that may be used to help overcome addictions.

Part VI: Drug Abuse Prevention Issues describes various drug abuse prevention programs and strategies used in the home, school, and workplace. In addition, it offers information about related cultural issues and other topics of concern in minority populations.

Part VII: Additional Help and Information includes a glossary of substance abuse terms, a dictionary of street terms, a resource guide for parents, and directories of other types of resources.

Bibliographic Note

This volume contains documents and excerpts from publications issued by the following U.S. government agencies: Center for Substance Abuse Prevention (CSAP); Centers for Disease Control and Prevention (CDC); Executive Office of the President, Office of National Drug Control Policy; National Clearinghouse for Alcohol and Drug Information; National Institute on Drug Abuse (NIDA); National Institutes of Health (NIH), Consensus Development Program; Substance Abuse and Mental Health Services Administration (SAMHSA); U.S. Department of Education; U.S. Department of Justice (DOJ); U.S. Department of Labor; U.S. General Accounting Office (GOA), and the United States Information Agency.

In addition, this volume contains copyrighted documents from the following organizations: American Psychiatric Association; American

School Health Association; Harvard Medical School; Indiana Prevention Resource Center; Manisses Communications Group, Inc.; Medquest Communications, Inc.; National Drug Strategy Network; and the Tennessee Statewide Clearinghouse. Copyrighted articles from *Alcoholism and Drug Abuse Week*, *Behavioral Health Management*, *Brown University Child and Adolescent Behavior Letter*, *Brown University Digest of Addiction Theory and Application*, *Patient Care*, and *Time Magazine* are also included.

Full citation information is provided on the first page of each chapter. Every effort has been made to secure all necessary rights to reprint the copyrighted material. If any omissions have been made, please contact Omnigraphics to make corrections for future editions.

Acknowledgements

In addition to the organizations listed above, special thanks are due to document engineer Bruce Bellenir, researchers Jenifer Swanson and Joan Margeson, verification assistant Dawn Matthews, and permissions specialist Maria Franklin.

Note from the Editor

This book is part of Omnigraphics' *Health Reference Series*. The series provides basic information about a broad range of medical concerns. It is not intended to serve as a tool for diagnosing illness, in prescribing treatments, or as a substitute for the physician/patient relationship. All persons concerned about medical symptoms or the possibility of disease are encouraged to seek professional care from an appropriate health care provider.

Our Advisory Board

The *Health Reference Series* is reviewed by an Advisory Board comprised of librarians from public, academic, and medical libraries. We would like to thank the following board members for providing guidance to the development of this series:

Dr. Lynda Baker,
Associate Professor of Library and Information Science,
Wayne State University, Detroit, MI

Nancy Bulgarelli,
William Beaumont Hospital Library, Royal Oak, MI

Karen Imarasio,
Bloomfield Township Public Library, Bloomfield Township, MI

Karen Morgan,
Mardigian Library, University of Michigan-Dearborn,
Dearborn, MI

Rosemary Orlando,
St. Clair Shores Public Library, St. Clair Shores, MI

Health Reference Series *Update Policy*

The inaugural book in the *Health Reference Series* was the first edition of *Cancer Sourcebook* published in 1992. Since then, the *Series* has been enthusiastically received by librarians and in the medical community. In order to maintain the standard of providing high-quality health information for the lay person, the editorial staff at Omnigraphics felt it was necessary to implement a policy of updating volumes when warranted.

Medical researchers have been making tremendous strides, and it is the purpose of the *Health Reference Series* to stay current with the most recent advances. Each decision to update a volume will be made on an individual basis. Some of the considerations will include how much new information is available and the feedback we receive from people who use the books. If there is a topic you would like to see added to the update list, or an area of medical concern you feel has not been adequately addressed, please write to:

Editor
Health Reference Series
Omnigraphics, Inc.
615 Griswold Street
Detroit, MI 48226

The commitment to providing on-going coverage of important medical developments has also led to some format changes in the *Health Reference Series*. Each new volume on a topic is individually titled and called a "First Edition." Subsequent updates will carry sequential edition numbers. To help avoid confusion and to provide maximum flexibility in our ability to respond to informational needs, the practice of consecutively numbering each volume has been discontinued.

Part One

Drug Use and Abuse

Chapter 1

Let's Talk Facts about Substance Abuse

The use of various substances to modify mood or behavior is generally regarded as normal and acceptable in our society, despite wide cultural differences. Many people drink coffee or tea for the stimulant effects of caffeine, or engage in the social drinking of alcohol. And certain drugs may be used medically to relieve tension or pain or to suppress appetite. When the symptoms and behavioral changes associated with regular use of these substances become maladaptive, however, substance use turns to substance abuse.

Substance abuse, the misuse of alcohol, cigarettes, and both illegal and legal drugs, is by far the predominant cause of premature and preventable illness, disability, and death in our society. Alcohol and drug abuse afflict an estimated 25.5 million Americans. When the effects on the families of abusers and people close to those injured or killed by intoxicated drivers are considered, such abuse affects untold millions more.

The annual cost of alcoholism is $89.5 billion for treatment and indirect losses such as reduced worker productivity, early death, and property damage resulting from alcohol-related accidents and crime each year. Drug abuse accounts for another $46.9 billion a year in direct and indirect costs to business and the economy. This economic toll amounts to over four times that of cancer and nearly a third greater than that of cardiovascular disease, according to a 1984 Research Triangle Institute report.

Among the disorders related to the misuse of these substances, a distinction is made between substance abuse and substance dependence. Substance abuse victims can't control their use of alcohol or other drugs. They become intoxicated on a regular basis, daily, every weekend, or in binges, and often need the drug for normal daily functioning. They repeatedly try to stop using the drug but fail, even though they know its use interferes with their family life, social relationships, and work performance, or that it causes or aggravates a psychological or physical problem.

Substance dependence victims suffer all the symptoms of abuse plus a tolerance for the drug so that increased amounts of it are necessary for the desired effects. Opioids, alcohol, and amphetamines also lead to physical dependence in which the person develops withdrawal symptoms when he or she stops using the drug.

Alcohol Use

For no other disease more than alcoholism has social stigma blocked the road to understanding. Society has long viewed the affliction as a psychological problem, the sign of a ravaged soul devoid of discipline or morality. Physicians are inclined to ignore its symptoms, and victims deny its existence.

Recent scientific breakthroughs, however, have begun to dramatically alter our views on alcoholism. The myth that alcoholism is always psychologically based is yielding under the weight of evidence that the disease is largely biologically determined. This news holds significant hope for the estimated 18 million adult victims of alcohol (10.6 million alcoholics and another 7.3 million with serious alcohol abuse problems), as well as the 56 million people directly affected by them. Such discoveries may eventually lead to prevention or detection of the disease before its damage becomes irreversible.

The following characteristics of alcoholism leave little doubt as to the devastating impact of the disease:

- Alcoholism is a progressive disease that generally first appears between the ages of 20 and 40, although children can become alcoholics.

- Drinking patterns vary by age and sex. At all ages, two to five times more males than females are heavy drinkers. For both males and females, drinking prevalence is highest and abstention lowest in the 21 to 34 age range. Among those 65 years and older, abstainers exceed drinkers in both sexes.

4

- Alcohol dependence tends to cluster in families.

- Alcohol dependence is often associated with depression, but the depression typically appears to be a consequence of the drinking rather than a cause.

- It takes five to 15 years for an adult to become an alcoholic; an adolescent can become an alcoholic, by contrast, in six to 18 months of heavy drinking.

- Generally, abuse occurs in one of three patterns: regular, daily intoxication; drinking large amounts of alcohol at specific times, such as every weekend; and long periods of sobriety interspersed with binges of heavy daily drinking that last for weeks or months.

- As drinking continues, dependence develops and sobriety brings serious withdrawal symptoms such as delirium tremens (DTs) that include physical trembling, delusions, hallucinations, sweating and high blood pressure.

- Long-term heavy drinking can cause dementia, in which the individual loses memory and the ability to think abstractly, to recall names of common objects, to use correct words to describe recognized objects or to follow simple instructions.

- Physical complications of chronic alcohol dependence include cirrhosis (liver damage), hepatitis, altered brain-cell functioning, nerve damage, gastritis (inflammation of the stomach), premature aging, impotence and infertility, and a variety of reproductive disorders. Some researchers suspect the hormonal imbalances caused by alcohol dependence actually fool the body into shutting off its supply of natural opiates (endorphins). Chronic alcohol dependence also increases the risk and severity of heart disease, pneumonia, tuberculosis, and neurological disorders.

Among the new techniques for detecting alcoholism is a computerized method of analyzing blood chemistries that could help to identify early-stage alcoholism before the liver is significantly damaged. Another experimental blood test promises to detect changes in the liver that forecast cirrhosis, an insidious killer that often progresses with no warning until the damage is fatal.

Researchers are also discovering other biological markers that could eventually identify many potential alcoholics. Preliminary studies indicate that alcoholics are born with a faulty liver enzyme system that may lead to their addiction, an encouraging twist to the existing knowledge that alcoholics do not metabolize alcohol normally. Still other studies reveal that the majority of alcoholics have abnormal brain waves and memory impairments. This appears to be true of their young children as well, even though the offspring may never have been exposed to alcohol.

Alcoholism is generally recognized as a multifaceted disorder involving psychological, environmental, biological, and cultural factors, and treatment programs for the condition may vary in emphasis. Most programs, however, include a variety of therapies geared toward abstinence and designed to approach the illness from all vantage points.

Psychotherapy helps patients understand their behavior and motivations, develop higher self-esteem and cope with stress. Because long-term support is considered essential, self-help groups such as Alcoholics Anonymous are often part of a rehabilitation program. Some programs also prescribe daily doses of disulfiram (Antabuse), which induces violent physical reactions to alcohol and thus discourages drinking.

Drug Use

The dramatic increase in illegal drug use over the last 25 years makes it hard for anyone 50 or older to appreciate how extensively the problem has invaded our society. Experience with illegal drugs rose from 2 percent or less of the population in most areas of the country in the early 1960s to more than a third of the population, 70.4 million Americans, in 1985, according to household surveys by the National Institute on Drug Abuse (NIDA).

The drugs discussed here include seven major classes: marijuana, cocaine, opiates, hallucinogens, inhalants, sedative-hypnotics, and nicotine. Not all are physically addictive, but all can lead to psychological addiction, in which the user needs the drug in order to function.

Marijuana (Cannabis)

Marijuana is the most widespread and frequently used illicit drug in the nation. Almost 62 million Americans had tried marijuana at least once in their lives at the time of a 1985 NIDA survey. Current use (past-month use) had decreased, however, by 1.8 million people.

Marijuana is typically used in combination with other substances, particularly alcohol and cocaine. One out of every four young adults who have used marijuana say they usually had an alcoholic drink at the same time. The combination of marijuana and alcohol accounted for more than half of the marijuana-related emergency-room cases in 1985. Cigarette smoking by very young children is another pattern strongly related to marijuana smoking. Young people age 15 to 17 who are current cigarette smokers are five times more likely to be current marijuana users.

Boys and girls (age 12 to 17) are equally likely to try marijuana, but current users in the 18 to 25 age group are almost one-and-a-half times as likely to be male. Many of the people who have tried marijuana use the drug extensively, and a substantial majority of heavy marijuana users will go on to try other illicit drugs. For example, 74 percent of those who have used marijuana 100 or more times have tried cocaine.

The health consequences of marijuana depend on the frequency, duration, and intensity of use and the age at which use begins. Marijuana has the following known and suspected health hazards that merit serious concern:

- At commonly used doses, marijuana impairs short-term memory, concentration, judgment, information processing, perception, and fine motor skills. The risk of accidents while driving or operating complex machinery thus increases for those intoxicated with marijuana. Even when marijuana use is discontinued, memory loss may continue for three to six months. Marijuana impairs driving skills for at least four to six hours after smoking a single cigarette.

- Smoking marijuana immediately accelerates the heartbeat and, in some individuals, increases blood pressure, posing a threat to those with abnormal heart and circulatory conditions.

- Specific psychiatric concerns include chronic anxiety, symptoms of depression, and changes in lifestyle. There is particular concern about long-term developmental effects of marijuana use by children and adolescents. The term "amotivational syndrome" has evolved to describe the changes observed in some marijuana users, such as apathy, loss of ambition and effectiveness, diminished ability to carry out long-term plans, difficulty in concentrating, and a decline in school or work performance.

- Although human lung cancer has not been linked solely to marijuana smoking, abnormalities suggestive of precancerous lesions have been reported. There are more known carcinogens in marijuana smoke than in cigarette smoke. However, since many marijuana users also smoke cigarettes, the combined carcinogenic effect must be investigated. Marijuana significantly reduces the capacity of the lungs to exchange gas, even more so than does tobacco.

- Marijuana may have serious effects on reproduction. Some studies have shown that women who smoked marijuana during pregnancy gave birth to babies with defects.

- In animals, marijuana has been shown to interfere with the body's immune response to certain infections and diseases. What significance this may have for humans is still being investigated.

Cocaine

In 1982, it was estimated that more than 20 million Americans had tried cocaine and more than four million were current users. Current users have increased to almost six million, and the number continues to rise dramatically. Moreover, current and frequent users are more likely to report symptoms of dependence on cocaine.

What exactly is this seductive substance that has gained such popularity in recent years? Cocaine is a white powder produced from the leaves of the South American coca plant. It is known by a variety of names: coke, C, snow, blow, toot, nose candy, and The Lady. Cocaine is a stimulant, a class of drugs that give a temporary illusion of limitless power and energy. Most cocaine users in this country snort the powdered drug through the nose, and some dissolve it and inject it into a muscle or vein, to experience the drug's fleeting "highs."

Crack is a form of cocaine that is chemically altered so that it can be smoked. It belongs to a category of cocaine known as "freebase," because the processing converts the drug into a chemical base as opposed to an acid or a salt. Smoking allows high doses of cocaine to reach the brain almost instantly. As a result, crack produces the most dramatic cocaine "high." This rapid "high" is followed, however, by a profound "low" that becomes a door to addiction.

Cocaine is one of the most potent drugs of abuse. It causes chemical changes in the brain that lead to an intense craving for more of the drug. Anyone who tries cocaine or crack risks addiction. Dependence on these drugs is so powerful that they come to rule all aspects of the user's life. Addiction can erode physical and mental health, sap financial resources, ruin careers, and drive off family and friends.

Users fall into no particular stereotype. Many are well-educated, successful, upwardly mobile professionals in their 20s and 30s. But a cocaine user can be anyone, old or young, rich or poor, man or woman.

Cocaine abuse and dependence follow one of two patterns of use: episodic use and chronic daily, or almost daily, use. Episodic use may occur on weekends, for example, and once or twice during the week. Among users who smoke cocaine or take it intravenously, "binges," compressed time periods of continuous high-dose use, are common. Binges terminate only when the user collapses from physical exhaustion or the supply of cocaine is depleted. An intense and unpleasant "crash" requiring at least two days of recuperation generally follows the binge. Chronic daily, or almost daily, use may be at high or low doses, and may occur throughout the day or only during restricted hours. Although wide fluctuations in the amount of cocaine used from day to day are unlikely, doses generally increase over time.

The effects of cocaine on the body are wide ranging. Immediate effects include increases in blood pressure, heart rate, breathing rate, and body temperature; dilated pupils; narrowing of blood vessels; loss of appetite; and insomnia. As use progresses, a loss of interest in physical appearance and frequent upper respiratory infections may become apparent. Those who snort cocaine may be bothered by a runny nose. As the effects wear off, the initial elevation of mood and sense of well-being fade into a depression characterized by disappointment, dullness, and edginess.

Besides addiction, cocaine can lead to serious medical problems:

- While users with heart problems or circulatory disease are at greatest risk of heart attack or heart failure from cocaine and crack, new evidence indicates the drugs can cause heart attacks even in young people with healthy hearts.

- Cocaine and crack can also trigger brain seizures, a disturbance in the brain's electrical signals, some of which regulate the heart and muscles that control breathing.

- The increase in blood pressure caused by the drug may rupture blood vessels in the brain, causing some addicts to suffer strokes.

- Psychological effects accompanying the use of cocaine can include violent, erratic, or paranoid behavior. This "cocaine psychosis" tends to appear sooner in crack smokers. Users are anxious and convinced they have superhuman powers, or they may become so suspicious and paranoid that they believe their lives are threatened and react in bizarre ways. Hallucinations are also common.

• Heavy cocaine users may experience fundamental personality changes, impaired thinking, confusion, anxiety or depression. Continued use of cocaine and crack can lead to a partial or total break with reality.

• Miscarriage or stillbirths may result from the use of cocaine or crack during the early months of pregnancy. Use at a later stage may cause premature labor or delivery. Sometimes, when the drug causes the placenta to separate early, the lives of both mother and baby are in danger from shock and bleeding.

• Babies exposed to cocaine in the womb may be generally irritable and unresponsive, failing to cuddle or nurse well. Some of these babies have suffered strokes before birth or heart attacks following delivery. Infants born to mothers who use cocaine may have malformed kidneys and genitals and may be at increased risk of seizures or crib death (sudden infant death syndrome). Because nursing mothers can pass cocaine to their babies through breast milk, babies fed milk containing cocaine may be prone to suffer some of the same heart and brain problems as adults.

Recovery is possible for cocaine and crack users, although the long-lasting craving for these drugs makes addiction difficult to beat without assistance. There are many treatment programs available throughout the country to help people kick their habits and stay off cocaine and crack.

The first step to treatment is admission by the abuser that he or she has a problem. This is often a major hurdle, for denial is a typical and powerful force with drug abuse.

If the abuser resists, it may be necessary for family members to take serious steps on their own behalf as well as that of the loved one. Cocaine users spend vast amounts of money on the drug, whatever it takes to support their habit. As drug use progresses, they may reject all former responsibilities, ignoring bills, selling household possessions, emptying savings accounts, even stealing from friends and family members or turning to embezzling, robbery, drug dealing, or prostitution to get cash. Clearly, then, the emotional health and stability of the abuser's family are threatened.

Family members may choose to intervene to help get a cocaine user into treatment. Many professionals recommend a method called a family action plan or intervention. After several meetings with an experienced drug counselor, social worker, psychologist, or other health professional, the family confronts the user and each member openly communicates how the user's behavior has affected him or her personally. Other participants in the intervention may include friends, employers or coworkers.

During the actual confrontation, often led by a professional counselor, family and friends make it clear that the time has come to choose between them and the drug. The intervention is designed to catch the addict off guard and to overcome the likely denial. A crucial aspect of the process is presenting the user with treatment alternatives that can be started as soon as the intervention is completed.

Detoxification, ridding the body of the drug, is the starting point of any treatment program. This may be followed by medication, such as antidepressants, which help control the craving and relieve the severe depression that accompanies cocaine or crack withdrawal.

Therapy programs also guide the recovering user toward other alternatives to curb craving for the drug. This help may be through a combination of individual, group, and family counseling as well as other techniques aimed at changing behavior. The ultimate goal of recovery programs is to improve self-image and promote healthful, drug-free living. Continued strength and support are also found by many recovering individuals by attending meetings of Cocaine Anonymous or Narcotics Anonymous, self-help groups modeled after the Alcoholics Anonymous program.

Professional support is also available to family members who need help for themselves as they strive to break out of the destructive environment the user's addiction has created. One option is a telephone call to an anonymous service like the nationwide hotline run by the National Institute on Drug Abuse (1-800-662-HELP). Family therapy is often helpful, as is individual support from a trusted friend, family doctor, clergy member, or counselor. Among the support groups formed recently for the families of drug users are Nar-Anon for people whose lives have been affected by a drug abuser, Families Anonymous for families of drug abusers. These groups have local chapters, which are usually listed in the phone book.

Opiates

Opiates, also referred to as narcotics, are a class of drugs used medically as pain relievers, anesthetics, or cough suppressants. Unfortunately, as a result of their powerful properties, they have a high potential for abuse.

11

Some opiates come from resin taken from seed pods of the Asian poppy. This group of drugs includes opium, morphine, heroin, and codeine. Other opiates such as meperidine (Demerol) are synthetics with morphine-like action.

Opium is in the form of dark brown chunks or a powder and is usually smoked or eaten. Heroin can be a white or brownish powder and is most often dissolved in water and then injected. Most street versions of heroin are diluted, or "cut," with sugar, quinine, or other substances to extend the supply and increase profits. Other types of opiates come in the form of tablets, capsules, solutions, syrups, and suppositories.

An illegal drug also known as "junk" or "smack," heroin accounts for 90 percent of the opiate abuse in the United States, according to National Institute on Drug Abuse figures. An estimated half a million Americans are addicted to heroin. Other opiates used for legal medicinal purposes may also be abused. These include morphine, meperidine, paregoric (which contains opium), and cough syrups containing codeine.

About half of those who abuse opiates develop a dependence or addiction. When someone becomes dependent, obtaining and using the drug become the main focus in life to the exclusion of all else. As the drug is increased over time, greater amounts are needed to achieve the same effects. This tolerance can reach remarkably high levels.

Opiates generally relax the user. When they are injected, the person experiences an immediate "rush." Other initial adverse effects include nausea, vomiting, and restlessness. The user may alternate between feeling alert and drowsy. In the case of extremely large doses, the user can't be awakened, pupils become smaller, and the skin becomes cold, damp, and bluish. Breathing slows down and death may occur.

Opiate withdrawal symptoms usually begin within four to six hours of when a dependent user stops taking the drug. These symptoms include nausea, diarrhea, abdominal cramps, chills, sweating, uneasiness, and runny nose and eyes. The intensity of the symptoms depends on the dose, how often the drug was taken, and for how long. For most opiates, withdrawal symptoms are stronger about 24 to 72 hours after they start and subside within a week to 10 days. Symptoms like insomnia and craving for the drug can last for months.

Most of the dangers of opiate abuse are associated with the use of unsterile needles, contamination of the drug itself, or mixing the drug with other substances. Eventually, opiate users may develop infections of the heart lining and valves, congested lungs, and skin abscesses.

Infections from unsterile solutions, syringes, and needles can lead to acquired immune deficiency syndrome (AIDS), liver disease, tetanus, and serum hepatitis.

Scientists estimate that nearly half the women who are dependent on opiates suffer heart disease, anemia, diabetes, pneumonia, or hepatitis during pregnancy and childbirth. These women have more spontaneous abortions, premature births, stillbirths, breech deliveries, and cesarean sections. And their babies often have withdrawal symptoms that may last several weeks or months. Many of these infants die.

Treatment is available for opiate addiction. Most programs offer one of four basic approaches:

- Detoxification in a hospital or as an outpatient. This involves supervised withdrawal from drug dependence, either with or without medication.

- Therapeutic communities where patients live in a highly structured, drug-free environment and are encouraged to help themselves.

- Outpatient drug-free programs, which emphasize various forms of counseling as the main treatment.

- Methadone maintenance, which uses methadone, a substitute for heroin, daily to help people lead productive lives while still in treatment. A synthetic drug, methadone does not produce the same "high" as illegal drugs such as heroin, but does prevent withdrawal and the craving for other opiates. It can thus successfully break the cycle of dependence on illegal drugs.

Hallucinogens

Hallucinogens include such drugs as lysergic acid diethylamide (LSD), mescaline, and peyote. These substances are taken orally and can cause the abuser to experience hallucinations, perceptions of objects that have no external cause. Phencyclidine (PCP) is sometimes referred to as a hallucinogen, although it rarely causes hallucinations in the true sense.

These drugs came into popular use by young people in the mid-sixties. Since then, however, there has been a steady decline in their use. In 1985, only 3.2 percent of American youths had ever tried hallucinogens compared to 5.2 percent in 1982. Recent users (past-year users) had also decreased from 3.6 percent to 2.6 percent for the same period.

Most people are introduced to hallucinogens by experimenting with the drugs in social situations. Some find the hallucinogenic experience extremely vexing or gloomy and lose interest right away, while others enjoy it and continue using the substance.

Use almost always occurs in intermittent episodes, because the mind-altering effects of these substances impair cognitive and perceptual functions to such an extent that the user generally has to set aside time from a daily routine to take the drug. Moreover, the frequent user may quickly develop a tolerance for the drug, which makes it virtually impossible to take enough of it on a daily basis to obtain the desired effects. For these reasons, abuse is far more common than dependence.

Hallucinogens are often contaminated with other drugs such as PCP and amphetamines. In addition, users frequently smoke marijuana and abuse alcohol. The course of use is unpredictable, but most people resume their previous lifestyle relatively quickly after a brief period of abuse or dependence.

Phencyclidine can be taken orally or intravenously, or it can be smoked or inhaled. This substance is sold on the street under a variety of names, the most common of which are PCP, PeaCe Pill, and angel dust. PCP is usually taken episodically in binges and "runs" that can last several days. However, some people chronically use the substance on a daily basis.

Inhalants

Inhalants are breathable chemicals that produce mind-altering vapors. This group of substances includes solvents, aerosols, some anesthetics, and other chemicals. Inhalants are not usually thought of as drugs because that's not how most of them were intended to be used.

Examples of inhalants are gasoline, glue, paint thinners, nail polish remover, and lighter and cleaning fluids. Aerosols used as inhalants include spray paints, hair sprays, and cookware coating agents. Anesthetics include halothane and nitrous oxide, also known as laughing gas.

Amyl nitrite and butyl nitrite are other commonly abused inhalants. Amyl nitrite is a clear, yellowish liquid used for heart patients and for diagnostic purposes because it dilates the blood vessels and speeds up the heart rate. The substance is sold in a cloth-covered, sealed bulb that, when broken, makes a snapping sound. Thus the nickname "snappers" or "poppers." Butyl nitrate is packaged in small bottles and sold under such names as "locker room" and "rush." It produces a high lasting from a few seconds to several minutes.

Young people between the ages of seven and 17 are the most common abusers of inhalants. About 9 percent of young people in this country had experimented with inhalants in 1985, while only 4 percent were current users.

These youths generally come from backgrounds reflecting family instability, separation, lack of supervision, or alcohol or other drug dependence. School or work adjustment problems such as delinquency, truancy, poor grades, dropping out of school, and unemployment are also common. Occasionally, young children misuse inhalant products unintentionally, since they are often found around the house.

Inhalants reach the lungs and bloodstream very quickly. They work in much the same way as anesthetics, which slow down the body's functions. Low doses can cause a feeling of slight stimulation; more of the substance may lead to reduced inhibitions and less control. At high doses, loss of consciousness can occur.

The immediate effects of inhalants include nausea, nosebleeds, coughing, sneezing, feeling and looking tired, bad breath, lack of coordination, and loss of appetite. Solvents and aerosols also decrease heart and breathing rates and affect judgment. The degree of these effects varies with the specific substance inhaled, the dose, and the personality and experience of the user.

More serious effects can result from deep breathing of inhalant vapors, or using large quantities over a short period of time. These effects may include loss of self-control, violent behavior, losing touch with one's surroundings, unconsciousness or death. Nausea and vomiting may also occur, and if the user is unconscious while vomiting, death from aspiration can result.

Sniffing high concentrations of inhalant fumes can produce heart failure and instant death. Such concentrations cause death from suffocation by displacing the oxygen in the lungs. Inhalants can also depress the central nervous system to the point that breathing slows down until it stops.

Long-term abuse of inhalants can cause fatigue, weight loss, electrolyte (salt) imbalance, and muscle fatigue. Repeated sniffing of concentrated vapors over several years can damage the liver, kidneys, blood, and bone marrow, and can also lead to permanent damage to the nervous system, causing major physical and mental deficits.

Sedative-Hypnotics

Sedative-hypnotics are a group of drugs referred to as tranquilizers and sleeping pills, or generally as sedatives. These drugs are used medically to relieve anxiety and promote sleep. When they are abused or taken at high doses, however, many of these drugs can lead to unconsciousness and death.

Although the nonmedical use of sedatives among the 18 to 25 age group declined from 8.7 percent in 1982 to 5.1 percent in 1985, use of tranquilizers and analgesics (pain relievers) by older adults increased from 1.1 percent in 1982 to 2.8 percent in 1985.

The two major categories of sedative-hypnotics are barbiturates, also known as "barbs" and "downers," and benzodiazepines. All of the drugs in these groups have similar chemical structures. Some commonly abused barbiturates include amobarbital (Amytal), secobarbital (Seconal) and pentobarbital (Nembutal). Diazepam (Valium), chlordiazepoxide (Librium) and clorazepate (Tranxene) are examples of benzodiazepines.

Several sedative-hypnotics fall into a separate category. They include methaqualone (Quaalude, Sopor), ethchlorvynol (Placidyl), chloral hydrate (Noctec) and meprobamate (Miltown).

All of these drugs can be extremely dangerous when not taken according to a physician's instructions. They can cause both physical and psychological dependence, and regular use over a long period of time may lead to tolerance. Withdrawal symptoms are also likely to occur when regular users suddenly stop taking large doses of these drugs. These symptoms can range from restlessness, insomnia, and anxiety to convulsions and death.

Large doses of barbiturates can cause unconsciousness and death. With barbiturates, there is less difference than with other sedatives between the amount that produces sleep and the amount that kills. Barbiturate overdose is a factor in close to one-third of all reported drug-related deaths, including suicides and accidental drug poisonings.

When barbiturates are abused, their effects are similar to the effects of alcohol. Small doses produce calmness and relax muscles. Slightly larger amounts can cause poor judgment, slurred speech, staggering gait, and slow, uncertain reflexes. It is easy to see why driving a car or operating machinery becomes very dangerous if one abuses these drugs.

Combining sedative-hypnotics with alcohol is especially dangerous. The use of these drugs with alcohol and other drugs that slow down body functions multiplies their effects and greatly increases the risk of death. Overdose deaths can result, whether deliberate or accidental, when barbiturates and alcohol are combined.

Women who abuse sedatives during pregnancy may give birth to babies who are physically dependent on the drugs and show withdrawal symptoms shortly after birth. Many sedatives pass easily through the placenta and are known to cause birth defects and behavior problems in the offspring of women who abuse these drugs while pregnant.

Nicotine

After years of controversy over the dangers of smoking, the latest report by the U.S. Surgeon General has confirmed that nicotine in tobacco products is an addictive drug comparable to heroin or morphine.

The report showed a 37 percent decrease in smoking from 1975 to 1985. While this decline is certainly encouraging news, the fact remains that close to 50 million Americans still smoke cigarettes. And 320,000 deaths a year in this country are the result of tobacco products.

The prevalence of smoking among males continues to be greater than that among females (29.5 percent for men; 23.8 percent for women), and figures remain higher for black smokers than for whites (28.4 percent for blacks; 26.4 percent for whites).

Anyone who has smoked regularly can attest to the difficulty of giving up the habit. Most people try repeatedly to give up smoking without success. Studies suggest that the relapse rate is greater than 50 percent in the first six months, and at least 70 percent in the first year. After a year of abstinence, however, subsequent relapse is far less likely.

The most common form of nicotine dependence is linked to the inhalation of cigarette smoke. The nicotine effects of cigarette smoking have a more rapid onset than with pipe and cigar smoking, tobacco chewing, and the use of snuff. The habit pattern is more intensive and difficult to break due to frequent reinforcement and greater physical dependence on the nicotine.

The unpleasantness of withdrawal may add to the difficulty of giving up smoking. The nicotine withdrawal syndrome includes craving for the drug, irritability, frustration or anger, anxiety, difficulty concentrating, weight gain, and decreased heart rate or appetite. Environmental cues such as the presence of other smokers and the widespread availability of cigarettes also surround the smoker with temptations.

Evidence that nicotine is addictive has resulted from studies of the drug's effects on the brain and other parts of the body. Nicotine acts on specific receptors in the brain and other parts of the nervous system. It also relaxes skeletal muscles and affects the heart, blood vessels, and hormonal system.

Smokers become addicted to the mood-altering, stress-reducing properties of nicotine. Their performance has been shown to improve on some cognitive tests after smoking a cigarette, even on tests requiring sustained attention. And the drug also apparently helps to suppress appetite.

Some smokers muster the determination and willpower to quit on their own. For others, the various stop-smoking programs offered by health care agencies, employers, and various private groups around the country have been the answer.

If we are to maintain momentum toward the goal of a smoker-free society, the Centers for Disease Control recommends that government agencies, private organizations, healthcare providers, and others work together to support programs and policies that encourage nonsmoking behavior. Possible steps toward the realization of this goal include the following:

- Offer smoking prevention and cessation programs in schools, worksites, healthcare facilities, and other institutions.

- Ban or restrict smoking in public places and worksites.

- Restrict the sale of tobacco products to minors.

- Ban all tobacco advertising.

- Provide reduced premiums for health and life insurance to non-smokers.

- Provide third-party reimbursement for smoking cessation programs.

- Raise the cigarette excise tax.

Bibliography

General Information

Breeden, Joann. *Love, Hope, and Recovery: Healing the Pain of Addiction*. Nevada City, CA: Blue Dolphin Pub., 1994.

Cocores, James. *The 800 Cocaine Book of Drug and Alcohol Recovery*. New York: Simon & Schuster, 1991.

Cohen, Irving. *Addiction: The High-Low Trap*. Santa Fe, NM: Health Press, 1995.

Gossop, Michael. *Living with Drugs*. Brookfield, VT: Ashgate, 1996.

Hendler, Sheldon. *The Purification Prescription*. New York: W. Morrow and Co., 1991.

Kwasnik, Tom. *While Dragons Sleep: How to Solve a Chemical Dependence Problem: The Official TPA Manual*. Canandaigua, NY: Able Press, 1991.

Robertson, Joel. *Help Yourself: A Revolutionary Alternative Recovery Program*. Nashville, TN: Oliver-Nelson, 1992.

Robson, Phillip. *Forbidden Drugs*. New York: Oxford University Press, 1999.

Books Published by the American Psychiatric Press, Inc.
1400 K Street, N.W.
Washington, DC 20005
(800) 368-5777

Practice Guideline for the Treatment of Patients with Substance Use Disorders: Alcohol, Cocaine, Opioids. 1995, 126 pages, $22.50.

Practice Guideline for the Treatment of Patients with Nicotine Dependence. 1996, 80 pages, $22.50.

Other Resources

American Academy of Child and Adolescent Psychiatry
3615 Wisconsin Avenue, N.W.
Washington, DC 20016
(202) 966-7300
Web site: www.aacap.org

American Academy of Psychiatrists in Alcoholism and Addictions
7301 Mission Road
Suite 252
Prairie Village, KS 66208
(913) 262-6161
Fax: (913) 262-4311
E-Mail: info@aaap.org
Web site: www.aaap.org

American Council on Drug Education
164 West 74ᵗʰ Street
New York, NY 10023
(800) 488-DRUG

American Society of Addiction Medicine
4601 N. Park Avenue
Arcade Suite 101
Chevy Chase, MD 20815
(301) 656-3920
Fax: (301) 656-3815

Association for Medical Education and Research in Substance Abuse
125 Whipple Street, Third Floor
Providence, RI 02908
(401) 785-8263

Drug Abuse Information and Treatment Referral Line
1-800-662-HELP; Spanish 1-800-66-AYUDA

National Association of State Alcohol and Drug Abuse Directors
808 17th Street, Suite 410
Washington, DC 20006
(202) 293-0090
Web site: www.nasadad.org

National Clearinghouse for Alcohol and Drug Information
P.O. Box 2345
Rockville, MD 20847-2345
Toll Free: (800) SAY-NOTO
Web site: www.health.org

National Council on Alcoholism and Drug Dependence
12 W. 21st St., 7th Fl.
New York, NY 10010
Toll Free: (800) NCA-CALL
Phone: (212) 206-6770
Fax: (212) 645-1690
E-Mail: national@ncadd.org
Web site: www.ncadd.org

National Family Partnership
2490 Coral Way, Suite 501
Miami, FL 33145-3449
(305) 856-4173
Toll Free: (800) 705-8997
Fax: (305) 856-4815
Web site: www.nfp.org

National Institute on Alcohol Abuse and Alcoholism
National Institutes of Health
6000 Executive Boulevard
Willco Building
Bethesda, Maryland 20892
Phone: (301) 443-3885
Web site: www.niaaa.nih.gov

National Institute on Drug Abuse
National Institutes of Health
6001 Executive Blvd.
Bethesda, MD 20892
Phone: (301) 662-1124
Web site: www.nida.nih.gov

National Self-Help Clearinghouse
Graduate School and University Center
City University of New York
365 Fifth Avenue, Suite 3300
New York, NY 10016
(212) 817-1822
Web site: www.selfhelpweb.org

Substance Abuse and Mental Health Services Administration
5600 Fishers Lane
Rockville, MD 20857
(301) 443-8956
Web site: www.samhsa.gov

Online Resources

Visit the American Psychiatric Association's site on the World Wide Web.
www.psych.org

Additional Resources

Information about other resources, including organizations and on-line sources, may be found in the end section of this book.

Chapter 2

Nationwide Trends in Drug Abuse

According to the preliminary results of the 1996 National Household Survey on Drug Abuse (NHSDA), the number of current illicit drug users did not change significantly from 1995 (12.8 million) to 1996 (13 million). The following are highlights from the preliminary results of the 1996 NHSDA and highlights from the December 1996 meeting of NIDA's Community Epidemiology Work Group (CEWG). CEWG is a network of researchers from 20 major U.S. metropolitan areas and selected foreign countries who meet semiannually to discuss the current epidemiology of drug abuse.

Extent of Use

Cocaine

Crack cocaine continues to dominate the Nation's illicit drug problem. The overall number of current cocaine users did not change significantly between 1995 and 1996 (1.45 million in 1995 and 1.75 million in 1996). This is down from a peak of 5.7 million in 1985. Nevertheless, there were still an estimated 652,000 Americans who used cocaine for the first time in 1995. Supplies remain abundant in nearly every city. Data indicate a leveling off in many urban areas: cocaine-related deaths were stable or up slightly in 9 of the 10 areas where such information was reported; emergency department (ED) mentions increased in only 4 of the 19 CEWG cities in the Drug Abuse Warning

National Institute on Drug Abuse (NIDA), Pub. No.13567, November 1999.

Network (DAWN); the percentage of treatment admissions for primary cocaine problems declined slightly or remained stable in twelve of the fourteen areas where data were available; and prices of cocaine remained stable in most areas. Although demographic data continue to show most cocaine users as older, inner-city crack addicts, isolated field reports indicate new groups of users: teenagers smoking crack with marijuana in blunts (cigars emptied of tobacco and refilled with marijuana, often in combination with another drug) in some cities, Hispanic crack users in Texas, and in the Atlanta area, middle-class suburban users of cocaine hydrochloride and female crack users in their thirties with no prior drug history.

Heroin

There has been an increasing trend in new heroin use since 1992, with an estimated 141,000 new heroin users in 1995. The estimated number of past month heroin users increased from 68,000 in 1993 to 216,000 in 1996. A large portion of these recent new users were smoking, snorting, or sniffing heroin, and most were under age 26. Additional quantitative indicators and field reports continue to suggest an increasing incidence of new users (snorters) in the younger age groups, often among women. In some areas, such as San Francisco, the recent initiates increasingly include members of the middle class. In Boston and Newark, heroin users are also found in suburban populations. One concern is that young heroin snorters may shift to needle injecting, because of increased tolerance, nasal soreness, or declining or unreliable purity. Injection use would place them at increased risk for HIV/ AIDS. Purity has, indeed, been declining or is inconsistent in some cities, such as Atlanta, Boston, and New York. Nevertheless, purity remains high, as does intranasal use, in the East and in some Midwestern cities, notably Chicago and Detroit. Supplies remain abundant. Aggressive marketing and price cutting has intensified in some cities, such as Boston, Detroit, and New York; heroin dealers often sell other drugs too, as in Miami, Minneapolis/St. Paul, St. Louis, and some Atlanta neighborhoods. Recent mortality figures have increased or are stable at elevated levels in five of the ten cities where trend data are available; rates of ED mentions have increased in eight of the nineteen cities in DAWN; and the percentage of those in treatment reporting heroin use has increased in eight of fourteen areas.

Marijuana

There were an estimated 2.4 million people who started using marijuana in 1995. The resurgence in marijuana use continues, especially among adolescents, with rates of ED mentions increasing in 10 cities, the percentage of treatment admissions increasing in thirteen areas, and the National Institute of Justice's Drug Use Forecasting (DUF) percentages increasing among juvenile arrestees at numerous sites. In several cities, such as Minneapolis/St. Paul, increasing treatment figures have been particularly notable among juveniles. Two factors may be contributing to the dramatic leap in adverse consequences: higher potency and the use of marijuana mixed with or in combination with other dangerous drugs. Marijuana cigarettes or blunts often include crack, a combination known by various street names, such as "3750s," "diablitos," "primos," "oolies," and "woolies." Joints and blunts are also frequently dipped in PCP and go by street names such as "happy sticks," "wicky sticks," "illies," "love boat," "wet," or "tical." Both types of combinations are reported in Boston, Chicago, and New York; the marijuana-crack combinations are also sold in St. Louis; and the marijuana-PCP combinations are reported in Philadelphia and parts of Texas. In several cities, such as Atlanta and Chicago, teenagers often drink malt liquor when smoking marijuana. Marijuana cigarettes are also sometimes dipped in embalming fluid, as reported in Boston (where they are known as "shermans") and areas of Texas.

Stimulants

Methamphetamine. In several western and midwestern cities, methamphetamine indicators, which had been steadily increasing for several years, appear mixed this reporting period. All indicators suggest increases in San Francisco and Seattle, while San Diego and Los Angeles indicators show stable or slightly declining trends. However, it is too soon to predict that the indicators in those areas have peaked. Increased methamphetamine availability and use is sporadically reported in diverse areas of the country, particularly rural areas, prompting some concern about its spread outside of the areas of endemic use (the west coast). Most methamphetamine comes from large-scale Mexican operations. Recent seizures in Florida have included powder cocaine, heroin, and flunitrazepam in the same shipment with methamphetamine. Additionally, local labs remain common, with seizures increasing in areas such as Seattle, Arizona, and rural Georgia, Michigan and Missouri. All four routes of administration—injecting, snorting, smoking (including "chasing the dragon" in San Francisco), and oral ingestion—are used but vary from city to city. Reports of violence related to methamphetamine persist in Honolulu and are now also occurring in Seattle.

Other Stimulants. Methylphenidate (Ritalin) abuse continues among heroin users in Chicago and adolescents in Detroit. Methcathinone ("cat" or "goobs") has been reported in several indicators in Detroit and Michigan's Upper Peninsula, including treatment admissions and one death in Detroit. Ephedrine-based products sold at convenience stores, truck stops, and health food stores are common among adolescents in Atlanta, Detroit, Minneapolis/St. Paul, and Texas. New York State recently banned the sale of such products in an attempt to curb escalating abuse among adolescents. Methylenedioxymethamphetamine (MDMA or "ecstasy") use was reported most often among young adults and adolescents at clubs, raves, and rock concerts in Atlanta, Miami, St. Louis, Seattle, and areas of Texas.

Depressants

Use of gamma hydroxybutrate (GHB) in the club scene is becoming more widespread throughout the country, notably in Atlanta, Detroit, Honolulu, Miami, New York City (where it is also reportedly used by fashion models), Phoenix, and Texas. Ketamine ("Special K") use in nightclubs has also been reported in several cities. A mixture of GHB, ketamine, and alcohol, called "Special K-lude" because of the similar effects produced by methaqualone (Quaalude), is reported in New York City. Flunitrazepam (Rohypnol) use continues in many areas of the country (with the exception of the Northeast), most notably in Texas and Florida. Its widespread availability has declined, however, since the Federal ban on its importation. Other medications from the same manufacturer are now being sold and abused as "roofies" in Miami, Minnesota, and Texas. These drugs include clonazepam (another pharmaceutical benzodiazepine, marketed in Mexico as Rivotril), which has the same distinguishing manufacturer's imprint as flunitrazepam. Clonazepam (marketed in the United States as Klonopin) is also used by addicts in Minneapolis/St. Paul and Atlanta to enhance the effects of methadone and other opiates.

Hallucinogens

According to field reports in numerous areas, such as Texas, Boston, Chicago, New York, Philadelphia, St. Louis, and Washington, D.C., phencyclidine (PCP) is often used in combination with other drugs. A frequently reported combination is joints or blunts containing marijuana mixed with or dipped into PCP. In other cities, such as Los Angeles and New Orleans, PCP is commonly purchased as a predipped cigarette. In New York City, PCP is combined with crack in "spaceballs." PCP ED mentions increased in 10 cities, but rates remain relatively low. Lysergic acid diethylamide (LSD) remains widely available in most CEWG cities, especially in suburban and rural areas. Use of psilocybin mushrooms has also been reported among adolescents and young adults in Boston, Minneapolis/St. Paul, and Philadelphia.

Perceived Risk and Availability of Drugs

More than half of youths age 12-17 reported that marijuana was easy to obtain in 1996, and about one quarter reported that heroin was easy to obtain. Fifteen percent of youths reported being approached by someone selling drugs in the month prior to being surveyed. In addition to demonstrating the accessibility of illicit drugs, youths showed a decrease in their perception of the risk in using illicit drugs. The percentage of youths who perceived great risk in using cocaine once a month decreased from 63 percent in 1994 to 54 percent in 1996. The percent of youths age 12-17 that perceived great risk in using marijuana once a month decreased from 1990 (40 percent) to 1994 (33 percent), but remained level from 1994 to 1996.

Notes

NHSDA is an annual survey conducted by the Substance Abuse and Mental Health Services Administration. Copies of the latest survey are available from the National Clearinghouse for Alcohol and Drug Information at 1-800-729-6686.

CEWG's most recent report is Epidemiologic Trends in Drug Abuse, Volumes I and II, December 1996.

The most recent available DAWN emergency room data are for 1995. Increases noted are for 1994 versus 1995 data and are included only when they are reliable. DAWN is conducted by the Substance Abuse and Mental Health Services Administration. Copies of the latest DAWN data are available from the National Clearinghouse for Alcohol and Drug Information at 1-800-729-6686.

Chapter 3

Prescription Drug Abuse Trends

Since millions of prescription pills enter the illicit drug market every year, some see a double standard in drug enforcement because of grants of leniency towards the doctors and their rich clientele who abuse the drugs (Dan Weikel, "Prescription Fraud: Abusing the System," *Los Angeles Times*, August 18, 1996, p. A1; Dan Weikel, "Prescription Fraud: Abusing the System," *Los Angeles Times* (Washington Edition), August 19, 1996, p. A1).

The DEA estimated that prescription drugs were sold for about $25 billion in 1993 in the illegal drug market, compared to an estimate of $31 billion spent that year on cocaine, including crack. About 2.6 million people in the U.S. use prescription drugs for "non-medical reasons"—more than the estimated number of users of heroin, crack and cocaine, according to surveys by the National Institute on Drug Abuse. According to the Drug Abuse Warning Network, prescription painkillers, sedatives, stimulants and tranquilizers are about 75% of the top 20 drugs mentioned in emergency room episodes each year.

The high likelihood of accurate dosage, purity, and lower price of prescription pills make them an attractive alternative to street drugs. Although some prescription drugs are smuggled into the country or stolen from distributors, a large portion comes from medical offices and pharmacies. The American Medical Association estimates that 1%

to 1.5% of physicians dishonestly prescribe drugs, and another 5% are grossly negligent in their prescribing. At the "other end of the stethoscope" are "doctor shoppers," who deceive conscientious doctors with fake injuries or ailments to get prescriptions. One example is Vicki J. Renalso, who tricked 42 San Diego area doctors and 26 pharmacies into giving her codeine tablets during an eight-month period.

In view of this cornucopia of illegally distributed "legal" painkillers, stimulants and tranquilizers, many narcotics agents, politicians, insurance companies, and others feel that the drug war on prescription fraud has only been a skirmish. Nationally, the federal government spends $13 billion to $14 billion on the war on drugs, but only $70 million goes to the DEA to investigate prescription drug offenses. "There are two kinds of justice in this system, one for doctors, and one for everybody else," said Paul K. King, a former California narcotics agent who investigated prescription fraud in Los Angeles County.

Pursuing doctors and pharmaceutical companies doesn't make the headlines that other drug arrests do. "There is just no glory in it—no guns, no piles of coke, and no bundles of cash to stack up for the TV cameras," said Special Agent Walter Allen III of the California Bureau of Narcotic Enforcement. Even when action is taken, the results are often small. In California, less than two dozen doctors, dentists and pharmacists are prosecuted annually for prescription fraud.

Even if convicted, sentences for doctors are small, compared to those implicated in the sale of cocaine, opiates, marijuana, etc. One case is that of Dr. Eric C. Tucker, who issued more than 7,000 questionable prescriptions for the stimulant Preludin® and another 7,600 for Dilaudid®. More Dilaudid®, sometimes called "drugstore heroin," was distributed from Tucker's office every year than from the LAC-USC Medical Center, the West Coast's largest public hospital. Tucker, then 59, pleaded guilty to two felony counts and lost his medical license, but was only sentenced to eight days in jail. In contrast, Daniel G. Siemianowski, who was prosecuted in Los Angeles at about the same time as Tucker, having been arrested with about four ounces of crack, a small fraction of the quantity of drugs the doctor distributed, received a year in prison.

Following the death of Hollywood producer Don Simpson, who died in January from a mix of cocaine and 20 prescription drugs, prescription abuse has gotten more attention in Los Angeles. "Abuse of prescription drugs is a serious problem in our society, but nobody pays attention until somebody big and powerful like Don Simpson drops dead," said Steve Simmons, the California Medical Board's senior investigator on the case. On August 16, federal law enforcement officials raided the offices of two doctors of more than a dozen suspected of unlawfully supplying Simpson with prescription drugs, and the home of another doctor was searched.

Assistant U.S. Attorney Alka Sager said that of the estimated 10 prescription fraud cases that she handled since 1990, one doctor received a short sentence; the rest pleaded guilty and were placed on probation. Part of the problem, according to law enforcement officials, is that medical practitioners are usually charged under laws that carry low prison penalties. Prosecutors say that the way the laws are written allows health care professionals to escape serious drug-trafficking charges if they have written a prescription, no matter how fraudulent.

Disciplinary records from state pharmacy and medical boards also reveal leniency to those who violate criminal and professional codes. Records show that about 75% of physicians convicted of prescription drug crime kept their license. Officials acknowledge the problems, but say that reforms made since the early 1990s ameliorate the problem. California law now requires the automatic suspensions of medical, dental and pharmacy licenses for such professionals if one is convicted of a felony. Medical and pharmacy board investigators added that they are seeking more court orders to suspend licenses after someone is arrested.

Chapter 4

Drug Use among American Teens

Drug Use Shows Slight Downward Trend

The prevalence of illicit drug use among America's teenagers dropped slightly in 1998. The decrease follows a leveling off in 1997, and suggests that the increasing use of drugs by teenagers that marked most of the 1990s may have begun to turn around.

Data compiled by the NIDA-supported Monitoring the Future study show that, overall, teenagers were less likely to use marijuana, hallucinogens, or inhalants last year than they had been the year before. Heroin use leveled off in 1998, following several years of slight increases. Among all illicit drugs included in the survey, only crack and tranquilizers were used by a significantly higher percentage of teenagers in any grade in 1998 than in 1997, according to the study.

The Monitoring the Future study, funded by NIDA and conducted annually by the Institute for Social Research at the University of Michigan in Ann Arbor, surveyed nearly 50,000 students—including equal numbers of males and females—in 8th, 10th, and 12th grades at more than 420 public and private schools across the country. Data from the most recent survey, conducted in the spring of 1998, were released by Secretary of Health and Human Services Dr. Donna E. Shalala at a press conference in December 1998.

This chapter includes text from "Drug Use among America's Teenagers Shows Slight Downward Trend," *NIDA Notes,* 1998 and "High School and Youth Trends," National Institute on Drug Abuse (NIDA), March 1999.

"These new findings are encouraging, since they represent a leveling off in teens' use of illicit drugs," Secretary Shalala said. "It's not easy to convince our young people that drug use is illegal, dangerous, and wrong, but it is absolutely critical to their future."

The survey also asked students about the risks associated with drug use. The percentage of students who said there is a "great risk" associated with drug use rose or remained unchanged for most illicit drugs.

"We seem to be in the middle of a turnaround in young people's use of most kinds of illicit drugs following an earlier period of sustained increases," Dr. Lloyd Johnston, principal investigator for the study, said. "These behaviors sometimes change very slowly, and often only after there has been some reassessment by young people of how dangerous these various drugs are. Such reassessment now appears to be occurring for many drugs, but very gradually."

Teenagers now are responding to increased knowledge of the facts about illicit drug use, NIDA Director Dr. Alan I. Leshner said. "The more that scientific research helps us understand what addiction is and how illicit drugs change the brain and behavior, the better able students and others will be to make informed decisions. The findings from this year's report suggest that many of our educational efforts are beginning to pay off," Dr. Leshner said.

Highlights of the 1998 Monitoring the Future Study

- **Marijuana.** Use declined among all three grades, and this accounted for most of the overall decline in 1998 drug use. Eighth-grade use declined for the second successive year. Nonetheless, marijuana use is still prevalent: 22 percent of 8th-graders and nearly half of 12th-graders surveyed reported that they have tried marijuana. However, the perceived risk of marijuana use has increased among 8th-graders.

- **Heroin.** Although use did not decline, it remained unchanged among all students in 1998: 1.3 percent of 8th-graders, 1.4 percent of 10th-graders, and 1.0 percent of 12th-graders reported using heroin at least once during the previous 12 months. This leveling in heroin use follows a rise in perceived risk over the previous 2 years.

- **Stimulants.** Use decreased for the second consecutive year to 7.2 percent among 8th-graders, showed a 1-year drop to 10.7 percent among 10th-graders, and leveled off at 10.1 percent among 12th-graders.

- **Hallucinogens.** Overall use decreased slightly at all grade levels—to 3.4 percent among 8th- graders, 6.9 percent among 10th-graders, and 9.0 percent among 12th-graders. Decreases in use of MDMA, or ecstasy, were recorded for the second year in a row for 10th- and 12th-grade students.

- **Crack Cocaine.** Among 8th-graders, use of crack cocaine increased to its highest level, 2.1 percent, since 1991, when the drug was first included in the 8th grade survey. Slight increases—also to their highest levels in recent years—were reported for crack use by 10th-graders, to 2.5 percent, and 12th-graders, to 2.5 percent.

- **Inhalants.** Use declined among all students for the third consecutive year. In 1998, 11.1 percent of 8th-graders, 8.0 percent of 10th-graders, and 6.2 percent of 12th-graders reported using inhalants at least once in the past year. This decrease follows an upward shift in 1996 in the proportion of students associating great risk with inhalant use.

- **Gender.** Overall, higher percentages of males than females reported using illicit drugs at least once during the previous year. As has been the case since 1991—the first year for which data are available—younger girls are more likely than boys to use illicit drugs other than marijuana, primarily due to their greater use of stimulants and tranquilizers; 12.1 percent of 8th-grade girls and 9.6 percent of boys reported using drugs other than marijuana. In 10th grade, 17.5 percent of girls and 15.6 percent of boys reported using drugs other than marijuana at least once during the previous year. Among 12th-graders, 21.7 percent of boys and 18.0 percent of girls reported using drugs other than marijuana.

—by Patrick Zickler, NIDA NOTES Staff Writer

Monitoring the Future Study (MTF)

Since 1975, the MTF has annually measured the extent of drug abuse among high school seniors. The survey was expanded in 1991 to include 8th- and 10th-grade students. It is funded by NIDA and is conducted by the University of Michigan's Institute for Social Research.

- Among the graduating class of 1997, 54.3 percent of students had used an illicit drug by the time they reached their senior year of high school, continuing an upward trend from 40.7 in 1992 but still far below the peak of 65.6 percent in 1981.

- After increasing significantly between 1992 and 1996, the use of illegal drugs by adolescents leveled off for most drugs in 1997. Illicit drug use among 8th graders remained stable or decreased for some substances in 1997. Use among 10th- and 12th-graders remained stable, however, lifetime use of some substances increased.

- Use of any illicit drug in the past year (annual use) by seniors increased from 27.1 percent in 1992 to 42.4 percent in 1997 after steadily declining from a peak of 54.2 percent in 1979. The percentage of seniors who had used an illicit drug within the past month (current use) increased from 14.4 percent in 1992 to 26.2 percent in 1997.

Students' Attitudes and Perceptions

- Adolescents perception of the harmfulness of drugs is a key predictor of increases and decreases in their subsequent use of drugs. For most drugs, perceived risk of harm remained stable between 1996 and 1997.

- In 1997, 43.1 percent of 8th-graders, 31.9 percent 10th-graders, and 24.7 percent of 12th-graders believed that people are at great risk of harming themselves by smoking marijuana occasionally.

- In 1997, 54.2 percent of 8th-graders, 80.5 percent of 10th-graders, and 89.6 percent of seniors said it would be "very easy" or "fairly easy" for them to get marijuana.

- There was an increase in the percentage of 8th-graders saying there is great risk in having five or more drinks once or twice each weekend (heavy drinking), increasing from 51.8 percent in 1996 to 55.6 percent in 1997.

- Moving in the wrong direction, however, are attitudes about drinking among 12th graders, specifically a decrease in the percentage of seniors saying there is great risk in heavy drinking (49.5 percent in 1996 to 43.0 percent in 1997).

For More Information

Additional information about the Monitoring the Future study can be obtained by calling NIDA Infofax at 1-888-NIH-NIDA (644-6432) or by accessing NIDA's home page on the World Wide Web at http://www.nida.nih.gov/ and clicking on Information on Drugs of Abuse. Information is also available from the Monitoring the Future home page at the Institute for Social Research at the University of Michigan: http://www.monitoringthefuture.org.

Chapter 5

Trends in Workplace Substance Abuse

Incidence of Substance Abuse in the Workplace

- Eight percent of full time workers employed as adults are current users of illicit drugs.[1]

    - The rate of illicit drug use among full-time workers is higher for:[1]

    - Construction workers: 16%

    - Food preparation, waitstaff, and bartenders: 11%

    - Handlers, helpers, or laborers: 11%

    - Machine operators or inspectors: 11%

- About 8% of the workforce are heavy drinkers, with significantly higher rates among:[1]

    - Construction workers: 17.6%

    - Food preparation, waitstaff, and bartenders: 12%

    - Handlers, helpers, or laborers: 16%

    - Machine operators or inspectors: 14%

- Seventeen percent of employees surveyed across five different work sites reported situations that imply prescription drug misuse.[2]

Center for Substance Abuse Prevention (CSAP), Substance Abuse and Mental Health Services Administration (SAMHSA), November 1998.

39

- Small businesses are more likely to have problems with illicit drugs.[3]

  - Employees in companies with fewer than 25 employees are twice as likely to use illicit drugs as employees in larger companies.

  - Illicit drug use among employees is linked to a lack of workplace drug policies; illicit drug users were less likely than employees from large establishments to report that their employer provided information, had written policies, or provided access to an employee assistance program (EAP).

- Fifteen percent of illicit drug users and 6% of heavy alcohol users report that they had gone to work high or a little drunk in the past year.[4]

- Seventy-five percent of people calling a cocaine hotline said they sometimes used cocaine on the job; 25% said they took cocaine on the job daily.[5]

- In a survey of 1,200 employees at five different work sites, 18% of persons reporting alcohol use and 12% of illicit drug users reported that their performance declined due to alcohol or illicit drug use.[2]

- Comprehensive data on the specific impact of workplace substance abuse are still being studied. Preliminary findings are compelling:[6]

  - Drug-using employees at GM average 40 days of sick leave each year, compared with 4.5 days for nonusers.

  - Employees testing positive on pre-employment drug tests at Utah Power & Light were five times more likely to be involved in a workplace accident than those who tested negative.

  - The State of Wisconsin estimates that expenses and losses related to substance abuse average 25% of the salary of each worker affected.

Cost to Employers of Employees with a Diagnosed Chemical Dependency Problem

- Alcoholism causes 500 million lost workdays each year.[6]

- Alcoholics are expensive to businesses in several different ways:[5]

  - Workplace accident rates are two or three times higher than normal;

40

- Alcoholics are five times more likely to file a worker's compensation claim; and

- Alcoholics are 2.5 times more likely to have absences of eight days or more.

- Employees diagnosed with a chemical dependency problem in a large manufacturing plant were found to have:[7]

  - Six times the number of absences;

  - Seven times the number of days missed from work; and

  - Higher incidence of injuries, hypertension, and mental disorders.

Workplace Factors Associated with Substance Use/ Alcohol Abuse

- Alienating work seems to increase problem drinking indirectly through contribution to job dissatisfaction, and then only when workers believe that alcohol is "an important and efficacious coping mechanism."[8]

- In data from a large assembly plant, positive team attitudes and positive supervisor relations are associated with less tolerance for drinking. Also, employees involved in teams that are more effective showed less permissive drinking norms.[9]

References

1. Hoffman, J.P.; Brittingham, A.; and Larison, C. (1996). Drug use among U.S. workers: Prevalence and trends by occupation and industry categories. Number DHHS Publ. No. (SMA) 96-3089. Rockville, MD: SAMHSA, Office of Applied Studies.

2. French, M.T.; Zarkin, G.A.; Hartwell, T.D.; and Bray, J.W. (1995). Prevalence and consequences of smoking, alcohol use, and illicit drug use at five worksites. *Public Health Rep.* 110:593-599.

3. Hoffman, J.P.; Larison, C.; and Sanderson, A. (1997). An analysis of worker drug use and workplace policies and programs. Rockville, MD, Substance Abuse and Mental Health Services Administration, Office of Applied Studies, A-2 Analytic Series.

4. National Household Survey on Drug Abuse: Main Findings 1991 (1993). Substance Abuse and Mental Health Services Administration, Rockville, MD.

5. "Drug abuse in the workplace: An employer's guide for prevention." *EAP Digest*.

6. Department of Labor. (1998). "Working partners for an alcohol- and drug-free American workplace," (http://www.dol.gov/dol/asp).

7. Bross, M.H.; Pace, S.K.; and Cronin, I.H. (1992). Chemical dependence: Analysis of work absenteeism and associated mental illness. *Journal of Occupational Medicine* 34(1):16-19.

8. Greenberg, E.S.; and Grunberg, L. (1995). Work alienation and problem alcohol behavior. *Journal of Health and Social Behavior* 36(1):83-102.

9. Delaney, W.P. and Ames, G. (1995). Work team attitudes, drinking norms, and workplace drinking. *The Journal of Drug Issues* 25(2):275-290.

Chapter 6

Pregnancy and Drug Use Trends

Drug abuse can occur at any stage in a woman's life. Of women who use illicit drugs, however, about half are in the childbearing age group of 15 to 44. In 1992/1993, NIDA conducted a nationwide hospital survey to determine the extent of drug abuse among pregnant women in the United States. This National Pregnancy and Health Survey still provides the most recent national data available.

The survey found that of the 4 million women who gave birth during the period, 757,000 women drank alcohol products and 820,000 women smoked cigarettes during their pregnancies. There was a strong link among cigarette, alcohol, and illegal drug use. Thirty-two percent of those who reported use of one drug also smoked cigarettes and drank alcohol.

Survey results showed that 221,000 women used illegal drugs during their pregnancies that year, with marijuana and cocaine being the most prevalent: 119,000 women reported use of marijuana and 45,000 reported use of cocaine. The survey estimated that the number of babies born to these women was 222,000, a close parallel to the number of mothers. Generally, rates of any illegal drug use were higher in women who were not married, had less than 16 years of formal education, were not working, and relied on some public source of funding to pay for their hospital stay.

Despite a generally decreasing trend in the use of drugs from 3 months before pregnancy and through the pregnancy, women did not discontinue drug use. However, findings from other NIDA research

National Institute on Drug Abuse (NIDA), Pub. No.13568, November 1999.

on women in treatment, for example, indicate that once women are successfully detoxified and enrolled in a treatment program, their motivator to stay drug free is their children.

The survey also pointed to issues of prevalence differences among ethnic groups. While the rates of illegal substance abuse were higher for African Americans, the estimated number of white women using drugs during pregnancy was larger at 113,000 than the number of African-American women at 75,000, or Hispanic women at 28,000.

As for the legal drugs, estimates of alcohol use were also highest among white women at about 588,000, compared to 105,000 among African-American women, and 54,000 among Hispanic women. Whites had the highest rates of cigarette use as well: 632,000 compared with 132,000 for African Americans and 36,000 for Hispanics.

Rates of marijuana use were highest among those under 25 and rates of cocaine use were higher among those 25 and older.

Note

To receive a complete copy of NIDA's National Pregnancy and Health Survey, call the National Clearinghouse for Alcohol and Drug Information (NCADI) at 1-800-729-6686. Information on general drug use trends among women is available from NCADI through Substance Abuse Among Women in the United States, printed in 1997 by the Substance Abuse and Mental Health Administration Office of Applied Studies, and other publications.

## Chapter 7

The Controlled Substances Act

The Controlled Substances Act (CSA), Title II of the Comprehensive Drug Abuse Prevention and Control Act of 1970, is the legal foundation of the government's fight against abuse of drugs and other substances. This law is a consolidation of numerous laws regulating the manufacture and distribution of narcotics, stimulants, depressants, hallucinogens, anabolic steroids, and chemicals used in the illicit production of controlled substances.

Controlling Drugs or Other Substances

Formal Scheduling

The CSA places all substances which were in some manner regulated under existing Federal law into one of five schedules. This placement is based upon the substance's medical use, potential for abuse, and safety or dependence liability. The Act also provides a mechanism for substances to be controlled, or added to a schedule; decontrolled, or removed from control; and rescheduled or transferred from one schedule to another. The procedure for these actions is found in Section 201 of the Act (21 U.S.C. 811).

Proceedings to add, delete, or change the schedule of a drug or other substance may be initiated by the Drug Enforcement Administration (DEA), the Department of Health and Human Services (HHS), or by

Excerpted from *Drugs of Abuse*, U.S. Department of Justice, Drug Enforcement Administration, 1997.

petition from any interested party: the manufacturer of a drug, a medical society or association, a pharmacy association, a public interest group concerned with drug abuse, a state or local government agency, or an individual citizen. When a petition is received by DEA, the agency begins its own investigation of the drug.

The agency also may begin an investigation of a drug at any time based upon information received from law enforcement laboratories, state and local law enforcement and regulatory agencies, or other sources of information.

Once DEA has collected the necessary data, the Administrator of DEA, by authority of the Attorney General, requests from HHS a scientific and medical evaluation and recommendation as to whether the drug or other substance should be controlled or removed from control. This request is sent to the Assistant Secretary of Health of HHS. HHS solicits information from the Commissioner of the Food and Drug Administration (FDA), evaluations and recommendations from the National Institute on Drug Abuse, and on occasion from the scientific and medical community at large. The Assistant Secretary, by authority of the Secretary, compiles the information and transmits back to DEA a medical and scientific evaluation regarding the drug or other substance, a recommendation as to whether the drug should be controlled, and in what schedule it should be placed.

The medical and scientific evaluations are binding on DEA with respect to scientific and medical matters. The recommendation on scheduling is binding only to the extent that if HHS recommends that the substance not be controlled, DEA may not control the substance.

Once DEA has received the scientific and medical evaluation from HHS, the Administrator will evaluate all available data and make a final decision whether to propose that a drug or other substance should be controlled and into which schedule it should be placed.

The threshold issue is whether the drug or other substance has potential for abuse. If a drug does not have a potential for abuse, it cannot be controlled. Although the term "potential for abuse" is not defined in the CSA, there is much discussion of the term in the legislative history of the Act. The following items are indicators that a drug or other substance has a potential for abuse:

1. There is evidence that individuals are taking the drug or other substance in amounts sufficient to create a hazard to their health or to the safety of other individuals or to the community; or

2. There is significant diversion of the drug or other substance from legitimate drug channels; or

3. Individuals are taking the drug or other substance on their own initiative rather than on the basis of medical advice from a practitioner licensed by law to administer such drugs; or

4. The drug is a new drug so related in its action to a drug or other substance already listed as having a potential for abuse to make it likely that the drug will have the same potential for abuse as such drugs, thus making it reasonable to assume that there may be significant diversions from legitimate channels, significant use contrary to or without medical advice, or that it has a substantial capability of creating hazards to the health of the user or to the safety of the community. Of course, evidence of actual abuse of a substance is indicative that a drug has a potential for abuse.

In determining into which schedule a drug or other substance should be placed, or whether a substance should be decontrolled or rescheduled, certain factors are required to be considered. Specific findings are not required for each factor. These factors are listed in Section 201 (c), [21 U.S.C. 811 (c)], of the CSA and are as follows:

1. The drug's actual or relative potential for abuse.

2. Scientific evidence of the drug's pharmacological effects. The state of knowledge with respect to the effects of a specific drug is, of course, a major consideration. For example, it is vital to know whether or not a drug has a hallucinogenic effect if it is to be controlled because of that. The best available knowledge of the pharmacological properties of a drug should be considered.

3. The state of current scientific knowledge regarding the substance. Criteria (2) and (3) are closely related. However, (2) is primarily concerned with pharmacological effects and (3) deals with all scientific knowledge with respect to the substance.

4. Its history and current pattern of abuse. To determine whether or not a drug should be controlled, it is important to know the pattern of abuse of that substance, including the socioeconomic

characteristics of the segments of the population involved in such abuse.

5. The scope, duration, and significance of abuse. In evaluating existing abuse, the Administrator must know not only the pattern of abuse but whether the abuse is widespread. In reaching his decision, the Administrator should consider the economics of regulation and enforcement attendant to such a decision. In addition, he should be aware of the social significance and impact of such a decision upon those people, especially the young, that would be affected by it.

6. What, if any, risk there is to the public health. If a drug creates dangers to the public health, in addition to or because of its abuse potential, then these dangers must also be considered by the Administrator.

7. The drug's psychic or physiological dependence liability. There must be an assessment of the extent to which a drug is physically addictive or psychologically habit-forming, if such information is known.

8. Whether the substance is an immediate precursor of a substance already controlled. The CSA allows inclusion of immediate precursors on this basis alone into the appropriate schedule and thus safeguards against possibilities of clandestine manufacture.

After considering the above listed factors, the Administrator must make specific findings concerning the drug or other substance. This will determine into which schedule the drug or other substance will be placed. These schedules are established by the CSA. They are as follows:

Schedule I

- The drug or other substance has a high potential for abuse.

- The drug or other substance has no currently accepted medical use in treatment in the United States.

- There is a lack of accepted safety for use of the drug or other substance under medical supervision.

- Some Schedule I substances are heroin, LSD, marijuana, and methaqualone.

Schedule II

- The drug or other substance has a high potential for abuse.
- The drug or other substance has a currently accepted medical use in treatment in the United States or a currently accepted medical use with severe restrictions.
- Abuse of the drug or other substance may lead to severe psychological or physical dependence.
- Schedule II substances include morphine, PCP, cocaine, methadone, and methamphetamine.

Schedule III

- The drug or other substance has a potential for abuse less than the drugs or other substances in Schedules I and II.
- The drug or other substance has a currently accepted medical use in treatment in the United States.
- Abuse of the drug or other substance may lead to moderate or low physical dependence or high psychological dependence.
- Anabolic steroids, codeine, and hydrocodone with aspirin or Tylenol®, and some barbiturates are Schedule III substances.

Schedule IV

- The drug or other substance has a low potential for abuse relative to the drugs or other substances in Schedule III.
- The drug or other substance has a currently accepted medical use in treatment in the United States.
- Abuse of the drug or other substance may lead to limited physical dependence or psychological dependence relative to the drugs or other substances in Schedule III.
- Included in Schedule IV are Darvon®, Talwin®, Equanil®, Valium® and Xanax®.

Schedule V

- The drug or other substance has a low potential for abuse relative to the drugs or other substances in Schedule IV.
- The drug or other substance has a currently accepted medical use in treatment in the United States.

- Abuse of the drug or other substances may lead to limited physical dependence or psychological dependence relative to the drugs or other substances in Schedule IV.

- Over-the-counter cough medicines with codeine are classified in Schedule V.

When the Administrator of DEA has determined that a drug or other substance should be controlled, decontrolled, or rescheduled, a proposal to take action is published in the *Federal Register*. The proposal invites all interested persons to file comments with DEA. Affected parties may also request a hearing with DEA. If no hearing is requested, DEA will evaluate all comments received and publish a final order in the *Federal Register*, controlling the drug as proposed or with modifications based upon the written comments filed. This order will set the effective dates for imposing the various requirements imposed under the CSA.

If a hearing is requested, DEA will enter into discussions with the party or parties requesting a hearing in an attempt to narrow the issue for litigation. If necessary, a hearing will then be held before an Administrative Law Judge. The judge will take evidence on factual issues and hear arguments on legal questions regarding the control of the drug. Depending on the scope and complexity of the issues, the hearing may be brief or quite extensive. The Administrative Law Judge, at the close of the hearing, prepares findings of fact and conclusions of law and a recommended decision which is submitted to the Administrator of DEA. The Administrator will review these documents, as well as the underlying material, and prepare his/her own findings of fact and conclusions of law (which may or may not be the same as those drafted by the Administrative Law Judge). The Administrator then publishes a final order in the *Federal Register* either scheduling the drug or other substance or declining to do so.

Once the final order is published in the *Federal Register*, interested parties have 30 days to appeal to a U.S. Court of Appeals to challenge the order. Findings of fact by the Administrator are deemed conclusive if supported by "substantial evidence." The order imposing controls is not stayed during the appeal, however, unless so ordered by the Court.

Emergency or Temporary Scheduling

The CSA was amended by the Comprehensive Crime Control Act of 1984. This Act included a provision which allows the Administrator of DEA to place a substance, on a temporary basis, into Schedule I when necessary to avoid an imminent hazard to the public safety.

This emergency scheduling authority permits the scheduling of a substance which is not currently controlled, is being abused, and is a risk to the public health while the formal rule making procedures described in the CSA are being conducted. This emergency scheduling applies only to substances with no accepted medical use. A temporary scheduling order may be issued for one year with a possible extension of up to six months if formal scheduling procedures have been initiated. The proposal and order are published in the *Federal Register* as are the proposals and orders for formal scheduling. [21 U.S.C. 811 (1)]

Controlled Substance Analogues

A new class of substances was created by the Anti-Drug Abuse Act of 1986. Controlled substance analogues are substances which are not controlled substances, but may be found in the illicit traffic. They are structurally or pharmacologically similar to Schedule I or II controlled substances and have no legitimate medical use. A substance which meets the definition of a controlled substance analogue and is intended for human consumption is treated under the CSA as if it were a controlled substance in Schedule I.

International Treaty Obligations

U. S. treaty obligations may require that a drug or other substance be controlled under the CSA, or rescheduled if existing controls are less stringent than those required by a treaty. The procedures for these scheduling actions are found in Section 201 (d) of the Act. [21 U.S.C. 811 (d)]

The United States is a party to the Single Convention on Narcotic Drugs of 1961, designed to establish effective control over international and domestic traffic in narcotics, coca leaf, cocaine, and cannabis. A second treaty, the Convention on Psychotropic Substances of 1971, which entered into force in 1976, is designed to establish comparable control over stimulants, depressants, and hallucinogens. Congress ratified this treaty in 1980.

Regulation

The CSA creates a closed system of distribution for those authorized to handle controlled substances. The cornerstone of this system is the registration of all those authorized by DEA to handle controlled substances. All individuals and firms that are registered are required to maintain complete and accurate inventories and records of all transactions involving controlled substances, as well as security for the storage of controlled substances.

Registration

Any person who handles or intends to handle controlled substances must obtain a registration issued by DEA. A unique number is assigned to each legitimate handler of controlled drugs: importer, exporter, manufacturer, distributor, hospital, pharmacy, practitioner, and researcher. This number must be made available to the supplier by the customer prior to the purchase of a controlled substance. Thus, the opportunity for unauthorized transactions is greatly diminished.

Recordkeeping

The CSA requires that complete and accurate records be kept of all quantities of controlled substances manufactured, purchased, and sold. Each substance must be inventoried every two years. Some limited exceptions to the recordkeeping requirements may apply to certain categories of registrants.

From these records it is possible to trace the flow of any drug from the time it is first imported or manufactured through the distribution level, to the pharmacy or hospital that dispensed it, and then to the actual patient who received the drug. The mere existence of this requirement is sufficient to discourage many forms of diversion. It actually serves large drug corporations as an internal check to uncover diversion, such as pilferage by employees.

There is one distinction between scheduled items for recordkeeping requirements. Records for Schedule I and II drugs must be kept separate from all other records of the handler; records for Schedule III, IV, and V substances must be kept in a "readily retrievable" form. The former method allows for more expeditious investigations involving the highly abusable substances in Schedules I and II.

Distribution

The keeping of records is required for distribution of a controlled substance from one manufacturer to another, from manufacturer to distributor, and from distributor to dispenser. In the case of Schedule I and II drugs, the supplier must have a special order form from the customer. This order form (DEA Form 222) is issued by DEA only to persons who are properly registered to handle Schedules I and II. The form is preprinted with the name and address of the customer. The drugs must be shipped to this name and address. The use of this device is a special reinforcement of the registration requirement; it makes doubly certain that only authorized individuals may obtain Schedule I and II drugs. Another benefit of the form is the special monitoring it permits. The form is issued in triplicate: the customer keeps one copy; two copies go to the supplier who, after filling the order, keeps a copy and forwards the third copy to the nearest DEA office.

For drugs in Schedules III, IV, and V, no order form is necessary. The supplier in each case, however, is under an obligation to verify the authenticity of the customer. The supplier is held fully accountable for any drugs which are shipped to a purchaser who does not have a valid registration.

Manufacturers must submit periodic reports of the Schedule I and II controlled substances they produce in bulk and dosage forms. They also report the manufactured quantity and form of each narcotic substance listed in Schedules III, IV, and V, as well as the quantity of synthesized psychotropic substances listed in Schedules I, II, III, and IV. Distributors of controlled substances must report the quantity and form of all their transactions of controlled drugs listed in Schedules I and II and narcotics listed in Schedule III. Both manufacturers and distributors are required to provide reports of their annual inventories of these controlled substances. This data is entered into a system called the Automated Reports and Consolidated Orders System (ARCOS). It enables DEA to monitor the distribution of controlled substances throughout the country, and to identify retail level registrants that receive unusual quantities of controlled substances.

Dispensing to Patients

The dispensing of a controlled substance is the delivery of the controlled substance to the ultimate user, who may be a patient or research subject. Special control mechanisms operate here as well. Schedule I drugs are those which have no currently accepted medical use in the United States; they may, therefore, be used in the United States only in research situations. They generally are supplied by only a limited number of firms to properly registered and qualified researchers. Controlled substances may be dispensed by a practitioner by direct administration, by prescription, or by dispensing from office supplies.

Records must be maintained by the practitioner of all dispensing of controlled substances from office supplies and of certain administrations. The CSA does not require the practitioner to maintain copies of prescriptions, but certain states require the use of multiple copy prescriptions for Schedule II and other specified controlled substances.

The determination to place drugs on prescription is within the jurisdiction of the FDA. Unlike other prescription drugs, however, controlled substances are subject to additional restrictions. Schedule II prescription orders must be written and signed by the practitioner; they may not be telephoned into the pharmacy except in an emergency. In addition, a prescription for a Schedule II drug may not be refilled; the patient must see the practitioner again in order to obtain more drugs. For Schedule III and IV drugs, the prescription order may be either written or oral (that is, by telephone to the pharmacy). In addition, the patient may (if authorized by the practitioner) have the prescription refilled up to five times and at anytime within six months from the date of the initial dispensing.

Schedule V includes some prescription drugs and many over-the-counter narcotic preparations, including antitussives and antidiarrheals. Even here, however, the law imposes restrictions beyond those normally required for the over-the-counter sales; for example, the patient must be at least 18 years of age, must offer some form of identification, and have his or her name entered into a special log maintained by the pharmacist as part of a special record.

Quotas

DEA limits the quantity of Schedule I and II controlled substances which may be produced in the United States in any given calendar year. By utilizing available data on sales and inventories of these controlled substances, and taking into account estimates of drug usage provided by the FDA, DEA establishes annual aggregate production quotas for Schedule I and II controlled substances. The aggregate production quota is allocated among the various manufacturers who are registered to manufacture the specific drug. DEA also allocates the amount of bulk drug which may be procured by those companies which prepare the drug into dosage units.

Security

DEA registrants are required by regulation to maintain certain security for the storage and distribution of controlled substances.

Manufacturers and distributors of Schedule I and II substances must store controlled substances in specially constructed vaults or highly rated safes, and maintain electronic security for all storage areas. Lesser physical security requirements apply to retail level registrants such as hospitals and pharmacies.

All registrants are required to make every effort to ensure that controlled substances in their possession are not diverted into the illicit market. This requires operational as well as physical security. For example, registrants are responsible for ensuring that controlled substances are distributed only to other registrants that are authorized to receive them, or to legitimate patients and consumers.

Penalties

The CSA provides penalties for unlawful manufacturing, distribution, and dispensing of controlled substances. The penalties are basically determined by the schedule of the drug or other substance, and sometimes are specified by drug name, as in the case of marijuana. As the statute has been amended since its initial passage in 1970, the penalties have been altered by Congress.

User Accountability/Personal Use Penalties

On November 19, 1988, Congress passed the Anti-Drug Abuse Act of 1988, P. L. 100690. Two sections of this Act represent the Federal Government's attempt to reduce drug abuse by dealing not just with the person who sells the illegal drug, but also with the person who buys it. The first new section is titled "User Accountability" and is codified at 21 U.S.C. § 862 and various sections of Title 42, U.S.C. The second involves "personal use amounts" of illegal drugs, and is codified at 21 U.S.C. § 844a.

User Accountability

The purpose of User Accountability is to not only make the public aware of the Federal Government's position on drug abuse, but to describe new programs intended to decrease drug abuse by holding drug abusers personally responsible for their illegal activities, and imposing civil penalties on those who violate drug laws.

It is important to remember that these penalties are in addition to the criminal penalties drug abusers are already given, and do not replace those criminal penalties.

The new User Accountability programs call for more instruction in schools, kindergarten through senior high, to educate children on the dangers of drug abuse. These programs will include participation by students, parents, teachers, local businesses and the local, state and Federal Government.

User Accountability also targets businesses interested in doing business with the Federal Government. This program requires those businesses to maintain a drug-free workplace, principally through educating employees on the dangers of drug abuse, and by informing employees of the penalties they face if they engage in illegal drug activity on company property.

There is also a provision in the law that makes public housing projects drug-free by evicting those residents who allow their units to be used for illegal drug activity, and denies Federal benefits, such as housing assistance and student loans, to individuals convicted of illegal drug activity. Depending on the offense, an individual may be prohibited from ever receiving any benefit provided by the Federal Government.

Personal Use Amounts

This section of the 1988 Act allows the government to punish minor drug offenders without giving the offender a criminal record if the offender is in possession of only a small amount of drugs. This law is designed to impact the "user" of illicit drugs, while simultaneously saving the government the costs of a full-blown criminal investigation. Under this section, the government has the option of imposing only a civil fine on individuals possessing only a small quantity of an illegal drug. Possession of this small quantity, identified as a "personal use amount" carries a civil fine of up to $10,000.

In determining the amount of the fine in a particular case, the drug offender's income and assets will be considered. This is accomplished through an administrative proceeding rather than a criminal trial, thus reducing the exposure of the offender to the entire criminal justice system, and reducing the costs to the offender and the government.

The value of this section is that it allows the government to punish a minor drug offender without saddling the offender with a criminal record. This section also gives the drug offender the opportunity to fully redeem himself or herself, and have all public record of the proceeding destroyed. If this was the drug offender's first offense, and the offender has paid all fines, can pass a drug test, and has not been convicted of a crime after three years, the offender can request that all proceedings be dismissed.

If the proceeding is dismissed, the drug offender can lawfully say he or she had never been prosecuted, either criminally or civilly, for a drug offense.

Congress has imposed two limitations on this section's use. It may not be used if (1) the drug offender has been previously convicted of a Federal or state drug offense; or (2) the offender has already been fined twice under this section.

Chapter 8

Drugs and Crime Facts

Most of the information presented in this chapter is collected from Bureau of Justice Statistics (BJS) reports and from other statistical agencies. The primary sources of information include:

- The National Crime Victimization Survey (NCVS) which asks victims of personal crimes if they believed the offenders had been using drugs.

- The Law Enforcement Management and Administrative Statistics (LEMAS) program which produces information on drug-related programs of State and local police agencies.

- Correctional programs which provide data on Federal and State prisoners, jail inmates, and incarcerated youth, including data on their histories of drug use and drug offenses.

- The Federal Justice Statistics Program which collects and publishes detailed data on drug law violators in the Federal justice system.

- *The Sourcebook of Criminal Justice Statistics* which presents data on drug use in the general population, on public opinion toward drugs and enforcement of drug laws, and administrative law enforcement data from agencies such as the Drug Enforcement Administration (DEA).

Excerpted from *Drugs and Crime Facts*, U.S. Department of Justice, Office of Justice Programs, Bureau of Justice Statistics, Document No. NCJ 165148, May 1999. The full text of this document may be found at www.ojp.usdoj.gov/bjs.

Drug-Related Crime

Overall, 16% of convicted jail inmates said they had committed their offense to get money for drugs. Of convicted property and drug offenders, about 1 in 4 had committed their crimes to get money for drugs. A higher percentage of drug offenders in 1996 (24%) than in 1989 (14%) were in jail for a crime committed to raise money for drugs.

In 1997, 19% of State prisoners and 16% of Federal inmates said they committed their current offense to obtain money for drugs. These percentages represent a slight increase from 1991, when 17% of State and 10% of Federal prisoners identified drug money as a motive for their current offense. (Source: BJS, *Substance Abuse and Treatment, State and Federal Prisoners*, 1997, NCJ 172871, January 1999.)

The Uniform Crime Reporting Program (UCR) of the Federal Bureau of Investigation (FBI) reported that in 1997, 5.1% of the 15,289 homicides in which circumstances were known were narcotics related. Those murders that occurred specifically during a narcotics felony, such as drug trafficking or manufacturing, are considered drug related.

Offenders Under the Influence at the Time of the Offense

Victim's Perception

On average each year from 1992 to 1995, according to the National Crime Victimization Survey, there were 11.1 million violent victimizations of residents age 12 or older. Victims of violence were asked to describe whether they perceived the offender to have been drinking or using drugs.

- About 16% of the victims of violence reported that the offender was using drugs, alone or in combination with alcohol.

- Based on victim perceptions, about 2.7 million violent crimes occurred each year in which victims were certain that the offender had been drinking. For about 1 in 5 of these violent victimizations involving alcohol use by the offender, victims believed the offender was also using drugs at the time of the offense.

American Indian Victims

Alcohol and drug use was a factor in more than half of violent crimes against American Indians.

Substantial differences can be found by race in the reports of victims of violence of their perceptions of drug and alcohol use by offenders.

Table 8.1. Percent of jail inmates who committed offense to get money for drugs.

Offense	1996	1989
Total	15.8 %	13.3 %
Violent	8.8	11.5
Property	25.6	24.4
Drugs	23.5	14.0
Public-order	4.2	3.3

Source: BJS, *Profile of Jail Inmates*, 1996, NCJ 164620, April 1998.

Table 8.2. Drug-related homicides.

Year	Number of homicides	Percent drug related
1986	19,257	3.9 %
1987	17,963	4.9
1988	17,971	5.6
1989	18,954	7.4
1990	20,273	6.7
1991	21,676	6.2
1992	22,716	5.7
1993	23,180	5.5
1994	22,084	5.6
1995	20,232	5.0
1996	15,848	4.9
1997	15,289	5.1

Note: Includes only those homicides where circumstances were known.

Source: Table constructed by ONDCP Drug Policy Information Clearinghouse staff from FBI, Uniform Crime Reports, *Crime in the United States*, annually.

Among those who could describe alcohol or drug use by offenders, American Indian victims of violence were the most likely to report such perceived use by the offender.

Table 8.3. Victims' perception of the use of alcohol or drugs by violent offenders, by victim-offender relationship, 1995

Victim-offender relationship	Total	Alcohol	Offender using: Drugs	Drugs or alcohol	Neither drugs nor alcohol
All victims of violence	100%	28%	7%	9%	56%
Intimate*	100	55	9	12	25
Nonmarital relative	100	38	14	12	36
Acquaintance	100	28	9	10	52
Stranger	100	24	6	7	63

Note: Excludes "don't know"" from calculations.

*Includes current or former spouse, boyfriend, and girlfriend.

Source: BJS, National Crime Victimization Survey as reported in *Alcohol and Crime*, NCJ 168632, April 1998.

Table 8.4. Violent crime, by the perceived drug or alcohol use of the offender and by race of victim, 1992-96.

Race of victim	Total	Perceived drug or alcohol use by offender Alcohol	Drugs	Both	Neither
Total	100%	28%	8%	7%	57%
American Indian	100	38	9	8	45
White	100	29	8	7	56
Black	100	21	7	7	65
Asian	100	20	3	2	75

Note: Table excludes those respondents who were unable to report whether or not they perceived the offender to have been using drugs or alcohol.

Source: BJS, *American Indians and Crime*, NCJ 173386, February 1999.

Overall, in 55% of American Indian violent victimizations, the victim said the offender was under the influence of alcohol, drugs, or both. The offender's use of alcohol and/or drugs was somewhat less likely in violent crimes committed against whites (44%) or blacks (35%).

Perspectives of Jail Inmates and State Probationers and Prisoners

Probationers

The first national survey of adults on probation, conducted in 1995, reported that 14% of probationers were on drugs when they committed their offense. (Source: BJS, *Substance Abuse and Treatment of Adults on Probation*, 1995, NCJ 166611, March 1998.)

Prisoners

In the 1997 Survey of Inmates in State and Federal Correctional Facilities, 33% of State prisoners and 22% of Federal prisoners said they had committed their current offense while under the influence of drugs. Drug offenders (42%) and property offenders (37%) reported the highest incidence of drug use at the time of the offense. (Source: BJS, *Substance Abuse and Treatment, State and Federal Prisoners*, 1997, NCJ 172871, January, 1999.)

Jail Inmates

- Thirty-six percent of convicted jail inmates said they were using drugs at the time of their offense in 1996, compared to 27% in 1989. Almost 2 in 10 were using marijuana in 1996, compared to 1 in 10 in 1989. Approximately 6% in 1996 and 2% in 1989 were using amphetamines or other stimulants. In both 1996 and 1989 about 15% were on cocaine or crack at the time of the offense.

- Those jail inmates convicted of drug trafficking (60%), drug possession (57%), fraud (45%), or robbery (44%) were most likely to have reported to be using drugs at the time of the offense.

Source: BJS, *Profile of Jail Inmates*, 1996, NCJ 164620, April 1998.

According to the Surveys of Inmates in State Correctional Facilities, 1991, and Inmates in local Jails, 1996, more than half of prison and jail inmates with an intimate victim had been drinking or using drugs when they committed the violent crime. (Source: BJS, *Violence by Intimates*, NCJ 167237, March 1998.)

Drug Use at Arrest

In 1997 the ADAM program found that the percentage of adult male arrestees testing positive for an illicit drug at the time of arrest ranged from 51% in San Jose to 80% in Chicago. Adult female arrestees testing positive ranged from 40% in New Orleans to 81% in Manhattan. Juvenile male detainees testing positive ranged from 43% in Portland to 66% in Washington, D.C. (Source: NIJ, *Arrestee Drug Abuse Monitoring (ADAM)*, formerly known as Drug Use Forecasting (DUF), annual report, 1997, NCJ 171672, July 1998.)

Between 1996 and 1997 levels of overall drug use among arrestees reported by ADAM sites appear to have changed little. In 9 of 23 sites, the percentages of both male and female arrestees who tested positive for at least one drug in 1997 remained the same or decreased slightly from rates reported in the prior year. Among them are the largest cities in the ADAM system—Manhattan, Chicago, Los Angeles, and Detroit—where overall cocaine rates have been moving downward since the early 1990's and marijuana use is currently leveling off. In other sites—San Jose, Omaha, St. Louis, and Denver—both cocaine and marijuana decreased. Data from the National Institute of Justice (NIJ) first annual Arrestee Drug Abuse Monitoring (ADAM) report, which is an expansion and re-engineering of the Drug Use Forecasting (DUF) program, describe tested urine samples collected from volunteers—selected adult male arrestees in 23 cities, adult female arrestees in 21 cities, and juvenile male detainees in 12 cities.

In 1997 data show some significant changes in drug use among juvenile male arrestees in the ADAM samples. (Source: NIJ, *Arrestee Drug Abuse Monitoring Program (ADAM)*, annual report, 1997, NCJ 171672, July 1998.)

Marijuana

The rate for increased marijuana use appears to be slowing down in this population, following 2 years of sharply rising rates.

In most sites, the percentage of marijuana positives was lower for juvenile males than for adult male arrestees 15-20 years old. For several sites the rates were higher for juvenile males than adult males— for Los Angeles, 9 percentage points higher; for Phoenix, 13 percentage points; and for San Diego, 5 percentage points higher.

Cocaine

A trend first noted in 1996 is that cocaine use appears to be expanding for juvenile males in some ADAM cities.

Several sites in the West and Southwest (Denver, Phoenix, and San Antonio) reported increasing positives for cocaine, among juvenile males. Rates for most sites remained relatively unchanged, although rates in Indianapolis dropped from 6% to 3%.

Prior Drug Use by Offenders

Probationers

In 1995 the first national survey of adults on probation reported:

* nearly 70% of probationers reported past drug use

* 32% said they were using illegal drugs in the month before their offense.

Marijuana (10%) was the most commonly used drug among probationers at the time of the offense.

Table 8.5. Prior drug use of adults on probation at the time of offense, by type of drugs, 1995.

Type of drug	Percent of adults on probation who were under the influence of drugs at the time of offense
Any drug	14%
Marijuana/hashish	10
Cocaine/crack	4
Heroin and other opiates	1
Barbiturates	1
Stimulants	2
Hallucinogens	1

Note: Excludes 11,712 probationers for whom information on drug use was not provided.

Source: BJS, *Substance Abuse and Treatment of Adults on Probation*, 1995, NCJ 166611, March 1998.

In 1995 adults on probation in the age categories under 45 (87% of all probationers) reported similar levels of prior drug abuse, and their incidence of drug use was consistently higher than that of older probationers. Over 70% of probationers under 45 reported some prior drug use, compared to 37% of those 45 or older. Thirty-five percent of probationers under 45—but 9% of older probationers—reported drug use in the month before their offense. (Source: BJS, *Substance Abuse and Treatment of Adults on Probation*, 1995, NCJ 166611, March 1998.)

Jail Inmates

Of those inmates held in local jails, only convicted offenders were asked if they had used drugs in the time leading up to their current offense. In 1996, 55% of convicted jail inmates reported they had used illegal drugs during the month before their offense, up from 44% in 1989. Use of marijuana in the month before the offense increased from 28% to 37% and of stimulants from 5% to 10%. Reported cocaine or crack use was stable at about 24%.

A higher percentage of jail inmates in 1996 than in 1989 reported ever using for every type of drug except cocaine or crack.

- marijuana rose from 71% to 78%

- stimulants (amphetamine and methamphetamine) from 22% to 34%

- hallucinogens, including LSD and PCP, from 24% to 32%

- depressants, including Quaalude, barbiturates, and tranquilizers without a doctor's prescription, from 21% to 30%

- heroin or other opiates from 19% to 24%.

Half of inmates in both years reported trying cocaine.
Overall, 82% of all jail inmates in 1996 said they had ever used an illegal drug, up from 78% in 1989.

State and Federal Prison Inmates

In the 1997 Survey of Inmates in State and Federal Correctional Facilities, over 570,000 of the Nation's prisoners (51%) reported the use of alcohol or drugs while committing their offense.

In 1991, 60% of Federal prisoners reported prior drug use, compared to 79% of State prisoners. In 1997 this gap in prior drug use was narrowed, as the percentage of Federal inmates reporting past drug use rose to 73%, compared to 83% of State inmates. This increase was mostly due to a rise in the percentage of Federal prisoners reporting prior use of marijuana (from 53% in 1991 to 65% in 1997) and cocaine-based drugs (from 37% in 1991 to 45% in 1997).

Most other drug types showed modest increases over this period. A fifth of Federal prisoners had used stimulants and hallucinogens, followed by depressants and opiates, including heroin (both 16%). About 1 in 12 Federal prisoners reported the prior use of inhalants.

Table 8.6. Prior drug use of jail inmates, by type of drug, 1996 and 1989.

Type of drug	Ever used drugs		Ever used drugs regularly[a]		Used drugs in the month before the offense		Used drugs at the time of the offense	
	1996	1989	1996	1989	1996	1989	1996	1989
Any drug[b]	82.4%	77.7%	64.2%	58.0%	55.0%	43.8%	35.6%	27.0%
Marijuana	78.2	70.7	54.9	47.8	36.8	28.0	18.5	9.0
Cocaine or crack	50.4	50.4	31.0	30.7	24.1	23.5	15.2	13.7
Heroin or opiates	23.9	18.6	11.8	11.8	8.8	7.2	5.6	4.9
Depressants[c]	29.9	21.1	10.4	9.0	5.9	3.9	2.4	1.2
Stimulants[d]	33.6	22.1	16.5	12.1	10.4	5.4	6.1	2.2
Hallucinogens[e]	32.2	23.7	10.5	9.4	4.6	3.2	1.6	1.6
Inhalants	16.8	—	4.8	—	1.0	—	0.3	—

Note: Detail add to more than total because inmates may have used more than one drug.

—Not reported.

[a] used drugs at least once week for a month.

[b] Other unspecified drugs are included in the totals.

[c] Includes barbiturates, tranquilizers, and Quaalude.

[d] Includes amphetamine and methamphetamine.

[e] Includes LSD and PCP.

Source: BJS, *Profile of Jail Inmates, 1996*, NCJ 164620, April 1998.

Although the proportion of Federal prisoners held for drug offenses rose from 58% in 1991 to 63% in 1997, the percentage of all Federal inmates who reported using drugs in the month before the offense rose more dramatically from 32% to 45%.

The proportion of State prison inmates reporting the past use of cocaine or crack remained stable between 1991 and 1997:

- Marijuana (77%) use had increased slightly since 1991 (74%), and remained the most commonly used drug.

- Past use of cocaine-based drugs remained unchanged at 49% since 1991.

- Twenty percent of all inmates reported the past use of intravenous drugs, down from 25% in 1991.

Table 8.7. Drug use by State prisoners, 1991 and 1997.

	Percent of inmates who had ever used drugs	
Type of drug	1997	1991
Any drug	83%	79%
Marijuana	77	74
Cocaine/crack	49	49
Heroin/opiates	24	25
Depressants	24	24
Stimulants	28	30
Hallucinogens	29	27

Source: BJS, *Substance Abuse and Treatment, State and Federal Prisoners, 1997*, NCJ 172871, January 1999.

Chapter 9

Emerging Drug Problems

Changes to Drug Detection Mechanisms

During the crack crisis of the 1980s, limitations in the drug detection system hampered the identification and monitoring of drug use activity in many geographic areas and for some high-risk populations. Timely analysis and dissemination of drug use prevalence data were also problems. Since the mid-1980s, a number of changes have been made to the drug use detection mechanisms to address some surveillance and monitoring limitations. New information sources have also been added.

The changes to the National Institute on Drug Abuse (NIDA)-sponsored drug use detection mechanisms were intended to improve geographic and population coverage and timeliness of drug use data. To obtain and help ensure a representative sample of hospital emergency departments in the Drug Abuse Warning Network (DAWN), a new representative sample was drawn and provisions were made for including new hospitals in the sampling frame each year. Adjustments for nonresponse patterns were also made. Monitoring the Future (MTF) was expanded to include a representative sample of 8th- and 10th-grade students in addition to the 12th-graders and young adults already being surveyed. The National Household Survey on Drug Abuse (NHSDA) was expanded to include civilians living on military

Excerpted from "Emerging Drug Problems: Despite Changes in Detection and Response Capability, Concerns Remain," U.S. General Accounting Office, Document No. GAO/HEHS98-130, July 1998.

69

bases and people living in noninstitutional quarters, such as college dormitories, rooming houses, and shelters. NHSDA was also expanded to include Alaska and Hawaii. To provide more timely national data, since 1990 NHSDA has been conducted every year, instead of every 2 to 3 years. There are also plans, promoted by ONDCP, to expand NHSDA to collect state-level drug use prevalence data. This expansion is expected to provide annual estimates for each state's household population and, specifically, for the population aged 12 to 17 and 18 to 25.

In addition to changes in DAWN, MTF, and NHSDA, several new drug use detection mechanisms have been developed. The Substance Abuse and Mental Health Services Administration (SAMHSA) has cited the particular importance of two of these mechanisms: the Arrestee Drug Abuse Monitoring (ADAM) program and the Treatment Episode Data Set (TEDS). ADAM, formerly the Drug Use Forecasting program, comprises an ongoing quarterly study of the drug use patterns of new arrestees at booking facilities in approximately 20 cities across the country. TEDS is a database of substance abuse client admissions to those publicly funded substance abuse treatment programs that receive some of their funding through a state alcohol and drug agency. In commenting on this report, SAMHSA officials stated that their Violence Data Exchange Teams (VDET) are in the process of creating a local-level system to track trends and changes in substance abuse-related violence. When fully operational, VDETs will assist local communities in the detection of drug abuse patterns as they are manifested through violence-related data. SAMHSA officials believe that such data can be used to serve as an early warning system.

In 1992, the Office of National Drug Control Policy (ONDCP) initiated "Pulse Check," a telephone survey (as well as a report of the survey results), to provide a quick and current snapshot of drug use and drug markets across the country. According to ONDCP officials, "Pulse Check," which was initially published quarterly but was changed to a biannual report, typically includes information on the availability of drugs, their purity, and their street prices; user demographics; methods of use; and user primary drug of choice. These data are obtained from different sources, including telephone interviews with drug ethnographers and epidemiologists, law enforcement agents, drug treatment providers across the nation, and Community Epidemiology Work Group (CEWG) reports. ONDCP officials said that surveillance data from "Pulse Check" and other sources have increased ONDCP's capability to perform quick analyses and special studies of changing drug use patterns as well as to identify problems in certain population groups and geographic areas.

ONDCP Was Charged with Developing and Coordinating a National Drug Control Strategy

Before the Anti-Drug Abuse Act of 1988, which created ONDCP, each federal agency involved with drug control had its own set of goals, objectives, targets, and measures, as well as congressional mandates. To coordinate the federal drug control effort, ONDCP was charged with developing an annual national drug control strategy. ONDCP officials have pointed out that achieving the goals will depend not only on federal agencies but also on state, local, and foreign governments; private entities; and individuals.

Two of ONDCP's programs focus on addressing the trend in drug use primarily among youth: a national media campaign and the Drug-free Communities Support Program. Moreover, ONDCP has taken the initiative to help focus attention on some recent changes in drug use trends that have emerged as potentially problematic. For example, ONDCP responded to changes in methamphetamine use in certain geographic areas by publishing a special issue of "Pulse Check" on these trends and cosponsoring a methamphetamine conference. In addition, ONDCP is now developing a national methamphetamine strategy. ONDCP officials admit, however, that they have no systematic approach or strategy for specifically addressing emerging drug use problems.

SAMHSA Was Created to Strengthen Drug Prevention and Treatment Services

SAMHSA was created to address concerns related to the availability and quality of drug prevention and treatment services. Specifically, SAMHSA was to develop national goals and model programs; coordinate federal policy related to providing prevention and treatment services; and evaluate the process, outcomes, and community impact of prevention and treatment services. In addition, SAMHSA was to ensure, through coordination with NIDA, the dissemination of relevant research findings to service providers to improve the delivery and effectiveness of prevention and treatment services. To carry out these responsibilities, SAMHSA initially established demonstration grant programs that supported individual grants, cooperative agreements, and contracts. SAMHSA also assumed responsibility for administering the separate Substance Abuse Prevention and Treatment (SAPT) block grant program.

In 1995, SAMHSA developed the Knowledge Development and Application (KD&A) program, consolidating SAMHSA's individual demonstration grant programs. According to SAMHSA officials, the program offers improved ways of generating and disseminating knowledge on the prevention and treatment of problems related to drug use and how to apply that knowledge to delivering services.

According to SAMHSA officials, the agency is not yet adequately positioned to deter emerging drug use that might result in future epidemics. The SAPT block grant is not designed to provide a rapid response to emerging drug problems. SAMHSA officials, however, have planned several initiatives to address emerging drug abuse trends. For example, the Center for Substance Abuse Prevention (CSAP) plans to continue its support of the HHS Secretary's Youth Substance Abuse Prevention Initiative.

Additionally, the Center for Substance Abuse Treatment (CSAT) plans to test the feasibility of implementing new approaches in treatment settings. For example, more individuals—particularly on the West Coast and in the Southwest—are seeking treatment for methamphetamine dependence; but, according to CSAT, there are no well-established treatment approaches for this drug. CSAT's Replicating Effective Treatment for Methamphetamine Dependence study is designed to develop knowledge of psychosocial treatment for methamphetamine dependence as well as to provide an opportunity to determine the problems involved in transferring this knowledge.

To help states put the infrastructure in place to respond to emerging drug use trends, CSAT plans to further strengthen its partnerships with state and local governments as well as with community-based treatment providers and the private sector to solve common problems. For example, the Targeted Treatment Capacity Expansion Program is designed to award grants to states, cities, and other government entities to create and expand comprehensive substance abuse treatment services and promote accountability. CSAT plans to support states, cities, and other partners in their efforts to identify gaps in the delivery system and, where current capacity within a treatment modality is insufficient, provide for expanded access to treatment.

In an effort to disseminate information to service providers and others, SAMHSA operates the National Clearinghouse for Alcohol and Drug Information. SAMHSA, NIDA, and other public health agencies provide posters, brochures, reports, booklets, audiotapes, and videotapes to aid in drug abuse prevention and awareness efforts.

NIDA Was Transferred to NIH to Strengthen Drug Abuse Research

With its transfer to the National Institutes of Health (NIH), NIDA was relieved of most of its direct service delivery functions with the intent of having it focus on conducting research on drug abuse and addiction. However, according to NIDA officials, the nature of research and the research grant approval process (which is often lengthy) limits the agency's immediate response to emerging drug problems. That is, it takes time to generate grants in a new priority area, conduct the research, publicize the research findings, and move these findings from the "lab" into practice. NIDA has a key role to play both in generating research-based prevention and treatment approaches and in training research scientists who potentially can be useful to the public health community in addressing drug control problems. The move to NIH also gave NIDA the opportunity to focus more on developing initiatives in public education and research training.

NIDA officials have indicated, however, that quickly focusing research on newly emerging drug problems is difficult, in part, because of the time it takes to generate grant applications and award grants in a new priority area. The extramural research grant application approval process has multiple stages and can take several months to complete.

Despite Changes, Concerns Remain

Despite changes to federal drug detection mechanisms and congressional efforts to better position federal public health agencies to respond to emerging drug crises, concerns remain. While federal entities now have an array of tools to detect drug use, there is concern about the overall efficiency and effectiveness of these efforts. In addition, questions remain about when and how to best respond to emerging drug use trends. This is also an issue for state and local substance abuse authorities, who are challenged with allocating resources to address both current and emerging drug use problems. Given competing demands on federal, state, and local resources, it is important that the most appropriate drug prevention and treatment strategies are developed and effectively implemented.

A More Defined Strategy for Responding to Emerging Drug Problems Is Still Needed

The usefulness of better and more timely information on emerging drug use problems is, in part, a function of the nation's ability to respond to those problems, which itself is affected by demands on federal, state, and local resources to address ongoing substance abuse concerns. Still, a more defined strategy for responding is needed. While we learned of different approaches the federal government uses to respond to changing drug use patterns, some of which address emerging drugs, no overall defined strategy for specifically addressing emerging drug use problems exists. Also, there is no agreed-upon set of operational definitions for key terms, such as "drug epidemic" or "drug crisis."

Determining an appropriate response to emerging drug use problems involves considering:

- the timing of a response to a detected change in drug use patterns;

- the nature of the response—that is, the most effective prevention and treatment approaches to address a drug use problem at different stages; and

- the magnitude of the response, taking into account resource limitations and uncertainties about the potential scale of the problem.

Determining the timing of a response is complicated by uncertainty about what point above the normative pattern of use warrants a response, either in a specific geographic area or nationwide. Several factors—including availability of information, public opinion, and political sensitivity—play a role in determining the timing of a response to a detected change in drug use patterns. In addition, the most accurate and useful data are not always available for immediate decisions on when to respond to a particular change.

Determining the nature of the response requires a better understanding of the extent to which various prevention and treatment approaches are effective in controlling specific drug use problems. A rise in marijuana use among youth and a shift in heroin use from injecting to smoking may require different approaches because of the drug, the population, or both.

Determining the magnitude of a response is complicated by the risk of misallocating scarce federal, state, and local resources to combat a problem that may not warrant the investment. There is also the risk of inadvertently promoting the use of a drug to risk-takers by creating too much publicity addressing its dangers. Consideration must also be given to the capacity of the system to treat those who currently seek or will seek treatment.

Strengthening Ties between Federal Agencies and States and Localities

Some researchers believe that to improve the chances of deterring the spread of emerging drug problems or epidemics, greater attention must be given to changes in drug use patterns at the local level, where such problems typically originate. Although SAMHSA has relationships with states through the block grant program, experts in the drug field describe less than adequate linkages between state and local communities and the three major federal agencies involved in drug abuse demand reduction efforts. ONDCP, SAMHSA, and NIDA do not currently have a well-established network with the many local entities associated with reducing drug use, and their relationships with states and local communities might not facilitate a response to an emerging drug problem at the local level. A defined strategy for addressing emerging drug problems would benefit from better linkages with state and local entities to capitalize on their experiences with local drug crises or epidemics.

Although addressing drug use problems is not necessarily the same as addressing infectious diseases, the networks and linkages with state and local entities that have been established by Centers for Disease Control and Prevention (CDC) may be worth considering for detecting and responding to emerging drug use problems. CDC is responsible for detecting and responding to potential health crises, such as outbreaks of infectious and chronic diseases. The agency has established relationships with states and local entities through a number of efforts, some of which follow:

- CDC's Epidemic Intelligence Service enables the agency to maximize its investigative capabilities. At any given time, CDC has up to 150 epidemiologists to call on to assess a potential public health epidemic or crisis. Through direct on-site public health surveillance, CDC can gain rapid and in-depth understanding of the initiation and spread of a public health problem. These investigations enable CDC to target specific individuals and groups affected and likely to be affected, identify the circumstances under which infections take place and spread, track the movement of the problem across geographic areas, and establish the time parameters governing the infection of each subsequent target group.

- Through collaboration with the Council of State and Territorial Epidemiologists, CDC is able to ensure broad geographic coverage, since the group includes representatives from all 50 states and the U.S. territories.

- CDC has established procedures with states for quick responses to perceived health crises. If a state public health agency is experiencing a problem in either identifying or managing a public health problem, CDC can be called on to provide immediate guidance and support. According to a CDC official, if the problem is not one that can be handled over the telephone, CDC is able to quickly dispatch appropriate staff to the scene to provide on-site public health surveillance and response support.

Conclusions

The public health agencies' approach to addressing drug use problems in the United States has changed since the mid-1980s. Given changes made in the drug use detection mechanisms, organizational changes in HHS' drug control agencies, and the creation of ONDCP, the federal capability to address emerging drug use problems has been enhanced. However, the benefits of these changes depend largely on how drug data are used and how well the agencies carry out their roles and responsibilities. For example, the complement of drug use detection mechanisms available to public health agencies and others now provides more timely data and broader geographic and population coverage. However, ONDCP's Subcommittee on Data, Evaluation, and Interagency Coordination and others have pointed out weaknesses that need to be addressed to improve the accuracy of drug data and to increase the efficiency and effectiveness of the nation's drug data collection systems.

ONDCP, NIDA, and SAMHSA officials report that some of their efforts are addressing emerging drug problems. However, these agencies have no overall defined strategy that addresses factors such as how to determine the timing, nature, and magnitude of a response to new patterns of drug use identified through the nation's surveillance systems. In addition, maintaining ongoing mechanisms with the capacity to link surveillance knowledge from local and national sources with knowledge about effective demand reduction approaches should increase our nation's capability to deter future drug crises. Developing a defined strategy for addressing emerging drug problems will be challenging because of data uncertainties and other factors, such as engaging federal, state, and local entities in collaborative response actions. However, the CDC approach to responding to emerging infectious diseases might offer some insights on establishing linkages with state and local entities and developing response protocols.

Since ONDCP is responsible for developing and coordinating a national drug control strategy, it could take the lead in improving the nation's drug data collection system and coordinating the development of a strategy to address future emerging drug use problems.

Chapter 10

Does Marijuana Have a Place in Medicine?

In the moral, legal, an medical realms, the use of medical marijuana is a hotly contested issue. What do we really know about its efficacy? When, if ever, is it recommended?

In the crude herb *Cannabis sativa* — more commonly known as marijuana, pot, or hemp — delta-9-tetrahydrocannabinol (THC) occurs as a sticky, extractable, resinous oil. In total, marijuana contains more than 60 cannabinoids, most of them poorly characterized. The major psychoactive ingredient appears to be THC, however. Whether marijuana is smoked, eaten, brewed in a tea, or swallowed in pill form, THC is the major ingredient affecting the central nervous system (CNS). This is also true of dronabinol, marijuana's chemically synthesized THC counterpart ("medical marijuana"), which is formulated in sesame oil and supplied in 2.5-, 5-, or 10-mg gelatin capsules.

Some argue that manufacturing dronabinol by extracting only one of many cannabinoids produces an agent that is less effective than the polypharmaceutical herb marijuana.[1] Others feel very strongly that as long as dronabinol is available, the Drug Enforcement Agency (DEA) does not need to reschedule crude marijuana as a medicinal drug. With the passage of bills in California and Arizona recognizing marijuana as a medication, there is increasing political and public pressure for a final decision on the legal status of smoked marijuana

"Does Marijuana Have a Place in Medicine?" by Lisa Capaldina, Donald Tashkin, William Vilensky, Lori D. Talarico in *Patient Care,* January 30, 1998, Vol. 32, No. 2, p. 41(6), ©1998 by Medical Economics Publishing. Reprinted with permission.

as a regulated substance prescribed for medicinal purposes. The few studies that have examined the medical efficacy of smoked marijuana were conducted in the 1970s and 1980s. While the debate rages, marijuana remains illegal, and dronabinol is the only legally available THC. With the advent of serotonin antagonists, the need for medicinal THC as an antiemetic is less clear than ever.

How Dronabinol Works

Dronabinol, a Schedule II (prescription only) controlled substance, affects receptors in the brain and the spinal cord. It is labeled for use in the treatment of anorexia associated with weight loss in patients with AIDS and for the nausea and vomiting associated with cancer chemotherapy in patients who have failed to respond adequately to conventional antiemetic treatment. Although it is an efficacious antiemetic, it may have significant side effects.[2] Dronabinol is often used as a rescue medication when other drugs do not work, rather than as a first-line treatment. It is prescribed primarily by oncologists, although other physicians use it off-label, either alone or as an adjunct, in treating glaucoma and epilepsy and to relieve tremor, ataxia, and muscular spasticity in patients with multiple sclerosis (MS).

Dronabinol is clearly most useful as a treatment option when nausea and vomiting are uncontrolled by other means, and its stimulating effect on the appetite may continue for 24 hours or longer after administration. It can also be administered with a variety of medications (e.g., many cytotoxic agents, anti-infective agents, sedatives, or opioid analgesics) without causing clinically significant drug interactions. Synthetic THC may interact with some medications, however, through both metabolic and pharmacodynamic mechanisms, at least theoretically. Dronabinol is highly protein-bound, for example, and therefore might displace other protein-bound drugs, and patients should be monitored for possible changes in dosage requirements.

Oral THC capsules have other disadvantages. A patient suffering from nausea and vomiting may be unable to swallow the pill or keep it down. A suppository form appears to have been successful in clinical trials, but it is not yet available. Trials with a dronabinol nasal inhaler are also under way.

It is difficult to titrate dronabinol because of its erratic bioavailability and relatively slow onset of action. Onset is delayed for approximately 30-60 minutes, with a peak effect at 2-4 hours. The psychoactive effects last for 4-6 hours, and side effects may be prolonged. Dronabinol-induced parasympatholytic-like activity may result in tachycardia or conjunctivitis. Effects on blood pressure are inconsistent, and some patients have experienced orthostatic hypotension or syncope [fainting].

Dronabinol must be taken on a regular schedule; treatment is initiated with a low dosage (2.5 mg/d), which is increased only as necessary. Possible psychoactive side effects, including impairment of coordination, mood, and perception, are the biggest drawback to the medical use of THC. They may be most severe in patients who are not experienced cannabinoid users. Tachyphylaxis and tolerance to some of the pharmacological effects develop with chronic use.

Alternatives to THC

At least seven controlled studies comparing prochlorperazine maleate with synthetic THC were performed more than a decade ago.[3] Several other antiemetics have come to the fore since then, but they have not been compared to THC in controlled clinical trials. These newer drugs include the serotonin antagonists ondansetron HCl dihydrate and granisetron HCl, which are more effective and cause fewer side effects than prochlorperazine and can be administered to children.

A number of dopamine receptor blockers are currently used to treat nausea, including metoclopramide HCl, haloperidol, and cisapride. Two studies comparing the antiemetic effects of oral THC and metoclopramide have yielded mixed results.[3, 4] Corticosteroids like dexamethasone and methylprednisolone acetate and minor tranquilizers, such as lorazepam, have proven safe and effective for the treatment of chemotherapy-induced nausea and vomiting, especially when used in conjunction with other antinausea medications such as scopolamine.[5] Even a combination sedative/antiemetic in the phenothiazine family, such as chlorpromazine HCl, can be used.

Inhaled Marijuana

Few of the more than 60 active cannabinoids found in crude marijuana have been studied. There is speculation that some of the non-THC cannabinoids may help confer the additional benefits reported by those who smoke or eat marijuana, although no human trials confirm this. Little information about the efficacy of inhaled marijuana has been derived from clinical trials, but an abundance of anecdotal and clinical reports exist. In fact, marijuana was widely prescribed by Western physicians in the mid-19th century for asthma, insomnia, dysmenorrhea, convulsions, and a number of other complaints.

Today, whole cannabis is thought to be effective in a wide range of conditions, including appetite enhancement for the wasting syndrome of AIDS, control of nausea and vomiting associated with cancer chemotherapy, relief of spasticity and pain associated with MS, a decrease in intraocular pressure in glaucoma, and control of migraine headaches and epileptic seizures. Many of the compounds contained in marijuana have demonstrated pain-relieving actions in animal tests, although few studies of cannabinoid effects on pain have been conducted in humans.[6] As is the case with dronabinol, these benefits come with possible psychotropic effects that can impair normal activities.

Inhaling smoke, which irritates the throat and lungs, can lead to respiratory problems. Marijuana use by patients with AIDS is discouraged since it is not known to what extent marijuana may further compromise the lungs' immune defenses and predispose the patient to opportunistic pulmonary infections.[7,8] The illegality of marijuana has made it difficult to scientifically document a connection with lung disease or the effects of passive exposure to marijuana smoke.

It has been suggested that alternate drug delivery devices and marijuana extracts be studied for use in lieu of smoking an unfiltered marijuana cigarette. Examples include different kinds of water pipes, filters, and vaporizing devices that could selectively remove potentially harmful elements from marijuana smoke. Water pipes have always been available as illegal drug paraphernalia. Research has shown that THC, the active antinausea agent in marijuana, is more quickly absorbed when marijuana is smoked rather than ingested. According to one study, a substantial proportion of practicing oncologists who responded to the survey regard smoked cannabis as a safe and effective antinausea agent.[1]

Comparing Dronabinol and Marijuana

Quality control is another factor to consider when comparing dronabinol with smoked marijuana. The synthetic THC found in dronabinol is manufactured under sterile, controlled conditions. There are numerous variables in the production of illegal marijuana. The quality of the herb is affected by soil conditions, water quality, and humidity and temperature control. For example, like all plants, cannabis accumulates metal from the soil, and soils in different parts of the country contain varying levels of mercury, lithium, cadmium, and copper.

Since the crop is produced illegally, contamination by unrestricted use or overuse of pesticides, herbicides, fungicides, or insecticides may occur. In addition, the marijuana plant is often plagued with patho-genic fungi, such as *Aspergillus* or *Fusarium*. It can also transmit other fungal infections such as histoplasmosis. This problem can be eradicated by proper sterilization, though, and baking marijuana kills *Aspergillus* spores with no effect on THC content.[9]

Dronabinol can be produced in specific potencies, but variations in growing climate and product preparation greatly affect available THC levels in marijuana. The more potent, resinous hemp is grown in hot, moist southern climates. Furthermore, the concentration of THC in a marijuana cigarette, commonly called a joint, which con-tains dried stems, leaves, and flowers, is much lower than the THC level in hashish—a preparation of the unadulterated resin scraped from the flowering tops of the female hemp plants. Hashish, or hash, is usually shaped like a bar of soap, and a piece is broken off and used in a pipe or water pipe, or sometimes crumbled up with marijuana and rolled into a cigarette. Like marijuana, it can be eaten.

Government-produced cigarettes sponsored by the National Insti-tute on Drug Abuse (NIDA) are reported to be bacteria- and fungus-free as well as consistent in THC level. Many supporters of marijuana for medical use, therefore, support governmental control of the pro-duction of cannabis for safety and consistency of THC levels and the elimination of fungi and bacteria.

The bioavailability of dronabinol and marijuana vary tremendously in individuals and from day to day in the same person. Even though synthetic THC is available in three strengths, it can be very difficult to define appropriate dose and determine what time day the patient needs to take it. Some studies suggest that smoking is a more effi-cient delivery system for THC than dronabinol because the patient gets near-immediate results and can self-titrate—although the abil-ity to self-titrate has been questioned.[10] Smoking marijuana appears to surpass eating crude marijuana in terms of control of titration. In addition, eating marijuana may be difficult for patients who are an-orectic, nauseated, or vomiting.[10, 11]

Smoking a cannabis cigarette is associated with a nearly five-fold increase in the carboxyhemoglobin concentration compared to that associated with smoking a tobacco cigarette. More tar is also inhaled and retained in the respiratory tract when smoking marijuana.[12] It's true too, however, that the medicinal use of inhaled marijuana en-tails smoking far fewer cigarettes than the number typically smoked by a tobacco user.

Cardiac effects such as tachycardia and hypotension are common with both dronabinol and smoked marijuana. Although these effects may be of minimal consequence in younger persons, elderly patients may be more sensitive to them. The adverse reactions can also be more prominent in the inexperienced marijuana user.

Proponents of smoked marijuana for medical use believe that government-approved marijuana would be less expensive than dronabinol or the new antiemetics. For example, ondansetron costs $120-$160 for oral administration but, because of nausea and vomiting, especially in AIDS patients, IV administration is often required at a cost of about $600.[13] Without the black market, the price of government-grown marijuana cigarettes could be quite low.

What's Next

Supporters of smoked marijuana for medical use believe that governmental control over marijuana as a Schedule I substance (no currently accepted medical use) has prevented an objective evaluation of the drug in controlled clinical trials. In fact, no major trials to assess marijuana's safety or efficacy have been conducted. Some people believe that the federal government should remove legal barriers to research, provide direct or indirect financial support to research, and, in the meantime, allow continued and expanded use of the drug on a compassionate-use basis.[14, 15]

Many physicians say that if cannabinoids are found to be as effective as other available medications, they would prescribe them. At the least, many physicians would like to put the issue to rest once and for all. Many doctors believe that the greatest danger in the medical use of marijuana is its illegality, which imposes much anxiety and expense on suffering people, forces them to bargain with illicit drug dealers, and exposes them to threats of criminal prosecution. Only clinical research comparing dronabinol to other tetrahydrocannabinoids and cannabinoids for therapeutic efficacy can clarify this controversy. The National Institutes of Health are open to receiving research grant applications for studies of the medical efficacy of marijuana, and they have recently provided a $1 million grant to the Institute of Medicine to review scientific and laboratory tests on marijuana.

References

1. Doblin RE, Kleiman MAR: Marijuana as antiemetic medicine: A survey of oncologists' experiences and attitudes. *J Clin Oncol* 1991;9:1314-1319.

2. Beal JE, Olson DO, Laubenstein L, *et al.*: Dronabinol as a treatment for anorexia associated with weight loss in patients with AIDS. *J Pain Symptom Manage* 1995;10:89-97.

3. Ekert H, Waters KD, Jurk IH, *et al.*: Amelioration of cancer chemotherapy-induced nausea and vomiting by delta-9-tetrahyrdocannabinol. *Med J Aust* 1979;2:657-659.

4. Gralia RJ, Tyson LB, Clark RA, *et al.*: Antiemetic trials with high dose metoclopramide: Superiority over THC, preservation of efficacy in subsequent chemotherapy courses, abstracted. *Proceedings of the American Society of Clinical Oncology* 1982;1:58.

5. Grunberg SM, Hesketh PJ: Control of chemotherapy-induced emesis. *N Engl J Med* 1993;24:1790-1796.

6. Hardman JG (ed): *Goodman and Gilman's: The Pharmacological Basis of Therapeutics, Ninth Edition*. New York, McGraw-Hill, 1996.

7. Sherman MP, Campbell LA, Gong H Jr, *et al.*: Antimicrobial and respiratory burst characteristics of pulmonary alveolar macrophages recovered from smokers of marijuana alone, smokers of tobacco alone, smokers of marijuana and tobacco, and nonsmokers. *Am Rev Respir Dis* 1991;144:1351-1356.

8. Baldwin GC, Tashkin DP, Buckley DM, et al: Marijuana and cocaine impair alveolar macrophage function and cytokine production. *Am J Respir Care Med* 1997;156:1606-1613.

9. Levitz SM, Diamond RD: Aspergillosis and marijuana. *Ann Intern Med* 1991; 115:578-579.

10. Matthias P, Tashkin DP, Marques-Magallanes JA, *et al.*: Effects of varying marijuana potency on deposition of tar and [Delta][9]-THC in the lung during smoking. *Pharmacol Biochem Behav* 1997;58:1045-1050.

11. Mattes RD, Engelman K, Shaw LM, *et al.*: Cannabinoids and appetite stimulation. *Pharmacol Biochem Behav* 1994;49:187-195.

12. Nahas G, Latour C: The human toxicity of marijuana. *Med J Aust* 1992; 156:495-497.

13. Nelan EH: Medical marijuana: Research priority, hoax or civil right? *Gay Men's Health Crisis Treatment Issues* 1997;11:1-3.

14. Kassirer JP: Federal foolishness and marijuana, editorial, *N Engl J Med* 1997; 336-336-367.

15. Annas GJ: Reefer madness: The federal response to California's medical-marijuana law. *N Engl J Med* 1997;337:435-439.

Suggested Reading

* Grinspoon L, Bakalar J: *Marijuana, the Forbidden Medicine*, New Haven, Conn, Yale Univ Pr, 1993.

* Rosenthal E, Mikuriya T, Gieringer D: *Marijuana Medical Handbook: A guide to therapeutic use*. Oakland, Calif, Quick American Archives, 1997.

* Schwartz RH, Beveridge RA: Marijuana as an antiemetic drug: How useful is it today? Opinions from clinical oncologists. *J Addict Dis* 1994;13:53-65.

* Schwartz RH, Voth EA, Sheridan MJ: Marijuana to prevent nausea and vomiting in cancer patients: A survey of clinical oncologists. *South Med J* 1997;90:167-172.

* Voth EA, Schwartz RH: Medicinal applications of delta-9-tetrahydrocannabinol and marijuana. *Ann Intern Med* 1997;126-791-798.

* Wu T-C, Tashkin DP, Djahed B, *et al.*: Pulmonary hazards of smoking marijuana as compared with tobacco. *N Engl J Med* 1988;318:347-351.

Consultants for This Article

Lisa Capaldina, MD, is Associate clinical Professor of Medicine, University of California, San Francisco, School of Medicine; and Director, Castro Medical Clinic, San Francisco.

Donald Tashkin, MD, is Professor of Medicine, Division of Pulmonary and Critical Care Medicine, Department of Medicine, University of California, Los Angeles, UCLA School of Medicine; and a researcher for the National Institute on Drug Abuse, Bethesda, Maryland.

William Vilensky, RPh, DO, is Clinical Associate Professor, Department of Family Medicine, Robert Wood Johnson Medical School, University of Medicine and Dentistry of New Jersey, Piscataway; Clinical Associate Professor, Department of Psychiatry. UMDMJ—New Jersey Medical School, Newark; and Executive Medical Director, Forensic and Educational Consultants, Margate, New Jersey.

—prepared by Lori D. Talarico,
Senior associate editor Patient Care

Part Two

The Nature of Addiction

Chapter 11

Addiction Is a Brain Disease

One of America's foremost experts on drug abuse discusses some of the latest knowledge about use, addiction, and treatment. Addictive drugs change the brain in fundamental ways, he says, producing compulsive, uncontrollable drug seeking and use.

Question: Are there particular personality types or socioeconomic conditions that predominate among those who try a drug in the first place?   ,

Leshner: There are different ways to approach this question. One, is to recognize that there are 72 risk factors for drug abuse and addiction that have been identified. They're not equally important. They operate either at the level of the individual, the level of the family, or the level of the community. These are, by the way, the same risk factors for everything else bad that can happen—poverty, racism, weak parenting, peer-group pressure, and getting involved with the wrong bunch of kids, for example. What these risk factors do is increase the probability that people with certain characteristics will, in fact, take drugs.

But you cannot generalize because the majority of people who have a lot of risk factors never do use drugs. In spite of the importance of these risk factors, they are not determinants.

"Addiction Is a Brain Disease," an interview with Dr. Alan Leshner, director of the National Institute of Drug Abuse, by Jerry Stilkind, in *USIA Electronic Journal*, Vol. 2, No. 3, June 1997.

So, what determines whether, say, Harry will use drugs, and whether Harry will become addicted to drugs? They're not the same question. Whether or not Harry will use drugs has to do with his personal situation—is he under stress, are his peers using drugs, are drugs readily available, what kind of pressure is there to use drugs, and does Harry have a life situation that, in effect, he wants to medicate? That is, does Harry feel that if he changed his mood he would feel better, he would have a happier life? People, at first, take drugs to modify their mood, their perception, or their emotional state. They don't use drugs to counteract racism or poverty. They use drugs to make them feel good. And we, by the way, know a tremendous amount about how drugs make you feel good, why they make you feel good, the brain mechanisms that are involved.

Now, there are individual differences, not only in whether or not someone will take drugs, but in how they will respond to drugs once they take them. A Harvard University study published [in 1997] demonstrated that there is a genetic component to how much you like marijuana. That's very interesting because the prediction, of course, is that the more you like it the more you would be prone to take it again, and the greater the probability you would become addicted. And so there's a genetic component to your initial response to it—whether you like it or not—and also to your vulnerability to becoming addicted once you have begun taking it. We know far more about this for alcohol than we do about other drugs.

Question: Do you mean that the genetic make-up of one person may be such that he gets more of a kick from taking cocaine than another individual? Is that what you mean by vulnerability?

Leshner: There's no question that there are individual differences in the experience of drug-taking—not everybody becomes addicted equally easily. There's a myth that I was taught when I was a kid, and that was if you take heroin once, you're instantly addicted for the rest of your life. It's not true. Some people get addicted very quickly, and other people become addicted much less quickly. Why is that? Well, it's probably determined by your genes, and by other unknown factors like your environment, social context, and who you are.

Question: Is this true for people around the world—in the United States, Western Europe, India, Colombia?

Leshner: The fundamental phenomenon of getting addicted is a biological event and, therefore, it's the same everywhere, and the underlying principles that describe the vulnerability, or the propensity to become addicted, are universal.

Question: What is addiction? How is it created in the body?

Leshner: There has long been a discussion about the difference between physical addiction, or physical dependence, and psychological dependence, behavioral forms of addiction. That is a useless and unimportant distinction. First of all, not all drugs that are highly addicting lead to dramatic physical withdrawal symptoms when you stop taking them. Those that do—alcohol and heroin, for example—produce a physical dependence, which means that when you stop taking them you have withdrawal symptoms—gastrointestinal problems, shaking, cramps, difficulty breathing in some people and difficulty with temperature control.

Drugs that don't have those withdrawal symptoms include some of the most addicting substances ever known—crack cocaine and methamphetamine are the two most dramatic examples. These are phenomenally addicting substances, and when you stop taking them you get depressed, you get sad, you crave the drug, but you don't have dramatic—what we call "florid" —withdrawal symptoms.

Second, when you do have those dramatic withdrawal symptoms with alcohol and heroin, we have medicines that pretty well control those symptoms. So, the important issue is not of detoxifying people. What is important is what we call clinical addiction, or the clinical manifestation of addiction, and that is compulsive, uncontrollable drug seeking and use. That's what matters. People have trouble understanding that uncontrollable, compulsive drug seeking—and the words "compulsive" and "uncontrollable" are very important—is the result of drugs changing your brain in fundamental ways.

Question: How do drugs change the brain? What is it that makes you feel good and wants you to have more?

Leshner: Let's, again, separate initial drug use from addiction. Although addiction is the result of voluntary drug use, addiction is no longer voluntary behavior, it's uncontrollable behavior. So, drug use and addiction are not a part of a single continuum. One comes from the other, but you really move into a qualitatively different state. Now, we know more about drugs and the brain than we know about anything else and the brain. We have identified the receptors in the brain for every major drug of abuse. We know the natural compounds that normally bind to those receptors in the brain. We know the mechanisms, by and large, by which every major drug of abuse produces its euphoric effects.

Question: Including tobacco, alcohol, marijuana?

Leshner: Tobacco, alcohol, marijuana, cocaine, heroin, barbiturates, inhalants—every abusable substance. We know a phenomenal amount. What we also know is that each of these drugs has its own receptor system—its own mechanism of action. But in addition to having idiosyncratic mechanisms of action, each also has common mechanisms of action. That common mechanism of action is to cause the release of dopamine, a substance in the base of the brain, in what is actually a circuit called the mesolimbic reward pathway. That circuit has a neurochemical neurotransmitter, which is dopamine.

We believe that the positive experience of drugs comes through the mesolimbic-dopamine pathway. We know that because if you block activation of that dopamine pathway, animals who had been giving themselves drugs no longer give themselves drugs. In addition to that, *Nature Magazine* (a British science and medicine journal) published a study showing that the greater the activation of the dopamine system following the administration of cocaine the greater the experience of the high. So we know that this is a critical element, and we know that every addicting substance modifies dopamine levels in that part of the brain. That is to say, alcohol, nicotine, amphetamines, heroin, cocaine, marijuana—all produce dopamine changes in the nucleus accumbens, in the mesolimbic pathway in the base of the brain.

We also know that in the connection between the ventral tegmentum and the nucleus accumbens—in the mesolimbic circuit—that at least cocaine, heroin, and alcohol produce quite similar changes at the biochemical level. That is, not only in terms of how much dopamine is produced but also in the similar effects these substances have long after you stop using the drug. So the point here is that we are close to understanding the common essence of addiction in the brain, and we care about this because it tells us how to develop medications for drug addiction. That is the goal—how to treat drug addiction.

Question: But over time, doesn't the brain of an addict release less and less dopamine? So how does he continue to feel good? How does he get his high if dopamine levels are reduced, rather than increased?

Leshner: Here is another indication of the difference between drug use and addiction. Initially, taking drugs increases dopamine levels, but over time, it actually has the reverse effect. That is, dopamine levels go down. And one of the reasons that we believe that most addicts have trouble experiencing pleasure is that dopamine is important to the experience of pleasure, and when the levels are low you don't feel so good. But once addicted, an individual actually does not take the drug to produce the high.

It is the case in heroin addiction that, initially, they take the drug for the high, but ultimately they take the drug to avoid being sick. The same is true, to some degree, in crack cocaine addiction. That is, we find that people coming off crack cocaine get depressed very badly, and so they are, in effect, medicating themselves, giving themselves crack cocaine to avoid the low. What they're trying to do is pump their dopamine levels up, which doesn't happen, but they keep trying to do it.

Question: Perhaps we should assure people that a certain level of dopamine is normally produced in the brain by pleasurable foods, or activities, and is necessary for human life. Is that correct?

Leshner: Dopamine is a very important substance in many different ways. It is, for example, involved in motor function. In order to maintain motor function, you must have a minimal amount of dopamine. Parkinson's disease is a deficit in dopamine levels, which results in motor problems. Both schizophrenia and depression have dopamine components to them, mostly schizophrenia. In fact, antipsychotic drugs work on dopamine levels. And so, what you need to be doing is balancing your dopamine, not raising it or lowering it. You're trying to maintain dopamine at a normal level. And again, we think that people who are addicted have trouble experiencing pleasure because their dopamine systems are altered.

Question: If the working of the brain changes during addiction, is this alteration permanent, or can other drugs administered by physicians, or behavioral changes in various programs, bring the brain back to an unaddicted, unaffected state?

Leshner: Drugs of abuse have at least two categories of effects. One is what I will call "brain damage." That is, they literally destroy cells or functions in the brain. For example, if you use inhalants, you literally destroy brain tissue. If you use large doses of methamphetamine, we believe you literally destroy both dopamine and serotonin neurons. In most cases, however, we believe changes in the brain associated with addiction are reversible in one way or another, or they can be compensated for. We know that the brain of an addicted individual is substantially different from the brain of a non-addicted individual, and we have many markers of those differences—changes in dopamine levels, changes in various structures and in various functions at the biochemical level. We know some of those changes, like the ability to produce dopamine, recover over time. What we don't know is if they recover to fully normal.

Secondly, we know that some medications can compensate, or can reverse some effects. If the change is reversible, your goal is to reverse. If it's not reversible, but you still need to get that person back to normal functioning, you need a mechanism to compensate for the change.

Question: That moves us into the question of prevention and treatment programs. First, what kinds of prevention programs are known to work?

Leshner: One problem in the prevention of drug abuse is that people think in terms of programs, rather than in terms of principles. But the truth is, like anything else that you study scientifically, stock programs that you apply anywhere around the world in exactly the same way do not work. Rather what you want are guiding principles. And we have now supported over 10 years of research into prevention, and have actually been able to derive a series of principles of what works in prevention, and have just issued the first ever science-based guide to drug-abuse prevention. And some of those principles are fairly obvious once you state them, but if you don't say them you don't do them. For example, prevention programs need to be culturally appropriate. Well, people say that all the time, and then they look at a prevention program and they say, "Oh good, I'm going to just take that one and put it in my country." Then they're shocked when it doesn't work. Well, you need to have the cultural context to whatever you do.

Another obvious principle is that programs need to be age appropriate. Everyone knows that youngsters early in adolescence are a different species from those late in adolescence. So, you need to deal with them differently. The messages have to be different. The advertisement industry has done a very good job with that.

In addition, people frequently like "one-shot" prevention programs. Go in, do something, and then the problem's solved. Well, they never work. You need to have sustained efforts with what we call "boosters." You make your first intervention, then you go back and give another intervention, and then another, and finally you successfully inoculate the individual. There are a whole series of principles outlined in a pamphlet we recently published—"Preventing Drug Use Among Children and Adolescents: A Research Based Guide"—and a checklist against which you could rate programs.

Question: Is this booklet on your web site?

Leshner: Yes. You can find this prevention booklet by going to—www.nida.nih.gov—and looking under publications. You can download the whole thing.

Question: Which have been found more effective in treating addicts—behavioral or medical programs? Or do they need to complement each other?

Leshner: I believe that addiction is a brain disease, but a special kind of brain disease—a brain disease that has behavioral and social aspects. Therefore, the best treatments are going to deal with the biological, the behavioral, and the social-context aspects. Now that's difficult for people to understand, I think, but it's a very important principle. We have studies that show that although behavioral treatment can be very effective, and biological treatment can be very effective, combining the two makes them more effective. In addition to that, remember that people who are addicted typically have been addicted for many, many years, and, therefore, they have to almost relearn how to live in society. And that's a part of treatment.

Question: Such a comprehensive approach sounds pretty expensive. Is it more expensive than a prevention program?

Leshner: The question boils down to whether you're going to try to compare treating an individual once addicted, which involves doing a cost-benefit analysis of what that individual's habit is costing society, versus a massive prevention program that might cost only three cents per person but which only affects the one or two people who would have used the drug in the first place. So, it's not a comparison that you can actually make. However, I can tell you that even the most expensive treatments—inpatient, therapeutic communities that cost, depending on the particular kind of program, between $13,000 and $20,000 a year per person, are a lot less than imprisoning people. Incarceration costs $40,000 a year per person. So the cost-benefit ratio always is in favor of the treatment approach.

Question: How many drug addicts are there in the United States and around the world?

Leshner: We believe that there are about 3.6 million individuals in the United States who are addicted to heroin, crack cocaine, amphetamine, marijuana—the illegal drugs. So, at least that many are in need of treatment. Then heavy users add to that number. It's impossible to know exactly the total number who are in need of treatment, but it's probably between four and six million people. I don't know what the comparable figures are internationally.

—by Jerry Stilkind

Jerry Stilkind writes on drugs, environment and other subjects for the United States Information Agency.

Chapter 12

The Addicted Brain: An Era of Scientific Breakthroughs

Though it may not rank with discovery of life on another planet, the discovery that the brain has an "addiction pathway" shared by nearly all substances of abuse is big news enough. It means that, for the first time, we are beginning to understand how addiction works in the brain at the cellular and molecular levels. It means deepening our understanding of addiction—of why craving occurs and why withdrawal is painful. And it means targeting the search for medications to counteract addiction. Most of the discoveries leading to this progress have occurred within the past year or two, largely under the auspices of the National Institute on Drug Abuse. NIDA Director Alan I. Leshner, PhD was asked by *Behavioral Health Management* Editorial Director Richard L. Peck to elaborate on these discoveries and to place them in the overall context of substance abuse treatment. That there is an overall context—one not relegated solely to "science-based" therapy—he acknowledges readily. It's just that the science these days is so replete with exciting breakthroughs.

Peck: Would you review some of the recent developments in addiction research?

Dr. Leshner: Within the past few years, particularly the last year or so, there has been a series of tremendous scientific advances that

"The Addicted Brain: An Era of Scientific Breakthroughs," by Richard L. Peck, in *Behavioral Health Management*, Vol. 16, No. 5, September-October 1996, p. 33(2), © 1996 Medquest Communications, Inc.; reprinted with permission.

have revolutionized our understanding of substance abuse and addiction.

In the field of neuroscience, we have identified and cloned the specific brain receptors for every major drug of abuse—the opiates, cocaine, marijuana, the benzodiazepines, LSD and nicotine. More recently, we have come to realize that almost all the major drugs of abuse affect a single brain circuit. It has traditionally been called the "reward center" of the brain, but we now know it to be the mesolimbic pathway. This runs from the ventral tegmentum (a rear, lower area of the brain) to the nucleus accumbens in the orbitofrontal area, with projections into the amygdala and other parts of the limbic system. PET scanning has shown that this pathway becomes highly active when impinged upon by all major drugs of abuse. This suggests that there is a common essence to all addiction.

The mesolimbic pathway is mediated by dopamine, a neurotransmitter associated with pleasurable feelings. Nicotine, marijuana, cocaine and the opiates all produce major increases in dopamine levels over the short term. Over the long term, however, continuous use of many of these substances (not all have been studied) leads to reduced dopamine availability. Many of us believe that these dopamine-related events and the cellular changes that accompany them may be the common essence of addiction.

Peck: Does the existence of a single pathway mean that there will be a single drug that will fix all this?

Dr. Leshner: I don't believe that there will ever be a "magic bullet." Let's not forget that there is a whole series of conditioning and learning phenomena going on with addiction, and I think there will always be a need for comprehensive treatment using not only biological, but behavioral and social context interventions as well.

Having said that, we are using a variety of approaches to developing new medications, ranging from looking at specific target sites for specific compounds to looking at ways to modulate the common pathway.

Peck: And in which of these areas would a new drug seem to be most imminent?

Dr. Leshner: We already have some medications for opiate and nicotine addiction, and we're getting close to medications that will complement methadone and LAAM in treating opiate addiction. We have nothing for cocaine addiction, and in fact I have declared this to be our top medication development priority. We have nothing to treat cocaine overdose, nothing to help people stop abusing cocaine and nothing to treat the craving that comes with withdrawal. We are looking at five or six science-based strategies—for example, dopamine modulators, reuptake transporter modulators, and even antibodies that could be used in vaccination. There may be "chemical cocktails" that would address multiple mechanisms involved in cocaine addiction. Altogether we have 26 compounds at various stages of clinical testing. In any event, though, we're talking about years before a usable drug becomes available.

Peck: Does behavioral treatment have a role in reversing some of these brain changes?

Dr. Leshner: Recent work by Lewis Baxter at UCLA produced interesting findings. He studied obsessive-compulsive disorder and, using PET, compared the effects on the brain of clomipramine vs. behavioral treatment. Both produced the same brain changes as the OCD symptomatology was reduced. This was important, because it showed that if you modify behavioral symptoms, you modify the brain.

Peck: Are the brain changes produced by addiction reparable by any form of treatment?

Dr. Leshner: We don't know whether we can ever fully restore the brain to normal. But, if treatment is working, we know that we are at least partially correcting the abnormalities.

Again, though, I don't want to take a reductionist view, I think we will always need behavioral treatments to help people become functional in society. It is analogous to stroke rehabilitation, which employs both biological and behavioral treatment to restore function.

Peck: What about the Alcoholics Anonymous approach, which emphasizes abstinence—would this have an impact on the brain?

Dr. Leshner: This has not been studied very systematically, but of course we know of many, many alcoholics who have reported being helped and supported by this approach. Self-help techniques have demonstrated their usefulness in a wide variety of domains. We know that abstinence will ultimately have a physiological impact on the brain, but we don't know what it is. We know of course, that the effects of addiction on the brain are long-lasting and that four or five months of abstinence produces profound changes in brain function, but we don't know how as yet.

Peck: Some wonder whether the description of long-lasting brain changes and the questions about physical healing of the brain might conceivably lead to addicted persons feeling hopeless about ever getting better, at least without long-lasting pain. How would you respond?

Dr. Leshner: I would respond that there is healing, and treatment accelerates the healing process. We have to remember that we are talking about chronic, relapsing disorders here—it is not analogous to treating a broken bone—therefore, we will need ongoing management of the disorder and at times repeated treatment episodes.

Peck: Which bespeaks a need for patience on the part of managed care, would you say?

Dr. Leshner: Very much so. We're talking about highly complex disorders—a brain disorder with truly embedded behavioral and social context effects requiring complex treatment strategies. This has been called "whole person treatment," and that is what we are talking about. Managed care will find it to be extremely cost-effective to take a longer-term, comprehensive perspective on this.

Peck: What do you foresee as the future of addictions treatment within, say, the next 10 years?

Dr. Leshner: We will have medications that are useful for specific drugs of abuse and as treatments applying to the common mechanisms of addiction. We will also have very specific behavioral treatments, to the point that they are manualized, as we are seeing today for depression and anxiety disorders.

There is a myth that behavioral treatments for addiction are ineffective. In fact, we have many effective treatments, and the issue is to match the appropriate treatment with the appropriate patient, and to apply treatment long enough to have an effect. That this does, in fact, work has been scientifically documented, and the published research confirming treatment efficacy is growing monthly.

Chapter 13

Why Do People Get Hooked?

Imagine you are taking a slug of whiskey, a puff of a cigarette, a toke of marijuana, a snort of cocaine, a shot of heroin. Put aside whether these drugs are legal or illegal. Concentrate, for now, on the chemistry. The moment you take that slug, that puff, that toke, that snort, that shot, trillions of potent molecules surge through your bloodstream and into your brain. Once there, they set off a cascade of chemical and electrical events, a kind of neurological chain reaction that ricochets around the skull and rearranges the interior reality of the mind.

Given the complexity of these events—and the inner workings of the mind in general—it's not surprising that scientists have struggled mightily to make sense of the mechanisms of addiction. Why do certain substances have the power to make us feel so good (at least at first)? Why do some people fall so easily into the thrall of alcohol, cocaine, nicotine, and other addictive substances, while others can, literally, take them or leave them?

The answer, many scientists are convinced, may be simpler than anyone has dared imagine. What ties all these mood-altering drugs together, they say, is a remarkable ability to elevate levels of a common substance in the brain called dopamine. In fact, so overwhelming has evidence of the link between dopamine and drugs of abuse become that the distinction (pushed primarily by the tobacco industry

"Addicted: Why Do People Get Hooked?" by J. Madeleine Nash, in *Time,* Vol. 149, No. 18, May 18, 1997. Reprinted with permission of Time Life Syndication.

and its supporters) between substances that are addictive and those that are merely habit-forming has very nearly been swept away.

The Liggett Group, smallest of the U.S.'s Big Five cigarette makers, broke ranks in March 1977 and conceded not only that tobacco is addictive but also that the company has known it all along. While RJR Nabisco and the others continue to battle in the courts—insisting that smokers are not hooked, just exercising free choice—their denials ring increasingly hollow in the face of the growing weight of evidence. Over the past year, several scientific groups have made the case that in dopamine-rich areas of the brain, nicotine behaves remarkably like cocaine. And in 1997 federal judge ruled for the first time that the Food and Drug Administration has the right to regulate tobacco as a drug and cigarettes as drug-delivery devices.

Now, a team of researchers led by psychiatrist Dr. Nora Volkow of the Brookhaven National Laboratory in New York has published the strongest evidence to date that the surge of dopamine in addicts' brains is what triggers a cocaine high. In the journal *Nature* they described how powerful brain-imaging technology can be used to track the rise of dopamine and link it to feelings of euphoria.

Like serotonin (the brain chemical affected by such antidepressants as Prozac), dopamine is a neurotransmitter—a molecule that ferries messages from one neuron within the brain to another. Serotonin is associated with feelings of sadness and well-being, dopamine with pleasure and elation. Dopamine can be elevated by a hug, a kiss, a word of praise or a winning poker hand—as well as by the potent pleasures that come from drugs.

The idea that a single chemical could be associated with everything from snorting cocaine and smoking tobacco to getting good grades and enjoying sex has electrified scientists and changed the way they look at a wide range of dependencies, chemical and otherwise. Dopamine, they now believe, is not just a chemical that transmits pleasure signals but may, in fact, be the master molecule of addiction.

This is not to say dopamine is the only chemical involved or that the deranged thought processes that mark chronic drug abuse are due to dopamine alone. The brain is subtler than that. Drugs modulate the activity of a variety of brain chemicals, each of which intersects with many others. "Drugs are like sledgehammers," observes Dr. Eric Nestler of the Yale University School of Medicine. "They profoundly alter many pathways."

Nevertheless, the realization that dopamine may be a common endpoint of all those pathways represents a signal advance. Provocative, controversial, unquestionably incomplete, the dopamine hypothesis provides a basic framework for understanding how a genetically encoded trait—such as a tendency to produce too little dopamine—might intersect with environmental influences to create a serious behavioral disorder. Therapists have long known of patients who, in addition to having psychological problems, abuse drugs as well. Could their drug problems be linked to some inborn quirk? Might an inability to absorb enough dopamine, with its pleasure-giving properties, cause them to seek gratification in drugs?

Such speculation is controversial, for it suggests that broad swaths of the population may be genetically predisposed to drug abuse. What is not controversial is that the social cost of drug abuse, whatever its cause, is enormous. Cigarettes contribute to the death toll from cancer and heart disease. Alcohol is the leading cause of domestic violence and highway deaths. The needles used to inject heroin and cocaine are spreading AIDS. Directly or indirectly, addiction to drugs, cigarettes, and alcohol is thought to account for a third of all hospital admissions, a quarter of all deaths, and a majority of serious crimes. In the U.S. alone the combined medical and social costs of drug abuse are believed to exceed $240 billion.

For nearly a quarter-century the U.S. has been waging a war on drugs, with little apparent success. As scientists learn more about how dopamine works (and how drugs work on it), the evidence suggests that we may be fighting the wrong battle. Americans tend to think of drug addiction as a failure of character. But this stereotype is beginning to give way to the recognition that drug dependence has a clear biological basis. "Addiction," declares Brookhaven's Volkow, "is a disorder of the brain no different from other forms of mental illness."

That new insight may be the dopamine hypothesis' most important contribution in the fight against drugs. It completes the loop between the mechanism of addiction and programs for treatment. And it raises hope for more effective therapies. Abstinence, if maintained, not only halts the physical and psychological damage wrought by drugs but in large measure also reverses it.

Genes and social forces may conspire to turn people into addicts but do not doom them to remain so. Consider the case of Rafael Rios, who grew up in a housing project in New York City's drug-infested South Bronx. For 18 years, until he turned 31, Rios, whose father died of alcoholism, led a double life. He graduated from Harvard Law School and joined a prestigious Chicago law firm. Yet all the while he was secretly visiting a shooting gallery once a day. His favored concoction: heroin spiked with a jolt of cocaine. Ten years ago, Rios succeeded in kicking his habit—for good, he hopes. He is now executive

105

director of A Safe Haven, a Chicago-based chain of residential facilities for recovering addicts.

How central is dopamine's role in this familiar morality play? Scientists are still trying to sort that out. It is no accident, they say, that people are attracted to drugs. The major drugs of abuse, whether depressants like heroin or stimulants like cocaine, mimic the structure of neurotransmitters, the most mind-bending chemicals nature has ever concocted. Neurotransmitters underlie every thought and emotion, memory and learning; they carry the signals between all the nerve cells, or neurons, in the brain. Among some 50 neurotransmitters discovered to date, a good half a dozen, including dopamine, are known to play a role in addiction.

The neurons that produce this molecular messenger are surprisingly rare. Clustered in loose knots buried deep in the brain, they number a few tens of thousands of nerve cells out of an estimated total of 100 billion. But through long, wire-like projections known as axons, these cells influence neurological activity in many regions, including the nucleus accumbens, the primitive structure that is one of the brain's key pleasure centers. At a purely chemical level, every experience humans find enjoyable—whether listening to music, embracing a lover, or savoring chocolate—amounts to little more than an explosion of dopamine in the nucleus accumbens, as exhilarating and ephemeral as a firecracker.

Dopamine, like most biologically important molecules, must be kept within strict bounds. Too little dopamine in certain areas of the brain triggers the tremors and paralysis of Parkinson's disease. Too much causes the hallucinations and bizarre thoughts of schizophrenia. A breakthrough in addiction research came in 1975, when psychologists Roy Wise and Robert Yokel at Concordia University in Montreal reported on the remarkable behavior of some drug-addicted rats. One day the animals were placidly dispensing cocaine and amphetamines to themselves by pressing a lever attached to their cages. The next they were angrily banging at the lever like someone trying to summon a stalled elevator. The reason? The scientists had injected the rats with a drug that blocked the action of dopamine.

In the years since, evidence linking dopamine to drugs has mounted. Amphetamines stimulate dopamine-producing cells to pump out more of the chemical. Cocaine keeps dopamine levels high by inhibiting the activity of a transporter molecule that would ordinarily ferry dopamine back into the cells that produce it. Nicotine, heroin and alcohol trigger a complex chemical cascade that raises dopamine levels. And a still unknown chemical in cigarette smoke, a group led by Brookhaven chemist Joanna Fowler reported last year, may extend the activity of dopamine by blocking a mopping-up enzyme, called MAO B, that would otherwise destroy it.

The evidence that Volkow and her colleagues present in *Nature* suggests that dopamine is directly responsible for the exhilarating rush that reinforces the desire to take drugs, at least in cocaine addicts. In all, 17 users participated in the study, says Volkow, and they experienced a high whose intensity was directly related to how extensively cocaine tied up available binding sites on the molecules that transport dopamine around the brain. To produce any high at all, she and her colleagues found, cocaine had to occupy at least 47% of these sites; the "best" results occurred when it took over 60% to 80% of the sites, effectively preventing the transporters from latching onto dopamine and spiriting it out of circulation.

Scientists believe the dopamine system arose very early in the course of animal evolution because it reinforces behaviors so essential to survival. "If it were not for the fact that sex is pleasurable," observes Charles Schuster of Wayne State University in Detroit, "we would not engage in it." Unfortunately, some of the activities humans are neurochemically tuned to find agreeable—eating foods rich in fat and sugar, for instance—have backfired in modern society. Just as a surfeit of food and a dearth of exercise have conspired to turn heart disease and diabetes into major health problems, so the easy availability of addictive chemicals has played a devious trick. Addicts do not crave heroin or cocaine or alcohol or nicotine per se but want the rush of dopamine that these drugs produce.

Dopamine, however, is more than just a feel-good molecule. It also exercises extraordinary power over learning and memory. Think of dopamine, suggests P. Read Montague of the Center for Theoretical Neuroscience at Houston's Baylor College of Medicine, as the proverbial carrot, a reward the brain doles out to networks of neurons for making survival-enhancing choices. And while the details of how this system works are not yet understood, Montague and his colleagues at the Salk Institute in San Diego, California, and M.I.T. have proposed a model that seems quite plausible. Each time the outcome of an action is better than expected, they predicted, dopamine-releasing neurons should increase the rate at which they fire. When an outcome is worse, they should decrease it. And if the outcome is as expected, the firing rate need not change at all.

As a test of his model, Montague created a computer program that simulated the nectar-gathering activity of bees. Programmed with a dopamine-like reward system and set loose on a field of virtual "flowers," some of which were dependably sweet and some of which were either very sweet or not sweet at all, the virtual bees chose the reliably sweet flowers 85% of the time. In laboratory experiments real bees behave just like their virtual counterparts. What does this have to do with drug abuse? Possibly quite a lot, says Montague. The theory is that dopamine-enhancing chemicals fool the brain into thinking drugs are as beneficial as nectar to the bee, thus hijacking a natural reward system that dates back millions of years.

The degree to which learning and memory sustain the addictive process is only now being appreciated. Each time a neurotransmitter like dopamine floods a synapse, scientists believe, circuits that trigger thoughts and motivate actions are etched onto the brain. Indeed, the neurochemistry supporting addiction is so powerful that the people, objects, and places associated with drug taking are also imprinted on the brain. Stimulated by food, sex, or the smell of tobacco, former smokers can no more control the urge to light up than Pavlov's dogs could stop their urge to salivate. For months Rafael Rios lived in fear of catching a glimpse of bare arms—his own or someone else's. Whenever he did, he remembers, he would be seized by a nearly unbearable urge to find a drug-filled syringe.

Indeed, the brain has many devious tricks for ensuring that the irrational act of taking drugs, deemed "good" because it enhances dopamine, will be repeated. PET-scan images taken by Volkow and her colleagues reveal that the absorption of a cocaine-like chemical by neurons is profoundly reduced in cocaine addicts in contrast to normal subjects. One explanation: the addicts' neurons, assaulted by abnormally high levels of dopamine, have responded defensively and reduced the number of sites (or receptors) to which dopamine can bind. In the absence of drugs, these nerve cells probably experience a dopamine deficit, Volkow speculates, so while addicts begin by taking drugs to feel high, they end up taking them in order not to feel low.

PET-scan images of the brains of recovering cocaine addicts reveal other striking changes, including a dramatically impaired ability to process glucose, the primary energy source for working neurons. Moreover, this impairment—which persists for up to 100 days after withdrawal—is greatest in the prefrontal cortex, a dopamine-rich area of the brain that controls impulsive and irrational behavior. Addicts, in fact, display many of the symptoms shown by patients who have suffered strokes or injuries to the prefrontal cortex. Damage to this region, University of Iowa neurologist Antonio Damasio and his colleagues have demonstrated, destroys the emotional compass that controls behaviors the patient knows are unacceptable.

Anyone who doubts that genes influence behavior should see the mice in Marc Caron's lab. These tireless rodents race around their cages for hours on end. They lose weight because they rarely stop to eat, and then they drop from exhaustion because they are unable to sleep.

Why? The mice, says Caron, a biochemist at Duke University's Howard Hughes Medical Institute laboratory, are high on dopamine. They lack the genetic mechanism that sponges up this powerful stuff and spirits it away. Result: there is so much dopamine banging around in the poor creatures' synapses that the mice, though drug-free, act as if they were strung out on cocaine.

For years scientists have suspected that genes play a critical role in determining who will become addicted to drugs and who will not. But not until now have they had molecular tools powerful enough to go after the prime suspects. Caron's mice are just the most recent example. By knocking out a single gene—the so-called dopamine-transporter gene—Caron and his colleagues may have created a strain of mice so sated with dopamine that they are oblivious to the allure of cocaine, and possibly alcohol and heroin as well. "What's exciting about our mice," says Caron, "is that they should allow us to test the hypothesis that all these drugs funnel through the dopamine system."

Several dopamine genes have already been tentatively, and controversially, linked to alcoholism and drug abuse. Inherited variations in these genes modify the efficiency with which nerve cells process dopamine, or so the speculation goes. Thus, some scientists conjecture, a dopamine-transporter gene that is superefficient, clearing dopamine from the synapses too rapidly, could predispose some people to a form of alcoholism characterized by violent and impulsive behavior. In essence, they would be mirror images of Caron's mice. Instead of being drenched in dopamine, their synapses would be dopamine-poor.

The dopamine genes known as d2 and d4 might also play a role in drug abuse, for similar reasons. Both these genes, it turns out, contain the blueprints for assembling what scientists call a receptor, a minuscule bump on the surface of cells to which biologically active molecules are attracted. And just as a finger lights up a room by merely flicking a switch, so dopamine triggers a sequence of chemical reactions each time it binds to one of its five known receptors. Genetic differences that reduce the sensitivity of these receptors or decrease their number could diminish the sensation of pleasure.

The problem is, studies that have purported to find a basis for addiction in variations of the d2 and d4 genes have not held up under scrutiny. Indeed, most scientists think addiction probably involves an intricate dance between environmental influences and multiple genes, some of which may influence dopamine activity only indirectly. This has not stopped some researchers from promoting the provocative theory that many people who become alcoholics and drug addicts suffer from an inherited condition dubbed the reward-deficiency syndrome. Low dopamine levels caused by a particular version of the d2 gene, they say, may link a breathtaking array of aberrant behaviors. Among them: severe alcoholism, pathological gambling, binge eating, and attention-deficit hyperactivity disorder.

The more science unmasks the powerful biology that underlies addiction, the brighter the prospects for treatment become. For instance, the discovery by Fowler and her team that a chemical that inhibits the mopping-up enzyme MAO B may play a role in cigarette addiction has already opened new possibilities for therapy. A number of well-tolerated MAO B-inhibitor drugs developed to treat Parkinson's disease could find a place in the antismoking arsenal. Equally promising, a Yale University team led by Eric Nestler and David Self has found that another type of compound—one that targets the dopamine receptor known as d1—seems to alleviate, at least in rats, the intense craving that accompanies withdrawal from cocaine. One day, suggests Self, a d1 skin patch might help cocaine abusers kick their habit, just as the nicotine patch attenuates the desire to smoke.

Like methadone, the compound that activates d1 appears to be what is known as a partial agonist. Because such medications stimulate some of the same brain pathways as drugs of abuse, they are often addictive in their own right, though less so. And while treating heroin addicts with methadone may seem like a cop-out to people who have never struggled with a drug habit, clinicians say they desperately need more such agents to tide addicts—particularly cocaine addicts—over the first few months of treatment, when the danger of relapse is highest.

Realistically, no one believes better medications alone will solve the drug problem. In fact, one of the most hopeful messages coming out of current research is that the biochemical abnormalities associated with addiction can be reversed through learning. For that reason, all sorts of psychosocial interventions, ranging from psychotherapy to 12-step programs, can and do help. Cognitive therapy, which seeks to supply people with coping skills (exercising after work instead of going to a bar, for instance), appears to hold particular promise. After just 10 weeks of therapy, before-and-after PET-scans suggest, some patients suffering from obsessive-compulsive disorder (which has some similarities with addiction) manage to result not only their behavior but also activity patterns in their brain.

In late 20th century America, where drugs of abuse are being used on an unprecedented scale, the mounting evidence that treatment works could not be more welcome. Until now, policymakers have responded to the drug problem as though it were mostly a criminal matter. Only a third of the $15 billion the U.S. earmarks for the war on drugs goes to prevention and treatment. "In my view, we've got things upside down," says Dr. David Lewis, director of the Center for Alcohol and Addiction Studies at Brown University School of Medicine. "By relying so heavily on a criminalized approach, we've only added to the stigma of drug abuse and prevented high-quality medical care."

Ironically, the biggest barrier to making such care available is the perception that efforts to treat addiction are wasted. Yet treatment for drug abuse has a failure rate no different from that for other chronic diseases. Close to half of recovering addicts fail to maintain complete abstinence after a year—about the same proportion of patients with diabetes and hypertension who fail to comply with their diet, exercise, and medication regimens. What doctors who treat drug abuse should strive for, says Alan Leshner, director of the National Institute on Drug Abuse, is not necessarily a cure but long-term care that controls the progress of the disease and alleviates its worst symptoms. "The occasional relapse is normal," he says, "and just an indication that more treatment is needed."

Rafael Rios has been luckier than many. He kicked his habit in one lengthy struggle that included four months of in-patient treatment at a residential facility and a year of daily outpatient sessions. During that time, Rios checked into 12-step meetings continually, sometimes attending three a day. As those who deal with alcoholics and drug addicts know, such exertions of will power and courage are more common than most people suspect. They are the best reason yet to start treating addiction as the medical and public health crisis it really is.

—by J. Madeleine Nash
with reporting by Alice Park / New York

Chapter 14

Studies Link Stress
and Drug Addiction

Drug-addicted patients who are trying to remain off drugs can often resist the cravings brought on by seeing reminders of their former drug life, NIDA-funded researcher Dr. Mary Jeanne Kreek of Rockefeller University in New York City has noted. "For 6 months or so, they can walk past the street corner where they used to buy drugs and not succumb to their urges. But then all of a sudden they relapse," she says. "When we ask them why they relapse, almost always they tell us something like, 'Well, things weren't going well at my job,' or 'My wife left me.' Sometimes, the problem is as small as 'My public assistance check was delayed,' or 'The traffic was too heavy.'"

Anecdotes such as these are common in the drug abuse treatment community. These anecdotes plus animal studies on this subject point toward an important role for stress in drug abuse relapse. In addition, the fact that addicts often relapse apparently in response to what most people would consider mild stressors suggests that addicts may be more sensitive than nonaddicts to stress.

This hypersensitivity may exist before drug abusers start taking drugs and may contribute to their initial drug use, or it could result from the effects of chronic drug abuse on the brain, or its existence could be due to a combination of both, Dr. Kreek has proposed. She has demonstrated that the nervous system of an addict is hypersensitive to chemically induced stress, which suggests that the nervous system also may be hypersensitive to emotional stress.

"Studies Link Stress and Drug Addiction," by Steven Stocker, in *NIDA Notes,* Vol. 14, No. 1, 1998; National Institute on Drug Abuse (NIDA).

How the Body Copes with Stress

The body reacts to stress by secreting two types of chemical messengers—hormones in the blood and neurotransmitters in the brain. Scientists think that some of the neurotransmitters may be the same or similar chemicals as the hormones but acting in a different capacity.

Some of the hormones travel throughout the body, altering the metabolism of food so that the brain and muscles have sufficient stores of metabolic fuel for activities, such as fighting or fleeing, that help the person cope with the source of the stress. In the brain, the neurotransmitters trigger emotions, such as aggression or anxiety, that prompt the person to undertake those activities.

Normally, stress hormones are released in small amounts throughout the day, but when the body is under stress the level of these hormones increases dramatically. The release of stress hormones begins in the brain. First, a hormone called corticotropin-releasing factor (CRF) is released from the brain into the blood, which carries the CRF to the pituitary gland, located directly underneath the brain. There, CRF stimulates the release of another hormone, adrenocorticotropin (ACTH), which, in turn, triggers the release of other hormones—principally cortisol—from the adrenal glands. Cortisol travels throughout the body, helping it to cope with stress. If the stressor is mild, when the cortisol reaches the brain and pituitary gland it inhibits the further release of CRF and ACTH, which return to their normal levels. But if the stressor is intense, signals in the brain for more CRF release outweigh the inhibitory signal from cortisol, and the stress hormone cycle continues.

Researchers speculate that CRF and ACTH may be among the chemicals that serve dual purposes as hormones and neurotransmitters. The researchers posit that if, indeed, these chemicals also act as neurotransmitters, they may be involved in producing the emotional responses to stress.

The stress hormone cycle is controlled by a number of stimulatory chemicals in addition to CRF and ACTH and inhibitory chemicals in addition to cortisol both in the brain and in the blood. Among the chemicals that inhibit the cycle are neurotransmitters called opioid peptides, which are chemically similar to opiate drugs such as heroin and morphine. Dr. Kreek has found evidence that opioid peptides also may inhibit the release of CRF and other stress-related neurotransmitters in the brain, thereby inhibiting stressful emotions.

How Addiction Changes the Body's Response to Stress

Heroin and morphine inhibit the stress hormone cycle and presumably the release of stress-related neurotransmitters just as the natural opioid peptides do. Thus, when people take heroin or morphine, the drugs add to the inhibition already being provided by the opioid peptides. This may be a major reason that some people start taking heroin or morphine in the first place, suggests Dr. Kreek. "Every one of us has things in life that really bother us," she says. "Most people are able to cope with these hassles, but some people find it very difficult to do so. In trying opiate drugs for the first time, some people who have difficulty coping with stressful emotions might find that these drugs blunt those emotions, an effect that they might find rewarding. This could be a major factor in their continued use of these drugs."

When the effects of opiate drugs wear off, the addict goes into withdrawal. Research has shown that, during withdrawal, the level of stress hormones rises in the blood and stress-related neurotransmitters are released in the brain. These chemicals trigger emotions that the addict perceives as highly unpleasant, which drive the addict to take more opiate drugs. Because the effects of heroin or morphine last only 4 to 6 hours, opiate addicts often experience withdrawal three or four times a day. This constant switching on and off of the stress systems of the body heightens whatever hypersensitivity these systems may have had before the person started taking drugs, Dr. Kreek says. "The result is that these stress chemicals are on a sort of hair-trigger release. They surge at the slightest provocation," she says.

Studies have suggested that cocaine similarly heightens the body's sensitivity to stress, although in a different way. When a cocaine addict takes cocaine, the stress systems are activated, much like when an opiate addict goes into withdrawal, but the person perceives this as part of the cocaine rush because cocaine is also stimulating the parts of the brain that are involved in feeling pleasure. When cocaine's effects wear off and the addict goes into withdrawal, the stress systems are again activated—again, much like when an opiate addict goes into withdrawal. This time, the cocaine addict perceives the activation as unpleasant because the cocaine is no longer stimulating the pleasure circuits in the brain. Because cocaine switches on the stress systems both when it is active and during withdrawal, these systems rapidly become hypersensitive, Dr. Kreek theorizes.

115

Evidence for the Link Between Stress and Addiction

This theory about stress and drug addiction is derived in part from studies conducted by Dr. Kreek's group in which addicts were given a test agent called metyrapone. This chemical blocks the production of cortisol in the adrenal glands, which lowers the level of cortisol in the blood. As a result, cortisol is no longer inhibiting the release of CRF from the brain and ACTH from the pituitary. The brain and pituitary then start producing more of these chemicals.

Physicians use metyrapone to test whether a person's stress system is operating normally. When metyrapone is given to nonaddicted people, the ACTH level in the blood increases. However, when Dr. Kreek and her colleagues administered metyrapone to active heroin addicts, the ACTH level hardly rose at all. When the scientists gave metyrapone to heroin addicts who were abstaining from heroin use and who were not taking methadone, the synthetic opioid medication that suppresses cravings for opiate drugs, the ACTH level in the majority of the addicts increased about twice as high as in nonaddicts. Finally, when the scientists gave metyrapone to heroin addicts maintained for at least 3 months on methadone, the ACTH level rose the same as in nonaddicts.

Addicts on heroin under-react because all the excess opioid molecules in the brain greatly inhibit the brain's stress system, Dr. Kreek explains. Addicts who are heroin-free and methadone-free overreact because the constant on-off of daily heroin use has made the stress system hypersensitive, she says, and heroin addicts who are on methadone react normally because methadone stabilizes this stress system. Methadone acts at the same sites in the brain as heroin, but methadone stays active for about 24 hours while the effects of heroin are felt for only 4 to 6 hours. Because methadone is long-acting, the heroin addict is no longer going into withdrawal three or four times a day. Without the constant activation involved in these withdrawals, the brain's stress system normalizes.

Recently, Dr. Kreek's group reported that a majority of cocaine addicts who are abstaining from cocaine use over-react in the metyrapone test, just like the heroin addicts who are abstaining from heroin and not taking methadone. As with heroin addicts, this over-reaction in cocaine addicts reflects hypersensitivity of the stress system caused by chronic cocaine abuse.

"We think that addicts may react to emotional stress in the same way that their stress hormone system reacts to the metyrapone test," says Dr. Kreek. At the slightest provocation, CRF and other stress-related neurotransmitters pour out into the brain, producing unpleasant emotions that make the addict want to take drugs again, she suggests. Since life is filled with little provocations, addicts in withdrawal are constantly having their stress system activated, she concludes.

Sources

Kreek, M.J., and Koob, G.F. Drug dependence: Stress and dysregulation of brain reward pathways. *Drug and Alcohol Dependence* 51:23-47, 1998.

Kreek, M.J., et al. ACTH, cortisol, and b-endorphin response to metyrapone testing during chronic methadone maintenance treatment in humans. *Neuropeptides* 5:277-278, 1984.

Schluger, J.H., et al. Abnormal metyrapone tests during cocaine abstinence. In: L.S. Harris, ed. *Problems of Drug Dependence, 1997: Proceedings of the 59th Annual Scientific Meeting, College on Problems of Drug Dependence, Inc.* NIDA Research Monograph Series, Number 178. NIH Publication No. 98-4305. Pittsburgh, PA: Superintendent of Documents, U.S. Government Printing Office, p. 105, 1998.

Schluger, J.H., et al. Nalmefene causes greater hypothalamic-pituitary-adrenal axis activation than naloxone in normal volunteers: Implications for the treatment of alcoholism. *Alcoholism: Clinical and Experimental Research* 22(7):1430-1436, 1998.

Chapter 15

Pain Medications and Addiction

Pain is the most common reason people visit a doctor. When treating pain, physicians have long wrestled with a dilemma: How can a doctor relieve a patient's suffering while avoiding the potential for that patient to become addicted to a powerful, opiate pain medication?

Today, the medical profession has concluded that many doctors under-prescribe powerful painkillers because they overestimate the potential for patients to become addicted to these painkillers, which include opiates (from opium) such as morphine and codeine, and substances that are structurally related to morphine. The term "opioids" is used to describe the entire class (both synthetic and natural) of chemicals structurally similar to morphine. Although these drugs carry an extreme risk of addiction for many people, many physicians are not aware that these drugs are rarely abused when used for medicinal purposes.

When doctors limit pain medication, thousands of patients suffer needlessly, according to a number of studies. This quandary over the prescription of powerful pain relievers continues while investigators search for new ways to control pain. National Institute on Drug Abuse (NIDA)-funded researchers are spearheading the exploration for new painkillers that are effective but nonaddicting.

Opium, the bitter dried juice of the opium poppy, has been used for centuries to relieve pain. Opium's analgesic properties come from morphine, opium's major active component.

National Institute on Drug Abuse (NIDA), Pub. No. 13553, November 1999.

119

In the 1970s and 1980s, researchers discovered morphine-like substances that occur naturally in the body, the endogenous opioid peptides.

However, the debilitating side effects that opiate medications can produce, such as nausea, sedation, confusion, and constipation, limit their effectiveness and contribute to the need for alternative analgesics.

NIDA-supported researchers are addressing this need through a number of experimental approaches. These include:

- Developing opioid compounds, synthetic derivatives of opiates, that promote pain relief without producing the euphoria, or "high," that can lead to addiction.

- Developing "promoter compounds" that enhance the pain-relieving effects of opioids so that smaller doses can be used.

- Developing nonopioid analgesics that function through different pain-relief processes and presumably will not produce the negative side effects of opioids.

Years of research have uncovered three categories of opioids:

1. agonists, such as Demerol and methadone, that mimic the effects of endogenous opioids;

2. antagonists, such as naloxone, that block certain effects of opioids; and

3. mixed agonist-antagonist opioid agents, such as buprenorphine and nalbuphine, that both activate and block specific opioid effects. These partial agonists—buprenorphine and nalbuphine—minimize the agonists' negative side effects, including sedation, respiratory problems, and abuse potential, while relieving pain.

Opiates, including morphine and codeine, and synthetic opioids, such as Demerol and fentanyl, work by mimicking the endogenous opioid peptides, pain-relieving chemicals produced in the body. These peptides bind chemically to opiate receptors, activating pain-relieving systems in the brain and spinal cord. But opioids can cause undesirable side effects such as nausea, sedation, confusion, and constipation. With prolonged use of opiates and opioids, individuals become tolerant to the drugs, require larger doses, and can become physically dependent on the drugs.

In recent years, research has shown that doctors' fears that patients will become addicted to pain medication, known as "opiophobia," are largely unfounded. Studies indicate that most patients who receive opioids for pain, even those undergoing long-term therapy, do not become addicted to these drugs. The very few patients who develop rapid and marked tolerance and addiction to opioids are usually those who have a history of psychological problems or prior substance abuse.

One study found that only four out of more than 12,000 patients who were given opioids for acute pain actually became addicted to the drugs. Even long-term therapy has limited potential for addiction. In a study of 38 chronic pain patients, most of whom received opioids for 4 to 7 years, only 2 patients actually became addicted, and both had a history of drug abuse.

The problem of under-prescription of opiates and opioids and the accompanying needless suffering for millions of patients has prompted official reaction. In 1992 the Federal Agency for Health Care Policy and Research issued guidelines for the treatment of pain. The recommendations encourage health professionals to ignore myths about addiction to pain medications and to cease groundless restrictions on the dispensing of opioid pain relievers. The guidelines also recommend greater use of intravenous drug "pumps," which allow nurses or patients themselves to control the timing and dosage of the drug being taken. Following the guidelines, the agency said, would not only relieve unnecessary suffering, but would speed patients' recovery and reduce hospital stays and costs.

For More Information

Questions may be directed to:

National Institute on Drug Abuse (NIDA) Infofax
P.O. Box 30652
Bethesda, MD 20824-0652
1-888-NIH-NIDA
Web site: www.drugabuse.gov

For additional information about NIDA send e-mail to Information @lists. nida.nih.gov.

Part Three

Drugs of Abuse

Chapter 16

Types of Drugs: An Overview

Narcotics

The term narcotic, derived from the Greek word for stupor, originally referred to a variety of substances that induced sleep. In a legal context, narcotic refers to opium, opium derivatives and their semisynthetic or totally synthetic substitutes. Cocaine and coca leaves, which are classified as "narcotics" in the Controlled Substances Act (CSA), are technically not narcotics and are discussed in the section on stimulants.

Narcotics can be administered in a variety of ways. Some are taken orally, transdermally (skin patches), or injected. They are also available in suppositories. As drugs of abuse, they are often smoked, sniffed, or self-administered by the more direct routes of subcutaneous ("skin popping") and intravenous ("mainlining") injection.

Drug effects depend heavily on the dose, route of administration, previous exposure to the drug and the expectation of the user. Aside from their clinical use in the treatment of pain, cough suppression, and acute diarrhea, narcotics produce a general sense of well-being by reducing tension, anxiety, and aggression. These effects are helpful in a therapeutic setting but contribute to their abuse.

Narcotic use is associated with a variety of unwanted effects including drowsiness, inability to concentrate, apathy, lessened physical activity, constriction of the pupils, dilation of the subcutaneous

Excerpted from *Drugs of Abuse*, U.S. Department of Justice, Drug Enforcement Administration, 1997.

125

blood vessels causing flushing of the face and neck, constipation, nausea and vomiting and, most significantly, respiratory depression. As the dose is increased, the subjective, analgesic, and toxic effects become more pronounced. Except in cases of acute intoxication, there is no loss of motor coordination or slurred speech as occurs with many depressants.

Among the hazards of illicit drug use is the ever increasing risk of infection, disease, and overdose. Medical complications common among narcotic abusers arise primarily from adulterants found in street drugs and in the non-sterile practices of injecting. Skin, lung, and brain abscesses, endocarditis, hepatitis, and AIDS are commonly found among narcotic abusers. Since there is no simple way to determine the purity of a drug that is sold on the street, the effects of illicit narcotic use are unpredictable and can be fatal.

With repeated use of narcotics, tolerance and dependence develop. The development of tolerance is characterized by a shortened duration and a decreased intensity of analgesia, euphoria, and sedation which creates the need to administer progressively larger doses to attain the desired effect. Tolerance does not develop uniformly for all actions of these drugs, giving rise to a number of toxic effects. Although the lethal dose is increased significantly in tolerant users, there is always a dose at which death can occur from respiratory depression.

Physical dependence refers to an alteration of normal body functions that necessitates the continued presence of a drug in order to prevent the withdrawal or abstinence syndrome. The intensity and character of the physical symptoms experienced during withdrawal are directly related to the particular drug of abuse, the total daily dose, the interval between doses, the duration of use, and the health and personality of the addict. In general, narcotics with shorter durations of action tend to produce shorter, more intense withdrawal symptoms, while drugs that produce longer narcotic effects have prolonged symptoms that tend to be less severe.

The withdrawal symptoms experienced from heroin/morphine-like addiction are usually experienced shortly before the time of the next scheduled dose. Early symptoms include watery eyes, runny nose, yawning, and sweating. Restlessness, irritability, loss of appetite, tremors, and severe sneezing appear as the syndrome progresses. Severe depression and vomiting are not uncommon. The heart rate and blood pressure are elevated. Chills alternating with flushing and excessive sweating are also characteristic symptoms. Pains in the bones and muscles of the back and extremities occur as do muscle spasms and kicking movements, which may be the source of the expression "kicking the habit." At any point during this process, a suitable narcotic can be administered that will dramatically reverse the withdrawal symptoms. Without intervention, the syndrome will run its course and most of the overt physical symptoms will disappear within 7 to 10 days.

The psychological dependence that is associated with narcotic addiction is complex and protracted. Long after the physical need for the drug has passed, the addict may continue to think and talk about the use of drugs. There is a high probability that relapse will occur after narcotic withdrawal when neither the physical environment nor the behavioral motivators that contributed to the abuse have been altered.

There are two major patterns of narcotic abuse or dependence seen in the U.S. One involves individuals whose drug use was initiated within the context of medical treatment who escalate their dose through "doctor shopping" or branch out to illicit drugs. A very small percentage of addicts are in this group.

The other more common pattern of abuse is initiated outside the therapeutic setting with experimental or recreational use of narcotics. The majority of individuals in this category may abuse narcotics sporadically for months or even years. These occasional users are called "chippers." Although they are neither tolerant of nor dependent on narcotics, the social, medical, and legal consequences of their behavior is very serious. Some experimental users will escalate their narcotic use and will eventually become dependent, both physically and psychologically. The earlier drug use begins, the more likely it is to progress to abuse and dependence. Heroin use among males in inner cities is generally initiated in adolescence and dependence develops in about 1 or 2 years.

Narcotics of Natural Origin

The poppy *Papaver somniferum* is the source for nonsynthetic narcotics. It was grown in the Mediterranean region as early as 5000 B.C., and has since been cultivated in a number of countries throughout the world. The milky fluid that seeps from incisions in the unripe seedpod of this poppy has, since ancient times, been scraped by hand and air dried to produce what is known as opium. A more modern method of harvesting is by the industrial poppy straw process of extracting alkaloids from the mature dried plant. The extract may be in liquid, solid, or powder form, although most poppy straw concentrate available commercially is a fine brownish powder. More than 500 tons of opium or its equivalent in poppy straw concentrate are legally imported into the U.S. annually for legitimate medical use.

Opium. There were no legal restrictions on the importation or use of opium until the early 1900s. In the United States, the unrestricted availability of opium, the influx of opium smoking immigrants from the Orient, and the invention of the hypodermic needle contributed to the more severe variety of compulsive drug abuse seen at the turn of the twentieth century. In those days, medicines often contained opium without any warning label. Today there are state, federal, and international laws governing the production and distribution of narcotic substances.

Although opium is used in the form of paragoric to treat diarrhea, most opium imported into the United States is broken down into its alkaloid constituents. These alkaloids are divided into two distinct chemical classes, phenanthrenes and isoquinolines. The principal phenanthrenes are morphine, codeine, and thebaine, while the isoquinolines have no significant central nervous system effects and are not regulated under the CSA.

Morphine. Morphine, the principal constituent of opium, can range in concentration from 4 to 21 percent (note: commercial opium is standardized to contain 10% morphine). It is one of the most effective drugs known for the relief of pain, and remains the standard against which new analgesics are measured. Morphine is marketed in a variety of forms including oral solutions (Roxanol), sustained-release tablets (MSIR and MS-Contin), suppositories and injectable preparations. It may be administered orally, subcutaneously, intramuscularly, or intravenously, the latter method being the one most frequently used by addicts. Tolerance and physical dependence develop rapidly in the user. Only a small part of the morphine obtained from opium is used directly; most of it is converted to codeine and other derivatives.

Codeine. This alkaloid is found in opium in concentrations ranging from 0.7 to 2.5 percent. Most codeine used in the U.S. is produced from morphine. Compared to morphine, codeine produces less analgesia, sedation, and respiratory depression and is frequently taken orally. Codeine is medically prescribed for the relief of moderate pain. It is made into tablets either alone or in combination with aspirin or acetaminophen (Tylenol). Codeine is an effective cough suppressant and is found in a number of liquid preparations. Codeine products are also used to a lesser extent, as an injectable solution for the treatment of pain. It is by far the most widely used naturally occurring narcotic in medical treatment in the world. Codeine products are encountered on the illicit market frequently in combination with glutethimide (Doriden) or carisoprodol (Soma).

Thebaine. A minor constituent of opium, thebaine is chemically similar to both morphine and codeine, but produces stimulatory rather than depressant effects. Thebaine is not used therapeutically, but is converted into a variety of compounds including codeine, hydrocodone, oxycodone, oxymorphone, nalbuphine, naloxone, naltrexone and buprenorphine. It is controlled in Schedule II of the CSA as well as under international law.

Semi-Synthetic Narcotics

The following narcotics are among the more significant substances that have been derived by modification of the phenanthrene alkaloids contained in opium:

Heroin. First synthesized from morphine in 1874, heroin was not extensively used in medicine until the beginning of the twentieth century. Commercial production of the new pain remedy was first started in 1898. While it received widespread acceptance from the medical profession, physicians remained unaware of its potential for addiction for years. The first comprehensive control of heroin in the United States was established with the Harrison Narcotic Act of 1914.

Pure heroin is a white powder with a bitter taste. Most illicit heroin is a powder which may vary in color from white to dark brown because of impurities left from the manufacturing process or the presence of additives. Pure heroin is rarely sold on the street. A "bag" —slang for a single dosage unit of heroin—may contain 100 mg of powder, only a portion of which is heroin; the remainder could be sugars, starch, powdered milk, or quinine. Traditionally the purity of heroin in a bag has ranged from 1 to 10 percent; more recently heroin purity has ranged from 1 to 98 percent, with a national average of 35 percent.

Another form of heroin known as "black tar" has also become increasingly available in the western United States. The color and consistency of black tar heroin result from the crude processing methods used to illicitly manufacture heroin in Mexico. Black tar heroin may be sticky like roofing tar or hard like coal, and its color may vary from dark brown to black. Black tar heroin is often sold on the street in its tar-like state at purities ranging from 20 to 80 percent. Black tar heroin is most frequently dissolved, diluted and injected.

The typical heroin user today consumes more heroin than a typical user did just a decade ago, which is not surprising given the higher purity currently available at the street level. Until recently, heroin in the United States almost exclusively was injected either intravenously, subcutaneously (skin-popping), or intramuscularly. Injection is the most practical and efficient way to administer low-purity heroin. The availability of higher purity heroin has meant that users now can snort or smoke the narcotic. Evidence suggests that heroin snorting is widespread or increasing in those areas of the country where high-purity heroin is available, generally in the northeastern United States. This method of administration may be more appealing to new users because it eliminates both the fear of acquiring syringe-borne diseases such as HIV/AIDS and hepatitis, and the historical stigma attached to intravenous heroin use.

Hydromorphone. Hydromorphone (Dilaudid) is marketed both in tablet and injectable forms. Its analgesic potency is from two to eight times that of morphine. Much sought after by narcotic addicts, hydromorphone is usually obtained by the abuser through fraudulent prescriptions or theft. The tablets are dissolved and injected as a substitute for heroin.

Oxycodone. Oxycodone is synthesized from thebaine. It is similar to codeine, but is more potent and has a higher dependence potential. It is effective orally and is marketed in combination with aspirin (Percodan) or acetaminophen (Percocet) for the relief of pain. Addicts take these tablets orally or dissolve them in water, filter out the insoluble material, and "mainline" the active drug.

Hydrocodone. Hydrocodone is an orally active analgesic and antitussive Schedule II narcotic which is marketed in multi-ingredient Schedule III products. The therapeutic dose of 5-10 mg is pharmacologically equivalent to 60 mg of oral morphine. Sales and production of this drug have increased significantly in recent years as have diversion and illicit use. Trade names include Anexsia, Hycodan, Hycomine, Lorcet, Lortab, Tussionex, Tylox, and Vicodin. These are available as tablets, capsules and/or syrups.

Synthetic Narcotics

In contrast to the pharmaceutical products derived directly or indirectly from narcotics of natural origin, synthetic narcotics are produced entirely within the laboratory. The continuing search for products that retain the analgesic properties of morphine without the consequent dangers of tolerance and dependence has yet to yield a product that is not susceptible to abuse. A number of clandestinely produced drugs as well as drugs that have accepted medical uses fall into this category.

Meperidine. Introduced as a potent analgesic in the 1930s, meperidine produces effects that are similar but not identical to morphine (shorter duration of action and reduced antitussive and antidiarrheal actions). Currently it is used for the relief of moderate to severe pain, particularly in obstetrics and post-operative situations. Meperidine is available in tablets, syrups, and injectable forms (Demerol). Several analogues of meperidine have been clandestinely produced. One noteworthy analogue is a preparation with a neurotoxic by-product that has produced irreversible Parkinsonism.

Methadone and Related Drugs. German scientists synthesized methadone during World War II because of a shortage of morphine. Although chemically unlike morphine or heroin, methadone produces many of the same effects. Introduced into the United States in 1947 as an analgesic (Dolophine), it is primarily used today for the treatment of narcotic addiction (Methadone). The effects of methadone are longer-lasting than those of morphine-based drugs. Methadone's effects can last up to 24 hours, thereby permitting administration only once a day in heroin detoxification and maintenance programs. Methadone is almost as effective when administered orally as it is by injection. Tolerance and dependence may develop, and withdrawal symptoms, though they develop more slowly and are less severe than those of morphine and heroin, are more prolonged. Ironically, methadone used to control narcotic addiction is frequently encountered on the illicit market and has been associated with a number of overdose deaths.

Closely related to methadone, the synthetic compound levo-alphacetylmethadol or LAAM (ORLAAM) has an even longer duration of action (from 48 to 72 hours), permitting a reduction in frequency of use. In 1994 it was approved as a treatment of narcotic addiction. Buprenorphine (Buprenex), a semi-synthetic Schedule V narcotic analgesic derived from thebaine, is currently being investigated as a treatment of narcotic addiction.

Another close relative of methadone is dextropropoxyphene, first marketed in 1957 under the trade name of Darvon. Oral analgesic potency is one-half to one-third that of codeine, with 65 mg approximately equivalent to about 600 mg of aspirin. Dextropropoxyphene is prescribed for relief of mild to moderate pain. Bulk dextropropoxyphene is in Schedule II, while preparations containing it are in Schedule IV. More than 100 tons of dextropropoxyphene are produced in the U.S. annually, and more than 25 million prescriptions are written for the products. This narcotic is associated with a number of toxic side effects and is among the top 10 drugs reported by medical examiners in drug abuse deaths.

Fentanyl. First synthesized in Belgium in the late 1950s, fentanyl was introduced into clinical practice in the 1960s as an intravenous anesthetic under the trade name of Sublimaze. Thereafter, two other fentanyl analogues were introduced: alfentanil (Alfenta), an ultra-short (5-10 minutes) acting analgesic, and sufentanil (Sufenta), an exceptionally potent analgesic for use in heart surgery. Today fentanyls are extensively used for anesthesia and analgesia. Illicit use of pharmaceutical fentanyls first appeared in the mid 1970s in the medical community and continues to be a problem in the U.S. To date, over 12 different analogues of fentanyl have been produced clandestinely and identified in the U.S. drug traffic. The biological effects of the fentanyls are indistinguishable from those of heroin with the exception that the fentanyls may be hundreds of times more potent. Fentanyls are most commonly used by intravenous administration, but like heroin, they may be smoked or snorted.

Pentazocine. The effort to find an effective analgesic that is less dependence-producing led to the development of pentazocine (Talwin). Introduced as an analgesic in 1967, it was frequently encountered in the illicit trade, usually in combination with tripelennamine and placed into Schedule IV in 1979. An attempt at reducing the abuse of this drug was made with the introduction of Talwin Nx. This product contains a quantity of antagonist sufficient to counteract the morphine-like effects of pentazocine if the tablets are dissolved and injected.

Depressants

Historically, people of almost every culture have used chemical agents to induce sleep, relieve stress, and allay anxiety. While alcohol is one of the oldest and most universal agents used for these purposes, hundreds of substances have been developed that produce central nervous system (CNS) depression. These drugs have been referred to as "downers," sedatives, hypnotics, minor tranquilizers, anxiolytics, and antianxiety medications. Unlike most other classes of drugs of abuse, depressants, except for methaqualone, are rarely produced in clandestine laboratories. Generally, legitimate pharmaceutical products are diverted to the illicit market.

Although a number of depressants (i.e., chloral hydrate, glutethimide, meprobamate, and methaqualone) have been important players in the milieu of depressant use and abuse, two major groups of depressants have dominated the licit and illicit market for nearly a century, first barbiturates and now benzodiazepines.

Barbiturates were very popular in the first half of this century. In moderate amounts, these drugs produce a state of intoxication that is remarkably similar to alcohol intoxication. Symptoms include slurred speech, loss of motor coordination, and impaired judgment. Depending on the dose, frequency, and duration of use, one can rapidly develop tolerance, physical dependence, and psychological dependence on barbiturates. With the development of tolerance, the margin of safety between the effective dose and the lethal dose becomes very narrow. That is, in order to obtain the same level of intoxication, the tolerant abuser may raise his or her dose to a level that can produce coma and death. Although many individuals have taken barbiturates therapeutically without harm, concern about the addiction potential of barbiturates and the ever-increasing numbers of fatalities associated with them led to the development of alternative medications. Today, only about 20% of all depressant prescriptions in the U.S. are for barbiturates.

Benzodiazepines were first marketed in the 1960s. Touted as much safer depressants with far less addiction potential than barbiturates, these drugs today account for about 30% of all prescriptions for controlled substances. It has only been recently that an awareness has developed that benzodiazepines share many of the undesirable side effects of the barbiturates. A number of toxic CNS effects are seen with chronic high dose benzodiazepine therapy. These include headache, irritability, confusion, memory impairment, depression, insomnia, and tremor. The risk of developing over-sedation, dizziness, and confusion increases substantially with higher doses of benzodiazepines. Prolonged use can lead to physical dependence even at recommended dosages. Unlike barbiturates, large doses of benzodiazepines are rarely fatal unless combined with other drugs or alcohol. Although primary abuse of benzodiazepines is well documented, abuse of these drugs usually occurs as part of a pattern of multiple drug abuse. For example, heroin or cocaine abusers will use benzodiazepines and other depressants to augment their "high" or alter the side effects associated with over-stimulation or narcotic withdrawal.

There are marked similarities among the withdrawal symptoms seen with all drugs classified as depressants. In its mildest form, the withdrawal syndrome may produce insomnia and anxiety, usually the same symptoms that initiated the drug use. With a greater level of dependence, tremors and weakness are also present, and in its most severe form, the withdrawal syndrome can cause seizures and delirium. Unlike the withdrawal syndrome seen with most other drugs of abuse, withdrawal from depressants can be life-threatening.

Chloral Hydrate

The oldest of the hypnotic (sleep inducing) depressants, chloral hydrate was first synthesized in 1832. Marketed as syrups or soft gelatin capsules, chloral hydrate takes effect in a relatively short time (30 minutes) and will induce sleep in about an hour. A solution of chloral hydrate and alcohol constituted the infamous "knockout drops" or "Mickey Finn." At therapeutic doses, chloral hydrate has little effect on respiration and blood pressure but, a toxic dose produces severe respiratory depression and very low blood pressure. Although chloral hydrate is still encountered today, its use declined with the introduction of the barbiturates.

Barbiturates

Barbiturates (derivatives of barbituric acid) were first introduced for medical use in the early 1900s. More than 2,500 barbiturates have been synthesized, and in the height of their popularity about 50 were marketed for human use. Today, only about a dozen are used. Barbiturates produce a wide spectrum of CNS depression, from mild sedation to coma, and have been used as sedatives, hypnotics, anesthetics, and anticonvulsants.

The primary differences among many of these products are how fast they produce an effect and how long those effects last. Barbiturates are classified as ultrashort, short, intermediate, and long-acting.

The ultrashort-acting barbiturates produce anesthesia within about one minute after intravenous administration. Those in current medical use are methohexital (Brevital), thiamylal (Surital) and thiopental (Pentothal).

Barbiturate abusers prefer the short-acting and intermediate-acting barbiturates: pentobarbital (Nembutal), secobarbital (Seconal), and amobarbital (Amytal). Other short- and intermediate- acting barbiturates are butalbital (Fiorinal, Fioricet), butabarbital (Butisol), talbutal (Lotusate) and aprobarbital (Alurate). After oral administration, the onset of action is from 15 to 40 minutes and the effects last up to 6 hours. These drugs are primarily used for sedation or to induce sleep. Veterinarians use pentobarbital for anesthesia and euthanasia.

Long-acting barbiturates include phenobarbital (Luminal) and mephobarbital (Mebaral). Effects of these drugs are realized in about one hour and last for about 12 hours and are used primarily for daytime sedation and the treatment of seizure disorders or mild anxiety.

Glutethimide and Methqualone

Glutethimide (Doriden) was introduced in 1954 and methaqualone (Quaalude, Sopor) in 1965 as safe barbiturate substitutes. Experience showed, however, that their addiction liability and the severity of withdrawal symptoms were similar to those of barbiturates. By 1972, "luding out," taking methaqualone with wine, was a popular college pastime. Excessive use leads to tolerance, dependence, and withdrawal symptoms similar to those of barbiturates. Overdose by glutethimide and methaqualone is more difficult to treat than barbiturate overdose, and deaths have frequently occurred. In the United States, the marketing of methaqualone pharmaceutical products stopped in 1984 and methaqualone was transferred to Schedule I of the CSA. In 1991, glutethimide was transferred into Schedule II in response to an upsurge in the prevalence of diversion, abuse and overdose deaths.

Meprobamate

Meprobamate was introduced as an antianxiety agent in 1955 and is prescribed primarily to treat anxiety, tension, and associated muscle spasms. More than 50 tons are distributed annually in the U.S. under its generic name and brand names such as Miltown and Equanil. Its onset and duration of action are similar to the intermediate acting barbiturates; however, therapeutic doses of meprobamate produce less sedation and toxicity than barbiturates. Excessive use can result in psychological and physical dependence.

135

Benzodiazepines

The benzodiazepine family of depressants are used therapeutically to produce sedation, induce sleep, relieve anxiety and muscle spasms, and to prevent seizures. In general, benzodiazepines act as hypnotics in high doses, as anxiolytics in moderate doses, and as sedatives in low doses. Of the drugs marketed in the United States that affect CNS function, benzodiazepines are among the most widely prescribed medications and, unfortunately, are frequently abused. Fifteen members of this group are presently marketed in the United States and an additional twenty are marketed in other countries.

Like the barbiturates, benzodiazepines differ from one another in how fast they take effect and how long the effects last. Shorter acting benzodiazepines, used to manage insomnia, include estazolam (ProSom), flurazepam (Dalmane), quazepam (Doral), temazepam (Restoril), and triazolam (Halcion).

Benzodiazepines with longer durations of action include alprazolam (Xanax), chlordiazepoxide (Librium), clorazepate (Tranxene), diazepam (Valium), halazepam (Paxipam), lorazepam (Ativan), oxazepam (Serax) and prazepam (Centrax). These longer acting drugs are primarily used for the treatment of general anxiety. Midazolam (Versed) is available in the U.S. only in an injectable form for an adjunct to anesthesia. Clonazepam (Klonopin) is recommended for use in the treatment of seizure disorders.

Flunitrazepam (Rohypnol), which produces diazepam-like effects, is becoming increasingly popular among young people as a drug of abuse. The drug is not marketed legally in the United States, but is smuggled in by traffickers.

Benzodiazepines are classified in the CSA as Schedule IV depressants. Repeated use of large doses or, in some cases, daily use of therapeutic doses of benzodiazepines is associated with physical dependence. The withdrawal syndrome is similar to that of alcohol withdrawal and is generally more unpleasant and longer lasting than narcotic withdrawal and frequently requires hospitalization. Abrupt cessation of benzodiazepines is not recommended and tapering-down the dose eliminates many of the unpleasant symptoms.

Given the number of people who are prescribed benzodiazepines, relatively few patients increase their dosage or engage in drug-seeking behavior. However, those individuals who do abuse benzodiazepines often maintain their drug supply by getting prescriptions from several doctors, forging prescriptions, or buying diverted pharmaceutical products on the illicit market. Abuse is frequently associated with adolescents and young adults who take benzodiazepines to obtain a "high." This intoxicated state results in reduced inhibition and impaired judgment. Concurrent use of alcohol or other depressants with benzodiazepines can be life-threatening. Abuse of benzodiazepines is particularly high among heroin and cocaine abusers. Approximately 50 percent of people entering treatment for narcotic or cocaine addiction also report abusing benzodiazepines.

Stimulants

Stimulants are sometimes referred to as "uppers" and reverse the effects of fatigue on both mental and physical tasks. Two commonly used stimulants are nicotine, found in tobacco products, and caffeine, an active ingredient in coffee, tea, some soft drinks, and many nonprescription medicines. Used in moderation, these substances tend to relieve malaise and increase alertness. Although the use of these products has been an accepted part of our culture, the recognition of their adverse effects has resulted in a proliferation of caffeine-free products and efforts to discourage cigarette smoking.

A number of stimulants, however, are under the regulatory control of the CSA. Some of these controlled substances are available by prescription for legitimate medical use in the treatment of obesity, narcolepsy, and attention deficit hyperactivity disorders. As drugs of abuse, stimulants are frequently taken to produce a sense of exhilaration, enhance self esteem, improve mental and physical performance, increase activity, reduce appetite, produce prolonged wakefulness, and to "get high." They are recognized as among the most potent agents of reward and reinforcement that underlie the problem of dependence.

Stimulants are both diverted from legitimate channels and clandestinely manufactured exclusively for the illicit market. They are taken orally, sniffed, smoked, and injected. Smoking, snorting, or injecting stimulants produces a sudden sensation known as a "rush" or a "flash." Abuse is often associated with a pattern of binge use, that is, consuming large doses of stimulants sporadically. Heavy users may inject themselves every few hours, continuing until they have depleted their drug supply or reached a point of delirium, psychosis, and physical exhaustion. During this period of heavy use, all other interests become secondary to recreating the initial euphoric rush. Tolerance can develop rapidly, and both physical and psychological dependence occur. Abrupt cessation, even after a weekend binge, is commonly followed by depression, anxiety, drug craving, and extreme fatigue ("crash").

Therapeutic levels of stimulants can produce exhilaration, extended wakefulness, and loss of appetite. These effects are greatly intensified when large doses of stimulants are taken. Physical side effects—including dizziness, tremor, headache, flushed skin, chest pain with palpitations, excessive sweating, vomiting, and abdominal cramps—may occur as a result of taking too large a dose at one time or taking large doses over an extended period of time. Psychological effects include agitation, hostility, panic, aggression, and suicidal or homicidal tendencies. Paranoia, sometimes accompanied by both auditory and visual hallucinations, may also occur. In overdose, unless there is medical intervention, high fever, convulsions, and cardiovascular collapse may precede death. Because accidental death is partially due to the effects of stimulants on the body's cardiovascular and temperature-regulating systems, physical exertion increases the hazards of stimulant use.

Cocaine

Cocaine, the most potent stimulant of natural origin, is extracted from the leaves of the coca plant (*Erythroxylon coca*) which is indigenous to the Andean highlands of South America. Natives in this region chew or brew coca leaves into a tea for refreshment and to relieve fatigue similar to the customs of chewing tobacco and drinking tea or coffee.

Pure cocaine was first isolated in the 1880s and used as a local anesthetic in eye surgery. It was particularly useful in surgery of the nose and throat because of its ability to provide anesthesia as well as to constrict blood vessels and limit bleeding. Many of its therapeutic applications are now obsolete due to the development of safer drugs.

Illicit cocaine is usually distributed as a white crystalline powder or as an off-white chunky material. The powder, usually cocaine hydrochloride, is often diluted with a variety of substances, the most common of which are sugars such as lactose, inositol, and mannitol, and local anesthetics such as lidocaine. The adulteration increases the volume and thus multiplies profits. Cocaine hydrochloride is generally snorted or dissolved in water and injected. It is rarely smoked.

"Crack," the chunk or "rock" form of cocaine, is a ready-to-use freebase. On the illicit market it is sold in small, inexpensive dosage units that are smoked. With crack came a dramatic increase in drug abuse problems and violence. Smoking delivers large quantities of cocaine to the lungs producing effects comparable to intravenous injection; these effects are felt almost immediately after smoking, are

138

very intense, and are quickly over. Once introduced in the mid-1980s, crack abuse spread rapidly and made the cocaine experience available to anyone with $10 and access to a dealer. In addition to other toxicities associated with cocaine abuse, cocaine smokers suffer from acute respiratory problems including cough, shortness of breath, and severe chest pains with lung trauma and bleeding.

The intensity of the psychological effects of cocaine, as with most psychoactive drugs, depends on the dose and rate of entry to the brain. Cocaine reaches the brain through the snorting method in three to five minutes. Intravenous injection of cocaine produces a rush in 15 to 30 seconds and smoking produces an almost immediate intense experience. The euphoric effects of cocaine are almost indistinguishable from those of amphetamine, although they do not last as long. These intense effects can be followed by a dysphoric crash. To avoid the fatigue and the depression of "coming down," frequent repeated doses are taken. Excessive doses of cocaine may lead to seizures and death from respiratory failure, stroke, cerebral hemorrhage, or heart failure. There is no specific antidote for cocaine overdose.

According to the 1993 Household Drug Survey, the number of Americans who used cocaine within the preceding month of the survey numbered about 1.3 million; occasional users (those who used cocaine less often than monthly) numbered at approximately 3 million, down from 8.1 million in 1985. The number of weekly users has remained steady at around a half million since 1983.

Amphetamines

Amphetamine, dextroamphetamine, and methamphetamine are collectively referred to as amphetamines. Their chemical properties and actions are so similar that even experienced users have difficulty knowing which drug they have taken.

Amphetamine was first marketed in the 1930s as Benzedrine in an over-the-counter inhaler to treat nasal congestion. By 1937 amphetamine was available by prescription in tablet form and was used in the treatment of the sleeping disorder narcolepsy and the behavioral syndrome called minimal brain dysfunction (MBD), which today is called attention deficit hyperactivity disorder (ADHD). During World War II, amphetamine was widely used to keep the fighting men going; both dextroamphetamine (Dexedrine) and methamphetamine (Methedrine) became readily available.

As use of amphetamines spread, so did their abuse. Amphetamines became a cure-all for helping truckers to complete their long routes without falling asleep, for weight control, for helping athletes to perform better and train longer, and for treating mild depression. Intravenous amphetamine abuse spread among a subculture known as "speed freaks." With experience, it became evident that the dangers of abuse of these drugs outweighed most of their therapeutic uses.

Increased control measures were initiated in 1965 with amendments to the federal food and drug laws to curb the black market in amphetamines. Many pharmaceutical amphetamine products were removed from the market and doctors prescribed those that remained less freely. In order to meet the ever-increasing black market demand for amphetamines, clandestine laboratory production mushroomed, especially methamphetamine laboratories on the West Coast. Today, most amphetamines distributed to the black market are produced in clandestine laboratories.

Amphetamines are generally taken orally or injected. However, the addition of "ice," the slang name for crystallized methamphetamine hydrochloride, has promoted smoking as another mode of administration. Just as "crack" is smokable cocaine, "ice" is smokable methamphetamine. Both drugs are highly addictive and toxic.

The effects of amphetamines, especially methamphetamine, are similar to cocaine, but their onset is slower and their duration is longer. In general, chronic abuse produces a psychosis that resembles schizophrenia and is characterized by paranoia, picking at the skin, preoccupation with one's own thoughts, and auditory and visual hallucinations. Violent and erratic behavior is frequently seen among chronic abusers of amphetamines.

Methcathinone

Methcathinone is one of the more recent drugs of abuse in the U.S. and was placed into Schedule I of the CSA in 1993. Known on the streets as "Cat," it is a structural analogue of methamphetamine and cathinone. Clandestinely manufactured, methcathinone is almost exclusively sold in the stable and highly water soluble hydrochloride salt form. It is most commonly snorted, although it can be taken orally by mixing it with a beverage or diluted in water and injected intravenously. Methcathinone has an abuse potential equivalent to methamphetamine, and produces amphetamine-like activity including superabundant energy, hyperactivity, extended wakefulness, and loss of appetite. Pleasant effects include a burst of energy, speeding of the mind, increased feelings of invincibility and euphoria. Unpleasant effects include anxiety, tremor, insomnia, weight loss, dehydration, sweating, stomach pains, pounding heart, nose bleeds, and body aches. Toxic levels may produce convulsions, paranoia, and hallucinations. Like other CNS stimulants, binges are usually followed by a "crash" with periods of variable depression.

Khat

For centuries, khat, the fresh young leaves of the *Cathula edulis* shrub, has been consumed where the plant is cultivated, primarily in East Africa and the Arabian peninsula. There, chewing khat predates the use of coffee and is used in a similar social context. Chewed in moderation, khat alleviates fatigue and reduces appetite. Compulsive use may result in manic behavior with grandiose delusions or in a paranoid type of illness, sometimes accompanied by hallucinations.

Khat has been brought into the U.S. and other countries for use by emigrants from the source countries. It contains a number of chemicals among which are two controlled substances, cathinone (Schedule I) and cathine (Schedule IV). As the leaves mature or dry, cathinone is converted to cathine which significantly reduces its stimulatory properties.

Methylphenidate (Ritalin)

The primary, legitimate medical use of methylphenidate (Ritalin) is to treat attention deficit disorders in children. As with other Schedule II stimulants, the abuse of methylphenidate may produce the same effects as the abuse of cocaine or the amphetamines. It has been reported that the psychosis of chronic methylphenidate intoxication is identical to the paranoid psychosis of amphetamine intoxication. Unlike other stimulants, however, methylphenidate has not been clandestinely produced, although abuse of this substance has been well documented among narcotic addicts who dissolve the tablets in water and inject the mixture. Complications arising from this practice are common due to the insoluble fillers used in the tablets. When injected, these materials block small blood vessels, causing serious damage to the lung and retina of the eye.

Anorectic Drugs

A number of drugs have been developed and marketed to replace amphetamines as appetite suppressants. These anorectic drugs include benzphetamine (Didrex), diethylproprion (Tenuate, Tepanil),

141

fenfluramine (Pondimin), mazindol (Sanorex, Mazanor), phendimetrazine (Bontril, Prelu-2, Plegine) and phentermine (Ionamin, AdipexP). They produce many of the effects of the amphetamines, but are generally less potent. All are controlled under the CSA because of the similarity of their effects to those of the amphetamines.

Hallucinogens

Hallucinogens are among the oldest known group of drugs that have been used for their ability to alter human perception and mood. For centuries, many of the naturally occurring hallucinogens found in plants and fungi have been used for medical, social, and religious practices. In more recent years, a number of synthetic hallucinogens have been produced, some of which are much more potent than their naturally occurring counterparts.

The biochemical, pharmacological and physiological basis for hallucinogenic activity is not well understood. Even the name for this class of drugs is not ideal, since hallucinogens do not always produce hallucinations. However, taken in nontoxic dosages, these substances produce changes in perception, thought, and mood. Physiological effects include elevated heart rate, increased blood pressure, and dilated pupils. Sensory effects include perceptual distortions that vary with dose, setting, and mood. Psychic effects include disorders of thought associated with time and space. Time may appear to stand still and forms and colors seem to change and take on new significance. This experience may be pleasurable or extremely frightening. It needs to be stressed that the effects of hallucinogens are unpredictable each time they are used.

Weeks or even months after some hallucinogens have been taken, the user may experience flashbacks—fragmentary recurrences of certain aspects of the drug experience in the absence of actually taking the drug. The occurrence of a flashback is unpredictable, but is more likely to occur during times of stress and seem to occur more frequently in younger individuals. With time, these episodes diminish and become less intense.

The abuse of hallucinogens in the United States reached a peak in the late 1960s. A subsequent decline in their use may be attributed to real or perceived hazards associated with taking these drugs. However, a resurgence of use of hallucinogens in the 1990s, especially at the junior high school level, is cause for concern.

There is a considerable body of literature that links the use of some of the hallucinogenic substances to neuronal damage in animals;

however, there is no conclusive scientific data that links brain or chromosomal damage to the use of hallucinogens in humans. The most common danger of hallucinogen use is impaired judgment that often leads to rash decisions and accidents.

Naturally Occurring Hallucinogens

Peyote and Mescaline. Peyote is a small, spineless cactus, *Lophophora williamsii*, whose principal active ingredient is the hallucinogen mescaline. From earliest recorded time, peyote has been used by natives in northern Mexico and southwestern United States as a part of traditional religious rites. The top of the cactus above ground—also referred to as the crown—consists of disc-shaped buttons that are cut from the roots and dried. These buttons are generally chewed or soaked in water to produce an intoxicating liquid. The hallucinogenic dose for mescaline is about 0.3 to 0.5 grams (equivalent to about 5 grams of dried peyote) and lasts about 12 hours. While peyote produced rich visual hallucinations which were important to the native peyote cults, the full spectrum of effects served as a chemically induced model of mental illness. Mescaline can be extracted from peyote or produced synthetically.

Psilocybin and Psilocyn. Psilocybin and psilocyn are both chemicals obtained from certain mushrooms found in Mexico and Central America. Like peyote, the mushrooms have been used in native rites for centuries. Dried mushrooms contain about 0.2 to 0.4 percent psilocybin and only trace amounts of psilocyn. The hallucinogenic dose of both substances is about 4 to 8 milligrams or about 2 grams of mushrooms with effects lasting for about six hours. Both psilocybin and psilocyn can be produced synthetically.

Dimethyltryptamine (DMT). Dimethyltryptamine, (DMT) has a long history of use worldwide as it is found in a variety of plants and seeds and can also be produced synthetically. It is ineffective when taken orally unless combined with another drug that inhibits its metabolism. Generally it is sniffed, smoked, or injected. The effective hallucinogenic dose in humans is about 50 to 100 milligrams and lasts for about 45 to 60 minutes. Because the effects last only about an hour, the experience was called a "businessman's trip."

A number of other hallucinogens have very similar structures and properties to those of DMT. Diethyltryptamine (DET), for example, is an analogue of DMT and produces the same pharmacological effects but is some what less potent than DMT. Alpha-ethyltryptamine (AET) is another tryptamine hallucinogen recently added to the list of Schedule I substances in the CSA.

Synthetic Hallucinogens

LSD. Lysergic acid diethylamide (LSD) is the most potent and highly studied hallucinogen known to man. It was originally synthesized in 1938 by Dr. Albert Hoffman, but its hallucinogenic effects were unknown until 1943 when Hoffman accidentally consumed some LSD. It was later found that an oral dose of as little as 0.025 mg (or 25 micrograms, equal to a few grains of salt) was capable of producing rich and vivid hallucinations.

Because of its structural similarity to a chemical present in the brain and its similarity in effects to certain aspects of psychosis, LSD was used as a research tool to study mental illness. Although there was a decline in its illicit use from its initial popularity in the 1960s, LSD is making a comeback in the 1990s. The average effective oral dose is from 20 to 80 micrograms with the effects of higher doses lasting for 10 to 12 hours. LSD is usually sold in the form of impregnated paper (blotter acid), tablets (microdots), or thin squares of gelatin (window panes).

Physical reactions may include dilated pupils, lowered body temperature, nausea, "goose bumps," profuse perspiration, increased blood sugar, and rapid heart rate. During the first hour after ingestion, the user may experience visual changes with extreme changes in mood. In the hallucinatory state, the user may suffer impaired depth and time perception accompanied by distorted perception of the size and shape of objects, movements, color, sound, touch, and the user's own body image. During this period, the user's ability to perceive objects through the senses is distorted. He may describe "hearing colors" and "seeing sounds." The ability to make sensible judgments and see common dangers is impaired, making the user susceptible to personal injury. He may also injure others by attempting to drive a car or by operating machinery.

After an LSD "trip," the user may suffer acute anxiety or depression for a variable period of time. Flashbacks have been reported days or even months after taking the last dose.

DOM, DOB, MDA, MDMA and 2C-B. Many chemical variations of mescaline and amphetamine have been synthesized for their "feel good" effects. 4-Methyl-2,5dimethoxyamphetamine (DOM) was introduced into the San Francisco drug scene in the late 1960s, and was nicknamed STP, an acronym for "Serenity, Tranquillity, and Peace." Doses of 1 to 3 milligrams generally produce mood alterations and minor perceptual alterations while larger doses can produce pronounced hallucinations that last from 8 to 10 hours.

Other illicitly manufactured analogues include 4-bromo-2,5-dimethoxyamphetamine (DOB), 3,4-methylenedioxyamphetamine (MDA), 3,4-methylenedioxymethamphetamine (MDMA, also referred to as Ecstasy or XTC) and 4-bromo-2,5-dimethoxyphenethylamine (2C-B, NEXUS). These drugs differ from one another in their potency, speed of onset, duration of action and their capacity to modify mood with or without producing overt hallucinations. These drugs are widely used at "raves." (Raves are large all-night dance parties held in unusual settings, such as warehouses or railroad yards, that feature computer-generated, high volume, pulsating music.) The drugs are usually taken orally, sometimes snorted, and rarely injected. Because they are produced in clandestine laboratories, they are seldom pure and the amount in a capsule or tablet is likely to vary considerably.

Phencyclidine (PCP) and Related Drugs. In the 1950s, phencyclidine was investigated as an anesthetic but, due to the side effects of confusion and delirium, its development for human use was discontinued. It became commercially available for use as a veterinary anesthetic in the 1960s under the trade name of Sernylan and was placed in Schedule III of the CSA. In 1978, due to considerable abuse of phencyclidine, it was transferred to Schedule II of the CSA and manufacturing of Sernylan was discontinued. Today, virtually all of the phencyclidine encountered on the illicit market in the U.S. is produced in clandestine laboratories. Phencyclidine, more commonly known as PCP, is illicitly marketed under a number of other names including Angel Dust, Supergrass, Killer Weed, Embalming Fluid, and Rocket Fuel, reflecting the range of its bizarre and volatile effects. In its pure form, it is a white crystalline powder that readily dissolves in water. However, most PCP on the illicit market contains a number of contaminates as a result of makeshift manufacturing causing the color to range from tan to brown and the consistency from powder to a gummy mass. Although sold in tablets and capsules as well as in powder and liquid form, it is commonly applied to a leafy material, such as parsley, mint, oregano, or marijuana, and smoked.

The drug's effects are as varied as its appearance. A moderate amount of PCP often causes the user to feel detached, distant, and estranged from his surroundings. Numbness, slurred speech, and loss of coordination may be accompanied by a sense of strength and invulnerability. A blank stare, rapid and involuntary eye movements, and an exaggerated gait are among the more observable effects. Auditory hallucinations, image distortion, severe mood disorders, and amnesia may also occur. In some users, PCP may cause acute anxiety and a feeling of impending doom, in others paranoia and violent hostility, and in some it may produce a psychosis indistinguishable from schizophrenia. PCP use is associated with a number of risks and many believe it to be one of the most dangerous drugs of abuse.

Cannabis

Cannabis sativa L. the hemp plant, grows wild throughout most of the tropic and temperate regions of the world. Prior to the advent of synthetic fibers, the cannabis plant was cultivated for the tough fiber of its stem. In the United States, cannabis is legitimately grown only for scientific research. In fact, since 1980, the United States has been the only country where cannabis is licitly cultivated for scientific research.

Cannabis contains chemicals called cannabinoids that are unique to the cannabis plant. Among the cannabinoids synthesized by the plant are cannabinol, cannabidiol, cannabinolidic acids, cannabigerol, cannabichromene, and several isomers of tetrahydrocannabinol. One of these, delta-9-tetrahydrocannabinol (THC), is believed to be responsible for most of the characteristic psychoactive effects of cannabis. Research has resulted in development and marketing of dronabinol (Marinol), a product containing synthetic THC, for the control of nausea and vomiting caused by chemotherapeutic agents used in the treatment of cancer and to stimulate appetite in AIDS patients.

Cannabis products are usually smoked. Their effects are felt within minutes, reach their peak in 10 to 30 minutes, and may linger for two or three hours. The effects experienced often depend upon the experience and expectations of the individual user as well as the activity of the drug itself. Low doses tend to induce a sense of well-being and a dreamy state of relaxation, which may be accompanied by a more vivid sense of sight, smell, taste, and hearing as well as by subtle alterations in thought formation and expression. This state of intoxication may not be noticeable to an observer. However, driving, occupational, or household accidents may result from a distortion of time and space relationships and impaired coordination. Stronger doses intensify reactions. The individual may experience shifting sensory imagery, rapidly fluctuating emotions, a flight of fragmentary thoughts

146

with disturbed associations, an altered sense of self-identity, impaired memory, and a dulling of attention despite an illusion of heightened insight. High doses may result in image distortion, a loss of personal identity, and fantasies and hallucinations.

Three drugs that come from cannabis—marijuana, hashish, and hashish oil—are currently distributed on the U.S. illicit market. Having no currently accepted medical use in treatment in the United States, they remain under Schedule I of the CSA. Today, cannabis is carefully illicitly cultivated, both indoors and out, to maximize its THC content, thereby producing the greatest possible psychoactive effect.

Marijuana

Marijuana is the most commonly used illicit drug in America today. The term marijuana, as commonly used, refers to the leaves and flowering tops of the cannabis plant.

A tobacco-like substance produced by drying the leaves and flowering tops of the cannabis plant, marijuana varies significantly in its potency, depending on the source and selection of plant materials used. The form of marijuana known as sinsemillia (Spanish, *sin semilla*: without seed), derived from the unpollinated female cannabis plant, is preferred for its high THC content.

Marijuana is usually smoked in the form of loosely rolled cigarettes called joints or hollowed out commercial cigars called blunts. Joints and blunts may be laced with a number of adulterants including phencyclidine (PCP), substantially altering the effects and toxicity of these products. Street names for marijuana include pot, grass, weed, Mary Jane, Acapulco Gold, and reefer.

Although marijuana grown in the U.S. was once considered inferior because of a low concentration of THC, advancements in plant selection and cultivation have resulted in highly potent domestic marijuana. In 1974, the average THC content of illicit marijuana was less than one percent; in early 1994, potency averaged 5 percent. The THC of today's sinsemilla ranges up to 17 percent.

Marijuana contains known toxins and cancer-causing chemicals which are stored in fat cells for as long as several months. Marijuana users experience the same health problems as tobacco smokers, such as bronchitis, emphysema, and bronchial asthma. Some of the effects of marijuana use also include increased heart rate, dryness of the mouth, reddening of the eyes, impaired motor skills, and concentration, and frequently hunger and an increased desire for sweets. Extended use increases risk to the lungs and reproductive system, as well as suppression of the immune system. Occasionally hallucinations, fantasies, and paranoia are reported.

Hashish

Hashish consists of the THC-rich resinous material of the cannabis plant, which is collected, dried, and then compressed into a variety of forms, such as balls, cakes, or cookie-like sheets. Pieces are then broken off, placed in pipes and smoked. The Middle East, North Africa, and Pakistan/Afghanistan are the main sources of hashish. The THC content of hashish that reached the United States, where demand is limited, averaged 6 percent in the 1990s.

Hash Oil

The term hash oil is used by illicit drug users and dealers but is a misnomer in suggesting any resemblance to hashish. Hash oil is produced by extracting the cannabinoids from plant material with a solvent. The color and odor of the resulting extract will vary, depending on the type of solvent used. Current samples of hash oil, a viscous liquid ranging from amber to dark brown in color, average about 15 percent THC. In terms of its psychoactive effect, a drop or two of this liquid on a cigarette is equal to a single "joint" of marijuana.

Steroids

Anabolic steroid abuse has become a national concern. These drugs are used illicitly by weight lifters, body builders, long distance runners, cyclists and others who claim that these drugs give them a competitive advantage and/or improve their physical appearance. Once viewed as a problem associated only with professional athletes, recent reports estimate that 5 percent to 12 percent of male high school students and 1 percent of female students have used anabolic steroids by the time they were seniors. Concerns over a growing illicit market and prevalence of abuse combined with the possibility of harmful long-term effects of steroid use, led Congress in 1991 to place anabolic steroids into Schedule III of the Controlled Substances Act (CSA).

The CSA defines anabolic steroids as any drug or hormonal substance chemically and pharmacologically related to testosterone (other than estrogens, progestins, and corticosteroids), that promotes muscle growth. Most illicit anabolic steroids are sold at gyms, competitions, and through mail order operations. For the most part, these substances are smuggled into this country. Those commonly encountered on the illicit market include: boldenone (Equipoise), ethylestrenol (Maxibolin), fluoxymesterone (Halotestin), methandriol, methandrostenolone (Dianabol), methyltestosterone, nandrolone (Durabolin, Deca-Durabolin), oxandrolone (Anavar), oxymetholone (Anadrol), stanozolol (Winstrol), testosterone and trenbolone (Finajet). In addition, a number of bogus or counterfeit products are sold as anabolic steroids.

A limited number of anabolic steroids have been approved for medical and veterinary use. The primary legitimate use of these drugs in humans is for the replacement of inadequate levels of testosterone resulting from a reduction or absence of functioning testes. In veterinary practice, anabolic steroids are used to promote feed efficiency and to improve weight gain, vigor, and hair coat. They are also used in veterinary practice to treat anemia and counteract tissue breakdown during illness and trauma.

When used in combination with exercise training and high protein diet, anabolic steroids can promote increased size and strength of muscles, improve endurance, and decrease recovery time between workouts. They are taken orally or by intramuscular injection. Users concerned about drug tolerance often take steroids on a schedule called a cycle. A cycle is a period of between 6 and 14 weeks of steroid use followed by a period of abstinence or reduction in use. Additionally, users tend to "stack" the drugs, using multiple drugs concurrently. Although the benefits of these practices are unsubstantiated, most users feel that cycling and stacking enhance the efficiency of the drugs and limit their side effects.

Yet another mode of steroid use is "pyramiding" in which users slowly escalate steroid use (increasing the number of drugs used at one time and/or the dose and frequency of one or more steroids) reaching a peak amount at mid-cycle and gradually tapering the dose toward the end of the cycle. The escalation of steroid use can vary with different types of training. Body builders and weight lifters tend to escalate their dose to a much higher level than do long distance runners or swimmers.

The adverse effects of large doses of multiple anabolic steroids are not well established. However, there is increasing evidence of serious health problems associated with the abuse of these agents, including cardiovascular damage, liver damage, and damage to reproductive organs.

Physical side effects include elevated blood pressure and cholesterol levels, severe acne, premature balding, reduced sexual function, and testicular atrophy. In males, abnormal breast development (gynecomastia) can occur. In females, anabolic steroids have a masculinizing effect resulting in more body hair, a deeper voice, smaller

149

breasts, and fewer menstrual cycles. Several of these effects are irreversible. In adolescents, abuse of these agents may prematurely stop the lengthening of bones resulting in stunted growth.

Inhalants

Inhalants are a chemically diverse group of psychoactive substances composed of organic solvents and volatile substances commonly found in adhesives, lighter fluids, cleaning fluids and paint products. Their easy accessibility, low cost and ease of concealment make inhalants, for many, one of the first substances abused. While not regulated under the CSA, a few states place restrictions on the sale of these products to minors. Studies have indicated that between 5 percent and 15 percent of young people in the United States have tried inhalants, although the vast majority of these youngsters do not become chronic abusers.

Inhalants may be sniffed directly from an open container or "huffed" from a rag soaked in the substance and held to the face. Alternatively, the open container or soaked rag can be placed in a bag where the vapors can concentrate before being inhaled. Although inhalant abusers may prefer one particular substance because of odor or taste, a variety of substances may be used because of their similar effects, availability, and cost. Once inhaled, the extensive capillary surface of the lungs allows rapid absorption of the substance and blood levels peak rapidly. Entry into the brain is so fast that the effects of inhalation can resemble the intensity of effects produced by intravenous injection of other psychoactive drugs.

The effects of inhalant intoxication resemble those of alcohol inebriation, with stimulation and loss of inhibition followed by depression at high doses. Users report distortion in perceptions of time and space. Many users experience headache, nausea or vomiting, slurred speech, loss of motor coordination, and wheezing. A characteristic "glue sniffer's rash" around the nose and mouth may be seen. An odor of paint or solvents on clothes, skin and breath is sometimes a sign of inhalant abuse.

The chronic use of inhalants has been associated with a number of serious health problems. Glue and paint thinner sniffing in particular produce kidney abnormalities, while the solvents, toluene and trichloroethylene, cause liver toxicity. Memory impairment, attention deficits, and diminished non-verbal intelligence have been associated with the abuse of inhalants. Deaths resulting from heart failure, asphyxiation, or aspiration have occurred.

Chapter 17

Amphetamines

Amphetamines are powerful stimulant drugs that increase activity in the central nervous system. Their effect is similar to that of the body's own adrenalin. Even though amphetamines mimic the effects of adrenalin, they act for a much longer time in the body.

Amphetamines can be acquired legally by prescription, although their medical uses are limited. They are used today to treat childhood hyperactivity, obesity and narcolepsy, a rare disorder in which persons are overcome by sudden attacks of deep sleep. Amphetamines can be taken orally in capsule form, snorted or injected. They may be referred to as speed, uppers, white crosses, dexies, bennies, black beauties, crystal and crank.

Amphetamines first were synthesized in 1887, but were not used medically until about 1930. Between 1930 and the early 1960s, amphetamines were prescribed to a variety of people with some experiencing no ill effects, while others showed relatively mild forms of amphetamine abuse. Significant abuse of the drug began to be seen in the United States in the 1960s, when amphetamines were injected intravenously, and dependence problems became evident.

The Controlled Substances Act reclassified amphetamines as a Schedule II Drug. This put tighter controls on manufacturing and prescribing amphetamines. Many doctors today prescribe "pseudo-amphetamines" instead of amphetamines. These are Schedule IV

Indiana Prevention Resource Center, © 1995, 1998 The Trustees of Indiana University; reprinted with permission.

drugs, which have looser controls, but their abuse potential is similar to that of amphetamines.

As a result of the tighter controls placed on amphetamines, many illegal labs now manufacture and sell homemade amphetamines, and some dealers have taken to selling quasi-legal fake amphetamines. This illicit market has created additional problems for users, because it is virtually impossible for a drug user to know if a capsule is genuine, homemade or a fake.

- "Look-alike drugs" are tablets or capsules that are made to look like real amphetamines and roughly imitate their effects. They usually contain varying amounts of legal substances such as caffeine, ephedrine and phenylpropanolamine, which are found in over-the-counter diet pills and decongestants. They are sold on the street as "uppers" or "speed" and often are purported by the sellers to be authentic amphetamines.

- Methamphetamine is the most potent form of amphetamine readily available with or without a prescription. Although pharmaceutical methamphetamine once widely was available in this country, its medical use is very restricted today. Almost all of today's methamphetamine is homemade and resembles a fine coarse powder, crystal or chunks. Its color varies from off-white to yellow, and it is furnished in plastic wrap, aluminum foil, capsules or tablets of various sizes and colors. It is taken into the body by swallowing, snorting or injecting intravenously. Methamphetamine is called by many names, including crank, crystal, meth, speed, go-fast, go, crystal meth, zip, chris, cristy, or ice.

- "Crystal" methamphetamine has experienced a revival on the black market as a replacement for cocaine or mixed with heroin. It is similar to cocaine in its euphoric effects, but is longer lasting. Crystal is sold as a powder that's injected, inhaled or taken orally. It is popular among some users because it is readily available, of a purer quality, has longer-lasting effects, and is less expensive than cocaine or heroin on the streets. In the past few years, police have uncovered several major crystal methamphetamine labs in Indiana. "Crank" is another name for methamphetamine.

- "Ice" or "Glass" is a concentrated form of methamphetamine that resembles tiny chunks of translucent glass. It is very potent crystal methamphetamine in a form that can be "smoked" rather than injected. Because the ice is vaporized and inhaled, and not actually burned, the term "smoking" is technically incorrect. As crack is to cocaine, ice is to methamphetamine. The intoxicating high may last from two to 20 hours, depending on how much is smoked. Because ice is odorless and has a colorless smoke, users of the drug may go virtually unnoticed. The use of ice in the United States began in Hawaii; however, its effects are being seen in California, and states such as Florida and Texas also have reported significant problems with the drug.

The physical effects of amphetamines are similar to those of other stimulant drugs. When amphetamines are taken by mouth, snorted or smoked, the user usually experiences feelings of euphoria, heightened alertness and greater energy. Heart, breathing and blood pressure rates increase, and sensations of hunger and fatigue are reduced. Heart palpitations may be experienced. The mouth is usually dry and swallowing is difficult, which makes eating food difficult. Urination is also difficult. The users' pupils are dilated, and reflexes are faster. Rapid speech often occurs, followed by slurred speech. Extremely high doses may cause people to flush or become pale, and cause a rapid or irregular heartbeat, loss of coordination and even physical collapse. Amphetamine injections create such an increase in blood pressure that strokes, high fevers or heart failure may result. As the drug wears off, feelings of fatigue or depression are experienced.

Amphetamines initially produce physical pleasure, so users easily are seduced into the repeated use of these drugs. Often users continually will take amphetamines to avoid the "down" mood they get when the drug wears off. Tissue tolerance develops quickly. It is not uncommon for some users to increase from 5 mg. to 1,000 mg. doses over a one-year period. "Speed freaks" are methamphetamine users who inject their drugs intravenously. Tissue tolerance develops very rapidly with them, as most methamphetamine users are compulsive/ addictive users who cannot control their drug taking.

Long-term heavy use of amphetamines may lead to malnutrition, skin disorders, ulcers and diseases resulting from vitamin deficiencies. Regular use may contribute to lack of sleep and weight loss. Intravenous users are at risk for serious, life-threatening diseases such as AIDS, lung and heart disease and other cardiovascular diseases.

Frequent use of large amounts of amphetamines may eventually result in mental illness, suicide and violent death. Amphetamine-induced psychosis is a paranoid state that may develop after ingestion or the injection of large doses of amphetamines.

Amphetamine use increases self-confidence, which often ignores the reality of personal limitations. Amphetamine users may experience "Superman Syndrome," in which they attempt to perform tasks they are incapable of performing. In well-rested persons, certain physical performances can improve with small doses of stimulant drugs. In tired users, stimulants cause most performance to deteriorate. Users often take unnecessary risks; truck drivers and motorists who use amphetamines are more likely to have accidents. Postponement of sleep due to amphetamine use may result in slower reaction times and decreased watchfulness.

Chapter 18

Cocaine

What is cocaine?

Cocaine is a powerfully addictive stimulant that directly affects the brain. Cocaine has been labeled the drug of the 1980s and '90s, because of its extensive popularity and use during this period. However, cocaine is not a new drug. In fact, it is one of the oldest known drugs. The pure chemical, cocaine hydrochloride, has been an abused substance for more than 100 years, and coca leaves, the source of cocaine, have been ingested for thousands of years.

Pure cocaine was first extracted from the leaf of the *Erythroxylon coca* bush, which grows primarily in Peru and Bolivia, in the mid-19th century. In the early 1900s, it became the main stimulant drug used in most of the tonics/elixirs that were developed to treat a wide variety of illnesses. Today, cocaine is a Schedule II drug, meaning that it has high potential for abuse, but can be administered by a doctor for legitimate medical uses, such as a local anesthetic for some eye, ear, and throat surgeries.

There are basically two chemical forms of cocaine: the hydrochloride salt and the "freebase." The hydrochloride salt, or powdered form of cocaine, dissolves in water and, when abused, can be taken intravenously (by vein) or intranasally (in the nose). Freebase refers to a

Excerpted from "Cocaine Abuse and Addiction," NIDA Research Report, National Institute on Drug Abuse (NIDA), May 1999. To obtain printed copies of the complete report including references, please call or write the National Clearinghouse for Alcohol and Drug Information, P.O. Box 2345, Rockville, MD 20852, 1-800-729-6686.

compound that has not been neutralized by an acid to make the hydrochloride salt. The freebase form of cocaine is smokable.

Cocaine is generally sold on the street as a fine, white, crystalline powder, known as "coke," "C," "snow," "flake," or "blow." Street dealers generally dilute it with such inert substances as cornstarch, talcum powder, and/or sugar, or with such active drugs as procaine (a chemically-related local anesthetic) or with such other stimulants as amphetamines.

What is crack?

Crack is the street name given to the freebase form of cocaine that has been processed from the powdered cocaine hydrochloride form to a smokable substance. The term "crack" refers to the crackling sound heard when the mixture is smoked. Crack cocaine is processed with ammonia or sodium bicarbonate (baking soda) and water, and heated to remove the hydrochloride.

Because crack is smoked, the user experiences a high in less than 10 seconds. This rather immediate and euphoric effect is one of the reasons that crack became enormously popular in the mid 1980s. Another reason is that crack is inexpensive both to produce and to buy.

What is the scope of cocaine use in the United States?

In 1997, an estimated 1.5 million Americans (0.7 percent of those age 12 and older) were current cocaine users, according to the 1997 National Household Survey on Drug Abuse (NHSDA). This number has not changed significantly since 1992, although it is a dramatic decrease from the 1985 peak of 5.7 million cocaine users (3 percent of the population). Based upon additional data sources that take into account users under represented in the NHSDA, the Office of National Drug Control Policy estimates the number of chronic cocaine users at 3.6 million.

Adults 18 to 25 years old have a higher rate of current cocaine use than those in any other age group. Overall, men have a higher rate of current cocaine use than do women. Also, according to the 1997 NHSDA, rates of current cocaine use were 1.4 percent for African Americans, 0.8 percent for Hispanics, and 0.6 percent for Caucasians.

Crack cocaine remains a serious problem in the United States. The NHSDA estimated the number of current crack users to be about 604,000 in 1997, which does not reflect any significant change since 1988.

The 1998 Monitoring the Future Survey, which annually surveys teen attitudes and recent drug use, reports that lifetime and past-year use of crack increased among eighth graders to its highest levels since 1991, the first year data were available for this grade. The percentage of eighth graders reporting crack use at least once in their lives increased from 2.7 percent in 1997 to 3.2 percent in 1998. Past-year use of crack also rose slightly among this group, although no changes were found for other grades.

Data from the Drug Abuse Warning Network (DAWN) showed that cocaine-related emergency room visits, after increasing 78 percent between 1990 and 1994, remained level between 1994 and 1996, with 152,433 cocaine-related episodes reported in 1996.

How is cocaine used?

The principal routes of cocaine administration are oral, intranasal, intravenous, and inhalation. The slang terms for these routes are, respectively, "chewing," "snorting," "mainlining," "injecting," and "smoking" (including freebase and crack cocaine). Snorting is the process of inhaling cocaine powder through the nostrils, where it is absorbed into the bloodstream through the nasal tissues. Injecting releases the drug directly into the bloodstream, and heightens the intensity of its effects. Smoking involves the inhalation of cocaine vapor or smoke into the lungs, where absorption into the bloodstream is as rapid as by injection. The drug can also be rubbed onto mucous tissues. Some users combine cocaine powder or crack with heroin in a "speedball."

Cocaine use ranges from occasional use to repeated or compulsive use, with a variety of patterns between these extremes. There is no safe way to use cocaine. Any route of administration can lead to absorption of toxic amounts of cocaine, leading to acute cardiovascular or cerebrovascular emergencies that could result in sudden death. Repeated cocaine use by any route of administration can produce addiction and other adverse health consequences.

How does cocaine produce its effects?

A great amount of research has been devoted to understanding the way cocaine produces its pleasurable effects, and the reasons it is so addictive. One mechanism is through its effects on structures deep in the brain. Scientists have discovered regions within the brain that, when stimulated, produce feelings of pleasure. One neural system that appears to be most affected by cocaine originates in a region, located deep within the brain, called the ventral tegmental area (VTA). Nerve cells originating in the VTA extend to the region of the brain known as the nucleus accumbens, one of the brain's key pleasure centers. In studies using animals, for example, all types of pleasurable stimuli, such as food, water, sex, and many drugs of abuse, cause increased activity in the nucleus accumbens.

Researchers have discovered that, when a pleasurable event is occurring, it is accompanied by a large increase in the amounts of dopamine released in the nucleus accumbens by neurons originating in the VTA. In the normal communication process, dopamine is released by a neuron into the synapse (the small gap between two neurons), where it binds with specialized proteins (called dopamine receptors) on the neighboring neuron, thereby sending a signal to that neuron. Drugs of abuse are able to interfere with this normal communication process. For example, scientists have discovered that cocaine blocks the removal of dopamine from the synapse, resulting in an accumulation of dopamine. This buildup of dopamine causes continuous stimulation of receiving neurons, probably resulting in the euphoria commonly reported by cocaine abusers.

As cocaine abuse continues, tolerance often develops. This means that higher doses and more frequent use of cocaine are required for the brain to register the same level of pleasure experienced during initial use. Recent studies have shown that, during periods of abstinence from cocaine use, the memory of the euphoria associated with cocaine use, or mere exposure to cues associated with drug use, can trigger tremendous craving and relapse to drug use, even after long periods of abstinence.

What are the short-term effects of cocaine use?

Cocaine's effects appear almost immediately after a single dose, and disappear within a few minutes or hours. Taken in small amounts (up to 100 mg), cocaine usually makes the user feel euphoric, energetic, talkative, and mentally alert, especially to the sensations of sight, sound, and touch. It can also temporarily decrease the need for food and sleep. Some users find that the drug helps them to perform simple physical and intellectual tasks more quickly, while others can experience the opposite effect.

The duration of cocaine's immediate euphoric effects depends upon the route of administration. The faster the absorption, the more intense the high. Also, the faster the absorption, the shorter the duration of action. The high from snorting is relatively slow in onset, and may last 15 to 30 minutes, while that from smoking may last 5 to 10 minutes.

The short-term physiological effects of cocaine include constricted blood vessels; dilated pupils; and increased temperature, heart rate, and blood pressure. Large amounts (several hundred milligrams or more) intensify the user's high, but may also lead to bizarre, erratic, and violent behavior. These users may experience tremors, vertigo, muscle twitches, paranoia, or, with repeated doses, a toxic reaction closely resembling amphetamine poisoning. Some users of cocaine report feelings of restlessness, irritability, and anxiety. In rare instances, sudden death can occur on the first use of cocaine or unexpectedly thereafter. Cocaine-related deaths are often a result of cardiac arrest or seizures followed by respiratory arrest.

What are the long-term effects of cocaine use?

Cocaine is a powerfully addictive drug. Once having tried cocaine, an individual may have difficulty predicting or controlling the extent to which he or she will continue to use the drug. Cocaine's stimulant and addictive effects are thought to be primarily a result of its ability to inhibit the reabsorption of dopamine by nerve cells. Dopamine is released as part of the brain's reward system, and is either directly or indirectly involved in the addictive properties of every major drug of abuse.

An appreciable tolerance to cocaine's high may develop, with many addicts reporting that they seek but fail to achieve as much pleasure as they did from their first experience. Some users will frequently increase their doses to intensify and prolong the euphoric effects. While tolerance to the high can occur, users can also become more sensitive (sensitization) to cocaine's anesthetic and convulsant effects, without increasing the dose taken. This increased sensitivity may explain some deaths occurring after apparently low doses of cocaine.

Use of cocaine in a binge, during which the drug is taken repeatedly and at increasingly high doses, leads to a state of increasing irritability, restlessness, and paranoia. This may result in a full-blown paranoid psychosis, in which the individual loses touch with reality and experiences auditory hallucinations.

What are the medical complications of cocaine abuse?

There are enormous medical complications associated with cocaine use. Some of the most frequent complications are cardiovascular effects, including disturbances in heart rhythm and heart attacks; such respiratory effects as chest pain and respiratory failure; neurological effects, including strokes, seizure, and headaches; and gastrointestinal complications, including abdominal pain and nausea.

Cocaine use has been linked to many types of heart disease. Cocaine has been found to trigger chaotic heart rhythms, called ventricular fibrillation; accelerate heartbeat and breathing; and increase blood pressure and body temperature. Physical symptoms may include chest pain, nausea, blurred vision, fever, muscle spasms, convulsions and coma.

Different routes of cocaine administration can produce different adverse effects. Regularly snorting cocaine, for example, can lead to loss of sense of smell, nosebleeds, problems with swallowing, hoarseness, and an overall irritation of the nasal septum, which can lead to a chronically inflamed, runny nose. Ingested cocaine can cause severe bowel gangrene, due to reduced blood flow. And, persons who inject cocaine have puncture marks and "tracks," most commonly in their forearms. Intravenous cocaine users may also experience an allergic reaction, either to the drug, or to some additive in street cocaine, which can result, in severe cases, in death. Because cocaine has a tendency to decrease food intake, many chronic cocaine users lose their appetites and can experience significant weight loss and malnourishment.

Research has revealed a potentially dangerous interaction between cocaine and alcohol. Taken in combination, the two drugs are converted by the body to cocaethylene. Cocaethylene has a longer duration of action in the brain and is more toxic than either drug alone. While more research needs to be done, it is noteworthy that the mixture of cocaine and alcohol is the most common two-drug combination that results in drug-related death.

Are cocaine abusers at risk for contracting HIV/AIDS and hepatitis B and C?

Yes. Cocaine abusers, especially those who inject, are at increased risk for contracting such infectious diseases as human immunodeficiency virus (HIV/AIDS) and hepatitis. In fact, use and abuse of illicit drugs, including crack cocaine, have become the leading risk factors for new cases of HIV. Drug abuse-related spread of HIV can result from direct transmission of the virus through the sharing of contaminated needles and paraphernalia between injecting drug users. It can also result from indirect transmission, such as an HIV-infected mother transmitting the virus perinatally to her child. This is particularly alarming, given that more than 60 percent of new AIDS cases are women. Research has also shown that drug use can interfere with judgement about risk-taking behavior, and can potentially lead to reduced precautions about having sex, the sharing of needles and injection paraphernalia, and the trading of sex for drugs, by both men and women.

Additionally, hepatitis C is spreading rapidly among injection drug users; current estimates indicate infection rates of 65 to 90 percent in this population. At present, there is no vaccine for the hepatitis C virus, and the only treatment is expensive, often unsuccessful, and may have serious side effects.

What is the effect of maternal cocaine use?

The full extent of the effects of prenatal drug exposure on a child is not completely known, but many scientific studies have documented that babies born to mothers who abuse cocaine during pregnancy are often prematurely delivered, have low birth weights and smaller head circumferences, and are often shorter in length.

Estimating the full extent of the consequences of maternal drug abuse is difficult, and determining the specific hazard of a particular drug to the unborn child is even more problematic, given that, typically, more than one substance is abused. Such factors as the amount and number of all drugs abused; inadequate prenatal care; abuse and neglect of the children, due to the mother's lifestyle; socioeconomic status; poor maternal nutrition; other health problems; and exposure to sexually transmitted diseases, are just some examples of the difficulty in determining the direct impact of perinatal cocaine use, for example, on maternal and fetal outcome.

Many may recall that "crack babies," or babies born to mothers who used cocaine while pregnant, were written off by many a decade ago as a lost generation. They were predicted to suffer from severe, irreversible damage, including reduced intelligence and social skills. It was later found that this was a gross exaggeration. Most crack-exposed babies appear to recover quite well. However, the fact that most of these children appear normal should not be over-interpreted as a positive sign. Using sophisticated technologies, scientists are now finding that exposure to cocaine during fetal development may lead to subtle, but significant, deficits later, especially with behaviors that are crucial to success in the classroom, such as blocking out distractions and concentrating for long periods of time.

What treatments are effective for cocaine abusers?

There has been an enormous increase in the number of people seeking treatment for cocaine addiction during the 1980s and 1990s. Treatment providers in most areas of the country, except in the West and Southwest, report that cocaine is the most commonly cited drug of abuse among their clients. The majority of individuals seeking treatment smoke crack, and are likely to be poly-drug users, or users of more than one substance. The widespread abuse of cocaine has stimulated extensive efforts to develop treatment programs for this type of drug abuse. Cocaine abuse and addiction is a complex problem involving biological changes in the brain as well as a myriad of social, familial, and environmental factors. Therefore, treatment of cocaine addiction is complex, and must address a variety of problems. Like any good treatment plan, cocaine treatment strategies need to assess the psychobiological, social, and pharmacological aspects of the patient's drug abuse.

Pharmacological approaches. There are no medications currently available to treat cocaine addiction specifically. Consequently, the National Institute on Drug Abuse (NIDA) is aggressively pursuing the identification and testing of new cocaine treatment medications. Several newly emerging compounds are being investigated to assess their safety and efficacy in treating cocaine addiction. For example, one of the most promising anti-cocaine drug medications to date, selegeline, is being taken into multi-site phase III clinical trials in 1999. These trials will evaluate two innovative routes of selegeline administration: a transdermal patch and a time-released pill, to determine which is most beneficial. Disulfiram, a medication that has been used to treat alcoholism, has also been shown, in clinical studies, to be effective in reducing cocaine abuse. Because of mood changes experienced during the early stages of cocaine abstinence, antidepressant drugs have been shown to be of some benefit. In addition to the problems of treating addiction, cocaine overdose results in many deaths every year, and medical treatments are being developed to deal with the acute emergencies resulting from excessive cocaine abuse.

Behavioral interventions. Many behavioral treatments have been found to be effective for cocaine addiction, including both residential and outpatient approaches. Indeed, behavioral therapies are often the only available, effective treatment approaches to many drug problems, including cocaine addiction, for which there is, as yet, no viable medication. However, integration of both types of treatments is ultimately the most effective approach for treating addiction. It is important to match the best treatment regimen to the needs of the patient. This may include adding to or removing from an individual's treatment regimen a number of different components or elements. For example, if an individual is prone to relapses, a relapse component should be added to the program. A behavioral therapy component that is showing positive results in many cocaine-addicted populations, is contingency management. Contingency management uses a voucher-based system to give positive rewards for staying in treatment and remaining cocaine free. Based on drug-free urine tests, the patients earn points, which can be exchanged for items that encourage healthy living, such as joining a gym, or going to a movie and dinner. Cognitive-behavioral therapy is another approach. Cognitive-behavioral coping skills treatment, for example, is a short-term, focused approach to helping cocaine-addicted individuals become abstinent from cocaine and other substances. The underlying assumption is that learning processes play an important role in the development and continuation of cocaine abuse and dependence. The same learning processes can be employed to help individuals reduce drug use. This approach attempts to help patients to recognize, avoid, and cope; i.e., recognize the situations in which they are most likely to use cocaine, avoid these situations when appropriate, and cope more effectively with a range of problems and problematic behaviors associated with drug abuse. This therapy is also noteworthy because of its compatibility with a range of other treatments patients may receive, such as pharmaco-therapy.

Therapeutic communities, or residential programs with planned lengths of stay of 6 to 12 months, offer another alternative to those in need of treatment for cocaine addiction. Therapeutic communities are often comprehensive, in that they focus on the resocialization of the individual to society, and can include on-site vocational rehabilitation and other supportive services. Therapeutic communities typically are used to treat patients with more severe problems, such as co-occurring mental health problems and criminal involvement.

Where can I get further scientific information about cocaine addiction?

To learn more about cocaine and other drugs of abuse, contact the National Clearinghouse for Alcohol and Drug Information (NCADI) at 1-800-729-6686. Information specialists are available to assist you in locating needed information and resources. Fact sheets on the health effects of drug abuse and other topics can be ordered free of charge, in English and Spanish, by calling NIDA INFOFAX at 1-888-NIH-NIDA (1-888-644-6432), or for hearing impaired persons, 1-888-TTY-NIDA (1-888-889-6432). Information can also be accessed through the NIDA World Wide Web site (http://www.nida.nih.gov/) or the NCADI Web site (http://www.health.org).

Chapter 19

GHB
(Gamma-Hydroxybutyrate)

What Is GHB?

GHB is gamma-hydroxybutyrate. It was originally developed as anaesthetic, but was withdrawn due to unwanted side effects. The only legal use of GHB has been as an investigational treatment for the treatment of narcolepsy. In Europe, GHB has been used as an anaesthetic and experimentally to treat alcohol withdrawal. It is being marketed in England as an anto-again medicine which allegedly increases the libido, decreases body fat, aids alcohol withdrawal, and induces sleep.

GHB is a chemical that has been promoted as a steroid alternative for body building and other uses for several years. Although recently, it has gained favor as a recreational drug because of its intoxicating effects. In the past GHB has undergone clinical testing for several indications, it has never been approved for sale as a medical product in this country.

Reports of use and abuse of GHB occurred about ten years ago, prompting the FDA to began an intensive investigation of distribution after numerous cases of GHB-related illness were reported. Recently, however, there appears to be a resurgence in the abuse of GHB; virtually all of the products now encountered have been produced in clandestine laboratories. This increase in use has been accompanied by an increase in reports of GHB-related injuries, including deaths.

The Tennessee Statewide Clearinghouse, 1999; reprinted with permission.

What does GHB look like and what are the effects?

GHB is an odorless, colorless, nearly tasteless, but slightly salty-tasting drug available in liquid, powder or capsule form. Liquid GHB is being used in nightclubs for effects similar to those of Rohypnol. On the club scene it is also known as "liquid ecstasy", "grievous bodily harm", "GBH", "somatomax", "Georgia Home Boy" or "scoop".

Coma and seizures can occur following abuse of GHB and, when combined with methamphetamine, there appears to be an increased risk of seizure. Combining use with other drugs such as alcohol can result in nausea and difficulty breathing. GHB may also produce withdrawal effects, including insomnia, anxiety, vertigo, seizures, vomiting and sweating. After excessive use, some users have experienced loss of consciousness, irregular and depressed respiration, tremors, or coma.

GHB is currently circulating within the dance music scene (at raves and night clubs) as an alternative to Ecstasy or Amphetamine Sulfate (speed).

In Atlanta, GHB is commonly used as synthetic steroid at fitness centers and gyms. There are reports that GHB is available in Tennessee and is used primarily by "rave club" party goers to enhance the effects of alcohol. As with Rohypnol and Clonazepam, GHB has been associated with sexual assault in cities throughout the country. To counteract this in 1996, Congress passed the "Drug-Induced Rape Prevention and Punishment Act of 1996". This legislation increased federal penalties for use of any controlled substance to aid in sexual assault.

For More Information

For more information or referral on GHB or other drugs and alcohol contact The Tennessee Statewide Clearinghouse (TSC) at 1-800-889-9789, 1 Vantage Way, Suite B-240, Nashville, TN 37228; web site: www.tnclearinghouse.com.

Chapter 20

Heroin

What is heroin?

Heroin is an illegal, highly addictive drug. It is both the most abused and the most rapidly acting of the opiates. Heroin is processed from morphine, a naturally occurring substance extracted from the seed pod of certain varieties of poppy plants. It is typically sold as a white or brownish powder or as the black sticky substance known on the streets as "black tar heroin." Although purer heroin is becoming more common, most street heroin is "cut" with other drugs or with substances such as sugar, starch, powdered milk, or quinine. Street heroin can also be cut with strychnine or other poisons. Because heroin abusers do not know the actual strength of the drug or its true contents, they are at risk of overdose or death. Heroin also poses special problems because of the transmission of HIV and other diseases that can occur from sharing needles or other injection equipment.

What is the scope of heroin use in the United States?

According to the 1996 National Household Survey on Drug Abuse, which may actually under estimate illicit opiate (heroin) use, an estimated 2.4 million people used heroin at some time in their lives, and

Excerpted from "Heroin Abuse and Addiction," NIDA Research Report, National Institute on Drug Abuse (NIDA), May 1999. To obtain printed copies of the complete report including references, please call or write the National Clearinghouse on Alcohol and Drug Information, P.O. Box 2345, Rockville, MD 20852, 1-800-729-6686.

167

nearly 216,000 of them reported using it within the month preceding the survey. The survey report estimates that there were 141,000 new heroin users in 1995, and that there has been an increasing trend in new heroin use since 1992. A large proportion of these recent new users were smoking, snorting, or sniffing heroin, and most were under age 26. Estimates of use for other age groups also increased, particularly among youths age 12 to 17: the incidence of first-time heroin use among this age group increased fourfold from the 1980s to 1995.

The 1996 Drug Abuse Warning Network (DAWN), which collects data on drug-related hospital emergency department (ED) episodes from 21 metropolitan areas, estimates that 14 percent of all drug-related ED episodes involved heroin. Even more alarming is the fact that between 1988 and 1994, heroin-related ED episodes increased by 64 percent (from 39,063 to 64,013).

The National Institute on Drug Abuse (NIDA)'s Community Epidemiology Work Group (CEWG), which provides information about the nature and patterns of drug use in 20 cities, reported in its December 1996 publication that heroin was the primary drug of abuse related to drug abuse treatment admissions in Newark, San Francisco, Los Angeles, and Boston, and it ranked a close second to cocaine in New York and Seattle.

How is heroin used?

Heroin is usually injected, sniffed/snorted, or smoked. Typically, a heroin abuser may inject up to four times a day. Intravenous injection provides the greatest intensity and most rapid onset of euphoria (7 to 8 seconds), while intramuscular injection produces a relatively slow onset of euphoria (5 to 8 minutes). When heroin is sniffed or smoked, peak effects are usually felt within 10 to 15 minutes. Although smoking and sniffing heroin do not produce a "rush" as quickly or as intensely as intravenous injection, NIDA researchers have confirmed that all three forms of heroin administration are addictive.

Injection continues to be the predominant method of heroin use among addicted users seeking treatment; however, researchers have observed a shift in heroin use patterns, from injection to sniffing and smoking. In fact, sniffing/snorting heroin is now a widely reported means of taking heroin among users admitted for drug treatment in Newark, Chicago, New York, and Detroit.

With the shift in heroin abuse patterns comes an even more diverse group of users. Older users (over 30) continue to be one of the largest user groups in most national data. However, several sources indicate an increase in new, young users across the country who are being lured by inexpensive, high-purity heroin that can be sniffed or smoked instead of injected. Heroin has also been appearing in more affluent communities.

What are the immediate (short-term) effects of heroin use?

Soon after injection (or inhalation), heroin crosses the blood-brain barrier. In the brain, heroin is converted to morphine and binds rapidly to opioid receptors. Abusers typically report feeling a surge of pleasurable sensation, a "rush." The intensity of the rush is a function of how much drug is taken and how rapidly the drug enters the brain and binds to the natural opioid receptors. Heroin is particularly addictive because it enters the brain so rapidly. With heroin, the rush is usually accompanied by a warm flushing of the skin, dry mouth, and a heavy feeling in the extremities, which may be accompanied by nausea, vomiting, and severe itching.

After the initial effects, abusers usually will be drowsy for several hours. Mental function is clouded by heroin's effect on the central nervous system. Cardiac functions slow. Breathing is also severely slowed, sometimes to the point of death. Heroin overdose is a particular risk on the street, where the amount and purity of the drug cannot be accurately known.

What are the long-term effects of heroin use?

One of the most detrimental long-term effects of heroin is addiction itself. Addiction is a chronic, relapsing disease, characterized by compulsive drug seeking and use, and by neurochemical and molecular changes in the brain. Heroin also produces profound degrees of tolerance and physical dependence, which are also powerful motivating factors for compulsive use and abuse. As with abusers of any addictive drug, heroin abusers gradually spend more and more time and energy obtaining and using the drug. Once they are addicted, the heroin abusers' primary purpose in life becomes seeking and using drugs. The drugs literally change their brains.

Physical dependence develops with higher doses of the drug. With physical dependence, the body adapts to the presence of the drug and withdrawal symptoms occur if use is reduced abruptly. Withdrawal may occur within a few hours after the last time the drug is taken. Symptoms of withdrawal include restlessness, muscle and bone pain, insomnia, diarrhea, vomiting, cold flashes with goose bumps ("cold turkey"), and leg movements. Major withdrawal symptoms peak between 24 and 48 hours after the last dose of heroin and subside after about a week. However, some people have shown persistent withdrawal signs for many months. Heroin withdrawal is never fatal to otherwise healthy adults, but it can cause death to the fetus of a pregnant addict.

At some point during continuous heroin use, a person can become addicted to the drug. Sometimes addicted individuals will endure many of the withdrawal symptoms to reduce their tolerance for the drug so that they can again experience the rush.

Physical dependence and the emergence of withdrawal symptoms were once believed to be the key features of heroin addiction. We now know this may not be the case entirely, since craving and relapse can occur weeks and months after withdrawal symptoms are long gone. We also know that patients with chronic pain who need opiates to function (sometimes over extended periods) have few if any problems leaving opiates after their pain is resolved by other means. This may be because the patient in pain is simply seeking relief of pain and not the rush sought by the addict.

What are the medical complications of chronic heroin use?

Medical consequences of chronic heroin abuse include scarred and/ or collapsed veins, bacterial infections of the blood vessels and heart valves, abscesses (boils) and other soft-tissue infections, and liver or

Table 20.1. Short- and Long-Term Effects of Heroin Use

Short-Term Effects	Long-Term Effects
"Rush"	Addiction
Depressed respiration	Infectious diseases, for example, HIV/AIDS and hepatitis B and C
Clouded mental functioning	Collapsed veins
Nausea and vomiting	Bacterial infections
Suppression of pain	Abscesses
Spontaneous abortion	Infection of heart lining and valves
	Arthritis and other rheumatologic problems

170

kidney disease. Lung complications (including various types of pneumonia and tuberculosis) may result from the poor health condition of the abuser as well as from heroin's depressing effects on respiration. Many of the additives in street heroin may include substances that do not readily dissolve and result in clogging the blood vessels that lead to the lungs, liver, kidneys, or brain. This can cause infection or even death of small patches of cells in vital organs. Immune reactions to these or other contaminants can cause arthritis or other rheumatologic problems.

Of course, sharing of injection equipment or fluids can lead to some of the most severe consequences of heroin abuse—infections with hepatitis B and C, HIV, and a host of other blood-borne viruses, which drug abusers can then pass on to their sexual partners and children.

How does heroin abuse affect pregnant women?

Heroin abuse can cause serious complications during pregnancy, including miscarriage and premature delivery. Children born to addicted mothers are at greater risk of SIDS (sudden infant death syndrome), as well. Pregnant women should not be detoxified from opiates because of the increased risk of spontaneous abortion or premature delivery; rather, treatment with methadone is strongly advised. Although infants born to mothers taking prescribed methadone may show signs of physical dependence, they can be treated easily and safely in the nursery. Research has demonstrated also that the effects of *in utero* exposure to methadone are relatively benign.

Why are heroin users at special risk for contracting HIV/ AIDS and hepatitis B and C?

Because many heroin addicts often share needles and other injection equipment, they are at special risk of contracting HIV and other infectious diseases. Infection of injection drug users with HIV is spread primarily through reuse of contaminated syringes and needles or other paraphernalia by more than one person, as well as through unprotected sexual intercourse with HIV-infected individuals. For nearly one-third of Americans infected with HIV, injection drug use is a risk factor. In fact, drug abuse is the fastest growing vector for the spread of HIV in the nation.

NIDA-funded research has found that drug abusers can change the behaviors that put them at risk for contracting HIV, through drug abuse treatment, prevention, and community-based outreach programs. They can eliminate drug use, drug-related risk behaviors such as needle sharing, unsafe sexual practices, and, in turn, the risk of exposure to HIV/AIDS and other infectious diseases. Drug abuse prevention and treatment are highly effective in preventing the spread of HIV.

What are the treatments for heroin addiction?

A variety of effective treatments are available for heroin addiction. Treatment tends to be more effective when heroin abuse is identified early. The treatments that follow vary depending on the individual, but methadone, a synthetic opiate that blocks the effects of heroin and eliminates withdrawal symptoms, has a proven record of success for people addicted to heroin. Other pharmaceutical approaches, like LAAM (levo-alpha-acetyl-methadol), and many behavioral therapies also are used for treating heroin addiction.

Detoxification. The primary objective of detoxification is to relieve withdrawal symptoms while patients adjust to a drug-free state. Not in itself a treatment for addiction, detoxification is a useful step only when it leads into long-term treatment that is either drug-free (residential or outpatient) or uses medications as part of the treatment. The best documented drug-free treatments are the therapeutic community residential programs lasting at least 3 to 6 months.

Methadone programs. Methadone treatment has been used effectively and safely to treat opioid addiction for more than 30 years. Properly prescribed methadone is not intoxicating or sedating, and its effects do not interfere with ordinary activities such as driving a car. The medication is taken orally and it suppresses narcotic withdrawal for 24 to 36 hours. Patients are able to perceive pain and have emotional reactions. Most important, methadone relieves the craving associated with heroin addiction; craving is a major reason for relapse. Among methadone patients, it has been found that normal street doses of heroin are ineffective at producing euphoria, thus making the use of heroin more easily extinguishable.

Methadone's effects last for about 24 hours—four to six times as long as those of heroin—so people in treatment need to take it only once a day. Also, methadone is medically safe even when used continuously for 10 years or more. Combined with behavioral therapies or counseling and other supportive services, methadone enables patients to stop using heroin (and other opiates) and return to more stable and productive lives.

LAAM and other medications. LAAM, like methadone, is a synthetic opiate that can be used to treat heroin addiction. LAAM can block the effects of heroin for up to 72 hours with minimal side effects when taken orally. In 1993 the Food and Drug Administration approved the use of LAAM for treating patients addicted to heroin. Its long duration of action permits dosing just three times per week, thereby eliminating the need for daily dosing and take-home doses for weekends. LAAM will be increasingly available in clinics that already dispense methadone.

Naloxone and naltrexone are medications that also block the effects of morphine, heroin, and other opiates. As antagonists, they are especially useful as antidotes. Naltrexone has long-lasting effects, ranging from 1 to 3 days, depending on the dose. Naltrexone blocks the pleasurable effects of heroin and is useful in treating some highly motivated individuals. Naltrexone has also been found to be successful in preventing relapse by former opiate addicts released from prison on probation.

Although not yet approved for the treatment of opioid addiction, buprenorphine is another medication being studied by NIDA as a treatment for heroin addiction. Buprenorphine is a particularly attractive treatment because it does not produce the same level of physical dependence as other opiate medications, such as methadone. Discontinuing buprenorphine is easier than stopping methadone treatment because there are fewer withdrawal symptoms. Several other medications with potential for treating heroin overdose or addiction are currently under investigation by NIDA.

Behavioral therapies. Although behavioral and pharmacologic treatments can be extremely useful when employed alone, science has taught us that integrating both types of treatments will ultimately be the most effective approach. There are many effective behavioral treatments available for heroin addiction. These can include residential and outpatient approaches. An important task is to match the best treatment approach to meet the particular needs of the patient. Moreover, several new behavioral therapies, such as contingency management therapy and cognitive-behavioral interventions, show particular promise as treatments for heroin addiction. Contingency management therapy uses a voucher-based system, where patients earn "points" based on negative drug tests, which they can exchange for items that encourage healthy living. Cognitive-behavioral interventions are designed to help modify the patient's thinking, expectancies, and behaviors and to increase skills in coping with various life stressors. Both behavioral and pharmacological treatments help to restore a degree of normalcy to brain function and behavior.

What are the opioid analogs and their dangers?

Drug analogs are chemical compounds that are similar to other drugs in their effects but differ slightly in their chemical structure. Some analogs are produced by pharmaceutical companies for legitimate medical reasons. Other analogs, sometimes referred to as "designer" drugs, can be produced in illegal laboratories and are often more dangerous and potent than the original drug. Two of the most commonly known opioid analogs are fentanyl and meperidine (marketed under the brand name Demerol, for example).

Fentanyl was introduced in 1968 by a Belgian pharmaceutical company as a synthetic narcotic to be used as an analgesic in surgical procedures because of its minimal effects on the heart. Fentanyl is particularly dangerous because it is 50 times more potent than heroin and can rapidly stop respiration. This is not a problem during surgical procedures because machines are used to help patients breathe. On the street, however, users have been found dead with the needle used to inject the drug still in their arms.

Where can I get further scientific information about heroin abuse and addiction?

To learn more about heroin and other drugs of abuse, contact the National Clearinghouse for Alcohol and Drug Information (NCADI) at 1-800-729-6686. Information specialists are available to assist you in locating needed information and resources. Information can be accessed also through the NIDA World Wide Web site (http://www.nida.nih.gov/) or the NCADI Web site (http://www.health.org).

174

Chapter 21

Inhalants

Inhalants are breathable chemical vapors that produce psychoactive (mind-altering) effects. Although people are exposed to volatile solvents and other inhalants in the home and in the workplace, many do not think of inhalable substances as drugs because most of them were never meant to be used in that way.

Young people are likely to abuse inhalants, in part because inhalants are readily available and inexpensive. Sometimes children unintentionally misuse inhalant products that are found in household products. Parents should see that these substances are monitored closely so that they are not inhaled by young children.

Inhalants fall into the following categories:

- Solvents

  - *industrial or household solvents* or solvent-containing products, including paint thinners or solvents, degreasers (dry-cleaning fluids), gasoline, and glues

  - *art or office supply solvents*, including correction fluids, felt-tip-marker fluid, and electronic contact cleaners

- Gases

  - *gases used in household or commercial products*, including butane lighters and propane tanks, whipping cream aerosols or dispensers (whippets), and refrigerant gases

National Institute on Drug Abuse (NIDA), Pub. No. 13549, November 1999.

- *household aerosol propellants* and associated solvents in items such as spray paints, hair or deodorant sprays, and fabric protector sprays

- *medical anesthetic gases*, such as ether, chloroform, halothane, and nitrous oxide (laughing gas)

- Nitrites

  - *aliphatic nitrites*, including cyclohexyl nitrite, which is available to the general public;

  - *amyl nitrite*, which is available only by prescription; and

  - *butyl nitrite*, which is now an illegal substance.

Health Hazards

Although different in makeup, nearly all abused inhalants produce effects similar to anesthetics, which act to slow down the body's functions. When inhaled via the nose or mouth into the lungs in sufficient concentrations, inhalants can cause intoxicating effects. Intoxication can last only a few minutes or several hours if inhalants are taken repeatedly. Initially, users may feel slightly stimulated; with successive inhalations, they may feel less inhibited and less in control; finally, a user can lose consciousness.

Sniffing highly concentrated amounts of the chemicals in solvents or aerosol sprays can directly induce heart failure and death. This is especially common from the abuse of fluorocarbons and butane-type gases. High concentrations of inhalants also cause death from suffocation by displacing oxygen in the lungs and then in the central nervous system so that breathing ceases. Other irreversible effects caused by inhaling specific solvents are as follows:

- Hearing loss—toluene (paint sprays, glues, dewaxers) and trichloroethylene (cleaning fluids, correction fluids)

- Peripheral neuropathies or limb spasms—hexane (glues, gasoline) and nitrous oxide (whipping cream, gas cylinders)

- Central nervous system or brain damage—toluene (paint sprays, glues, dewaxers)

- Bone marrow damage—benzene (gasoline).

Serious but potentially reversible effects include:

- Liver and kidney damage—toluene-containing substances and chlorinated hydrocarbons (correction fluids, dry-cleaning fluids).

- Blood oxygen depletion—organic nitrites ("poppers," "bold," and "rush") and methylene chloride (varnish removers, paint thinners).

Death from inhalants usually is caused by a very high concentration of fumes. Deliberately inhaling from an attached paper or plastic bag or in a closed area greatly increases the chances of suffocation. Even when using aerosols or volatile products for their legitimate purposes (i.e., painting, cleaning), it is wise to do so in a well-ventilated room or outdoors.

Amyl and butyl nitrites have been associated with Kaposi's sarcoma (KS), the most common cancer reported among AIDS patients. Early studies of KS showed that many people with KS had used volatile nitrites. Researchers are continuing to explore the hypothesis of nitrites as a factor contributing to the development of KS in HIV-infected people.

Extent of Use

Initial use of inhalants often starts early. Some young people may use inhalants as a cheap, accessible substitute for alcohol. Research suggests that chronic or long-term inhalant abusers are among the most difficult to treat and they may experience multiple psychological and social problems.

Monitoring the Future Study (MTF)*

The National Institute on Drug Abuse (NIDA)'s national survey of drug use among high school students provides estimates of the percentage of seniors using inhalants since 1976. The annual rate of inhalant use among seniors steadily rose from 3.0 percent in 1976 to a peak of 8.0 percent in 1995. In 1997, 6.7 percent of seniors reported past year inhalant use.

The MTF also includes 8th- and 10th-graders, providing estimates of drug use among a younger population. In 1997, 21.0 percent of 8th-graders and 18.3 percent of 10th-graders had used inhalants at least once in their lives; 11.8 percent of 8th-graders and 8.7 percent of 10th-graders had used inhalants in the past year.

The perceived harmfulness of inhalants varies among high school students. In 1997, almost 40.1 percent of 8th-graders and 47.5 percent of 10th-graders said there is great risk in trying inhalants once or twice; 68.7 percent of 8th-graders and 74.5 percent of 10th-graders saw great risk in taking inhalants regularly.

Table 21.1. Inhalant Use by Students, 1997: Monitoring the Future Study

	8th-Graders	10th-Graders	12th-Graders
Ever Used	21.0%	18.3%	16.1%
Used in Past Year	11.8	8.7	6.7
Used in Past Month	5.6	3.0	2.5

National Household Survey on Drug Abuse (NHSDA)**

Data from the National Household Survey on Drug Abuse show that in 1996, 5.9 percent of adolescents (1.3 million) reported use of inhalants at least once in their lifetimes, and 4 per cent (900,000) reported using inhalants in the past year.

Notes

* MTF is an annual survey on drug use and related attitudes of America's adolescents that began in 1975. The survey is conducted by the University of Michigan's Institute for Social Research and is funded by NIDA. Copies of the latest survey are available from the National Clearinghouse for Alcohol and Drug Information at 1-800-729-6686.

** NHSDA is an annual survey conducted by the Substance Abuse and Mental Health Services Administration. Copies of the latest survey are available from the National Clearinghouse for Alcohol and Drug Information at 1-800-729-6686.

Chapter 22

Ketamine

Ketamine, an anesthetic for human and veterinary use, is a legitimately manufactured product that is being abused with increasing frequency. On the street, the drug is often called "K" or "Special K." It produces effects similar to those produced by phencyclidine (PCP), and the visual effects of LSD. Drug users say "Special K" produces a better high than PCP or LSD because its effects last an hour or less. The drug, however, can affect the senses, judgment, and coordination for 18 to 24 hours.

Ketamine hydrochloride is used as an anesthetic for both humans and animals. Vets use it primarily to immobilize cats or monkeys. Its use in human surgery has declined with introduction of safer, more effective products. The synthesis of ketamine is complicated, and to date, diversion of the legitimate product is the only known source on the street.

Ketamine hydrochloride powder can look very similar to pharmaceutical grade cocaine HCl. Ketamine powder can be snorted like cocaine, mixed into drinks, or smoked. The liquid is either injected, applied to smokable materials, or consumed in drinks.

Veterinarians pay a retail price of about $7 per vial of liquid. Middlemen may pay $30-$45 per vial, and drug users may pay $100-$200 per vial. A pharmaceutical vial of liquid contains the equivalent of about one gram of powder. A smaller quantity, called a "bump," is about 0.2 gram and costs about $20.

U.S. Department of Justice, Drug Enforcement Administration, February 4, 1997.

179

Ketamine can produce a very wide range of effects, and users adjust the dosage depending on the effect desired. The drug's effect can be influenced by body size, built-up tolerance, the presence of alcohol or other drugs, the method of administration, and the setting in which the drug is consumed. In the past several years, law enforcement has encountered ketamine powder packaged in small plastic bags, folded paper, aluminum foil, and capsules. These packets commonly contain 0.2 gram, and more recently, 0.07 gram.

Some users inhale about 0.02 grams in each nostril, repeated in 5-10 minute intervals until the desired state is reached. A dose of 0.07 gram may produce intoxication. A larger dose of 0.2 gram may result in "K-land," a "mellow, colorful wonder-world." A dose of 0.5 grams can produce a so-called "K-hole" or "out-of-body, near-death experience." With repeated daily exposure, users can develop tolerance and psychological dependence.

Ketamine abuse has been reported at teen "rave" parties. Law enforcement agencies are encountering ketamine abuse when stopping drivers for what appears to be driving while intoxicated. Veterinary clinics have been burglarized for ketamine. These are among the factors that have caused the DEA to re-evaluate the control status of the drug. Since it is a controlled substance only in California, Connecticut, New Mexico and Oklahoma, most law enforcement data collection systems do not have record instances of ketamine abuse.

Since 1993, the DEA Office of Diversion Control has been collecting data on ketamine and its abuse. Reports of encounters with ketamine may be faxed to (202) 307-8570, or mailed to:

Drug Enforcement Administration
Drug and Chemical Evaluation Section
Office of Diversion Control
700 Army Navy Drive
Arlington, VA 22202

Chapter 23

LSD
(Lysergic Acid Diethylamide)

LSD (lysergic acid diethylamide) is one of the major drugs making up the hallucinogen class. LSD was discovered in 1938 and is one of the most potent mood-changing chemicals. It is manufactured from lysergic acid, which is found in ergot, a fungus that grows on rye and other grains.

LSD, commonly referred to as "acid," is sold on the street in tablets, capsules, and, occasionally, liquid form. It is odorless, colorless, and has a slightly bitter taste and is usually taken by mouth. Often LSD is added to absorbent paper, such as blotter paper, and divided into small decorated squares, with each square representing one dose.

The Drug Enforcement Administration reports that the strength of LSD samples obtained currently from illicit sources ranges from 20 to 80 micrograms of LSD per dose. This is considerably less than the levels reported during the 1960s and early 1970s, when the dosage ranged from 100 to 200 micrograms, or higher, per unit.

Health Hazards

The effects of LSD are unpredictable. They depend on the amount taken; the user's personality, mood, and expectations; and the surroundings in which the drug is used. Usually, the user feels the first effects of the drug 30 to 90 minutes after taking it. The physical effects include dilated pupils, higher body temperature, increased heart rate and blood pressure, sweating, loss of appetite, sleeplessness, dry mouth, and tremors.

National Institute on Drug Abuse (NIDA), Pub. No. 13550, November 1999.

Sensations and feelings change much more dramatically than the physical signs. The user may feel several different emotions at once or swing rapidly from one emotion to another. If taken in a large enough dose, the drug produces delusions and visual hallucinations. The user's sense of time and self changes. Sensations may seem to "cross over," giving the user the feeling of hearing colors and seeing sounds. These changes can be frightening and can cause panic.

Users refer to their experience with LSD as a "trip" and to acute adverse reactions as a "bad trip." These experiences are long—typically they begin to clear after about 12 hours.

Some LSD users experience severe, terrifying thoughts and feelings, fear of losing control, fear of insanity and death, and despair while using LSD. Some fatal accidents have occurred during states of LSD intoxication.

Many LSD users experience flashbacks, recurrence of certain aspects of a person's experience, without the user having taken the drug again. A flashback occurs suddenly, often without warning, and may occur within a few days or more than a year after LSD use. Flashbacks usually occur in people who use hallucinogens chronically or have an underlying personality problem; however, otherwise healthy people who use LSD occasionally may also have flashbacks.

Bad trips and flashbacks are only part of the risks of LSD use. LSD users may manifest relatively long-lasting psychoses, such as schizophrenia or severe depression. It is difficult to determine the extent and mechanism of the LSD involvement in these illnesses.

Most users of LSD voluntarily decrease or stop its use over time. LSD is not considered an addictive drug since it does not produce compulsive drug-seeking behavior as do cocaine, amphetamine, heroin, alcohol, and nicotine. However, like many of the addictive drugs, LSD produces tolerance, so some users who take the drug repeatedly must take progressively higher doses to achieve the state of intoxication that they had previously achieved. This is an extremely dangerous practice, given the unpredictability of the drug. NIDA is funding studies that focus on the neurochemical and behavioral properties of LSD. This research will provide a greater understanding of the mechanisms of action of the drug.

Extent of Use

*Monitoring the Future Study (MTF)**

Since 1975, MTF researchers have annually surveyed almost 17,000 high school seniors nationwide to determine trends in drug use and to measure attitudes and beliefs about drug abuse. Over the past 2 years, the percentage of seniors who have used LSD has remained relatively stable. Between 1975 and 1997, the lowest lifetime use of LSD was reported by the class of 1986, when 7.2 percent of seniors reported using LSD at least once in their lives. In 1997, 13.6 percent of seniors had experimented with LSD at least once in their lifetimes. The percentage of seniors reporting use of LSD in the past year nearly doubled from a low of 4.4 percent in 1985 to 8.4 percent in 1997.

In 1997, 34.7 percent of seniors perceived great risk in using LSD once or twice, and 76.6 percent said they saw great risk in using LSD regularly. More than 80 percent of seniors disapproved of people trying LSD once or twice, and almost 93 percent disapproved of people taking LSD regularly.

Almost 51 percent of seniors said it would have been fairly easy or very easy for them to get LSD if they had wanted it.

Table 23.1. LSD Use by Students, 1997: Monitoring the Future Study

	8th Graders	10th Graders	12th Graders
Ever Used	4.7%	9.5%	13.6%
Used in Past Year	3.2	6.7	8.4
Used in Past Month	1.5	2.8	3.1

National Household Survey on Drug Abuse (NHSDA)**

NHSDA reports the nature and extent of drug use among the American household population aged 12 and older. In the 1996 NHSDA estimates, the percentage of the population aged 12 and older who had ever used LSD (the lifetime prevalence rate) had increased to 7.7 percent from 6.0 percent in 1988. Among youths 12 to 17 years old, the 1996 LSD lifetime prevalence rate was 4.3 percent, and for those aged 18 to 25, the rate was 13.9 percent. The rate for past-year use of LSD among the population ages 12 and older was 1 percent in 1996. Past-year prevalence was highest among the age groups 12 to 17 (2.8 percent) and 18 to 25 (4.6 percent). The rate of current LSD use in 1996 for those aged 18 to 25 was 0.9 percent, and it was 0.8 percent for 12- to 17-year-old youths.

Notes

*MTF is an annual survey on drug use and related attitudes of America's adolescents that began in 1975. The survey is conducted by the University of Michigan's Institute for Social Research and is funded by NIDA. Copies of the latest survey are available from the National Clearinghouse for Alcohol and Drug Information at 1-800-729-6686.

**NHSDA is an annual survey conducted by the Substance Abuse and Mental Health Services Administration. Copies of the latest survey are available from the National Clearinghouse for Alcohol and Drug Information at 1-800-729-6686.

Chapter 24

Marijuana

Marijuana is a green or gray mixture of dried, shredded flowers and leaves of the hemp plant *Cannabis sativa*. There are over 200 slang terms for marijuana including "pot," "herb," "weed," "boom," "Mary Jane," "gangster," and "chronic." It is usually smoked as a cigarette (called a joint or a nail) or in a pipe or bong. In recent years, marijuana has appeared in blunts, which are cigars that have been emptied of tobacco and refilled with marijuana, often in combination with another drug, such as crack. Some users also mix marijuana into foods or use it to brew tea.

The main active chemical in marijuana is THC (delta-9-tetrahydrocannabinol). In 1988, it was discovered that the membranes of certain nerve cells contain protein receptors that bind THC. Once securely in place, THC kicks off a series of cellular reactions that ultimately lead to the high that users experience when they smoke marijuana. The short term effects of marijuana use include problems with memory and learning; distorted perception; difficulty in thinking and problem-solving; loss of coordination; and increased heart rate, anxiety, and panic attacks.

Scientists have found that whether an individual has positive or negative sensations after smoking marijuana can be influenced by heredity. A recent study demonstrated that identical male twins were more likely than non-identical male twins to report similar responses to marijuana use, indicating a genetic basis for their sensations. Identical twins share all of their genes, and fraternal twins share about half.

National Institute on Drug Abuse (NIDA), Pub. No. 13551, February 1999.

Environmental factors such as the availability of marijuana, expectations about how the drug would affect them, the influence of friends and social contacts, and other factors that differentiate identical twins' experiences also were found to have an important effect; however, it also was discovered that the twins' shared or family environment before age 18 had no detectable influence on their response to marijuana.

Health Hazards

Effects of Marijuana on the Brain

Researchers have found that THC changes the way in which sensory information gets into and is processed by the hippocampus. The hippocampus is a component of the brain's limbic system that is crucial for learning, memory, and the integration of sensory experiences with emotions and motivations. Investigations have shown that neurons in the information processing system of the hippocampus and the activity of the nerve fibers in this region are suppressed by THC. In addition, researchers have discovered that learned behaviors, which depend on the hippocampus, also deteriorate via this mechanism.

Recent research findings also indicate that long-term use of marijuana produces changes in the brain similar to those seen after long-term use of other major drugs of abuse.

Effects on the Lungs

Someone who smokes marijuana regularly may have many of the same respiratory problems as tobacco smokers. These individuals may have daily cough and phlegm, symptoms of chronic bronchitis, and more frequent chest colds. Continuing to smoke marijuana can lead to abnormal functioning of lung tissue injured or destroyed by marijuana smoke.

Regardless of the THC content, the amount of tar inhaled by marijuana smokers and the level of carbon monoxide absorbed are three to five times greater than among tobacco smokers. This may be due to the marijuana users' inhaling more deeply and holding the smoke in the lungs and because marijuana smoke is unfiltered.

Effects on Heart Rate and Blood Pressure

Recent findings indicate that smoking marijuana while shooting up cocaine has the potential to cause severe increases in heart rate and blood pressure. In one study, experienced marijuana and cocaine users were given marijuana alone, cocaine alone, and then a combination of both. Each drug alone produced cardiovascular effects; when they were combined, the effects were greater and lasted longer. The heart rate of the subjects in the study increased 29 beats per minute with marijuana alone and 32 beats per minute with cocaine alone. When the drugs were given together, the heart rate increased by 49 beats per minute, and the increased rate persisted for a longer time. The drugs were given with the subjects sitting quietly. In normal circumstances, an individual may smoke marijuana and inject cocaine and then do something physically stressful that may significantly increase the risk of overloading the cardiovascular system.

Effects of Heavy Marijuana Use on Learning and Social Behavior

A study of college students has shown that critical skills related to attention, memory, and learning are impaired among people who use marijuana heavily, even after discontinuing its use for at least 24 hours. Researchers compared 65 "heavy users," who had smoked marijuana a median of 29 of the past 30 days, and 64 "light users," who had smoked a median of 1 of the past 30 days. After a closely monitored 19- to 24-hour period of abstinence from marijuana and other illicit drugs and alcohol, the undergraduates were given several standard tests measuring aspects of attention, memory, and learning. Compared to the light users, heavy marijuana users made more errors and had more difficulty sustaining attention, shifting attention to meet the demands of changes in the environment, and in registering, processing, and using information. These findings suggest that the greater impairment among heavy users is likely due to an alteration of brain activity produced by marijuana.

Longitudinal research on marijuana use among young people below college age indicates those who used marijuana have lower achievement than the non-users, more acceptance of deviant behavior, more delinquent behavior and aggression, greater rebelliousness, poorer relationships with parents, and more associations with delinquent and drug-using friends.

Research also shows more anger and more regressive behavior (thumb sucking, temper tantrums) in toddlers whose parents use marijuana than among the toddlers of non-using parents.

Effects on Pregnancy

Any drug of abuse can affect a mother's health during pregnancy, making it a time when expectant mothers should take special care of

Table 24.1. Percentage of 8th-Graders Who Have Used Marijuana: Monitoring the Future Study, 1999

	1991	1992	1993	1994	1995	1996	1997	1998	1999
Ever Used	10.2%	11.2%	12.6%	16.7%	19.9%	23.1%	22.6%	22.2%	22.0%
Used in Past Year	6.2	7.2	9.2	13.0	15.8	18.3	17.7	16.9	16.5
Used in Past Month	3.2	3.7	5.1	7.8	9.1	11.3	10.2	9.7	9.7
Daily Use in Past Month	0.2	0.2	0.4	0.7	0.8	1.5	1.1	1.1	1.4

Table 24.2. Percentage of 10th-Graders Who Have Used Marijuana: Monitoring the Future Study, 1999

	1991	1992	1993	1994	1995	1996	1997	1998	1999
Ever Used	23.4%	21.4%	24.4%	30.4%	34.1%	39.8%	42.3%	39.6%	40.9%
Used in Past Year	16.5	15.2	19.2	25.2	28.7	33.6	34.8	31.1	32.1
Used in Past Month	8.7	8.1	10.9	15.8	17.2	20.4	20.5	18.7	19.4
Daily Use in Past Month	0.8	0.8	1.0	2.2	2.8	3.5	3.7	3.6	3.8

Table 24.3. Percentage of 12th-Graders Who Have Used Marijuana: Monitoring the Future Study, 1999

	1979	1985	1991	1992	1993	1994	1995	1996	1997	1998	1999
Ever Used	60.4%	54.2%	36.7%	32.6%	35.3%	38.2%	41.7%	44.9%	49.6%	49.1%	49.7%
Used in Past Year	50.8	40.6	23.9	21.9	26.0	30.7	34.7	35.8	38.5	37.5	37.8
Used in Past Month	36.5	25.7	13.8	11.9	15.5	19.0	21.2	21.9	23.7	22.8	23.1
Daily Use in Past Month	10.3	4.9	2.0	1.9	2.4	3.6	4.6	4.9	5.8	5.6	6.0

themselves. Drugs of abuse may interfere with proper nutrition and rest, which can affect good functioning of the immune system. Some studies have found that babies born to mothers who used marijuana during pregnancy were smaller than those born to mothers who did not use the drug. In general, smaller babies are more likely to develop health problems.

A nursing mother who uses marijuana passes some of the THC to the baby in her breast milk. Research indicates that the use of marijuana by a mother during the first month of breast-feeding can impair the infant's motor development (control of muscle movement).

Addictive Potential

A drug is addicting if it causes compulsive, often uncontrollable drug craving, seeking, and use, even in the face of negative health and social consequences. Marijuana meets this criterion. More than 120,000 people enter treatment per year for their primary marijuana addiction. In addition, animal studies suggest marijuana causes physical dependence, and some people report withdrawal symptoms.

Extent of Use

Monitoring the Future Study (MTF)*

The National Institute on Drug Abuse (NIDA)-funded MTF provides an annual assessment of drug use among 12th, 10th, and 8th grade students and young adults nationwide. After decreasing for over a decade, marijuana use among students began to increase in the early 1990s. From 1998 to 1999, use of marijuana at least once (lifetime use) increased among 12th- and 10th-graders, continuing the trend seen in recent years. The seniors' rate of lifetime marijuana use is higher than any year since 1987, but all rates remain well below those seen in the late 1970s and early 1980s. Past year and past month marijuana use did not change significantly from 1998 to 1999 in any of the three grades, suggesting the sharp increases of recent years may be slowing. Daily marijuana use in the past month increased slightly among all three grades as well.

Community Epidemiology Work Group (CEWG)**

In 1998, marijuana indicators continued an upward trend in most of the 20 CEWG metropolitan areas. Rates of emergency department mentions of marijuana increased significantly in seven sites, with the largest increases occurring in Dallas (emergency room mentions increased to 63.9 percent), Boston (to 44.1 percent), Denver (to 40 percent), San Diego (to 35.1 percent), and Atlanta (to 31.7 percent). The highest percent increase in emergency room mentions comparing the first half of 1997 and the first half of 1998 was among 12- to 17-year olds.

Treatment data for primary abuse of marijuana increased in six CEWG sites and remained stable elsewhere. Marijuana treatment admissions were highest in Denver (41 percent of all admissions), Miami (30 percent), New Orleans (22 percent), and Minneapolis/ St. Paul (20 percent). Half of the treatment admissions for marijuana in Minneapolis/St. Paul were under age 18.

In six of the CEWG sites, juvenile arrestees testing positive for marijuana ranged from a low of 40.3 percent in St. Louis to a high of 63.7 percent in Phoenix. More than 50 percent of juvenile arrestees in Los Angeles, Denver, and Washington, D.C. tested positive for marijuana, and 48.9 percent in San Diego. Among all arrestees, Seattle was the only site where women were more likely than men (37.9 percent vs. 35.4 percent) to test positive for marijuana.

National Household Survey on Drug Abuse (NHSDA)***

Marijuana remains the most commonly used illicit drug in the United States. There were an estimated 2.1 million people who started using marijuana in 1998. According to data from the 1998 NHSDA, more than 72.0 million Americans (33 percent) 12 years of age and older have tried marijuana at least once in their lifetimes, and almost 18.7 million (8.6 percent) had used marijuana in the past year. In 1985, 56.5 million Americans (29.4 percent) had tried marijuana at least once in their lifetimes, and 26.1 million (13.6 percent) had used marijuana within the past year.

Notes

* MTF is an annual survey on drug use and related attitudes of America's adolescents that began in 1975. The survey is conducted by the University of Michigan's Institute for Social Research and is funded by NIDA. Copies of the latest survey are available from the National Clearinghouse for Alcohol and Drug Information at 1-800-729-6686.

** CEWG is a NIDA-sponsored network of researchers from 20 major U.S. metropolitan areas and selected foreign countries who meet semiannually to discuss the current epidemiology of drug abuse. CEWG's most recent report is Epidemiologic Trends in Drug Abuse, Advance Report, June 1999.

*** NHSDA is an annual survey conducted by the Substance Abuse and Mental Health Services Administration Copies of the latest survey are available from the National Clearinghouse for Alcohol and Drug Information at 1-800-729-6686.

Chapter 25

MDMA (Ecstasy)

MDMA, called "Adam," "ecstasy," or "XTC" on the street, is a synthetic, psychoactive (mind-altering) drug with amphetamine-like and hallucinogenic properties. Its chemical structure (3-4 methylenedioxymethamphetamine) is similar to two other synthetic drugs, MDA and methamphetamine, which are known to cause brain damage.

Health Hazards

Beliefs about MDMA are reminiscent of the claims made about LSD in the 1950s and 1960s, which proved to be untrue. According to its proponents, MDMA can make people trust each other and can break down barriers between therapists and patients, lovers, and family members.

Many of the risks users face with MDMA use are similar to those found with the use of amphetamines and cocaine. They are:

- Psychological difficulties, including confusion, depression, sleep problems, drug craving, severe anxiety, and paranoia—during and sometimes weeks after taking MDMA (even psychotic episodes have been reported).

- Physical symptoms such as muscle tension, involuntary teeth clenching, nausea, blurred vision, rapid eye movement, faintness, and chills or sweating.

National Institute on Drug Abuse (NIDA), Pub. No. 13547, February 2000.

- Increases in heart rate and blood pressure, a special risk for people with circulatory or heart disease.

Recent research findings also link MDMA use to long-term damage to those parts of the brain critical to thought and memory. It is thought that the drug causes damage to the neurons that use the chemical serotonin to communicate with other neurons. In monkeys, exposure to MDMA for 4 days caused brain damage that was evident 6 to 7 years later. This study provides further evidence that people who take MDMA may be risking permanent brain damage.

Also, there is evidence that people who develop a rash that looks like acne after using MDMA may be risking severe side effects, including liver damage, if they continue to use the drug.

MDA, the parent drug of MDMA, is an amphetamine-like drug that has also been abused and is similar in chemical structure to MDMA. Research shows that MDA destroys serotonin-producing neurons in the brain, which play a direct role in regulating aggression, mood, sexual activity, sleep, and sensitivity to pain. It is probably this action on the serotonin system that gives MDA its purported properties of heightened sexual experience, tranquillity, and conviviality.

MDMA also is related in its structure and effects to methamphetamine, which has been shown to cause degeneration of neurons containing the neurotransmitter dopamine. Damage to these neurons is the underlying cause of the motor disturbances seen in Parkinson's disease. Symptoms of this disease begin with lack of coordination and tremors and can eventually result in a form of paralysis.

Extent of Use

Community Epidemiology Work Group (CEWG)*

MDMA is used most often by young adults and adolescents at clubs, raves (large, all-night dance parties), and rock concerts.

Its abuse is increasingly reported in the 20 metropolitan areas included in the CEWG.

In Kings County, Washington, a recently completed survey of young men who have sex with men showed that MDMA was among the frequently used drugs (20 percent of the sample).

In Boston, a 1996-97 survey of public schools in Boston found that about 14 percent of male and 7 percent of female 12th graders had used MDMA during their lifetime. Increased use of MDMA among youth was also reported in Seattle.

Information about MDMA from other CEWG areas include the following:

- In Atlanta, MDMA is reported as a popular stimulant.

- In Chicago, it's use is common in the rave and club scenes, especially in the North Side.

- In Miami, large-scale sales of drugs such as MDMA are occurring at raves.

- In New Jersey, it is available across the state, particularly in college towns.

National Household Survey on Drug Abuse (NHSDA)**

Each year, NHSDA reports on the nature and extent of drug use among the American household population aged 12 and older. The 1998 survey found that an estimated 1.5 percent (3.4 million) of Americans at least 12 years old had used MDMA at least once during their lifetime. By age group, the heaviest use (5 percent or 1.4 million people) was reported for those between 18 and 25 years old.

Monitoring the Future Study (MTF)***

In 1996, MTF began to collect data on MDMA use among students. Rates of use remained relatively stable from 1996 to 1999 for students in the 8th-grade. While usage among 10th- and 12th-graders has increased.

Table 25.1. Ecstasy Use by Students, 1999: Monitoring the Future Study

	8th-Graders	10th-Graders	12th-Graders
Ever Used	2.7%	6.0%	8.0%
Used in Past Year	1.7	4.4	5.6
Used in Past Month	0.8	1.8	2.5

"Ever used" refers to use at least once during a respondent's lifetime. "Past year" refers to an individual's drug use at least once during the year preceding their response to the survey. "Past month" refers to an individual's drug use at least once during the month preceding their response to the survey.

The number of 12th-graders that had used MDMA in their lifetime increased from 5.8 percent in 1998 to 8.0 percent in 1999. Use in the past year also increased from 3.6 percent in 1998 to 5.6 percent in 1999. In addition, 12th-graders use of MDMA in the past month also increased from 1.5 percent in 1998 to 2.5 percent in 1999.

On the other hand, the largest change for 10th-graders occurred in past year use, which increased from 3.3 percent in 1998 to 4.4 percent in 1999.

Notes

* CEWG is a NIDA-sponsored network of researchers from 21 major U.S. metropolitan areas and selected foreign countries who meet semi-annually to discuss the current epidemiology of drug abuse. CEWG's most recent report is Epidemiologic Trends in Drug Abuse, Advance Report, June 1999.

** NHSDA is an annual survey conducted by the Substance Abuse and Mental Health Services Administration. Copies of the latest survey are available from the National Clearinghouse for Alcohol and Drug Information at 1-800-729-6686.

*** MTF is an annual survey on drug use and related attitudes of America's adolescents that began in 1975. In 1996, MTF began to collect data on MDMA use among students. The survey is conducted by the University of Michigan's Institute for Social Research and is funded by NIDA. Copies of the latest survey are available from the National Clearinghouse for Alcohol and Drug Information at 1-800-729-6686.

Chapter 26

Methcathinone (Cat)

The scenario seems right out of some science fiction nightmare. A dangerous addictive drug that is cheap and easy to manufacture appears out of nowhere and creates a potential drug crisis. The drug is concocted from a "witches brew" of battery acid, Drano, and over-the-counter asthma medication, and can be manufactured in home kitchens.

Unfortunately, it isn't science fiction. It isn't fiction. It is methcathinone. Since 1991 or 1992, this new drug has emerged as a cheap substitute for methamphetamine. Since it is so new, all of the risks have not yet been assessed.

Slang Terms Associated with Methcathinone

- Cat
- Goob
- Jeff
- Speed
- Bathtub speed
- Mulka
- Gagers, gaggers
- The C
- Wild cat
- Wonder star
- Cadillac express
- Ephedrone

Ingredients Used in Methcathinone Synthesis

The ingredients used in various recipes for home-made methcathinone include:

197

- ephedrine or pseudoephedrine (found in some over-the-counter asthma and cold medications)
- acetone (explosive paint solvent)
- muriatic acid (used in sandblasting and cleaning mortar off bricks)
- sulfuric acid (usually purchased from auto supply stores as battery acid)
- lye (usually in the form of a crystal drain cleaner such as Drano)
- sodium dichromate or potassium dichromate
- sodium hydroxide
- toulene (explosive paint thinner)

History of Methcathinone

Methcathinone is a derivative of a naturally-occurring stimulant drug, cathinone, which is found in the "khat" plant, *Cathula edulis*, which is native to the horn of Africa and southern Arabian peninsula. It was first synthesized in Germany in 1928, and used in the Soviet Union as an anti-depressant during the 1930's and 1940's. Abuse of methcathinone, also known as "ephedrone," "Jeff," or "Mulka," has been reported in the Soviet Union since the late 1960's.

In the mid-1950's, American pharmaceutical manufacturer Parke Davis & Company conducted preliminary studies on methcathinone to determine if it had any medicinal potential. Although Parke Davis soon abandoned its methcathinone research, after determining that there were unacceptable safety risks and substantial side effects, their studies revealed that it had physiologic effects similar to amphetamine. Methcathinone reemerged in this country in 1989, when a University of Michigan student who was interning at Parke Davis stumbled across and stole samples of the drug and documentation of the manufacturing process. In 1990, associates of that student began manufacturing and selling the drug in clandestine laboratories in northern Michigan. Its use became popular in the Upper Peninsula of Michigan in 1990 and 1991, and quickly spread statewide. As of 1995, methcathinone laboratories have been discovered in ten states, from Colorado through the midwest. It has quickly become one of the biggest challenges faced by the U.S. Drug Enforcement Administration.

Methcathinone was classified as a Schedule I controlled substance under the federal Controlled Substances Act on May 1, 1992, under the emergency scheduling procedure. The classification was made permanent effective October 15, 1993.

Effects of Methcathinone Intoxication

The most common means of taking methcathinone is snorting (nasal insufflation). Other routes of administration include taking it by mouth (oral ingestion) mixed in a liquid such as coffee or soft drinks, intravenous injection, and smoking it either in a crack pipe or added to tobacco or marijuana cigarettes. Methcathinone is often used in binges lasting from two to six days, during which methcathinone is used repeatedly.

Effects of short term intoxication are similar to those produced by crack cocaine or methamphetamine: stimulation of heart rate and respiration; feeling of euphoria; loss of appetite; increased alertness; pupils may be dilated; body temperature may be slightly elevated. Acute intoxication at higher doses may also result in: insomnia, tremors and muscle twitching, fever, headaches, convulsions, irregular heart rate and respirations, anxiety, restlessness, paranoia, and hallucinations and delusions.

Problems Associated with Methcathinone Use

While research on the long-term effects of methcathinone use is just beginning in the United States, anecdotal reports from users in treatment in this country, and from published research in Russia, paint a similar picture. Chronic use of methcathinone produces a range of problems typical of addiction to powerful stimulant drugs including:

• paranoia and delusions

• hallucinations, including a sensation of bugs crawling under the skin

• anxiety followed by depression

• tremors and convulsions

• anorexia, malnutrition, and weight loss

• sweating, dehydration, and electrolyte imbalance

• stomach pains and nausea

- nose bleeding and eventual destruction of nasal tissues and erosion of the nasal septum
- elevated blood pressure and heart rate
- body aches

In addition, following a binge, users report a "crash" that often includes severe psychological depression, and suicide ideation.

Anecdotal reports from patients in treatment facilities in Michigan and Wisconsin suggest that methcathinone is highly addictive, similar to crack cocaine, and some users report developing tolerance and withdrawal symptoms after just one incident of binging (six to ten days) on methcathinone. Addiction to methcathinone appears to be as difficult to treat as addiction to crack cocaine.

Data from Russia report that many methcathinone addicts suffer permanent brain damage and exhibit symptoms similar to Parkinson's disease.

In extreme cases, deaths have been reported, and are related to heart failure, lethal overdoses, drug-related violence, and manufacturing accidents.

—by William J. Bailey

Chapter 27

Methamphetamine

Background Information

Methamphetamine, a derivative of amphetamine, is a powerful stimulant that affects the central nervous system. Amphetamine was originally intended for use in nasal decongestants and bronchial inhalers and has limited medical applications, including the treatment of narcolepsy, weight control, and attention deficit disorder. Methamphetamine can be smoked, snorted, orally ingested, or injected. It is accessible in many different forms and may be identified by color, which ranges from white or yellow to darker colors such as red or brown. Methamphetamine comes in a powder form that resembles granulated crystals and in a rock form known as "ice," which is preferred by those who smoke methamphetamine. According to the National Institute on Drug Abuse (NIDA), users have been known to use cocaine, marijuana, morphine, and alcohol in combination with methamphetamine.

Methamphetamine is a Schedule II narcotic under the Controlled Substances Act, Title II of the Comprehensive Drug Abuse Prevention and Control Act of 1970. If a person is convicted of trafficking

"Methamphetamine," Executive Office of the President, Office of National Drug Control Policy (ONDCP), Drug Policy Information Clearinghouse, May 1999. For further information about this text or about other drug policy issues, call: 1-800-666-3332 or write the Drug Policy Information Clearinghouse, P.O. Box 6000, Rockville, MD 20849-6000, or visit the World Wide Web site at: www.whitehousedrugpolicy.gov.

methamphetamine, depending on the amount of methamphetamine and if a person was injured or killed during the crime, the trafficker can receive 5 to 20 years in prison and a fine not to exceed $10 million for the first offense. In addition to being a Schedule II drug itself, methamphetamine is made from chemicals that are regulated under the Comprehensive Methamphetamine Control Act of 1996. This act broadens controls on drugs such as ephedrine and pseudoephedrine, which are used in the manufacturing of methamphetamine. It also increases penalties for trafficking and possession of such chemicals without registration.

Effects

Methamphetamine use produces increases in energy and alertness and a decrease in appetite. An intense rush is felt, almost instantaneously, when a user smokes or injects methamphetamine. Snorting methamphetamine affects the user in approximately 5 minutes, whereas orally ingesting methamphetamine takes about 20 minutes for the user to feel the effects. The intense rush and high felt from methamphetamine results from the release of high levels of dopamine into the section of the brain that controls the feeling of pleasure. The effects of methamphetamine can last up to 12 hours. Side effects of methamphetamine use are convulsions, dangerously high body temperature, stroke, cardiac arrhythmia, stomach cramps, and shaking.

Long-term use of methamphetamine may result in addiction. Methamphetamine abuse can also cause violent behavior, anxiety, and insomnia, as well as psychotic behavior such as paranoia, hallucinations, mood swings, and delusions. The user can also develop a tolerance to the drug, which requires the user to take increasing amounts to induce the desired effects. Chronic users of methamphetamine are also characterized as having poor hygiene, a gaunt or pale complexion, and, at times, sores on their bodies from scratching at "crank bugs," which is a common delusion that bugs are crawling under their skin. Additionally, long-term use of methamphetamine can cause damage to the dopamine-producing cells of the brain.

Methamphetamine Use and User Characteristics

The statistical measures used to track drug use indicate that methamphetamine use is stable or rising. These studies show that the majority of methamphetamine users are male, Caucasian, and over age 26. However, NIDA reports certain regions of the country exhibiting an increase in use among youth. The University of Michigan's *Monitoring the Future Study* reported that 5.3% of high school seniors from the class of 1998 had tried "ice" or crystal methamphetamine at least once in their life, up from 4.4% for the class of 1997. The study also found that 1.2% of seniors in the class of 1998 used "ice" in the past month, up from 0.8% in 1997. According to the Substance Abuse and Mental Health Services Administration (SAMHSA), 1.2% of the 12 to 17 age group used methamphetamine at least once in their life in 1997, up from 0.6% in 1996. SAMHSA also showed 2.5% of the U.S. population reported using methamphetamine in 1997, up from 2.3% in 1996 (see Table 27.1).

Table 27.1. Percentage reporting use of methamphetamine, at least once in lifetime, in the U.S. population aged 12 and over: 1994–1997.

Year	12–17	18–25	26–34	35 and older	Total
1994	0.6	1.7	0.6	1.6	1.8
1995	0.8	1.9	3.8	2.1	2.2
1996	0.6	2.5	4.2	2.0	2.3
1997	1.2	2.3	2.7	2.6	2.5

Source: U.S. Department of Health and Human Services, Office of Applied Studies, Substance Abuse and Mental Health Services Administration, *Preliminary Results from the 1995–1997 National Household Survey on Drug Abuse,* August 1996, July 1997, August 1998.

The National Association of State Alcohol and Drug Abuse Directors (NASADAD) reports that there were 44,593 admissions to State-supported treatment facilities for methamphetamine abuse in 1995. Methamphetamine admissions made up 5.1% of all admissions, which was the fourth highest percentage after cocaine (38.3%), heroin (25.5%), and marijuana (19.1%). SAMHSA's Drug Abuse Warning Network (DAWN) reported 5,236 methamphetamine emergency department mentions in 1990; in 1994 the number peaked at 17,655 before dropping to 11,002 in 1996. DAWN also reported the number of methamphetamine-related deaths at 487 in 1996; the majority of the decedents were Caucasian males over the age of 26 (see Table 27.2).

Between 1990 and 1998, approximately 250,000 adult arrestees were tested for drug use through the National Institute of Justice's Arrestee Drug Abuse Monitoring (ADAM) program. Table 27.3 shows the percentage of arrestees who tested positive for methamphetamine

Table 27.2. Number of methamphetamine-related deaths* by gender, race/ethnicity, and age: 1992–1996.

	1992	1993	1994	1995	1996
Total	234	382	492	488	487
Mentions†					
Gender					
Male	182	307	394	375	380
Female	50	71	97	94	94
Race/Ethnicity					
Caucasian	191	304	394	375	380
Black	12	21	26	24	20
Hispanic	22	43	59	75	68
Other	8	5	13	14	19
Age					
6–17	2	4	9	9	8
18–25	28	54	80	67	71
26–34	76	133	156	148	122
35 or older	127	190	243	258	280

* Excludes data on homicides, deaths in which AIDS was reported, and deaths in which "drug unknown" was the only substance mentioned.

† Includes episodes for which gender, race/ethnicity, and age were unknown or not reported.

Source: U.S. Department of Health and Human Services, Office of Applied Studies, Substance Abuse and Mental Health Services Administration, *Drug Abuse Warning Network, Annual Medical Examiner Data 1992–1996,* 1994, 1995, 1996, May 1997, July 1998.

in selected cities and years. The cities on the West Coast (e.g., San Diego) had a much higher percentage of arrestees who tested positive compared with cities on the East Coast (e.g., New York or Philadelphia).

Availability, Production, and Trafficking of Methamphetamine

According to the U.S. Drug Enforcement Administration (DEA), methamphetamine production and trafficking are rampant in the West and Midwest areas of the United States, and increasing in the Southeast and Northeast regions of the United States. In the Northeast, production and trafficking operations have increased and the principal traffickers are outlaw motorcycle gangs. The majority of methamphetamine was transported into the Northeast from outside sources. In the Southeast methamphetamine availability has increased significantly, and there has been an increase in seizures and

Table 27.3. Percentage of Arrestees Testing Positive for Methamphetamine, Selected Cities: 1990, 1994, 1997, and 1998.

	1990		1994		1997		1998	
Site	M	F	M	F	M	F	M	F
Atlanta	0.0%	0.0%	0.1%	0.3%	0.6%	0.7%	0.0%	—
Dallas	1.9	4.0	3.5	5.2	2.6	2.8	3.3	4.0
Denver	0.7	1.6	2.1	2.1	5.0	4.6	5.2	4.6
New York City	0.0	0.4	0.3	0.0	0.0	0.0	0.0	0.0
Omaha	0.6	—	3.3	2.7	9.7	13.3	10.2	13.6
Philadelphia	0.9	1.1	0.1	0.7	0.6	0.0	0.6	0.3
Phoenix	6.7	6.6	25.4	26.0	16.4	25.6	16.4	22.4
Portland	10.9	10.9	16.3	21.4	15.9	20.7	18.1	22.3
St. Louis	0.2	0.0	0.5	0.0	0.4	2.1	0.3	2.5
San Diego	27.3	31.8	41.0	53.0	39.6	42.2	33.2	33.3
San Jose	8.9	5.4	19.9	23.3	18.4	24.9	19.7	21.1
Washington, D.C.	0.1	0.6	0.1	0.0	0.3	0.0	0.0	0.5

Source: U.S. Department of Justice, National Institute of Justice, *1998 Annual Report on Methamphetamine Use Among Arrestees*, April 1999.

investigations by law enforcement officials. The majority of the methamphetamine in this part of the United States was supplied from West Coast and Mexican drug-trafficking organizations rather than produced in the region.

The Midwest region has experienced a tremendous growth in methamphetamine trafficking and production, especially in portions of Iowa and Missouri. The main source of methamphetamine in the Midwest is Mexican-controlled trafficking organizations based in California and Mexico. There has also been an increase of clandestine laboratory production in the region. The West—especially California, Arizona, and Utah—continues to be the region in the United States with the most methamphetamine trafficking, production, and use. The majority of methamphetamine operations in this region are controlled by Mexican drug-trafficking organizations, based along the California-Arizona border. In the West, there is also a high rate of methamphetamine-related violence, including driveby shootings, murders, kidnappings, and assaults. This region also has the most clandestine laboratories in operation.

Law enforcement statistics for methamphetamine, such as drug seizure and arrest data, have increased in the United States. In fiscal year 1995, the DEA seized 958 kilograms of methamphetamine, which is the largest total amount seized by the DEA in 1 year. In the same year, the DEA also made nearly 2,700 arrests as a result of methamphetamine investigations; this is an increase of 23% over fiscal year 1994.

The price of methamphetamine is also on the rise. In 1995 a pound of methamphetamine ranged in price from $3,000 to $20,000. In 1997 the price for a pound increased from $3,500 to $30,000. An ounce of methamphetamine in 1997 cost from $400 to $2,800, and the cost of a gram ranged from $37 to $200.

Slang Terms for Methamphetamine

- Blue Mollies
- Chalk
- Crank
- Crystal
- Glass
- Go-Fast
- Ice
- LA Glass

- Meth Yellow Bam
- Methlies Quick
- Mexican Crack
- Quartz
- Shabu
- Sketch
- Speed
- Stove Top

- West Coast

Clandestine Laboratories

Methamphetamine can be easily manufactured in clandestine laboratories (meth labs) using ingredients purchased in local stores. Over-the-counter cold medicines containing ephedrine or pseudoephedrine and other materials are "cooked" in meth labs to make methamphetamine. Manufacturing methamphetamine or "cooking" a batch releases toxic materials into the air as well as produces toxic waste after the drug is made. This situation can be very costly and dangerous for local authorities to deal with. As well as creating potential toxic waste dumps, meth labs have been known to be booby-trapped and lab operators are often well armed. Meth labs can be portable; they are easily dismantled, stored, or moved. This portability helps methamphetamine manufacturers avoid law enforcement authorities. Meth labs have been found in many different types of locations including apartments, hotel rooms, rented storage spaces, and trucks. The DEA and State and local law enforcement authorities seized 879 methamphetamine laboratories in 1996; this figure rose to 1,435 in 1997.

Summary

Available statistics show that production, trafficking, and use of the dangerous drug methamphetamine has increased, not only among the adult population, but also with the Nation's youth. Trafficking, production, and accessibility of methamphetamine have spread across the country, and have proved to be detrimental to the health of the Nation. Methamphetamine use can damage the user's brain and body, and production of the drug creates a hazard to law enforcement personnel, the community, and the producers of the drug. Increasing popularity and availability of methamphetamine, combined with the ease of manufacture and mobility of meth labs, present a costly and complex problem to Federal, State, and local authorities.

Sources

Executive Office of the President, Office of National Drug Control Policy, *Pulse Check: National Trends in Drug Abuse,* Winter 1998. http://www. white housedrugpolicy.gov/drugfact/pulsechk/winter98/contents.html

Executive Office of the President, Office of National Drug Control Policy, ONDCP Drug Policy Information Clearinghouse, *Street Terms: Drugs and the Drug Trade,* September 1997. http://www.whitehousedrug policy .gov/drugfact/terms/terms.html

National Association of State Alcohol and Drug Abuse Directors, Gustafson, John S., et al., *State Responses and Services Related to Alcohol and Other Drug Problems for Fiscal Year 1995,* March 1996. http://www.nasadad.org

National Institute on Drug Abuse, Community Epidemiology Work Group, *Epidemiologic Trends in Drug Abuse, Volume I: Highlights and Executive Summary,* June 1997. http://www.cdmgroup.com/CEWG

University of Michigan, Institute for Social Research, *National Survey Results on Drug Use from the Monitoring the Future Study,* December 1998. http://www.isr.umich.edu/src/mtf

U.S. Department of Health and Human Services, National Institute on Drug Abuse, *Research Report Series: Methamphetamine Abuse and Addiction,* April 1998. http://www.nida.nih.gov/ResearchReports/ Methamph/Methamph.html

U.S. Department of Health and Human Services, Office of Applied Studies, Substance Abuse and Mental Health Services Administration, *Drug Abuse Warning Network, Annual Medical Examiner Data 1992–1996,* 1994, 1995, 1996, 1997, and July 1998. http://www. samhsa .gov/OAS/dawn/dwnfiles.htm

U.S. Department of Health and Human Services, Office of Applied Studies, Substance Abuse and Mental Health Services Administration, *Preliminary Results from the 1995–1997 National Household Survey on Drug Abuse,* and August 1996, July 1997, and August 1998. http://www.samhsa.gov/OAS/nhsda/nhsdafls.htm

U.S. Department of Health and Human Services, Substance Abuse and Mental Health Services Administration, *Mid-Year 1997 Preliminary Emergency Department Data from the Drug Abuse Warning Network,* September 1998. http://www.samhsa.gov/OAS/dawn/dwnfiles.htm

U.S. Department of Justice, Drug Enforcement Administration, *Annual Statistical Report, FY 1995,* January 1996. U.S. Department of Justice, Drug Enforcement Administration, *Drugs of Abuse,* 1996. http://www.usdoj.gov/dea/pubs/abuse/contents.htm

U.S. Department of Justice, Drug Enforcement Administration, *Illegal Drug Price/Purity Report, United States: January 1993–December 1996,* June 1997.

U.S. Department of Justice, Drug Enforcement Administration, *The NNICC Report 1997: The Supply of Illicit Drugs to the United States,* November 1998. http://www.usdoj.gov/dea/pubs/intel/nnicc97.htm

U.S. Department of Justice, Drug Enforcement Administration, *Provisions of the Comprehensive Methamphetamine Control Act of 1996,* October 1996. http://www.usdoj.gov/dea/programs/diverson/divpub/substanc/compmeth.htm

U.S. Department of Justice, National Drug Intelligence Center, *Effects of D-Methamphetamine: Baseline Assessment, Mexico Unit,* December 1996. http://www.usdoj.gov/ndic/publications/effects_of_dmeth amphetamine/294.htm

U.S. Department of Justice, National Institute of Justice, *1998 Annual Report on Methamphetamine Use Among Arrestees,* April 1999. http://www.ncjrs.org/pdffiles1/175660.pdf

Chapter 28

Methylphenidate (Ritalin)

Ritalin, the trade name for methylphenidate, is a medication prescribed for children with an abnormally high level of activity or with attention-deficit hyperactivity disorder (ADHD) and is also occasionally prescribed for treating narcolepsy. It stimulates the central nervous system, with effects similar to but less potent than amphetamines and more potent than caffeine.

Although we do not understand fully how it works, Ritalin has a notably calming effect on hyperactive children and a "focusing" effect on those with ADHD. When taken as prescribed, Ritalin is a valuable medicine. Further, research funded by the National Institute of Mental Health has shown that people with ADHD do not get addicted to their stimulant medications at treatment dosages.

Because of its stimulant properties, however, in recent years there have been reports of its abuse by people for whom it is not a medication. At their December 1996 meeting, members of NIDA's Community Epidemiology Work Group (CEWG)* noted that:

- Illicit methylphenidate appears to be more available in Texas and Michigan than elsewhere in the country, with Michigan historically having one of the highest per capita levels of distribution.

- In Chicago, some stimulant users mix Ritalin (or "West Coast") with heroin, or with both cocaine and heroin for a more potent effect.

National Institute on Drug Abuse (NIDA), Pub. No. 13555, November 1999.

- In Detroit and Minneapolis/St. Paul, middle and high school students crush and inhale the drug or take the pill orally.

- In Phoenix, some adults have been admitted to treatment programs for abusing the drug from their children's prescriptions.

- In Boston, according to reports by youth treatment providers, adolescents continue to abuse the drug, which is most easily available through diverted prescriptions. Drug abuse treatment staffs in Boston also report an increase in abuse among adults.

Because stimulant medicines such as Ritalin do have potential for abuse, the U.S. Drug Enforcement Administration (DEA) has placed stringent controls on their manufacture, distribution, and prescription. For example, DEA requires special licenses for these activities, and prescription refills are not allowed. States may impose further regulations, such as limiting the number of dosage units per prescription.

In January 1996, the U.S. Food and Drug Administration (FDA) announced that in studies of rodents given methylphenidate (Ritalin), the drug produced a "weak signal" for the potential to cause liver cancer. The cancer occurred in male mice, but not in female mice or rats. FDA continues to regard Ritalin as a safe and effective drug, but says the potential risk needs to be considered and further studied because of the increasing and often long-term use of Ritalin in children. The FDA also noted that the kind of liver tumor found in mice is extremely rare in people, and its occurrence in recent years has not increased despite an increase in the use of Ritalin.

For more information on treating ADHD, please call the National Institute of Mental Health, National Institutes of Health, at 301-443-4513 or visit their internet address at http://www.nimh.nih.gov.

Note

* CEWG is a NIDA-sponsored network of researchers from 20 major U.S. metropolitan areas and selected foreign countries who meet semi-annually to discuss the current epidemiology of drug abuse. CEWG's most recent report is Epidemiologic Trends in Drug Abuse, Volumes I and II, December 1996.

Chapter 29

PCP (Phencyclidine)

PCP (phencyclidine) was developed in the 1950s as an intravenous anesthetic. Use of PCP in humans was discontinued in 1965, because it was found that patients often became agitated, delusional, and irrational while recovering from its anesthetic effects. PCP is illegally manufactured in laboratories and is sold on the street by such names as "angel dust," "ozone," "wack," and "rocket fuel." "Killer joints" and "crystal supergrass" are names that refer to PCP combined with marijuana. The variety of street names for PCP reflects its bizarre and volatile effects.

PCP is a white crystalline powder that is readily soluble in water or alcohol. It has a distinctive bitter chemical taste. PCP can be mixed easily with dyes and turns up on the illicit drug market in a variety of tablets, capsules, and colored powders. It is normally used in one of three ways: snorted, smoked, or eaten. For smoking, PCP is often applied to a leafy material such as mint, parsley, oregano, or marijuana.

Health Hazards

PCP is addicting; that is, its use often leads to psychological dependence, craving, and compulsive PCP-seeking behavior. It was first introduced as a street drug in the 1960s and quickly gained a reputation as a drug that could cause bad reactions and was not worth the risk. Many people, after using the drug once, will not knowingly

National Institute on Drug Abuse (NIDA), Pub. No. 13554, November 1999.

use it again. Yet others use it consistently and regularly. Some persist in using PCP because of its addicting properties. Others cite feelings of strength, power, invulnerability and a numbing effect on the mind as reasons for their continued PCP use.

Many PCP users are brought to emergency rooms because of PCP's unpleasant psychological effects or because of overdoses. In a hospital or detention setting, they often become violent or suicidal, and are very dangerous to themselves and to others. They should be kept in a calm setting and should not be left alone.

At low to moderate doses, physiological effects of PCP include a slight increase in breathing rate and a more pronounced rise in blood pressure and pulse rate. Respiration becomes shallow, and flushing and profuse sweating occur. Generalized numbness of the extremities and muscular incoordination also may occur. Psychological effects include distinct changes in body awareness, similar to those associated with alcohol intoxication. Use of PCP among adolescents may interfere with hormones related to normal growth and development as well as with the learning process.

At high doses of PCP, there is a drop in blood pressure, pulse rate, and respiration. This may be accompanied by nausea, vomiting, blurred vision, flicking up and down of the eyes, drooling, loss of balance, and dizziness. High doses of PCP can also cause seizures, coma, and death (though death more often results from accidental injury or suicide during PCP intoxication). Psychological effects at high doses include illusions and hallucinations. PCP can cause effects that mimic the full range of symptoms of schizophrenia, such as delusions, paranoia, disordered thinking, a sensation of distance from one's environment, and catatonia. Speech is often sparse and garbled.

People who use PCP for long periods report memory loss, difficulties with speech and thinking, depression, and weight loss. These symptoms can persist up to a year after cessation of PCP use. Mood disorders also have been reported. PCP has sedative effects, and interactions with other central nervous system depressants, such as alcohol and benzodiazepines, can lead to coma or accidental overdose.

Extent of Use

Monitoring the Future Study (MTF)

National Institute on Drug Abuse (NIDA)'s 1997 MTF shows that use of PCP by high school seniors has declined steadily since 1979, when 7.0 percent of seniors had used PCP in the year preceding the survey. In 1997, however, 2.3 percent of seniors used PCP at least once in the past year, up from a low of 1.2 percent in 1990. Past month use among seniors decreased from 1.3 percent in 1996 to 0.7 percent in 1997.

Table 29.1. Percentage of 12th-graders who have used PCP: Monitoring the Future Study

	1979	1985	1991	1992	1993	1994	1995	1996	1997
Ever Used	12.8%	4.9%	2.9%	2.4%	2.9%	2.8%	2.7%	4.0%	3.9%
Used in Past Year	7.0	2.9	1.4	1.4	1.4	1.6	1.8	2.6	2.3
Used in Past Month	2.4	1.6	0.5	0.6	1.0	0.7	0.6	1.3	0.7

National Household Survey on Drug Abuse (NHSDA)

According to the 1996 NHSDA, 3.2 percent of the population aged 12 and older have used PCP at least once. Lifetime use of PCP was higher among those aged 26 through 34 (4.2 percent) than for those 18 through 25 (2.3 percent) and those 12 through 17 (1.2 percent).

Chapter 30

Rohypnol

What Is Rohypnol?

Rohypnol, the trade name for flunitrazepam, is a drug produced by La Roche Pharmaceuticals. It is manufactured for use as a presurgery relaxant and is given to patients before they undergo anesthesia. Although use of Rohypnol is not legal in the United States, DEA officials say that Rohypnol is illegally coming into the U.S. from Mexico, Columbia, and Europe.

The DEA has classified Rohypnol as a schedule IV drug, which means that large does over a long period of time can lead to physical or psychological dependence.

Because of its rapid spread across the country, and because of its mind-altering and addictive effects, the DEA is trying to upgrade Rohypnol to a Schedule I drug, which would put it in the same class as heroin and LSD.

What Are Some of the Slang Names for Rohypnol?

Rohypnol is known by many different names on the street:

* Rophies
* Roofies
* Rope
* Ruffies
* Roach

* The "date rape "drug
* Mexican valium
* Costa Rican Quaaludes
* Forget pill or
* Forget me pill

The Tennessee Statewide Clearinghouse, 1999; reprinted with permission.

What Are the Effects of Rohypnol?

It produces sedative-hypnotic effects including muscle relaxation and amnesia; sleep, and memory loss. It can also produce physical and psychological dependence. People may unknowingly be given the drug which, when mixed with alcohol, (mostly beer) can incapacitate a victim and prevent them from resisting sexual assault.

Rohypnol intoxication is generally associated with impaired judgment and impaired motor skills, and the combination of alcohol and Rohypnol is also particularly hazardous because together, their effects on memory and judgment are greater that the effects resulting from either taken alone. It is commonly reported that persons who become intoxicated on a combination of alcohol and rohypnol have "blackouts" lasting 8 to 24 hours following ingestion.

Once physical dependence has developed, abrupt termination of the drug will result in withdrawal symptoms, such as:

- Extreme anxiety
- Headache
- Muscle pain
- Restlessness
- Tension
- Confusion and irritability

Higher doses may induce insomnia.

Rohypnol sells for about $2.50 to $5.00 per pill and is packaged in a foil bubble package that makes it seem clean and safe. Officials say "Roofies" have been used by some school children 8 to 10 years old in the past five years.

For More Information

For more information or referral on Rohypnol or other drugs and alcohol contact The Tennessee Statewide Clearinghouse (TSC) at 1-800-889-9789, 1 Vantage Way, Suite B-240, Nashville, TN 37228; web site: www.tnclearinghouse.com.

Chapter 31

Steroids

Anabolic steroids are synthetic derivatives of the male hormone testosterone. The full name is androgenic (promoting masculine characteristics) anabolic (building) steroids (the class of drugs). These derivatives of testosterone promote the growth of skeletal muscle and increase lean body mass. Anabolic steroids were first abused by athletes seeking to improve performance. Today, athletes and others abuse anabolic steroids to enhance performance and also to improve physical appearance.

Anabolic steroids are taken orally or injected, and athletes and other abusers take them typically in cycles of weeks or months, rather than continuously, in patterns called cycling. Cycling involves taking multiple doses of steroids over a specific period of time, stopping for a period, and starting again. In addition, users frequently combine several different types of steroids to maximize their effectiveness while minimizing negative effects, a process known as stacking.

Health Hazards

Reports indicate that use of anabolic steroids produces increases in lean muscle mass, strength, and ability to train longer and harder, but long-term, high-dose effects of steroid use are largely unknown. Many health hazards of short-term effects are reversible. In addition, people who inject anabolic steroids run the added risk of contracting or transmitting hepatitis or the HIV virus that leads to AIDS.

National Institute on Drug Abuse (NIDA), Pub. No. 13557, November 1999.

The major side effects of anabolic steroid use include liver tumors, jaundice (yellowish pigmentation of skin, tissues, and body fluids), fluid retention, high blood pressure, increases in LDL (bad cholesterol) and decreases in HDL (good cholesterol); others are severe acne and trembling. Additional side effects include the following:

- For men—shrinking of the testicles, reduced sperm count, infertility, baldness, development of breasts.

- For women—growth of facial hair, changes in or cessation of the menstrual cycle, enlargement of the clitoris, deepened voice.

- For adolescents—growth halted prematurely through premature skeletal maturation and accelerated puberty changes.

NIDA-supported research shows that aggression and other psychiatric side effects may result from anabolic steroid abuse. Many users report feeling good about themselves while on anabolic steroids, but researchers report that anabolic steroid abuse can cause wild mood swings including manic-like symptoms leading to violent, even homicidal, episodes. Depression often is seen when the drugs are stopped and may contribute to steroid dependence. Researchers reported also that users may suffer from paranoid jealousy, extreme irritability, delusions, and impaired judgment stemming from feelings of invincibility.

Extent of Use

Anabolic steroids are abused primarily by boys, but since the early 1990s, their abuse by girls has dramatically increased.

In 1997, about 175,000 teenage girls reported taking anabolic steroids at least once within the past year, an increase of 100 percent since 1991.

The rate among teenage boys has also continued to rise, to the current estimated level of 325,000.*

*Monitoring the Future Study (MTF)***

The MTF assesses drug use among adolescents and young adults across the country. Because of growing professional and public concern over the misuse and abuse of anabolic steroids by adolescents and young adults, questions regarding anabolic steroid use were added to the MTF in 1989 to afford a better understanding of the extent of the problem.

- Between 1989 and 1998, lifetime prevalence of anabolic steroid use among high school seniors fluctuated between a 3 percent high in 1989 and a 1.9 percent low in 1996. Annual prevalence rates for this period remained relatively stable.

- Among the class of 1998, 2.7 percent of high school seniors had used anabolic steroids at least once in their lifetimes—up from the class of 1997's 2.4 percent lifetime use. The rates also increased for past year and past month use from 1.4 percent in 1997 to 1.7 percent in 1998 and from 1.0 percent in 1997 to 1.1 in 1998, respectively.

- In 1998, 2.3 percent of 8th graders and 2.0 percent of 10th graders had used anabolic steroids at least once in their lifetimes, and 1.2 percent of 8th and 10th graders had used anabolic steroids within the past year.

In addition to data regarding use, the 1998 survey reported seniors' attitudes toward steroid use. Students' perceptions about the harmfulness of taking steroids and the trends in their disapproval of the use of steroids have remained relatively stable in the 1990s.

- 68.1 percent of 12th-graders perceive great risk in taking steroids.

- 91.4 percent of seniors say they disapprove of people who use steroids.

- 44.5 percent of seniors feel it would be fairly or very easy for them to get steroids.

Table 31.1. Anabolic Steroid Use by Students, 1998: Monitoring the Future Study

	8th-Graders	10th-Graders	12th-Graders
Ever Used	2.3%	2.0%	2.7%
Used in Past Year	1.2	1.2	1.7
Used in Past Month	0.5	0.6	1.1

"Lifetime" refers to use at least once during a respondent's lifetime. "Past year" refers to an individual's drug use at least once during the year preceding their response to the survey. "Past month" refers to an individual's drug use at least once during the month preceding their response to the survey.

Notes

* The Youth Risk and Behavioral Survey System monitors six categories of priority health-risk behaviors among youth and young adults— behaviors that contribute to unintentional and intentional injuries; tobacco use; alcohol and other drug use; sexual behaviors that contribute to unintended pregnancy and sexually transmitted diseases (STDs) (including human immunodeficiency virus [HIV] infection); unhealthy dietary behaviors; and physical inactivity. The YRBSS includes a national school-based survey conducted by CDC as well as state, territorial, and local school-based surveys conducted by education and health agencies. This report summarizes results from the national survey, 33 state surveys, 3 territorial surveys, and 17 local surveys conducted among high school students from February through May 1997.

** MTF is an annual survey on drug use and related attitudes of America's adolescents that began in 1975. The survey is conducted by the University of Michigan's Institute for Social Research and is funded by NIDA. Copies of the latest survey are available from the National Clearinghouse for Alcohol and Drug Information at 1-800-729-6686.

Part Four

Drug-Related Health Risks: Recent Research

Chapter 32

Drug Use and HIV Transmission

Sharing needles for drug injection is a well known route of HIV transmission, yet injection drug use contributes to the epidemic's spread far beyond the circle of those who inject. People who have sex with an injection drug user (IDU) also are at risk for infection through sexual HIV transmission. And, children born to mothers who contracted HIV through injecting drugs or having sex with an IDU may become infected as well.

Since the epidemic began, injection drug use has directly and indirectly accounted for more than one-third (36%) of AIDS cases in the United States. This disturbing trend appears to be continuing. Of the 60,634 new cases of AIDS reported in 1997, 19,463(32%) were IDU-associated.

- 76% of these cases were among people whose only reported risk factor was injection drug use.

- 12% were among male IDUs who also reported having sex with other men.

- 11% were among men and women whose sex partners were IDUs.

- 1% were among children born to mothers who were either IDUs or the sex partners of IDUs.

National Center for HIV, STD, and TB Prevention, Centers for Disease Control and Prevention (CDC), June 1998.

Racial and ethnic minority populations in the United States bear the heaviest burden of HIV disease related to drug injection. In 1997, IDU-associated AIDS cases made up 38% of all cases among African Americans and 37% of all cases among Hispanics, compared with 22% of all cases among whites.

Likewise, IDU-associated AIDS has a greater impact on women than on men. Since 1981, at least 61% of all AIDS cases among women have been attributed to injection drug use or sex with partners who inject drugs, compared with 31% of cases among men.

Noninjection drugs (such as "crack" cocaine) also contribute to the spread of the epidemic when users trade sex for drugs or money, or when they engage in risky sexual behaviors that they might not engage in when sober. One study of over 1,000 young adults in three inner-city neighborhoods found that crack smokers were three times more likely to be infected with HIV than non-smokers.

What Is Needed to Prevent HIV Transmission among Drug Users?

Comprehensive HIV prevention interventions for substance abusers must provide education on how to prevent transmission through sex. Numerous studies have documented that drug users are at risk for HIV through both drug-related and sexual behaviors, which places their partners at risk as well. Comprehensive programs must provide the information, skills, and support necessary to reduce both risks. Researchers have found that many interventions aimed at reducing sexual risk behaviors among drug users have significantly increased the practice of safer sex (e.g., using condoms, avoiding unprotected sex) among participants.

Substance abuse treatment *is* HIV prevention, but lack of drug treatment slots complicates prevention efforts. In the United States, about half a million drug treatment slots are available at any given time; however, the nation has an estimated 1.5 million active IDUs, and many others who use noninjection drugs or abuse alcohol. Clearly, the need for substance abuse treatment vastly outstrips our capacity to provide it. Effective treatment that helps people stop using drugs not only eliminates the risk of HIV transmission from sharing contaminated syringes, but, for many, reduces the risk of engaging in risky behaviors that might result in sexual transmission.

For injection drug users who cannot or will not stop inject-ing drugs, the once-only use of sterile needles and syringes remains the safest, most effective approach for limiting HIV transmission. To minimize the risk of HIV transmission, IDUs must have access to interventions that can help them protect their health. They must be advised to always use sterile injection equipment; warned never to reuse needles, syringes, and other injection equip-ment; and told that using syringes that have been cleaned with bleach or other disinfectants is not as safe as using new, sterile syringes.

The availability of new, sterile syringes varies across the country. HIV prevention strategies for IDUs who continue to inject have in-cluded various approaches to increasing the availability of sterile sy-ringes, reducing the risk of HIV transmission through needle sharing, and increasing access to drug treatment.

- In some communities, drug paraphernalia laws have been modi-fied to exclude syringes, syringe prescription laws have been re-pealed, and pharmacy regulations and practice guidelines restricting the sale of sterile syringes have been changed. Ef-forts to reduce HIV risk through these types of policy changes have been evaluated and found to be effective. For example, both New York and Connecticut reported significant reductions in the sharing of drug injection equipment after implementation of policies that increased access to sterile injection equipment through pharmacies and other outlets.

- In other communities, needle exchange programs have been es-tablished to increase the availability of sterile syringes. A re-view of extensive scientific evidence has shown that needle exchange programs can be an effective part of a comprehensive strategy to reduce HIV transmission. The evidence also demon-strates that these programs do not encourage the use of illegal drugs. Many needle exchange programs also provide drug users with referrals to drug counseling, drug treatment, and medical services and risk-reduction education. The most effective needle exchange programs have had the strong support of their com-munities, including appropriate state and local public health of-ficials. In addition to offering linkages to appropriate treatment and medical services, effective needle exchange programs make needles available on a replacement basis only.

Having access to sterile injection equipment is important, but it is not enough. Preventing the spread of HIV through injection drug use requires a wide range of approaches, including programs to prevent initiation of drug use, to provide high quality substance abuse treatment options to drug users, to provide outreach services to drug users and their sex partners, to provide prevention services in jails and prisons and to educate those at risk about preventive options.

Better integration of all prevention and treatment services is critically needed. HIV prevention and treatment, substance abuse prevention, and sexually transmitted disease treatment and prevention services must be better integrated to take advantage of the multiple opportunities for intervention—first, to help the uninfected stay that way; second to help infected people stay healthy; and third, to help infected individuals initiate and sustain behaviors that will keep themselves safe and prevent transmission to others.

CDC's Role in HIV Prevention for IDUs

CDC is the lead federal agency responsible for monitoring the epidemic and preventing HIV/AIDS. In cooperation with other federal agencies and offices responsible for addressing drug use—for example, the Center for Substance Abuse Prevention (CSAP) and the Center for Substance Abuse Treatment (CSAT) of the Substance Abuse and Mental Health Services Administration, the National Institute on Drug Abuse (NIDA) of the National Institutes of Health, and the White House's Office of National Drug Control Policy (ONDCP)—CDC works to address the HIV/AIDS risks presented by illicit drug use.

CDC's role is to provide communities with the best available science to guide comprehensive HIV prevention programs. As part of this process, CDC conducts an ongoing research synthesis process that seeks to identify the most recent and relevant scientific findings from around the world, both published and unpublished, and make them available to prevention program planners. CDC constantly combs the scientific literature, reviews domestic and international scientific databases, and speaks with colleagues around the world to identify effective interventions for all populations at risk, including IDUs.

CDC also provides financial and technical assistance to communities to help them address the unique prevention needs of IDUs, their sex partners, and their children. For example, CDC directly funds 94 community-based HIV prevention programs that provide prevention services in minority communities and other populations at high risk, many of whom are IDUs. Through the HIV Prevention Cooperative Agreements, CDC awards funds to health departments in 50 states,

6 cities, 7 territories, and the District of Columbia. These funds support the provision of services at state and local levels to high-risk populations (including IDUs). Services include health education and risk-reduction activities, such as street outreach programs, as well as HIV counseling, testing, referral, and partner counseling. Prevention needs are prioritized through the HIV Prevention Community Planning process. CDC also funds many national and regional organizations to provide technical assistance to local programs across the country.

In addition, CDC conducts research that provides information used to develop effective prevention programs for IDUs. This includes not only surveillance data on populations at greatest risk, but findings from behavioral and evaluation studies to identify the most effective approaches to prevention.

Chapter 33

Cocaine before Birth

The first research on infants exposed to cocaine in the womb appeared in 1985, when crack smoking was becoming epidemic in the inner cities. Especially as interpreted by the mass media, the reports suggested that we were witnessing the birth of hundreds of thousands of children who would be unteachable, incapable of affection, and a burden to themselves and society all their lives. As more evidence accumulated, a reaction against the horror stories (or predictions) set in, at least among medical and psychiatric researchers. As early as 1992, editorial commentators in the *Journal of the American Medical Association* were complaining about a "rush to judgment" and warning against self-fulfilling prophecies. By that time the subject was no longer news, and the press and television largely abandoned it, leaving only a vague impression in many people's minds that these children had suffered serious and irreparable damage. But researchers have quietly continued their work, and now, as some of the first cocaine babies reach adolescence, we have a much better idea of what to expect, what to fear, and what to do.

Mechanisms

Cocaine can harm a fetus in several ways. By constricting blood vessels in the umbilical cord and placenta, it may block the flow of

Excerpted from *Harvard Mental Health Letter*, December 1998,Vol 15, issue 6. © 1999, President and Fellows of Harvard College; reprinted with permission.

oxygen and nutrients to growing fetal tissue and alter hormone levels in pregnant women. Cocaine also interferes with the action of the neurotransmitters serotonin and dopamine—the main source of its pleasurable effects and addictive powers. These substances appear early in the development of the brain and apparently help to regulate the growth of nerve cells and their branchings and connections. When neurons in a laboratory dish are bathed in cocaine, their dopamine receptors do not communicate adequately with G-proteins, substances in the interior of the cell that are needed to complete the process of transmission. In a rat fetus, high doses of cocaine reduce levels of serotonin, lower the number of cerebral nerve fibers containing it, and delay the differentiation of nerve cells. It is difficult to say whether these mechanisms operate when cocaine is taken by human beings in normal doses. Changes found in the brains of rats are subtle and the effects uncertain, and according to some reports, serotonin activity returns to normal soon after birth. The amount of cocaine needed to sustain damage in a human fetus is not known. According to one recent study, although cocaine and nicotine are both vasoconstrictors and can cause oxygen deprivation, nicotine may be more dangerous because it is used more continuously and neurons do not have time to recover from its effects between doses.

Physical Effects

Hypothetical mechanisms matter only if there are physical and psychological symptoms to explain. The physical effects of prenatal cocaine exposure have not been the center of interest, although they can be serious when the mother is severely addicted. Rats subjected to high doses sometimes develop skeletal deformities and a malformed heart. In various studies, cocaine use during pregnancy has been associated with higher than average rates of sudden infant death syndrome, malformations of the urinary tract, spontaneous abortion, premature birth, stillbirth, and abruptio placentae (a rare condition involving premature separation of the placenta from the uterus). There have also been reports of cardiac abnormalities, poor control of the heart rate (in newborns), and small brain hemorrhages. But researchers have discovered nothing that resembles the distinct pattern of deformities found in fetal alcohol syndrome.

Infants exposed to cocaine before birth tend to be smaller and thinner than average (although the vast majority are in the normal size range), and in some studies they are found to have smaller than average heads at age one or two, although this difference is not correlated with lower IQ scores. It is not clear how these characteristics distinguish them from children prenatally exposed to other drugs, or from other children whose parents neglect their own and the child's health. It is important to note that the vast majority of these children are physically normal; for example, a study of 1,300 New York City infants born to women who had used cocaine during pregnancy found no increase in the rate of congenital abnormalities.

Mental and Behavioral Effects

The most widely publicized fears for these children concern their minds, emotions, and behavior. They are not mentally retarded; investigators agree that even the children of crack addicts show the same intellectual development as others living in similar social conditions. Many reports suggest that as newborns, they are unresponsive and cranky—stiffening at a mother's touch, crying at the sound of voices. Their sleep is said to be disturbed and their regulation of body temperature and blood pressure unreliable—all possible effects of drug withdrawal or residual drug traces. But these symptoms are not universal, and they usually disappear in a few days or weeks. In one study researchers concluded that exposure to cocaine during pregnancy had no effect on a mother's view of her child's temperament at six months.

Nevertheless, there may be problems as the children grow older. They often have symptoms of attention deficit disorder—impulsiveness, distractibility, and hyperactivity. They have been described as intolerant of frustration, easily startled, and both difficult to arouse and too easily overexcited once they are aroused. One study found impaired habituation—inability to ignore a repeated stimulus and recover interest when a new one is introduced.

As in the research on physical risks, almost every result has been challenged or contradicted. In a 1996 study of 28 women who admitted "light to moderate" cocaine use, there were no effects on the children's growth, intellectual ability, classroom behavior, or academic achievement at age six, although they performed slightly worse than average on a test of attention administered by a computer. In another study, monkeys were constantly given increasing doses of cocaine by injection three times a day, five days a week before conception and throughout pregnancy. When their infants were compared with controls given salt water injections, investigators found no effects on reflexes or behavior. Some researchers believe that more sensitive tests of attention and impulsiveness or more careful distinctions between heavy and light use will provide clearer evidence. Another possibility is that delayed effects on learning and motivation, subtle but serious, will appear as the children grow older.

Research Obstacles

If the evidence is difficult to interpret, that is partly because this kind of research is not easy. Even fetal alcohol syndrome, despite its relatively obvious symptoms of physical deformity and mental retardation, was identified and named only 30 years ago. One obstacle is finding out whether a woman has taken drugs during pregnancy, which drugs, and how much. None of the methods used for this purpose are entirely reliable or always practical. It is sometimes uncertain whether the infants chosen for study are typical, since investigators are more likely to suspect and uncover drug use if the baby or the mother has problems. The mother may not answer questions honestly because of guilt, shame, poor recall—or, in the case of an illicit drug like cocaine, fear of imprisonment or losing custody of the child. Many of these women lead chaotic lives that make it difficult for them to cooperate with research.

Looking for physical traces of cocaine does not always help. Because it remains in the body for only a few days, a urine test at birth reveals little about long-term use (newer methods include testing the hair, which retains the drug longer, and the meconium, or first stool passed by the newborn). In one study, an interview alone missed 24% of the women who had used cocaine during pregnancy, and a urine test alone missed 47%. It has been difficult to distinguish light or intermittent from heavy or continuous use—a distinction that may be crucial, since a recreational cocaine sniffer has little in common with a crack addict.

Assuming that researchers know whether a woman has used cocaine during pregnancy, and even assuming (usually contrary to fact) that they know when she used it, how often, and how much, they have to separate cocaine effects from all the other influences on the lives of these mothers and their children. Most of them, especially the crack addicts, are desperately poor.

Most use other illicit drugs, tobacco, and alcohol. If they are crack addicts, the effect of smoking itself has to be considered. If they trade sex for drugs, they may transmit syphilis or AIDS to the child. The father is probably absent and the child's nutrition and medical care inadequate.

With an addicted mother who is depressed, demoralized, and concerned mainly about her next fix, the healthiest infant might become a problem child.

Infants may be no better off if they have to remain in the hospital for weeks after birth and are then placed in institutions or foster care. In a follow-up to the first study that revealed deficiencies in infants exposed to cocaine, the researchers found that a mother's use of cocaine during pregnancy was ultimately much less important for the child's development than whether she continued to abuse drugs and alcohol afterward.

In the best studies, investigators try to match each child prenatally exposed to cocaine with another who is otherwise similar for comparison; but they can never be sure that the matching is adequate. This limitation is especially serious when the effects are apparently subtle and can be detected only by statistical analysis. Animal experiments are not always revealing, because the structure and development of the fetus and the effects of cocaine differ in different species, and because human patterns of drug use are not duplicated in animals. One way to improve the reliability of the research would be to monitor the drug intake of cocaine users throughout pregnancy. Another approach would be to compare two children of the same mother, only one of whom has been prenatally exposed to cocaine. Some researchers have also suggested studying the Aymara and Quechua Indians of Bolivia and Peru, where women who follow the custom of chewing coca leaves and drinking coca tea are not socially marginal and not regarded as self-destructive addicts.

Given the little that is known and the much that is not, what is to be done? Politicians have occasionally recommended punishing pregnant women who use cocaine by prosecuting them for child abuse or "delivering drugs" to the child. But people working in the field agree that fear of imprisonment or losing custody of the child only prevents women from seeking help. Charges have been pressed in a few highly publicized cases, but these prosecutions have been unsuccessful, and they are unlikely to set a precedent or start a trend.

Addicted mothers need good prenatal care and drug treatment, but too often they lack the will to seek or the opportunity to receive either one. After birth, most studies suggest that the earlier mothers and children get help, the better. One program described in a recent report was designed for high school girls who had used cocaine and other drugs while pregnant. One group received no special treatment.

The others, beginning at the child's birth, were given four months of vocational counseling, parenting education, and drug rehabilitation (including group therapy, counseling, urine tests, a self-help group, and muscle relaxation and visual imagery exercises). The mothers were interviewed about their emotional and social problems, and the children were given standard tests of infant development. When the children were three and six months old, researchers videotaped them with their mothers at play to judge the quality of their communication.

When compared with a control group of infants whose mothers did not use drugs during pregnancy, the newborn children of drug users seemed similar in most respects (even, surprisingly, in physical size), although they showed some signs of stress, irritability, poor orientation, and poor habituation. After three months, mothers and children in the treated group were communicating as well as those in the control group and better than those in the untreated group. At six months, they were indistinguishable in every way from the controls, and after a year they were better off. The mothers were under less stress, more likely to be in school, and less likely to have become pregnant again. On average, the children were taller and heavier, their intellectual development was more advanced, and mother and child had a more harmonious relationship. The researchers point out that a similar program has been equally effective for teenage mothers diagnosed as depressed, and they believe that depression was also the main problem for these young women and their children. Programs like this one might be less successful with older, more profoundly addicted mothers.

It is obviously not good for a child to be exposed to cocaine in the womb, but by far the greater risk is being born to or raised by a crack addict.

Prenatal exposure to cocaine is a far less serious social and health problem than prenatal exposure to alcohol or nicotine. There is no crack baby syndrome in the same sense that there is a fetal alcohol syndrome.

Most children whose mothers used cocaine during pregnancy develop normally, considering their upbringing and the conditions in which many of them live.

They do not need specialized treatment and rehabilitation programs. The long run is always uncertain, and research will continue as these children move into adolescence. Meanwhile, their lives should not be made more difficult by a stigma that causes unnecessary fear and rejection.

For Further Reading

Kenneth A. DeVille and Loretta M. Kopelman. Moral and social issues regarding pregnant women who use and abuse drugs. *Obstetrics and Gynecology Clinics of North America* 25(1) 237-254 (March 1998).

Fonda Davis Eyler, Mary Lou Behnke, Michael Conlon, et al. Birth outcome from a prospective, matched study of prenatal crack/cocaine use: I. Interactive and dose effects on health and growth. II. Interactive and dose effects on neurobehavioral assessment. *Pediatrics* 101 229-237 and 237-241 (February 1998).

Tiffany M. Field, Frank Scafidi, Jeffrey Pickens, et al. Polydrug-using adolescent mothers and their infants receiving early intervention. *Adolescence* 33: 116-143 (Spring 1998).

Mark A. Plessinger and James R. Woods, Jr. Cocaine in pregnancy: Recent data on maternal and fetal risks. *Obstetrics and Gynecology Clinics of North America* 25(1) 99-112 (March 1998).

Donald Scherling. Prenatal cocaine exposure and childhood psychopathology: A developmental analysis. *American Journal of Orthopsychiatry* 64(1): 9-19 (January 1994).

Joseph J. Volpe. Effect of cocaine use on the fetus. *New England Journal of Medicine* 327(6):399-407 (August 6, 1992).

Chapter 34

Cocaine Abuse May Lead to Strokes and Mental Deficits

In 1977, a 43 year-old man came to an emergency room in New York City after having injected cocaine into a muscle in his left arm. Between 1 and 2 hours after the injection, he had begun having trouble speaking and was weak in his right arm and leg. After performing a brain scan, doctors at the hospital determined that the man had had a stroke on the left side of the brain. Although the man also abused other drugs, the fact that the stroke had occurred shortly after he had injected cocaine suggested that cocaine had contributed to the stroke. This case was one of the earliest verified reports of a stroke associated with cocaine use. In their report, the doctors concluded, "If, in fact, cocaine played a causal role in the stroke, we anticipate that more strokes will be seen among the many abusers of this agent in American cities."

Their prediction turned out to be correct. In subsequent years, cocaine-related strokes became more frequent, particularly in the mid-1980s after the advent of crack cocaine. These strokes involved sudden dramatic reductions in blood flow to areas of the brain, resulting in neurological symptoms, such as paralysis, loss of speech, and dementia.

In the late 1980s, researchers began noticing another type of blood flow disturbance associated with cocaine use. This second type involved less dramatic but more persistent reductions in cerebral blood flow that could lead to difficulties concentrating, slowed thought processes, and memory deficits.

"Cocaine Abuse May Lead to Strokes and Mental Deficits," by Steven Stocker, in *NIDA Notes*, Vol.13, No. 3, 1998, National Institute on Drug Abuse (NIDA).

Until recently, scientists could only theorize about how cocaine was causing these cerebral blood flow disturbances. Now NIDA-supported scientists have learned more about how cocaine causes strokes and produces the persistent blood flow deficits. Other NIDA-funded researchers have observed that the brain damage caused by these deficits interferes with drug treatment, and they are studying how to modify treatment to accommodate patients with this type of brain damage.

Short-Term Reductions in Blood Flow

Using magnetic resonance angiography (MRA), an imaging technique that shows blood flow in large and medium-sized arteries in the brain, NIDA-funded researchers Dr. Marc Kaufman and Dr. Jonathan Levin and their colleagues at McLean Hospital in Belmont, Massachusetts, have demonstrated that cocaine use temporarily narrows arteries in the brain, thereby reducing the blood supply to various brain regions. Researchers had suspected this for many years because they knew that cocaine could cause vasoconstriction, or narrowing of blood vessels, in the heart and other regions of the body. This study conclusively demonstrated this effect in the human brain.

The researchers administered either cocaine or a placebo solution to 24 men, ages 24 to 34. The volunteers had used cocaine occasionally but were not dependent on the drug. The cocaine doses administered were relatively low, resulting in cocaine blood levels that were at the low end of the range typically experienced during cocaine abuse.

Images of the brain were obtained before and 20 minutes after the cocaine was administered. By comparing before and after images, the researchers could see where blood vessels were narrowed. Among the 7 men who received the placebo, only 1 showed blood vessel narrowing, but among the 9 men who received the lowest dose of cocaine, 3 had vasoconstriction in several brain arteries. Among the 8 men who received a higher dose, 5 showed this effect. The vasoconstrictions ranged from small reductions in blood vessel diameter to more significant obstructions of blood flow.

The more often the men had used cocaine in the past, the more likely the drug was to narrow blood vessels, which suggests that cocaine has a cumulative effect on brain arteries. "This cumulative effect may start with as few as 5 to 10 exposures to cocaine," says Dr. Kaufman. "As a result, people who use cocaine many times probably have a high incidence of vasoconstriction in their brains."

One possible outcome of cocaine's cumulative effect may be a stroke. As a result of many cocaine exposures, brain arteries may be more reactive to the chemical stimuli that normally cause them to constrict, Dr. Kaufman says. This constriction could substantially reduce the blood supply to a region for several minutes, thereby damaging nerve cells and possibly causing stroke-like symptoms. A more likely outcome of the cumulative effect would be persistent blood flow reductions to large areas of the brain. These reductions are less substantial than those that occur in a stroke and may not kill nerve cells, but they could cause thinking and memory deficits, says Dr. Kaufman.

Long-Term Reductions in Blood Flow

Scientists began to observe that cocaine could cause persistent blood flow deficits in the brain in the mid-1980s. NIDA-funded scientist Dr. Nora Volkow and her colleagues at the Brookhaven National Laboratory in Upton, New York, and at the University of Texas Health Science Center in Houston used another imaging technique called positron emission tomography (PET), which can show the flow of blood in the brain tissue rather than in the brain arteries, as MRA does. When the researchers compared PET scans of young adult cocaine-abusing men with scans of normal volunteers, they found that most of the abusers had less blood flow in some areas of the brain. When the researchers performed PET scans again 10 days later, the blood flow deficits were still there, even though the abusers had stopped using cocaine. Many of the volunteers had difficulties concentrating and performing simple calculations, which the researchers concluded were associated with the blood flow deficits.

Subsequently, other scientists verified that cocaine abusers had blood flow deficits in the brain and that these deficits persisted long after the individuals stopped abusing cocaine. Using a technique similar to PET called single photon emission computed tomography (SPECT), Dr. Tony Strickland of Charles R. Drew University of Medicine and Science in Los Angeles and the University of California, Los Angeles, School of Medicine and his colleagues took brain images of cocaine abusers who had abstained from cocaine for at least 6 months before evaluation. Even after this long period of abstinence, the images showed that the abusers still had blood flow deficits compared to control subjects, suggesting that the deficits may be long-term or perhaps even permanent.

In addition to taking brain images with SPECT, Dr. Strickland's group also administered neuropsychological tests to the cocaine abusers. These tests detected many abnormalities that seemed to be associated with reduced activity in the parts of the brain affected by the reduced blood flow. These abnormalities included deficits in attention, memory, concept formation, and mental flexibility. The tests also showed that long-term cocaine abusers had trouble inhibiting inappropriate behaviors, a condition psychologists call disinhibition.

Dr. Levin, who worked on the MRA study with Dr. Kaufman, thinks that chronic cocaine abuse may lead to strokes and long-term blood flow deficits by accelerating atherosclerosis in brain arteries. Atherosclerosis is a thickening on the inside of blood vessels that some researchers believe makes the vessels more likely to go into vasospasm, which is a vasoconstriction that lasts for minutes rather than seconds. "Let's say a blood vessel in a person's brain has atherosclerosis as a result of some injury to the blood vessel. If the person takes a compound such as cocaine that causes vasoconstriction, the part of the blood vessel that is likely to go into spasm is the part with the atherosclerosis," explains Dr. Levin. This vasospasm may then damage the inner lining of the blood vessel, which would further promote the development of atherosclerosis. If the person continues to take cocaine, more vasospasms would occur and hence more atherosclerosis. "It becomes a vicious cycle," he says.

This would explain how cocaine could cause strokes. Eventually, the vasospasms induced by cocaine last so long that nerve cells die from a lack of blood. The explanation for the persistent blood flow deficits might be that the atherosclerosis is slowly clogging the inside of the blood vessels, thereby reducing blood flow. One piece of evidence in favor of this theory is that aspirin has been shown to reverse temporarily the cerebral blood flow deficits caused by cocaine. Aspirin inhibits the formation of blood clots that are part of the atherosclerotic process.

Using a technology called transcranial Doppler sonography (TCD), Dr. Ronald Herning, Dr. Jean Lud Cadet, and colleagues in NIDA's Division of Intramural Research in Baltimore have found evidence that cocaine abusers do indeed have significant atherosclerosis in their brain arteries. In TCD, very high frequency sound waves are bounced off the blood flowing in large arteries in the brain, and the characteristics of the reflected sound waves can be used to estimate the constriction of the arteries. "Our data suggest that cocaine abusers in their thirties have arteries that are as constricted as those of normal subjects in their sixties," says Dr. Herning.

Mental Deficits

Drug treatment providers should be aware that mental deficits that develop in cocaine abusers as a result of reduced blood flow may hamper the ability of these patients to benefit from treatment, says Dr. Strickland. Some patients have trouble paying attention or remembering conversations; others disrupt the therapy by being disinhibited. They constantly interrupt the therapist, they begin tasks without waiting for all the instructions, and they may become aggressive.

Dr. Strickland recommends giving new drug abuse patients neuropsychological screening tests to identify their deficits. Once these deficits are identified, the therapist can modify the drug treatment to accommodate the deficits, he suggests. For example, if the patient has trouble paying attention and remembering, the therapist could present information in small segments and repeat each segment until the patient learns it.

A major component of therapy is simply informing these patients that their long-term drug abuse has changed the way their brains function, Dr. Strickland says. "Some of these patients know that something is wrong but don't know what it is," he says. "They are relieved to learn that they're not 'crazy' and that the source of their problems is that drugs have altered the way their brains process information. They also are relieved to learn that they can take steps to enhance their performance."

"Compared to patients who have brain injury from motorcycle accidents, gunshot wounds, or other causes, drug abuse patients have considerably less impairment," notes Dr. Strickland. "We're successful in helping traumatic brain injury patients, and so the chances of helping patients with drug-induced brain injury are comparatively good."

In addition to modifying drug abuse treatment to accommodate the mental deficits of cocaine abusers, NIDA scientists are also investigating the possibility of treating their blood flow and mental deficits with medications. TCD will be particularly useful for monitoring the blood flow effects of medications, says Dr. Herning. "TCD is a quick, easy, relatively inexpensive measure that can be used repeatedly, so you can give your subjects medications and monitor them weekly, which you cannot do with PET or SPECT."

Sources

Brust, J.C.M.; and Richter, R.W. Stroke associated with cocaine abuse? *New York State Journal of Medicine* 77:1473-1475, 1977.

Herning, R.I.; King, D.E.; Better, W.; and Cadet, J.L. Cocaine dependence: A clinical syndrome requiring neuroprotection. *Annals of the New York Academy of Sciences* 825:323-327, 1997.

Kaufman, M.J., et al. Cocaine-induced cerebral vasoconstriction detected in humans with magnetic resonance angiography. *The Journal of the American Medical Association* 279(5):376-380, 1998.

Kosten, T.R.; Malison, R.; and Wallace, E. Neuropsychological abnormalities in cocaine abusers: Possible correlates in SPECT neuroimaging. In: Majewska, M.D., ed. *Neurotoxicity and Neuropathology Associated with Cocaine Abuse.* NIDA Research Monograph Series, Number 163. NIH Publication No. 96-4019. Pittsburgh, PA: Supt. of Docs., U.S. Govt. Print. Off., 1996, pp. 175-192.

Strickland, T.L., et al. Cerebral perfusion and neuropsychological consequences of chronic cocaine use. *Journal of Neuropsychiatry* 5(4):419-427, 1993.

Strickland, T.L.; Stein, R.A.; Khalsa-Denison, M.E.; and Andre, K. Neuropsychological effects of chronic cocaine use following sustained abstinence. *Archives of Clinical Neuropsychology* 11(5):456-457, 1996.

Volkow, N.D.; Mullani, N.; Gould, K.L.; Adler, S.; and Krajewski, K. Cerebral blood flow in chronic cocaine users: A study with positron emission tomography. *British Journal of Psychiatry* 152:641-648, 1988.

—by Steven Stocker

Chapter 35

Cocaine and Long-Lasting Impaired Function

The detrimental effects of heavy cocaine use on an individual's manual dexterity, problem solving, and other critical skills can last for up to a month after the drug was taken, according to a study reported in the Summer [1999] issue of *The Journal of Neuropsychiatry and Clinical Neurosciences*. The study, which was conducted by researchers at the Intramural Research Program of the National Institute on Drug Abuse (NIDA) and Johns Hopkins University School of Medicine, found that heavy cocaine users were outperformed by moderate users and non-users on most tests measuring verbal memory, manual dexterity, and other cognitive skills. Heavy cocaine use was defined as two or more grams a week.

NIDA Director Dr. Alan I. Leshner says, "This study adds to the accumulating—and worrisome—evidence that heavy use of cocaine can result in persistent deficits in the skills needed to succeed in school and on the job. Cocaine users are risking their futures. For them, prevention and effective treatment become critical public health priorities."

"These findings underscore the connection between cocaine use and neurobehavioral effects," says Dr. Karen I. Bolla, Associate Professor of Neurology at Johns Hopkins. "While the intensity (grams per week) of cocaine use was more closely associated with decreased performance than the duration of use, all cocaine users in the study experienced reduced cognitive function."

National Institute on Drug Abuse (NIDA), August 1999.

This is the second recent study in which Dr. Bolla has identified persistent cognitive problems in former heavy drug users. In the December 1998 issue of *Neurology*, she published results showing memory impairment associated with the heavy use of the drug Ecstasy, also known as MDMA. In that study, too, the problem was related to the amount of the drug taken and lasted at least two weeks after stopping use.

Dr. Bolla and Jean Lud Cadet, M.D., Clinical Director and Chief of Neuropsychiatry at the NIDA Intramural Research Program, studied 30 individuals who had used cocaine at least four times a month for one year or longer and gave a urine sample positive for cocaine at the time of admission into the study. This group was compared to a control group of 21 individuals with no history of drug use except perhaps nicotine, who said they had not had more than 4 drinks of alcohol in the past 30 days. Cocaine users and controls were similar with respect to age, education, and intelligence. None had any current or past history of psychiatric disorder.

The cocaine users were interviewed about how long they had been using cocaine, how many times per week they used it, and their weekly intake in grams. They were admitted to the NIDA Clinical Inpatient Research Unit, where they remained drug free for 30 days.

The cocaine users were given a battery of neuropsychological tests on the 28th or 29th day after admission to the research unit. Those who reported the heaviest use, as measured by grams per week, performed much worse in most aspects of the testing than did light or moderate cocaine users and non-users. Dose-related effects were seen primarily on tasks involving the prefrontal cortex, which is the area of the brain most responsible for attention/concentration, planning, and reasoning. The heaviest cocaine users showed slower median reaction times and poorer attention and concentration.

Chapter 36

"Ecstasy" and Long Term Brain Injury

The designer drug "Ecstasy," or MDMA, causes long-lasting damage to brain areas that are critical for thought and memory, according to new research findings in the June 15 [1999] issue of *The Journal of Neuroscience*. In an experiment with red squirrel monkeys, researchers at The Johns Hopkins University demonstrated that 4 days of exposure to the drug caused damage that persisted 6 to 7 years later. These findings help to validate previous research by the Hopkins team in humans, showing that people who had taken MDMA scored lower on memory tests.

"The serotonin system, which is compromised by MDMA, is fundamental to the brain's integration of information and emotion," says Dr. Alan I. Leshner, director of the National Institute on Drug Abuse (NIDA), National Institutes of Health, which funded the research. "At the very least, people who take MDMA, even just a few times, are risking long-term, perhaps permanent, problems with learning and memory."

The researchers found that the nerve cells (neurons) damaged by MDMA are those that use the chemical serotonin to communicate with other neurons. The Hopkins team had also previously conducted brain imaging research in human MDMA users, in collaboration with the National Institute of Mental Health, which showed extensive damage to serotonin neurons.

MDMA (3,4-methylenedioxymethamphetamine) has a stimulant effect, causing similar euphoria and increased alertness as cocaine

National Institute on Drug Abuse (NIDA), June 1999.

and amphetamine. It also causes mescaline-like psychedelic effects. First used in the 1980s, MDMA is often taken at large, all-night "rave" parties.

In this new study, the Hopkins researchers administered either MDMA or salt water to the monkeys twice a day for 4 days. After 2 weeks, the scientists examined the brains of half of the monkeys. Then, after 6 to 7 years, the brains of the remaining monkeys were examined, along with age-matched controls.

In the brains of the monkeys examined soon after the 2-week period, Dr. George Ricaurte and his colleagues found that MDMA caused more damage to serotonin neurons in some parts of the brain than in others. Areas particularly affected were the neocortex (the outer part of the brain where conscious thought occurs) and the hippocampus (which plays a key role in forming long-term memories).

This damage was also apparent, although to a lesser extent, in the brains of monkeys who had received MDMA during the same 2-week period but who had received no MDMA for 6 to 7 years. In contrast, no damage was noticeable in the brains of those who had received salt water.

"Some recovery of serotonin neurons was apparent in the brains of the monkeys given MDMA 6 to 7 years previously," says Dr. Ricaurte, "but this recovery occurred only in certain regions, and was not always complete. Other brain regions showed no evidence of recovery whatsoever."

Other authors of the study are Dr. George Hatzidimitriou and Dr. Una McCann.

Chapter 37

Effects of Marijuana on the Lung and Its Immune Defenses

Abstract

Habitual marijuana use may lead to the following effects on the lung:

- acute and chronic bronchitis;

- extensive microscopic abnormalities in the cells lining the bronchial passages (bronchial epithelium), some of which may be premalignant;

- overexpression of genetic markers of progression to lung cancer in bronchial tissue;

- abnormally increased accumulation of inflammatory cells (alveolar macrophages) in the lung; and

- impairment in the function of these immune-effector cells (reduced ability to kill microorganisms and tumor cells) and in their ability to produce protective inflammatory cytokines.

Clinically, the major pulmonary consequences that may ensue from regular marijuana use (approximately one "joint" per day on the average) are pulmonary infections and respiratory cancer. Infections of the lung are more likely in marijuana users due to a combination of

From *Secretary's Youth Substance Abuse Prevention Initiative: Resource Papers,* March 1997, Center for Substance Abuse Prevention (CSAP), pp. 33-51.

smoking-related damage to the ciliated cells in the bronchial passages (the lung's first line of defense against inhaled microorganisms) and marijuana-related impairment in the function of alveolar macrophages (the principal immune cells in the lung responsible for defending it against infection). Patients with preexisting immune deficits due to AIDS or cancer chemotherapy might be expected to be particularly vulnerable to marijuana-related pulmonary infections. Finally, biochemical, cellular, genetic, animal, and human studies all suggest that marijuana is an important risk factor for the development of respiratory cancer. However, proof that habitual use of marijuana does in fact lead to respiratory cancer must await the results of well-designed case-control epidemiologic studies. Such studies should now be feasible after the passage of 30 years since the initiation of widespread marijuana use among young individuals in our society in the mid-1960s.

Introduction

Marijuana is the second most widely smoked substance in our society after tobacco (Johnston et al. 1995, 1996). Since marijuana is smoked, the lung is more exposed to higher concentrations of the inhaled smoke constituents than any other tissue, causing concern about possible harmful effects of marijuana on the lung by analogy with the well-known detrimental effects of tobacco on the lung (U.S. Department of Health, Education, and Welfare 1979). Pulmonary consequences of regular tobacco smoking include:

1. lung cancer;

2. chronic obstructive pulmonary disease (COPD), which consists of chronic bronchitis and emphysema; and

3. an increased incidence of respiratory tract infection due to smoking-related impairment in the lung's host defenses.

The importance to public health of these pulmonary consequences of tobacco is underscored by the fact that lung cancer accounts for over 125,000 deaths each year in the United States; COPD causes approximately 90,000 deaths per year and more chronic disability than any other medical illness; and respiratory tract infection (acute bronchitis and pneumonia) is a frequent cause of impairment in activities of daily living, increased utilization of health care resources, and even mortality. In this report, the evidence concerning the potential for habitual use of marijuana to produce adverse effects on the lung comparable to those caused by tobacco will be reviewed.

Smoke Contents of Marijuana and Tobacco

Analysis of the smoke contents of marijuana and tobacco reveals much the same gas phase constituents, including chemicals known to be toxic to respiratory tissue (Hoffmann et al. 1975; Novotny et al. 1982). Moreover, these gas phase components are present in somewhat similar concentrations in the smoke generated from the same quantity of marijuana and tobacco. The particulate phase (tar) constituents of marijuana and tobacco smoke are also generally similar, with the major exception that marijuana contains tetrahydrocannabinol (THC) and scores of other THC-like (cannabinoid) compounds not found in tobacco, while tobacco tar contains nicotine not found in marijuana. With regard to the carcinogenic potential of marijuana, it is noteworthy that the tar phase of marijuana smoke contains many of the same carcinogenic compounds contained in tobacco smoke, including polycyclic aromatic hydrocarbons, such as benzpyrene, which was recently identified as a key factor promoting human lung cancer (Denissenko et al. 1996).

Animal Studies

Animal and human studies provide the biologic evidence that regular exposure of the lung to the noxious components in marijuana smoke is, in fact, injurious to lung tissue. Studies in animals exposed to varying doses of marijuana smoke for from 12 to 30 months have shown extensive damage in dogs (Roy et al.1976) and monkeys (Fligiel et al. 1991) to the smaller airways, which are the major site of injury due to tobacco-related COPD, as well as acute and chronic pneumonia in rats (Fleischman et al. 1979; Rosenkrantz and Pleischman 1979) and monkeys (Fligiel et al. 1991). On the other hand, rats exposed for 1 year to increasing doses of marijuana smoke failed to demonstrate any anatomic or functional evidence of emphysema, whereas such evidence was apparent in tobacco-exposed rats (Huber and Mahajan 1988).

Human Studies

Early human studies yielded mixed results: some reported an association between regular marijuana use and chronic bronchitis and emphysema (Chopra 1973; Hall 1975), while others failed to find such a relationship (Boulougouris et al. 1976; Rubin and Comitas 1975). These studies may be criticized because of deficiencies in experimental design, including (1) failure to control for the important confounding variable of tobacco, (2) only small numbers of participants, and (3) probable selection biases.

Chronic Respiratory Symptoms

Subsequently, Tashkin and colleagues (1987) reported the following findings in a large sample of volunteers recruited from the Los Angeles area, including 144 heavy, habitual smokers of marijuana only (MS) and 135 smokers of marijuana plus tobacco (MTS), as well as 70 smokers of tobacco only (TS) and 97 nonsmokers (NS). Compared to NS, a significantly higher proportion of MS (15-20 percent) acknowledged symptoms of chronic bronchitis (chronic cough and phlegm production). While 20-25 percent of TS also reported symptoms of chronic bronchitis, the proportion of symptomatic TS did not differ significantly from that of symptomatic MS (despite a marked disparity in the amount of each substance smoked per day: 3 joints of marijuana vs. more than 20 cigarettes of tobacco), and no additive effects of marijuana and tobacco were noted. Similar findings were reported by Bloom and coworkers (1987) in a randomly stratified sample of young individuals (15–40 years of age) residing in the Tucson area with the exception that these investigators noted an additive effect of marijuana and tobacco that was not observed in the Los Angeles study.

Lung Function

In the Tucson study (Bloom et al. 1987), regular marijuana use (approximately 1 joint/day on the average) by young persons was associated with significant impairment in measurements that reflect the function of the small airways—the major site of COPD. These changes were even greater than those noted in young regular tobacco smokers, and the effects of both marijuana and tobacco appeared to be additive. The authors concluded that regular marijuana smoking was a risk factor for the development of COPD, which, in its advanced stages, is characterized by disabling shortness of breath. In contrast, the Los Angeles study (Tashkin et al. 1987) failed to find any impairment in small airways function in association with even heavier regular use of marijuana (3 joints per day), although mild, statistically significant narrowing of large, central airways was noted in the marijuana users.

Recently, a longitudinal analysis of the lung function results obtained in Los Angeles (Tashkin et al. 1997) revealed an accelerated rate of decline in lung function with age (as is characteristic of tobacco smokers who are destined to develop symptomatic COPD) in the tobacco-smoking participants but failed to find such an effect in the marijuana smokers. The mixed findings from these two studies leave open the question as to whether habitual smoking of marijuana, in the absence of tobacco, can lead to COPD.

Bronchoscopic Findings

Bronchoscopy was performed in 53 NS, 40 MS, 31 TS, and 44 MTS who participated in the Los Angeles study (Fligiel et al. in press; Gong et al. 1987) to ascertain whether regular smoking of marijuana with or without tobacco might cause damage to the airways and lung that might not be reflected by abnormalities in lung function. Visual inspection of the appearance of the large, central airways showed that a large proportion of smokers of marijuana or tobacco alone (but rarely nonsmokers) showed evidence of increased redness (erythema) and swelling (edema) of the airway tissues and increased mucous secretions, and the findings in the combined smokers of both marijuana and tobacco appeared additive (Roth et al. 1996). These visual findings were correlated with microscopic evidence of increased numbers and size of small blood vessels in the bronchial wall, tissue edema, and replacement of the normal ciliated surface lining cells (ciliated columnar epithelial cells) by mucus-secreting goblet cells. These observations may explain the relatively high proportion of marijuana smokers who complain of chronic cough and phlegm. Overproduction of mucus by the increased numbers of mucus-secreting cells in the face of diminished numbers of ciliated cells (cells with hair-like projections) that normally function to transport the mucus toward the mouth by rapid ciliary motion might leave cough as the only mechanism to remove mucus from the airways.

Microscopic findings in biopsies of the bronchial mucosa (superficial layer of cells) revealed that a much higher proportion of MS than NS (and a proportion comparable to, if not greater than, that of TS) exhibited a variety of cellular abnormalities. The latter included abnormal proliferation of cells (reserve cells, goblet cells), transformation of normal ciliated cells into abnormal cells resembling skin (squamous metaplasia), accumulation of inflammatory cells, and abnormalities in the cell nuclei (Fligiel et al. in press; Gong et al. 1987). Some of these changes (e.g., nuclear alterations and squamous metaplasia) have been described as precursors to the subsequent development of lung cancer in tobacco smokers (Auerbach et al. 1961) and thus may be considered to be premalignant. Smokers of both marijuana and tobacco exhibited these microscopic cellular abnormalities to the greatest extent, suggesting an additive injurious effect of marijuana and tobacco on airway tissue. These findings in healthy, largely nonsymptomatic, young marijuana smokers confirm and extend previous bronchoscopic observations of Tennant (1980) in symptomatic U.S. servicemen who smoked cannabis (in the form of hashish) heavily.

Genetic Markers of Precancer Progression

A specific combination of genes (oncogenes, tumor suppressor genes) that are responsible for regulating cell growth must be activated and/or mutated for lung cells to transform into cancerous cells. Bronchoscopic biopsies from 63 participants in the Los Angeles study (12 MS, 9 MTS, 14 TS, and 28 NS), none of whom used crack cocaine, were examined for alterations in some of the genes known to be involved in the development of lung cancer. Immunohistology was used to detect the overexpression of the protein products of these genes by epithelial cells in the bronchial biopsies (Roth et al. 1996). Protein products for two of the three genes examined were markedly overexpressed in the biopsies from MS compared to NS (and even to a greater extent than in the biopsies from TS), and the effects of marijuana and tobacco were additive. Expression of the third gene, the p53 oncogene, which may play a role in as many as 75 percent of all lung cancers, was found only in a smoker of marijuana plus tobacco, as well as in one of 12 combined smokers of marijuana, cocaine, and tobacco who were also examined. These results indicate genetic evidence of extensive growth dysregulation in these relatively young smokers of marijuana alone and, particularly, in the combined smokers of marijuana and tobacco, implying an important role of marijuana use in progression to lung cancer.

Structure and Function of Alveolar Macrophages

Alveolar macrophages are the principal immune-effector (inflammatory) cells in the lung and are primarily responsible for protecting the lung against infectious microorganisms. A saline (salt water) rinse was used in participants in the Los Angeles study at the time of bronchoscopy to harvest cells from the air spaces in the lung (over 90 percent of which are alveolar macrophages). Approximately two and three times as many alveolar macrophages were obtained from the lungs of marijuana or tobacco smokers, respectively, as from non-smokers, and the effects of smoking both substances were additive (Barbers et al. 1987). These observations indicate that regular marijuana use produces an inflammatory response, i.e., an accumulation of increased numbers of alveolar macrophages, in the lung. Under the electron microscope, alveolar macrophages from marijuana or tobacco smokers showed a striking increase in size and complexity of inclusion bodies in their cytoplasm (probably due to ingestion by these cells of particulate material in the smoke), and macrophages from combined smokers of marijuana and tobacco were nearly completely filled by these inclusions (Bears et al. 1989). It might be expected that the padding of these important cells with large inclusion bodies would interfere with their function.

Various aspects of alveolar macrophage function have been evaluated by contributing researchers in the Los Angeles study. Compared to NS, alveolar macrophages of both MS and TS showed a significantly reduced ability to kill a common fungal organism (*Candida albicans*) (Sherman et al. 1991). Moreover, alveolar macrophages of MS, but not TS, showed a significant impairment in (1) their ability to ingest and kill an important bacterial pathogen (*Staphylococcus aureus*); (2) their ability to kill tumor cell targets; and (3) their ability to produce a variety of proinflammatory cytokines, which play a key role in immunologic responses to infection and malignancy (Baldwin et al. 1996).

Role of Marijuana in Cancer

The following lines of evidence suggest that marijuana may play an important role in the development of respiratory cancer.

- The tar phase of marijuana smoke, as already noted, contains many of the same carcinogenic compounds contained in tobacco smoke, including nitrosamines, reactive aldehydes, and up to a 50 percent higher concentration of carcinogenic polycyclic hydrocarbons, including benzpyrene (Hoffmann et al. 1975). Benzpyrene, which has recently been shown to promote mutations in the p53 oncogene (Denissenko et al. 1996), is believed to play an important role in human cancer.

- One marijuana cigarette was shown by Wu and colleagues (1988) to deposit four times as much tar in the lung as a single filtered tobacco cigarette of approximately the same weight. The higher content of carcinogenic polycyclic hydrocarbons in marijuana tar and the greater deposition of marijuana tar in the lung act together to amplify exposure of the marijuana smoker to the carcinogens in the tar phase.

• Painting tar from marijuana smoke on the skin of mice produced lesions correlated with malignancy (Cottrell et al. 1973).

• Marijuana tar induced comparable numbers of mutations to those produced by tar from the same quantity of tobacco in a common bacterial assay for mutagenicity (Wehner et al. 1980).

• Exposure of hamster lung cell cultures to marijuana or tobacco smoke over a period of 2 years led to accelerated malignant transformation within 3-6 months of marijuana exposure compared to control (unexposed) cell cultures. Moreover, the changes in the cells exposed to marijuana smoke were more impressive than those in the tobacco-exposed cells (Leuchtenberger and Leuchtenberger 1976).

• Biopsies of bronchial lining tissue of habitual marijuana smokers demonstrated extensive cellular alterations, some of which may be considered premalignant. Effects of smoking both marijuana and tobacco on these cellular changes appeared to be additive (Fligiel et al. in press).

• Bronchial immunohistology revealed overexpression of genetic markers of lung tumor progression in smokers of marijuana (Roth et al. 1996).

• Preliminary findings suggest that marijuana smoke activates cytochrome P4501A1, the enzyme that converts polycyclic hydrocarbons, such as benzpyrene, into active carcinogens (Roth preliminary data).

• Alveolar macrophages from marijuana-only smokers have reduced ability to kill tumor cell targets (Baldwin et al. 1996).

• Pretreatment of mice with THC for 2 weeks prior to implanting Lewis lung cancer cells (a non-small-cell immunogenic carcinoma) into the animals caused larger, faster-growing tumors, a finding that was correlated with the increased immunosuppressive cytokine produced by the tumor cells, transforming growth factor-beta (Zhu et al. 1997). These findings suggest a THC-related impairment in immune responsiveness to tumor antigens.

• Several case-series reports indicate an unexpectedly large proportion of marijuana users among cases of lung cancer (Sridhar et al. 1994; Taylor 1988) and upper aerodigestive tract cancers (cancers of the oral cavity, pharynx, and larynx); (Donald 1991; Endicott et al. 1993; Taylor 1988) that occurred before age 45 years. These case-series reports suggest that marijuana may play a role in the development of human respiratory cancer. Without a control group, however, the effect of marijuana use on cancer risk cannot be estimated, nor can the potentially confounding effect of tobacco and other risk factors be controlled.

Taken together, the observations from a number of biochemical, cellular, genetic, tissue, animal, and clinical studies provide a biologically plausible basis for the hypothesis that marijuana is a risk factor for human cancer. What is lacking is epidemiologic evidence that marijuana indeed increases the risk of developing respiratory cancer. Because of the long period of time (latency period) required for induction of human carcinomas and the infrequent use of marijuana in the general U.S. population prior to 1966, there are currently no published epidemiologic studies that examine the association between marijuana and cancer. However, at the present time, epidemiologic investigation of this association may have become feasible since approximately 30 years have elapsed since the start of widespread marijuana use in the United States among teenagers and young adults, who are currently reaching an age when respiratory cancers are more common.

Effects of Marijuana on the Immune System

In Vitro and Animal Studies

The recent finding of cannabinoid receptors (to which THC binds) on white blood cells (Bouaboula et al.1993) is consistent with observations that THC is capable of influencing immune responses. *In vitro* and animal studies suggest that THC has a general immunosuppressive effect on a variety of immune cells, including macrophages, natural killer cells, and T cells (Burnette-Curley and Cabral 1995; Huber et al. 1975, 1980; Klein et al. 1991; Kusher et al. 1994). Mice exposed to D9THC were unable to develop protective immunity against lung infection by *Legionella pneumophilia*, an opportunistic pathogen (Newton et al. 1994).

Immune Deficits in Marijuana Smokers

As noted above, alveolar macrophages from the lungs of healthy, habitual marijuana smokers were suppressed in their ability to kill fungal and bacterial organisms, as well as tumor cells. Moreover, the same cells were suppressed in their ability to release proinflammatory cytokines. These findings suggest that marijuana is an immunosuppressant with clinically significant effects on host defense, which could have potentially serious health consequences in patients with preexisting immune deficits due to AIDS, organ transplantation (receiving immunosuppressive therapy to prevent rejection of the transplant), or cancer (receiving immunosuppressive chemotherapy). The latter possibility is supported by reports of fungal and bacterial pneumonias in patients with AIDS or organ transplantation who used marijuana (Caiaffa et al. 1994; Denning et al. 1991). Moreover, among HIV-positive individuals, active marijuana use has been found to be a significant risk factor for rapid progression from HIV infection to AIDS and acquisition of opportunistic infections and/or Kaposi's sarcoma (Tindall et al. 1988).

Summary

The evidence for the harmful consequences of marijuana smoking is preliminary and requires long-term study. In the interim, prudent advice must serve where substantial clinical evidence is lacking. Habitual marijuana use, as often as one joint per day, may result in serious pulmonary consequences. In the short term, breathing may be restricted, coughing may be increased, and resistance may be lowered to opportunistic infections of the lungs such as pneumonia. Respiratory cancer is a likely result in the long term. Heavier use of marijuana is likely to have more potent, adverse health consequences.

References

Auerbach, O.; Stout, A.P.; Hammond, E.D.; and Garfinkel, A. (1961). Changes in bronchial epithelium in relation to cigarette smoking and in relation to lung cancer. *New England Journal of Medicine* 265:253-267.

Baldwin, G.C.; Buckley, D.M.; Roth, M.D.; Dubinett, S.M.; and Tashkin D.P. (1996). Alveolar macrophages derived from the lungs of tobacco, marijuana and cocaine users are functionally compromised. In: Harris, L.S., ed. Problems of Drug Dependence. *Proceedings of the 57th Annual Scientific Meeting of the College on Problems of Drug Dependence.* NIDA Research Monograph Series 162. Rockville, MD: U.S. Department of Health and Human Services, p. 192.

Barbers, R.G.; Gong, H., Jr.; Tashkin, D.P.; Oishi, J.; and Wallace, J.M. (1987). Differential examination of bronchoalveolar lavage cells in tobacco cigarette and marijuana smokers. *American Review of Respiratory Diseases* 135:1271-1275.

Beals, T.F.; Fligiel, S.E.G.; Stuth, S.; and Tashkin, D.P. (1989). Morphological alterations of alveolar macrophages from marijuana smokers. *American Review of Respiratory Diseases* 139 (part 2):A336.

Bloom, J.W.; Kaltenborn, W.T.; Paoletti, P.; Camilli, A.; and Lebowitz, M.S. (1987). Respiratory effects of non-tobacco cigarettes. *British Medical Journal* 295:1516-1518.

Bouaboula, M.; Rinaldi M.; Carayon, P.; Carillon, C.; Delpech, B.; Shire, D.; LeFur, G.; and Casellas, P. (1993). Cannabinoid-receptor expression in human leukocytes. *European Journal Biochemistry* 214:173-180.

Boulougouris, J.C.; Panayiotopoulos, C.P.; Antypas, E.; Liakos, E.; and Stefanis, C. (1976). Effects of chronic hashish use on medical status in 44 users compared with 38 controls. *Annals of the New York Academy of Sciences* 282:168-172.

Burnette-Curley, D., and Cabral, G.A. (1995). Differential inhibition of RAW264.7 macrophage tumoricidal activity by delta-9-tetrahydrocannabinol. *Proceedings of the Society for Experimental Biology and Medicine* 210:64-76.

Caiaffa, W.T.; Vlahov, D.; Graham, N.M.; Astemborski, J.; Solomon, L.; Nelson, K.E.; and Munoz, A. (1994). Drug smoking, *Pneumocystis carinii* pneumonia, and immunosuppression increase risk of bacterial pneumonia in human immunodeficiency virus–seropositive infection drug users. *American Journal of Respiratory and Critical Care Medicine* 150(6 part 1):1493-1498.

Chopra, G.S. (1973). Studies on psycho-clinical aspects of long-term marijuana use in 124 cases. *International Journal of the Addictions* 8:1015-1026.

Cottrell, J.C.; Sohn, S.S.; and Vogel, W.H. (1973). Toxic effects of marijuana tar on mouse skin. *Archives of Environmental Health* 26(5):277-278.

Denning, D.W.; Follansbee, S.E.; Scolaro, M.; Norris, S.; Edelstein, H.; and Stevens, D.A. (1991). Pulmonary aspergillosis in the acquired immunodeficiency syndrome. *New England Journal of Medicine* 324:654-662.

Denissenko, M.F.; Pao, A.; Tang, M-S.; and Pfeifer, G.P. (1996). Preferential formation of benzpyrene adducts at lung cancer mutational hotspots in p53. Science 274:430-32.

Donald, P.J. (1991). Advanced malignancy in the young marijuana smoker. *Advances in Experimental Medicine and Biology* 288:33-56.

Endicott, J.N.; Skipper, P.; and Hernandez, L. (1993). Marijuana and head and neck cancer. *Advances in Experimental Medicine and Biology* 335:107-113.

Fleischman, RW.; Baker, J.R.; and Rosenkrantz, H. (1979). Pulmonary pathologic changes in rats exposed to marijuana smoke for one year. *Toxicology and Applied Pharmacology* 47:557-566.

Fligiel, S.E.G.; Beals, T.F.; Tashkin, D.P.; Paule, M.G.; Scallet, A.C.; Ali, S.F.; Bailey, J.R.; and Slikker, W. Jr. (1991). Marijuana exposure and pulmonary alterations in primates. *Pharmacology, Biochemistry and Behavior* 40:637-642.

Fligiel, S.E.G; Roth, M.D.; Kleerup, E.C.; Barsky, S.H.; Simmons, M.S.; and Tashkin, D.P. (in press). Tracheobronchial histopathology in habitual smokers of cocaine, marijuana and/or tobacco. *Chest*.

Gong, H., Jr.; Fligiel, S.; Tashkin, D.P.; and Barbers, R.G. (1987). Tracheobronchial changes in habitual, heavy smokers of marijuana with and without tobacco. *American Review of Respiratory Diseases* 136:142-149.

Hall, J.A.S. (1975). Testimony in marijuana-hashish epidemic and its impact on United States security. In: *Hearings of the Committee on the Judiciary, United States Senate*. Washington, DC: U.S. Government Printing Office, pp. 147-154.

Hoffmann, D.; Brunneman, D.K.; Gori, G.B.; and Wynder, E.L. (1975). On the carcinogenicity of marijuana smoke. *Recent Advances in Phytochemistry* 9:63-81.

Huber, G.L.; Simmons, G.A.; McCarthy, C.R.; Cuffing, M.B.; Laguarda, R.; and Pereira, W. (1975). Depressant effect of marijuana smoke on antibactericidal activity of pulmonary alveolar macrophages. *Chest* 68:769-773.

Huber, G.L., and Mahajan, V.K. (1988). The comparative response of the lung to marihuana or tobacco smoke inhalation. In: Chesher, G.; Consroe,

P.; and Musty, R. eds. *Marijuana: An International Research Report. Proceedings of Melbourne Symposium on Cannabis 2 - September, 1987*. National Campaign Against Drug Abuse. Monograph Series No. 7. Canberra: Australian Government Publishing Service, pp. 19-24.

Johnston, L.D.; O'Malley, P.M.; and Bachman, J.G. (1995). *National Survey Results on Drug Use from the Monitoring the Future Study, 1975-1994. Volume I, Secondary School Students*. National Institute on Drug Abuse, NIH Publication No. 95-4206. Washington, DC: U.S. Government Printing Office.

Johnston, L.D.; O'Malley, P.M.; and Bachman, J.G. (1996). *National Survey Results on Drug Use from the Monitoring the Future Study, 1975-1994. Volume II, College Students and Young Adults*. National Institute on Drug Abuse, NIH Publication No. 95-4207. Washington, DC: U.S. Government Printing Office.

Klein, T.S.; Kawakami, Y.; Newton, C.; and Friedman, H. (1991). Marijuana components suppress induction and cytolytic function of murine cytotoxic T cells *in vitro* and *in vivo*. *Journal of Toxicology and Environmental Health* 32:465-477.

Kusher, D.I.; Dawson, L.O.; Taylor, A.C.; and Djeu, J.Y. (1994). Effect of the psychoactive metabolite of marijuana, delta-9-tetrahydrocannabinol (THC), on the synthesis of tumor necrosis factor by human large granular lymphocytes. *Cellular Immunology* 154:99-108.

Leuchtenberger, C., and Leuchtenberger, R (1976). Cytological and cytochemical studies of the effects of fresh marijuana cigarette smoke on growth and DNA metabolism of animal and human lung cultures. In: Braude, M.C., and Szara, S., eds. *The Pharmacology of Marijuana*. New York: Raven Press, pp. 596-612.

Newton, C.A.; Klein, T.W.; and Friedman, H. (1994). Secondary immunity to *Legionaella pneumophilia* and Th1 activity are suppressed by 9-tetrahydrocannabinol injection. *Infection and Immunity* 62:4015-20.

Novotny, M.; Merli F.; Weisler, D.; Fend, M; and Saeed, T. (1982). Fractionation and capillary gas chromatographic-mass spectrometric characterization of the neutral components in marijuana and tobacco smoke concentrates. *Journal of Chromatography* 238:141-150.

Rosenkrantz, H., and Fleischman, R.W. (1979). Effects of cannabis on lung. In: Nahas, G.G., and Payton, W.D.H., eds. *Marijuana: Biological Effects*. Oxford, England: Pergamon Press, pp. 279-299.

Roth, M.D.; Kleerup, E.C.; Arora, A.; Barsky, S.; and Tashkin, D.P. (1996). Endobronchial injury in young tobacco and marijuana smokers as evaluated by visual, pathologic and molecular criteria. *American Journal of Respiratory and Critical Care Medicine* 153 (part 2):100.

Roy, P.E.; Magnan-Lapointe, F.; Huy, N.D.; and Boutet, M. (1976). Chronic inhalation of marijuana and tobacco in dogs: Pulmonary pathology. *Research Communications in Chemical Pathology and Pharmacology* 14:305-317.

Rubin, V., and Comitas, L. (1975). Respiratory function and hematology. In: *Ganja in Jamaica: A Medical Anthropological Study of Chronic Marijuana Use*. The Hague: Mouton, pp. 87-102.

Sherman, M.P.; Campbell, L.A.; Gong, H. Jr.; Roth, M.D.; and Tashkin, D.P. (1991). Antimicrobicidal and respiratory burst characteristics of pulmonary alveolar macrophages recovered from smokers of marijuana alone, smokers of tobacco alone, smokers of marijuana and tobacco and nonsmokers. *American Review of Respiratory Disease* 144:1351-1356.

Sridhar, K.S.; Raub, W.A.; Weatherby, N.L.; Metsch, L.R; Surratt, H.L.; Inciardi, J.A.; Duncan, R.C.; Anwyl, RS.; and McCoy, C.B. (1994). Possible role of marijuana smoking as a carcinogen in the development of lung cancer at a young age. *Journal of Psychoactive Drugs* 26:285-288.

Tashkin, D.P.; Coulson, A.H.; Clark, V.A.; Simmons, M.; Bourque, L.B.; Duann, S.; Spivey, G.H.; and Gong, H. (1987). Respiratory symptoms and lung function in habitual, heavy smokers of marijuana alone, smokers of marijuana and tobacco, smokers of tobacco alone, and nonsmokers. *American Review of Respiratory Disease* 135:209-216.

Tashkin, D.P.; Simmons, M.S.; Sherrill, D.; and Coulson, A.H. (1997). Heavy habitual marijuana smoking does not cause an accelerated decline in FEV1 with age: a longitudinal study. *American Journal of Respiratory and Critical Care Medicine* 155:141-148.

Taylor, F.M., III. (1988). Marijuana as a potential respiratory tract carcinogen: A retrospective analysis of a community hospital population. *Southern Medical Journal* 81:1213-1216.

Tennant, F.S., Jr. (1980). Histopathologic and clinical abnormalities of the respiratory system in chronic hashish smokers. *Substance and Alcohol Actions / Misuse* 1:93-100.

Tindall, B.; Cooper, D.A.; Donovan, B.; Barnes, T.; Philpot, C.R.; Gold, J.R.; and Penny, R. (1988). The Sydney AIDS Project: Development of acquired immunodeficiency syndrome in a group of HIV seropositive homosexual men. *Australian and New Zealand Journal of Medicine* 18(1):8-15.

U.S. Department of Health, Education, and Welfare. (1979). *Smoking and Health. A Report of the Surgeon General.* DHHS Publication No. (PHS) 79-50066. Washington, DC: U.S. Government Printing Office.

Wehner, F.C.; Van Rensburg, S.J.; and Theil, P.F. (1980). Mutagenicity of marijuana and Transkei tobacco smoke condensates in the Salmonella/microsome assay. *Mutation Research* 77:135-147.

Wu, T-C.; Tashkin, D.P.; Djahed, B.; and Rose, J.E. (1988). Pulmonary hazards of smoking marijuana as compared with tobacco. *New England Journal of Medicine* 318:347-351.

Zhu, L.; Sharma, S.; Stolina, M.; Chen, K.; Park, A.; Roth, M.; Tashkin, D.P.; and Dubinett, S.M. (1997). "THC-mediated Inhibition of the Antitumor Immune Response." Paper presented at the 19th Southern California Pulmonary Research Conference, Palm Springs, CA, January.

— by Donald P. Tashkin, M.D., UCLA School of Medicine

Donald P. Tashkin, M.D., is a professor of Medicine in the division of pulmonary and critical care medicine at the UCLA School of Medicine.

Chapter 38

Depression and Substance Use Can Be a Lethal Combination for Teens

The teen years are a period of turmoil for just about everyone. Learning new social roles, developing new relationships, getting used to bodily changes, making decisions about the future—all of these things can be overwhelming. With neither the comforting dependence of childhood nor the full-fledged membership in adulthood, teens often feel as if they were floating in limbo—isolated, confused, scared, and alone.

It is not surprising then, that depression is a common illness among adolescents. The feelings of helplessness and hopelessness that accompany depression can fuel a downward spiral of health and self-esteem, which can have potentially deadly results: In one study of teenage suicides, 60 to 70 percent of the teens had been diagnosed with a depressive illness prior to their deaths. An alarming 90 percent of the sample had some form of psychiatric diagnosis—depression, mood disorder, or substance abuse disorder.

According to David Shaffer, M.D., adolescent depression often is complicated further by substance use problems. In one study, nearly 45 percent of the teens who had committed suicide in a two-year period, had been abusing alcohol at the time of their deaths.

The Brown University Child and Adolescent Behavior Letter, Vol.12, No, 1 p. 51(2), © 1996 Manisses Communications Group Inc.; reprinted with permission of Manisses Communications Group.

What to Look for

Teens who are contemplating suicide often show symptoms of depression and/or substance use. The following symptoms typically indicate a problem:

- sleep disturbances—fatigue, frequent napping, early waking
- change in appetite—sudden noticeable weight loss or gain
- restlessness, inability to concentrate
- dramatic mood changes
- feelings of hopelessness, helplessness, despair
- withdrawal from friends and previously enjoyed activities

Teens who are depressed and abuse substances are at high risk for attempting suicide. If you think that your teen might be at risk, contact a professional immediately. Early intervention can prevent suicide attempts, and your teen can receive treatment for depression and for substance use.

Other Risk Factors

Young people who have attempted suicide in the past or who talk about suicide are at greater risk for future attempts. Listen for hints like, "I'd be better off dead," or "I won't be a problem for you much longer," or "Nothing matters; it's no use."

Adolescents who consider suicide generally feel alone, hopeless, and rejected. They are more vulnerable to having these feelings if they have been abused, feel that they have been humiliated recently in front of family or friends, or have chaotic, disorganized family lives.

Teenagers who are planning to commit suicide might "clean house" by giving away their favorite possessions, cleaning their rooms, or throwing things away. They also may become suddenly cheerful after a period of depression, because they think that they have found a solution by deciding to commit suicide.

One of the most dangerous times of a teen's life is when he or she has suffered a loss or humiliation of some kind—loss of self-esteem by doing poorly on an important test, breakup with a boyfriend or girlfriend, parents' divorce, for example.

What You Can Do

Most people who are depressed or who are thinking about suicide don't or won't talk about how they're feeling. They deny their emotions or think that talking about it will be a burden on others because no one cares. Or they are afraid other people will criticize or make fun of them. If your child brings up the subject of suicide with you, take it seriously and take some time to talk about it.

Reassure your child that he or she has someone to turn to. Remind the child of all the people who care about him or her—friends, family members, school counselors, physicians, or teachers. Don't lecture or point out all the reasons your child has to live. Instead, listen and reassure your child that the depression and suicidal tendencies can be treated.

Get help immediately. Don't wait for the symptoms to worsen. Contact one of the resources listed here, or check the yellow pages for the local chapter of the American Psychiatric Association. Don't attempt to solve the problem alone, and don't assume that the child is not serious. Any mention of suicide, even in what appears to be jest, should be considered seriously.

Source: "Let's Talk Facts about Teen Suicide," a publication of the American Psychiatric Association, 1400 K Street, NW, Washington, DC 20005.

Chapter 39

Substance Abuse and Violent Death

The victims of violent death—either homicide or suicide—are more likely to abuse alcohol or drugs than are their age, race, and gender-matched controls, according to a study published in the *Journal of the American Medical Association*. In addition, homicide victims are also more likely to live in a household where substances are abused, researchers say.

Investigators Frederick P. Rivara, M.D., and colleagues from the University of Washington in Seattle reached this conclusion after conducting a study of homicides and suicides in three large US. metropolitan areas: Shelby County, Tenn., King County, Wash., and Cuyahoga County, Ohio.

The investigators identified homicides and suicides taking place in the victim's home between 1987 and 1992 through medical examiner and police reports in the three counties. They then contacted proxies living in the home—usually relatives—and interviewed them regarding the history of substance use by the victim and by other family members.

Investigators also identified a group of matched controls, about whom information was obtained through a relative proxy, if possible; if this was impossible, the control subject was interviewed.

The investigators found that most homicide and suicide victims were likely to be male; suicides were highly likely to be white, while

The Brown University Digest of Addiction Theory and Application, Vol. 16, No. 12, p.4(2), © 1997 Manisses Communications Group, Inc.; reprinted with permission of Manisses Communications Group.

homicide victims were likely to be African American. In addition, homicide victims tended to be slightly younger than suicides (median age ranges 35-44 and 45-54, respectively).

Surveys revealed that substance use markedly increased the risk of both homicide and suicide. Being in trouble at work due to drinking, being hospitalized for a drinking problem, use of illicit drugs, and arrest for use of illicit drugs all placed subjects "at increased risk of violent death by homicide." Having a psychiatric problem or depression increased the risk for death by homicide 3-fold.

The same factors seemed to affect the risk of suicide. Drinking, problem drinking, hospitalization, and illicit drug use all increased subjects' risk of committing suicide. Psychiatric illness or depression, even when subjects were receiving medication for the problem, increased the risk of 107 times.

The investigators also found that living situation affected the risk of homicide and suicide. Subjects who lived alone were at increased risk for homicide whether or not they drank alcohol; for those who lived in households where others drank, the risk of homicide was increased by 3.5. Living in a household where others used illicit drugs had an especially strong impact increasing the risk of homicide 13.7 times.

Risk of suicide was higher among those who either drank or used illicit drugs and lived alone.

Study Limits

This study has a number of important limitations, including:

- the study was limited to homicides and suicides taking place in the home

- information was gathered from proxy respondents; it is possible (although unlikely) that some of the proxies in cases of homicide may have been perpetrators

- data were gathered in urban areas and may not be generalizable to rural areas

- the mechanism associating drinking/drug use with violent death are not clear.

In spite of these limitations, the authors conclude that "a history of alcohol and drug use by the subject was strongly associated with increased risks of both homicide and suicide."

Authors' Recommendations

These data indicate the need to address the relationship of alcohol and drug abuse and violent death as part of a multifaced approach to decreasing societal violence. Screening for substance abuse problems in emergency rooms and mental health settings, and designing appropriate treatments may help to reduce violent deaths.

In addition, the authors says, "our concept of the individual at risk for violent death should be broadened to include not only the substance abuser, but also those who may be at risk because of the presence of others within the household who are substance abusers."

Suggested Readings:

Cornelius, J.R., Salloum, I.M., et al. Disproportionate suicidiality in patients with comorbid major depression and alcoholism. *American Journal of Psychiatry*, 152:358-364, 1995.

Murdoch, D., Phil, R.O, Ross, D. Alcohol and crimes of violence: Present issues. *International Journal of Addiction*, 25:1065-1081, 1990.

Frederick P. Rivara, Beth A. Mueller, Grant Somes, Carmen T. Mendoza, Norman B. Rushforth, Arthur L. Kellermann. Alcohol and illicit drug abuse and the risk of violent death in the home. *Journal of the American Medical Association*, 278.-569-575, 1997

Part Five

Drug Abuse Treatment Issues

Chapter 40

Detoxification

Goals of Detoxification

The term detoxification implies a clearing of toxins. For many alcohol and other drug (AOD)-dependent people, removal of drugs from their bodies is indeed part of the detoxification process. In the context of treating patients who are physically dependent on alcohol or other drugs, detoxification also includes the period of time during which the body's physiology is adjusting to the absence of drugs.

Length of Detoxification

Because detoxification often entails a more intensive level of care than other types of AOD treatment, there is a practical value in defining a period during which a person is "in detoxification." There is no simple way to do this. Usually, the detoxification period is defined as the period during which the patient receives detoxification medications.

Another way of defining the detoxification period is by measuring the duration of withdrawal signs or symptoms. However, the duration of these symptoms may be difficult to determine in a correctly medicated patient because symptoms of withdrawal are largely suppressed by the medication.

Excerpted from *Detoxification from Alcohol and Other Drugs*, Treatment Improvement (TIP) Series 19, Substance Abuse and Mental Health Services Administration, Center for Substance Abuse Treatment, DHHS Publication No. (SMA) 95-3046, 1995.

The Role of Detoxification in AOD Abuse Treatment

For many AOD-dependent patients, detoxification is the beginning phase of treatment. It can entail more than a period of physical readjustment. It can also be a time when patients begin to make the psychological readjustments necessary for ongoing treatment. Offering detoxification alone, without follow-up to an appropriate level of care, is an inadequate use of limited resources. People who have severe problems that predate their AOD dependence or addiction—such as family disintegration, lack of job skills, illiteracy, or psychiatric disorders—may continue to have these problems after detoxification unless specific services are available to help them deal with these factors.

Detoxification Protocols

Some detoxification procedures are specific to particular drugs of dependence; others are based on general principles of treatment and are not drug specific. In this chapter, the general principles are presented first, followed by specific treatment regimens for each category.

Principles of Detoxification

- Detoxification alone is rarely adequate treatment for AOD dependencies.

- When using medication regimens or other detoxification procedures, clinicians should use only protocols of established safety and efficacy.

- Providers must advise patients when procedures are used that have not been established as safe and effective.

- During detoxification, providers should control patients' access to medication to the greatest extent possible.

- Initiation of withdrawal should be individualized.

- Whenever possible, clinicians should substitute a long-acting medication for short-acting drugs of addiction.

- The intensity of withdrawal cannot always be predicted accurately.

- Every means possible should be used to ameliorate the patient's signs and symptoms of AOD withdrawal.

- Patients should begin participating as soon as possible in follow-up support therapy such as peer group therapy, family therapy, individual counseling or therapy, 12-step recovery meetings, and AOD recovery educational programs.

Withdrawal from Opiates

All opiates—heroin, morphine, hydromorphone (Dilaudid), codeine, and methadone—produce similar withdrawal signs and symptoms. However, the time of onset and the duration of the abstinence syndrome vary. The severity of the withdrawal syndrome depends on many factors, including the drug used, the total daily dose, the interval between doses, the duration of use, and the health and personality of the addict.

Symptoms of withdrawal from opiates may be divided into four classes: (1) gastrointestinal distress, including diarrhea and, less frequently, nausea or vomiting; (2) pain, typically either arthralgias or myalgias or abdominal cramping; (3) anxiety, and (4) insomnia.

Opiate Abstinence Syndromes

Signs and symptoms of withdrawal from heroin or morphine begin 8 to 12 hours following the patient's last dose. They subside over a period of 5 to 7 days.

Signs and symptoms of withdrawal from methadone begin 12 hours after the patient's last dose. The peak intensity occurs on the third day of abstinence or later. Symptoms gradually subside, but may continue for 3 weeks or longer. Methadone abstinence syndrome develops more slowly and is more prolonged but usually less intense than other opiate abstinence syndromes.

In July 1993, the Food and Drug Administration (FDA) approved levo-alpha-acetylmethadol (LAAM) for use as a maintenance medication. It is a Schedule II controlled substance, which categorizes it as a medication with medical uses but also with a high potential for abuse. Few studies have addressed the medically supervised withdrawal of LAAM patients to a drug-free state. Withdrawal from LAAM produces similar symptoms to those produced by withdrawal from methadone.

Medication Treatment for Opiate Withdrawal

Clonidine. Clonidine (Catapres), a medication marketed for the treatment of hypertension, has been used for treatment of the symptoms of opiate withdrawal since 1978. Although clonidine has not yet been

277

approved by the FDA for treatment of opiate withdrawal, its use has become standard clinical practice.

Clonidine has some practical advantages over methadone for treating narcotic withdrawal, particularly in drug-free programs. These advantages include the following:

- It is not a scheduled medication.

- The use of opiates can be discontinued immediately in preparation for naltrexone induction or admission to a drug-free treatment program (e.g., a therapeutic community).

- It does not produce opiate euphoria, and patients' need for drugs is therefore reduced.

Although clonidine alleviates some symptoms of opiate withdrawal, it is not effective for muscle aches, insomnia, or drug craving. These symptoms require additional medication.

Methadone. Methadone can be used for withdrawal from heroin, fentanyl, or any other opiate. For certain patient populations, including those with many treatment failures, methadone is the treatment of choice. Methadone generally is not used with adolescents because FDA regulations prohibit its use with this age group (except in rare exceptions). In this population, there are high risks of addiction and promotion of drug-seeking behavior.

Methadone can be administered for detoxification only in a hospital or in an outpatient program that is licensed for methadone detoxification. Opiate-dependent inpatients who are being treated for an acute medical illness can be administered methadone for prevention of opiate withdrawal if opiate withdrawal would complicate treatment of their medical conditions.

LAAM. As mentioned previously, in July, 1993 the FDA approved LAAM for use as a maintenance medication. The trade name of LAAM is ORLAAM. Until August, 1993, LAAM was a Schedule I controlled substance, which is defined as a drug with a high abuse potential but with no recognized medical use. In August, 1993 the Drug Enforcement Administration (DEA) reclassified it as a Schedule II controlled substance, defined as a medication with medical uses as well as a high potential for abuse.

FDA methadone regulations have been revised to allow use of LAAM. The regulations for LAAM are similar to those for methadone, with two exceptions: Take-home doses of LAAM are not allowed, and LAAM cannot be administered to pregnant women. Patients who need take-home doses must be switched to methadone. Like methadone, LAAM may be dispensed only by licensed AOD abuse treatment clinics.

LAAM is a prodrug with little opiate activity. This means that its opiate effects are produced by its long-acting metabolites, nor-LAAM and dinor-LAAM. Since LAAM itself is not a potent opiate, oral ingestion or intravenous injection of LAAM does not produce rapid onset of opiate effects as does the ingestion of methadone, heroin, morphine, and most other opiates.

Buprenorphine. The FDA has approved buprenorphine for the treatment of pain, and it is being investigated as a treatment for opiate dependence and detoxification. Buprenorphine is a potent analgesic that is available by prescription as a sublingual tablet in many parts of the world. In the United States, it is available by prescription as an analgesic in an injectable form (Buprenex). The doses of buprenorphine under investigation for maintenance treatment are considerably higher than those commonly prescribed for treatment of pain.

Buprenorphine has an unusual pharmacological profile that makes it attractive for the treatment of opiate dependence, and its potential was recognized as early as 1978. The level of physical dependence produced by buprenorphine is not as great as that produced by methadone or heroin; therefore, most patients find buprenorphine easier to discontinue than methadone. Some patients can eventually be switched from buprenorphine maintenance to treatment with an opiate antagonist such as naltrexone.

Buprenorphine is safer than methadone or LAAM if an overdose is ingested. Its opiate effects appear to plateau at 16 mg. Although it is used intravenously by heroin addicts in countries where the sublingual tablet is legally available as an analgesic, its abuse potential appears to be substantially less than that of methadone or heroin. And though it is currently an experimental drug with regard to its use in detoxification, buprenorphine may soon be approved by the FDA. [See Chapter 45 for additional information regarding the use of buprenorphine for opiate detoxification.]

Dextropropoxyphene. In the 1970s, dextropropoxyphene (Darvon) was among the medications used for opiate withdrawal. Because of abuse of dextropropoxyphene by addicts, the DEA reclassified it as a

Schedule IV narcotic. The narcotic classification prohibits its use for treatment of opiate dependency in routine clinical practice.

Terminating Opiate Maintenance Treatment

Patients on opiate maintenance are sometimes discontinued from medication for disciplinary reasons. This situation is often awkward for both the program and the patient, particularly if the patient is abusive, threatening, and/or potentially violent.

Involuntary Termination of Opiate Maintenance. The program manager should develop and post prominently on the program premises at least one copy of a written policy covering criteria for involuntary termination from treatment. This policy should describe patients' rights and responsibilities as well as those of program staff. At the time a patient enters treatment, a staff member designated by the program director should inform the patient about the policy and where it is posted. The staff person should inform patients of the conditions under which they might be involuntarily terminated from treatment and of their rights under the termination procedure.

The medication discontinuation should not occur so rapidly that the patient experiences severe opiate withdrawal symptoms. Treatment staff should taper the methadone dosage until the patient is receiving 30 to 40 mg a day. At this point, treatment with clonidine and other medications may begin.

Voluntary Termination of Opiate Maintenance. Patients in methadone treatment, like others who are receiving daily medication on a long-term basis, should be evaluated periodically regarding the risks and benefits of their therapy. For some persons, eventual withdrawal from methadone maintenance is a realistic goal.

Research and clinical experience have not yet identified all the critical variables that determine when a patient can be withdrawn from methadone and remain drug-free. A decision to withdraw voluntarily from methadone maintenance must, therefore, be left to the patient and to the clinical judgment of the physician. Staff should encourage the patient to remain in the program for as long as necessary.

Patient Care and Comfort

Patient comfort is a primary consideration during detoxification, regardless of the detoxification agent. A complete physical examination should be conducted. The patient should be checked for tuberculosis; symptoms of acquired immune deficiency syndrome and opportunistic infections; hepatitis A, B, and C; and sexually transmitted diseases. Patients should be monitored for anxiety, sweating, chills, nutritional intake, diarrhea and gastrointestinal distress, sleep dysfunction, muscle cramps, aches, and bowel function.

Skin care is also important. Guidelines should be in place for management of conditions such as skin and subcutaneous abscesses due to needle use.

A few patients may remain in bed for several hours or for as long as a day during detoxification; however, most do not need to do so. Opiate addicts generally have less cognitive impairment than do alcoholics. During detoxification, they may view videotapes and participate in group activities.

If the patient might be pregnant, appropriate testing is essential. It is important to evaluate the safety of withdrawing a pregnant woman from opiates because of the potential effects on the fetus. Often it is best to put the pregnant patient on methadone maintenance.

Alternatives to Medication

Acupuncture. While some clinicians consider acupuncture an acceptable primary detoxification treatment for opiate abusers, there are few controlled studies that support this. Acupuncture can be a useful treatment adjunct to methadone or clonidine detoxification.

Auricular (ear) acupuncture has been used in treatment of opiate withdrawal since 1972, and it is done in clinics throughout the world. It is difficult to conduct rigorous double-blind controlled studies with acupuncture because the acupuncturist must insert the needles into very precise locations.

One study (Washburn, A.M., Fullilove, R.E., Fullilove, M.T., et al. Acupuncture heroin detoxification: a single-blind clinical trial. *Journal of Substance Abuse Treatment*, 1993, 10:345-351)) compared standard acupuncture with "sham" acupuncture. Dropout rates were high in both groups; however, more subjects were retained in the standard than in the "sham" group. Until controlled clinical data indicate otherwise, acupuncture must be viewed as an adjunctive treatment to detoxification.

Electrostimulation. Although some studies have shown that neuroelectric therapy (NET) reduces chronic withdrawal period for some opiate abusers, a recent study found that NET is no more effective than use of a placebo in opiate and cocaine detoxification. NET is therefore not recommended.

Withdrawal from Benzodiazepines and Other Sedative-Hypnotics

For therapeutic use, barbiturates and the older sedative-hypnotics have been largely replaced by the benzodiazepines. The withdrawal syndromes from benzodiazepines and other sedative-hypnotics are similar, and the pharmacotherapy treatment strategies apply to both. This section focuses on the benzodiazepines and adds information about treatment of other types of sedative-hypnotic dependence when appropriate.

Dependence on benzodiazepines and other sedative-hypnotics usually develops in the context of medical treatment. Benzodiazepines have many therapeutic uses: As therapy for some conditions, such as panic disorder, long-term treatment is appropriate medical practice. Physical dependency is sometimes unavoidable. Benzodiazepine dependency that develops during pharmacotherapy is not necessarily a substance use disorder. When the dependency results from patients taking the prescribed doses as directed by a physician, the term "therapeutic discontinuation" is preferable to the term "detoxification."

Abusers of heroin and stimulants often misuse benzodiazepines and other sedative-hypnotics, sometimes to the extent that they develop a physical dependence. In such cases, it is appropriate to think of withdrawal from the sedative-hypnotic as detoxification.

Use of either benzodiazepines or sedative-hypnotics at doses above the therapeutic range for a month or more produces physical dependence. Without appropriate medical treatment, withdrawal from benzodiazepines or other sedative-hypnotics can be severe and life threatening. Withdrawal from benzodiazepines or other sedative hypnotics produces a similar withdrawal syndrome, described below under high-dose sedative-hypnotic withdrawal.

Some people will develop withdrawal symptoms after stopping therapeutic doses of benzodiazepines or other sedative-hypnotics after they have been used daily for 6 months or more. With "low-dose" withdrawal, the benzodiazepines and other sedative-hypnotics can produce qualitatively different withdrawal syndromes. These are described as high-dose sedative- hypnotic withdrawal syndrome and low-dose benzodiazepine withdrawal syndrome.

High-Dose Sedative-Hypnotic Withdrawal Syndrome

Signs and symptoms of high-dose sedative-hypnotic withdrawal include anxiety, tremors, nightmares, insomnia, anorexia, nausea, vomiting, orthostatic hypotension, seizures, delirium, and hyperpyrexia. The syndrome is qualitatively similar for all sedative-hypnotics; however, the time course of symptoms depends upon the particular drug. With short-acting sedative-hypnotics (e.g., pentobarbital [Nembutal], secobarbital [Seconal], meprobamate [Miltown, Equanil], and methaqualone) and short-acting benzodiazepines (e.g., oxazepam [Serax], alprazolam [Xanax], and triazolam [Halcion]), withdrawal symptoms typically begin 12 to 24 hours after the last dose and reach peak intensity between 24 and 72 hours after the last dose. Patients who have liver disease or who are elderly may develop symptoms more slowly because of decreased drug metabolism. With long-acting drugs (e.g., phenobarbital, diazepam [Valium], and chlordiazepoxide [Librium]), withdrawal symptoms peak on the fifth to eighth day after the last dose.

The withdrawal delirium may include confusion and visual and auditory hallucinations. The delirium generally follows a period of insomnia. Some patients may have only delirium, others only seizures; some may have both.

Low-Dose Benzodiazepine Withdrawal Syndrome

In the literature of addiction medicine, low-dose benzodiazepine withdrawal syndrome may be referred to as "therapeutic-dose withdrawal," "normal-dose withdrawal," or "benzodiazepine-discontinuation syndrome." Knowledge about low-dose dependency is based on clinical observations and is still sketchy and controversial. As a practical matter, often it is impossible to know with certainty whether symptoms are caused by withdrawal or whether they mark a return of symptoms that were ameliorated by the benzodiazepine. Patients who are treated with benzodiazepines may have had symptoms such as anxiety, insomnia, or muscle tension before taking the benzodiazepine. When they stop taking the benzodiazepine, these symptoms may reappear.

Some people who have taken benzodiazepines in therapeutic doses for months to years can abruptly discontinue the drug without developing symptoms. Others, taking similar amounts of a benzodiazepine, develop symptoms ranging from mild to severe when the benzodiazepine is stopped or the dosage is substantially reduced.

The risk factors associated with withdrawal are not completely understood. Patients who develop the severe form of low-dose benzodiazepine withdrawal syndrome include those with a family or personal history of alcoholism, those who use alcohol daily, or those who concomitantly use other sedatives. According to one study, "higher doses of benzodiazepine lead to increases of withdrawal severity." This study found that the short-acting, high-potency benzodiazepines appear to produce a more intense low-dose withdrawal syndrome than the long-acting, low-potency ones (Rickels, K., Schweizer, E., Case, W.G., Greenblatt, D.J. Long-term therapeutic use of benzodiazepines: I. Effects of abrupt discontinuation. *Archives of General Psychiatry*, 1990; 47;899-907).

During the 1980s, many clinical studies and case reports were published concerning withdrawals that were attributed to therapeutic dose discontinuation. Most patients experienced only a transient increase in symptoms for 1 to 2 weeks after termination of the benzodiazepine. This transient increase is called "symptom rebound."

Protracted Withdrawal, Severe Form. A few patients experience a severe, long-lasting withdrawal syndrome, which includes symptoms such as paresthesia and psychoses, never experienced before the benzodiazepines were taken. It is this condition, which may be quite disabling and may last many months, that has generated much of the concern about the long-term safety of the benzodiazepines. However, many psychiatrists believe that the symptoms that occur after discontinuation of therapeutic doses of benzodiazepines are not a withdrawal syndrome but a reemergence or unmasking of the patient's psychopathology.

Protracted Withdrawal, Mild Form. One additional form of withdrawal is sometimes attributed to the benzodiazepines and other sedative-hypnotics as well as to alcohol and opiates. This is a mild form of protracted withdrawal. Its symptoms include irritability, anxiety, insomnia, and mood instability. The symptoms may persist for months following the beginning of abstinence

Medication Treatment for Benzodiazepine Withdrawal

The physician's response during benzodiazepine withdrawal is critical to a successful outcome. Some physicians interpret patients' escalating symptoms as evidence of their need for additional benzodiazepine treatment. Consequently, they prescribe a benzodiazepine, often at higher doses, or switch the patient to another benzodiazepine. Reinstitution of any benzodiazepine agonist may not achieve satisfactory symptom control and may in fact prolong the recovery process.

Another common response is to declare patients addicted to benzodiazepines and refer them to primary chemical dependency treatment. Such a referral is not appropriate unless the patient has a substance use disorder.

Treatment of High-Dose Benzodiazepine Withdrawal. Abrupt discontinuation of a sedative-hypnotic in patients who are severely physically dependent on it can result in serious medical complications and even death. For this reason, medical management is always needed, and treatment is best provided in a hospital. There are three general medication strategies for withdrawing patients from sedative-hypnotics, including benzodiazepines: (1) the use of decreasing doses of the agent of dependence; (2) the substitution of phenobarbital or another long-acting barbiturate for the addicting agent and the gradual withdrawal of the substitute medication; and (3) the substitution of a long-acting benzodiazepine, such as chlordiazepoxide (Librium), which is tapered over 1 to 2 weeks. The method selected depends on the particular benzodiazepine, the involvement of other drugs of dependence, and the clinical setting in which detoxification takes place.

Substituting phenobarbital is the best choice for patients who have lost control of their benzodiazepine use or who are polydrug dependent. Phenobarbital substitution has the broadest use for all sedative-hypnotic drug dependencies and is widely used in drug treatment programs.

The patient's average daily sedative-hypnotic dose is converted to phenobarbital equivalents, and the daily amount is divided into three doses. The computed phenobarbital equivalent dosage is given in three or four doses daily. If the patient is using significant amounts of other sedative-hypnotics, including alcohol, the amounts of all the drugs are converted to phenobarbital equivalents and added.

Unless the patient develops signs and symptoms of phenobarbital toxicity or sedative-hypnotic withdrawal, phenobarbital is decreased by 30 mg per day. Should signs of phenobarbital toxicity develop during withdrawal, the daily phenobarbital dose is decreased by 50 percent, and the 30 mg per day withdrawal is continued from the reduced phenobarbital dose. Should the patient have objective signs of sedative-hypnotic withdrawal, the daily dose is increased by 50 percent, and the patient is restabilized before continuing the withdrawal.

Treatment of Low-Dose Benzodiazepine Withdrawal. Clinicians should make decisions regarding the treatment of low-dose withdrawal based on the patient's symptoms. Withdrawal seizures are not usually expected. Patients with an underlying seizure disorder must be maintained on full doses of anticonvulsant medications, and medications that lower seizure threshold should be avoided. Patients may need much reassurance that the symptoms are transient and that with continued abstinence they will eventually subside.

Patients who have the severe form of withdrawal may need psychiatric hospitalization if symptoms become intolerable. Phenobarbital, in doses of 200 mg per day, generally provides considerable reduction in symptoms. Phenobarbital is slowly tapered over several months.

Withdrawal From Stimulants (Cocaine, Crack Cocaine, Amphetamines, and Methamphetamine)

The two most commonly abused stimulants are cocaine and methamphetamine. Intermittent binge use of both agents is common. The withdrawal symptoms that occur after a 2- to 3-day binge are different than those that occur after chronic, high-dose use. The withdrawal syndromes are similar.

Following a 2- to 3-day binge, stimulant abusers are dysphoric, exhausted, and somnolent for 24 to 48 hours. Because cocaine abusers commonly take alcohol, marijuana, or even heroin with cocaine to reduce the irritability caused by high-dose stimulant abuse, the withdrawal may be in response to the combination of drugs. The patient also may have become dependent on more than one drug.

Following regular use, the withdrawal syndrome consists of dysphoria, irritability, difficulty sleeping, and intense dreaming. Often stimulant abusers experience signs and symptoms of the abuse of multiple drugs. The symptoms subside over 2 to 4 days of drug abstinence.

There is no specific treatment for stimulant withdrawal. Mild sedation with phenobarbital or chloral hydrate for sleep may ameliorate patients' distress.

In the medical literature, descriptions of cocaine withdrawal can be confusing because some authors define cocaine craving as a prominent withdrawal symptom. Scientists are not yet certain that craving is a withdrawal symptom. Cocaine craving usually rapidly diminishes in inpatient cocaine abusers when they are unable to get the drug and no longer come in contact with the environmental stimuli associated with cocaine use.

Although the mechanism of drug craving is not well understood, recent studies have demonstrated that environmental and other stimuli can trigger the physiological process of craving. Therefore, exposure to stimuli (which include other drugs) must be controlled.

Withdrawal from Other Drugs

Marijuana

There is no acute abstinence syndrome associated with withdrawal from marijuana. Some patients are irritable and have difficulty sleeping for a few days when they discontinue chronic use of marijuana. Persons withdrawing from marijuana, like those withdrawing from cocaine, benefit from a supportive environment during detoxification.

Nicotine

Two issues regarding tobacco smoking merit consideration by staff of AOD detoxification programs. The first is the program management's desire to establish a smoke-free treatment environment to comply with workplace ordinances and to safeguard the health and comfort of patients from exposure to second-hand smoke. The second issue is the patient's dependence on nicotine as a drug of abuse.

Many programs have implemented smoke-free environments. Some programs treat nicotine as a drug of abuse and require that patients stop smoking as part of their chemical dependency treatment. Most programs provide education about nicotine and encourage patients to quit smoking. Some provide nicotine patches or other medication to manage physiological withdrawal symptoms.

Hallucinogens

Lysergic acid diethylamide (LSD), dimethyltryptamine (DMT), psilocybin, mescaline, 3,4methylenedioxy-amphetamine (MDA), and 3,4,-methylenedioxy-methamphetamine (MDMA, also called XTC or "ecstasy") do not produce physical dependence.

Treatment professionals have noted a recent resurgence in the use of hallucinogenic drugs such as LSD, phencyclidine (PCP), and MDMA. These drugs produce no acute withdrawal syndrome.

PCP

Chronic use of PCP (phencyclidine) can cause a toxic psychosis that takes days or weeks to clear; however, PCP does not have a withdrawal syndrome.

Inhalants / Solvents

Individuals may become physically dependent on hydrocarbons, which include gasoline, glue, and aerosol sprays (including paint, waterproofing material, etc.) and paint thinner. There is clinical evidence that withdrawal from inhalant use is similar to that experienced by persons withdrawing from alcohol. Phenobarbital may be prescribed during detoxification.

Polydrug Use

Addicts rarely use just one drug. Typical combinations and the preferred modes of treatment are shown as follows:

- Alcohol and stimulant: Treat alcohol abuse
- Alcohol and benzodiazepine: Treat with phenobarbital
- Cocaine and benzodiazepine: Treat benzodiazepine withdrawal
- Cocaine and opiate: Treat opiate dependence
- Cocaine and amphetamine: No detoxification protocol is known

Opiate-Barbiturate Dependence

Symptoms of withdrawal from opiates and barbiturates have some common features, making it difficult to assess the patient's clinical condition when both drugs are withdrawn at the same time. Many clinicians prefer to gradually withdraw the sedative-hypnotic first, while administering methadone to prevent opiate withdrawal. When the patient is barbiturate-free, the methadone is withdrawn at a level of 5 mg per day. If the sedative-hypnotic was a benzodiazepine (diazepam or chlordiazepoxide), some clinicians prefer to begin with a partial reduction of the sedative-hypnotic. While the patient is still receiving a partial dosage of the sedative, methadone is withdrawn. Finally, the sedative-hypnotic is totally withdrawn.

Chapter 41

Legal and Ethical Issues for Detoxification Programs

Consent to Treatment

Adults generally have the right to consent to or to refuse treatment—a right that is grounded in State law, judicial decision, and the United States Constitution. The right to consent to or refuse treatment—in other words, to make an informed choice—is normally based upon a process: The treatment provider presents the patient with a diagnosis, a prognosis, a description of available alternative treatments and their risks and benefits, and a prediction of the likely outcome if there is no treatment. This process requires that the patient have the ability, sometimes called "decisional capacity," to make an informed choice.

Intoxicated or Incapacitated Patients

Detoxification programs, perhaps more than any other kind of AOD abuse treatment program, deal with patients whose capacity to make rational decisions may be impaired. Persons who are intoxicated often demonstrate diminished mental capacity. Individuals who are incapacitated by AODs may be unconscious, or their judgment may

Excerpted from *Detoxification from Alcohol and Other Drugs*, Treatment Improvement (TIP) Series 19, Substance Abuse and Mental Health Services Administration, Center for Substance Abuse Treatment, DHHS Publication No. (SMA) 95-3046, 1995. Note: The purpose of this chapter is merely to introduce some of the issues surrounding this topic; it is not intended as legal advice.

be so impaired that they are incapable of making a rational decision about their basic needs, including their need for treatment.

Staff should assess each patient in order to determine whether he or she is able to give informed consent. If a patient is not able to do so because he or she is intoxicated or incapacitated by AOD use, the program should obtain consent as soon as the patient has regained his or her faculties. In the meantime, the program may obtain consent to treat from a relative or parent, if the patient is accompanied to the program. (In obtaining consent, the program must be aware of the Federal confidentiality laws, as described later in this chapter.) The validity of a third party's consent may depend on State law.

Minor Patients

Many States have passed laws permitting minors to consent to AOD abuse treatment without parental involvement. Program staff should become familiar with the laws in their State, by consulting either with their single State agency (SSA) or an attorney familiar with the law in this area.

In those States that require parental consent for treatment, programs must be aware that the Federal confidentiality regulations require them to obtain a minor's consent before they contact the minor's parent. Thus, if a minor seeks treatment but refuses to authorize the program to speak to his or her parent, the program may inform the minor that it cannot provide services unless he or she consents to have the program contact the parent.

The Federal regulations do contain one exception. A program director may communicate with a minor's parents without his or her consent provided that:

- The program director believes that the minor, because of extreme youth or medical condition, does not have the capacity to decide rationally whether to consent to the notification; and

- The program director believes the disclosure is necessary to cope with a substantial threat to the life or well-being of the minor or someone else.

If these two conditions do not exist, the program must explain to the minor that, while he or she has the right to refuse to consent to any communication with a parent, the program can provide no services without such communication and parental consent.

Medication and Drug Control

Use of Medication during Detoxification

Programs often use medications, including some scheduled drugs, to help patients through the detoxification process. Program staff must be aware of Federal and State laws and regulations governing the dispensing, storage, and inventory of all medications. These laws and regulations often require that medications be dispensed by certain classes of professionals. Separate provisions often govern the storage, prescription, and dispensing of scheduled drugs.

Drugs Brought into the Program by Patients

Patients sometimes enter AOD detoxification with drugs on their person or in their luggage. Staff may wish to search all newly admitted patients and the belongings they bring with them. The safest approach is to tell the patient at admission that this is a standard part of the process and that he or she must agree to the search in order to enter detoxification. The program also may incorporate this notice in its admission papers, thereby ensuring that the patient agrees to it in writing.

If a staff member finds drugs on a patient or in a patient's luggage, what should the program do? State regulations sometimes govern how a program may dispose of drugs. They may require, for example, that the drugs be flushed down the toilet, destroyed, or turned over to the police. (The Federal confidentiality laws and regulations, however, prohibit programs from turning patients who are in possession of drugs over to the police.) If a program does destroy drugs brought into treatment by patients, it is advisable for staff members responsible for such destruction to carry it out under observation and maintain a record of the act, so that a patient cannot later make a false accusation about what occurred. State regulations also govern the methods for handling prescription and over-the-counter medications that patients bring into treatment.

Drugs Brought into the Program by Visitors

Although programs cannot turn patients with illegal drugs over to the police, no such restrictions apply to visitors who enter the program facility with drugs. As long as no disclosure is made about a patient, such persons may be reported to the police. A program that plans to search visitors for drugs must obtain their consent, although it may make visiting privileges contingent on consent to search. The use of force should be avoided, as a visitor could sue the program for battery or false imprisonment.

Federal Law Protecting Patient's Right to Confidentiality

Two Federal laws and a set of Federal regulations guarantee the strict confidentiality of information about all persons receiving AOD abuse prevention and treatment services. They are designed to protect privacy rights and thereby attract individuals into treatment. The regulations are more restrictive of communications than are those governing the doctor-patient relationship or the attorney-client privilege.

Types of Programs Covered by the Regulations

Any program that specializes, in whole or in part, in providing detoxification, treatment, counseling and assessment, and referral services, or a combination thereof, for patients with alcohol or other drug problems must comply with the Federal confidentiality regulations. It is the kind of services provided, not the label, that determines whether a program must comply with the Federal law. Calling itself a "prevention program" does not insulate a program that also offers treatment services from the need to comply with confidentiality regulations. Although the Federal regulations apply only to programs that receive Federal assistance, the word "assistance" is broadly interpreted and includes indirect forms of Federal aid such as tax-exempt status or State or local funding that is derived, in whole or in part, from the Federal Government.

Federal Confidentiality Laws

The Federal confidentiality laws and regulations protect any information about a patient if the patient has applied for or received any alcohol- or drug-abuse-related services—including assessment, diagnosis, detoxification, counseling, group counseling, treatment, and referral for treatment—from a covered program. The restrictions on disclosure apply to any information that would identify the patient as an AOD abuser, either directly or by implication. The rule applies from the moment the patient makes an appointment. It applies to patients who are civilly or involuntarily committed, minor patients, patients who are mandated into treatment by the criminal justice system, and former patients. Finally, the rule applies whether or not the person making the inquiry already has the information, has other ways of getting it, enjoys official status, is authorized by State law, or comes armed with a subpoena or search warrant.

Conditions under which Confidential Information May Be Shared

Information that is protected by the Federal confidentiality regulations may always be disclosed after the patient has signed a proper consent form. (As explained earlier in this chapter, if the patient is a minor, parental consent must also be obtained in some States.) The regulations also permit disclosure without the patient's consent in several situations, including communicating information to medical personnel during a medical emergency or reporting child abuse to the authorities.

The most commonly used exception to the general rule prohibiting disclosures is for a program to obtain the patient's consent. The regulations' requirements regarding consent are somewhat unusual and strict and must be carefully followed.

Rules Governing Communication of Information

Seeking Information from Collateral and Referral Sources

Making inquiries of parents, other relatives, health care providers, employers, schools, or criminal justice agencies might seem at first glance to pose no risk to a patient's right to confidentiality, particularly if the person or entity approached for information referred the patient to treatment. Nonetheless, it does.

When a program that screens, assesses, or treats a patient asks a relative or parent, a doctor, an employer, or a school to verify information it has obtained from the patient, it is making a "patient-identifying disclosure." Patient-identifying information is information that identifies someone as an AOD abuser. In other words, when program staff seek information from other sources, they are letting these sources know that the patient has asked for detoxification services. The Federal regulations generally prohibit this kind of disclosure, unless the patient consents.

Communications with Insurance Carriers

Programs must obtain a patient's written consent on the form required by the Federal regulations in order to communicate with any third-party payer who may be responsible for funding the patient's treatment.

If a patient does not want the insurance carrier to be notified and is unable to pay for treatment, the program may refer the patient to a publicly funded program, if one is available. Programs should consult State law to learn whether they may refuse to admit a patient who is unable to pay and who will not consent to the necessary disclosures to his or her insurance carrier.

Insurance carriers, particularly managed care entities, are demanding more and more information about the patients covered by their policies and the treatment provided to those patients. Programs need to be sensitive about the amount and kind of information they disclose, because the insurer may use this information to deny benefits to the patient. For example, if, in response to a request from the insurer, the program releases the patient's entire chart, the insurer may learn from the intake notes that the patient's substance abuse problem included both alcohol and illegal drugs. The insurer may then deny benefits, arguing that since its policy does not cover treatment for abuse of drugs other than alcohol, it will not reimburse for treatment when abuse of both alcohol and drugs is involved. As a second example, the insurer may learn that the patient began drinking at age 11 and deny benefits for a "preexisting condition." Treatment notes may contain personal information about the patient's family life that is extraneous for insurance company review, the sole purpose of which is to determine whether treatment should be covered and, if so, what kind.

Communication among Agencies

Detoxification programs sometimes need to maintain ongoing communication with the referral source or with other professionals providing services to patients. The best way to proceed is to get the patient's consent.

When a staff member of a detoxification program refers a patient to another treatment program and makes an appointment for the patient, he or she is making a disclosure covered by the Federal regulations—a disclosure that the patient has sought or received detoxification services. A consent form is, therefore, required. If the detoxification program is part of a larger program to which the patient is being referred, a consent form may not be necessary under the Federal rules, since there is an exception for information disclosed to staff within the same program.

Detoxification programs, particularly those with limited medical resources, often must transfer patients to a hospital for intensive medical management and care. How should programs handle such transfers, since they involve a disclosure of patient-identifying information?

Programs may deal with this issue in two ways. First, they may ask all patients admitted to detoxification to sign a consent form permitting disclosure to the cooperating hospital, should hospitalization be required. Second, they may take advantage of a provision in the Federal regulations that permits a program to make disclosures in a "medical emergency" to medical personnel "who have a need for information about a patient for the purpose of treating a condition which poses an immediate threat to the health of any individual." The regulations define "medical emergency" as "a condition which poses an immediate threat to the health of any individual and which requires immediate medical intervention." If a patient's condition requires emergency treatment, the program may use this exception to communicate with medical personnel at a hospital. Whenever a disclosure is made to cope with a medical emergency, the program must document in the patient's records the name and affiliation of the recipient of the information, the name of the individual making the disclosure, the date and time of the disclosure, and the nature of the emergency.

Mandatory Reporting to Public Health Authorities

All States require that new cases of acquired immune deficiency syndrome (AIDS) be reported to public health authorities, which submit this information to the Federal Centers for Disease Control and Prevention. In some cases, they also use it for other purposes. Some States also require the reporting of new cases of human immunodeficiency virus (HIV) infection. States also require reporting of certain infectious diseases, such as tuberculosis and sexually transmitted diseases. The public health authority often uses reports of infectious diseases to engage in "contact tracing," that is, finding others to whom an infected person may have spread the disease.

The types of information that must be reported and for which diseases, who must report, and the purposes to which the information is put vary from State to State. Therefore, program directors must examine their State laws to discover (1) whether they or any member of their staff is a mandated reporter, (2) when reporting is required, (3) what information must be reported and whether it includes patient-identifying information, and (4) what will be done with the information reported.

If State law permits the use of a code rather than a patient's name, the program may make the report without the patient's consent, since no patient-identifying information is being revealed.

If patient-identifying information must be reported, there are a number of ways programs can comply with State mandatory reporting laws without violating the Federal confidentiality regulations. They include the following:

- *Obtaining consent.* The easiest way to comply with a State law that mandates reporting of patient-identifying information to a public health authority is to obtain the patient's consent. The information reported by the program may not be redisclosed by the public health authority unless the consent form is drafted to permit redisclosure.

- *Reporting without making a patient-identifying disclosure.* If the program is part of another health care facility (e.g., a general hospital or mental health program), it can include the patient's name in reports if it does so under the name of the parent agency, as long as no information is released that would link the patient with AOD abuse treatment.

- *Using a Qualified Service Organization Agreement (QSOA).* A detoxification program that is required to report patients' names to a public health department also may enter into a QSOA with a general medical care facility or a laboratory that conducts testing or other services for the program. The QSOA permits the detoxification program to report the names of patients to the medical care facility or laboratory, which may then report the information, including patient names, to the public heath department. However, no information is provided that would link those names with AOD abuse treatment.

- *Reporting under the audit and evaluation exception.* One of the exceptions to the general rule prohibiting disclosure without patient consent permits programs, under certain conditions, to disclose information to auditors and evaluators. The U.S. Department of Health and Human Services (DHHS) has written two opinion letters that approve the use of the audit and evaluation exception to report HIV-related information to public health authorities. Read together, these two letters suggest that AOD programs may report patient-identifying information even if that information will be used by the public health department to conduct contact tracing, as long as the health department does not disclose the name of the patient to the "contacts" it approaches. The letters also suggest that the public health authorities could use the information to contact the infected patient directly.

Telephone Calls to Patients

If someone telephones a patient at a detoxification program, the staff may not reveal that the patient is at the program unless the program has a written consent form signed by a patient to make a disclosure to that particular caller.

Patients Mandated into Treatment by the Criminal Justice System

Detoxification programs treating patients who are required to enter and participate in treatment as part of a criminal justice sanction must follow the Federal confidentiality rules. In addition, some special rules apply when a patient is in treatment as an official condition of probation, sentence, dismissal of charges, release from detention, or other disposition of any criminal proceeding, and information is being disclosed to the mandating agency.

A consent form or court order is still required before any disclosure may be made about an offender who is mandated into assessment or treatment. However, the rules concerning the length of time that a consent remains valid are different, and a "criminal justice system consent" may not be revoked before its expiration event or date.

Duty to Warn

Patient Threats. For most treatment professionals, the decision whether to report a patient's threat to commit a crime is a troubling one. Many professionals believe that they have an ethical, professional, or moral obligation to prevent a crime when they are in a position to do so, particularly if the crime is a serious one. Although these issues may not arise often, programs may face questions about their "duty to warn" someone of a patient's threatened suicide, a patient's threat to harm another, or a patient's insistence on driving while impaired.

There is a developing trend in the law to require therapists who have learned that a patient presents a "serious danger of violence to another" to take "reasonable steps" to protect an intended victim. This trend started with the case of *Tarasoff v. Regents of the Univ. of Cal.*, 17 Cal.3d 425 (1976), in which the California Supreme Court held a psychologist liable for monetary damages because he failed to warn a potential victim his patient threatened to, and then did, kill. The court ruled that if a psychologist knows that a patient poses a serious risk of violence to a particular person, the psychologist has a duty "to warn the intended victim or others likely to apprise the victim of the danger, to notify the police, or to take whatever other steps are reasonably necessary under the circumstances."

While strictly speaking the *Tarasoff* ruling applies only in California, courts in a number of other States have followed it in finding therapists and others liable for damages when they failed to warn a potential victim of threats disclosed during therapy by their patients. Most of these cases are limited to situations where patients threaten a specific victim; they do not generally apply where a patient makes a threat without identifying the intended target. States that have enacted laws on the subject have similarly limited the duty to warn to situations in which the identity of the potential victim has been revealed.

Driving while Impaired. Suppose that an intoxicated patient arrives at a detoxification program but decides not to enter treatment. If the patient is not in condition to drive home, what should the program do? First, it can offer the patient a ride home or taxi fare for a ride home. Second, it can maintain a room where such a person can "sleep it off." (The program would be wise to obtain the person's consent to alert his or her family.) This strategy can also be used by detoxification programs that do not admit patients who are inebriated.

What if the patient refuses both offers and leaves the premises, intending to drive home? Does the program have a duty to call the police to prevent an accident? Does it risk a lawsuit if it fails to do so? This is a question of State law.

In most States, it is unlikely that the program would be liable, particularly if it had made an effort to stop the patient from driving. As noted above, in States that follow the *Tarasoff* doctrine, liability has generally been limited to those situations where a patient threatens to harm a specific person. Liability has generally not been imposed in situations where a patient poses a threat to the community in general.

Liability concerns aside, the program may nonetheless believe it is obligated to call the police if its attempts to prevent the patient from driving fail. In doing so, it must take care not to violate the patient's confidentiality. For example, the program can call the police and tell them that the driver of a 1991 tan Nissan with a license number "XYZ 123," who is heading downtown from the intersection of Maple and Third streets, is not in a condition to operate a vehicle. The program should ask the police to respond immediately. The program may not tell the police that the patient has a substance abuse problem. This means it may not tell the police that the patient is impaired by alcohol or drugs and cannot reveal the program's name, since to do so would tell the police that the patient has a substance abuse problem.

Dealing with Police

Arrest Warrants. An arrest warrant gives police the authority to search the program facilities; however, the program is not authorized to help the police by pointing out the offender. The unfortunate result is that the confidentiality of all patients in the program may be compromised when the police enter and search for a fugitive. There is no solution to this problem, unless the police secure a court order, which would authorize the program to disclose the identity of the patient. If the program cannot convince the police to obtain a court order, it can try to convince the patient to surrender voluntarily. (Voluntary surrender by a patient is a disclosure by the patient, not the program.) It is usually in the patient's best interest to surrender voluntarily, since arrest is probably inevitable and cooperation may positively influence the prosecutor and judge when the question of bail arises. The risk is that the patient will attempt to escape, which might expose the program to a charge of assisting unlawful escape. To reduce this possibility, the program should work with the police so that law enforcement personnel have secured the area around the program.

Search Warrants. A search warrant does not authorize the program to permit the police to enter the premises. Even if signed by a judge, a search warrant is not the kind of "court order" that the Federal regulations require before the program can allow anyone to enter and see patients or patient records when patients have not consented. Law enforcement officials are unlikely to know about the restrictions of the Federal regulations, however, and they will probably believe that a search warrant permits them to enter and search the program. What should a program do?

Presented with a search warrant, program staff should show the officer a copy of the Federal regulations and explain their restrictions. Staff can suggest that the officer obtain a court order that will authorize the program to make the disclosure called for in the search warrant. No harm will ordinarily be caused by resultant delay (although the police may not agree with this view). The program should call its lawyer and let him or her talk with the police. Failing that, a program could try to call the prosecutor who has sent the police, explain the regulations, and point out that any evidence seized without the proper court order may be excluded at trial, since it will have been seized illegally.

If none of these steps works, the program must permit the police to enter. Refusal to obey a direct order of the police may be a crime, even if the police are wrong, and forcible resistance would be unwise. If the program has made a good faith effort to convince the law enforcement authorities to pursue the proper route, it is unlikely that it would be held liable for allowing entry when argument fails.

Reporting Criminal Activity by Patients

Threatened Criminal Activity. A program generally does not have a duty to warn another person or the police about a patient's intended actions, unless the patient presents a serious danger of violence to an identifiable individual. Petty crimes like shoplifting are important issues, but they should be dealt with therapeutically. They are not something a program should necessarily report to the police.

Past Criminal Activity. Suppose that a patient admits during a counseling session that he killed someone during a robbery 3 months ago. Does the program have a responsibility to report that?

In a situation where a program thinks it might have to report a past crime, three questions must be answered:

1. Is there a legal duty under State law to report the past criminal activity to the police? In most States, there is no duty to report to the police a crime committed in the past.

2. Does State law permit a counselor to report the crime to law enforcement authorities if he or she wants to? Whether or not there is a legal obligation to report past crimes to the police, State law may protect conversations between counselors of detoxification programs and their patients and may exempt counselors from any requirement to report past criminal activity by patients. Such laws are designed to protect the special counselor-patient relationship. State laws vary widely on the protection they accord communications between patients and counselors. In some States, admissions of past crimes

may be considered privileged, and counselors may be prohibited from reporting them; in others, admissions may not be privileged. Moreover, each State uniquely defines the kinds of relationships protected. Whether a communication about past criminal activity is privileged (and therefore cannot be reported) may depend on the counselor's profession and whether he or she is State-licensed or certified.

3. If State law requires a report, or if it permits one and the program decides to make a report, how can the program comply with the Federal confidentiality regulations and State law? Any program that decides to make a report to law enforcement authorities about a patient's prior criminal activity must do so without violating either the Federal confidentiality regulations or State laws. It may comply with the Federal regulations by following one of three methods:

- It can make a report in a way that does not identify the individual as a patient in a detoxification program.
- If the crime is sufficiently serious, it can obtain a court order permitting it to make a report.
- If the patient is an offender who has been mandated into treatment by a criminal justice agency, the program can make a report to that agency, provided it has a criminal justice system consent form signed by the patient that is worded broadly enough to allow disclosure of this sort of information.

Crimes on Program Premises or Against Program Personnel. When a patient has committed or threatens to commit a crime on program premises or against program personnel, the regulations are more straightforward. They permit the program to report the crime to a law enforcement agency or to seek its assistance. Without any special authorization, the program can disclose the circumstances of the incident, including the suspect's name, address, last known whereabouts, and status as a patient at the program.

Reporting Child Abuse and Neglect. All 50 States have statutes requiring reporting when there is reasonable cause to believe or suspect child abuse or neglect. While many State statutes are similar, each has different rules about what kinds of conditions must be reported, who must report and when, and how reports must be made.

Most States now require not only physicians but also educators and social service workers to report child abuse. Most States require an immediate oral report, and many have toll-free numbers to facilitate reporting. Half of the States require both oral and written reports. All States extend immunity from prosecution to persons reporting child abuse and neglect. Most States provide for penalties for failure to report.

The Federal confidentiality regulations permit programs to comply with State laws that require the reporting of child abuse and neglect. This exception to the general rule prohibiting disclosure of any information about a patient, however, applies only to initial reports of child abuse or neglect. Unless the patient consents or the appropriate court issues a special court order, programs may not respond to follow-up requests for information, or even to subpoenas, even if the records are sought for use in civil or criminal proceedings resulting from the program's initial report.

Conducting Research

Research about and evaluation of the efficacy of different methods of detoxification are essential if advances in treatment are to be made. But can detoxification programs share patient-identifying information with researchers and program evaluators? The confidentiality regulations do permit programs to disclose patient-identifying information to researchers, auditors, and evaluators without patient consent, providing certain safeguards are met.

Research. Detoxification programs may disclose patient-identifying information to persons conducting "scientific research" if the program director determines that the researcher (1) is qualified to conduct the research, (2) has a protocol under which patient-identifying information will be kept in accordance with the regulations' security provisions, and (3) has provided a written statement from a group of three or more independent individuals who have reviewed the protocol and determined that it protects patients' rights. Researchers are prohibited from identifying an individual patient in any report or from otherwise disclosing any patient identities, except back to the program.

Audit and Evaluation. Federal, State, and local government agencies that fund or are authorized to regulate a program, private entities that fund or provide third-party payments to a program, and peer review entities performing a utilization or quality control review may review patient records on the program premises in order to conduct an audit or evaluation.

Any person or entity that reviews patient records to perform an audit or conduct an evaluation must agree in writing that it will use the information only to carry out the audit or evaluation and that it will redisclose patient information only (1) back to the program, (2) in accordance with a court order to investigate or prosecute the program, or (3) to a Government agency overseeing a Medicare or Medicaid audit or evaluation. Any other person or entity that is determined by the program director to be qualified to conduct an audit or evaluation and that agrees in writing to abide by the restrictions on redisclosure also may review patient records.

Follow-up Research. Research that follows patients for any period of time after they leave treatment presents a special challenge under the Federal regulations. The detoxification program, researcher, or evaluator who seeks to contact former patients to gain information about how they are faring after leaving treatment must do so without disclosing to others any information about their connection to the detoxification program. If follow-up contact is attempted by telephone, the caller must make sure he or she is talking to the patient before identifying himself or herself or mentioning a connection to the detoxification program. For example, asking for "Willy Woe," when his wife or child has answered the phone, and announcing that one is calling from the "ABC Detoxification Program" (or the "Drug Research Corporation") violates the regulations. The program or research agency may form another entity, without a hint of detoxification (or drugs or alcohol) in its name (e.g., Health Research, Inc.) that can contact former patients without worrying about disclosing information simply by giving its name. When a representative of such an entity calls former patients, however, care must be taken that the patient is actually on the line before revealing any connection with the detoxification program.

If follow-up is done by mail, the return address should not disclose any information that could lead someone seeing the envelope to conclude that the addressee had been in treatment.

Other Requirements

Patient Notice and Access to Records

The Federal confidentiality regulations require programs to notify patients of their right to confidentiality and to give them a written summary of the regulations' requirements. The notice and summary should be handed to patients when they enter the program or shortly thereafter. The regulations contain a sample notice that may be used for this purpose.

Unless State law grants the right of patient access to records, programs have the right to decide when to permit patients to view or obtain copies of their records. The Federal regulations do not require programs to obtain written consent from patients before permitting them to see their own records.

Security of Records

The Federal regulations require programs to keep written records in a secure room, locked file cabinet, safe, or other similar container. The program should establish written procedures that regulate access to and use of patient records. The program director or a single staff person should be designated to process inquiries and requests for information.

Conclusion

Administrators and staff members of AOD detoxification programs should become thoroughly familiar with the many legal issues affecting their work. Such knowledge can prevent costly mistakes. Because legal requirements often vary by State and change over time, it is also essential that programs find a reliable source to whom they may turn for up-to-date information, advice, and training.

Chapter 42

Treatment Methods and Medications

Treatment Methods

Drug addiction is a treatable disorder. Through treatment that is tailored to individual needs, patients can learn to control their condition and live normal, productive lives. Like people with diabetes or heart disease, people in treatment for drug addiction learn behavioral changes and often take medications as part of their treatment regimen.

Behavioral therapies can include counseling, psychotherapy, support groups, or family therapy. Treatment medications offer help in suppressing the withdrawal syndrome and drug craving and in blocking the effects of drugs. In addition, studies show that treatment for heroin addiction using methadone at an adequate dosage level combined with behavioral therapy reduces death rates and many health problems associated with heroin abuse.

In general, the more treatment given, the better the results. Many patients require other services as well, such as medical and mental health services and HIV prevention services. Patients who stay in treatment longer than 3 months usually have better outcomes than those who stay less time. Patients who go through medically assisted withdrawal to minimize discomfort but do not receive any further treatment, perform about the same in terms of their drug use as those

The chapter includes text from the following documents produced by the National Institute on Drug Abuse (NIDA): "Treatment Methods," Pub. No. 13559, November 1999; "Treatment Medications," Pub. No. 13560, November 1999; and "Behavioral Change through Treatment," Pub. No. 13561, November 1999.

who were never treated. Over the last 25 years, studies have shown that treatment works to reduce drug intake and crimes committed by drug-dependent people. Researchers also have found that drug abusers who have been through treatment are more likely to have jobs.

Types of Treatment Programs

The ultimate goal of all drug abuse treatment is to enable the patient to achieve lasting abstinence, but the immediate goals are to reduce drug use, improve the patient's ability to function, and minimize the medical and social complications of drug abuse.

There are several types of drug abuse treatment programs. Short-term methods last less than 6 months and include residential therapy, medication therapy, and drug-free outpatient therapy. Longer term treatment may include, for example, methadone maintenance outpatient treatment for opiate addicts and residential therapeutic community treatment.

In maintenance treatment for heroin addicts, people in treatment are given an oral dose of a synthetic opiate, usually methadone hydrochloride or levo-alpha-acetyl methadol (LAAM), administered at a dosage sufficient to block the effects of heroin and yield a stable, noneuphoric state free from physiological craving for opiates. In this stable state, the patient is able to disengage from drug-seeking and related criminal behavior and, with appropriate counseling and social services, become a productive member of his or her community.

Outpatient drug-free treatment does not include medications and encompasses a wide variety of programs for patients who visit a clinic at regular intervals. Most of the programs involve individual or group counseling. Patients entering these programs are abusers of drugs other than opiates or are opiate abusers for whom maintenance therapy is not recommended, such as those who have stable, well-integrated lives and only brief histories of drug dependence.

Therapeutic communities (TCs) are highly structured programs in which patients stay at a residence, typically for 6 to 12 months. Patients in TCs include those with relatively long histories of drug dependence, involvement in serious criminal activities, and seriously impaired social functioning. The focus of the TC is on the resocialization of the patient to a drug-free, crime-free lifestyle.

Short-term residential programs, often referred to as chemical dependency units, are often based on the "Minnesota Model" of treatment for alcoholism. These programs involve a 3- to 6-week inpatient treatment phase followed by extended outpatient therapy or participation in

12-step self-help groups, such as Narcotics Anonymous or Cocaine Anonymous. Chemical dependency programs for drug abuse arose in the private sector in the mid-1980s with insured alcohol/cocaine abusers as their primary patients. Today, as private provider benefits decline, more programs are extending their services to publicly funded patients.

Drug treatment programs in prisons can succeed in preventing patients' return to criminal behavior, particularly if they are linked to community-based programs that continue treatment when the client leaves prison. Some of the more successful programs have reduced the rearrest rate by one-fourth to one-half. For example, the "Delaware Model," an ongoing study of comprehensive treatment of drug-addicted prison inmates, shows that prison-based treatment including a therapeutic community setting, a work release therapeutic community, and community-based aftercare reduces the probability of rearrest by 57 percent and reduces the likelihood of returning to drug use by 37 percent.

Drug abuse has a great economic impact on society—an estimated $67 billion per year. This figure includes costs related to crime, medical care, drug abuse treatment, social welfare programs, and time lost from work. Treatment of drug abuse can reduce those costs. Studies have shown that from $4 to $7 are saved for every dollar spent on treatment. It costs approximately $3,600 per month to leave a drug abuser untreated in the community, and incarceration costs approximately $3,300 per month. In contrast, methadone maintenance therapy costs about $290 per month.

Treatment Medications

Treatment for people who abuse drugs but are not yet addicted to them most often consists of behavioral therapies, such as psychotherapy, counseling, support groups, or family therapy. But treatment for drug-addicted people often involves a combination of behavioral therapies and medications. Medications, such as methadone or LAAM (levo-alpha-acetyl-methadol), are effective in suppressing the withdrawal symptoms and drug craving associated with narcotic addiction, thus reducing illicit drug use and improving the chances of the individual remaining in treatment.

The primary medically assisted withdrawal method for narcotic addiction is to switch the patient to a comparable drug that produces milder withdrawal symptoms, and then gradually taper off the substitute medication. The medication used most often is methadone, taken by mouth once a day. Patients are started on the lowest dose that prevents the more severe signs of withdrawal and then the dose is gradually reduced. Substitutes can be used also for withdrawal from sedatives. Patients can be switched to long-acting sedatives, such as diazepam or phenobarbital, which are then gradually reduced.

Once a patient goes through withdrawal, there is still considerable risk of relapse. Patients may return to taking drugs even though they no longer have physical withdrawal symptoms. A great deal of research is being done to find medications that can block drug craving and treat other factors that cause a return to drugs.

Patients who cannot continue abstaining from opiates are given maintenance therapy, usually with methadone. The maintenance dose of methadone, usually higher than that used for medically assisted withdrawal, prevents both withdrawal symptoms and heroin craving. It also prevents addicts from getting a high from heroin and, as a result, they stop using it. Research has shown that maintenance therapy reduces the spread of AIDS in the treated population. The overall death rate is also significantly reduced.

Within various methadone programs, those that provide higher doses of methadone (usually a minimum of 60 mg.) have better retention rates. Also, those that provide other services, such as counseling, therapy, and medical care, along with methadone generally get better results than the programs that provide minimal services.

Another drug recently approved for use in maintenance treatment is LAAM, which is administered three times a week rather than daily, as is the case with methadone. The drug naltrexone is also used to prevent relapse. Like methadone, LAAM and naltrexone prevent addicts from getting high from heroin. However, naltrexone does not eliminate the drug craving, so it has not been popular among addicts. Naltrexone works best with highly motivated patients.

There are currently no medications approved by the Food and Drug Administration (FDA) for treating addiction to cocaine, LSD, PCP, marijuana, methamphetamine and other stimulants, inhalants, or anabolic steroids. There are medications, however, for treating the adverse health effects of these drugs, such as seizures or psychotic reactions, and for overdoses from opiates. Currently, NIDA's top research priority is the development of a medication useful in treating cocaine addiction.

Behavioral Change through Treatment

Recovery from the disease of drug addiction is often a long-term process, involving multiple relapses before a patient achieves prolonged abstinence. Many behavioral therapies have been shown to help patients achieve initial abstinence and maintain prolonged abstinence. One frequently used therapy is cognitive behavioral relapse prevention in which patients are taught new ways of acting and thinking that will help them stay off drugs. For example, patients are urged to avoid situations that lead to drug use and to practice drug refusal skills. They also are taught to think of the occasional relapse as a "slip" rather than as a failure. Cognitive behavioral relapse prevention has proven to be a useful and lasting therapy for many drug addicted individuals.

One of the more well-developed behavioral techniques in drug abuse treatment is contingency management, a system of rewards and punishments to make abstinence attractive and drug use unattractive. Ultimately, the aim of contingency management programs is to make a drug-free, pro-social lifestyle more rewarding than a drug-using lifestyle. The community reinforcement approach is a comprehensive contingency management approach that has proven to be extremely helpful in promoting initial abstinence in cocaine addicts.

Once drug use is under control, education and job rehabilitation become crucial. Rewarding lifestyle options must be found for people in drug recovery to prevent their return to the old environment and way of life.

For More Information

For information on hotlines or counseling services, please call the Center for Substance Abuse Treatment's National Drug and Alcohol Treatment Service at 1-800-662-4357.

Chapter 43

Effective Medical Treatment for Opiate Addiction

Abstract

Opiate dependence is a brain-related medical disorder that can be effectively treated with significant benefits for the patient and society, and society must make a commitment to offer effective treatment for opiate dependence to all who need it. All opiate-dependent persons under legal supervision should have access to methadone maintenance therapy, and the U.S. Office of National Drug Control Policy and the U.S. Department of Justice should take the necessary steps to implement this recommendation. There is a need for improved training for physicians and other health care professionals and in medical schools in the diagnosis and treatment of opiate dependence. The unnecessary regulations of methadone maintenance therapy and other long-acting opiate agonist treatment programs should be reduced, and coverage for these programs should be a required benefit in public and private insurance programs.

Introduction

In the United States before 1914, it was relatively common for private physicians to treat opiate-dependent patients in their practices by

Excerpted from *Effective Medical Treatment of Opiate Addiction*. NIH Consensus Statement 1997 November 17-19; 15(6):1-38. NIH Consensus Statements and related materials are available by writing to the NIH Consensus Program Information Center, P.O. Box 2577, Kensington, MD 20891; by calling toll-free 1-888-NIH-CONSENSUS; or by visiting the NIH Consensus Development Program home page on the World Wide Web at http://consensus.nih.gov.

prescribing narcotic medications. While the passage of the Harrison Act did not prohibit the prescribing of a narcotic by a physician to treat an addicted patient, this practice was viewed as problematic by Treasury officials charged with enforcing the law. Physicians who continued to prescribe were indicted and prosecuted. Because of withdrawal of treatment by physicians, various local governments and communities established formal morphine clinics for treating opiate addiction. These clinics were eventually closed when the AMA [American Medical Association], in 1920, stated that there was unanimity that prescribing opiates to addicts for self-administration (ambulatory treatment) was not an acceptable medical practice. For the next 50 years, opiate addiction was basically managed in this country by the criminal justice system and the two Federal Public Health Hospitals in Lexington, Kentucky, and Fort Worth, Texas. The relapse rate for opiate use from this approach was close to 100 percent. During the 1960s, opiate use reached epidemic proportions in the United States, spawning significant increases in crime and in deaths from opiate overdose. The increasing number of younger people entering an addiction lifestyle indicated that a major societal problem was emerging. This stimulated a search for innovative and more effective methods for treating the growing number of individuals dependent upon opiates. This search resulted in the emergence of drug-free therapeutic communities and the use of the opiate agonist methadone to maintain those with opiate dependence. Furthermore, a multimodality treatment strategy was designed to meet the needs of the individual addict patient. These three approaches remain the main treatment strategies being used to treat opiate dependence in the United States today.

Opiate dependence has long been associated with increased criminal activity. For example, in 1993 more than one-quarter of the inmates in State and Federal prisons were incarcerated for drug offenses (234,600), and prisoners serving drug sentences were the largest single group (60 percent) in Federal prisons.

In the past 10 years, there has been a dramatic increase in the prevalence of human immunodeficiency virus (HIV), hepatitis B and C viruses, and tuberculosis among intravenous opiate users. From 1991 to 1995, in major metropolitan areas, the annual number of opiate-related emergency room visits increased from 36,000 to 76,000, and the annual number of opiate-related deaths increased from 2,300 to 4,000. This associated morbidity and mortality further underscore the human, economic, and societal costs of opiate dependence.

During the last two decades, evidence has accumulated on the neurobiology of opiate dependence. Whatever conditions may lead to opiate exposure, opiate dependence is a brain-related disorder with the requisite characteristics of a medical illness. Thus, opiate dependence as a medical illness will have varying causative mechanisms. There is a need to identify discrete subgroups of opiate-dependent persons and the most relevant and effective treatments for each subgroup. The safety and efficacy of narcotic agonist (methadone) maintenance treatment has been unequivocally established. Although there are other medications (e.g., levo-alpha acetylmethadol [LAAM] and naltrexone, an opiate antagonist) that are safe and effective in the treatment of opiate addicts, the focus of this consensus development conference was primarily on methadone maintenance treatment (MMT). MMT is effective in reducing illicit opiate drug use, in reducing crime, in enhancing social productivity, and in reducing the spread of viral diseases such as AIDS and hepatitis.

Approximately 115,000 of the estimated 600,000 opiate-dependent persons in the United States are in MMT. Science has not yet overcome the stigma of addiction and the negative public perception about MMT. Some leaders in the Federal Government, public health officials, members of the medical community, and the public at large frequently conceive of opiate dependence as a self-inflicted disease of the will or as a moral flaw. They also regard MMT as an ineffective narcotic substitution and believe that a drug-free state is the only valid treatment goal. Other obstacles to MMT include Federal and State government regulations that restrict the number of treatment providers and patient access. Some of these Federal and State regulations are driven by disproportionate concerns about methadone diversion, concern about premature (e.g., in 12-year-olds) initiation of maintenance treatment, and concern about provision of methadone without any other psychosocial services.

Although a drug-free state represents an optimal treatment goal, research has demonstrated that this goal cannot be achieved or sustained by the majority of opiate-dependent people. However, other laudable treatment goals, including decreased drug use, reduced criminal activity, and gainful employment can be achieved by most MMT patients.

What Is the Scientific Evidence to Support a Conceptualization of Opiate Dependence as a Medical Disorder?

The Natural History of Opiate Dependence

Individuals addicted to opiates often become dependent on these drugs by their early twenties and remain intermittently dependent for decades. Biological, psychological, sociological, and economic factors determine when an individual will start taking opiates. However, it is clear that when use begins, it often escalates to abuse (repeated use with adverse consequences) and then to dependence (opioid tolerance, withdrawal symptoms, compulsive drug-taking). Once dependence is established, there are usually repeated cycles of cessation and relapse extending over decades. This "addiction career" is often accompanied by periods of imprisonment.

Treatment can alter the natural history of opiate dependence, most commonly by prolonging periods of abstinence from illicit opiate abuse. Of the various treatments available, MMT, combined with attention to medical, psychiatric, and socioeconomic issues, as well as drug counseling, has the highest probability of being effective.

Addiction-related deaths, including accidental overdose, drug-related accidents, and many illnesses directly attributable to chronic drug dependence explain one-fourth to one-third of the mortality in an opiate-addicted population. As a population of opiate addicts ages, there is a decrease in the percentage who are still addicted.

There is clearly a natural history of opiate dependence, but causative factors are poorly understood. It is especially unclear for a given individual whether repeated use begins as a medical disorder (e.g., a genetic predisposition) or whether socioeconomic and psychological factors lead an individual to try, and then later to compulsively use, opiates. However, there is no question that once the individual is dependent on opiates, such dependence constitutes a medical disorder.

Diagnosis of Opioid Dependence

Opioid dependence (addiction) is defined as a cluster of cognitive, behavioral, and physiological symptoms in which the individual continues use of opiates despite significant opiate-induced problems. Opioid dependence is characterized by repeated self-administration that usually results in opioid tolerance, withdrawal symptoms, and compulsive drug-taking. Dependence may occur with or without the physiological symptoms of tolerance and withdrawal. Usually, there is a long history of opioid self-administration, typically via intravenous injection in the arms or legs, although recently the intranasal route or smoking also is used. Often there is a history of drug-related crimes, drug overdoses, and family, psychological, and employment problems. There may be a history of physical problems, including skin infections, hepatitis, HIV infection, or irritation of the nasal and pulmonary mucosa. Physical examination usually reveals puncture marks along veins in the arms and legs and "tracks" secondary to sclerosis of veins. If the patient has not taken opiates recently, he or she may also demonstrate symptoms of withdrawal, including anxiety, restlessness, runny nose, tearing, nausea, and vomiting. Tests for opioids in saliva and urine can help support a diagnosis of dependence. However, by itself, neither a positive nor a negative test can rule dependence in or out. Further evidence for opioid dependence can be obtained by a naloxone (Narcan) challenge test to induce withdrawal symptoms.

Evidence That Opioid Dependence Is a Medical Disorder

For decades, opioid dependence was viewed as a problem of motivation, willpower, or strength of character. Through careful study of its natural history and through research at the genetic, molecular, neuronal, and epidemiological levels, it has been proven that opiate addiction is a medical disorder characterized by predictable signs and symptoms. Other arguments for classifying opioid dependence as a medical disorder include:

- Despite varying cultural, ethnic, and socioeconomic backgrounds, there is clear consistency in the medical history, signs, and symptoms exhibited by individuals who are opiate-dependent.

- There is a strong tendency to relapse after long periods of abstinence.

- The opioid-dependent person's craving for opiates induces continual self-administration even when there is an expressed and demonstrated strong motivation and powerful social consequences to stop.

- Continuous exposure to opioids induces pathophysiologic changes in the brain.

What Are the Consequences of Untreated Opiate Dependence to Individuals, Families, and Society?

Of the estimated total opiate-dependent population of 600,000, only 115,000 are known to be in methadone maintenance treatment (MMT) programs. Research surveys indicate that the untreated population of opiate-addicted people is younger than those in treatment. They are typically in their late teens and early to middle twenties, during their formative, early occupational, and reproductive years. The financial costs of untreated opiate dependence to the individual, the family, and society are estimated to be approximately $20 billion per year. The costs in human suffering are incalculable.

Mortality

Before the introduction of MMT, annual death rates reported in four American studies of opiate dependence varied from 13 per 1,000 to 44 per 1,000, with a median of 21 per 1,000. Although it cannot be causally attributed, it is interesting to note that after the introduction of MMT, the death rates of opiate-dependent persons in four American studies had a narrower range, from 11 per 1,000 to 15 per 1,000, and a median of 13 per 1,000. The most striking evidence of the positive impact of MMT on death rates is studies directly comparing these rates in opiate-dependent persons, on and off methadone. Every study showed that death rates were lower in opiate-dependent persons maintained on methadone compared with those who were not. The median death rate for opiate-dependent persons in MMT was 30 percent of the death rate of those not in treatment. A clear consequence of not treating opiate dependence, therefore, is a death rate that is more than three times greater than that experienced by those engaged in MMT.

Illicit Drug Use

Multiple studies conducted over several decades and in different countries demonstrate clearly that MMT results in a marked decrease in illicit opiate use. In addition, there is also a significant and consistent reduction in the use of other illicit drugs, including cocaine and marijuana, and in the abuse of alcohol, benzodiazepines, barbiturates, and amphetamines.

Criminal Activity

Opiate dependence in the United States is unequivocally associated with high rates of criminal behavior. More than 95 percent of opiate-dependent persons report committing crimes during an 11-year at-risk interval. These crimes range in severity from homicides to other crimes against people and property. Stealing in order to purchase drugs is the most common criminal offense. Over the past two decades, clear and convincing evidence has been collected from multiple studies showing that effective treatment of opiate dependence markedly reduces the rates of criminal activity. Therefore, it is clear that significant amounts of crime perpetrated by opiate-dependent persons are a direct consequence of untreated opiate dependence.

Health Care Costs

Although the general health status of people with opiate dependence is substantially worse than that of their contemporaries, they do not routinely use medical services. Typically, they seek medical care in hospital emergency rooms only after their medical conditions are seriously advanced. The consequences of untreated opiate dependence include a much higher incidence of bacterial infections, including endocarditis, thrombophlebitis, and skin and soft tissue infections; tuberculosis; hepatitis B and C; AIDS and sexually transmitted diseases; and alcohol abuse. Because those who are opiate-dependent present for medical care late in their diseases, medical care is generally more expensive. Health care costs related to opiate dependence have been estimated to be $1.2 billion per year.

Joblessness

Opiate dependence prevents many users from maintaining steady employment. Much of their time each day is spent in drug-seeking and drug-taking behavior. Therefore, many seek public assistance because they are unable to generate the income needed to support themselves and their families. Long-term outcome data show that opiate-dependent persons in MMT earn more than twice as much money annually as those not in treatment.

Outcomes of Pregnancy

A substantial number of pregnant women who are dependent on opiates also have HIV/AIDS. On the basis of preliminary data, women who receive MMT are more likely to be treated with zidovudine. It has been well established that administration of zidovudine to HIV-positive pregnant women reduces by two-thirds the rate of HIV transmission to their infants. Comprehensive MMT, along with sound prenatal care, has been shown to decrease obstetrical and fetal complications as well.

What Is the Efficacy of Current Treatment Modalities in the Management of Opiate Dependence and What Is the Scientific Evidence for the Most Effective Use of Opiate Agonists in the Treatment of Opiate Dependence?

The Pharmacology of Commonly Prescribed Opiate Agonists and Antagonists

The most frequently used agent in medically supervised opiate withdrawal and maintenance treatment is methadone. Methadone's half-life is approximately 24 hours and leads to a long duration of action and once-a-day dosing. This feature, coupled with its slow onset of action, blunts its euphoric effect, making it unattractive as a principal drug of abuse. LAAM, a less commonly used opiate agonist, has a longer half-life and may prevent withdrawal symptoms for up to 96 hours. An emerging treatment option, buprenorphine, a partial opioid agonist, appears also to be effective for detoxification and maintenance.

Naltrexone is a non-addicting specific "mu" antagonist with a long half-life, permitting once-a-day administration. It effectively blocks the cognitive and behavioral effects of opioids, and its prescription does not require special registration. The opioid-dependent person considering treatment should be informed of the availability of naltrexone maintenance treatment. However, in actively using opiate addicts, it produces immediate withdrawal symptoms with potentially serious effects.

Medically Supervised Withdrawal

Methadone can also be used for detoxification. This can be accomplished over several weeks after a period of illicit opiate use or methadone maintenance. If methadone withdrawal is too rapid, abstinence symptoms are likely. They may lead the opiate-dependent person to illicit drug use and relapse into another cycle of abuse. Buprenorphine holds promise as an option for medically supervised withdrawal because its prolonged occupation of "mu" receptors attenuates withdrawal symptoms.

More rapid detoxification options include use of opiate antagonists alone; the alpha-2 agonist clonidine alone; or clonidine followed by naltrexone. Clonidine reduces many of the autonomic signs and symptoms of opioid withdrawal. These strategies may be used in both inpatient and outpatient settings and allow medically supervised withdrawal from opioids in as little as 3 days. Most patients successfully complete detoxification using these strategies, but information concerning relapse rates is not available.

The Role of Psychosocial Treatments

Nonpharmacologic supportive services are pivotal to successful MMT. The immediate introduction of these services as the opiate-dependent patient applies for MMT leads to significantly higher retention and more comprehensive and effective treatment. Comorbid psychiatric disorders require treatment. Other behavioral strategies have been successfully used in substance abuse treatment. Ongoing substance abuse counseling and other psychosocial therapies enhance program retention and positive outcome. Stable employment is an excellent predictor of clinical outcome. Therefore, vocational rehabilitation is a useful adjunct.

Efficacy of Opiate Agonists

It is now generally agreed that opiate dependence is a medical disorder and that pharmacologic agents are effective in its treatment. Evidence presented to the panel indicates that availability of these agents is severely limited and that large numbers of patients with this disorder have no access to treatment.

The greatest experience with such agents has been with the opiate agonist methadone. Prolonged oral treatment with this medication diminishes and often eliminates opiate use, reduces transmission of many infections, including HIV and hepatitis B and C, and reduces criminal activity. Evidence is now accumulating suggesting that LAAM and buprenorphine are effective in such patients.

For more than 30 years, the daily oral administration of methadone has been used to treat tens of thousands of individuals dependent upon opiates in the United States and abroad. The effectiveness of MMT is dependent on many factors, including adequate dosage, duration plus continuity of treatment, and accompanying psychosocial services. A dose of 60 mg given once daily may achieve the desired treatment goal: abstinence from opiates. But higher doses are often required by many patients. Continuity of treatment is crucial—patients who are treated for fewer than 3 months generally show little or no improvement, and most, if not all, patients require continuous treatment over a period of years and perhaps for life. Therefore, the program has come to be termed methadone "maintenance" treatment (MMT). Patient attributes that have sometimes been linked to better outcomes include older age, later age of dependence onset, less abuse of other substances including cocaine and alcohol, and less criminal activity. Recently, it has been reported that high motivation for change has been associated with positive outcomes.

The effectiveness of MMT is often dependent on the involvement of a knowledgeable and empathetic staff and the availability of psychotherapy and other counseling services.

The latter are especially important since individuals with opiate dependence are often afflicted with comorbid mental and personality disorders.

Because methadone-treated patients generally are exposed to much less or no intravenous opiates, they are much less likely to transmit and contract HIV and hepatitis. This is especially important since recent data have shown that up to 75 percent of new instances of HIV infection are attributable to intravenous drug use. Since for many patients a major source of financing the opiate habit is criminal behavior, MMT generally leads to much less crime.

Although methadone is the primary opioid agonist used, other full and partial opioid agonists have been developed for treatment of opiate dependence. An analogue of methadone, levo-alpha acetylmethadol (LAAM), has a longer half-life than methadone and therefore can be administered less frequently. A single dose of LAAM can prevent withdrawal symptoms and drug craving for 2 to 4 days. Buprenorphine, a recently developed partial opiate agonist, has an advantage over methadone; its discontinuation leads to much less severe withdrawal symptoms. The use of these medications is at an early stage, and it may be some time before their usefulness has been adequately evaluated.

What Are the Important Barriers to Effective Use of Opiate Agonists in the Treatment of Opiate Addiction in the United States?

Misperceptions and Stigmas

Many of the barriers to effective use of MMT in the treatment of opiate dependence stem from misperceptions and stigmas attached to opiate dependence, the people who are addicted, those who treat them, and the settings in which services are provided. Opiate-dependent persons are often perceived not as individuals with a disease but as "other" or "different." Factors such as racism play a large role here but so does the popular image of dependence itself. Many people believe that dependence is self-induced or a failure of willpower and that efforts to treat it will inevitably fail. Vigorous and effective leadership is needed to inform the public that dependence is a medical disorder that can be effectively treated with significant benefits for the patient and society.

Increasing Availability of Effective Services

Unfortunately, MMT programs are not readily available to all who could and wish to benefit from them. We as a society must make a commitment to offering effective treatment for opiate dependence to all who need it. Accomplishing that goal will require:

- Making treatment as cost-effective as possible without sacrificing quality.

- Increasing the availability and variety of treatment services.

- Including and ensuring wider participation by physicians trained in substance abuse who will oversee the medical care.

- Providing additional funding for opiate dependence treatments and coordinating these services with other necessary social services and medical care.

Training Physicians and Other Health Care Professionals

One barrier to availability of MMT is the shortage of physicians and other health care professionals prepared to provide treatment for opiate dependence. Practitioners of all primary care medical specialties (including general practice, internal medicine, family practice, obstetrics and gynecology, geriatrics, pediatrics, and adolescent medicine) should be taught the principles of diagnosing and treating patients with opiate dependence. Nurses, social workers, psychologists, physician assistants, and other health care professionals should also be trained in these areas. The greater the number of trained physicians and other health care professionals, the greater the supply not only of professionals who can competently treat the opiate dependent but also of members of the community who are equipped to provide leadership and public education on these issues.

Reducing Unnecessary Regulation

Of critical importance in improving MMT of opiate dependence is the recognition that, as in every other area of medicine, treatment must be tailored to the needs of the individual patient. Current Federal regulations make this difficult if not impossible. By prescribing MMT procedures in minute detail, FDA's regulations limit the flexibility and responsiveness of the programs, require unproductive paperwork, and impose administrative and oversight costs greater than those necessary for many patients. Yet these regulations seem to have little if any effect on quality of MMT care. We know of no other area where the Federal Government intrudes so deeply and coercively into the practice of medicine. For example, although providing a therapeutic dose is central to effective treatment and the therapeutic dose is now known to be higher than had previously been understood, FDA's regulations discourage such higher doses. However well intended the FDA's treatment regulations were when written in 1972, they are no longer helpful. We recommend that these regulations be eliminated. Alternative means, such as accreditation, for improving quality of MMT programs should be instituted. The U.S. Department of Health and Human Services can more effectively, less coercively, and much less expensively discharge its statutory obligation to provide treatment guidance to MMT programs, physicians, and staff by means of publications, seminars, Web sites, continuing medical education, and the like.

We also believe current laws and regulations should be revised to eliminate the extra level of regulation on methadone compared with other Schedule II narcotics. Currently, methadone can be dispensed only from facilities that obtain an extra license and comply with extensive extra regulatory requirements. These extra requirements are unnecessary for a medication that is not often diverted to individuals for recreational or casual use but rather to individuals with opiate dependence who lack access to MMT programs.

If extra levels of regulation were eliminated, many more physicians and pharmacies could prescribe and dispense methadone, making treatment available in many more locations than is now the case. Not every physician will choose to treat opiate-dependent persons, and not every methadone-treated person will prefer to receive services from an individual physician rather than to receive MMT in a clinic setting. But if some additional physicians and groups treat a few patients each, aggregate access to MMT would be expanded.

We also believe that State and local regulations and enforcement efforts should be coordinated. We see little reason for separate State and Federal inspections of MMT programs. State and Federal regulators should coordinate their efforts, agree about which programs each will inspect to avoid duplication, and target "poor performers" for the most intensive scrutiny while reducing scrutiny for MMT programs that consistently perform well. The States should address the problem of slow approval (at the State level) of FDA-approved medications. LAAM, for example, has not yet been approved by many States. States should harmonize their requirements with those of the Federal Government.

We would expect these changes in the current regulatory system to reduce unnecessary costs both to MMT programs and to enforcement agencies at all levels. The savings could be used to treat more patients.

In the end, an infusion of additional funding will be needed—funding sufficient to provide access to treatment for all who require treatment. We strongly recommend that legislators and regulators recognize that providing MMT is both cost-effective and compassionate and that it constitutes a health benefit that should be a component of public and private health care.

What Are the Future Research Areas and Recommendations for Improving Opiate Agonist Treatment and Improving Access?

* What initiates opiate use?

* Define genetic predispositions.

* Do some individuals take opiates to treat a preexisting disorder?

* Which of the multiple psychological, sociological, and economic factors believed to predispose individuals to try opiates are most important as causative factors?

* If the above are known, can one prevent opiate dependence?

* What are the changes in the human brain that result in dependence when individuals repeatedly use opiates?

* What are the underlying anatomical and neurophysiological substrates of craving?

* What are the differences between individuals who can successfully terminate opiate dependence and those who cannot?

* A scientifically credible national epidemiological study of the prevalence of opiate dependence in the United States is strongly recommended.

* Rigorous study of the economic costs of opiate dependence in the United States and the cost-effectiveness of methadone maintenance therapy is also needed.

* Longer term follow-up studies of patients who complete rapid detoxification are necessary.

* The feasibility of alternative routes of administration for agonist and antagonist therapy should be explored.

* Systematic pharmacokinetic studies of methadone during MMT maintenance therapy are essential.

- Physiologic factors that may influence adequate methadone dose in pregnant women need to be defined.

- The effects of reduction of entitlement programs for those patients on MMT must be assessed.

- The effects of the early and systematic introduction of rehabilitation services in MMT should be evaluated.

- Variables that determine barriers must be defined.

- Research on changing attitudes of the public, of health professionals, and of legislators is needed.

- Research on improving educational methods for health professionals should be performed.

- Research on prevention methods is necessary.

- Research on efficacy of other opiate agonists/antagonists should be compared with that of methadone.

Conclusions and Recommendations

- Vigorous and effective leadership is needed within the Office of National Drug Control Policy (ONDCP) (and related Federal and State agencies) to inform the public that dependence is a medical disorder that can be effectively treated with significant benefits for the patient and society.

- Society must make a commitment to offering effective treatment for opiate dependence to all who need it.

- The panel calls attention to the need for opiate-dependent persons under legal supervision to have access to MMT. The ONDCP and the U.S. Department of Justice should implement this recommendation.

- The panel recommends improved training of physicians and other health care professionals in diagnosis and treatment of opiate dependence. For example, we encourage the National Institute on Drug Abuse and other agencies to provide funds to improve training for diagnosis and treatment of opiate dependence in medical schools.

- The panel recommends that unnecessary regulation of MMT and all long-acting agonist treatment programs be reduced.

- Funding for MMT should be increased.

- We advocate MMT as a benefit in public and private insurance programs, with parity of coverage for all medical and mental disorders.

- We recommend targeting opiate-dependent pregnant women for MMT.

- MMT must be culturally sensitive to enhance a favorable outcome for participating African American and Hispanic persons.

- Patients, underrepresented minorities, and consumers should be included in bodies charged with policy development guiding opiate dependence treatment.

- We recommend expanding the availability of opiate agonist treatment in those States and programs where this treatment option is currently unavailable.

For Additional Information

To receive a copy of the complete report from which this text was excerpted, write to the NIH Consensus Program Information Center, P.O. Box 2577, Kensington, MD 20891; or call toll-free 1-888-NIH-CONSENSUS; or by visit the NIH Consensus Development Program home page on the World Wide Web at http://consensus.nih.gov. The full report includes a list of Consensus Development Panel members, Speakers, Planning Committee members, names of Lead and Supporting Organizations, and a bibliography.

Chapter 44

Higher Doses of Methadone Found to be Safe and Effective

Researchers have demonstrated that methadone can be used safely at dose levels higher than those often considered standard, and that the higher dosages significantly improve treatment outcomes. They also showed that addicts receiving even low doses of the medication are more likely to remain in a treatment program than those receiving no methadone. The study, supported by the National Institute on Drug Abuse (NIDA), National Institutes of Health, is reported in the March 17, 1999 issue of the *Journal of the American Medical Association.*

Despite decades of use in the treatment of opiate addicts, the "optimal" dose for methadone has never been agreed upon. Prescribed doses may be as low as 20-30 mg/d, and current U.S. laws discourage use above 100 mg/d. "This study," says Dr. Alan I. Leshner, Director of NIDA, "indicates that doses greater than 40-50 mg/d significantly improve treatment outcomes for clients in methadone maintenance therapy. But the finding that clients on lower doses have better treatment outcomes than those not on methadone also indicates that a comprehensive treatment program, including behavioral as well as pharmacological therapies, is the most effective treatment regimen for opiate addiction."

Dr. Eric C. Strain, lead author and a member of the Johns Hopkins University School of Medicine study team, agrees that "We found that methadone treatment, even over a very broad range of doses, significantly improves clinical outcomes for opiate addicts. But some addicts

National Institute on Drug Abuse (NIDA), March 1999.

may need doses in excess of 100 mg/d." In an earlier clinical trial, the Hopkins researchers found that low (20-25 mg) daily doses of methadone were less effective than moderate (50-80 mg) doses in reducing opioid use and in retaining patients in treatment, but that, even at the lower doses, addicts receiving methadone showed decreased heroin use. This new study was designed to ascertain whether large doses (greater than 80 mg) were more effective than moderate doses in reducing illicit drug use.

The study team recruited 192 addicts seeking treatment for opioid dependence. The study subjects had to be over the age of 18, be currently dependent on intravenous opioids, have a history of prior methadone treatment, and have a positive urine sample for opioids. The patients were admitted to a 40-week methadone treatment program and randomly assigned to 1 of 2 methadone dose schedules. Ninety-seven patients received 40-50 mg of methadone each day, and 95 received 80 to 100 mg per day. All patients received concurrent substance abuse counseling.

Prior to their admission to the study, the patients reported that they had used opioids an average of 24 times a week. During the latter part of the study, the high-dose group reported using illicit opioids once or fewer times a week, while the moderate-dose group reported using such drugs 2 to 3 times a week.

Through week 30, patients in the high-dose group had lower rates (53 percent) of opioid-positive urine samples, compared to patients in the moderate-dose group (61.9 percent). The average number of days each remained in treatment was virtually identical for the two groups: 159 days out of a possible 210 days for the high-dose group, and 157 days for the moderate-dose group. One third of the patients in the high dose group, and 11 percent of the patients in the moderate-dose group, completed the detoxification program in weeks 31 to 40.

These findings, coupled with the results of the earlier clinical trial, indicate that addicts benefit from methadone during treatment, and that improvements in keeping them in treatment occur as the methadone dose is increased at least to a moderate range (50 mg/d).

Chapter 45

Buprenorphine Update

Is buprenorphine (alone and in combination) a safe and effective treatment for drug addiction?

While the ultimate decision concerning safety and efficacy rests with the Food and Drug Administration (FDA), NIDA has funded many studies that support the safety and efficacy of buprenorphine and the buprenorphine/naloxone combination for the treatment of opiate dependence. During the time NIDA has studied this medication, we have been impressed with its safety and efficacy as a treatment for opiate dependence. Over the last five years NIDA has worked with Reckitt & Colman Pharmaceuticals, Inc., under a Cooperative Research and Development Agreement in an attempt to bring buprenorphine (which the FDA has designated as an orphan product), to a marketable status in the United States. These studies have been submitted by Reckitt & Colman to the FDA in support of a New Drug Application for buprenorphine products in the treatment of opiate dependence. The major studies of relevance have shown that buprenorphine is more effective than a low dose of methadone (Johnson et al, *JAMA*, 1992), and that an orderly dose effect of buprenorphine on reduction of opiate use occurred (Ling et al, *Addiction*, 1998).

Most recently, buprenorphine tablets (either buprenorphine alone or the combination with naloxone) were shown in a large clinical trial to be superior to placebo treatment in reducing opiate use (Fudala et al, *CPDD*, 1998). Additional clinical studies have shown that the addition

National Institute on Drug Abuse (NIDA), March 1999.

of naloxone to the buprenorphine tablet decreased the response to buprenorphine when the combination is injected under controlled conditions. This means that when persons attempt to dissolve the tablets and inject them, they will either experience withdrawal or a diminished buprenorphine effect. These properties will make buprenorphine combined with naloxone undesirable for diversion to illicit use, especially when compared with other existing illegal and legal opiate products.

Pharmacologically, buprenorphine is related to morphine but is a partial agonist (possesses both agonist and antagonist properties). Partial agonists exhibit ceiling effects (i.e., increasing the dose only has effects to a certain level). Therefore, partial agonists usually have greater safety profiles than full agonists (such as heroin or morphine and certain analgesic products chemically related to morphine). This means that buprenorphine is less likely to cause respiratory depression, the major toxic effect of opiate drugs, in comparison to full agonists such as morphine or heroin. We believe this will translate into a greatly reduced chance of accidental or intentional overdose. Another benefit of buprenorphine is that the withdrawal syndrome seen upon discontinuation with buprenorphine is, at worst, mild to moderate and can often be managed without administration of narcotics.

Do current regulations properly set forth the rules for administration, delivery, and use of these drugs?

There are no current regulations which address the use of buprenorphine or buprenorphine/naloxone for the treatment of opiate dependence because these products are not yet approved for this purpose by the FDA. The current regulations (21 CFR 291) for administration and delivery of narcotic medications in the treatment of narcotic dependent persons were written for the use of full agonist medications such as methadone with demonstrated abuse potential and do not take into account the unique pharmacological properties of these drugs. Therefore, these regulations would need to be re-examined and substantially rewritten in order to recognize the unique possibilities posed by buprenorphine/naloxone. Among these are the potential to administer buprenorphine and buprenorphine/naloxone in settings and situations other than the formal Narcotic Treatment Programs (NTPs) which have existed to date under existing regulations. NTPs are the most highly regulated form of medicine practiced in the U.S., as they are subject to Federal, State, and local regulation. Under this regulatory burden, expansion of this system has been static for many years. This has resulted in a "treatment gap," which is defined as the difference between the number of opiate dependent persons and those in treatment. The gap currently is over 600,000 persons and represents 75-80% of all addicts.

It may be useful to note the status of the last new product introduced to the opiate dependence treatment market (levo-alpha-acetylmethadol, trade name ORLAAM). ORLAAM was an orphan product developed by NIDA and a U.S. small business in the early 1990s for narcotic dependence. ORLAAM was approved by the FDA as a treatment medication for opiate dependence in July 1993. In the five years since its approval and dispensing under the more restrictive rules relating to the use of full agonist medications (21 CFR 291), ORLAAM has been poorly utilized to increase treatment for narcotic dependence. It is estimated that 2,000 of the estimated 120,000 patients in narcotic treatment programs are receiving ORLAAM. The failure of ORLAAM to make an appreciable impact under the more restrictive rules suggests that if buprenorphine is to make an appreciable impact on the "treatment gap" it must be delivered under different rules and regulations.

The issue then becomes why should buprenorphine products be delivered differently from ORLAAM and methadone. First, buprenorphine's different pharmacology should be kept in mind when rules and regulations are promulgated. The regulatory burden should be determined based on a review of the risks to individuals and society of this medication being dispensed by prescription and commensurate with its safety profile, as is the case with evaluation of all controlled substances. It is our understanding that the Drug Enforcement Administration has recognized the difference between buprenorphine treatment products and those currently subject to 21 CFR 291. Second, there are many narcotic addicts who refuse treatment under the current system. In a recent NIDA funded study (NIDA/VA1008), approximately 50% of the subjects had never been in treatment before. Of that group, fully half maintained that they did not want treatment in the current narcotic treatment program system. The opportunity to participate in a new treatment regimen (buprenorphine) was a motivating factor. Fear of stigmatization is a very real factor holding back narcotic dependent individuals from entering treatment. Third, narcotic addiction is spreading from urban to suburban areas. The current system, which tends to be concentrated in urban areas, is a poor fit for the suburban spread of narcotic addiction. There are many communities whose zoning will not permit the establishment of narcotic treatment facilities, which has in part been responsible for the treatment gap described above. While narcotic treatment capacity has been static, there has been an increase in the amount of heroin of high purity. The high purity of this heroin has made it possible to nasally ingest (snort) or smoke heroin. This change in the route of heroin administration removes a major taboo, injection and its attendant use of needles, from initiation and experimentation with heroin use. The result of these new routes of administration is an increase in the number of younger Americans experimenting with, and becoming addicted to, heroin. The incidence of first-time use of heroin in the 12 to 17 year old group has increased fourfold from the 1980s to 1995. Treatment for adolescents should be accessible, and graduated to the level of dependence exhibited in the patient. Buprenorphine products will likely be the initial medication(s) for most of the heroin-dependent adolescents.

Should more physicians be permitted to dispense these drugs under controlled circumstances?

More treatment should be made more widely available for the reasons stated above. The safety and effectiveness profiles for buprenorphine and buprenorphine/naloxone suggest they could be dispensed under controlled circumstances that would be delineated in the product labeling and associated rules and regulations. As currently envisioned, buprenorphine and buprenorphine/naloxone would be prescription, Schedule V controlled substances. The treatment of patients by physicians or group practice would allow office-based treatment to augment the current system, while placing an adequate level of control on the dispensing of these medications. Given the increased need for treatment, the relative safety and efficacy of the treatment product, and the development of a regulatory scheme satisfactory to the Department of Health and Human Services, these goals could be accomplished in a timely and effective manner.

Chapter 46

Blood-Borne Medications Could Intercept Drugs before They Reach the Brain

The damage done by cocaine and other drugs of abuse takes place among neurons deep in the brain, but the drugs are transported to these nerve cells by the blood. A number of researchers are investigating possible medications that could intercept and neutralize cocaine and other drugs in the bloodstream, preventing them from initiating the neurochemical reactions that lead to abuse and addiction.

"This represents a different approach to therapeutic research, which has most often focused on interfering with a drug's activity in the brain. This strategy is aimed at preventing the drug from reaching the brain," says Dr. Steven Sparenborg of NIDA's Medications Development Division.

Blood-borne medications, referred to as peripheral blockers, would offer several advantages over other pharmacological approaches to addictions, notes Dr. David Gorelick of NIDA's Intramural Research Program. They do not require knowledge of how or where the abused drug acts in the brain, they would be effective against drugs with multiple sites of action in the brain, and they could protect against a drug's actions—such as cardiovascular toxicity—at sites outside the central nervous system.

Peripheral blockers are modeled after the enzymes and antibodies of the body's natural defense system, according to Dr. Sparenborg.

"Blood-Borne Medications Could Intercept Drugs before They Reach the Brain," by Patrick Zickler, in *NIDA Notes*, Vol. 14, No. 2, 1999, National Institute on Drug Abuse (NIDA).

One peripheral blocker approach would bind drugs like cocaine, phencyclidine (PCP), or nicotine to antibodies, creating a drug-antibody complex that is too large to move through blood vessel walls into the brain. This would trap the drug within the bloodstream until it could be eliminated from the body through normal kidney activity. Another approach would enhance the rate at which naturally occurring enzymes break down drug molecules into inactive byproducts. A third method under investigation employs an engineered antibody that both binds to and breaks down drugs. Although individuals might overcome the action of these peripheral blockades by taking more of the drug and overwhelming the antibody or enzyme, effective blood-borne medications would serve as valuable components of treatment programs that protect against relapse or counteract acute toxic effects from drugs of abuse.

"There is still a long way to go with this research, but the validity of the approach has been demonstrated in animal tests. First-phase clinical trials of an active cocaine vaccine are under way now, and we're encouraged by the progress," says Dr. Sparenborg.

Immunization

Molecules as small as cocaine typically do not trigger the body's immune system to create antibodies. However, Dr. Barbara Fox and her colleagues at ImmuLogic Pharmaceutical Corporation in Waltham, Massachusetts, have developed a technique that links cocaine derivatives to a larger protein molecule, or carrier, to stimulate an immune reaction. Animals vaccinated with the cocaine-carrier combination develop cocaine-specific antibodies that bind with cocaine in the blood, preventing most of the drug from reaching the brain. These results suggest that catalytic antibodies have the unique potential both to treat the acute effects of cocaine overdose and to block some of the chronic reinforcing effects of abuse.

"In mice, the vaccine induced an antibody response that kept cocaine from reaching its targets in the central nervous system," says Dr. Fox, now with Addiction Therapies, Inc., in Wayland, Massachusetts. "And it appears to be long-lasting. Periodic boosters maintained the response for more than a year, which is a significant portion of a mouse's life."

The vaccine, which is currently being studied in first-phase human trials by researchers with Cantab Pharmaceuticals, uses a protein that generates a strong antibody response as a carrier. More than two dozen fragments of the cocaine molecule are bound to the carrier.

When injected into animals, the large protein molecules stimulate the production of antibodies that recognize the cocaine fragments. Moreover, the antibodies also bind to norcocaine, one of cocaine's minor but pharmacologically active metabolites, or byproducts, but do not bind to the more abundant but inactive ones. "This means that the antibodies don't become saturated with inactive metabolites and lose the capacity to bind with cocaine," Dr. Fox says.

Dr. Fox and her colleagues found that injecting cocaine into rats immunized with the compound resulted in significantly higher levels of cocaine in the blood, and correspondingly lower levels in the brain, than did injecting the same amount of cocaine into nonimmunized animals. As much as 63 percent of administered cocaine was bound in the blood as soon as 30 seconds after administration. In addition, immunized rats were much less likely to self-administer cocaine than were nonimmunized rats. This finding, Dr. Fox notes, suggests that the vaccine could help prevent relapse in patients in drug treatment programs. "This is not a 'magic bullet' treatment. Patients could overcome it by taking more drug. But for motivated patients it could be a very valuable part of a comprehensive treatment program," Dr. Fox says.

Enzymes

Naturally occurring enzymes can break down cocaine and other drugs before they reach the brain, but they cannot rapidly neutralize the amounts of drugs that are typically ingested by drug abuse patients. Studies involving cocaine abusers suffering acute toxic reactions show a significant relationship between activity levels in the blood of butyrylcholinesterase (BChE), an enzyme produced in the liver, and the severity of cocaine toxicity. Patients with severe reactions to cocaine tend to have lower levels of BChE. NIDA-supported research has demonstrated that enhancing BChE activity can lead to improved treatment of cocaine overdose.

Gilberto Carmona, a doctoral student in NIDA's Intramural Research Program, has shown that the metabolism of cocaine in the blood can be dramatically increased and the drug's effects decreased by raising BChE activity. Mr. Carmona and his colleagues demonstrated that cocaine half-life—the time needed for half the drug to be cleared from the blood—dropped from more than 5 hours to less than 5 minutes in rats pretreated with purified BChE that raised the enzyme's blood activity 400-fold. The increase in BChE activity significantly decreased the increased motor activity caused by a cocaine injection and changed the pattern of cocaine metabolism, resulting in production of predominantly nontoxic byproducts rather than pharmacologically active ones.

NIDA-supported researcher Dr. Oksana Lockridge at the University of Nebraska in Omaha has found that naturally occurring variations in human BChE have different capacities for cocaine metabolism. "People who don't have the typical variant may react to a 'standard' dose of cocaine as though it were an overdose," Dr. Lockridge says. "Other variants exist at levels as low as one-third of normal levels, and people with these variants are probably at very high risk for cocaine toxicity."

Building on this knowledge of BChE variants, Dr. Lockridge and her colleagues engineered a mutant form of BChE—designated A328Y—that demonstrated four times the catalytic activity of normal BChE when tested in the laboratory. Dr. Kenneth Dretchen at Georgetown University in Washington, D.C., is conducting animal trials of A328Y to determine if the more active variant can be used as a treatment for cocaine overdose. "We know that the butyrylcholinesterase can reduce cocaine-induced convulsions, hyperactivity, and hypertension, and we know that A328Y will act much more aggressively to break cocaine down into inactive metabolites. A328Y could prove to be a valuable 'crash cart' tool for treating acute cocaine toxicity in emergency room situations," he says.

Catalytic Antibodies

Dr. Donald Landry, a researcher at Columbia University College of Physicians and Surgeons in New York City, has developed a cocaine-specific catalytic antibody—a compound that combines features of antibodies that bind to cocaine molecules with features of enzymes that break the drug down into inactive fragments.

The catalytic antibody developed by Dr. Landry and his colleagues uses a molecule that mimics the structure of a cocaine molecule in its transition state—the shape of a cocaine molecule undergoing a chemical reaction. When the catalytic antibody binds to cocaine, the drug molecule takes on the configuration of the transition state. "This accelerates the rate of cocaine hydrolysis to inactive fragments. The antibody then releases the fragments and is free to bind to another cocaine molecule and initiate another cycle," Dr. Landry explains.

"Each molecule of the most potent antibody we have developed breaks down more than 2 cocaine molecules per minute and retains more than 95 percent of its activity through at least 200 turnovers," Dr. Landry says.

Animal tests of the antibody—designated mAB 15A10—demonstrate that it can reduce the toxic effects of cocaine overdose. Other tests show that pretreatment with the compound will prevent rats from self-administering cocaine.

"These results suggest that catalytic antibodies have the unique potential both to treat the acute effects of cocaine overdose and to block some of the chronic reinforcing effects of abuse," Dr. Landry says. "A humanized version of the antibody mAB 15A10 could be useful either as an emergency treatment for overdose or as part of a broader treatment program for addiction."

Sources

Carmona, G.N., et al. Attenuation of cocaine-induced locomotor activity by butyrylcholinesterase. *Experimental and Clinical Psychopharmacology* 6(3):274-279, 1998.

Fox, B.S., et al. Efficacy of a therapeutic cocaine vaccine in rodent models. *Nature Medicine* 2(10):1129-1132, 1996.

Fox, B.S. Development of a therapeutic vaccine for the treatment of cocaine addiction. *Drug and Alcohol Dependence* 48:153-158, 1997.

Gorelick, D.A. Enhancing cocaine metabolism with butyrylcholinesterase as a treatment strategy. *Drug and Alcohol Dependence* 48:159-165, 1997.

Landry, D.W. Immunotherapy for cocaine addiction. *Scientific American* 276(2):42-45, 1997.

Mattes, C.E.; Belendiuk, G.W.; Lynch, T.J.; Brady, R.O.; and Dretchen, K.L. Butyrylcholinesterase: An enzyme antidote for cocaine intoxication. *Addiction Biology* 3:171-188, 1998.

Mets, B.; Winger, G.; Cabrera, C.; Seo, S.; Jamdar, S.; Yang, G.; Zhao, K.; Briscoe, R.J.; Almonte, R.; Woods, J.H.; and Landry, D.W. A catalytic antibody against cocaine prevents cocaine's reinforcing and toxic effects in rats. *Proceedings of the National Academy of Sciences* 95:10176-10181, 1998.

Sparenborg, S.; Vocci, F.; and Zukin, S. Peripheral cocaine-blocking agents: New medications for cocaine dependence. *Drug and Alcohol Dependence* 48:149-151, 1997.

Xie, W.; Altimirano, C.V.; Bartels, C.F.; Speirs, R.J.; Cashman, J.R.; and Lockridge, O. An improved cocaine hydrolase: The A328Y mutant of human butyrylcholinesterase is 4-fold more efficient. *Molecular Pharmacology* 55(1):83-91, 1999.

Chapter 47

Antistress Medications May Help Drug Abuse Patients Avoid Relapse

A class of medications currently being developed by several pharmaceutical companies may help drug abuse patients avoid relapse after experiencing stress. Called CRF antagonists, the compounds block the action of corticotropin-releasing factor (CRF), a naturally occurring chemical in the brain. Scientists think that CRF may play a key role in producing arousal, anxiety, and other emotional responses to stress.

Dr. Yavin Shaham, formerly of the University of Toronto and now in NIDA's Intramural Research Program in Baltimore; NIDA grantee Dr. Jane Stewart of Concordia University in Montreal; and their colleagues at Concordia University and the Addiction Research Foundation in Toronto have conducted a series of studies to determine whether CRF antagonists can prevent stress-induced relapse to drug-seeking in rats. In these studies, rats were trained to press a lever to receive a dose of cocaine or heroin. After the rats learned this behavior, the supply of drugs was terminated so that pressing the lever no longer resulted in a dose of drug. As a result, the rats reduced their lever pressing to practically nothing. However, when the rats were given mild intermittent footshocks for 10 to 15 minutes, they started to press the lever again as soon as it became available, even though they did not receive any drug. This indicates that stress can reinstate drug seeking in rats, just as it is reported to do in human addicts, says Dr. Stewart.

NIDA Notes, Vol. 14, No. 1, 1999, National Institute on Drug Abuse (NIDA).

The researchers found that giving the rats a CRF antagonist prior to giving them footshocks could greatly reduce the rate at which the rats would press the lever again. However, the compound had no effect when the rats were pressing a lever to receive a drop of sugar solution that they could drink. "This suggests that the CRF antagonist blocks stress-induced relapse to drug seeking specifically and does not produce its effects by interfering with the animal's ability to press the lever," says Dr. Stewart.

Results such as these have interested staff in NIDA's Medications Development Division (MDD) in the potential of CRF antagonists for treating drug abuse relapse. "What's so interesting about CRF antagonists is that evidence suggests that they may be useful in treating relapse to a variety of drugs, including cocaine, heroin, and nicotine," says Dr. Jane Acri of MDD. "This is particularly important considering that people who abuse drugs often abuse a number of different drugs."

Source

Shaham, Y.; Erb, S.; Leung, S.; Buczek, Y.; and Stewart, J. CP-154,526, a selective, non-peptide antagonist of the corticotropin-releasing factor 1 receptor attenuates stress-induced relapse to drug seeking in cocaine- and heroin-trained rats. *Psychopharmacology* 137:184-190, 1998.

Chapter 48

Serotonin Agonist Reduces Craving in Cocaine Addicts

Evidence suggests that serotonin may play a role in cocaine craving among substance abusers, according to an article published in *The American Journal on Addictions*.

Investigators Laure Buydens-Branchey, M.D., and colleagues from the SUNY Health Science Center in Brooklyn, say that the administration of meta-chlorophenylpiperazine (m-CPP), a serotonin agonist, can significantly reduce feelings of craving in cocaine addicts, suggesting that serotonin systems play a role in the complex experience called craving. Studies in laboratory rats have shown that manipulations of the serotonin brain system will reduce cocaine self-administration.

The investigators studied response to m-CPP in a group of 31 male cocaine addicts who were hospitalized in an inpatient drug rehabilitation unit.

Subjects who had been drug free for a period of 12 to 19 days participated in two test sessions conducted 48 hours apart. During the sessions, subjects received identical looking capsules containing either m-CPP or a placebo. The investigators rated side effects on a four-point scale. In addition, they asked subjects to "assess the chance the would use cocaine if they were not in the "hospital and had unlimited financial resources" by placing a mark on a 100-mm line with 0 indicating no chance, and 100 indicating certain cocaine use.

The Brown University Digest of Addiction Theory and Application, Vol. 16, No. 8, August 1997, p. 1(3), © 1997 Manisses Communications Group Inc.; reprinted with permission of Manisses Communication Group.

These assessments took place 30 minutes before and 30, 90, 150, and 210 minutes after m-CPP or placebo administration. The investigators assessed side effects as well as psychological changes using a modified version of the NIMH self-rating scale, which measures anxiety, activation-euphoria, depressive affect, dysphoria, altered self-reality, and functional deficit.

Responses indicated that subjects experienced side effects after m-CPP administration, including nausea, chills, and dizziness. In addition, those who received m-CPP reported psychological changes as reflected in increased scores on the NIMH self-report in anxiety, activity-euphoria, and altered self-reality.

Sixteen subjects reported feeling craving for cocaine before administering both placebo and m-CPP and are included in the primary analysis. The remaining 15 subjects did not consistently report craving in the test setting. While "there seemed to be a moderate decline in craving in the course of the placebo test sessions," the investigators say that "the decrease in craving after m-CPP, on the other hand, appeared to be more dramatic." In fact, by 90 minutes after m-CPP administration, "craving had decreased to 20% of its initial value."

Analyses showed that the changes in craving were not associated with other drug side effects or self-reported psychological changes. In addition, there was no correlation between baseline craving and other variables, including time since last cocaine intake, average daily amount and maximum daily amount of cocaine use during the month before admission, or frequency of cocaine use during the same period.

Authors' Conclusions

The investigators conclude that "patients" craving for cocaine decreased significantly after the administration of the 5-HT [serotonin] partial agonist m-CPP."

The small decline in craving reported by subjects in the placebo group "could be attributed to either a placebo effect or to circadian variations in craving." In subjects receiving m-CPP, the decline in craving was much more significant, lasted until the end of the test period, and was not influenced by drug induced changes in the subjects' physical and psychological state.

What this means, the authors say, is that "it would appear that multiple factors can influence cocaine craving. Although the role of internal cues (such as dysphoria) or environmental cues (such as those bringing to mind previous drug use) has been demonstrated, a modulation of craving by neurotransmitters, and by 5-HT in particular, should be considered as well."

Additional Reading

Pickens, R.W., Johanson, C.E. Craving: Consensus of status and agenda for future research. *Drug and Alcohol Dependency*, 30:127-131, 1992.

Satel, S.L., Krystal, J.H., et al. Tryptophan depletion and attenuation of cue-induced craving for cocaine. *American Journal of Psychiatry*, 152:778-782, 1995.

Laure Buydens-Branchey, Marc Branchey. Paul Fergeson, Jeffrey Hudson, Craig McKernin. Craving for cocaine in addicted users: Role of serotonergic mechanisms. *The American Journal on Addictions*, 665-73, 1997.

Chapter 49

Methylphenidate Reduces Drug Cravings in Cocaine Users with Attention Deficit/ Hyperactivity Disorder

A new study has shown that methylphenidate (Ritalin), a stimulant used to treat attention-deficit/hyperactivity disorder (ADHD), may also be effective in reducing drug cravings in cocaine users. Investigators from New York State Psychiatric Institute (NYSPI), writing in the *Journal of Clinical Psychiatry*, say that after a three-month follow-up, cocaine users treated with methylphenidate were less likely to have relapsed.

Frances R. Levin and colleagues tested methylphenidate in a sample of cocaine users who also had ADHD. Potential subjects were recruited by advertisements, and were subsequently screened for ADHD using two self-report ratings of ADHD, the Wender Utah Rating Scale (WURS) and the Adult Behavior Checklist (ABC). Subjects with elevated scores on one or both of these screens were further assessed using the Structured Clinical Interview for *DSM-IV* Axis I and II Disorders (SCID I and SCID-II).

The ten subjects who met criteria received 40 to 80 mg/day of sustained release methylphenidate, which they received during visits to the NYSPI cocaine clinic. Throughout the study, ADHD symptoms were assessed weekly using the Targeted Attention Deficit Disorder Symptoms Scale (TADDS) and the ABC. Substance abuse was assessed at baseline, at weeks six and 12, and at three-month follow-up

"Methylphenidate reduces drug cravings in cocaine users with ADHD," by F.R. Levin; S.M. Evans; D.M. McDowell; and H.D. Kleber in *The Brown University Digest of Addiction Theory and Application*, Vol. 16, No. 8, January 1999, p. 5(1), © 1999 Manisses Communications Group Inc.; reprinted with permission of Manisses Communications Group.

using the Addiction Severity Index (ASI) and through regular urine samples. Throughout the study, subjects also received standardized, individual relapse prevention therapy.

Investigators found that there were significant improvements in ADHD symptoms as observed using the TADDS and the ABC. Mood lability was the only symptom that did not show significant improvement during the study period.

Investigators found that cocaine use among subjects also decreased, from 9.8 days in the four weeks before study entry to 1.1 days in the last four weeks of study enrollment. Among seven patients who were available for three-month follow-up, three who were still being treated with methylphenidate gave urine samples that were negative for cocaine. Two of the remaining four subjects tested positive for cocaine use.

Study Limits

The authors note that the effectiveness of methylphenidate in this study may have been influenced or produced by the study's open, rather than double-blind, design; by support the subjects received through interaction with staff; and, by the therapeutic benefit of relapse prevention therapy. In fact, several previously seemingly promising medications for cocaine dependence have failed when subjected to the rigor of a double-blind study.

Authors' Conclusions

The authors conclude that "sustained release methylphenidate, in daily doses up to 80 mg, may reduce ADHD symptoms, cocaine craving and cocaine use among cocaine users with ADHD."

Authors' Recommendations

More double-blind studies of methylphenidate for this population are warranted. In an interview, Levin told *The Brown University Digest of Addiction Theory and Application* that studies are under way on the comorbidity of cocaine dependence and other psychiatric conditions including depression, bipolar disorder and schizophrenia.

Suggested Reading

Mannuzza S., Klein R.G., Bonagura N., et al.: Adult outcome of hyperactive boys: educational achievement, occupational rank and psychiatric status. *Archives of General Psychiatry* 1993: 48:77-83.

Schubiner H., Tzelepis A., Issacson J.H., et al.: The dual diagnosis of attention-deficit/hyperactivity disorder and substance abuse: case reports and literature review. *Journal of Clinical Psychiatry* 1995; 56:146-150.

Levin F.R., Evans S.M., McDowell D.M., Kleber H.D.: Methylphenidate treatment for cocaine abusers with adult attention-deficit/hyperactivity disorder: a pilot study. *Journal of Clinical Psychiatry* 1998; 59:300-305.

Chapter 50

The Changing Face of Addictions Treatment

As with so many aspects of behavioral health treatment, treatment of substance abuse disorders is undergoing basic change. What is intensifying this change are evolving client needs and programmatic priorities. Clinical practices are being challenged by clients who are "multi-needy" —often presenting with concurrent personality disorders, mental health issues, developmental impairments, polysubstance dependency, and often greater need for primary health care services. These are altering conventional approaches to treatment and are prompting the establishment of specialized addictions programming services.

Polydrug-addicted clients' needs have forced skills development and cognitive behavioral therapy to the forefront of treatment programming. Relapse initiatives at all levels of treatment have become an essential ingredient to a new "harm reduction" model—a concept that accents the idea that polydrug clients will more than likely relapse but will not, as in past years, face automatic discharge or referral to higher levels of care.

The new "addictions therapist" needs to work with a collaborative treatment team to provide a seamless continuum of addictions, mental health, and primary health care. And this requires new therapeutic skills and competencies.

"The Changing Face of Addictions Treatment: With Society's Help, the Field Is Reinventing Itself to Meet Today's Needs," by Richard C. Washousky and George A. Thomas in *Behavioral Health Management*, Vol. 16, No. 2, March-April 1996, p. 30(2), © 1996 Medquest Communications, Inc.; reprinted with permission.

Beyond this, however, Medicaid managed care, insurance plan gatekeeping and health reform proposals are stressing client access, improved treatment quality, customer satisfaction, outcomes accountability and cost-effectiveness. We no longer have a treatment system that divides providers according to licensure definition of alcohol abuse, substance abuse, or mental health treatment. Nor do we have a treatment system in which 70% of Federal funding should be directed toward a winless war on drugs.

Today's System Needs

- A seamless continuity of care that links or networks agencies into an operational, comprehensive partnership treatment system, based primarily on outpatient intensive services.

- New treatment programming models which emphasize polydrug addictions treatment modalities, including urge management, relapse prevention, changing the addict's subculture identity, and managing protracted drug withdrawal symptomatology.

- Early introduction of vocational rehabilitation activities, comprehensive child and family services, and a strong emphasis on drug-intensive day rehabilitation services as an alternative to inpatient care.

- Increases in alternatives to incarceration programs, with liaison with local drug court systems and networking with mandated addictions service agencies.

- Standardized criteria for client placement, continued stay and discharge.

- Increased professional growth opportunities for clinicians to enhance skills and competencies, while experimenting with new treatment approaches within a clinical environment emphasizing cultural sensitivity and diversity.

Alternatives to incarceration are including inpatient and outpatient programs that address structured accountability, basic client habilitation and rehabilitation needs, with a strong emphasis on group experiential therapy. The essential components of treatment-related drug courts today include mandated periodic drug testing, compliance safeguards, offender management, and closely monitored collaborative continue care services and relapse prevention skills training.

There is no question, of course, that there are significant resisters to change among addictions professionals, due to possible lack of skills, provider burnout, and/or simple fear of change. Recognizing this should in no way impede support for an addictions treatment field pursuing constructive change.

There must be a reallocation of Federal dollars toward effective and efficient comprehensive models for prevention, intervention, and treatment. There must be less emphasis, especially in today's era of fiscal restraint, on criminal justice enforcement, and more support for alternatives to incarceration. The addictions treatment system must move beyond bureaucratic realignments and ecopolitics to the credentialing of a "new polydrug addictions treatment professional" who has the ability to service the high-risk clients who are now the case load norm for most addictions agencies.

The level of staff development and inservice training will have to be emphasized to more effectively service these special clients, to emphasize the relationships and congruence among individual, group, and specialty therapy activities, to develop case management strategies, and to instill cultural and gender sensitivity into clinical practices and operations.

Privileging or credentialing of professional staff must reflect cross-disciplinary training, awareness of community-based domestic violence counseling, holistic case management, *DSM-IV* standards, and increasing knowledge of how to treat clients with multiple disorders. The traditional philosophical dichotomies between mental health providers and addictions treatment counselors must be reduced. Most importantly, certification of clinicians must address the issues of polydrug addiction rather than the conventional separation of alcohol and substance abuse treatment.

Accountability and cost effectiveness will necessitate maintaining a functional, comprehensive partnership-based treatment system—from detoxification through supportive structured living for those addicted. All levels of prevention activity must be pursued within school systems, community agencies, and treatment programs.

Inpatient and outpatient services will have to add standardized assessment tools, such as the Substance Disorder Diagnostic Schedule (SUDDS), the Recovery Attitude Treatment Evaluator (RATE), and the Addictions Severity Index (ASI) Standardized, and computer-based screening, assessment and pre- and post-treatment evaluation instruments.

Access to limited charity dollars will be more and more competitive and focused. Foundations require more justification of need, using outcomes documentation. No longer will treatment agencies receive continuous demonstration funding. Fiscal management, cost containment, and cost effectiveness are new bench marks for addictions treatment providers. The ability to integrate quality care with financial livelihood can, and should, reduce the demands for Federal, state, and local grant dollars. Monies no longer needed to sustain operations can be redirected (one would hope) to under-serviced populations and new methodologies.

In sum, the changes currently underway and the transformations that they will bring about are exciting to contemplate—and also, at times, exasperating, if not frustrating.

Nevertheless, if we are willing to invest in altering our present paradigms, we will model a new, coordinated approach to addictions treatment for the 21st century—one that is, indeed, "keeping up with the times."

About the Authors

Richard C. Washousky, MS, CRC, NCC is Executive Director for the Erie County (New York) Medical Center, Division of Chemical Dependency. He has over 21 years of experience working with alcoholism and chemical dependency. He is also the Professor/Department Head for Erie Community College's Mental Health Assistant: Alcohol and Substance Abuse Degree Program.

George A. Thomas, MA is the Management Consultant to the Division of Chemical Dependency's Outpatient Services and has implemented Total Quality Management throughout the Department's Administrative, Programmatic and Clinical Operations. He is the former Vice President of Academic Affairs for Erie Community College.

Chapter 51

Clinician Adds Cultural Element to Relapse Prevention Model

In recent years, many addiction treatment administrators responded to the need to have a strategy to combat client relapse for each person entering treatment. Experience is now teaching the field that one size does not necessarily fit all patients when it comes to preventing relapse.

The work of an African-American clinician and a leading expert in relapse prevention has generated a culturally specific relapse prevention model that, while targeted to African-American clients, could help treatment programs identify relapse triggers in a variety of special populations.

The model builds on the Chicago-based CENAPS Corp.'s relapse prevention strategy, which supports ongoing identification and management of relapse warning signs in community recovery settings. Roland Williams, clinical coordinator for outpatient services at Good Samaritan Hospital in San Jose, California, has worked with CENAPS owner Terence T. Gorski to create a model tailored to the African-American community's needs.

As an African-American in the addiction treatment field, Williams was particularly frustrated that African-American clients were experiencing a disproportionately high number of relapses. "I had a lot of concerns about what alcohol and drug dependence were doing to the

Alcoholism & Drug Abuse Week, Vol. 10, No. 5, February 2, 1998, p. 1(3), © Manisses Communications Group; reprinted with permission of Manisses Communications Group.

black community," he told *Alcoholism & Drug Abuse Week (ADAW)*. "It's pretty heartbreaking."

A lack of insurance and a dearth of treatment centers in African-American neighborhoods have contributed to a high number of second- and third-generation drug users in the black community, said Williams, who is also president of the Free Life Enterprises counseling and consulting service. And for those who can get to treatment, the care they receive too often ignores issues unique to the African-American community, he said.

Similarly, Gorski noticed that the African-American clients he was seeing were discontinuing aftercare at a rate approaching a staggering 80 to 90 percent. In a number of centers where he worked, programs that were set up to treat a predominantly white, middle-class clientele, "Our black clients tended to either be more quiet and reserved or they were angry and acted out."

"There are issues that people from the outside can't get a handle on," Gorski told *ADAW*, emphasizing that while a member of the dominant culture can in theory understand the existence of racial differences, he or she still may not be able to identify with the feelings of a minority group member.

His observations helped Gorski decide that the CENAPS model—which always had been offered as culturally neutral—needed to be tailored to minority populations, which research is showing have their own set of relapse triggers.

Williams set out to develop a model that not only would take into account factors specific to the African-American client population, but that also could be used as a template for developing relapse prevention models for other groups, such as Hispanics, gays, or health care professionals.

In his book *Relapse Prevention Counseling for African-Americans: A Culturally Specific Model*, Williams outlines his initial research with 200 African-Americans in successful recovery. "The results [of Williams' survey] surprised me about the degree to which race and cultural issues interfered with recovery," Gorski said.

Working from his research, his own clinical experiences, meetings with other African-American clinicians and the original CENAPS warning-signs list compiled by Gorski in 1973, Williams developed a list of 22 culturally specific relapse warning signs for African-Americans. Many involve self-esteem issues that, while similar to those seen in white addicts, are experienced differently in the black community.

"Most clinicians already have good counseling skills. What they need are vehicles to connect with their clients," Williams said. "I'm not trying to replace anyone's clinical style, but simply to enhance it. I'm trying to build a bridge."

Williams is quick to point out that while some clients experience one or two of the 22 warning signs, some experience 20. Likewise, he emphasizes that they occur in no predictable order. The warning signs take into account a number of cultural pressures unique to African-Americans, Williams said, and generally fall into categories such as victimization, aggression, acting out, and holding on. In many cases, societal pressures are intertwined with the black addict's feelings of alienation and low self-esteem.

Williams defines his mission as fostering "discussion in which [patients] don't sound like they are pointing fingers or playing the part of victims." He says race and the nation's history of racism must be taken into account in treating an African-American addict because these factors are central to the black experience.

He likens treatment of African-Americans to that of the dually diagnosed: In order for treatment to be effective, it can't focus on just one element of a client's personality.

Although Williams believes race must be taken into consideration in the healing process, he warns that it shouldn't become the sole focus of treatment. "Addicts would rather talk about anything but their alcohol and drug problems," he said. "Clinicians sometimes get suckered off into left field when the race card gets played."

Henry Culbreth, chief executive of the Culbreth & Culbreth counseling and training center in Washington, D.C., has used Williams' modification of the CENAPS model, and is pleased with what he has seen.

"It deals with the touchy issues that society has been willing not to face," Culbreth told *ADAW*. "It goes exactly where the African-American lives, especially when it talks about feelings of inadequacy." And Culbreth added, simply identifying that race may be linked with an addict's problems can mark a significant step toward successful recovery.

Note

Copies of *Relapse Prevention Counseling for African-Americans: A Culturally Specific Model and Relapse Warning Signs for African-Americans: A Culturally Specific Model* are available by calling (800) 767-8181.

Chapter 52

Treatment Methods for Women

Addiction to drugs is a serious, chronic, and relapsing health problem for both women and men of all ages and backgrounds. Among women, however, drug abuse may present different challenges to health, may progress differently, and may require different treatment approaches.

Understanding Women Who Use Drugs

It is possible for drug-dependent women, of any age, to overcome the illness of drug addiction. Those that have been most successful have had the help and support of significant others, family members, friends, treatment providers, and the community. Women of all races and socioeconomic status suffer from the serious illness of drug addiction. And women of all races, income groups, levels of education, and types of communities need treatment for drug addiction, as they do for any other problem affecting their physical or mental health.

Many women who use drugs have faced serious challenges to their well-being during their lives. For example, research indicates that up to 70 percent of drug-abusing women report histories of physical and sexual abuse. Data also indicate that women are far more likely than men to report a parental history of alcohol and drug abuse. Often, women who use drugs have low self-esteem and little self-confidence and may feel powerless. In addition, minority women may face additional

National Institute on Drug Abuse (NIDA), Pub. No. 13562, November 1999.

cultural and language barriers that can affect or hinder their treatment and recovery.

Many drug-using women do not seek treatment because they are afraid: They fear not being able to take care of or keep their children, they fear reprisal from their spouses or boyfriends, and they fear punishment from authorities in the community. Many women report that their drug-using male sex partners initiated them into drug abuse. In addition, research indicates that drug-dependent women have great difficulty abstaining from drugs, when the lifestyle of their male partner is one that supports drug use.

Consequences of Drug Use for Women

Research suggests that women may become more quickly addicted than men to certain drugs, such as crack cocaine, even after casual or experimental use. Therefore, by the time a woman enters treatment, she may be severely addicted and consequently may require treatment that both identifies her specific needs and responds to them.

These needs will likely include addressing other serious health problems—sexually transmitted diseases (STDs) and mental health problems, for example. More specifically, health risks associated with drug abuse in women are:

- Poor nutrition and below-average weight
- Low self-esteem
- Depression
- Physical abuse
- If pregnant, preterm labor or early delivery
- Serious medical and infectious diseases (e.g., increased blood pressure and heart rate, STDs, HIV/AIDS)

Drug Abuse and HIV/AIDS

AIDS is now the fourth leading cause of death among women of childbearing age in the United States. Substance abuse compounds the risk of AIDS for women, especially for women who are injecting drug users and who share drug paraphernalia, because HIV/AIDS often is transmitted through shared needles, and other shared items, such as syringes, cotton swabs, rinse water, and cookers. In addition, under the influence of illicit drugs and alcohol, women may engage in unprotected sex, which also increases their risk for contracting or transmitting HIV/AIDS.

From 1993 to 1994, the number of new AIDS cases among women decreased 17 percent. Still, as of January 1997, the Centers for Disease Control and Prevention had documented almost 85,500 cases of AIDS among adolescent and adult women in the United States. Of these cases,

- About 62 percent were related either to the woman's own injecting drug use or to her having sex with an injecting drug user.

- About 37 percent were related to heterosexual contact, and almost half of these women acquired HIV/AIDS by having sex with an injecting drug user.

Treatment for Women

Research shows that women receive the most benefit from drug treatment programs that provide comprehensive services for meeting their basic needs, including access to the following:

- Food, clothing, and shelter
- Transportation
- Job counseling and training
- Legal assistance
- Literacy training and educational opportunities
- Parenting training
- Family therapy
- Couples counseling
- Medical care
- Child care
- Social services
- Social support
- Psychological assessment and mental health care
- Assertiveness training
- Family planning services

Traditional drug treatment programs may not be appropriate for women because those programs may not provide these services. Research also indicates that, for women in particular, a continuing relationship with a treatment provider is an important factor throughout treatment. Any individual may experience lapses and relapses as expected steps of the treatment and recovery process; during these periods, women particularly need the support of the community and encouragement of those closest to them. After completing a drug treatment program, women also need services to assist them in sustaining their recovery and in rejoining the community.

Extent of Use

The National Household Survey on Drug Abuse (NHSDA)* provides yearly estimates of drug use prevalence among various demographic groups in the United States. Data are derived from a nationwide sample of household members aged 12 and older.

- In 1996, 29.9 percent of U.S. women (females over age 12) had used an illicit drug at least once in their lives—33.3 million out of 111.1 million women. More than 4.7 million women had used an illicit drug at least once in the month preceding the survey.

- The survey showed 30.5 million women had used marijuana at least once in their lifetimes. About 603,000 women had used cocaine in the preceding month; 241,000 had used crack cocaine. About 547,000 women had used hallucinogens (including LSD and PCP) in the preceding month.

- In 1996, 56,000 women used a needle to inject drugs, and 856,000 had done so at some point in their lives.

- In 1996, nearly 1.2 million females aged 12 and older had taken prescription drugs (sedatives, tranquilizers, or analgesics) for a nonmedical purpose during the preceding month.

- In the month preceding the survey, more than 26 million women had smoked cigarettes, and more than 48.5 million had consumed alcohol.

Note

* NHSDA is an annual survey conducted by the Substance Abuse and Mental Health Services Administration. Copies of the latest survey are available from the National Clearinghouse for Alcohol and Drug Information at 1-800-729-6686.

Chapter 53

Treatment Is Effective but Benefits May Be Overstated

Research Issues Make Assessment of Treatment Effectiveness Difficult

The study of drug treatment programs is complicated by a number of challenging methodological and implementation issues. Evaluations of treatment effectiveness can use one of several methodologies, depending on the specific questions to be addressed. Thus, the appropriateness of the study design and how well the evaluation is conducted determine the confidence to be placed in the research findings. In particular, studies of the validity of self-reported data demonstrate that information on treatment outcomes collected by self-report should be interpreted with some caution. The ability to compare the results of effectiveness studies is also influenced, and often limited, by differences in how outcomes are measured, how programs are operated, and client variables.

Quality of Evidence Varies by Study Design

Drug treatment effectiveness research conducted over the past 2 decades has used a variety of designs, including randomized clinical trials, simple or controlled observation, and quasiexperimental designs. Selection of the study design depends on a number of factors,

Excerpted from "Drug Abuse: Research Shows Treatment Is Effective, but Benefits May be Overstated," United States General Accounting Office (GAO), Doc. No. GAO/HEHS-98-72, March 1998.

including the questions being addressed and the resources available to fund the study. Methodologists agree that randomized clinical trials are the most rigorous study designs and therefore offer the strongest support for their findings. Studies that rely on a simple observational design produce less definitive findings but can provide a good indication of the operation of drug treatment programs as well as information on treatment outcomes. A quasiexperimental design, the most frequently used in field settings, falls somewhere in between.

Randomized clinical studies are designed to isolate the effects of a treatment by randomly assigning individuals to either a control group—receiving no treatment or an alternative treatment—or to a group that receives the treatment being studied. This study design has been used in the assessment of methadone maintenance for treating heroin addiction. Randomized trials are often used to study the efficacy of a treatment, asking the question, "Can it work?" Although such studies provide the most definitive information about whether particular treatments are effective, they are not widely used in drug treatment research. According to an analysis by the Lewin Group, among the reasons cited for the limited use of randomized trials are the difficulties in obtaining informed consent from drug abusers and the perceived ethical issue of randomly assigning people who are seeking drug treatment to a control group in which no treatment or a treatment regimen not of the client's choice is provided.

Simple and controlled observation designs typically employ a repeated-measures methodology, whereby the researchers collect information on drug use patterns and other criteria from clients before, during, and after treatment. Generally, controlled observation studies examine multiple treatment groups, and simple observation studies follow a single treatment group without a nontreatment comparison group. Observational studies provide information about the effectiveness of treatments when implemented in uncontrolled, or real-world, conditions. Observational design has been used to assess treatment provided in all four of the major treatment settings: residential therapeutic communities and outpatient methadone maintenance, outpatient drug-free, and inpatient chemical dependency programs.

Quasiexperimental study designs generally have a comparison group, a key feature of strong research design, but an investigator does not randomly assign individuals to treatment and comparison groups. Instead, comparisons are made between possibly nonequivalent client groups or by using statistical techniques that adjust for known differences in client characteristics. Even in a quasiexperimental design, a repeated-measures methodology might be used in comparing the behaviors of the same group of drug abusers before, during, and after treatment. A quasiexperimental design is often applied in evaluations of naturally occurring events, such as introducing a new treatment approach or closing a treatment program. Such a design allows greater confidence (than observation alone) that any differences detected are due to treatment but not as much confidence as random assignment of clients to treatment and comparison groups. Quasi-experimental study designs have been used to assess the effectiveness of both methadone maintenance programs and therapeutic communities as well as outpatient drug-free programs.

Treatment Evaluations Define and Measure Outcomes Differently

Treatment program goals generally include a wide range of issues, such as reducing drug use, reducing criminal behavior, and improving employment status. Most researchers have agreed that reducing drug use from the level it would have been without treatment (harm reduction) is a valid goal of drug treatment and an indication of program success. In addressing this issue, researchers acknowledge that abstinence from illicit drug consumption is the central goal of all drug treatment, but they contend it is not the only acceptable goal of treatment, since total abstinence from drug use may be unrealistic for many users. According to the Institute of Medicine, "an extended abstinence, even if punctuated by slips and short relapses, is beneficial in itself and may serve as a critical intermediate step toward lifetime abstinence and recovery."

Another issue related to measuring treatment outcomes is concern about the time frame for client follow-up. Since drug addiction is commonly viewed as a life-long disease, many argue that long-term follow-up is needed to fully assess treatment outcomes. However, many of those who complete treatment programs are lost in the follow-up assessment period.

Reliance on Self-Reported Data Has Limitations

With all types of study designs, data collection issues can hamper assessments of treatment effectiveness. The central debate regarding data collection on the use of illicit drugs surrounds the common use of self-reported data. A recent National Institute on Drug Abuse (NIDA) review of current research on the validity of self-reported drug use highlights the limitations of data collected in this manner. According to this review, recent studies conducted with criminal justice clients (such as people on parole, on probation, or awaiting trial) and former treatment clients suggest that 50 percent or fewer current users accurately report their drug use in confidential interviews. In general, self-reports are less valid for the more stigmatized drugs, such as cocaine; for more recent rather than past use; and for those involved with the criminal justice system.

The largest studies of treatment effectiveness, which have evaluated the progress of thousands of people in drug treatment programs, have all relied on self-reported data. That is, the drug abuser is surveyed when entering treatment, and then again at a specified follow-up interval. In general, individuals are asked, orally or in writing, to report their drug use patterns during the previous year. Self-reports of drug use may be subject to bias both prior to and following treatment and can be either over- or understated. Drug abusers may inflate their current level of drug use when presenting for treatment if they believe that higher levels of use will increase the likelihood of acceptance into treatment. Drug use may also be under-reported at treatment intake or follow-up. Motivations cited for under-reporting include the client's desire to reflect a positive outcome from treatment and the perception of a strong societal stigma associated with the use of particular drugs.

As questions have developed about the accuracy of self-reported data, researchers have begun using objective means to validate the data collected in this manner, although these methods also have limitations. Generally, a subgroup of the individuals surveyed after treatment is asked to provide either a urine sample or a hair sample, which is then screened for evidence of drug use. The results from the urinalysis or hair analysis are then compared against self-reports of drug use. Some researchers believe that it may be possible to systematically adjust self-reported data to correct for the biases exposed by urinalysis or hair analysis, although this technique is not currently in use.

Variation in Program Operations and Client Factors Makes Comparisons Difficult

Research results often do not account for the tremendous variation in program operations, such as differences in standards of treatment, staff levels and expertise, and level of coordination with other services. For example, surveys of the dosages used in methadone maintenance programs have shown that a large proportion of programs use suboptimal or even subthreshold dosages, which would likely result in poorer treatment outcomes than those of programs that provide optimal dosage levels to their clients. Similarly, outpatient drug-free programs operate with different numbers and quality of staff and have varying levels of coordination with local agencies that offer related services that are generally needed to support recovering abusers. An outpatient drug-free program that has close ties with local services, such as health clinics and job training programs, is likely to have better treatment outcomes than a program without such ties.

Assessing treatment effectiveness is also complicated by differences in client factors. Researchers recognize that client motivation and readiness for treatment, as well as psychiatric status, can significantly affect the patient's performance in treatment. For example, unmotivated clients are less likely than motivated ones to adhere to program protocols and to continue treatment. In studies of pharmacotherapy for opiate addiction, researchers have found that patients with high motivation to remain drug-free—such as health professionals, parolees, and work-release participants—have better treatment outcomes.

Studies Indicate Benefits from Treatment, but Evidence Varies on Best Approaches for Specific Groups

Major studies have shown that drug treatment is beneficial, although concerns about the validity of self-reported data suggest that the degree of success may be overstated. In large-scale evaluations conducted over the past 20 years, researchers have concluded that treatment reduces the number of regular drug users as well as criminal activity. In addition, these studies demonstrate that longer treatment episodes are more effective than shorter ones. Research also indicates that the amount and strength of evidence available to support particular treatment approaches for specific groups of drug abusers vary.

Consistent Evidence Shows Drug Treatment Is Beneficial, but Outcomes May Be Overstated

Numerous large-scale studies that examined the outcomes of treatment provided in a variety of settings have found drug treatment to be beneficial. Clients receiving treatment report reductions in drug use and criminal activity, with better treatment outcomes associated with longer treatment duration. However, studies examining the validity of self-reported data suggest that a large proportion of individuals do not report the full extent of drug use following treatment. Therefore, the findings from these major studies of treatment effectiveness—all of which relied on self-reported data as the primary data collection method—may be somewhat inflated.

Major Studies Report Reductions in Drug Use and Crime Following Treatment

Comprehensive analyses of the effectiveness of drug treatment have been conducted by several major studies over a period of nearly 30 years: Drug Abuse Treatment Outcome Study (DATOS; sponsored by the National Institute on Drug Abuse), National Treatment Improvement Evaluation Study (NTIES; sponsored by the Substance Abuse and Mental Health Services Administration), Treatment Outcome Prospective Study (TOPS; sponsored by the National Institute on Drug Abuse), and the Drug Abuse Reporting Program (DARP; sponsored by the National Institute of Mental Health). These large, multisite studies were designed to assess drug abusers on several measures before, during, and after treatment. These studies are generally considered by the Institute of Medicine and the drug treatment research community to be the major evaluations of drug treatment effectiveness, and much of what is known about typical drug abuse treatment outcomes comes from these studies.

These federally funded studies were conducted by research organizations independent of the groups operating the treatment programs being assessed. Although the characteristics of the studies vary somewhat, all are based on observational or quasiexperimental designs. The most recently completed study, DATOS, is a longitudinal study that used a prospective design and a repeated-measures methodology to study the complex interactions of client characteristics and treatment elements as they occur in typical community-based programs. NTIES, completed in March 1997, was a congressionally mandated, 5-year study that examined the effectiveness of treatment provided in public programs supported by SAMHSA.

All of these studies relied on self-report as the primary data collection method. That is, drug abusers were interviewed prior to entering treatment and again following treatment, and asked to report on their use of illicit drugs, their involvement in criminal activity, and other drug-related behaviors. As described previously in this report, studies examining the validity of self-reported data suggest that many individuals do not report the full extent of drug use following treatment. Since results from the major studies of treatment effectiveness

366

were not adjusted for the likelihood of under-reported drug use (as revealed by urinalysis substudies), the study results may overstate reductions in drug use achieved by drug abusers. Researchers contend that the bias in self-reports on current drug use is greater than the bias in self-reports on past year use and that therefore the overall findings of treatment benefits are still valid.

The major studies also found that criminal activity declined after treatment. DATOS found that reports of criminal activity declined by 60 percent for cocaine users in long-term residential treatment at the 1-year follow-up. Only 17 percent of NTIES clients reported arrests in the year following treatment—down from 48 percent during the year before treatment entry. Additionally, the percentage of clients who reported supporting themselves primarily through illegal activities decreased from 17 percent before treatment to 9 percent after treatment. DARP found reported reductions in criminal activity for clients who stayed in treatment at least 3 months.

Longer Treatment Episodes Have Better Outcomes, but Treatment Duration Is Limited by Client Drop-Out

Another finding across these studies is that clients who stay in treatment longer report better outcomes. For the DATOS clients that reported drug use when entering treatment, fewer of those in treatment for more than 3 months reported continuing drug use than those in treatment for less than 3 months. DATOS researchers also found that the most positive outcomes for clients in methadone maintenance were for those who remained in treatment for at least 12 months.

Earlier studies reported similar results. Both DARP and TOPS found that reports of drug use were reduced most for clients who stayed in treatment at least 3 months, regardless of the treatment setting. In fact, DARP found that treatment lasting 90 days or less was no more effective than no treatment at facilitating complete abstinence from drug use and criminal behavior during the year following treatment.

Although these studies show better results for longer treatment episodes, they found that many clients dropped out of treatment long before reaching the minimum length of treatment episode recommended by those operating the treatment program. For example, a study of a subset of DATOS clients found that all of the participating methadone maintenance programs recommend 2 or more years of treatment, but the median treatment episode by clients was about 1 year. Long-term residential programs participating in DATOS generally recommended a treatment duration of 9 months or longer, while outpatient drug-free programs recommended at least 6 months in treatment; for both program types, the median treatment episode was 3 months. TOPS found that in the first 3 months of treatment, 64 percent of outpatient drug-free program clients and 55 percent of therapeutic community clients discontinued treatment. For clients receiving methadone maintenance treatment, drop-out rates were somewhat lower— 32 percent—in the first 3 months.

Researchers note that drug abuse treatment outcomes should be considered comparable to those of other chronic diseases; therefore, significant dropout rates should not be unexpected. These results are similar to the levels of compliance with treatment regimens for people with chronic diseases such as diabetes and hypertension. A review of over 70 outcome studies of treatment for diabetes, hypertension, and asthma found that less than 50 percent of people with diabetes fully comply with their insulin treatment schedule, while less than 30 percent of patients with hypertension or asthma comply with their medication regimens.

Evidence Varies on the Best Treatment Approaches for Specific Groups of Drug Abusers

Research provides strong evidence to support methadone maintenance as the most effective treatment for heroin addiction. However, research on the most effective treatment interventions for other groups of drug abusers is less definitive. Promising treatment approaches for other groups include cognitive-behavioral therapy for treatment of cocaine abuse and family-based therapy for adolescent drug users.

Research Supports Methadone Maintenance as the Most Effective Treatment for Heroin Addiction

A number of approaches have been used in treating heroin addiction. Methadone maintenance, however, is the treatment most commonly used, and numerous studies have shown that those receiving methadone maintenance treatment have better outcomes than those who go untreated or use other treatment approaches—including detoxification with methadone. Methadone maintenance has been shown to reduce heroin use and criminal activity and improve social functioning. HIV risk is also minimized, since needle usage is reduced. Proponents of methadone maintenance also argue that reductions in the use of illicit drugs and associated criminal behavior help recovering drug abusers focus on their social and vocational rehabilitation and become reintegrated into society.

However, outcomes among methadone programs have varied greatly, in part because of the substantial variation in treatment practices across the nation. Many methadone clinics have routinely provided clients dosage levels that are lower than optimum—or even subthreshold—and have discontinued treatment too soon. In late 1997, an NIH (National Institutes of Health) consensus panel concluded that people who are addicted to heroin or other opiates should have broader access to methadone maintenance treatment programs and recommended that federal regulations allow additional physicians and pharmacies to prescribe and dispense methadone [see Chapter 43].

Similarly, several studies conducted over the past decade show that when counseling, psychotherapy, health care, and social services are provided along with methadone maintenance, treatment outcomes improve significantly. However, the recent findings from DATOS suggest that the provision of these ancillary services—both the number and variety—has eroded considerably during the past 2 decades across all treatment settings. DATOS researchers also noted that the percentage of clients reporting unmet needs was higher than that in previous studies.

There are other concerns associated with methadone maintenance. For example, methadone is often criticized for being a substitute drug for heroin, which does not address the underlying addiction. Additional concerns center on the extent to which take-home methadone doses are being sold or exchanged for heroin or other drugs.

Cognitive-Behavioral Treatments Show Promise for Cocaine Addiction

Evidence of treatment effectiveness is not as strong for cocaine addiction as it is for heroin addiction. No pharmacological agent for treating cocaine addiction or reducing cocaine craving has been found. However, an accumulating body of research points to cognitive-behavioral therapies as promising treatment approaches for cocaine addiction.

Family Therapy Is Under Study for Adolescent Drug Abusers

Adolescent drug abusers are similar to adult drug abusers in that they are likely to use more than one type of illicit drug and to have coexisting psychiatric conditions. In other ways, they differ from adult drug abusers. Adolescents may have a shorter history of drug abuse and thus less severe symptoms of tolerance, craving, and withdrawal. In addition, they usually do not show the long-term physical effects of drug abuse. Despite a number of studies on the topic, little is known about the best way to treat adolescent drug abusers. Researchers believe that adolescents have special treatment needs; however, research has not shown any one method or approach to be consistently superior to others in achieving better treatment outcomes for adolescents. Among the wide variety of treatment approaches and settings used for adolescents, family-based therapies show promise.

Conclusions

With an annual expenditure of more than $3 billion, the federal investment in drug abuse treatment is an important component of the nation's drug control efforts, and monitoring the performance of treatment programs can help ensure that progress toward the nation's goals is being achieved. Research on the effectiveness of drug abuse treatment, however, is highly problematic, given the methodological challenges and numerous factors that influence the results of treatment. Although studies conducted over nearly three decades consistently show that treatment reduces drug use and crime, current data collection techniques do not allow accurate measurement of the extent to which treatment reduces the use of illicit drugs. Furthermore, research literature has not yet yielded definitive evidence to identify which approaches work best for specific groups of drug abusers.

Part Six

Drug Abuse
Prevention Issues

Chapter 54

Growing Up Drug Free: A Parent's Guide to Prevention

The teen years can be trying for families. It is not always easy to communicate with those you love. But the stakes are high. If teens can navigate these years without drinking, smoking, or taking drugs, chances are that they won't use or abuse these substances as adults. Your influence early on can spare your child the negative experiences associated with illegal drug use, and even save your child's life.

Laying the Groundwork

Children learn by example. They adopt the values we demonstrate through our actions. As they grow, they're impressed by our concern for others when we bring soup to a sick neighbor and by our honesty when we admit making a mistake.

Although we believe these traits are important, it's not always easy to be consistent. Telling a friend you're younger than you really are sends a confusing message to your child—isn't it wrong to lie? If you forbid smoking in the house, how can you allow your friends to break the rules? If you say that drinking alcohol is a serious matter, how can you laugh uproariously at TV and movie drunks? Because

Excerpted from *Growing Up Drug-Free: How to Teach Your Child About Drugs*, U.S. Department of Education, 1998. To order free printed copies of this guide, call the Department of Education's toll-free number: 1-877-4EDPUBS, or send your name and address to: Growing Up Drug-Free, Pueblo, CO 81009. The full text of this document is also available on line at http://www.ed.gov/offices/OESE/SDFS.

alcohol is off-limits for children, even asking them to fetch a beer from the refrigerator or to mix drinks at an adult party can be confusing.

Children who decide not to use alcohol or other drugs often make this decision because they have strong convictions against the use of these substances—convictions based on a value system. You can make your family's values clear by explaining why you choose a particular course of action and how that choice reflects your values. If you're walking down the street together and spot a blind person attempting to cross, you can both offer to help him and then take the opportunity to discuss why it's important to support those in need. You can also explore moral issues by posing hypothetical questions at the dinner table or in the car—for example, "What would you do if the person ahead of you in the movie line dropped a dollar bill?" or "What would you do if your friend wanted you to skip class with him and play video games instead?" Concrete examples like these make the abstract issue of values come alive.

What to Say When Your Child Asks: "Did You Ever Use Drugs?"

Among the most common drug-related questions asked of parents is "Did you ever use drugs?" Unless the answer is "no," it's difficult to know what to say because nearly all parents who used drugs don't want their children to do the same thing. Is this hypocritical? No. We all want the best for our children, and we understand the hazards of drug use better than we did when we were their age and thought we were invincible. To guide our children's decisions about drugs, we can now draw on credible real-life examples of friends who had trouble as a result of their drug use: the neighbor who caused a fatal car crash while high; the family member who got addicted; the teen who used marijuana for years, lost interest in school, and never really learned how to deal with adult life and its stresses.

Some parents who used drugs in the past choose to lie about it, but they risk losing their credibility if their children discover the truth. Many experts recommend that when a child asks this question, the response should be honest.

This doesn't mean that parents need to recount every moment of their experiences. As in conversations about sex, some details should remain private, and you should avoid providing more information than is actually sought by your child. Ask clarifying questions to make sure you understand exactly why and what a child is asking before answering questions about your past drug use, and limit your response to that information.

This discussion provides a good opportunity for parents to speak frankly about what attracted them to drugs, why drugs are dangerous, and why they want their children to avoid making the same mistake. There's no perfect way to get this message across, only approaches that seem more fitting than others.

Making Your Position Clear

When it comes to dangerous substances like alcohol, tobacco, and other drugs, don't assume that your children know where you stand. They want you to talk to them about drugs. State your position clearly; if you're ambiguous, children may be tempted to use. Tell your children that you forbid them to use alcohol, tobacco, and drugs because you love them. (Don't be afraid to pull out all the emotional stops. You can say, "If you took drugs it would break my heart.") Make it clear that this rule holds true even at other people's houses. Will your child listen? Most likely. According to research, when a child decides whether or not to use alcohol, tobacco, and other drugs, a crucial consideration is "What will my parents think?"

Also discuss the consequences of breaking the rules—what the punishment will be and how it will be carried out. Consequences must go hand-in-hand with limits so that your child understands that there's a predictable outcome to his choosing a particular course of action. The consequences you select should be reasonable and related to the violation. For example, if you catch your son smoking, you might "ground" him, restricting his social activities for two weeks. You could then use this time to show him how concerned you are about the serious health consequences of his smoking, and about the possibility that he'll become addicted, by having him study articles, books, or video tapes on the subject.

Contrary to some parents' fears, your strict rules won't alienate your children. They want you to show you care enough to lay down the law and to go to the trouble of enforcing it. Rules about what's acceptable, from curfews to insisting that they call in to tell you where they are, make children feel loved and secure. Rules about drugs also give them reasons to fall back on when they feel tempted to make bad decisions. A recent poll showed that drugs are the number-one concern of young people today. Even when they appear nonchalant, our children need and want parental guidance. It does not have to be preachy. You will know best when it is more effective to use an authoritarian tone or a gentler approach.

Always let your children know how happy you are that they respect the rules of the household by praising them. Emphasize the things your children do right instead of focusing on what's wrong. When parents are quicker to praise than to criticize, children learn to feel good about themselves, and they develop the self-confidence to trust their own judgment.

Talking with Your Children Effectively

As soon as your child begins to talk, the questions come: "Why is the grass green?" "What's wrong with that man sitting in the park?" If you show your child that you're ready to give answers at any time, even if the topics make you uncomfortable, you'll forge a trusting relationship, and your child will feel comfortable coming to you with concerns because she knows you take her seriously.

Being a good listener also gives you insight into your child's world. Your child will tell you about the sights and sounds that influence him every day—he's the expert about fashion, music, TV, and movies that people his age follow. Ask him what music groups are popular and what their songs are about, what his friends like to do after school, what's cool and what's not and why. Encourage him with phrases such as "That's interesting" or "I didn't know that," and by asking follow-up questions.

In these conversations, you can steer the talk to drugs and why they're harmful. If you can ingrain this information in your children well before they are faced with making difficult choices, experts say they'll be more likely to avoid rather than use. In fact, teenagers who say they've learned a lot about the risks of drugs from their parents are much less likely to try marijuana than those who say they learned nothing from them. You needn't fear that by introducing the topic of drugs, you're "putting ideas" into your children's heads, any more than talking about traffic safety might make them want to jump in front of a car. You're letting them know about potential dangers in their environment so that when they're confronted with them, they'll know what to do.

To introduce the topic, ask your child what he's learned about drugs in school and what he thinks of them. He may even mention people who might be using them. If you hear something you don't like (perhaps a friend smokes marijuana or your child confesses to trying beer at a party), it is important not to react in any way that cuts off further discussion. If he seems defensive or assures you that he doesn't know anyone who uses drugs, ask him why he thinks people use them. Discuss whether the risks are worth what people may get out of using them and whether he thinks it would be worth it to take the risks.

Even without addiction, experimentation is too great a gamble. One bad experience, such as being high and misjudging how long it takes to cross a busy street, can change—or end—a life forever. If something interrupts your conversation, pick it up the next chance you get.

When There's a Family History of Alcoholism or Drug Abuse

If your family had a tendency for high blood pressure, you'd tell your children they might inherit it. In the same way, they need to know about recurring patterns of substance abuse, particularly if you, your spouse, or their grandparents have had problems with alcohol or other drugs. Children of substance abusers are much more likely to become addicted if they use drugs; they may have inherited genes that make them react to alcohol and drugs differently, and they may have had more difficult upbringings. When you use the example of a family member to illustrate why your children should be careful about trying alcohol and other drugs, you make a compelling argument.

Try to find a positive perspective. If substance abuse is a persistent problem in your family, you might tell your children that being aware of the challenge that the future holds better equips them to plan ahead and avoid potentially unhealthy situations.

Your Child's Perspective

Why a Child Uses Drugs

Understandably, some parents of drug users think that their child might have been pressured into taking drugs by peers or drug dealers. But children say they choose to use drugs because they want to:

- relieve boredom
- feel good
- forget their troubles and relax
- have fun
- satisfy their curiosity
- take risks
- ease their pain
- feel grown-up
- show their independence
- belong to a specific group
- look cool.

Rather than being influenced by new friends whose habits they adopt, children and teens often switch peer groups so they can hang around with others who have made the same lifestyle choices.

Parents know their children best and are therefore in the best position to suggest healthy alternatives to doing drugs. Sports, clubs, music lessons, community service projects, and after-school activities not only keep children and teens active and interested, but also bring them closer to parents who can attend games and performances. To develop a positive sense of independence, you could encourage babysitting or tutoring. For a taste of risk-taking, suggest rock-climbing, karate, or camping.

How to Teach Your Child about Drugs

Preschoolers

It may seem premature to talk about drugs with preschoolers, but the attitudes and habits that they form at this age have an important bearing on the decisions they will make when they're older. At this early age, they are eager to know and memorize rules, and they want your opinion on what's "bad" and what's "good." Although they are old enough to understand that smoking is bad for them, they're not ready to take in complex facts about alcohol, tobacco, and other drugs. Nevertheless, this is a good time to practice the decision-making and problem-solving skills that they will need to say "no" later on.

Here are some ways to help your preschool children make good decisions about what should and should not go into their bodies:

- Discuss why children need healthy food. Have your child name several favorite good foods and explain how these foods contribute to health and strength.

- Set aside regular times when you can give your son or daughter your full attention. Get on the floor and play with him; learn about her likes and dislikes; let him know that you love him; say that she's too wonderful and unique to do drugs. You'll build strong bonds of trust and affection that will make turning away from drugs easier in the years to come.

- Provide guidelines like playing fair, sharing toys, and telling the truth so children know what kind of behavior you expect from them.

- Encourage your child to follow instructions, and to ask questions if he does not understand the instructions.

- When your child becomes frustrated at play, use the opportunity to strengthen problem-solving skills. For example, if a tower of blocks keeps collapsing, work together to find possible solutions. Turning a bad situation into a success reinforces a child's self-confidence.

- Whenever possible, let your child choose what to wear. Even if the clothes don't quite match, you are reinforcing your child's ability to make decisions.

- Point out poisonous and harmful substances commonly found in homes, such as bleach, kitchen cleanser, and furniture polish, and read the products' warning labels out loud. Explain to your children that not all "bad" drugs have warnings on them, so they should only eat or smell food or a prescribed medicine that you, a grandparent, or a babysitter give them.

- Explain that prescription medications are drugs that can help the person for whom they are meant but that can harm anyone else—especially children, who must stay away from them.

Kindergarten through Third Grade (5-8 Years Old)

A child this age usually shows increasing interest in the world outside the family and home. Now is the time to begin to explain what alcohol, tobacco, and drugs are, that some people use them even though they are harmful, and the consequences of using them. Discuss how anything you put in your body that is not food can be extremely harmful. How drugs interfere with the way our bodies work and can make a person very sick or even cause them to die. (Most children of this age have had real-life experiences with a death of a relative or the relative of someone at school.) Explain the idea of addiction—that drug use can become a very bad habit that is hard to stop. Praise your children for taking good care of their bodies and avoiding things that might harm them.

By the time your children are in third grade, they should understand:

- how foods, poisons, medicines, and illegal drugs differ;

- how medicines prescribed by a doctor and administered by a responsible adult may help during illness but can be harmful if misused, so children need to stay away from any unknown substance or container;

- why adults may drink but children may not, even in small amounts—it's harmful to children's developing brains and bodies.

Grades Four through Six (9-11 Years Old)

Continue to take a strong stand about drugs. At this age, children can handle more sophisticated discussion about why people are attracted to drugs. You can use their curiosity about major traumatic events in people's lives (like a car accident or divorce) to discuss how drugs can cause these events. Children this age also love to learn facts, especially strange ones, and they want to know how things work. This age group can be fascinated by how drugs affect a user's brain or body. Explain how anything taken in excess—whether it's cough medicine or aspirin—can be dangerous.

Friends—either a single best friend or a group of friends—are extremely important during this time, as is fitting in and being seen as "normal." When children enter middle or junior high school, they leave their smaller, more protective surroundings and join a much larger, less intimate crowd of preteens. These older children may expose your child to alcohol, tobacco, or drugs. Research shows that the earlier children begin using these substances, the more likely they are to experience serious problems. It is essential that your child's anti-drug attitudes be strong before entering middle school or junior high.

Before leaving elementary school, your children should know:

- the immediate effects of alcohol, tobacco, and drug use on different parts of the body, including risks of coma or fatal overdose;

- the long-term consequences—how and why drugs can be addicting and make users lose control of their lives;

- the reasons why drugs are especially dangerous for growing bodies;

- the problems that alcohol and other illegal drugs cause not only to the user, but the user's family and world.

Rehearse potential scenarios in which friends offer drugs. Have your children practice delivering an emphatic "That stuff is really bad for you!" Give them permission to use you as an excuse: "My mom will kill me if I drink a beer!" " "Upsetting my parents" is one of the top reasons preteens give for why they won't use marijuana.

Teach your children to be aware of how drugs and alcohol are promoted. Discuss how advertising, song lyrics, movies, and TV shows bombard them with messages that using alcohol, tobacco, and other drugs is glamorous. Make sure that they are able to separate the myths of alcohol, tobacco, and other drug use from the realities, and praise them for thinking for themselves.

Get to know your children's friends, where they hang out, and what they like to do. Make friends with the parents of your children's friends so you can reinforce each others' efforts. You'll feel in closer touch with your child's daily life and be in a better position to recognize trouble spots. (A child whose friends are all using drugs is very likely to be using them, too.) Children this age really appreciate this attention and involvement.

The Transition Years

Your child's transition from elementary school to middle school or junior high calls for special vigilance. Children are much more vulnerable to drugs and other risky behavior when they move from sixth to seventh grade than when they were younger.

Continue the dialogue on drugs that you began when your child was younger, and stay involved in your child's daily life by encouraging interests and monitoring activities. Use the specific actions below to significantly reduce the chance of your child becoming involved with drugs. Some of these actions, like being sure your child is supervised in the hours after school, may seem like common sense. And some may meet with resistance from preteens who are naturally striving to achieve independence from their parents. But all the measures listed below are critically important in making sure that your child's life is structured in such a way that drugs have no place in it.

- If possible, arrange to have your children looked after and engaged from three to five p.m. Encourage them to get involved with youth groups, arts, music, sports, community service and academic clubs.

- Make sure children who are unattended for periods during the day feel your presence. Give them a schedule and set limits on their behavior. Give them household chores to accomplish. Enforce a strict phone-in-to-you policy. Leave notes for them around the house. Provide easy-to-find snacks.

- Get to know the parents of your child's friends. Exchange phone numbers and addresses. Have everyone agree to forbid each others' children from consuming alcohol, tobacco, and other drugs in their homes, and pledge that you will inform each other if one of you becomes aware of a child who violates this pact.

- Call parents whose home is to be used for a party. Make sure they can assure you that no alcoholic beverages or illegal substances will be dispensed. Don't be afraid to check out the party yourself to see that adult supervision is in place.

- Make it easy for your child to leave a place where substances are being used. Discuss in advance how to contact you or another designated adult in order to get a ride home. If another adult provides the transportation, be up and available to talk about the incident when your child arrives home.

- Set curfews and enforce them. Weekend curfews might range from 9 p.m. for a fifth-grader to 12:30 a.m. for a senior in high school.

- Encourage open dialogue with your children about their experiences. Tell your child, "I love you and trust you, but I don't trust the world around you, and I need to know what's going on in your life so I can be a good parent to you."

Grades Seven through Nine (12-14 Years Old)

A common stereotype holds that teenagers are rebellious, are ruled by peer pressure, and court danger even to the point of self-destructiveness. Although teens do often seem unreceptive to their parents as they struggle to become independent, teens need parental support, involvement, and guidance more than ever.

Young teens can experience extreme and rapid shifts in their bodies, emotional lives, and relationships. Adolescence is often a confusing and stressful time, characterized by mood changes and deep insecurity, as teens struggle to figure out who they are and how to fit in while establishing their own identities. It's not surprising that this is the time when many young people try alcohol, tobacco, and other drugs for the first time.

Parents may not realize that their young teens feel surrounded by drug use. Nearly nine out of ten teens agree that "it seems like marijuana is everywhere these days." Teens are twice as likely to be using marijuana as parents believe they are, and teens are getting high in the places that parents think are safe havens, such as around school, at home, and at friends' houses.

Although teens may not show they appreciate it, parents profoundly shape the choices their children make about drugs. Take advantage of how much young people care about social image and appearance to point out the immediate, distasteful consequences of tobacco and marijuana use—for example, that smoking causes bad breath and stained teeth and makes clothes and hair smell. At the same time, you should discuss drugs' long-term effects:

- the lack of crucial social and emotional skills ordinarily learned during adolescence;

- the risk of lung cancer and emphysema from smoking;

- fatal or crippling car accidents and liver damage from heavy drinking;

- addiction, brain coma, and death

Grades Ten through Twelve (15-17 Years Old)

Older teens have already had to make decisions many times about whether to try drugs or not. Today's teens are savvy about drug use, making distinctions not only among different drugs and their effects, but also among trial, occasional use, and addiction. They witness many of their peers using drugs—some without obvious or immediate consequences, others whose drug use gets out of control.

To resist peer pressure, teens need more than a general message not to use drugs. It's now also appropriate to mention how alcohol, tobacco, and other drug consumption during pregnancy has been linked with birth defects in newborns. Teens need to be warned of the potentially deadly effects of combining drugs. They need to hear a parent's assertion that anyone can become a chronic user or an addict and that even non-addicted use can have serious permanent consequences.

Because most high school students are future oriented, they are more likely to listen to discussions of how drugs can ruin chances of getting into a good college, being accepted by the military, or being hired for certain jobs. Teenagers tend to be idealistic and enjoy hearing about ways they can help make the world a better place. Tell your teens that drug use is not a victimless crime, and make sure they understand the effect that drug use has on our society. Appeal to your teen by pointing out how avoiding illegal drugs helps make your town a safer, better place, and how being drug-free leaves more energy to volunteer after school for tutoring or coaching younger kids—activities the community is counting on.

What to Do If You Think Your Child Might Be Using Drugs

Signs That Your Child Might Be Using Drugs

Since mood swings and unpredictable behavior are frequent occurrences for preteens and teenagers, parents may find it difficult to spot signs of alcohol and drug abuse. But if your child starts to exhibit one or more of these signs (which apply equally to sons and daughters), drug abuse may be at the heart of the problem:

- She's withdrawn, depressed, tired, and careless about personal grooming.
- He's hostile and uncooperative; he frequently breaks curfews.
- Her relationships with family members have deteriorated.
- He's hanging around with a new group of friends.
- Her grades have slipped, and her school attendance is irregular.
- He's lost interest in hobbies, sports, and other favorite activities.
- Her eating or sleeping patterns have changed; she's up at night and sleeps during the day.
- He has a hard time concentrating.
- Her eyes are red-rimmed and/or her nose is runny in the absence of a cold.
- Household money has been disappearing.

The presence of pipes, rolling papers, small medicine bottles, eye drops, or butane lighters in your home signal that your child may be using drugs. Other clues include homemade pipes and bongs (pipes that use water as a filter) made from soda cans or plastic beverage containers. If any of these indicators show up, parents should start discussing what steps to take so they can present a united front. They may also want to seek other family members' impressions.

Acting on Your Suspicions

If you suspect that your child is using drugs, you should voice your suspicions openly—avoiding direct accusations—when he or she is sober or straight and you're calm.

This may mean waiting until the next day if he comes home drunk from a party, or if her room reeks of marijuana. Ask about what's been going on—in school and out—and discuss how to avoid using drugs and alcohol in the future. If you encounter reluctance to talk, enlist the aid of your child's school guidance counselor, family physician, or a local drug treatment referral and assessment center—they may get a better response. Also explore what could be going on in your child's emotional or social life that might prompt drug use.

Taking the time to discuss the problem openly without turning away is an important first step on the road to recovery. It shows that your child's well-being is crucial to you and that you still love him, although you hate what he's doing to himself. But you should also show your love by being firm and enforcing whatever discipline your family has agreed upon for violating house rules. You should go over ways to regain the family's trust such as calling in, spending evenings at home, and improving grades.

Even in the face of mounting evidence, parents often have a hard time acknowledging that their child has an alcohol, tobacco, or drug problem. Anger, resentment, guilt, and a sense of failure are all common reactions, but it is important to avoid self-blame. Drug abuse occurs in families of all economic and social backgrounds, in happy and unhappy homes alike. Most important is that the faster you act, the sooner your child can start to become well again.

Addiction

No one who begins to use drugs thinks he or she will become addicted. Addiction is a disease characterized by compulsive drug-seeking behavior regardless of the consequences. Research conducted by the National Institute on Drug Abuse clearly shows that virtually all drugs that are abused have a profound effect on the brain. Prolonged use of many drugs including cocaine, heroin, marijuana and amphetamines can change the brain in fundamental and long-lasting ways, resulting in drug craving and addiction.

If and when a drug abuser becomes addicted depends on the individual. Research shows that children who use alcohol and tobacco are more likely to use marijuana than children who do not use these substances. Children who use marijuana are more likely to use other addictive drugs. Certain genetic, social, and environmental risk factors make it more likely that certain individuals will become addicted to alcohol, tobacco, and other drugs. These include:

- children of alcoholics who, according to several studies, may have inherited genes that make them more prone to addiction, and who may have had more stressful upbringings;

- sensation-seekers who may like the novelty of feeling drunk or high;

- children with psychological problems, such as conduct disorders, who self-medicate to feel better;

- children with learning disabilities, and others who find it difficult to fit in or become frustrated learning;

- children of poverty who lack access to opportunities to succeed and to resources when they're in trouble.

The more risk factors children have, the greater their vulnerability. And everyone has a different ability to tolerate drugs and alcohol—what if your child's tolerance is very low?

Regardless of how "cool" drugs may look, there is nothing glamorous about the reality of addiction, a miserable experience for the addict and everyone around him. Addiction causes an all-consuming craving for drugs, leading an otherwise responsible, caring person to destroy relationships, work, and family life.

Finding the Right Treatment

Certified drug and alcohol counselors work with families to find the program best suited to a child's needs. To find a good certified counselor you can consult your child's doctor, other parents whose children have been treated for drug abuse, the local hospital, a school social worker, the school district's substance abuse coordinator, or the county mental health society.

You can also call the U. S. Department of Health and Human Services Center for Substance Abuse Treatment (800) 662-HELP for referrals. Counselors will discuss treatment options such as individual or group out-patient programs, prescription medication, and residential programs. Counselors may also have information on whether a particular treatment center will accept third-party, partial or no payment for services. (Some residential centers reserve a number of government-financed beds for patients who are unable to afford treatment.) Counselors may also be able to suggest support groups that can steer families to sources of funding such as local church programs.

Addiction is a treatable disease. The success of any treatment approach depends on a variety of factors such as the child's temperament and willingness to change, and the extent and frequency of use. Drug addiction is now understood to be a chronic, relapsing disease.

It is not surprising, then, that parents may have to make a number of attempts at intervention before their child can remain drug-free, and they should not despair if their first try does not produce long-lasting results. Even if it is not apparent at the time, each step brings the child closer to being healthy.

Getting Involved and Staying Involved

Parent-School Partnerships

Parents do not need to feel they are alone in helping their children stay drug-free. For the first time ever, there are preventative intervention programs that have been proven to be effective and are available to schools, families and communities.

Children have the best prospects for leading healthy, drug-free lives when schools support parents in their anti-drug message. There should be nothing confusing or contradictory in what children learn about drugs from the adults in their lives, and school policies need to reflect the same attitude toward alcohol and drugs that you express at home: Drug use is not acceptable. Drugs diminish a child's ability to concentrate and follow through on academic responsibilities, they cause loss of motivation and absenteeism, and students who use them can be disruptive and drain teachers' time and energy. The best way to ensure that the anti-drug policies at your child's school are strong is to be involved. You can:

- Learn about the current policies regarding alcohol and other drugs at your child's school. If there's no anti-drug policy in place, attend PTA or curriculum review meetings, or schedule an interview with the principal to help develop a policy. The policy should specify what constitutes an alcohol, tobacco, or other drug offense, spell out the consequences for failing to follow the rules, and describe procedures for handling violations.

- Familiarize yourself with how drug education is being taught in your child's school. Are the faculty members trained to teach about alcohol, tobacco, and other drug use? Is drug education taught in an age-appropriate way at each grade level throughout the year or only once during a special week? Is drug education taught during health class, or do all the teachers incorporate anti-drug information into their classes? Is there a parent education component? Is the school's program based on current research?

- Immerse yourself in the school's drug education program at home. Ask your child to show you any materials distributed during or outside class and take the opportunity to review them together.

- Find out if your child's school conducts assessments of its drug problem and whether these results are used in the program.

- Ask what happens to those who are caught abusing drugs. Does the school offer a list of referrals for students who need special help?

- Request and examine any existing materials. Do they contain a clear message that alcohol, tobacco, and other drug use is wrong and harmful? Is the information accurate and up to date?

- Investigate whether your school's drug program is being evaluated for success. Research indicates that some of the most effective programs emphasize the value of life skills such as coping with anxiety, being assertive, and feeling comfortable socially. When these lessons are combined with drug education and media literacy (being able to critically evaluate the media's messages), students confronted with drugs are better equipped to resist them.

Help from the Community

Drug-free sons and daughters not only strengthen their families but their communities, too. As a result, many towns have found ways to help local young people stay healthy. Some offer teens alternatives to familiar rituals, such as alcohol- and drug-free proms, and special dry events such as First Night festivities on New Year's Eve. Others support student-run clubs where teens can hang out, listen to music, and play sports in the evening.

Reclaiming Neighborhoods

Contrary to a common misperception, drug-use rates for urban African-American children have typically been lower than rates for the population as a whole. But children in less affluent urban areas are more often exposed to drugs and the street-level drug culture. When dealers make themselves at home in a neighborhood, they often bring with them a number of other blights: crime, truancy, a higher drop-out rate, increased drug use, the physical deterioration of buildings and common areas, and despair. Residents, however, often don't realize the tools at their command to discourage drug dealing. Dealers tend to avoid neighborhoods in which the community stands united against them. Here's how we can demonstrate our commitment to reclaiming our streets:

- Form a community patrol, block association, or Neighborhood Watch. Members can take turns patrolling the streets and recording license-plate numbers of cars cruising for drugs.

- Increase two-way communication with the police by inviting them to neighborhood meetings and by keeping them informed about suspicious drug activities, which can be reported anonymously.

- Fill the streets with volleyball games, block parties, and other events that make a strong, united showing to dealers.

- Call the city public works department for help in cleaning up. Blazing lights, litter-free streets, and newly-planted flowers tell drug dealers that residents care too much about their neighborhood to hand it over.

- Provide positive outlets for the energies of local young people so they won't be attracted to drug-dealing—an activity that increases the likelihood that they'll become users.

- Continue to reassure our children that we love them and don't want them to do drugs. Even in neighborhoods where a walk to the grocery store can mean exposure to a drug dealer, children whose parents reinforce strong anti-drug attitudes stand a better chance of growing up drug-free.

Parents Supporting Each Other

Parents have no stronger allies in their fight against drug abuse than each other. Many parents find it useful to meet regularly in support of each other. It's helpful to be able to turn to other parents at the same stage of child-rearing with questions like "My daughter wants to go to a party where the chaperone will be a 20-year-old cousin—are you allowing your son to go?" If you haven't met many parents in your area with whom you can share anti-drug plans, you might want to contact a parent or community group with resources for parents. These organizations also provide interested families with information about drug prevention and referrals for treatment.

No matter how good school and community anti-drug efforts are, a parent's prevention campaign is still the most powerful. Gail Amato Baker, former president of Bowling Green Parents for Drug-Free Youth, who is now a community service representative for the Passage Group in Knoxville, Tennessee, tells why: "People often ask me why I think parents are the answer, and I think it's because we have the most to lose. Schools can help, churches can help, law enforcement can help, but no one can replace the family. Being involved with drug and alcohol prevention lets our children know that we care. It strengthens the family and helps us to be the kind of parents our children need us to be."

Chapter 55

Preventing Inhalant Abuse

Inhalant Abuse: It's Deadly

Inhalant abuse can kill. It can kill suddenly, and it can kill those who sniff for the first time.

Every year, young people in this country die of inhalant abuse. Hundreds suffer severe consequences, including permanent brain damage, loss of muscle control, and destruction of the heart, blood, kidney, liver, and bone marrow.

Today more than 1,000 different products are commonly abused. The National Institute on Drug Abuse (NIDA) reported in 1996 that one in five American teenagers have used inhalants to get high.

Many youngsters say they begin sniffing when they're in grade school. They start because they feel these substances can't hurt them, because of peer pressure, or because of low self-esteem. Once hooked, these victims find it a tough habit to break.

These questions and answers will help you identify inhalant abuse and understand what you can do to prevent or stop this problem.

What is inhalant abuse?

Inhalant abuse is the deliberate inhalant or sniffing of common products found in homes and schools to obtain a "high."

"A Parent's Guide to Preventing Inhalant Abuse," an undated fact sheet developed by the U.S. Consumer Product Safety Commission available from the National Clearinghouse for Alcohol and Drug Information.

What are the effects of inhalant abuse?

Sniffing can cause sickness and death. For example, victims may become nauseated, forgetful, and unable to see things clearly. Victims may lose control of their body, including the use of arms and legs. These effects can last 15 to 45 minutes after sniffing.

In addition, sniffing can severely damage many parts of the body, including the brain, heart, liver, and kidneys.

Even worse, victims can die suddenly—without any warning. "Sudden Sniffing Death" can occur during or right after sniffing. The heart begins to overwork, beating rapidly but unevenly, which can lead to cardiac arrest. Even first-time abusers have been known to die from sniffing inhalants.

What products are abused?

Ordinary household products, which can be safely used for legitimate purposes, can be problematic in the hands of an inhalant abuser. The following categories of products are reportedly abused: glues/adhesives, nail polish remover, marking pens, paint thinner, spray paint, butane lighter fluid, gasoline, propane gas, typewriter correction fluid, household cleaners, cooking sprays, deodorants, fabric protectors, whipping cream aerosols, and air conditioning coolants.

Information for Parents

How can you tell if a young person is an inhalant abuser?

If someone is an inhalant abuser, some or all these symptoms may be evident:

- Unusual breath odor or chemical odor on clothing.
- Slurred or disoriented speech.
- Drunk, dazed, or dizzy appearance.
- Signs of paint or other products where they wouldn't normally be, such as on the face or fingers.
- Red or runny eyes or nose.
- Spots and/or sores around the mouth.
- Nausea and/or loss of appetite.
- Chronic inhalant abusers may exhibit such symptoms as anxiety, excitability, irritability, or restlessness.

What could be other telltale behaviors of inhalant abuse?

Inhalant abusers also may exhibit the following signs:

- Sitting with a pen or marker near nose.
- Constantly smelling clothing sleeves.
- Showing paint or stain marks on the face, fingers, or clothing.
- Hiding rags, clothes, or empty containers of the potentially abused products in closets and other places.

What is a typical profile of an inhalant abuser in the U.S.?

There is no typical profile of an inhalant abuser. Victims are represented by both sexes and all socioeconomic groups throughout the U.S. It's not unusual to see elementary and middle-school age youths involved with inhalant abuse.

How does a young person who abuses inhalants die?

There are many scenarios for how young people die of inhalant abuse. Here are some of them:

- A 13 year-old boy was inhaling fumes from cleaning fluid and became ill a few minutes afterwards. Witnesses alerted the parents, and the victim was hospitalized and placed on life support systems. He died 24 hours after the incident.

- An 11 year-old boy collapsed in a public bathroom. A butane cigarette lighter fuel container and a plastic bag were found next to him. He also had bottles of typewriter correction fluid in his pocket. CPR failed to revive him, and he was pronounced dead.

- A 15 year-old boy was found unconscious in a backyard. According to three companions, the four teenagers had taken gas from a family's grill propane tank. They put the gas in a plastic bag and inhaled the gas to get high. The victim collapsed shortly after inhaling the gas. He died on the way to the hospital.

Guidelines for Preventing Inhalant Abuse

What can parents do to prevent inhalant abuse?

One of the most important steps you can take is to talk with your children or other youngsters about not experimenting even a first time with inhalants. In addition, talk with your children's teachers, guidance counselors, and coaches. By discussing this problem openly and stressing the devastating consequences of inhalant abuse, you can help prevent a tragedy.

If you suspect your child or someone you know is an inhalant abuser, what can you do to help?

Be alert for symptoms of inhalant abuse. If you suspect there's a problem, you should consider seeking professional help.

Contact a local drug rehabilitation center or other services available in your community, or:

National Inhalant Prevention Coalition
1-800-269-4237
or on the World Wide Web at www.inhalants.org

National Drug and Alcohol
Treatment Referral Service
1-800-662-HELP

National Clearinghouse for Alcohol and Drug Information
1-800-729-6686
or www.health.org

Chapter 56

How to Establish a Workplace Substance Abuse Program

There is no absolute "model" substance abuse program that is right for all companies. The program will depend largely on a company's circumstances, needs, location, culture, resources, and alcohol and other drug abuse experiences. However, first and foremost, a program should reflect a company's commitment to establishing and maintaining a workplace free of substance abuse.

A workplace substance abuse program should include those components that employers and employees identify as important to the company. There are five standard components of a comprehensive workplace substance abuse program that should be considered. They are a written policy statement, supervisor training, employee, education and awareness, employee assistance for providing help, and drug and alcohol testing.

A comprehensive program including all five components is the most effective way to address substance abuse problems in the workplace.

Step One: Writing a Substance Abuse Policy

Before developing a substance abuse policy, there are a number of important steps that should be taken. A needs assessment survey, however informal, may help to better understand the company's current situation and determine exactly what the program needs to accomplish. Enlisting the assistance and input of employees will not only

U.S. Department of Labor (DoL), November 1998.

395

help to develop the best policy possible but will also secure employees' support. Workers should be allies in this effort.

There are three basic parts to a written policy.

1. An explanation of why the program is being implemented. An important consideration may be the safety of employees, customers, and the general public. Other reasons may include workers' and dependents' health, product quality, productivity, public liability, and legal requirements.

2. A clear description of substance abuse-related behaviors that are prohibited. This should, at a minimum, include the use, possession, transfer, or sale of illegal drugs. Unacceptable behavior may also include employees under the influence of alcohol or other drugs while at work.

3. A thorough explanation of the consequences for violations of the policy.

A policy needs to identify all the elements of the substance abuse program. For example, if a company's program includes an employee assistance program (EAP), this needs to be stated in the policy. Essentially, the policy should specify everything that will affect employees and the options available to them should a substance abuse problem occur.

Step Two: Training Supervisors

The level of support supervisors give to the company's substance abuse program, combined with the fairness of the program and the firmness of the commitment, will greatly influence its potential for success. Many of the problems encountered when implementing a program can be avoided if the full support and participation of supervisors and managers is enlisted.

Supervisors are responsible for identifying and addressing performance problems when they occur which may, on occasion, be the result of substance abuse. However, supervisors should not be expected to diagnose possible substance abuse problems. Employees can, however, expect supervisors to identify the signs of poor job performance and follow standard company procedures for dealing with them.

The key to having effective supervisory support for a substance abuse program is to make sure all supervisors have been trained to understand the company's substance abuse policy and procedures, to identify and help resolve employee performance problems, and to know how to refer employees to available assistance so that any personal problems that may be affecting performance can be addressed.

An effective training program will allow supervisors to do the following:

- Know the company's policy and understand their role in its implementation and maintenance;

- Observe and document unsatisfactory job performance;

- Confront workers about unsatisfactory job performance according to company procedures;

- Understand the effects of substance abuse in the workplace; and,

- Know how to refer an employee suspected of having a substance abuse problem to those who are qualified to make a specific diagnosis and to offer assistance.

Step Three: Educating Employees

Educating all workers about substance abuse and the company's substance abuse program is a critical step in actually achieving the objectives of the program. A substance abuse education and awareness program will differ from those of other companies according to a company's specific needs. However, a basic program should achieve the following objectives:

- Provide information about the dangers of alcohol and other drugs and how they can affect individuals and families;

- Describe the impact that substance abuse can have on safety at work as well as the company's productivity, product quality, absenteeism, health care costs, accident rates, and the overall bottom line;

- Explain in detail how the workplace policy applies to every employee of the company and the consequences for violations of the policy;

- Describe how the basic components of the overall program work, including employee assistance program and drug and/or alcohol testing if these are part of the program; and,

- Explain how employees and their dependents, if included, can get help for their substance abuse problems including how to access the company's EAP or how to obtain services available from the community.

An effective education and awareness program is not a one-time effort. New workers should be informed immediately about a substance abuse policy and what is expected of them. Because of the regular turnover that many companies experience and the occasional changes and updates to the policy that may occur, education efforts will need to be undertaken periodically. If a company is unionized, the union representatives can provide valuable assistance in the development and maintenance of an education and awareness program.

Step Four: Providing Employee Assistance

Many employers are unsure whether they can or should offer or provide assistance to employees who have alcohol or other drug problems. Often they are concerned about the cost of providing assistance and their ability to continue to meet work demands while employees are getting help.

Terminating employees with alcohol and other drug problems and hiring a new worker may seem to be the most cost-effective approach. In some cases, starting fresh may be the best course of action. However, in most cases it actually makes better sense—from a business point of view as well as a humanitarian one—to help employees overcome personal problems. This is when providing some type of employee assistance comes into play.

An employee assistance program (EAP) is a job-based program intended to assist workers whose job performance is being negatively affected by personal problems. Workers' personal problems may be caused by any number of factors including substance abuse. Many employers have discovered that EAPs are cost-effective because they help reduce accidents, workers' compensation claims, absenteeism, and employee theft and contribute to improved productivity and employee morale.

Before including employee assistance as part of a program, it may be helpful to take the following steps:

- Contact other companies in the area that provide some type of employee assistance and learn about their programs—what they offer, how the service is provided, and the costs and results they are getting from the program.

- Determine whether there is an EAP consortium available in the community that local businesses can join to receive EAP services at prices typically only available to larger companies.

In order for an EAP to be successful, it must be seen by employees as a confidential source of help. They must believe that they will not jeopardize their employment or future opportunities with the company by seeking help from the EAP. Conversely, they must also understand that the EAP will not shield them from disciplinary action for continued poor performance or violations of company policy.

Almost any size company can offer its employees the services of an EAP. EAPs can be tailored to address the specific needs of a work force. With a strong commitment from the management of the company, quality EAP professionals, and a clear understanding by all that employee assistance services do not offer "quick fixes," an EAP can be a valuable component of a comprehensive workplace substance abuse program.

It is not always necessary to have a formal employee assistance program (EAP). For many companies, particularly small businesses, it is economically unrealistic to consider providing a formal program. However, the services that such a program provides are available in a variety of alternative ways—often within the budget of many small businesses. Regardless of how formal or informal employee assistance services are, they can be a valuable component to a program.

Step Five: Drug and Alcohol Testing

Drug and alcohol testing by itself is not a substance abuse program. However, many companies believe that, when combined with the other components of a comprehensive substance abuse program, testing can be an effective deterrent to substance abuse and an important tool to help employers identify workers who need help.

Though setting up a testing program is not a simple process, every year more and more companies of all sizes are doing so. Some establish programs because they are required to do so by state or federal laws or regulations. Others test to take advantage of incentive programs made available through the state or an insurance provider. Still, others do so because it is the right business decision for them.

Before implementing a drug or alcohol testing program, the following questions should be considered.

- Who will be tested? (Job applicants? All employees? Selected employees? Employees only at certain job sites?)

- When will tests be conducted? (After all accidents or only after some? When there is reason to believe an employee is using drugs? As part of periodic physical examinations? Randomly?)

- For what substances will testing be done? (For only the five drugs required by many federal government agencies—marijuana, opiates, amphetamines, cocaine, and PCP? Only for marijuana and cocaine because they are the most commonly abused illegal substances? For alcohol because it is the number one abused substance in American workplaces? For other legal substances that are commonly abused, such as prescription drugs, that can affect job performance?)

- What consequences will employees and job applicants face if they test positive?

- Who will conduct the testing program?

Drug testing has been gaining in popularity in the private sector for the past decade. During that time, many safeguards and confidentiality measures have been developed to ensure the quality and accuracy of drug testing. In addition, laws and regulations have been passed that govern how many programs must be set up and run. Before implementing a testing program, it is a good idea to contact an individual or organization with expertise in drug and alcohol testing issues to help establish the program.

It also is important to remember that drug testing is a mandatory subject of collective bargaining when employees are represented by a union.

Chapter 57

Prevalence of Drug Testing in the Workplace

Drug testing continues to develop as a popular strategy to control substance abuse in the workplace; the incidence of testing is partially based on the type of worksite, characteristics of employees, and policies of the company.

Substance abuse has compelled many U.S. firms to create strategies that would help keep it out of the workplace. Some firms have sponsored elaborate and extensive programs to control alcohol and drug misuse.[1] However, these programs have tended to rely on a supervisor's, a coworker's, or an employee's judgment about the presence of substance abuse in another individual or themselves. In the 1980s, some firms began to adopt drug and alcohol testing as an objective strategy to detect and control substance abuse. Advocates of this approach assert that an employee's positive test results can be linked to impairments in job performance, safety risks, and absenteeism.[2]

While drug testing programs span many segments of society (including suspected criminal offenders and automobile operators), this chapter focuses on the prevalence and characteristics of drug testing programs in private-sector workplaces within the United States. First, we describe the proliferation of drug tests as evidenced in earlier studies. We then present our findings from a national telephone survey conducted in 1993, which estimated the prevalence and characteristics

Excerpted from "Prevalence of Drug Testing in the Workplace," by Tyler D. Hartwell, Paul D. Steele, and Nathaniel F. Rodman, in *Monthly Labor Review*, Vol. 119, No. 11, November 1996, p. 35(8), U.S. Department of Labor (DoL).

of testing programs, and descriptors of worksites most likely to implement them. We discuss the implementation of various types of programs (that is, preemployment, random, regular), the types of worksites that conduct such tests, and the employees who are eligible to be tested in those worksites. Research findings are discussed within the context of social policy and the findings of earlier research studies. Lastly, we offer some comments regarding the future of testing and its integration with other workplace substance abuse control strategies.

Drug Testing Trends

Surveys of worksite respondents indicate a growing trend in the implementation of drug testing programs from the mid-1980s to the present. For example, one study finds that 18 percent of Fortune 500 companies tested their employees in 1985, but by 1991, the proportion had more than doubled to 40 percent.[3] A survey conducted by the American Management Association in 1988 indicated increases in the testing of both applicants and current employees for drugs. Thirty-eight percent of all the organizations in the survey tested job applicants, compared with 28 percent of those in 1987; 36 percent tested current employees, compared with 28 percent in 1986.[4] By 1991, 48 percent of Fortune 1000 firms engaged in some type of drug testing.[5] Another study found that up to 63 percent of surveyed employers performed some type of testing in 1992.[6] And, in a survey of 342 large firms (that is, firms that have more than 200 workers) in the State of Georgia, Terry Blum, and others report that 77 percent of the companies engaged in some type of drug testing between 1991 and 1992.[7] In addition to these relatively small surveys, representative national surveys conducted by the Bureau of Labor Statistics (BLS) indicate that 31.9 percent of worksites with more than 250 employees had drug testing programs in 1988, and by 1990, that proportion had increased to 45.9 percent.[8] Even with the methodological differences among these studies, it seems reasonable to conclude that the drug testing of job applicants and current employees has become much more common in recent years.

Worksites Linked to Testing

Previous research indicates that drug testing programs are implemented differently, according to company size and industry type. For example, a study conducted by the American Management Association in 1987 reported that while 43 percent of large corporate respondents (sales over $500 million) indicated that they test job applicants, only 16 percent of smaller corporate respondents (less than $50 million in sales) reported any type of drug testing.[9] In the BLS Survey of Employer Anti-Drug Programs, conducted in the summer of 1988, 43 percent of the largest worksites (with 1,000 employees or more) had drug testing programs, compared with 2 percent of the smallest worksites (fewer than 50 employees).[10] Furthermore, the BLS follow-up survey, conducted in 1990, showed an increase in the percentage of larger companies, but no significant increase in the percentage of small firms with drug testing programs.[11]

Firms implementing drug testing programs also can be distinguished by type of industry. The 1989 Conference Board survey showed that three-fourths of the companies with drug testing programs were manufacturers or gas and electric utilities, while nearly half of the companies that reported not having a drug testing program were in banking, insurance, and other financial service industries.[12] The 1988 BLS survey also showed that worksites in mining, communications, public utilities, and transportation were most likely to have testing programs, reaffirming the findings reported by the Conference Board.[13]

Worksites least likely to have testing programs were those in the retail trade and services industries. Worksites in the latter industries tended to be small, however, confounding the relationship between the existence of testing programs and specific industry type.

Differences in Programs

Three primary distinctions among drug testing programs relate to the persons or groups subject to testing, the scheduling of tests, and the substances for which they are tested. The groups that are subject to testing are usually job applicants or current employees. Testing of new applicants appears to be a more common policy than any form of testing of current employees. For example, the Conference Board survey reports that almost half of all organizations screened job applicants by using a drug test.[14] In addition, the study by Blum and her colleagues found that job applicants were not often subjected to drug testing among the large firms in Georgia.[15] The firms that did test current employees, but not applicants were rare, and were probably located in communities with limited labor markets.

The scheduling of tests among current employees is usually classified as random, comprehensive, or for reasonable cause (including followup testing). Random testing is completed with all or a specific segment of employees at a particular worksite, on an unannounced, variable schedule. Random testing seems to be the approach most commonly implemented by firms affected by Department of Transportation regulations.[16] The proportion of larger firms engaged in random testing of employees has increased rapidly. In fact, one study found an increase from 2 percent in 1987 to 30 percent in 1991.[17] Blum and colleagues found that 18 percent of the firms in the American Management survey conducted random tests in 1988.[18]

On a regular basis, companies are likely to conduct testing as a part of a routinely scheduled annual physical examination. Alternatively, they may otherwise announce testing dates, or periods in which tests will be conducted, to employees. This pattern of testing is likely to be conducted with all workers, and unlike random testing, does not seem to have a detrimental effect on employee morale (the administrators are tested along with subordinates). Regular testing is usually more acceptable to workers and organized labor, and it can enhance the firm's image in the community. It is less effective than random testing in detecting substance misuse, however, because employees are usually notified when the test will be scheduled.[19]

Among companies that test current employees, testing for reasonable cause has been the most common practice, and is based on suspicion of substance misuse (resulting from unsafe or nonproductive practices, observation of erratic behavior, possession, or other indications of intoxication or policy violation).[20] If detected, substance abusers are given the opportunity to seek treatment by the firm and retain their jobs. They could be subjected to return-to-work and followup testing as a condition of employment, for a period of time.

Employers have the option of selecting substances for which employees are tested, threshold levels of various chemicals in the body that would constitute a positive drug test, and the option of retesting in the case of a positive result. Of particular interest is the inclusion of alcohol testing in a comprehensive drug testing program.[21] While practically all companies that conduct alcohol tests also test for drugs, only a small proportion of all drug testing programs screen for alcohol misuse.[22]

Other Corporate Responses

According to the 1989 Conference Board survey, drug testing programs were typically part of an integrated substance abuse strategy, which included a written substance abuse policy, an employee assistance program, and a drug education and awareness program.[23] Coordinated efforts to deal with alcohol and drug misuse in the workplace were far less common in corporations without drug testing programs. Similarly, one study found that 60 percent of companies with a drug testing program also had a comprehensive treatment and education program.[24] Another study reported that more than one-half of companies with drug testing programs also had Employee Assistance Programs.[25] Other research has indicated that organizations with drug testing programs are significantly more likely to also have Employee Assistance Programs than those without drug testing programs.[26]

Results

Table 57.1 presents national estimates of drug and alcohol testing for worksites and employees by worksite size, type of industry, and region. Approximately 48 percent of all private worksites in the United States with 50 or more full-time employees conduct drug tests, and approximately 23 percent test employees for alcohol misuse. The prevalence of worksite drug testing increased approximately 32 percent (that is, from 16 percent to 48 percent) from the 1988 BLS survey to the period of our survey, 1992-93.[27]

Worksite Size

Table 57.1 also shows a positive relationship between worksite size and the prevalence of a drug or an alcohol testing program. Approximately 71 percent of worksites with more than 1,000 employees conduct drug tests and 42 percent test for alcohol misuse. In contrast, 40.2 percent of worksites with 50 to 99 employees conduct drug tests and 16.5 percent test for alcohol misuse.

Because of the relatively greater prevalence of drug and alcohol testing programs in larger worksites, most employees in the United States are in worksites with these programs. As shown in Table 57.1, about 62 percent of all employees in private-sector worksites (with 50 or more workers) are employed by firms which conduct drug tests and approximately 33 percent are employed by firms which test for alcohol misuse. Compared with the BLS survey, this coverage rate is greater in all worksite size categories.[28]

Type of Industry

The prevalence of drug and alcohol testing varies across industry groups. As Table 57.1 shows, the manufacturing (60.2 percent); wholesale and retail trade (53.7 percent); communications, utilities, and transportation (72.4 percent); and mining and construction (69.6 percent) industries have the highest prevalence of drug testing, compared

Table 57.1. National estimates of the prevalence of drug and alcohol testing among worksites and employees, by selected characteristics of the worksite, 1992-93, in percent. (NOTE: Standard errors appear in parentheses.) (Continued on next page)

| | Worksites* | | |
Characteristic	Total (In thousands)	Test for drug use	Test for alcohol use
All worksites	162.8 (-)	48.4 (1.2)	23.0 (1.0)
Worksites size			
50-99 employees	61.6 (1.7)	40.2 (2.1)	16.5 (1.6)
100-249 employees	66.0 (1.8)	48.2 (1.9)	22.9 (1.7)
250-999 employees	29.0 (.9)	61.4 (2.1)	32.7 (2.1)
1,000+ employees	6.2 (.3)	70.9 (3.4)	42.1 (3.5)
Type of Industry			
Manufacturing	54.0 (1.0)	60.2 (2.2)	28.3 (2.0)
Wholesale and retail	32.2 (1.1)	53.7 (3.3)	22.1 (2.7)
Communications, utilities, and transportation	13.5 (.8)	72.4 (3.3)	34.9 (3.0)
Finance, insurance, and real estate	14.2 (0.5)	22.6 (2.1)	7.8 (1.3)
Mining and construction	5.6 (.4)	69.6 (4.1)	28.6 (3.5)
Services	43.3 (1.2)	27.9 (2.0)	17.4 (1.7)
Region			
Northeast	33.0 (1.5)	33.3 (2.4)	12.9 (1.7)
Midwest	40.7 (1.8)	50.3 (2.5)	24.0 (2.1)
South	59.1 (19)	56.3 (2.0)	26.3 (1.8)
West	30.0 (1.6)	46.8 (2.9)	26.0 (2.5)

* Worksites of private nonagricultural firms with more than 50 full-time employees at the time of survey.

Table 57.1. (continued) National estimates of the prevalence of drug and alcohol testing among worksites and employees, by selected characteristics of the worksite, 1992-93, in percent. (NOTE: Standard errors appear in parentheses.)

Characteristic	Total (In thousands)	Employees In worksites that test for drug use	In worksites that test for alcohol use
All worksites	41,127 (1,271)	62.3 (1.6)	32.7 (2.1)
Worksites size			
50-99 employees	4,319 (124)	40.7 (2.2)	16.7 (1.6)
100-249 employees	9,612 (265)	48.9 (1.9)	23.2 (1.7)
250-999 employees	12,520 (404)	62.8 (2.1)	33.5 (2.2)
1,000+ employees	14,675 (1,282)	77.1 (3.4)	43.0 (5.0)
Type of Industry			
Manufacturing	14,058 (554)	73.5 (2.2)	37.5 (2.8)
Wholesale and retail	4,901 (236)	57.3 (3.0)	27.7 (3.2)
Communications, utilities, and transportation	4,202 (435)	85.8 (2.6)	43.9 (5.3)
Finance, insurance, and real estate	4,369 (563)	50.2 (6.7)	12.2 (3.1)
Mining and construction	801 (49)	77.7 (3.2)	32.2 (3.1)
Services	12,796 (998)	47.5 (4.5)	32.7 (5.2)
Region			
Northeast	9,356 (617)	49.1 (3.6)	19.3 (2.6)
Midwest	10,190 (616)	62.4 (3.1)	34.4 (3.2)
South	14,986 (1,168)	71.8 (2.6)	36.9 (4.4)
West	6,594 (460)	59.4 (3.3)	39.7 (3.9)

with the finance, real estate, and insurance (22.6 percent) and services (27.9 percent) industries, which have the lowest. A similar pattern is demonstrated for alcohol testing programs with the communications, utilities, and transportation (34.9 percent) industries having the highest prevalence rates and the finance, real estate, and insurance industries (7.8 percent) having the lowest rates. Approximately, the same ranking orders apply when percentage of worksite data are compared with percentage of employees (Table 57.1).

Regional Areas

The highest prevalence for drug and alcohol testing in worksites, by regional area (as defined by the Bureau of the Census) is in the South (56.3 percent for drugs and 26.3 percent for alcohol), while the lowest is in the Northeast (33.3 percent for drugs and 12.9 percent for alcohol). The Midwestern and Western regions have similar prevalence rates (approximately 48 percent for drugs and 25 percent for alcohol). (The remainder of this chapter pertains to drug testing programs only.)

Worksites and Employees[29]

Of all employees in worksites with 50 or more full-time employees, 12.7 percent are represented by a union. However, worksites with a larger percentage of union employees are more likely to have a drug testing program than not to have one (16.3 percent, versus 9.2 percent). A similar relationship exists with the percentage of full-time employees. Worksites with a larger percentage of full-time employees are more likely to have drug testing. A reverse relationship exists with the percentage of employees who have a college degree and are under age 30. Worksites with larger percentages of these employees are less likely to have drug testing programs. Neither the percentage of minority employees at a worksite nor those with a high school diploma is related to having a drug testing program.

The worksite characteristics indicate the following: when a worksite conducts drug testing, it is more likely to have a written alcohol and drug use policy (96.0 percent) and it is more likely to have an Employee Assistance Program (45.9 percent).

Who Gets Tested?

In addition to the overall prevalence of drug testing programs in worksites, we also examined which employees were subject to testing.

Statistical data show 48.4 percent of worksites with more than 50 full-time employees have some type of drug testing program. Of this group, 23.6 percent subject all employees to testing, 14.0 percent test only applicants, and 3.6 percent test only employees regulated by the Department of Transportation. Interesting to note, is that 0.8 percent of the worksites test only safety or security employees and 6.4 percent test other combinations of groups (for example, job applicants and employees regulated by the Department of Transportation only).

Thus, most programs are designed to test all employees or applicants only. In general, the percentage of worksites that test all employees and applicants only increases by worksite size. The mining and construction industries have the largest percentage of worksites where all employees are subject to testing (49.0 percent), and the manufacturing industry has the largest percentage that test new employees only (21.4 percent). As expected, the communications, utility, and transportation industries have the largest percentage of worksites that test only employees who are regulated by the Department of Transportation (13.4 percent). Of the four regions, the South has the largest percentage of worksites that test all employees (32.7 percent).

Frequency

Table 57.2 presents the percentage of drug testing worksites that test on a regular or random basis. Generally, less than 15 percent of these worksites actually conduct such tests on a regular basis. In contrast, approximately 47 percent of these worksites test on a random basis. The percentage of random testing decreases with worksite size and is the highest in the communication, utilities, and transportation industries (76.1 percent). Regular testing does not appear to be related to worksite size and is highest in the mining and construction industries (20.7 percent). The South has the highest percentage of random testing (53.8 percent), while regular testing is highest in the Midwest (16.2 percent). The West has the lowest percentages for both random (32.7 percent) and regular testing (11.0 percent).

Who Conducts the Tests?

Overall, outside contractors are responsible for testing at approximately 79 percent of worksites, while a medical department within a company conducts tests for approximately 11 percent and a personnel or human resources department tests for 6.4 percent. As worksite employment size increases, outside contractors are used less frequently

Table 57.2. Frequency of drug testing for worksites that test current employees, by characteristics of the worksite[1], 1992-93. (Note: Standard errors appear in parentheses.)

Characteristic	On regular basis	On random basis
All worksites with drug testing program[2]	13.7 (1.4)	46.7 (2.0)
Worksite size		
50-99 employees	15.3 (2.6)	54.3 (4.1)
100-249 employees	12.8 (2.3)	46.4 (3.3)
250-999 employees	12.5 (2.3)	38.2 (3.3)
1,000+ employees	14.6 (3.6)	38.0 (4.6)
Type of industry		
Manufacturing	11.6 (2.2)	35.9 (3.3)
Wholesale and retail	12.8 (3.5)	51.3 (5.4)
Communications, utilities, and transportation	15.9 (2.5)	76.1 (3.5)
Finance, insurance, and real estate	5.8 (4.2)	32.4 (7.2)
Mining and construction	20.7 (4.5)	55.1 (5.2)
Services	16.2 (3.6)	38.8 (4.5)
Region		
Northeast	14.7 (3.5)	45.4 (5.5)
Midwest	16.2 (2.8)	44.4 (4.0)
South	13.0 (2.1)	53.8 (3.1)
West	11.0 (3.1)	32.7 (4.4)

[1]*Worksites that test only job applicants are not included in this table.*

[2]*Worksites of private nonagricultural firms with more than 50 full-time employees at the time of survey.*

(for example, 86.9 percent for worksites with 50-99 employees, versus 46.3 percent for worksites with 1,000 or more employees), while the use of a medical department increases dramatically (for example, 5.0 percent for worksites with 50-99 employees, versus 40.4 percent for worksites with 1,000 or more employees). Thus, compared with smaller worksites, the larger worksites are more likely to conduct tests internally. The wholesale/retail trade industry reported the largest percentage of tests done by an outside contractor (91.2 percent), while the services industry reported the lowest percentage (69.0 percent). The Northeast had the largest percentage of drug tests done by a medical department (16.8 percent), while there was no noticeable pattern across regions for the percentage of testing by an outside contractor.

Conclusion

Drug testing is widely implemented in worksites throughout the United States, and is partially based on the characteristics of the worksite, the characteristics of its employees, and the implementation of other strategies and policies to control substance misuse. Drug testing programs are continually added to worksite policies, as well as the proportion of the labor force subject to testing. Programs that test for illicit drug use are more than twice as prevalent as those that test for alcohol use. This is ironic, in that alcohol misuse is by far the more common personal problem related to impaired job performance.[30] However, testing for alcohol use is a more complex social and legal issue because alcohol use per se does not constitute a violation of law or company personnel policies.[31]

However, the results of this study confirm that drug testing continues to develop as a preferred strategy to control substance abuse in the workplace. Programs are most prevalent in larger worksites, those industries affected by drug testing legislation, and those employing high risk or unionized labor forces. Random drug testing has emerged as the most common form of testing, and most often, all employees and applicants are now included in testing programs. Drug testing is commonly conducted by external firms, but larger worksites are significantly more likely than their smaller counterparts to conduct testing within their worksites. Proliferation of the number and scope of programs, coupled with the movement towards random testing suggests continued strengthening of the employers' dedication to systematically identify and intervene in cases of drug and, to a lesser degree, alcohol abuse at their worksites. Drug testing has joined with other programs and policies (such as Employee Assistance Programs, health promotion programs, and written drug and alcohol use policies) to form more comprehensive responses to workplace substance abuse. Additional research is recommended to further define the integration of strategies to control worksite substance abuse and to examine the outcomes and effectiveness of these efforts.

Notes

1. See William Sonnenstuhl and Harrison Trice, *Strategies for Employee Assistance Programs: the Crucial Balance, Second Revised* (Ithaca, NY, ILR Press, 1990); Harrison Trice and Janice Beyer, "Work-related outcomes of constructive confrontation strategies in a job-based alcoholism program," Vol. 45, *Journal of Studies on Alcohol*, 1984, pp. 393-104; and Harrison Trice and Mona Schonbrunn, "A history of job-based alcoholism programs; 1900-1955," Vol. 11, *Journal of Drug Issues*, 1981, pp. 171-98.

2. Steven Gust and J. Michael Walsh, eds., *Drugs in the workplace: research and evaluation*, Research Monograph 91 (National Institute of Drug Abuse, Washington, DC, 1989).

3. D. Ackerman, "A history of drug testing" in R. H. Coombs and L. J. West, eds., *Drug Testing: Issues and Options* (New York, Oxford University Press, 1991), pp. 3-21.

4. Terry Blum, S. Fields, S. Mine, and C. Spell, "Workplace drug testing programs: a review of research and a survey of worksites," Vol. 1, No. 2, *Journal of Employee Assistance Research*, 1992, pp. 315-49.

5. J. Guthrie and J. Olian, "Drug and alcohol testing programs: do firms consider their operating environment," Vol. 14, *Human Resource Planning*, 1991, p. 221.

6. M. Harris and L. Heft, "Alcohol and drug use in the workplace: issues, controversies, and directions for future research," Vol. 18, *Journal of Management*, 1992, pp. 239-66.

7. Blum and others, "Workplace drug testing programs."

8. "Survey of Employer Anti-drug Programs," Report 760 (Bureau of Labor Statistics, January 1989); and Howard Hayghe, "Anti-drug programs in the workplace—are they here to stay?" *Monthly Labor Review*, April 1991, pp. 26-29.

9. E. Greenberg, "Workplace testing: results of a new AMA survey," Vol. 65, *Personnel*, 1988, p. 36.

10. "Survey of Employer Anti-drug Programs," Report 760.

11. Hayghe, "Anti-drug programs."

12. The Conference Board, "Surveys reach different conclusions about prevalence of drug testing," Vol. 21, *Compensation and Benefits Review*, 1989, p. 13.

13. Hayghe, "Anti-drug programs."

14. The Conference Board, "Surveys reach different conclusions."

15. Blum and others, "Workplace drug testing programs."

16. U.S. Department of Transportation, Drug and alcohol testing programs: proposed rules, Vol. 57, *Federal Register*, 1992, p. 241.

17. K. Murphy and G. Thornton, "Characteristics of employee drug testing policies," Vol. 6, *Journal of Business and Psychology*, 1990, p. 295.

18. Blum and others, "Workplace drug testing programs."

19. Harrison Trice and Paul Steele, "Impairment testing: issues and convergence with employee assistance programs," *Journal of Drug Issues*, 1995, in press.

20. See Blum and others, "Workplace drug testing programs;" Murphy and Thornton, "Characteristics of employee drug testing policies;" and D. Masi, "Company responses to drug abuse from AMA's nationwide survey," Vol. 64, *Personnel*, 1987, p. 40.

21. Trice and Steele, "Impairment testing."

22. P. Greenfield, R. Karren, and J. Giacobbe, "Drug testing in the workplace: an overview of legal and philosophical issues," Vol. 2, *Employee Responsibilities and Rights Journal*, 1989, pp. 1-10.

23. The Conference Board "Surveys reach different conclusions."

24. E. Greenberg, "Workplace testing: results of a new AMA survey."

25. Terry Blum, "The presence and integration of drug abuse intervention in human resources management," in Steven Gust and J. Michael Walsh, eds., *Drugs in the Workplace: Research and*

Evaluation Data, NIDA Research Monograph 91 (Rockville, MD, National Institute on Drug Abuse, 1989), pp. 245-70.

26. Blum and others, "Workplace drug testing programs."

27. Survey of Employer Anti-drug Programs, Report 760.

28. Ibid.

29. For the employee characteristics, our questionnaire asked for the percentage of the employee population with the given characteristic and our analysis involved comparing means of these percentages. For the worksite characteristics, our questionnaire asked "Do you have this characteristic?, yes/no." Our analysis involved analyzing 2x2 contingency tables.

30. Terry Blum and Paul Roman, "A description of clients using employee assistance programs," Vol. 16, *Alcohol Health and Research World*, 1992, pp. 120-28; and Lee Kobins and D. Regier, *Psychiatric Disorders in America: The Epidemiologic Area Study* (New York, The Free Press, 1991).

31. Trice and Steele, "Impairment testing."

About the Authors

Tyler D. Hartwell is a senior statistician at the Research Triangle Institute, Triangle Park, NC; Paul D. Steele is Director of Research at Vera Institute of Justice, New York, NY; Michael T. French, is Research Associate Professor, University of Miami, Coral Gables, FL; and Nathaniel F. Rodman is research statistician at Research Triangle Institute.

Chapter 58

A Review of the Evaluation of 47 Drug Abuse Prevention Curricula Available Nationally

Drug prevention efforts during the past two decades relied largely on classroom curricula, usually designed for elementary and middle school children. The General Accounting Office estimates that the nation's schools spend $125 million on drug abuse prevention curricula each year.[1] A survey of school districts in Wisconsin[2] revealed that almost two-thirds had purchased a drug abuse prevention curriculum.

A growing consensus in the drug abuse prevention field suggests certain types of school-based programs effectively can reduce drug use in adolescence. This opinion, reflected in recent literature reviews,[3-6] is supported by several meta-analyses.[1,7-13] Specifically, prevention curricula which give students training in social resistance skills or how to recognize influences and resist them effectively, and normative education positing that drug use is not the norm have been shown to reduce substance use behavior. In addition, training in broader personal and social skills such as decision-making, anxiety reduction, communication, and assertiveness appears to enhance program effectiveness.

Unfortunately, while research has shown that certain prevention curricula are effective, Hansen, Rose, and Dryfoos[1] suggest that most of the money in this country is not spent on curricula proven to work,

"A Review of the Evaluation of 47 Drug Abuse Prevention Curricula Available Nationally," by Linda Dusenbury; Antonia Lake; Mathea Falco, in *Journal of School Health*, Vol. 67, No. 4, April 1997, p127(6), © 1997 American School Health Association; reprinted with permission. American School Health Association, Kent, Ohio.

but on aggressively marketed programs that have not been evaluated, or worse, have been shown not to work.

This review determined how many drug prevention curricula available to schools have been shown in rigorous research studies to reduce substance use behavior. Previous reviews of the literature do not answer this question. They identified promising prevention approaches,[3-6] but they did not limit themselves to drug abuse prevention curricula available to schools. Indeed, many studies evaluated experimental curricula not available to the general population. This review is unique in that it focuses on the universe of programs available to schools and asks which of these have been shown to effectively reduce substance use.

Identifying Curricula and Evaluations

The project's first step involved identifying drug abuse prevention curricula. Curricula meeting four criteria were included:

1. they focused on primary prevention of alcohol and/or drug use, and not simply on tobacco use,

2. they were classroom-based curricula designed for any grade level P-12,

3. they were nationally and currently available, and

4. program distributors were willing to provide samples of curriculum materials to determine drug abuse prevention content.

Six procedures were followed to create an exhaustive list of currently available drug abuse prevention curricula:

1. review of the literature on drug abuse prevention curricula,

2. queries to experts in drug abuse prevention to identify programs they knew about and to review the list for omissions,

3. queries to federal agencies involved in drug abuse prevention research and practice,

4. queries to publishers of health education curricula and review of their catalogs,

5. announcements at drug abuse and health education conferences and meetings, and

416

6. review of published and unpublished guides to drug abuse prevention.

Forty-eight curricula met the criteria; one (Me-Me) declined to participate. Table 58.1 contains a list of 47 curricula reviewed.

Curriculum distributors and developers also were contacted by mail and in follow-up telephone calls to request full evaluation reports of each curriculum. Evaluation summaries or abstracts were not sufficient.

The quality of evaluations of drug abuse prevention curricula was found to be quite variable, ranging from process evaluations which may have asked teachers or students to comment on the appeal of curriculum materials or activities at one extreme, all the way to rigorous outcome evaluations involving large longitudinal field trials at the other extreme. In between were a multitude of types of evaluations, including small and large outcome studies, some sound while others had dubious research designs or major methodological flaws. Some evaluations assessed knowledge or attitudes about drugs, but not drug use behavior.

Since the goal was to determine effectiveness of curricula in reducing substance use behavior, three criteria were used to identify adequate and acceptable evaluations. These criteria are similar to those established for meta-analysis:[12,14]

1. pretest-post-test control group designs,

2. outcome measures of substance use behavior, and

3. published in peer-reviewed journals to select studies which have solid research designs and methodologies.

Of 47 drug abuse prevention curricula identified, 10 (21%) were found to have been subjected to sufficiently rigorous evaluations. Results of evaluations for these 10 curricula are summarized below (information is adapted from *Making the Grade: A Guide to School Drug Prevention Programs.* Washington, DC: Drug Strategies; 1996):

Alcohol Misuse Prevention Program.[15-18] There are two versions of the Alcohol Misuse Prevention Program, which is a social resistance skills curriculum focusing specifically on alcohol prevention. The stronger, and more complete version is for students in grades six-eight, with eight sessions in the first year, five sessions in the second year,

Table 58.1. Listing of Drug Abuse Prevention Curricula Currently Available (continued on next page)

Comprehensive Health Programs	Grade Level
Actions for Health	K-6
Comprehensive Health	5-9
Discover: Decisions for Health	7-12
Entering Adulthood	9-12
Great Body Shop	K-6
*Growing Healthy	K-6
Health Skills for Life	K-12
*Know Your Body	K-6
Michigan Model	K-8
Quest: Skills for Growing	K-5
Quest: Skills for Adolescence	6-8
Quest: Skills for Action	9-12
Science for Life and Living	K-6
*Teenage Health Teaching Modules	6-12

K-12 Programs	Grade Level
BABES	P-12
Choosing for Yourself II	K-12
*DARE	K-12
Discover Skills for Life	K-12
Here's Looking at Your, 2000	K-12
Learning About Alcohol and Other Drugs	K-12
Learning to Live Drug Free	K-12
Project Oz	K-12
That's Life	K-10

Table 58.1. (continued) Listing of Drug Abuse Prevention Curricula Currently Available

Elementary and Middle School Programs	Grade Level
CounterAct	4, 5, or 6
Facts, Feelings, Family, and Friends	K-6
Growing Up Strong	P-6
Growing Up Well	K-8
I'm Special	3 or 4
McGruff	P-6
Paper People	P-3
Positive Action	K-8
Project Charlie	K-6
Starting Early	K-6

Middle and High School Programs	Grade Level
Al-Co-Hol	7-9
*Alcohol Misuse Prevention Program	6-8
Drug Proof	6-8
From Peer Pressure to Peer Support	7-12
Healthy for Life	6-8
*Life Skills Training	6-8 or 7-9
Ombudsman	5-9
*Project Alert	6, 7, or 7,8
Project All-Stars	6,7
*Project Northland	6-8
Setting Norms for Refusal	6, 7, or 8
*Social Competence Promotion Program	5, 6, or 7
*STAR	5-8
Talking with Your Students About Alcohol	5-12

* Curriculum have been evaluated adequately

and four sessions in the third year. This review examined the most complete version of the Alcohol Misuse Prevention Project.

Grade level: 6-8

Length of longest evaluation: 2 years

# of different research studies: 1

Sample size in longest evaluation: 1,725 sixth grade students

Changes in ATOD use: reduced misuse of alcohol in high-risk students

Duration of behavioral changes: 2 years

Evaluated with different cultural groups: 5% minority (2% black, 3% other)

Comments: increased knowledge about alcohol.

Contact: Youth and Social Issues, University of Michigan, Institute for Social Research, Room 2311, 426 Thompson Street, Ann Arbor, MI 48106-1248, (734) 763-5043

DARE.[19-22] DARE, the most widely used drug prevention approach in the United States, is a social resistance skills training curriculum which covers some broader personal and social skills. It is designed for use in grades K-12, though the core curriculum is 17 sessions implemented in the fifth or sixth grade. DARE is implemented by law enforcement officers.

Grade level: K-12

Length of longest evaluation: 2 years

# of different research studies: 4

Sample size in longest evaluation: 1,334 fifth/sixth grade students

Changes in ATOD use: Studies have yielded inconsistent findings

Duration of behavioral changes: immediate post-test

Evaluated with different cultural groups: 46% minority (22% black, 9% Hispanic,15% other); substantial minority samples in other studies

Comments: no consistent results; some studies show affect on knowledge and attitudes about ATOD and more favorable attitudes toward police.

Contact: DARE America, P.O. Box 512090, Los Angeles, CA 90051-0090, (800) 223-DARE; web site: www.dare.com

Growing Healthy.[23] Growing Healthy covers broader personal and social skills in a comprehensive health program consisting of 40 or more sessions per year for grades K-6.

Grade level: K-6

Length of longest evaluation: 2 years

# of different research studies: 1

Sample size in longest evaluation: 30,000 fourth-seventh grade students

Changes in ATOD use: reduced tobacco use 29% by ninth grade

Duration of behavioral changes: 2 years

Evaluated with different cultural groups: 19% minority (15% black, 2% Hispanic, 2% other)

Comments: significant affect on knowledge and attitudes related to health.

Contact: Growing Healthy, National Center for Health Education, 72 Spring St., Suite 208, New York, NY 10012-4019, (800) 551-3488

Know Your Body.[24] Know Your Body covers broader personal and social skills in a comprehensive health program with an average of 60 sessions per year for grades K-6.

Grade level: K-6

Length of longest evaluation: six years

# of different research studies: 1

Sample size in longest evaluation: 1,105 fourth grade students

Changes in ATOD use: Reduced tobacco use 73% in ninth grade

Duration of behavioral changes: 6 years

Evaluated with different cultural groups: 21% minority (14% black, 2% Hispanic, 5% other)

Comments: greater reductions in use for males. Increased health knowledge (including cigarette and drug information) for nine years. Positive effects on attitudes.

Contact: Know Your Body, American Health Foundation, 675 Third Ave., 11th floor, New York, NY 10017, (212) 551-2509

Life Skills Training.[25-30] The Life Skills Training Program is a broader personal and social skills training program for middle school students designed to prevent tobacco, alcohol, and drug use. It has 15 sessions the first year, 10 sessions in the second year, and eight sessions the third year.

Grade level: 6-8 or 7-9

Length of longest evaluation: 6 years

# of different research studies: 10

Sample size in longest evaluation: 4,466 seventh grade students

Changes in ATOD use: Reduced smoking, alcohol, and marijuana use at seventh grade post-test up to 50% to 75%. By end of high school, results erode only slightly with 44% reductions in tobacco, alcohol, or marijuana use and 66% reduction in use of all three

Duration of behavioral changes: 6 years

Evaluated with different cultural groups: 75% minority in four of 10 studies; combination of black (11% to 87%) and Hispanic (10% to 74%)

Comments: significant effect on knowledge and attitudes about ATOD at thee years (six year data on knowledge and attitudes not yet analyzed).

Contact: Life Skills Training, Institute for Prevention Research, Cornell University Medical, Rm. 201, 411 E. 69th St., New York, NY 10021, (212) 746-1270; web site: www.lifeskillstraining.com

Project Alert.[31-33] Project Alert is a social resistance skills training program for students in grades six and seven, or seven and eight. Project Alert consists of 11 sessions the first year, and three the second.

Grade level: 6-7 or 7-8

Length of longest evaluation: 6 years

# of different research studies: 1

Sample size in longest evaluation: 3,852 seventh grade students)

Changes in ATOD use: reduced drinking up to 50% at post-test. Reduced marijuana use 33% to 60% in eighth grade. Reduced tobacco use 17% to 55% in eighth grade.

Duration of behavioral changes: 15 months

Evaluated with different cultural groups: 30% minority (10% Asian, 9% Hispanic, 3% other)

Comments: Some negative effects for high-risk youth. Significant effect on attitudes, some effects on belief about harm of drugs and normative perceptions lasting six years.

Contact: Project Alert, Best Foundation, 725 S. Figueroa St., Suite 1615, Los Angeles, CA 90017, (800) ALERT-10; web site: www.best.org

Project Northland.[34] Project Northland is a social resistance skills training approach to alcohol prevention. Project Northland consists of eight sessions per year for grades six-eight.

Grade level: 6-8

Length of longest evaluation: 3 years

# of different research studies: 1

Sample size in longest evaluation: 1,901 sixth grade students

Changes in ATOD use: reduced alcohol use 27%. Reduced tobacco use 37%. Reduced marijuana use 50%.

Duration of behavioral changes: 3 years

Evaluated with different cultural groups: 5% minority (4% Native American, 1% other)

Comments: Significant effect on perceived norms among students who did not drink at baseline.

Contact: Project Northland, University of Minnesota, Division of Epidemiology, School of Public Health, 1300 S. Second St., Suite 300, Minneapolis, MN 55445-1015, (612) 624-1818; web site: www.epi.umn.edu/projectnorthland

Social Competence Promotion Program.[35] The Social Competence Promotion Program is a 27-session social problem-solving program with a nine-session drug abuse prevention module. It includes social resistance skills training within the context of broader personal and social skills.

Grade level: 5, 6, or 7

Length of longest evaluation: immediate post-test

# of different research studies: 1

Sample size in longest evaluation: 282 sixth and seventh grade students

Changes in ATOD use: reduced heavy alcohol use

Duration of behavioral changes: immediate post-test

Evaluated with different cultural groups: 73% minority (66% black, 6% Hispanic, 1% other)

Comments: Significant effect on intentions to use alcohol.

Contact: Social Competence Promotion Program, Dept. of Psychology, (M/C 285), University of Illinois at Chicago, 1007 W. Harrison St., Chicago, IL 60607-7137, (312) 996-3037

STAR.[36] STAR is a two-year social resistance skills training approach for students in grades five-eight. It has 10-13 sessions the first year and five the second year.

Grade level: 5-8

Length of longest evaluation: 3 years

# of different research studies: 1

Sample size in longest evaluation: 4,978 sixth and seventh grade students

Changes in ATOD use: reduced tobacco, alcohol, and marijuana use 30% at one year

Duration of behavioral changes: 3 years

Evaluated with different cultural groups: 22% minority (17% black, 2% Hispanic, 1% Asian, 2% other). Study involved multi-component intervention (school, family, media).

Comments: Significant effect on beliefs about drug use at 1½ year follow-up. More recent data not yet analyzed.

Contact: STAR, Institute for Prevention Research, 1000 S. Fremont Ave., Rm. 1810, Alhambra, CA 91803, (323) 442-2600

Teenage Health Teaching Modules.[37] Teenage Health Teaching Modules is a comprehensive health program with 40-70 sessions per year for grades 7-12. Depending on the modules implemented, Teenage Health Teaching Modules covers social resistance skills training in the context of broader personal and social skills.

Grade level: 6-12

Length of longest evaluation: immediate post-test

# of different research studies: 1

Sample size in longest evaluation: 4,806 (high school juniors and seniors)

Changes in ATOD use: moderate reductions in ATOD use for senior high school students

Duration of behavioral changes: immediate post-test

Evaluated with different cultural groups: 26% minority (12% Hispanic, 10% black, 3% Asian, 1% Native American)

Comments: Significant effect on knowledge and attitudes related to health for junior and senior high school students.

Contact: Teenage Health Teaching Modules, Educational Development Center, 55 Chapel St., Newton, MA 02458-1060, (800) 225-4276

Data Presentation and Methods

Considerable variability existed in the way data were presented in the evaluation studies of these curricula. Where possible, results are presented in above in terms of percent reductions of substance use. Research groups that evaluated these curricula were contacted to confirm the summaries accurately reflected their findings. However, no standard exists for presenting data in drug abuse prevention evaluations.

Some evaluators summarize results in terms of percent reductions in drug use, as does this evaluation. Percent reductions are easy to calculate. They involve subtracting mean rate of drug use in the experimental group from mean rate of drug use in the control group, then dividing the difference by the mean rate of the control group. If the experimental group had a post-test drug use rate of 2%, and the control group had a rate of 4%, a 50% reduction occurred in drug use.

However, some experts feel this approach to presenting results is misleading since it exaggerates the size of the difference between the experimental and control group. An alternative approach simply discusses difference between the control group and the experimental group as a straight percentage. The difference between 2% and 4% is 2%, or a 2% reduction. However, this approach is equally misleading since it minimizes the difference.

The best technical solution may involve calculating an effect size for each study, since an effect size standardizes the data. Effect sizes are used in meta-analyses. The mathematical formula for calculating an effect size involves subtracting the mean of the control group from the mean of the experimental group and dividing the difference by the standard deviation of the control group. An effect size of .2 is considered small, an effect size of .5 is considered moderate, and an effect size of .8 is considered large. The difficulty with calculating effect sizes, and the reason effect sizes are not used here (except when that was the only result provided in an evaluation) is that evaluators do not always report the standard deviation of the control group, making the effect size impossible to calculate. Moreover, since studies are often five or more years old, it was not possible for many researchers to locate that information when asked.

Evaluations that met the inclusion criteria were of variable quality. Most were large: nine of 10 involved samples of at least 1,000 students. Evaluation of Social Competence Promotion Program was the exception, with less than 300 students participating. Eight of 10 curricula were evaluated in studies which followed students at least two years. Exceptions were the Social Competence Promotion Program and Teenage Health Teaching Modules, which only measured outcomes at the immediate post-test. Eight of 10 included measures of alcohol and/or use of marijuana or other illicit substances. Evaluations of two curricula, Growing Healthy and Know Your Body, only measured tobacco use.

Evaluation studies of the different curricula had varying lengths of follow-up, ranging from immediate post-test only in two cases (the Social Competence Promotion Program and the Teenage Health Teaching Modules) to six-year follow-ups in three cases (Know Your Body, Life Skills Training, and Project Alert). Of the three curricula evaluated in six-year studies, two (Know Your Body and Life Skills Training) showed curriculum effects on behavior lasting the duration of the study. In the remaining case (Project Alert), positive behavioral effects disappeared after 15 months.

Finally, curricula had been evaluated in different numbers of studies. Life Skills Training had been evaluated in 10 separate studies which met the criteria. DARE had been evaluated in four separate studies. The Alcohol Misuse Prevention project has two curricula, and each had been evaluated in a separate study. The remaining curricula all had been evaluated in a single study.

Project Findings

Evaluations summarized above suggest that substance abuse prevention curricula effectively can reduce substance use. At least eight programs have been effective at reducing tobacco or drug use, in at least some studies. One program (Life Skills Training) has been shown to have effects into young adulthood. Evaluations of Life Skills Training included measures of tobacco, alcohol, and marijuana. Six of the 10 curricula (Alcohol Misuse Prevention Project, Growing Healthy, Know

Your Body, Life Skills Training, Project Northland, and STAR) have been shown to have effects lasting for at least two years after the pretest. Two curricula (Social Competence Promotion Program and Teenage Health Teaching Modules) have not been evaluated beyond the post-test, so it is impossible to know whether their effectiveness will last.

Two programs (Project Alert and DARE) did not appear to have sustained effects on drug use, though they had variable success at reducing substance use early on. Project Alert showed an effect on substance use for the first 15 months of the evaluation, but positive effects on behavior disappeared beyond that point. In addition, Project Alert increased substance use among some groups of high-risk youth, although these effects disappeared after 10th grade.

DARE appeared to produce effects on substance use at the immediate post-test in some studies, though the results are not consistent. One of four studies evaluating DARE showed no effects of the curriculum on substance use at any time.[22] However, three of the four studies[19-21] did find at least some reductions in use of some substances or for some subgroups of the study population, although these effects disappeared in the two studies[19,20] that followed students beyond the initial post-test. The third study did not follow students beyond the initial post-test.[21]

While DARE and Project Alert do not appear to have a lasting affect on substance use behavior, these programs still may make an important contribution to drug abuse prevention, if done within the context of ongoing and sustained prevention efforts. Prevention programming must have adequate coverage and sufficient follow-up—students must receive a sufficient dose—if these efforts are to have lasting effects. When programs are brief, it is not surprising that effects diminish over time.

Research has not yet determined exactly how many sessions constitute adequate coverage, or how many years of intervention constitute adequate follow-up. The authors have proposed[38] that curricula should be at least 10 sessions long in the first year (Project Alert is eight), and five sessions long in the second year (the emphasis in DARE has typically been on the core sessions which are presented in one year). Reinforcement and follow-up are critical to the success of prevention programs, and no one should be surprised when effects disappear after prevention programming ends.

Conclusions and Recommendations

Of 47 curricula available to schools, only 10 (21%) have been evaluated in rigorous studies. Meanwhile schools are purchasing the other

37 with no real information about their effectiveness. It is possible that many of these programs are effective. However, without adequate evaluations, schools are buying products that have no guarantee of success.

If curricula are marketed as substance abuse prevention curricula, curriculum developers and distributors have a responsibility to evaluate the effect of their programs on substance use behavior and to make the results of their evaluations available. Schools should insist on evaluations that assess curriculum affect on behavior.

Research has confirmed that certain approaches to drug abuse prevention are effective. Yet some of the best and most thoroughly evaluated in terms of tobacco, alcohol, and marijuana (Life Skills Training, Project Northland, and STAR) are not being marketed aggressively. In large part, this lack is because these curricula were developed by researchers, who may feel some conflict of interest in marketing a program they also evaluate, or may simply not know how to promote a curriculum. One solution would be for the federal agencies which funded the research of these curricula either to promote them or to facilitate partnerships with publishers effective at marketing.

Another strategy would encourage the federal government to promote or even require evaluation of curricula being used in schools. Federal and state research funding could be set aside to evaluate these curricula.

In addition, guidelines should be established to provide minimum acceptable standards for evaluation. Begin with the criteria used here for acceptable evaluation: pretest-post-test, control group designs with measures of substance use behavior, and published in peer-reviewed journals. However, evaluation standards also might set some minimum follow-up period such as one or two years. Adequate sample sizes also could be determined such as more than 1,000. Standardized measures of substance use behavior could be determined, and should include alcohol use, marijuana use, and other drug use in addition to tobacco use.

Presentation of data should be standardized. Evaluation studies could be required to report results in terms of percent reductions, and they could be required to calculate effect sizes.

Such guidelines also could require that in evaluation studies the whole school should be assigned to condition, rather than classes within a school, to avoid contamination across the experimental and control groups. This requirement would raise statistical problems when the unit of assignment (school) did not match the unit of analysis (usually the individual). One solution is to treat schools as the unit of analysis as well, but this approach requires enormous studies, since so many schools would be required to have sufficient sample sizes for the analysis. Another solution is to simply decide to have a unit of assignment (school) that does not match the unit of analysis (individual), and accept the fact that some assumptions of the analysis have been violated.

References

1. Hansen WB, Rose LA, Dryfoos JC. *Causal Factors, Interventions and Policy Considerations in School-Based Substance Abuse Prevention*. Washington, DC: U.S. Congress, Office of Technology Assessment; May 26, 1993.

2. Fredisdorf M. Alcohol and drug abuse prevention in Wisconsin public schools. *J Sch Health*. 1989;59:21-24.

3. Botvin GJ, Botvin EM. School-based and community-based prevention approaches. In Lowinson J, Ruiz P, Millman R, eds. *Comprehensive Textbook of Substance Abuse*. Baltimore, MD: Williams & Wilkins; 1992:910-927.

4. Hansen WB. School-based substance abuse prevention: A review of the state of the art in curriculum, 1980-1990. *Health Educ Res*. 1992;7:403-430.

5. Hansen WB. School-based alcohol prevention programs. *Alc Health Res World*. 1993;17:54-60.

6. Perry CL, Kelder SH. Models for effective prevention. *J Adol Health*. 1992;13:355-363.

7. Bangert-Drowns RL. The effects of school-based substance abuse education—A meta-analysis. *J Drug Educ*. 1988;18:243-264.

8. Bruvold WH. A meta-analysis of the California school based risk reduction program. *J Drug Educ*. 1990;20:139-152.

9. Bruvold WH. A meta-analysis of adolescent smoking prevention programs. *Am J Public Health* 1993;83:872-880.

10. Bruvold WH, Rundall TG. A meta-analysis and theoretical review of school based tobacco and alcohol intervention programs. *Psych Health*. 1988;2:53-78.

11. Rundall TG, Bruvold WH. A meta-analysis of school-based smoking and alcohol use prevention programs. *Health Educ Q*. 1988;15:317-334.

12. Tobler NS. Drug prevention programs can work: Research findings. *J Addict Dis*. 1992; 11:1-28.

13. Tobler NS. Analyses of school-site strategies: Updated meta-analysis of adolescent drug prevention programs: Conference proceedings. In Montoya CF, Ringwalt C, Ryan BE, Zimmerman R, eds. *Evaluating School-linked Prevention Strategies: Alcohol, Tobacco and other Drugs*. San Diego, Calif: University of California at San Diego; 1993.

14. Ennett S. Tobler NS, Ringwalt CL, Flewelling RL. How effective is Project DARE? A meta-analysis of outcome evaluations. *Am J Public Health*. 1994;84.

15. Dielman TE, Kloska DD, Leech SL, Schulenberg JE, Shope J. Susceptibility to peer pressure as an explanatory variable for the differential effectiveness of an alcohol misuse prevention program in elementary schools. *J Sch Health*. 1992;62:233-237.

16. Dielman TE, Shope JT, Leech SL, Butchart AT. Differential effectiveness of an elementary school-based alcohol misuse prevention program. *J Sch Health*. 1989;59:255-263.

17. Shope JT. Dielman TE, Butchart AT, Campanelli PC, Kloska DD. An elementary school-based alcohol misuse prevention program: A follow-up evaluation. *J Stud Alc*. 1992;53:106-121.

18. Shope JT. Kloska DD, Dielman TE, Maharg R. Longitudinal evaluation of an enhanced alcohol misuse prevention study (AMPS) curriculum for grades six-eight. *J Sch Health*. 1994;64:160-166.

19. Clayton RR, Cattarello A, Walden KP. Sensation seeking as a potential mediating variable for school-based intervention: A two-year follow-up of DARE. *Health Commun*. 1991;3:229-239.

20. Ennett S. Rosenbaum DP. Flewelling RL. Bieler GS, Ringwalt CL, Bailey SL. Long-term evaluation of drug abuse resistance education. *Addict Behav*. 1994;19:113-125.

21. Harmon MA. Reducing the risk of drug involvement among early adolescents: An evaluation of Drug Abuse Resistance Education (DARE). *Eval Rev.* 1993;17:221-239.

22. Ringwalt C, Ennett ST, Holt KD. An outcome evaluation of Project DARE (Drug Abuse Resistance Education). *Health Educ Res.* 1991;6:327-337.

23. Connell DB, Turner RR, Mason EF. Summary of findings of the School Health Education Evaluation: Health promotion effectiveness, implementation, and costs. *J Sch Health.* 1985; 55:316-321.

24. Walter HJ, Vaughan RD, Wynder EL. Primary prevention of cancer among children: Changes in cigarette smoking and diet after six years of intervention. *J Nat Cancer Institute.* 1989; 81:995-998.

25. Botvin GJ, Baker E, Dusenbury L, Botvin E, Diaz T. Long-term follow-up results of a randomized drug abuse prevention trial in a white middle-class population. *JAMA.* 1995;273: 1106-1112.

26. Botvin GI, Baker E, Dusenbury L, Tortu S, Botvin EM. Preventing adolescent drug abuse through a multimodal cognitive-behavioral approach: Results of a 3-Year study. *J Consult Clinical Psychol.* 1992;58:437-446.

27. Botvin GI. Batson HW, Witts-Vitale S, Bess V, Baker E, Dusenbury L. A psychosocial approach to smoking prevention for urban black youth. *Public Health Rep.* 1989;104:573-582.

28. Botvin GJ, Dusenbury L, Baker E, James-Ortiz S, Kerner J. A skills training approach to smoking prevention among Hispanic youth. *J Behav Med.* 1989;12:279-296.

29. Botvin GJ, Dusenbury LD, Baker E, Ortiz S, Botvin E, Kerner J. Smoking prevention among urban minority youth: Assessing effects on outcome and mediating variables. *Health Psychol.* 1992;11:290-299.

30. Botvin GJ, Schinke SP, Epstein JA, Diaz T. Effectiveness of culturally focused and generic skills training approaches to alcohol and drug abuse prevention among minority youths. *Psychol Addict Behav.* 1994;8:116-127.

31. Bell RM, Ellickson PL, Harrison ER. Do drug prevention effects persist into high school? How Project ALERT did with ninth graders. *Prev Med*. 1993;22:463-483.

32. Ellickson PL, Bell RM. Drug prevention in junior high: A multi-site longitudinal test. *Science*. 1990;247:1299-1305.

33. Ellickson PL, Bell RM, McGuigan K. Preventing adolescent drug use: Long-term results of a junior high program. *Am J Public Health*. 1993;83:856-861.

34. Perry CL, Williams CL, Veblen-Mortenson S, Toomey TL, Komro KA, et al. Outcomes of a community-wide alcohol use prevention program during early adolescence: Project Northland. *Am J Public Health*. 1996;86:956-965.

35. Caplan M, Weissberg RP, Grober JS, Sivo PJ, Grady K, Jacoby C. Social competence promotion with inner-city and suburban young adolescents: Effects on social adjustment and alcohol use. *J Consult Clin Psychol*. 1992;60:56-63.

36. Pentz MA, Dwyer IH, MacKinnon DP, Flay BR, Hansen WB, et al. A multicommunity trial for primary prevention of adolescent drug abuse. *JAMA*. 1989;261:3259-3266.

37. Errecart MT, Walberg HJ, Ross JG, Gold RS, Fielder JL, Kolbe LJ. Effectiveness of Teenage Health Teaching Modules. *J Sch Health*. 1991 ;61 :26-30.

38. Dusenbury L, Falco M. Eleven components of effective drug abuse prevention curricula. *J Sch Health*. 1995;65:420-425.

Chapter 59

Lessons from Prevention Research

In more than 20 years of drug abuse research, the National Institute on Drug Abuse (NIDA) has identified important principles for prevention programs in the family, school, and community. NIDA-supported researchers have tested these principles in long-term drug abuse prevention programs and have found them to be effective.

- Prevention programs should be designed to enhance "protective factors" and move toward reversing or reducing known "risk factors." Protective factors are those associated with reduced potential for drug use. Risk factors are those that make the potential for drug use more likely:

  - Protective factors include strong and positive bonds within a prosocial family; parental monitoring; clear rules of conduct that are consistently enforced within the family; involvement of parents in the lives of their children; success in school performance; strong bonds with other prosocial institutions, such as school and religious organizations; and adoption of conventional norms about drug use.

  - Risk factors include chaotic home environments, particularly in which parents abuse substances or suffer from mental illnesses; ineffective parenting, especially with children with difficult temperaments or conduct disorders; lack of mutual attachments and nurturing; inappropriately shy or

National Institute on Drug Abuse (NIDA), Doc. No. 13563, November 1999.

433

aggressive behavior in the classroom; failure in school performance; poor social coping skills; affiliations with deviant peers or peers displaying deviant behaviors; and perceptions of approval of drug-using behaviors in family, work, school, peer, and community environments.

- Prevention programs may target a variety of drugs of abuse, such as tobacco, alcohol, inhalants, and marijuana or may target a single area of drug abuse such as the misuse of prescription drugs.

- Prevention programs should include general life skills training and training in skills to resist drugs when offered, strengthen personal attitudes and commitments against drug use, and increase social competency (e.g., in communications, peer relationships, self-efficacy, and assertiveness).

- Prevention programs for children and adolescents should include developmentally appropriate interactive methods, such as peer discussion groups and group problem solving and decision making, rather than didactic teaching techniques alone.

- Prevention programs should include parents' or caregivers' components that train them to use appropriate parenting strategies, reinforce what the children are learning about drugs and their harmful effects, and that open opportunities for family discussions about the use of legal and illegal substances and family policies about their use.

- Prevention programs should be long-term (throughout the school career), with repeat interventions to reinforce the original prevention goals. For example, school-based efforts directed at elementary and middle school students should include booster sessions to help with the critical transitions such as from middle to high school.

- Family-focused prevention efforts have a greater impact than strategies that focus on parents only or children only.

- Community programs that include media campaigns and policy changes, such as new regulations that restrict access to alcohol, tobacco, or other drugs, are more effective when they are accompanied by school and family interventions.

- Community programs need to strengthen norms against drug use in all drug abuse prevention settings, including the family, the school, the workplace and the community.

- Schools offer opportunities to reach all populations and also serve as important settings for specific subpopulations at risk for drug abuse, such as children with behavior problems or learning disabilities and those who are potential dropouts.

- Prevention programming should be adapted to address the specific nature of the drug abuse problem in the local community.

- The higher the level of risk of the target population, the more intensive the prevention effort must be and the earlier it must begin.

- Prevention programs should be age-specific, developmentally appropriate, and culturally sensitive.

- Effective prevention programs are cost-effective. For every $1 spent on drug use prevention, communities can save $4 to $5 in costs for drug abuse treatment and counseling.*

The following are critical areas for prevention planners to consider when designing a program:

- *Family Relationships:* Prevention programs can teach skills for better family communication, discipline, and firm and consistent rulemaking to parents of young children. Research also has shown that parents need to take a more active role in their children's lives, including talking with them about drugs, monitoring their activities, getting to know their friends, and understanding their problems and personal concerns.

- *Peer Relationships:* Prevention programs focus on an individual's relationship to peers by developing social-competency skills, which involve improved communications, enhancement of positive peer relationships and social behaviors, and resistance skills to refuse drug offers.

- *The School Environment:* Prevention programs also focus on enhancing academic performance and strengthening students' bonding to school, by giving them a sense of identity and achievement and reducing the likelihood of their dropping out of school. Most curriculums include the support for positive peer relationships (described above) and a normative education component designed to correct the misperception that most students are using drugs. Research has also found that when children understand the negative effects of drugs (physical, psychological, and social), and when they perceive their friends' and families' social disapproval of drug use, they tend to avoid initiating drug use.

* *The Community Environment:* Prevention programs work at the community level with civic, religious, law enforcement, and governmental organizations and enhance antidrug norms and prosocial behavior through changes in policy or regulation, mass media efforts, and community-wide awareness programs. Community-based programs might include new laws and enforcement, advertising restrictions, and drug-free school zones—all designed to provide a cleaner, safer, drug-free environment.

For more information on these principles and on programs that incorporate them, please order *Preventing Drug Use Among Children and Adolescents: A Research-Based Guide for the Community.* This publication is available from the National Clearinghouse for Alcohol and Drug Information (NCADI) at 1-800-729-6686.

Note

* Pentz, M.A. "Costs, benefits, and cost effectiveness of comprehensive drug abuse prevention." In W. J. Bukoski, ed. *Cost Effectiveness and Cost Benefit Research of Drug Abuse Prevention: Implications for Programming and Policy.* NIDA Research Monograph. In Press.

Chapter 60

Ethnic Identification and Cultural Ties May Help Prevent Drug Use

Among Puerto Ricans, African Americans, and Asians, cultural influences and ethnic identification may significantly influence drug use. Studies conducted by National Institute on Drug Abuse (NIDA) researchers in New York City suggest that Puerto Rican and African-American adolescents who strongly identify with their communities and cultures are less vulnerable to risk factors for drug use and benefit more from protective factors than do adolescents without this identification. In San Francisco, NIDA-supported research demonstrated different patterns of drug use among different subgroups of the Asian community. These findings suggest that incorporating ethnic and cultural components into drug abuse prevention programs can make these programs more effective.

In one study, Dr. Judith Brook at the Mount Sinai School of Medicine in New York City examined the extent to which ethnic and cultural factors influenced drug-related behavior in Puerto Rican adolescents. She and her colleagues interviewed 275 males and 280 females aged 16 to 24. The researchers asked the participants to describe the importance in their lives of cultural and ethnic factors such as observation of Hispanic holidays and customs, preference for speaking Spanish or English, feelings of attachment to their ethnic group, ethnic affiliation of their friends, and the value placed on the family. The participants also answered questions designed to assess their personal

"Ethnic Identification and Cultural Ties May Help Prevent Drug Use," by Patrick Zickler, *NIDA Notes*, Vol. 14, No. 3, 1999, National Institute on Drug Abuse (NIDA).

risk for drug use; these risk factors included the use of drugs by parents or siblings, peer use or tolerance of drug use, perception of the riskiness of drug use, and the availability of illegal drugs in their environment. The participants were categorized into stages of drug use: no reported drug use, used alcohol or tobacco only, used marijuana but no other illicit drug, or used illicit drugs other than or in addition to marijuana.

"Other studies have looked at ethnic identification in isolation, not as an interactive part of a young person's cultural and social context," Dr. Brook says. "We wanted to determine the extent to which ethnic and cultural factors might mitigate risk factors or enhance protective factors and lead to lower stages of drug use. We found that strong ethnic identification acts to offset some risks, resulting in less drug use.

"For example, strong identification with Puerto Rican cultural factors offsets drug risks such as a father's drug use, peer tolerance of drugs, and the availability of drugs. Identification with Puerto Rican friends offsets risks associated with family tolerance for drug use and drug availability," Dr. Brook notes.

Ethnic identification also serves to amplify the effect of protective factors, Dr. Brook says. For example, among participants whose siblings were not drug users, those with a strong Puerto Rican affiliation were significantly more likely to be in a lower stage of drug use than those whose affiliation was weaker.

In a related study that focused on late-adolescent African Americans in New York City, Dr. Brook and her colleagues found a similar interaction between ethnic and cultural identification and drug use. The study involved 627 participants—259 male and 368 female—aged 16 to 25 years.

The researchers found that components of ethnic identity—such as awareness of African-American history and tradition, identification with African-American friends, or participation in African-American cultural activities such as Kwanzaa—interacted with other factors to reduce risk or to enhance protection.

"In isolation, few specific components of ethnic identity play a role as main effects on drug use. Instead, they act in combination with family, personality, or peer influences to blunt the negative impact of risk factors and magnify the positive value of protective factors," Dr. Brook says.

"Together, the research with Puerto Rican and African-American populations points out the importance of incorporating ethnic identity into drug programs," Dr. Brook concludes. "It can be a valuable part of drug prevention programs in communities and can also be applied to individual treatment programs."

Cultural Differences Lead to Different Patterns of Drug Use

In another NIDA-supported study, Dr. Tooru Nemoto and his colleagues at the University of California, San Francisco, have identified patterns of drug use among Asian drug users that are unique to ethnicity, gender, age group, and immigrant status.

"Large multiracial studies have not distinguished between Asian ethnic groups," Dr. Nemoto says. "The purpose of our study was to describe the patterns of drug use in Chinese, Filipino, and Vietnamese groups and to assess the relationship between cultural factors and drug use among the groups."

The San Francisco study was based on qualitative interviews with 35 Chinese, 31 Filipino, and 26 Vietnamese drug users who were not enrolled in treatment programs. All participants were 18 years or older, with an average age of 32.5, and had used illicit drugs more than three times per week during the preceding 6 months. Overall, immigrants and women represented 66 percent and 36 percent, respectively. However, all Vietnamese were immigrants.

Overall, participants born in the U.S. began using drugs at an earlier age—15 years—than did immigrant Asians—19 years—and were more likely than immigrants to use more than one drug. In general, women started drug use at about the same age as men—about 17.5 years—but ethnic groups showed a varied pattern. Chinese women began earlier—at 15.2 years—than Chinese men—at 18.5 years. Filipino women began using drugs later—at 15.5 years—than Filipino men—at 13.1 years. Vietnamese women in the study started drug use much later—at 27.8 years—than did Vietnamese men—at 19.9 years.

Dr. Nemoto and his colleagues identified differences in drug use among the ethnic groups. Filipino drug users were most likely to have begun drug use with marijuana, while Vietnamese drug users in the study most often started with crack or powder cocaine. Chinese and Vietnamese were twice as likely as Filipinos to be using crack as their current primary drug. Filipinos were four times more likely to be using heroin than were Chinese or Vietnamese. Filipino study participants were more likely than Chinese or Vietnamese to be injecting and less likely to be smoking drugs. There were also significant differences in the characteristics of drug user networks among the ethnic groups.

For example, Filipinos were more than twice as likely as Chinese or Vietnamese participants to use drugs in groups that included members of other races or ethnic groups.

"These differences among ethnic groups have important implications for the way we design programs aimed at Asian drug users," Dr. Nemoto says. "Prevention programs should address the common factors among Asian drug users, such as stigma associated with injection drug use, but we should also be careful to incorporate factors that are unique to each target group."

Sources

Brook, J.S., et al. Drug use among African Americans: Ethnic identity as a protective factor. *Psychological Reports* 83:1427-1446, 1998.

Brook, J.S.; Whiteman, M.; Balka, E.B.; Win, P.T.; and Gursen, M.D. Drug use among Puerto Ricans: Ethnic identity as a protective factor. *Hispanic Journal of Behavioral Sciences* 20(2):241-254, 1998.

Nemoto, T., et al. Drug use behaviors among Asian drug users in San Francisco. *Addictive Behavior* (in press).

Chapter 61

Prevention Strategies for Specific Populations

Prevention Strategies for Youth

Prevention strategies targeting youth have evolved over the past 20 years as evaluation research reveals more about what works. Several strategies are used effectively, especially in combination:

- *Information dissemination.* This strategy provides awareness and knowledge of the nature and extent of alcohol, tobacco, and other drug use, abuse, and addiction and their effects on individuals, families, and communities, as well as information to increase perceptions of risk. It also provides knowledge and awareness of prevention policies, programs, and services. It helps set and reinforce norms (for example, underage drinking and drug dealers will not be tolerated in this neighborhood).

- *Prevention education.* This strategy aims to affect critical life and social skills, including decision making, refusal skills, critical analysis (for example, of media messages), and systematic and judgmental abilities.

- *Alternatives.* This strategy provides for the participation of targeted populations in activities that exclude alcohol, tobacco, and other drug use by youth. Constructive and healthy activities offset

Excerpted from *Prevention Primer: An Encyclopedia of Alcohol, Tobacco, and Other Drug Prevention Terms*, National Clearinghouse for Alcohol and Drug Information, 1993.

441

the attraction to, or otherwise meet the needs usually filled by, alcohol, tobacco, and other drug use.

- *Problem identification and referral.* This strategy calls for identification, education, and counseling for those youth who have indulged in age-inappropriate use of tobacco products or alcohol, or who have indulged in the first use of illicit drugs. Activities under this strategy would include screening for tendencies toward substance abuse and referral for preventive treatment for curbing such tendencies.

- *Community-based process.* This strategy aims to enhance the ability of the community to provide prevention and treatment services to alcohol, tobacco, and other drug use disorders more effectively. Activities include organizing, planning, enhancing efficiency and effectiveness of services implementation, interagency collaboration, coalition building, and networking. Building healthy communities encourages healthy lifestyle choices.

- *Environmental approach.* This strategy sets up or changes written and unwritten community standards, codes, and attitudes—influencing incidence and prevalence of alcohol, tobacco, and other drug use problems in the general population. Included are laws to restrict availability and access, price increases, and community-wide actions.

College and University Students

Alcohol has long been the drug of choice among U.S. college students, who drink at higher rates than their non-college counterparts. College students spend approximately $4.2 billion annually to purchase 430 million gallons of alcoholic beverages, including over 4 billion cans of beer. Students have particularly high rates of heavy drinking compared to the general population.

Student drinking is the number one health problem on college and university campuses throughout the Nation. Alcohol consumption contributes to a range of problems among college students, including academic problems, trauma, date rape, and vandalism. College students are at a higher risk for alcohol-related problems because they have high rates of heavy consumption, tend to drink more recklessly than others, are vulnerable to other risks that are exacerbated by alcohol (e.g., suicide, automobile crashes, and falls), and are heavily targeted by the advertising and promotions of the alcoholic beverage industry.

Surveys on alcohol and other drug use by college students have found:

- 41 percent report binge drinking in the last 2 weeks;
- Nearly 4 percent drink daily;
- Approximately one-third have used marijuana in the past year;
- 5.6 percent have used cocaine in the past year, 0.6 percent used crack, 4.3 percent used LSD, and a combined total of 3.3 percent used heroin and/or opiates.

Alcohol is associated with missed classes and poor performance on tests and projects. The number of alcoholic drinks per week is clearly related to lower GPAs. In the Core Alcohol and Drug Survey of 56,000 college students, students who reported D and F grade point averages consumed an average of 11 alcoholic drinks per week, while those who earned mostly As consumed only 3 drinks per week.

While many institutions have been working for many years to prevent alcohol and other drug problems, colleges and universities received additional impetus to review existing campus alcohol and other drug policies with the implementation of the U.S. Drug-Free Schools and Communities Act Amendments of 1989 (Public Law 101-226). It requires that institutions of higher learning receiving Federal funds attest that they have adopted and implemented a drug prevention program for students and employees.

The following describes what some campuses are doing to reduce alcohol and other drug problems:

- *Enforcement.* According to one study, to discourage the use of false identification to purchase alcohol 58 percent of colleges impose a fine or probation, 9 percent suspend students, and 22 percent report the offenses to law enforcement authorities and/or the motor vehicles bureau.

- *Availability.* Virtually every college campus in America regulates alcohol availability in some manner. Beer is banned on 25 percent of the campuses, and 33 percent do not allow distilled spirits on campus. Other restrictions on availability include requirements that parties with alcoholic beverages be registered with campus officials and meet minimum standards of responsible hosting. The Core Survey found that 67 percent of non-bingeing students would prefer an alcohol-free campus environment and almost 94 percent would prefer a drug-free environment.

- *Pricing.* Because the availability of cheap alcohol contributes to high risk drinking, some campuses have restricted or banned campus advertisements that promote reduced priced drinks at happy hours for students. Others have imposed strict controls on keg parties that promote "all you can drink" for a fixed price.

- *Peer Counseling.* Many colleges train peer counselors to educate groups and individuals about the dangers of alcohol use. For example, fraternity and sorority members reach out to fellow fraternity and sorority members, an especially important group. Studies have shown that fraternity members drink more frequently and at higher levels than other college students.

- *Advertising / Sponsorship.* Some colleges limit or ban alcohol advertising in student newspapers and sponsorship of student events by alcoholic beverage companies. The Fraternity Insurance Purchasing Group (FIPG), the largest insurer to fraternities nationwide, adopted a risk management policy that, among other provisions, includes a prohibition of cosponsorship of fraternity events with an alcohol distributor or tavern.

- *Alcohol-Free Residence Halls.* The California State University at Chico banned alcohol in residences. An emerging trend is for colleges to establish residence halls where students sign pledges that they will not use alcohol, tobacco, or other drugs.

The Department of Education sponsors The Network of Colleges and Universities Committed to the Elimination of Drug and Alcohol Abuse, which includes over 1,300 institutions of higher education. Also, DoEd supports grants to many schools through the Fund for the Improvement of Postsecondary Education (FIPSE).

There is a small, but significant downward trend in the prevalence of alcohol and other drug use among college students. This trend mirrors a similar pattern of a small, national reduction in consumption.

Gay, Lesbian, and Bisexual Youth and Adults

Research has found that gay, lesbian, and bisexual Americans are at increased risk for alcohol and other drug problems. Although this audience comprises more than 10 percent of people at risk for problems, alcohol and other drug programs generally do not address their prevention needs.

Because of the historical stigmatization of gay, lesbian, and bisexual people, few prevention programs are inclusive of gay and lesbian culture.

If community norms are intolerant of sexual diversity, separate prevention strategies may be necessary. A systematic approach to alcohol and other drug problem prevention requires an understanding of the risk factors for this audience. They include:

- History of family alcohol and other drug problems
- Physical, sexual, or psychological abuse and victimization
- School drop-out
- Attempted suicide
- Low self esteem/efficacy
- Inadequate social services
- Homelessness
- Pro-use norms in the community
- Lack of role models

It is not enough to assume that gay, lesbian, and bisexual youth and adults are included in other high-risk category prevention and treatment programs. Their vulnerability to alcohol and other drug use is unique and exacerbated by feelings of rejection by their environment and self. They often feel rejected because of their sexual orientation, over which they have no control. Prevention efforts that are not affirming of gay, lesbian, and bisexual persons are not only nonproductive, they may increase problems.

Prevention strategies recommended for the gay, lesbian, and bisexual communities include:

- Providing training on issues for this community to police, social service staff, foster care families, teachers, principals, religious leaders, health care providers, and others.

- Increasing community understanding and acceptance of homosexuality.

- Supporting families of gay, lesbian, and bisexual youth and involving them in prevention efforts.

- Educating community members about the link between alcohol and other drug use with AIDS, sexually transmitted disease, date rape, and family violence.

- Providing peer support and recovery groups in the gay, lesbian, and bisexual community.

445

- Sponsoring alcohol, tobacco, and other drug-free events.

- Providing structured workshops on "coming out."

- Involving established gay, lesbian, and bisexual organizations in prevention efforts.

Like other communities, the gay, lesbian, and bisexual community is typified by its own history, customs, values, and social and behavioral norms. It has clearly identified festivals, holidays, rituals, symbols, heroes, language, art, music, songs, and literature. Effective prevention efforts must both reflect and mobilize the culture of the gay, lesbian, and bisexual community.

African-American Youth

Contrary to commonly held beliefs, use of alcohol and other drugs is low among urban African Americans under age 16 who stay in school. Although these youths tend to delay starting the use of alcohol and other drugs for a longer period of time (into their late to mid teens) than their white, Hispanic/Latino, and American Indian peers, they are at risk for developing heavy patterns of drug use by virtue of a number of negative environmental factors. Those factors include daily exposure to alcohol and other drugs, often at the hands of friends and family, and the lure of the drug trade and the drug culture that surrounds them.

The messages conveyed to young people are important factors affecting the community environment surrounding alcohol, tobacco, and other drug use. For example, inner-city communities are often targets of alcohol and tobacco promotional activities. In New York and Philadelphia, prevention activists like Reverend Calvin O. Butts and Reverend Jesse Brown have mobilized community protests against billboard advertising of alcohol and tobacco products. In Detroit, prevention activists like Alberta Tinsley-Williams were successful in removing billboard advertisements for a popular brand of rolling papers, often used for marijuana cigarettes, from African-American neighborhoods.

A key element of any prevention initiative is communicating messages that reflect social norms to promote healthy behaviors. *Communicating About Alcohol and Other Drugs: Strategies for Reaching Populations at Risk*, Center for Substance Abuse and Prevention (CSAP) Monograph 5, makes recommendations for prevention strategies focused on African-American youth. They are:

1. Encourage personal, one-on-one mentoring of young urban African Americans by positive role models. Community-wide mass media campaigns could promote the positive benefits that can result from the involvement of African-American adults with youths as mentors and positive role models.

2. Call attention to the need for improved parenting skills and reduced teen pregnancies. With the proliferation of teenage pregnancy and poor single parent families, there is a need to challenge normative beliefs among young African Americans who consider getting pregnant at early ages as acceptable. Communications activities to address teenage pregnancy and improve parenting skills could include church-based parent training workshops and seminars; using drama such as plays, skits, and rap songs as ways to reach teens; television documentaries and town meetings to focus community attention on the importance and benefits of improved parenting; and television documentaries highlighting success stories about the adoption of African-American children.

3. Encourage African-American churches to become involved. The African-American church has a historical role in addressing social and political issues of the community. Provided with appropriate information and training about alcohol, tobacco, and other drugs, they can better identify strategies to address these problems within the context of the African-American spirituality.

4. Communicate to more young African Americans their rich cultural heritage. All prevention and treatment programs need to communicate the inherent dignity of each human being and, in the case of young urban African Americans, the rich cultural heritage they share with people of African ancestry all over the world.

5. Persuade television program decision-makers to be more sensitive in their portrayals of African Americans. Because much of alcohol and tobacco advertising is targeted specifically to African-American consumers, media strategies are needed to serve as countermeasures. Citizens concerned about the quantity and content of alcohol advertisements targeted at African Americans may want to write or call their local stations to complain and encoura ge airing counter messages and information about the adverse consequences of alcohol use, particularly for young people.

6. Use African-American radio. Urban areas often have several radio stations that target and reach African-American audiences. Popular activities that can be used include:

- Call-in talk shows;

- Locally produced public service announcements (PSAs);

- Disk jockeys who introduce issues, inform listeners, promote activities, and invite commentary; and

- Letters and telephone calls to station general managers, urging more attention to developing solutions to alcohol, tobacco, and other drug problems affecting the community, and highlighting the successes of youth in the community.

7. Work with the business community, especially in high-density urban areas, to increase advertising for prevention messages. A number of African-American organizations are beginning to focus on the issue of alcohol and tobacco advertising targeted to African Americans. These organizations have begun an appeal to the African-American media to rethink their ad content because of a concern about alcohol, tobacco, and other drug problems in the African-American community. While they recognize that alcohol and tobacco advertising is a major source of income for many African-American publications, they want to explore ways to replace alcohol ads with ads for other products.

8. Mobilize local citizens to demand removal of offensive alcohol, tobacco, and other drug paraphernalia ads from billboards. Studies have shown that there is a higher rate of alcohol and tobacco billboard advertising in inner-city neighborhoods. Some community leaders are seeking bans on such advertising. Counter-advertising on billboards can also be an effective strategy.

9. Use media that involve youths. Much creative talent can be found among African-American youth. Youths can contribute in meaningful ways to developing messages and communicating ideas through video documentaries, poster and rap contests, music videos, and plays and skits.

10. Make information available where youths congregate. Examples of such environments include:

- *Movie theaters:* Movie makers and theater owners can be encouraged to devote PSA space for alcohol, tobacco, and other drug prevention messages as lead-ins to feature presentations.

- *Recreation centers:* Many urban African-American youths frequent recreation centers, which are ideal places to distribute prevention materials.

- *Corner grocery stores:* Many inner-city neighborhoods are served by small family-operated grocery stores. Store owners can be enlisted to help distribute prevention materials.

11. Encourage corporations to take a more active role in prevention efforts. Some corporations are beginning to realize it is more cost effective to help urban African-American youths develop into productive adults than to face the enormous economic and social consequences of benign neglect. Communication strategies can be developed to increase the awareness of the benefits of helping these youths through programs like Adopt-A-School and Summer Jobs.

12. Develop materials targeted to African-American youths. Materials should feature African Americans in good visual materials including billboards, posters, and brochures. Materials developed should be culturally as well as age-appropriate. Where appropriate, low-literacy materials should be developed.

Hispanic/Latino

The Hispanic/Latino community is often considered by prevention practitioners a hard-to-reach population, implying that their language or cultural differences represent a barrier to prevention information and outreach. However, for many of the Nation's largest consumer products manufacturers and retailers, the Hispanic/Latino community is highly accessible, and represents strong growth markets.

According to CSAP's Prevention Monograph 5: *Communicating About Alcohol and Other Drugs: Strategies for Reaching Populations at Risk*, the challenge to those in the prevention field is to move away from regarding Hispanic/Latinos as hard-to-reach and toward an approach that builds on research and demonstration findings regarding successful communication strategies aimed at this large and growing population group. While knowledge about effective ways to prevent alcohol, tobacco, and other drug problems among Hispanic/Latinos is not entirely definitive, there is a growing body of promising approaches. In addition, communications networks serving primarily

Hispanic/Latino communities are valuable, but currently under-used resources for prevention practitioners.

When developing prevention initiatives directed at the Hispanic/Latino community, it is important to recognize that it represents a population group that:

- Consists of diverse subgroups, including Mexican Americans, Puerto Ricans, Central Americans, South Americans, and Cubans;

- Has experienced dramatic population growth in the United States;

- Includes a large proportion of young people;

- Includes a high proportion of female-headed households, compared to the general population;

- Includes proportionately fewer married couples than the general population;

- Places high importance on the family;

- May experience conflict between generations related to differences in acculturation; and

- Is at a higher risk for teen pregnancy and juvenile incarceration than youth in the general population.

Over the past 20 years, the Hispanic/Latino community has emerged as one of the fastest growing segments of the United States population. The high growth rate is projected to continue. Data from the Census Bureau suggest that the Hispanic/Latino population will grow at a rate of approximately five times the non-Hispanic/Latino white population in upcoming years. Consequently, prevention practitioners must understand the knowledge, attitudes, and practices of Hispanic/Latinos regarding alcohol, tobacco, and other drug use and problems.

While information is limited, studies on alcohol, tobacco, and other drug use in the Hispanic/Latino populations indicate that:

- Hispanic/Latinos in general may have lower rates than non-Hispanic/Latino whites of lifetime use of alcohol, PCP, hallucinogens, and stimulants;

- Hispanic/Latino youths ages 12 to 17 may have higher rates of cocaine use than their non-Hispanic/Latino counterparts;

- Puerto Rican and Cuban youths may have the highest rates of cocaine use among Hispanic/Latinos;

- Mexican Americans ages 12 to 17 may have higher rates of marijuana use than non-Hispanic/Latino whites;

- Hispanic/Latino children have extensive exposure at an early age to alcohol and other drug use;

- Younger Hispanic/Latino women in general use alcohol much less than Hispanic/Latino men;

- Younger Hispanic/Latino women may use alcohol more than the women in their parents' generation, perhaps as a result of acculturation;

- Hispanic/Latinos in general may believe that drinking is an acceptable way to celebrate and have fun; and

- May believe that drinking is a primary source of inappropriate behavior.

Prevention programs or strategies should neither begin nor end with information campaigns. Activities should focus on building the desire, resources, and mechanisms to promote healthy behaviors and environments.

While appropriate national roles exist for developing leadership, research and data, and prototypes of programs, a community-based commitment to prevention is necessary for the national prevention component to fulfill its potential.

For prevention practitioners, working with Hispanic/Latino communities requires an appreciation of the dynamics of change—diversification of subgroups within geographic areas; evolving values and norms; shifts in family structure and religious affiliation; and transitions in attitudes toward and use of alcohol, tobacco, and other drugs. An appreciation of change should be combined with an understanding of deeply rooted beliefs and values that lie at the core of the Hispanic/Latino experience. Together, they can bring relevance and power to prevention efforts targeting Hispanic/Latino communities.

Asian/Pacific Islander Americans

The term Asian/Pacific Islander comprises more than 60 separate ethnic/racial groups and subgroups. These groups represent diverse populations in terms of their histories and experiences in the United

States, languages and dialect, religions, cultures, socioeconomic status, and places of birth. There are also vast differences in the degree in which these groups are acculturated and assimilated into the mainstream culture. While alcohol and other drug use does not appear to be as extensive among the Asian/Pacific Islander population as it is in other population groups, there are significant differences in use and problems among the different ethnic/racial groups and subgroups.

Little research has been conducted on alcohol and other drug use among Asian/Pacific Islander Americans. Research that has been conducted suggests that numerous high-risk factors are common to both Asian and non-Asian youth. However, Asian youths and adults experience added personal, family, and social problems by virtue of their immigration status, economic stress, racism, and discrimination.

Prevention programs for Asian/Pacific Islander Americans will be most effective if they reflect the values and norms of the culture group being served. It is also important to understand how alcohol, tobacco, and other drugs are viewed, and used, within that culture. The cultural context approach to Asian/Pacific Islander Americans' alcohol, tobacco, and other drug use is the one most widely used by prevention practitioners. However, it has limitations in that it fails to account for the vast differences among these groups.

The National Asian Pacific American Families Against Substance Abuse, Inc. (NAPAFASA), a national umbrella organization, has been successful in drawing attention to alcohol and other drug problems in the Asian/Pacific Islander American population. NAPAFASA has implemented several CSAP community-based prevention efforts that provide important information on both the level of problems and promising strategies for prevention among this fast growing, diverse racial group.

American Indians and Native Alaskans

While overall rates of alcohol and other drug use are high in American Indian/Native Alaskan groups, the prevalence varies tremendously from tribe to tribe and by age and sex within tribes. However, American Indians/Native Alaskans die more frequently than members of other ethnic/racial groups from suicide, homicide, and unintentional injuries or accidents, most of which are related to alcohol. These causes, along with cirrhosis of the liver and alcoholism, account for more than a third of all American Indian deaths. For this group as a whole, death rates from alcohol-related causes are more than three times higher than other groups.

452

Marijuana is the next most widely used drug after alcohol. It is estimated that about half (41 to 62 percent) of American Indian youths have tried marijuana, compared with less than half (28 to 50 percent) of other youths, although there is wide intertribal variation.

A task force convened by the U.S. Office for Minority Health reports that American Indians/Native Alaskans have had their traditional way of life disrupted, often resulting in a sense of powerlessness and hopelessness which may be related to the high incidence of alcohol and other drug problems in this population.

But American Indians/Native Alaskans also often draw upon traditional sources of strength to cope with stress, including the family, the tribe, and the land itself. As with other population groups, the use of culturally appropriate strategies is important for the success of prevention programs. It is also important to understand the diversity of American Indian/Native Alaskan tribes. In addition, as American Indian/Native Alaskan tribes are often sovereign political entities with specific powers of self-governance, it is important to include tribal leaders and other important community members in all phases of prevention initiatives.

Many groups on and off reservations are beginning to carry out alcohol and other drug prevention and intervention strategies that are community controlled and empowered. Unlike 10 years ago, there are now pow-wows, rodeos, and other gatherings at which alcohol and other drugs are expressly forbidden.

Part Seven

Additional Help and Information

Chapter 62

Glossary of
Substance Abuse Terms

Abstinence facilitation: An outpatient treatment strategy designed to help persons who are addicted to drugs stop using them. Commonly used in association with the medical treatment of cocaine abuse.

Acute abstinence syndrome: The aggregate of withdrawal signs and symptoms that occur shortly after a person who is physically dependent on a drug stops taking it. The adjective "acute" distinguishes this variant from the "protracted" or "chronic" drug withdrawal or abstinence syndrome.

Acute psychosis: A disturbance in thinking that is often accompanied by delusions and visual or auditory hallucinations. An acute psychosis may be caused by alcohol or other drug (AOD) withdrawal, drug toxicity (most commonly in conjunction with abuse of cocaine, methamphetamine, or psychedelic agents), or schizophrenia.

Addiction: A chronic, relapsing disease, characterized by compulsive drug-seeking and use and by neurochemical and molecular changes in the brain.

Terms in this glossary were excerpted from *Detoxification from Alcohol and Other Drugs*, Treatment Improvement (TIP) Series 19, Substance Abuse and Mental Health Services Administration, Center for Substance Abuse Treatment, DHHS Publication No. (SMA) 95-3046, 1995; "Cocaine Abuse and Addiction," NIDA Research Report, National Institute on Drug Abuse (NIDA), May 1999; and "Heroin Abuse and Addiction," NIDA Research Report, National Institute on Drug Abuse (NIDA), May 1999.

457

Agonist: A chemical compound that mimics the action of a natural neurotransmitter.

Analgesia: Relief from pain.

Analog: A chemical compound that is similar to another drug in its effects but differs slightly in its chemical structure.

Anesthetic: An agent that causes insensitivity to pain.

Anhedonia: Absence of pleasure from acts that would ordinarily be enjoyable.

Anorexia: Diminished appetite; aversion to food.

Antagonist: A drug that counteracts or blocks the effects of another drug.

Antidepressants: A group of drugs used in treating depressive disorders.

Arthralgia: Joint pain.

Ataxia: Unsteady walking or staggering, caused by an inability to coordinate the muscles.

Authorizing order: An order issued by a court that permits an AOD abuse treatment program to make a disclosure about a patient that would otherwise be forbidden.

Buprenorphine: A mixed agonist/antagonist medication being studied for the treatment of heroin addiction.

Cellulitis: Inflammation of the cellular or connective tissues.

Chronic obstructive pulmonary disease (COPD): A combination of chronic bronchitis and emphysema. Characterized by persistent disruption of the flow of air in and out of the lungs.

Clouded sensorium: Confusion.

Coca: The plant, *Erythroxylon*, from which cocaine is derived. Also refers to the leaves of this plant.

Cocaethylene: Potent stimulant created when cocaine and alcohol are used together.

Cold turkey: Popular term used to describe the process of opiate withdrawal that is not treated with medication. During withdrawal, the person's skin is covered with goose bumps and resembles that of a turkey.

Crack: Short term for a smokable form of cocaine.

Craving: A powerful, often uncontrollable desire for drugs.

Decisional capacity: The ability of a patient to make an informed choice.

Delirium tremens: A severe form of alcohol withdrawal characterized by confusion, auditory or visual hallucinations, and severe shakiness. Commonly called "DTs."

Delirium: A state of mental confusion characterized by difficulty in responding to stimuli and an absence of orientation to place and time. May be accompanied by auditory, visual, or tactile hallucinations. May be caused by drug withdrawal or severe intoxication with phencyclidine.

Delusions: Fixed, irrational ideas not shared by others and not responding to a logical argument.

Designer drug: An analog of a restricted drug that has psychoactive properties (*see also* Analog).

Detoxification: A process of allowing the body to rid itself of a drug while managing the symptoms of withdrawal; often the first step in a drug treatment program.

Diaphoresis: Profuse sweating that is not in response to high temperature or exercise. A common symptom of opiate or sedative-hypnotic withdrawal.

Dopamine: A neurotransmitter present in regions of the brain that regulate movement, emotion, motivation, and the feeling of pleasure.

Drug receptors: Specialized areas on the surface of brain cells to which drugs attach and through which they produce their effects.

Drug tolerance: The body's ability to endure increasing quantities of a drug. As the brain cells adapt to the presence of a drug, more of the drug is required to produce the same effect.

Dual diagnosis: The presence of both an AOD abuse problem and a psychiatric disorder.

Duty to warn: The legal obligation of a health care provider to notify law-enforcement officials or the potential victim when a patient presents a serious danger of violence to an identifiable individual.

Dysphoria: An unpleasant mood.

Electrolytes: Compounds in the blood that conduct electricity and can be decomposed by it. They include, for example, sodium, potassium, and chloride ions. Electrolyte imbalance can be caused by protracted vomiting, diarrhea, or dehydration. It also may result from failure to administer the correct type or quantity of intravenous fluids.

Encephalopathy: Any disease or disorder that affects the brain.

Fentanyl: A medically useful opioid analog that is 50 times more potent than heroin.

Grand mal seizures: A type of seizure in which a person falls to the ground unconscious and suffers generalized muscle contractions. The person usually remains unconscious for a time and may have no recall of the episode on awakening. Petit mal seizures, by contrast, are characterized by a momentary loss of awareness; an observer may think the person experiencing the seizure is simply daydreaming.

Hyperpyrexia: Extremely high fever.

Hyperreflexia: An exaggerated response of muscle reflexes that indicates that the nervous system is in a pathologically excited state. May occur during withdrawal from sedative-hypnotic agents or alcohol.

Hypertension: Abnormally high blood pressure. Usually defined as a resting blood pressure greater than 140 mm hg (systolic) and 90 mm hg (diastolic).

Involuntary commitment: Process by which patients who have not committed any crime are brought into treatment against their wishes by relatives or the police or through a court proceeding. Involuntary commitment is also known as "protective custody" or "emergency commitment."

Levo-alpha-acetyl-methadol (LAAM): An FDA-approved medication for heroin addiction that patients need to take only three to four times a week.

Medical comorbidity: Presence of two serious illnesses at once; for example, drug addiction and acquired immune deficiency syndrome (AIDS).

Medical emergency: A condition that poses an immediate threat to the health of any individual and that requires immediate medical intervention.

Medically debilitated: Term used to describe an individual who is both AOD-dependent and who has a chronic or severe medical disease such as emphysema.

Medication discontinuation: The process through which therapeutic doses of a prescribed medication are tapered or withdrawn. Detoxification, by contrast, refers to discontinuation of the use of an illicit drug or a self-administered prescription medication.

Meperidine: A medically approved opioid available under various brand names (e.g., Demerol).

Methadone: A long-acting synthetic medication shown to be effective in treating heroin addiction.

Myalgia: Muscle pain. A common complaint during opiate withdrawal.

Narcotic treatment program: According to Federal methadone guidelines, an organization (or a person, including a private physician) that administers or dispenses a narcotic drug to an addict for maintenance or detoxification treatment; provides, when appropriate or necessary, a comprehensive range of medical and rehabilitative services, is approved by the State authority and the Food and Drug Administration; and is registered with the Drug Enforcement Administration to use a narcotic drug for the treatment of narcotic addiction.

Narcotic-dependent: According to Federal methadone guidelines, a term used to describe an individual who physiologically needs heroin or a morphine-like drug to prevent the onset of signs of withdrawal.

Neuroadaptation: The process by which the function of the brain cells changes in response to exposure to drugs. These adaptive changes may include increases in the number of receptor sites, alterations in the shape of the receptors, or changes in the chemical functioning of the cell.

Neuron: A nerve cell in the brain.

Nonmalignant pain: Chronic pain that is not caused by cancer. Also called "chronic benign pain."

Nystagmus: A jerky movement of the eyes. May be seen in persons who are intoxicated as a result of ingestion of alcohol, sedative-hypnotic agents, or phencyclidine.

Orthostatic hypotension: A rapid drop in blood pressure (usually defined as 10 mm hg or greater) that occurs when a person stands up. Such an individual may become dizzy or even faint. May be a sign of sedative-hypnotic withdrawal or opiate intoxication. Also called "postural hypotension."

Pancreatitis: Inflammation of the pancreas. Alcohol abuse is the most common cause of chronic pancreatitis and a principal cause of acute pancreatitis.

Paresthesia: An abnormal burning, pricking, tickling, or tingling sensation.

Pentobarbital challenge: A method of assessing physical dependence on alcohol or other sedative-hypnotic agents. The challenge consists of administering standard doses of pentobarbital to a patient and observing the effects. Patients who become intoxicated on 200 mg or less of pentobarbital do not have substantial tolerance to sedatives and are presumed not to be physically dependent on these substances.

Physical dependence: A condition in which the brain cells have adapted as a result of repeated exposure to a drug and consequently require the drug in order to function. If the drug is suddenly made unavailable, the cells become hyperactive. The hyperactive cells produce the signs and symptoms of drug withdrawal.

Poly-drug user: An individual who uses more than one drug.

Protracted abstinence syndrome: The aggregate of signs and symptoms of drug withdrawal. These signs and symptoms may continue for weeks or months after cessation of drug use (*see also* Acute abstinence syndrome).

Recrudescence: Reappearance of symptoms after a period of remission.

Relapse prevention: In common usage, any strategy or activity designed to assist a drug user who has become abstinent from returning to drug use.

Rush: A surge of pleasure that rapidly follows administration of some drugs.

Signs: Observable or measurable changes in a patient's physiology; for example, increased blood pressure or dilated pupils. Such changes may not be perceived by the patient.

Somnolence: Sleepiness, drowsiness.

Symptom rebound: Transient, intensified return of symptoms following termination of therapeutic doses of a benzodiazepine; the most common withdrawal consequence of prolonged benzodiazepine use.

Symptoms: Subjective changes in mood, feelings, or bodily sensations.

Tachycardia: Rapid heartbeat (generally more than 100 beats per minute).

Therapeutic dosage: The amount of a drug required to produce a beneficial effect.

Tolerance: A condition in which higher doses of a drug are required to produce the same effect as during initial use; often is associated with physical dependence.

Triage: Process by which patients are assessed to determine the type of services and level of care they will require.

Up-regulation: An increase in the number of receptors on the brain cells that is caused by continuous contact with drugs.

Vertigo: The sensation of dizziness.

Withdrawal: A variety of symptoms that occur after use of an addictive drug is reduced or stopped.

Chapter 63

Dictionary of Street Terms

Numbers

151: crack cocaine

2-for-1 sale: a marketing scheme designed to promote and increase crack sales

24-7: crack cocaine

45 minute psychosis: Dimethyltryptamine

A

A: LSD; amphetamine

A la canona: abrupt ("cold turkey") withdrawal from heroin*

Abe: $5 worth of drugs

Abe's cabe: $5 bill

Abolic: veterinary steroid

A-bomb: marijuana and heroin smoked in cigarette*

Acapulco gold: marijuana from S.W. Mexico

Acapulco red: marijuana

Ace: marijuana cigarette*; PCP

Acid cube: sugar cube containing LSD

Acid freak: heavy user of LSD

Acid head: LSD user

Acid: LSD

Acido: LSD

AD: PCP

Ad: drug addict

Adam: MDMA

Adam and Eve: MDMA and MDEA combo*

Afgani Indica: marijuana

This dictionary includes terms from *Street Terms: Drugs and The Drug Trade*, Executive Office of the President, Office of National Drug Control Policy (ONDCP), Drug Policy Information Clearinghouse, at whitehousedrugpolicy.gov; and "Drug Slang Dictionary" Indiana Prevention Resource Center (IPRC), at http://prc-ntserv.idap.indiana.edu. Terms from IPRC are marked with asterisks (*) and are reprinted with permission.

African black: marijuana
African bush: marijuana
African woodbine: marijuana
  cigarette
African: marijuana
Agonies: withdrawal symptoms
A-head: frequent amphetamine
  user*
Ah-pen-yen: opium
Aimies: amphetamine; amyl ni-
  trite
AIP: heroin from Afghanistan,
  Iran, and Pakistan
Air blast: inhalant
Air head: marijuana user
Airplane: marijuana
Alice B. Toklas: marijuana
  brownie
All lit up: under the influence of
  drugs
All star: user of multiple drugs
All-American drug: cocaine
Alpha-ET: alpha-ethyltyptamine
Ames: amyl nitrite
Amidone: methadone
Amoeba: PCP
Amp: amphetamine; marijuana
  dipped in formaldehyde and
  smoked
Amp joint: marijuana cigarette
  laced with some form of nar-
  cotic
Amped (verb): stimulated by
  drugs, especially cocaine or
  amphetamine*
Amped-out: fatigue after using
  amphetamines
Amping: accelerated heartbeat
AMT: dimethyltryptamine
Amys: amylnitrite; Amytal*
Anadrol: oral steroid
Anatrofin: injectable steroid

Anavar: oral steroid
Angel dust: PCP
Angel hair: PCP
Angel mist: PCP
Angel poke: PCP
Angel: PCP
Angie: cocaine
Angola: marijuana
Animal tranq: PCP
Animal tranquilizer: PCP
Animal: LSD
Ant: small-time drug dealer*
Antifreeze: heroin
Anywhere: holding or possessing
  drugs*
Apache: fentanyl
Apple jacks: crack
Aries: heroin
Aroma of men: isobutyl nitrite
Artillery: equipment for inject-
  ing drugs
Ashes: marijuana
Assassin of Youth: marijuana
  (from 1930's film of same
  name)*
Astro turf: marijuana
Atom bomb: marijuana and
  heroin
Atshitshi: marijuana
Aunt Hazel: heroin
Aunt Mary: marijuana
Aunt Nora: cocaine
Aunti: opium
Aunti Emma: opium
Aurora borealis: PCP
Author: a doctor who writes ille-
  gal prescriptions

B

B: amount of marijuana to fill a matchbox

B-40: cigar laced with marijuana and dipped in malt liquor

B.J.'s: crack

Babe: drug used for detoxification

Baby: minor heroin habit*

Baby bhang: marijuana

Baby habit: occasional use of drugs

Baby T: crack

Babysit: guide someone through first drug experience

Back breakers: LSD and strychnine

Back dex: amphetamine

Back door: residue left in a pipe

Back jack: injecting opium

Back off: injecting drug partially into a vein, then withdrawing blood into syringe before re-injecting*

Back to back: smoking crack after injecting heroin or heroin used after smoking crack

Backtrack: allow blood to flow back into a needle during injection

Backup: prepare vein for injection

Backwards: depressant

Bad: crack cocaine

Bad bundle: inferior quality heroin

Bad go: bad reaction to a drug

Bad pizza: PCP*

Bad seed: peyote; heroin; marijuana

Badrock: crack cocaine

Bag: container for drugs

Bag bride: crack-smoking prostitute

Bag man: person who transports money

Bagging: using inhalant

Bah-say: freebase cocaine; cocaine paste (basuco)*

Bale: marijuana

Ball: crack; crack cocaine; Mexican black tar heroin

Balling: vaginally implanted cocaine

Balloon: heroin supplier

Ballot: heroin

Bam: depressant; amphetamine

Bamba: marijuana

Bambalacha: marijuana

Bambs: depressant

Bammy: marijuana*

Banano: marijuana or tobacco cigarettes laced with cocaine*

Bang: to inject a drug; inhalant

Bank bandit pills: depressant

Banker: drug financier who assumes little risk of arrest*

Bar: marijuana

Barb: depressant

Barbies: depressant

Barbs: barbiturates*; cocaine

Barrels: LSD

Bart Simpson: heroin

Base: cocaine; crack

Base crazies: searching on hands and knees for crack

Base head: person who bases

Base house: place for smoking freebase cocaine or crack*

Base pipe: pipe for smoking freebase cocaine or crack*

Baseball: crack; freebase cocaine*

Baseballing: smoking freebase cocaine*

Bash: marijuana

Basing: crack cocaine

Basuco: cocaine; coca paste residue sprinkled on marijuana or regular cigarette

Bathtub speed: methcathinone

Batt: IV needle

Battery acid: LSD

Batu: smokable methamphetamine

Bazooka: coca paste and marijuana*; cocaine; crack

Bazulco: cocaine

B-bombs: amphetamines

Beam: cocaine

Beam me up Scottie: crack dipped in PCP; taking an additional dose of cocaine*

Beamer: crack user

Beamers: crack cocaine

Beans: amphetamine; crack cocaine; depressant; mescaline

Beast: heroin; LSD

Beat: crack cocaine

Beat artist: person selling bogus drugs

Beat vials: vials containing sham crack to cheat buyers

Beautiful boulders: crack

Beavis & Butthead: LSD

Bebe: crack

Bedbugs: fellow addicts

Beedies: cigarettes from India (resemble marijuana joints/vehicle for other drugs)

Beemers: crack

Behind the scale: to weigh and sell cocaine

Beiging: chemicals altering cocaine to make it appear a higher purity

Belladonna: PCP

Belly habit: heroin addiction resulting in stomach symptoms*

Belt: effects of drugs

Belushi: cocaine and heroin

Belyando spruce: marijuana

Bender: drug party

Bennies: Benzedrine (amphetamine sulfate)*

Benny and the Jets: Benzedrine (amphetamine sulfate)*

Bens: amphetamine

Bent: intoxicated on narcotic or psychedelic*

Benz: Benzedrine (amphetamine sulfate)*

Benzidrine: amphetamine

Bernice: cocaine

Bernie: cocaine

Bernie's flakes: cocaine

Bernie's gold dust: cocaine

Bhang: marijuana, Indian term

Big 8: 1/8 kilogram of crack

Big bag: heroin

Big bloke: cocaine

Big C: cocaine

Big Chief: mescaline*

Big D: LSD

Big flake: cocaine

Big H: heroin

Big Harry: heroin

Big man: drug supplier

Big O: opium

Big rush: cocaine

Bikers coffee: methamphetamine and coffee

Bill Blass: crack

Billie hoke: cocaine

Bindle: small packet of drug powder; heroin

Bing: enough of a drug for one injection

Bingers: crack addicts
Bingo: to inject a drug
Bings: crack
Biphetamine: amphetamine
Birdhead: LSD
Birdie powder: heroin; cocaine
Biscuit: 50 rocks of crack
Bite one's lips: to smoke marijuana
Biz: bag or portion of drugs; injection paraphernalia (as in business)*
Bjs: crack cocaine
Black: opium; marijuana
Black acid: LSD; LSD and PCP
Black and white: amphetamine
Black bart: marijuana
Black beauties: Biphetamine (amphetamine/dextroamphetamine) capsules*
Black birds: amphetamine
Black bombers: amphetamine
Black Cadillacs: amphetamine
Black dust: PCP
Black ganga: marijuana resin
Black gold: high potency marijuana
Black gungi: marijuana from India
Black gunion: marijuana
Black hash: opium and hashish
Black mo/black moat: highly potent marijuana
Black mollies: amphetamine
Black mote: marijuana mixed with honey
Black pearl: heroin
Black pill: opium pill
Black rock: crack
Black Russian: hashish mixed with opium; very potent hashish*

Black star: LSD
Black stuff: black tar opium*; heroin
Black sunshine: LSD
Black tabs: LSD
Black tar heroin: potent heroin from Mexico*
Black tar opium: tar-like opium for smoking*
Black whack: PCP
Blacks: amphetamine
Blanca: cocaine
Blanco: heroin
Blanket: marijuana cigarette
Blanks: low quality drugs
Blast: to smoke marijuana; to smoke crack; cocaine
Blast a joint: to smoke marijuana
Blast a roach: to smoke marijuana
Blast a stick: to smoke marijuana
Blasted: under the influence of drugs
Blizzard: white cloud in a pipe used to smoke cocaine
Block busters: depressant
Block: crude opium*
Block: cube of morphine*
Block: marijuana
Blockbuster: 50mg Nembutal (pentobarbital) capsules*
Blonde: marijuana
Blotter acid: LSD
Blotter cube: LSD
Blotter: LSD; cocaine
Blow: cocaine; to inhale cocaine; to smoke marijuana
Blow a fill: smoke opium*
Blow a fix/blow a shot/blow the vein: injection misses the vein and is wasted in the skin

469

Blow a stick: to smoke marijuana

Blow blue: to inhale cocaine

Blow coke: to inhale cocaine

Blow one's roof: to smoke marijuana

Blow smoke: to inhale cocaine

Blow up: crack cut with lidocaine to increase size, weight, and street value

Blow your mind: become intoxicated on a psychedelic drug*

Blowcaine: crack diluted with cocaine

Blowing smoke: marijuana

Blowout: a party at which alcohol and/or drugs are used to excess*; crack

Blows: heroin

Blue: depressant; crack

Blue acid: LSD

Blue and clears: Fastin (phentermine) (blue and clear capsule filled with blue and white balls)*

Blue angels: depressant

Blue barrels: LSD

Blue birds: Amytal (amobarbital sodium) capsules*

Blue blood: one who injects drugs intravenously*

Blue boy: amphetamine

Blue bullets: depressant

Blue caps: mescaline

Blue chairs: LSD

Blue cheers: LSD

Blue de hue: marijuana from Vietnam

Blue devil: depressant

Blue dolls: depressant

Blue heaven: LSD

Blue heavens: Amytal (amobarbital)*

Blue madman: PCP

Blue meth: methamphetamine

Blue microdot: LSD

Blue mist: LSD

Blue mollies: amphetamine

Blue moons: LSD

Blue sage: marijuana

Blue sky blond: high potency marijuana from Columbia

Blue star: a type of blotter LSD*

Blue tabs: LSD*

Blue tips: depressant

Blue velvet: combination of elixir terpin hydrate with codeine and tripelennamine (as weak heroin substitute); combination of paregoric and PBZ (pyribenzamine or tripelennamine) used as a weak heroin substitute*

Blue vials: LSD

Blues: Amytal (amobarbital sodium) (blue-colored capsule)*

Blues and reds: Amytal (amobarbital) and Seconal (secobarbital) capsules; barbiturates*

Blunt: marijuana inside a cigar; marijuana and cocaine inside a cigar

Bo: marijuana

Boat: PCP

Bobo bush: marijuana

Bobo: crack

Bo-bo: marijuana

Body packer: person who ingests crack or cocaine to transport it

Body packing: smuggling or hiding drugs inside body cavities*

Body stuffer: person who ingests crack vials to avoid prosecution

Bogart a joint: salivate on a marijuana cigarette; refuse to share

Bohd: marijuana; PCP

Bolasterone: injectable steroid

Bolivian marching powder: cocaine

Bolivian: cocaine

Bolo: crack

Bolt: isobutyl nitrite

Bomb: crack; heroin; large marijuana cigarette; high potency heroin

Bomb squad: crack-selling crew

Bomber: marijuana cigarette

Bombido: injectable amphetamine; heroin; depressant

Bombita: amphetamine; heroin; depressant; Desoxyn (methamphetamine) in solution for injection*

Bombs away: heroin

Bone: marijuana; $50 piece of crack

Bonecrusher: crack

Bones: crack

Bong: pipe used to smoke marijuana

Bonita: heroin

Boo boo bama: marijuana

Boo: marijuana

Boogie: to travel for the purpose of smuggling drugs*

Book: 100 dosage units of LSD

Boom: marijuana

Boomers: psilocybin/psilocin

Boost: to inject a drug; to steal; crack cocaine

Boost and shoot: steal to support a habit

Booster: to inhale cocaine

Boot the gong: to smoke marijuana

Boot: to inject a drug

Booted: under the influence of drugs

Booting: injecting drug partially into a vein, then withdrawing blood into syringe before re-injecting*

Boppers: amyl nitrite

Botray: crack

Bottles: crack vials; amphetamine

Boubou: crack

Boulder: crack; $20 worth of crack

Boulya: crack

Bouncing powder: cocaine

Boxed: in jail

Boy: heroin; cocaine

Bozo: heroin

Brain damage: heroin

Brain ticklers: amphetamine

Brea: heroin

Break night: staying up all night until day break

Breakdowns: $40 crack rock sold for $20

Brewery: place where drugs are made

Brick gum: heroin

Brick: 1 kilogram of marijuana; crack

Bridge up or bring up: ready a vein for injection

Britton: peyote

Broccoli: marijuana

Brody: to fake an illness to obtain a prescription*

Broja: heroin

Broker: go-between in a drug deal

Brother: heroin*

Brown: heroin; marijuana

Brown and clears: Dexedrine (dextroamphetamine) Spansules (brown and clear capsules filled with white and brown beads)*

Brown bombers: LSD

Brown crystal: heroin

Brown dots: LSD

Brown rhine: heroin

Brown sugar: heroin

Brownies: amphetamines, especially Dexedrine (dextroamphetamine) Spansules (brown capsule)*

Browns: amphetamine

Bubble gum: cocaine; crack

Buck: shoot someone in the head

Bud: marijuana

Buda: a high-grade marijuana joint filled with crack

Buddha: potent marijuana spiked with opium*

Buffer: crack smoker; a woman who exchanges oral sex for crack

Bugged: annoyed; to be covered with sores and abscesses from repeated use of unsterile needles

Bull: narcotics agent or police officer

Bullet: isobutyl nitrite

Bullia capital: crack

Bullion: crack

Bullyon: marijuana

Bumblebees: amphetamine

Bummer trip: unsettling and threatening experience from PCP intoxication

Bump: crack; fake crack; cocaine; boost a high; hit of ketamine ($20)

Bundle: heroin

Bunk: fake cocaine; crack cocaine

Burese: cocaine

Burn one: to smoke marijuana

Burn the main line: to inject a drug

Burn: to sell fake drugs or to take money without delivering a drug during a sale; to report a drug user or dealer to the police*

Burned out: collapse of veins from repeated injections; permanent impairment from drug abuse

Burned: purchase fake drugs

Burnese: cocaine

Burnie: marijuana

Burnout: heavy abuser of drugs

Burnt: intoxicated*

Burrito: marijuana*

Bush: cocaine; marijuana

Business: injection paraphernalia*

Businessman's LSD: dimethyltryptamine

Businessman's special: dimethyltryptamine

Businessman's trip: dimethyltryptamine

Busted: arrested

Busters: depressant

Busy bee: PCP

Butt naked: PCP

Butter flower: marijuana

Butter: marijuana; crack

Buttons: mescaline

Butu: heroin

Buzz: slight or mild intoxication*; under the influence of drugs

472

Buzz bomb: device for inhaling nitrous oxide from small canisters*; nitrous oxide

C

C: cocaine

C, the: methcathinone; amphetamine

C&M: cocaine and morphine

C joint: place where cocaine is sold

C.S.: marijuana

Caballo: heroin

Cabello: cocaine

Caca: heroin

Cactus: mescaline

Cactus buttons: mescaline

Cactus head: user of peyote*

Cad/Cadillac: 1 ounce

Cadillac express: methcathinone

Cadillac: PCP; cocaine

Caine: cocaine; crack

Cakes: round discs of crack

Calbo: heroin

California cornflakes: cocaine

California sunshine: LSD

Cam trip: high potency marijuana

Cambodian red/Cam red: marijuana from Cambodia

Came: cocaine

Can: marijuana; 1 ounce

Canadian black: marijuana

Canamo: marijuana

Canappa: marijuana

Cancelled stick: marijuana cigarette

Candy: cocaine; crack; depressant; amphetamine; illegal drugs in general*

Candy C: cocaine

Candy cane: cocaine*

Candy flipping: combining or sequencing LSD with MDMA

Candy flipping on a string: LSD

Candy man: drug pusher*

Candycaine: cocaine*

Cannabinol: PCP

Cannabis tea: marijuana

Cap: crack; LSD

Cap up: transfer bulk form drugs to capsules

Capital H: heroin

Caps: capsules, pills in general*; crack; heroin; psilocybin/psilocin

Capsula: crack

Captain Cody: codeine*

Carburetor: crack stem attachment

Carga: heroin

Carmabis: marijuana

Carne: heroin

Carnie: cocaine

Carpet patrol: crack smokers searching the floor for crack

Carrie: cocaine

Carrie Nation: cocaine

Cartucho: package of marijuana cigarettes

Cartwheels: amphetamine

Casper: crack cocaine

Casper the ghost: crack

Cat valium: ketamine

Cat: methcathinone

Catnip: marijuana cigarette

Cat's pee: crack cocaine*

Caviar: crack

Cavite all star: marijuana

C-dust: cocaine

Cecil: cocaine

Cest: marijuana

C-game: cocaine

Chalk: methamphetamine; amphetamine; crack cocaine

Chalked up: under the influence of cocaine

Chalking: chemically altering the color of cocaine so it looks white

Champagne of drugs: cocaine hydrochloride*

Chandoo/chandu: opium

Channel: vein into which a drug is injected

Channel swimmer: one who injects heroin

Chapopote: heroin

Charas: marijuana from India

Charge: marijuana

Charged up: under the influence of drugs

Charley: heroin

Charlie: cocaine

Chase: to smoke cocaine; to smoke marijuana

Chaser: compulsive crack user

Chasing the dragon: inhaling vapors of heroin or cocaine heated on tin foil*

Chasing the tiger: to smoke heroin

Chatarra: heroin

Cheap basing: crack

Check: personal supply of drugs

Cheeba: marijuana

Cheeo: marijuana

Chemical: crack

Cheroot: smoking cigar-shaped object (tobacco or marijuana or mixture)*

Chewies: crack

Chiba chiba: high potency marijuana from Columbia

Chicago black: marijuana, term from Chicago

Chicago green: marijuana

Chick: heroin*

Chicken powder: amphetamine

Chicken scratch: searching on hands and knees for crack

Chicken sh*t habit: small heroin habit, usually not addicted*

Chicle: heroin

Chief: LSD; mescaline

Chieva: heroin

Chillums: marijuana*

China cat: high potency heroin

China girl: fentanyl

China town: fentanyl

China white: very pure form of heroin, alternately a fentanyl analog used as a heroin substitute*

Chinese molasses: opium

Chinese red: heroin

Chinese tobacco: opium

Chip: heroin

Chipper: occasional Hispanic user

Chipping: using drugs occasionally

Chippy: cocaine

Chips: tobacco or marijuana cigarettes laced with PCP*

Chira: marijuana

Chiva: heroin

Chocofan: brown tar heroin

Chocolate: opium; amphetamine; marijuana

Chocolate chips: LSD

Chocolate ecstasy: crack made brown by adding chocolate milk powder during production

Choe: cocaine

Cholly: cocaine

Chorals: depressant

Christina: amphetamine

Christmas rolls: depressant

Christmas tree: marijuana; depressant; amphetamine

Christmas trees: Dexamyl (dextroamphetamine and amobarbital combo) (green and clear capsules with white balls inside)*

Chronic: marijuana; marijuana mixed with crack

Chucks: hunger following withdrawal from heroin

Chunky: marijuana

Churus: marijuana

CIBAs: Doriden (glutethimide)*

Cid: LSD

Cigarette paper: packet of heroin

Cigarrode cristal: PCP

Citrol: high potency marijuana, from Nepal

CJ: PCP

Clarity: MDMA

Clear up: stop drug use

Clicker: crack and PCP; marijuana dipped in formaldehyde and smoked

Cliffhanger: PCP

Climax: crack; isobutyl nitrite; heroin

Climb: marijuana cigarette

Clips: rows of vials heat-sealed together

Clocking paper: profits from selling drugs

Closet baser: user of crack who prefers anonymity

Cloud: crack

Cloud nine: crack

Cluck: crack smoker

Coasting: under the influence of drugs

Coasts to coasts: amphetamine

Coca: cocaine

Cocaine blues: depression after extended cocaine use

Cochornis: marijuana

Cocktail: cigarette laced with cocaine or crack; partially smoked marijuana cigarette inserted in regular cigarette

Coco rocks: dark brown crack made by adding chocolate pudding during production

Coco snow: benzocaine used as cutting agent for crack

Cocoa puff: to smoke cocaine and marijuana

Coconut: cocaine

Cod: large amount of money

Cody: codeine*

Coffee: LSD

Coke: cocaine; crack

Coke bar: bar where cocaine is openly used

Coke bugs: tactile hallucination after using cocaine which creates the illusion of bugs burrowing under the skin*

Cola: cocaine

Colas: marijuana flowing tops*

Cold bust: unplanned arrest for drugs after a police stop for another crime*

Cold turkey: sudden withdrawal from drugs

Coli: marijuana

Coliflor tostao: marijuana

Colorado cocktail: marijuana

Columbian: marijuana

Columbo: PCP

Columbus black: marijuana

Combol: cocaine

Come home: end a "trip" from LSD

Comeback: benzocaine and mannitol used to adulterate cocaine for conversion to crack

Conductor: LSD

Connect: purchase drugs; supplier of illegal drugs

Contact lens: LSD

Contraband chemist: who makes or prepares drugs*

Cook: mix heroin with water; heating heroin to prepare it for injection

Cook down: process in which users liquify heroin in order to inhale it

Cooker: to inject a drug; person that makes methamphetamine

Cookies: crack

Cooler: cigarette laced with a drug

Coolie: cigarette laced with cocaine

Cop: obtain drugs

Co-pilot: amphetamine; sober companion for one who is intoxicated, especially on LSD*

Copping zones: specific areas where buyers can purchase drugs

Coral: depressant

Coriander seeds: cash

Corine: cocaine

Cork the air: to inhale cocaine

Corrinne: cocaine

Cosa: marijuana

Cotics: heroin

Coties: codeine

Cotton: currency

Cotton brothers: cocaine, heroin, and morphine

Cotton fever: septicemia caused by injecting small amounts of cotton fibers with the drugs*

Cotton habit: infrequent use of narcotics*

Cotton shooter: desperate addict who injects the residue from cotton used to filter heroin*

Courage pills: heroin; depressant

Course note: bill larger than $2

Cozmo's: PCP

Crack: cocaine

Crack attack: craving for crack

Crack back: crack and marijuana

Crack cooler: crack soaked in wine cooler

Crack gallery: place where crack is bought and sold

Crack house: place where crack cocaine is sold and smoked*

Crack kits: glass pipe and copper mesh

Crack pipe: pipe for smoking crack cocaine*

Crack spot: area where people can purchase crack

Cracker jacks: crack smokers

Crackers: crack cocaine*; LSD

Cracking: gesturing as if cracking a whip, as a means of advertising crack for sale*

Crank: methamphetamine; amphetamine; methcathinone; heroin

Crank bugs: tactile hallucination after using stimulants which creates the illusion of bugs burrowing under the skin*

Cranking up: to inject a drug

Crankster: person who uses or manufactures methamphetamine

Crash: sleep off effects of drugs

Crazy coke: PCP

Crazy Eddie: PCP

Crazy weed: marijuana

Cream and crimsons: Dalmane (a red and white sleeping pill capsule)*

Credit card: crack stem

Crib: crack

Crimmie: cigarette laced with crack

Crink: methamphetamine

Cripple: marijuana cigarette

Cris: methamphetamine

Crisscross: amphetamine

Crisscrossing: the practice of setting up a line of cocaine next to a line of heroin. The user places a straw in each nostril and snorts about half of each line. Then the straws are crossed and the remaining lines are snorted.

Cristal: MDMA

Cristina: methamphetamine

Cristy: smokable methamphetamine

Croak: crack and methamphetamine

Crop: low quality heroin

Cross tops: amphetamine

Crossles: methamphetamine

Crossroads: amphetamine

Crown crap: heroin

Crumbs: tiny pieces of crack

Crunch & Munch: crack

Cruz: opium from Veracruz, Mexico

Crying weed: marijuana

Cryppie: marijuana

Crypto: methamphetamine

Cryptonie: marijuana

Crystal: methamphetamine; PCP; amphetamine; cocaine

Crystal joint: PCP

Crystal meth: methamphetamine

Crystal methadrine: amphetamine

Crystal T: PCP

Crystal tea: LSD

Cube: 1 ounce; LSD; morphine*

Cubes: marijuana tablets; crack cocaine

Culican: high potency marijuana from Mexico

Cupcakes: LSD

Cura: heroin

Cushion: vein into which a drug is injected

Cut: adulterate drugs

Cut-deck: heroin mixed with powdered milk

Cycline: PCP

Cyclones: PCP

D

D: LSD; PCP

Dabble: use drugs occasionally

Dagga: marijuana

Dama blanca: cocaine

Dance fever: fentanyl

Dank: marijuana

Dark blooded (person): one who injects drugs into an artery*

Dawamesk: marijuana

Daytime: high on drugs, especially heroin*

Dead on arrival: heroin

Debs: amphetamine

Decadence: MDMA

Deca-duabolin: injectable steroid

Deck: 1 to 15 grams of heroin, also known as a bag; packet of drugs

Deeda: LSD

Delatestryl: injectable steroid

Demo: crack stem; sample-size quantity of crack

Demolish: crack

Dep-testosterone: injectable steroid

Desocins: methamphetamine

Desocsins: methamphetamine

Desogtion: methamphetamine

DET: dimethyltryptamine

Detox: detoxification*

Detroit pink: PCP

Deuce: $2 worth of drugs; heroin

Devil, the: crack

Devil's dandruff: crack

Devil's dick: crack pipe

Devil's drug: crack cocaine

Devil's dust: PCP

Devilsmoke: crack

Dew: marijuana

Dews: $10 worth of drugs

Dex: amphetamine

Dexedrine: amphetamines

Dexies: Dexedrine (dextroamphetamine); Dexamyl (dextroamphetamine/ amobarbital combo)*

Diablito: combination of crack cocaine and marijuana in a joint

Diambista: marijuana

Diamonds: amphetamines

Dianabol: veterinary steroid

Dice: crack cocaine

Diesel: heroin

Diet pills: amphetamine

Dihydrolone: injectable steroid

Dilaudid cowboys: person who scams physicians into prescribing Dilaudid (hydromorphone) by faking severe pain symptoms*

Dillys: Dilaudid (hydromophone)*

Dimba: marijuana from West Africa

Dime: crack; $10 worth of crack

Dime bag: $10 worth of drugs

Dime special: crack cocaine

Dime store high: glue sniffing*

Dime's worth: amount of heroin to cause death

Ding: marijuana

Dinkie dow: marijuana

Dinosaurs: populations of heroin users in their forties and fifties

Dip: crack

Dip and dab: experiment, especially with heroin*

Dipper: PCP

Dipping out: crack runners taking a portion of crack from vials

Dirt: heroin

Dirt grass: inferior quality marijuana

Dirty basing: crack

Dirty drop: drugs found in urine after drug test*

Dirty joints: combination of crack cocaine and marijuana

Dirty urine: drugs found in urine after drug test*

Disco biscuits: depressant; MDMA; Quaalude (methaqualone)*

Disease: drug of choice
Ditch: marijuana
Ditchweed: low potency marijuana that grows wild*
Djamba: marijuana
DMT: Dimethyltryptamine
Do a joint: to smoke marijuana
Do a line: to inhale cocaine
Do it Jack: PCP
Do up: inject a drug, especially heroin*
Do: use drugs*
DOA: PCP; crack
Doctor: MDMA
Dog: good friend
Dog food: heroin
Dogie: heroin
Dollar: $100 worth of drugs
Dollies: methadone (from the brand name Dolophine)*
Dolls: depressant; amphetamines
Domes: LSD
Domestic: locally grown marijuana; marijuana
Domex: PCP and MDMA
Dominoes: amphetamine
Don jem: marijuana
Don Juan: marijuana
Dona Juana: marijuana
Dona Juanita: marijuana
Doob: marijuana
Doobee: marijuana
Doobie/dubbe/duby: marijuana
Doogie/doojee/dugie: heroin
Dooley: heroin
Doors: Doriden (glutethimide)*
Doors and fours: Doriden (gluthethimide) and codeine*
Dope: heroin; marijuana; any other drug
Dope fiend: crack addict

Dope smoke: to smoke marijuana
Dopium: opium
Doradilla: marijuana
Dors and 4's: combination of Doriden and Tylenol 4
Dots: LSD
Doub: $20 rock of crack
Double breasted dealing: dealing cocaine and heroin together
Double bubble: cocaine
Double cross: amphetamine
Double dome: LSD
Double rock: crack diluted with procaine
Double trouble: Tuinal (amobarbital/secobarbital combination);*
Double up: when a crack dealer delivers an extra rock as a marketing ploy to attract customers
Double ups: a $20 rock that can be broken into two $20 rocks
Double yoke: crack
Dove: $35 piece of crack
Dover's powder: opium
Down: under the influence of a depressant drug; depressant; period of depression after "crashing" when an intoxicating drug wears off*
Down and dirtys: Quaalude (methaqualone)*
Down and out: (after drug wears off) no longer high, drug supply is exhausted (out of drugs)*
Downer: depressant
Downie: depressant
Dr. Feelgood: heroin

Draf weed: marijuana
Drag weed: marijuana
Draw up: to inject a drug
Dream gum: opium
Dream stick: opium
Dream: cocaine
Dreamer: morphine
Dreams: opium
Dreck: heroin
Drink: PCP
Drivers: amphetamine
Dropper: to inject a drug
Drowsy high: depressant
Drug store cowboy: person who steals drugs from pharmacies*
Drug store dope: morphine*
Druggies: college students deeply involved with drugs*
Dry high: marijuana
Drying out: detoxification*
Dub: when a crack dealer delivers an extra rock as a marketing ploy to attract more customers
Dube: marijuana
Duby: marijuana
Duct: cocaine
Due: residue of oils trapped in a pipe after smoking base
Duji: heroin
Dummy dust: PCP
Durabolin: injectable steroid
Durog: marijuana
Duros: marijuana
Dust joint: PCP
Dust of angels: PCP
Dust: heroin; cocaine; PCP; marijuana mixed with various chemicals
Dusted parsley: PCP
Dusting: adding PCP, heroin, or another drug to marijuana

Dusty roads: cocaine and PCP mixture for smoking*
Dymethzine: injectable steroid
Dynamite: heroin and cocaine
Dyno: heroin
Dyno-pure: heroin

E

Earth: marijuana cigarette
Easing powder: opium
Eastside player: crack
Easy score: obtaining drugs easily
Eating: taking a drug orally
Ecstasy: MDMA
Egg: crack
Eight ball: 1/8 ounce of drugs
Eightball: crack and heroin
Eighth: heroin
El diablito: marijuana, cocaine, heroin and PCP
El diablo: marijuana, cocaine and heroin
Electric Kool Aid: LSD
Elephant: PCP; marijuana
Elephant tranquilizer: PCP
Elvis: LSD
Embalming fluid: PCP
Embroidery: scars left over veins from frequent injections*
Emergency gun: instrument used to inject other than syringe
Emsel: morphine
Endo: marijuana
Energizer: PCP
Enoltestovis: injectable steroid
Ephedrone: methcathinone
Equipose: veterinary steroid
Erth: PCP

Esra: marijuana
Essence: MDMA
Estuffa: heroin
ET: alpha-ethyltyptamine
Eve: MDMA
Evening: onset of heroin withdrawal (start of night time)*
Everclear: cocaine
Ex: ecstasy (MDMA)*
Explorers club: group of LSD users
Extasy: ecstasy (MDMA)*
Eye opener: crack; amphetamine

F

Factory: place where drugs are packaged, diluted, or manufactured
Fake STP: PCP
Fall: arrested
Fallbrook redhair: marijuana, term from Fallbrook, CA
Famous dimes: crack
Fantasia: dimethyltryptamine
Fastin: amphetamine
Fat bags: crack
Fatty: marijuana cigarette
Feds: federal narcotics officers*
Feed bag: container for marijuana
Feeling: marijuana
Feenies: phenobarbital*
Felix the Cat: LSD
Ferry dust: heroin
Fi-do-nie: opium
Fields: LSD
Fiend: drug addict who lacks control*; someone who smokes marijuana alone
Fifteen cents: $15 worth of drugs
Fifty-one: crack

Finajet/finaject: veterinary steroid
Fine stuff: marijuana
Finger lid: marijuana
Finger: marijuana cigarette; stick-shaped piece of hashish; condom filled with drugs and swallowed to facilitate drug smuggling*
Fir: marijuana
Fire it up: to smoke marijuana
Fire up: smoke marijuana*
Fire: to inject a drug; crack and methamphetamine
Firing the ack ack gun: technique for smoking heroin by dipping tip of a tobacco cigarette in heroin (Asian slang)*
First line: morphine
Fish scales: crack
Fit: paraphernalia for injecting drugs*
Five C note: $500 bill
Five cent bag: $5 worth of drugs
Five dollar bag: $50 worth of drugs
Fives: amphetamine
Fix: to inject a drug
Fizzies: methadone
Flag: appearance of blood in the vein
Flake: cocaine
Flakes: PCP
Flaky: addicted to cocaine*
Flame cooking: smoking cocaine base by putting the pipe over a stove flame
Flamethrowers: cigarette laced with cocaine and heroin
Flash: glue (for sniffing)*; LSD
Flashback: recurring hallucinations long after LSD use*
Flashing: sniffing glue*

481

Flat blues: LSD

Flat chunks: crack cut with benzocaine

Flea powder: low purity heroin

Flip out: psychotic reaction after using a drug*

Floating: high on a drug, especially heroin*

Florida snow: cocaine; look-alike cocaine*

Flower tops: marijuana

Flower: marijuana

Fluff: filtering heroin or cocaine through cloth (often a stocking) to increase its apparent bulk*

Fly agaric: amanita muscaria mushrooms*

Fly Mexican airlines: to smoke marijuana

Flying saucers: variety of psychedelic morning glory seeds*

Flying: under the influence of drugs

Following that cloud: searching for drugs

Foo foo stuff: heroin; cocaine

Foo-foo dust: cocaine

Foolish powder: heroin; cocaine

Footballs: Diphetamine tablets; Diaudid (hydromorphone) tablets*

Forget me drug: rohypnol

Forget pill: rohypnol

Forwards: amphetamine

Four doors: Doriden (glutethimide) and codeine*

Four D's: drinkin', druggin', datin' and dinin'*

Four ways: LSD, methamphetamine, strychnine, and STP combo*

Fours: Tylenol with Codeine No. 4, a prescription painkiller containing 60 mg. codeine plus acetominophen; or Empirin Compound with Codeine No. 4*

Fraho/frajo: marijuana

Freak out: panic or psychotic reaction, particularly to LSD or another psychedelic*

Free trips: psychedelic flashbacks*

Freebase: smoking cocaine; crack

Freebee: psychedelic flashback; inhaling freon*

Freeze: cocaine; renege on a drug deal

French blue: amphetamine

French fries: crack

Fresh: PCP

Fried: intoxicated*

Friend: fentanyl

Fries: crack

Frios: marijuana laced with PCP

Frisco special: cocaine, heroin and LSD

Frisco speedball: cocaine, heroin and LSD

Friskie powder: cocaine

Fry: crack

Fry daddy: crack and marijuana; cigarette laced with crack

Fu: marijuana

Fuel: marijuana mixed with insecticides; PCP

Fuete: hypodermic needle

Full moon: large piece of peyote cactus*

Fuma d'Angola: marijuana

Fungus: psilocybin (from mushrooms)*

Funk: marijuana*
Funny stuff: marijuana*
Furra: heroin
Fuzz: police officer; narcotics officer*

G

G: $1000 or 1 gram of drugs; term for an unfamiliar male
G.B.: depressant
G.I. gin: elixir of terpin hydrate with codeine*
Gaffel: fake cocaine
Gaffus: hypodermic needle
Gage/gauge: marijuana
Gagers: methcathinone
Gaggers: methcathinone
Gaggler: amphetamine
Galloping horse: heroin
Gallup: heroin
Gamot: heroin
Gange: marijuana
Gangster: marijuana; person who uses or manufactures methamphetamine
Gangster pills: depressant
Ganja: marijuana from Jamaica
Gank: fake crack
Garbage: inferior quality drugs
Garbage head: addict who will take anything to become intoxicated; one who is not particular about which drug s/he uses*; users who buy crack from street dealers instead of cooking it themselves
Garbage rock: crack
Gas: nitrous oxide*
Gash: marijuana
Gasper: marijuana cigarette
Gato: heroin

Gauge butt: marijuana
GB: barbiturate (from "goofball")*
Gee head: user of paregoric*
Gee: opium; paregoric*
Geek joints: cigarettes or cigars filled with tobacco and crack
Geek: crack and marijuana
Geekers: crack user
Geeze: to inhale cocaine
Geezer: to inject a drug
Geezin a bit of dee gee: injecting a drug
George smack: heroin
George: heroin
Georgia home boy: GHB
Geronimo: alcoholic beverage (especially wine) mixed with a barbiturate sleeping pill*
Get a gage up: to smoke marijuana
Get a gift: obtain drugs
Get down: to inject a drug
Get high: to smoke marijuana
Get lifted: under the influence of drugs
Get off houses: private places heroin users can purchase and use heroin for a fee
Get off: to inject a drug; get "high"
Get on: smoke marijuana*
Get the wind: to smoke marijuana
Get through: obtain drugs
Get your own: cocaine*
Getting roached: using Rohypnol
Ghana: marijuana
Ghanja: marijuana*
GHB: gamma hydroxy butyrate
Ghost: LSD

Ghost busting: smoking cocaine; searching for white particles in the belief that they are crack

Gick monster: crack smoker

Gift-of-the-sun: cocaine

Giggle smoke: marijuana

Giggle weed: marijuana

Gimmick: drug injection equipment

Gimmie: crack and marijuana

Gin: cocaine

Girl: cocaine; crack; heroin

Girlfriend: cocaine

Giro house: non-bank financial institutions for businesses frequently used by drug traffickers to launder drug proceeds

Give wings: inject someone or teach someone to inject heroin

Glacines: heroin

Glad stuff: cocaine

Glading: using inhalant

Glass: hypodermic needle; amphetamine; heroin

Glass gun: hypodermic needle

Glo: crack

Gluey: person who sniffs glue

G-men: government officers, often FBI or DEA agents*

Go into a sewer: to inject a drug

Go loco: to smoke marijuana

Go on a sleigh ride: inhale cocaine

Go: amphetamines

Goblet of jam: marijuana

God's drug: morphine

God's flesh: psilocybin/psilocin

God's medicine: opium

Go-fast: methcathinone; crank; methamphetamine

Gold: marijuana; crack; heroin

Gold dust: cocaine

Gold star: marijuana

Golden dragon: LSD

Golden girl: heroin

Golden leaf: very high quality marijuana

Golden: marijuana

Golf ball: crack

Golf balls: depressant

Golpe: heroin

Goma: morphine*; opium; black tar heroin

Gondola: opium

Gong: marijuana; opium

Gonj: marijuana

Goob: methcathinone

Good: PCP; heroin

Good and plenty: heroin

Good butt: marijuana cigarette

Good giggles: marijuana

Good go: proper amount of drugs for the money paid

Good H: heroin

Good horse: heroin

Good lick: good drugs

Good sick: nausea following heroin injection*

Good stuff: high potency drug, especially marijuana*

Goodfellas: fentanyl

Goods: any drug, especially heroin*

Goody-goody: marijuana

Goof butt: marijuana cigarette

Goofball: barbiturate*; cocaine and heroin

Goofers: barbiturate*

Goofing: intoxicated on barbiturates*

Goofy's: LSD

Goon: PCP

Goon dust: PCP
Gooney birds: LSD*
Gopher: person paid to pickup
 drugs
Goric: opium
Gorilla biscuits: PCP
Gorilla pills: barbiturate sleep-
 ing pills*
Gorilla tab: PCP
Got it going on: fast sale of
 drugs
Graduate: completely stop using
 drugs or progress to stronger
 drugs
Gram: hashish
Granulated orange: metham-
 phetamine
Grape parfait: LSD
Grass: marijuana
Grass brownies: marijuana
Grasshopper: marijuana
Grata: marijuana
Gravel: crack
Gravy: to inject a drug; heroin
Grease: currency
Great bear: fentanyl
Great tobacco: opium
Green: inferior quality mari-
 juana; PCP; ketamine
Green and clears: Dexamyl (dex-
 troamphetamine and
 amobarbital combo) (green
 and clear capsules with white
 balls inside)*
Green buds: marijuana
Green double domes: LSD
Green dragons: depressant
Green frog: depressant
Green goddess: marijuana
Green gold: cocaine
Green goods: paper currency
Green leaves: PCP

Green single domes: LSD
Green tea: PCP
Green wedge: LSD
Greenies: amphetamines
Greens/green stuff: paper cur-
 rency
Greeter: marijuana
Grefa: marijuana*
Greta: marijuana
Grey shields: LSD
Griefo: marijuana
Griefs: marijuana
Grievous bodily harm: GHB
 (gamma hydroxy butyric
 acid)*
Grifa: marijuana
Griff: marijuana
Griffa: marijuana
G-riffic: GHB (gamma hydroxy
 butyric acid)*
Griffo: marijuana
Grit: crack
Groceries: crack
Grocery store high: nitrous ox-
 ide*
G-rock: one gram of rock cocaine
Groovy: intoxicated by a drug*
Groovy lemon: yellow LSD tab-
 let*
Ground control: sober compan-
 ion for one who is intoxi-
 cated, especially on LSD*
Ground man: sober companion
 for one who is intoxicated, es-
 pecially on LSD*
G-shot: small dose of drugs used
 to hold off withdrawal symp-
 toms until full dose can be
 taken
Guide: experienced drug user
 who teaches novice users how
 to use drugs, especially LSD*

Gum: opium refined for smoking*

Guma: opium

Gun: to inject a drug; needle

Gunga: marijuana

Gungeon: marijuana

Gungeon: potent Jamaican marijuana*

Gungun: marijuana

Gunja: marijuana

Gunney: marijuana*

Gunney sack: marijuana (from sacks made with hemp fiber)*

Gutter: veins on inside of elbow where addict injects drugs*

Gutter glitter: cocaine; drugs in general*

Gutter junkie: addict who relies on others to obtain drugs

Gyve: marijuana cigarette

H

H: heroin

H&C: heroin and cocaine

H Caps: heroin

Hache: heroin

Hail: crack

Haircut: marijuana

Hairy: heroin

Half a football field: 50 rocks of crack

Half G: $500

Half load: 15 bags (decks) of heroin

Half moon: peyote

Half piece: 1/2 ounce of heroin or cocaine

Half track: crack

Half: 1/2 ounce

Half-a-C: $50 bill

Hamburger helper: crack

Hand-to-hand: direct delivery and payment

Hand-to-hand man: transient dealers who carry small amounts of crack

Hanhich: marijuana

Hanyak: smokable methamphetamine

Happy cigarette: marijuana cigarette

Happy dust: cocaine

Happy powder: cocaine

Happy sticks: PCP

Happy trails: cocaine

Hard ball: crack cocaine

Hard candy: heroin

Hard line: crack

Hard on: amyl nitrite*

Hard rock: crack

Hard stuff: opium; heroin

Hardware: isobutyl nitrite

Harry Jones: heroin*

Harry: heroin

Harsh: marijuana

Has: marijuana

Hash: hashish*

Hats: LSD

Have a dust: cocaine

Haven dust: cocaine

Hawaiian: very high potency marijuana

Hawaiian black: marijuana

Hawaiian homegrown hay: marijuana

Hawaiian sunshine: LSD

Hawk: LSD

Hay: marijuana

Hay butt: marijuana cigarette

Haze: LSD

Hazel: heroin

HCP: PCP

Head drugs: amphetamine

Head shop: drug paraphernalia store*

Headlights: LSD

Heads: frequent drug users*

Heart-on: inhalant

Hearts: amphetamine

Heaven: cocaine; heroin

Heaven & Hell: PCP

Heaven dust: heroin; cocaine

Heavenly blue: LSD; variety of psychedelic morning glory seeds*

Heavy stuff: heroin or cocaine*

Heeled: having plenty of money

Helen: heroin

Hell dust: heroin

Hell: crack cocaine

He-man: fentanyl

He-man: iso-butyl nitrite (brand name)*

Hemp: marijuana

Henpicking: searching on hands and knees for crack

Henry: heroin

Henry VIII: cocaine

Her: cocaine

Hera: heroin (Hispanic communities)

Herb: marijuana

Herb and Al: marijuana and alcohol

Herba: marijuana

Herms: PCP

Hero: heroin

Hero of the underworld: heroin

Heroina: heroin

Herone: heroin

Hessle: heroin

Hi speeds: amphetamines*

High: intoxicated*

High speed: amphetamines*

Highbeams: the wide eyes of a person on crack

Hikori: peyote

Hikuli: peyote

Him: heroin

Hinkley: PCP

Hippie crack: inhalant

Hironpon: smokable mehamphetamine

Hit: a single dose of an illegal drug; a single puff on a marijuana cigarette; a single puff on a pipe (any drug)*

Hit house: house where users go to shoot up and leave the owner drugs as payment

Hit the hay: to smoke marijuana

Hit the main line: to inject a drug

Hit the needle: to inject a drug

Hit the pit: to inject a drug

Hitch up the reindeers: to inhale cocaine

Hitter: little pipes designed for only one hit

Hitting up: injecting drugs

Hocus: opium; marijuana

Hog: PCP

Holding: possessing drugs

Hombre: heroin

Hombrecitos: psilocybin

Homegrown: marijuana

Homer: freebase cocaine*

Honey: currency

Honey blunts: marijuana cigars sealed with honey

Honey oil: ketamine; inhalant

Honeymoon: early stages of drug use before addiction or dependency develops

Hong-yen: heroin in pill form

Hooch: marijuana

Hookah: a Middle Eastern water pipe used for smoking tobacco or marijuana*

Hooked: addicted

Hooking: working as female prostitute to pay for drugs*

Hooter: cocaine; marijuana

Hop: opium for smoking*

Hop dog: opium addict*

Hophead: opium addict*

Hopped up: under the influence of drugs

Horn: snorting a drug; using an inhalant*; to inhale cocaine; crack pipe

Horning: heroin; to inhale cocaine

Horse: heroin

Horse heads: amphetamine

Horse tracks: PCP

Horse tranquilizer: PCP

Horsebite: heroin

Hospital heroin: Diluadid

Hot bust: drug arrest based upon informant or undercover officer*

Hot dope: heroin

Hot heroin: heroin poisoned to give to a police informant

Hot ice: smokable methamphetamine

Hot load/hot shot: lethal injection of an opiate

Hot rolling: liquefying methamphetamine in an eye dropper and then inhaling it

Hot stick: marijuana cigarette

Hotcakes: crack

House fee: money paid to enter a crackhouse

House piece: crack given to the owner of a crackhouse or apartment where crack users congregate

How do you like me now?: crack

Hows: morphine

HRN: heroin

Hubba: crack cocaine

Hubba, I am back: crack

Hubba pigeon: crack user looking for rocks on a floor after a police raid

Hubbas: crack

Huff: inhalant

Huffer: inhalant abuser

Huffing: using an inhalant*

Hug drug: MDMA*

Huggers: MDMA*

Hulling: using others to get drugs

Hunter: cocaine

Hustle: attempt to obtain drug customers

Hustling: working as a male prostitute to pay for drugs*

Hyatari: peyote

Hydro: amphetamine; marijuana

Hype: heroin addict; an addict

Hype stick: hypodermic needle

I

I am back: crack

Iboga: amphetamine

Ice: cocaine; crack cocaine into a single joint; methamphetamine; smokeable methamphetamine; PCP; MDMA

Ice cream habit: occasional use of drugs

Ice cube: crack

Icing: cocaine

Idiot pills: barbiturates*

Ill: PCP

Illies: beedies dipped in PCP

Illy momo: PCP

In: connected with drug suppliers

In transit: on an LSD trip*

Inbetweens: depressant; amphetamine

Inca message: cocaine

Incentive: cocaine*

Indian boy: marijuana

Indian hay: marijuana from India

Indian hemp: marijuana

Indiana ditchweed: low-potency wild marijuana, grows wild from seeds originally bred for hemp rope*

Indiana hay: marijuana*

Indians: mescaline*

Indica: species of cannabis, found in hot climate, grows 3.5 to 4 feet

Indo: marijuana, term from Northern CA

Indonesian bud: marijuana; opium

Instaga: marijuana

Instagu: marijuana

Instant zen: LSD

Interplanetary mission: travel from one crackhouse to another in search of crack

Isda: heroin

Issues: crack

J

J: marijuana cigarette

Jab/job: to inject a drug

Jack: steal someone else's drugs

Jack back: injecting drug partially into a vein, then withdrawing blood into syringe before reinjecting*

Jack off: injecting drug partially into a vein, then withdrawing blood into syringe before reinjecting*

Jacking: stealing*

Jackpot: fentanyl

Jack-Up: to inject a drug

Jag: prolonged intoxication*

Jam: amphetamine; cocaine

Jam cecil: amphetamine

Jamaican gold: marijuana

Jammed up: overdosed on drugs*

Jane: marijuana

Jay smoke: marijuana

Jay: marijuana cigarette

Jee gee: heroin

Jeff: methcathinone*

Jefferson airplane: used match cut in half to hold a partially smoked marijuana cigarette

Jejo: cocaine

Jellies: chloral hydrate*

Jelly: cocaine

Jelly baby: amphetamine

Jelly bean: amphetamine; depressant

Jelly beans: chloral hydrate*; crack

Jerk off: injecting drug partially into a vein, then withdrawing blood into syringe before reinjecting*

Jet: ketamine

Jet fuel: PCP

Jim Jones: marijuana laced with cocaine and PCP

Jive: heroin; marijuana; drugs

Jive doo jee: heroin

Jive stick: marijuana

Joe Fridays: Quaalude (meth-aqualone—from the Sgt. Friday's badge number on *Dragnet*, and the numeric code on the Quaalude tablet: 714)*

Joharito: heroin

Johnson: crack

Johnson grass: low potency Texas marijuana (as in Lyndon Johnson)*

Joint: marijuana cigarette

Jojee: heroin

Jolly bean: amphetamine

Jolly green: marijuana

Jolly pop: casual user of heroin

Jolt: to inject a drug; strong reaction to drugs

Jones: heroin

Jones, the: drug addiction; withdrawal symptoms*

Jonesing: need for drugs

Jonesing a fix: obtaining small amount of drugs when unable to pay*

Joy: heroin

Joy flakes: heroin

Joy juice: choral hydrate in an alcoholic beverage*

Joy plant: opium

Joy pop: to inject a drug

Joy popping: occasional use of drugs

Joy powder: heroin; cocaine

Joy smoke: marijuana

Joy stick: marijuana cigarette

Juan Valdez: marijuana

Juanita: marijuana

Judas: heroin (a friend that betrays you)*

Juggle: sell drugs to another addict to support a habit

Juggler: teen-aged street dealer

Jugs: amphetamine

Juice: steroids; PCP

Juice joint: marijuana cigarette sprinkled with crack

Juja: marijuana

Ju-ju: marijuana cigarette

Jum: sealed plastic bag containing crack

Jumbos: large vials of crack sold on the streets

Junco: heroin

Junk: cocaine; heroin

Junkie kits: glass pipe and copper mesh

Junkie: addict

K

K: ketamine*; PCP

Kabayo: heroin

Kabuki: crack pipe made from a plastic rum bottle and a rubber sparkplug cover

Kaksonjae: smokable methamphetamine

Kalakit: marijuana

Kali: marijuana

Kangaroo: crack

Kansas grass: marijuana

Kaps: PCP

Karachi: heroin

Kat: khat, leaves of the *Cathula edulis* plant (a stimulant)*

Kate bush: marijuana

Kaya: marijuana

K-blast: PCP

Kee: kilogram of a drug*; marijuana

Kentucky blue: marijuana

Key: kilogram of a drug*; marijuana

Keys to the kingdom: LSD*

KGB (killer green bud): marijuana

Khat: amphetamine; leaves of the *Cathula edulis* plant (a stimulant)*

K-hole: periods of ketamine-induced confusion

Ki: marijuana

Kibbles & Bits: small crumbs of crack; Talwin (pentazocine) and Ritalin combo*

Kick: getting off a drug habit; inhalant

Kick cold turkey: withdraw from narcotics (from the gooseflesh sensation as symptom of withdrawal syndrome)*

Kick stick: marijuana cigarette

Kick the habit: withdraw from narcotics (from leg tremors and convulsions as symptoms of withdrawal syndrome); withdraw from any drug*

Kicking: withdrawing from drugs*

Kiddie dope: prescription drugs

Kif: hashish, potent Moroccan marijuana*

Kiff: marijuana

Killer: high potency drug*; marijuana; PCP

Killer green bud: marijuana

Killer joints: PCP

Killer weed (1960s): marijuana

Killer weed (1980s): marijuana and PCP

Kilo: 2.2 pounds; kilogram of a drug*

Kilo connection: drug dealer who sells in kilogram quantities*

Kilter: marijuana

Kind: marijuana

King: cocaine

King bud: marijuana

King ivory: fentanyl

King Kong pills: barbiturate sleeping pills*

King Kong: major heroin habit*

Kingpin: major drug dealer who imports or sells drugs in large quantities*

King's habit: cocaine

Kissing: the exchange of plastic wrapped rocks (crack) by kissing (mouth to mouth transfer)

Kit: equipment used to inject drugs

KJ: PCP

Kleenex: MDMA

Klingons: crack addicts

Knockout drops: chloral hydrate; choral hydrate mixed in an alcoholic beverage*

Kokomo: crack

Kools: PCP

Krypt tonight: isobutyl nitrite (brand name)*

Kryptonite: crack

Krystal: PCP

Krystal joint: PCP

Kumba: marijuana

KW: PCP

L

L: LSD

L.A.: long-acting amphetamine

L.A. glass: smokable methamphetamine

L.A. ice: smokable methamphetamine

L.A. turnarounds: amphetamines, especially Biphetamine (amphetamine/dextroamphetamine combo)*

L.B.: a pound of drugs*

L.B.J.: JB 226-N-Methyl-3 Piperidyl benzitate hydrochloride (a psychedelic drug)*

L.L.: marijuana

La Buena: heroin

Lace: cocaine and marijuana

Lace (verb): incorporating or mixing one drug in another*

Lady: cocaine

Lady caine: cocaine

Lady snow: cocaine

Lakbay diva: marijuana

Lamborghini: crack pipe made from plastic rum bottle and a rubber sparkplug cover

Lamb's bread: marijuana*

Lame: non-user of drugs*

Las mujercitas: psilocybin

Lason sa daga: LSD

Late night: cocaine

Laugh and scratch: to inject a drug

Laughing gas: nitrous oxide

Laughing grass: marijuana

Laughing weed: marijuana

Lay: smoke opium*

Lay back: depressant

Lay down: smoke opium in reclining position; use drugs*

Layout: paraphernalia for using drugs, especially for smoking opium*

LBJ: LSD; PCP; heroin

Leaf: marijuana; cocaine

Leaky bolla: PCP

Leaky leak: PCP

Leapers: amphetamine

Leaping: under the influence of drugs

Lebanese: hashish from Lebanon*

Legal speed: over-the-counter asthma drug; trade name-MiniThin

Lemmon 714: Quaalude (methaqualone)*

Lemon: weak or impotent dose of drugs*

Lemon 714: PCP

Lemon drop: methamphetamine with a dull yellow tint

Lemonade: heroin; poor quality drugs

Lemons: Quaalude (methaqualone)*

Lennons: Quaalude (methaqualone)*

Leño: marijuana

Lenos: PCP

Lens: LSD

Lethal weapon: PCP

Lettuce: money

Lewds: Quaalude (methaqualone)*

Lib (Librium): depressant

Lid proppers: amphetamine

Lid: 1 ounce of marijuana

Light stuff: marijuana

Light up: smoke marijuana*

Lightning: amphetamine

Lima: marijuana

Limbo: marijuana*

Lime acid: LSD

Line: main vein in the arm used for injecting drugs; single dose for snorting cocaine hydrochloride*

Lip poppers: amphetamines*

Lipton tea: inferior quality drugs

Liquid ecstacy: GHB (gamma hydroxy butyric acid)*

Liquid X: GHB (gamma hydroxy butyric acid)*

Lit up: under the influence of drugs

Little bomb: amphetamine; heroin; depressant

Little ones: PCP

Little smoke: marijuana; psilocybin/psilocin

Live ones: PCP

Llesca: marijuana

Load: 25 bags of heroin

Loaded: intoxicated on any drug*

Loads: Doriden (glutethimide) and codeine combo*

Loaf: marijuana

Lobo: marijuana

Locker room: isobutyl nitrite

Loco: marijuana

Locoweed: marijuana

Log: PCP; marijuana cigarette

Logor: LSD

Look-alike drug: counterfeit drug that mimics the appearance of a controlled substance*

Loony Toons: LSD

Loused: covered by sores and abscesses from repeated use of unsterile needles

Love affair: cocaine

Love: crack

Love boat: marijuana dipped in formaldehyde; PCP; blunts mixed with marijuana and heroin

Love drug: MDMA; depressant; Quaalude (methaqualone)*

Love pearls: alpha-ethyltyptamine

Love pills: alpha-ethyltyptamine

Love trip: MDMA and mescaline

Love weed: marijuana

Lovelies: marijuana laced with PCP

Lovely: PCP

Lovers: Quaalude (methaqualone)*

LSD: lysergic acid diethylamide

Lubage: marijuana

Lucas: marijuana*

Lucy: LSD*

Lucy in the sky with diamonds: LSD

Ludes: Quaalude (methaqualone)*

Luding out: intoxicated on Quaalude (methaqualone)*

Luds: depressant

Lumber: marijuana stems and wastes*

Lunch money drug: rohypnol

M

M: marijuana; morphine

M&Ms: Seconal (secobarbital); MDMA*

M.J.: marijuana

M.O.: marijuana

M.S.: morphine

M.U.: marijuana

Machinery: marijuana

Macon: marijuana

Maconha: marijuana

Mad dog: PCP

Madman: PCP

Mafu: marijuana

Magic: PCP

Magic dust: PCP

Magic mushroom: psilocybin/psilocin

Magic smoke: marijuana
Main line: to inject a drug
Mainliner: person who injects into the vein
Make up: need to find more drugs
Mama coca: cocaine
Man: heroin; drug dealer; the police*
Manhattan silver: marijuana
Manteca: heroin
MAO: amphetamines
Marathons: amphetamine
Marching dust: cocaine
Marching powder: cocaine
Mari: marijuana cigarette
Marimba: marijuana
Marley: marijuana*
Marshmallow reds: depressant
Mary: marijuana
Mary and Johnny: marijuana
Mary Ann: marijuana
Mary Jane: marijuana
Mary Jonas: marijuana
Mary Warner: marijuana
Mary Weaver: marijuana
Maserati: crack pipe made from a plastic rum bottle and a rubber sparkplug cover
Matchbox: 1/4 ounce of marijuana or 6 marijuana cigarettes
Matsakow: heroin
Maui wauie: marijuana from Hawaii
Maui-wowie: marijuana; methamphetamine
Max: gamma hydroxy butyrate dissolved in water and mixed with amphetamines
Maxibolin: oral steroid
Mayo: cocaine; heroin

MDM: MDMA
MDMA: methylenedioxy-methamphetamine
Mean green: PCP
Medusa: inhalant
Meg: marijuana
Megg: marijuana cigarette
Meggie: marijuana
Mellow drug of America: MDMA*
Mellow yellow: LSD
Merchandise: drugs
Merck: pharmaceutical cocaine (from the manufacturer)*
Merk: cocaine
Mesc: mescaline
Mescal: an intoxicating distilled beverage, from the maguey plant*; mescaline
Mese: mescaline
Messorole: marijuana
Meth: methamphetamine
Meth head: regular user of methamphetamine
Meth monster: person who has a violent reaction to methamphetamine
Meth speed ball: methamphetamine combined with heroin
Methatriol: injectable steroid
Methedrine: amphetamines
Methlies Quik: methamphetamine
Methyltestosterone: oral steroid
Mexican brown: heroin; marijuana
Mexican crack: methamphetamine with the appearance of crack
Mexican green: marijuana
Mexican horse: heroin
Mexican locoweed: marijuana

Mexican mud: heroin
Mexican mushroom: psilocybin/ psilocin
Mexican red: marijuana
Mexican reds: depressant
Mexican valium: rohypnol
Mezc: mescaline
Mickey Finn: choral hydrate mixed in an alcoholic beverage*
Mickey's: depressant
Microdot: LSD
Midnight oil: opium
Mighty Joe Young: depressant
Mighty mezz: marijuana cigarette
Mighty Quinn: LSD
Mike: microgram of a drug (one-millionth of a gram)*
Mikes: microdot LSD*
Miltown: meprobamate, a tranquilizer*
Mind detergent: LSD
Mini beans: amphetamine
Minibennie: amphetamine
Mint leaf: PCP
Mint weed: PCP
Mira: opium
Miss: to inject a drug
Miss Emma: morphine
Missile basing: crack liquid and PCP
Mission: trip out of the crackhouse to obtain crack
Mist: PCP; crack smoke
Mister blue: morphine
Mister Brownstone: hashish, brown heroin*
Mister Natural: LSD*
Mixed jive: crack cocaine
Mo: marijuana
Modams: marijuana

Mohasky: marijuana
Mojo: cocaine; heroin; morphine*
Monkey: drug dependency; cigarette made from cocaine paste and tobacco
Monkey dust: PCP
Monkey on one's back: addiction to a drug, especially heroin or opium*
Monkey tranquilizer: PCP
Monoamine oxidase: amphetamine
Monos: cigarette made from cocaine paste and tobacco
Monster: cocaine
Monte: marijuana from South America
Mooca/moocah: marijuana
Moocher: one who uses other people's drugs without paying*
Moon gas: inhalant
Moon: mescaline
Moonrock: crack and heroin
Mooster: marijuana
Moota/mutah: marijuana
Mooters: marijuana cigarette
Mootie: marijuana
Mootos: marijuana
Mor a grifa: marijuana
More: PCP
Morf: morphine
Morning shot: amphetamine
Morning wake-up: first blast of crack from the pipe
Morotgara: heroin
Morphina: morphine*
Morpho: morphine
Morphy: morphine*
Mortal combat: high potency heroin
Mosquitos: cocaine
Mota/moto: marijuana

Mother: a drug pusher*; marijuana

Mother's little helper: Valium (diazepam)*

Mouth worker: one who takes drugs orally

Movie star drug: cocaine

Mow the grass: to smoke marijuana

Mu: marijuana

Mud: morphine*; opium; heroin

Muggie: marijuana

Muggles: marijuana

Mujer: cocaine

Mule: carrier of drugs

Munchies: symptoms of intense hunger after marijuana use*

Murder 8: fentanyl

Murder one: heroin and cocaine

Murotugora: heroin

Murphy: morphine*

Mushrooms: psilocybin/psilocin

Musk: psilocybin/psilocin

Muta: marijuana

Mutha: marijuana

Muzzle: heroin

N

Nail: hypodermic syringe*; marijuana cigarette

Nailed: arrested

Nanoo: heroin

Narc/nark: pejorative term for narcotics officer*

Narco: pejorative term for narcotics officer*

Nebbies: Nembutal (pentobarbital)*

Needle: hypodermic syringe*

Needle freak: drug user who is enamored with injection*

Nemish: Nembutal (pentobarbital)*

Nemmies: depressant

New acid: PCP

New addition: crack cocaine

New Jack Swing: heroin and morphine

New magic: PCP

Nice and easy: heroin

Nickel bag: $5 worth of drugs; heroin

Nickel deck: heroin

Nickel note: $5 bill

Nickelonians: crack addicts

Nie: nitrous oxide*

Niebla: PCP

Nieve: cocaine

Nigh: nitrous oxide*

Night time: heroin withdrawal*

Nigra: marijuana

Nimbies: Nembutal (pentobarbital)*

Nineteen: amphetamine

Nitro: nitrous oxide*

Nitrogen: nitrous oxide*

Nix: stranger among the group

Nixon: low potency heroin*

Nod: effects of heroin

Noise: heroin

Nontoucher: crack user who doesn't want affection during or after smoking crack

Nose: heroin; cocaine

Nose candy: cocaine

Nose drops: liquified heroin

Nose powder: cocaine

Nose stuff: cocaine

Nubs: peyote

Nugget: amphetamine

Nuggets: crack

Number: marijuana cigarette

Number 3: cocaine; heroin

Number 4: heroin
Number 8: heroin

O

O: opium
O.D.: drug overdose*
O.J.: marijuana
O.P.: opium
O.P.P.: PCP
Ocean: Aqua Net hair spray (high alcohol content) in milk*
Ocean Spray: salt water in mister bottle used to spray nasal passages after snorting cocaine or other drugs*
Octane: PCP laced with gasoline
Off: high on a drug*
Ogoy: heroin
Oil: hashish oil*; heroin; PCP
Old Steve: heroin
On a mission: searching for crack
On a trip: under the influence of drugs
On ice: in jail
On the bricks: walking the streets
On the nod: under the influence of narcotics or depressant
On the pine: smoking freebase cocaine*
On the street: out of drugs, out looking for more; immersed in the drug culture*
One and one: snorting cocaine using both nostrils*
One box tissue: one ounce of crack
One on one house: where cocaine and heroin can be purchased

One plus one sales: selling cocaine and heroin together
One way: LSD
One-fifty-one: crack
Oolies: marijuana cigarettes laced with crack
Ope: opium
Optical illusions: LSD
Orange: Desoxyn (methamphetamine)*
Orange barrels: LSD
Orange crystal: PCP
Orange cubes: LSD
Orange cupcakes: LSD, methamphetamine, strychnine, and STP combo*
Orange haze: LSD
Orange micro: LSD
Orange wedges: LSD
Oranges: amphetamine
Ounce man: dealer who sells in one ounce quantities*
Outerlimits: crack and LSD
Outfit: paraphernalia for injecting drugs*
Overjolt: overdose*
Owsley: LSD
Owsley's acid: LSD
Oyster stew: cocaine
Oz: an ounce of a drug*; inhalant
Ozone: PCP
Ozzie's stuff: LSD (apparent reference to Ozzie Osborne)*

P

P: peyote; PCP
P.F.: crack cocaine in aspirin-sized tablets as a disguise*
P.G.: paregoric*
P.R. : Panama red marijuana*

497

Paca lolo: marijuana (Hawaiian term)*

Pack a bowl: marijuana

Pack of rocks: marijuana cigarette

Pack: heroin; marijuana

Pakalolo: marijuana

Pakistani black: marijuana

Panama cut: marijuana

Panama gold: marijuana

Panama red: marijuana

Panatella: large marijuana cigarette

Pancakes and syrup: combination of glutethimide and codeine cough syrup

Pane: LSD

Pangonadalot: heroin

Panic: drugs not available

Paper: a dosage unit of heroin

Paper acid: LSD

Paper bag: container for drugs

Paper blunts: marijuana within a paper casing

Paper boy: heroin peddler

Parabolin: veterinary steroid

Parachute: crack and PCP smoked; heroin

Paradise: cocaine

Paradise white: cocaine

Paregoric: camphorated tincture of opium, lightly regulated*

Parker: one who fails to share a marijuana cigarette*

Parlay: crack

Parsley: marijuana; PCP

Partying: using a drug, especially heroin; getting drunk*

Paste: crack

Pasto: marijuana

Pat: marijuana

Patico: crack

Paz: PCP

PCP: phencyclidine

PCPA: PCP

P-dope: 20-30% pure heroin

Peace: LSD; PCP

Peace pill: PCP

Peace tablets: LSD

Peace weed: marijuana with PCP*; PCP

Peaches: Benzedrine (amphetamine) tablets*

Peaking: point of highest intensity in an LSD trip*

Peanut: depressant

Peanut butter: PCP mixed with peanut butter; methamphetamine

Peanuts: barbiturate sleeping pills*

Pearl: cocaine

Pearls: amyl nitrite

Pearly gates: LSD; variety of psychedelic morning glory seeds*

Pebbles: crack

Peddlar: drug supplier

Pee wee: crack; $5 worth of crack

Peep: PCP

Peg: heroin

Pellets: LSD

Pen yan: opium

People, the: high level heroin distributors*

Pep pills: amphetamine

Pepsi habit: occasional use of drugs

Percia/percio: cocaine

Percs/perks: Percodan (oxycodone)*

Perfect high: heroin

Perlas: street dealer (heroin)

Perp: fake crack made of candle wax and baking soda

Peruvian: cocaine

Peruvian flake: cocaine

Peruvian lady: cocaine

Peter Pan: PCP

Peter: choral hydrate*

Peth: Demerol (meperidine)*

Petrol: gasoline (for sniffing)*

Peyote: mescaline

P-funk: heroin; crack and PCP

Phennies: phenobarbital*

Phenos: phenobarbital*

Phillies Blunt: cigar hollowed out and filled with marijuana*

Pianoing: using the fingers to find lost crack

Picked up: smoked marijuana*

Piece: 1 ounce; cocaine; crack

Piedra: crack

Pig killer: PCP

Piles: crack

Pillhead: heavy user of barbiturates or amphetamines*

Pimp: cocaine

Pimp your pipe: lending or renting your crack pipe

Pin gon: opium

Pin yen: opium

Pin: marijuana; thinly-rolled marijuana cigarettes*

Pineapple: heroin and Ritalin or amphetamine*

Ping-in-wing: to inject a drug

Pingus: rohypnol

Pinhead: thinly-rolled marijuana cigarettes*

Pink blotters: LSD

Pink hearts: amphetamine

Pink ladies: depressant

Pink panther: LSD

Pink robots: LSD

Pink spoons: Percodan (oxycodone)*

Pink wedge: LSD

Pink witches: LSD

Pinks: Seconal (secobarbital) tablets*

Pinned: high on narcotics (from pinpoint pupils)*

Pipe: crack pipe; marijuana pipe; vein into which a drug is injected; mix drugs with other substances

Pipero: crack user

Pit: PCP

Pixies: amphetamine

Plant: drugs placed by others to incriminate a suspect*; hiding place for drugs

Platters: hashish*

Pocket rocket: marijuana

Pod: marijuana

Point: hypodermic needle or syringe*

Poison: heroin; fentanyl

Poison people: heroin addicts*

Poke: marijuana; to smoke a marijuana cigarette*

Pollutants: amphetamines

Polo: mixture of heroin and motion sickness drug

Polvo: heroin; PCP

Polvo blanco: cocaine

Polvo de angel: PCP

Polvo do estrellas: PCP

Pony: crack

Poor man's pot: inhalant

Poor man's speedball: heroin and methamphetamine combo*

Pop: drug arrest*; to inhale cocaine

Poppers: isobutyl nitrite; amyl nitrite

Popping: injecting drugs subcutaneously*

Poppy: heroin

Pot liquor: tea brewed from marijuana waste*

Pot: marijuana

Potato chips: crack cut with benzocaine

Potato: LSD

Potlikker: marijuana; tea brewed from marijuana waste*

Potten bush: marijuana

Powder: heroin; amphetamine; cocaine HCL

Powder diamonds: cocaine

Power puller: rubber piece attached to crack stem

Pox: opium

Predator: heroin

Preludes: Preludin (phenmetrazine hydrochloride)*

Prescription: marijuana cigarette

Press: cocaine; crack

Pretendica: marijuana

Pretendo: marijuana

Prime time: crack cocaine

Primo: crack; marijuana mixed with crack

Primobolan: injectable and oral steroid

Primos: cigarettes laced with cocaine and heroin

Product: crack cocaine

Proviron: oral steroid

Pseudocaine: phenylpropanolamine, an adulterant for cutting crack

Puff: to smoke, especially opium*

Puff the dragon: to smoke marijuana

Puffer: crack smoker

Puffy: PCP

Pulborn: heroin

Pullers: crack users who pull at parts of their bodies excessively

Pumping: selling crack

Pure: heroin

Pure love: LSD

Purple: ketamine

Purple barrels: LSD

Purple flats: LSD

Purple haze: LSD

Purple hearts: LSD; amphetamine; depressant; Luminal tablets*

Purple ozoline: LSD

Purple rain: PCP

Push: sell drugs

Push shorts: to cheat or sell short amounts

Pusher: one who sells drugs; metal hanger or umbrella rod used to scrape residue in crack stems

Q

Q: Quaalude (methaqualone)*

Q'at: khat, leaves of the *Cathula edulis* plant (a stimulant)*

Qat: methcathinone

Qua: Quaalude (methaqualone)*

Quaa: Quaalude (methaqualone)*

Quack: Quaalude (methaqualone)*

Quad: Quaalude (methaqualone)*

Quarter: 1/4 ounce or $25 worth of drugs

Quarter bag: $25 worth of drugs

Quarter moon: hashish

Quarter piece: 1/4 ounce

Quartz: smokable methamphetamine

Quas: Quaaludes (methaqualone)*

Queen Ann's lace: marijuana

Quicksilver: isobutyl nitrite

Quill: methamphetamine; heroin; cocaine

Quinolone: injectable steroid

R

R and R: Seconal (secobarbital) and Ripple wine (reds and Ripple)*

R2: rohypnol

Racehorse charlie: cocaine; heroin

Ragweed: inferior quality marijuana; heroin

Rail: single dose for snorting cocaine hydrochloride*

Railroad weed: marijuana

Rainbow: LSD

Rainbows: Tuinal (amobarbital/ secobarbital combo) (a multicolored striped capsule)*

Rainy day woman: marijuana

Rambo: heroin

Rane: cocaine; heroin

Rangood: marijuana grown wild

Rap: criminally charged; to talk with someone

Raspberry: female who trades sex for crack or money to buy crack

Rasta weed: marijuana

Rat: addict-turned-informer*

Rave: party designed to enhance a hallucinogenic experience through music and behavior

Raw: crack

Raw fusion: heroin

Raw hide: heroin

Razed: under the influence of drugs

Ready rock: cocaine; crack; heroin

Recompress: change the shape of cocaine flakes to resemble "rock"

Recycle: LSD

Red: under the influence of drugs

Red and blues: Tuinal (amobarbital/secobarbital combo)*

Red birds: Seconal (secobarbital) (red capsules)*

Red bud: marijuana

Red bullets: Seconal (secobarbital) (red capsules)*

Red caps: crack

Red chicken: Chinese heroin*

Red cross: marijuana

Red devil: depressant; PCP

Red dirt: marijuana

Red eagle: heroin

Red lips: LSD

Red phosphorus: smokable speed

Red rum: potent form of heroin (murder spelled backward)*

Redneck cocaine: methamphetamine

Reds: Seconal (secobarbital) (red capsules)*

Reds and Ripple: Seconal (secobarbital) and Ripple wine*

Reefer: marijuana

Regular P: crack

Reindeer dust: heroin
Rest in peace: crack cocaine
Reynolds: rohypnol
Rhine: heroin
Rhythm: amphetamine
Rib: rohypnol
Riding the wave: under the influence of drugs
Rig: equipment used to inject drugs
Righteous bush: marijuana
Ringer: good hit of crack
Rip: marijuana
Ripped: intoxicated*
Rippers: amphetamine
Roach: butt of marijuana cigarette
Roach clip: holds partially smoked marijuana cigarette
Roacha: marijuana
Roaches: rohypnol
Road dope: amphetamine
Roapies: rohypnol
Roasted: intoxicated*
Roasting: smoking marijuana
Robutal: rohypnol
Roca: crack; MDMA
Rochas dos: rohypnol
Roche: rohypnol
Rock(s): cocaine; crack
Rock attack: crack
Rock house: place where crack is sold and smoked
Rock star: female who trades sex for crack or money to buy crack
Rocket caps: dome-shaped caps on crack vials
Rocket fuel: PCP
Rockets: marijuana cigarette
Rockette: female who uses crack

Rocks of hell: crack
Rocky III: crack
Roid rage: aggressive behavior caused by excessive steroid use
Roller: to inject a drug
Rollers: police
Rolling: MDMA
Roofies: rohypnol
Rooms: psilocybe mushrooms*
Rooster: crack
Root: marijuana
Rope: marijuana; rohypnol
Rophies: rohypnol
Rophy: rohypnol
Roples: rohypnol
Rosa: amphetamine
Rose marie: marijuana
Roses: Benzedrine (amphetamine) tablets*
Rough stuff: marijuana
Row-shay: rohypnol
Rox: crack
Roxanne: cocaine; crack
Royal blues: LSD
Roz: crack
Rubia: marijuana
Ruderalis: species of cannabis, found in Russia, grows 1 to 2.5'
Ruffies: rohypnol
Ruffles: rohypnol
Runners: people who sell drugs
Running: MDMA
Rush: initial euphoria at the onset of drug use*; isobutyl nitrite; cocaine
Rush snappers: isobutyl nitrite
Russian sickles: LSD

S

Sack: heroin

Sacrament: LSD

Sacred mushroom: psilocybin

Salt: heroin

Salt and pepper: marijuana

Sam: federal narcotics agent

Sancocho: to steal

Sandoz: LSD

Sandwich: two layers of cocaine with a layer of heroin in the middle

Santa Marta: marijuana

Sasfras: marijuana

Satan's secret: inhalant

Satch: papers, letters, cards, clothing, etc., saturated with drug solution (used to smuggle drugs into prisons or hospitals)

Satch cotton: fabric used to filter a solution of narcotics before injection

Sativa: species of cannabis, found in cool, damp climate, grows up to 18 feet

Scaffle: PCP

Scag: heroin

Scat: heroin

Scate: heroin

Schmack: heroin*

Schmeck: cocaine; heroin*

Schmecker: heroin user*

Schoolboy: cocaine; codeine

Schoolboy scotch: codeine in scotch whisky*

Schoolcraft: crack

Scissors: marijuana

Scooby snacks: MDMA

Scoop: GHB (gamma hydroxy butyric acid)*

Score: price of a bundle of drugs, especially heroin*; purchase drugs

Scorpion: cocaine

Scott: heroin

Scottie: cocaine

Scotty: cocaine; crack cocaine; the high from crack

Scrabble: crack cocaine

Scramble: crack

Scrape and snort: to share crack by scraping off small pieces for snorting

Scratch: addict (from an addict's habit of scratching self)*; money

Scrip/script: prescription*

Scrubwoman's kick: cleaning fluid inhaled, especially naptha*

Scruples: crack

Scuffle: PCP

Seccy: Seconal (secobarbital)*

Second to none: heroin

Seeds: marijuana

Seggy: Seconal (secobarbital)*

Sen: marijuana

Seni: peyote

Serenity, tranquility, and peace: STP*

Serenity: STP*

Serial speedballing: sequencing cocaine, cough syrup, and heroin over a 1-2 day period

Sernyl: PCP

Serpico 21: cocaine

Server: crack dealer

Sess: marijuana

Set: place where drugs are sold

Set up: use of informants to obtain a drug conviction; drugs planted by police prior to a drug raid*

Sets: Talwin (pentazocine) and PBZ (pyribenzamine)*

Sevenup: cocaine; crack

Sewer: vein into which a drug is injected

Sezz: marijuana

Sh*t: Heroin

Shabu: ice; crack cocaine; methamphetamine

Shake: marijuana

Shaker/baker/water: materials needed to freebase cocaine; shaker bottle, baking soda, water

Sharps: needles

She: cocaine

Sheet rocking: crack and LSD

Sheets: PCP

Sherm: tobacco cigarette laced with PCP*

Sherman: tobacco cigarette laced with PCP*

Shermans: PCP

Sherms: PCP; crack

Shlook: a puff of a marijuana cigarette*

Shmeck/schmeek: heroin

Shoot: heroin

Shoot the breeze: nitrous oxide

Shoot/shoot up: to inject a drug

Shooting gallery: place where drugs are used

Short count: short weight of drug as a result of cheating*

Short go: short weight of drug as a result of cheating*

Shot: to inject a drug

Shot down: under the influence of drugs

Shotgun: inhaling marijuana smoke forced into one's mouth by another's exhaling*

Shrooms: psilocybin/psilocin

Siddi: marijuana

Sightball: crack

Silly Putty: psilocybin/psilocin

Simple Simon: psilocybin/psilocin

Sinse: marijuana

Sinsemilla: potent variety marijuana

Sixty second trip: amyl nitrite*

Sixty-two: 2 1/2 ounces of poor quality crack

Skag: heroin

Skee: opium

Skeegers/skeezers: crack-smoking prostitute

Sketch: methamphetamine

Sketching: coming down from a speed induced high

Skid: heroin

Skied: under the influence of drugs

Skin: marijuana rolling paper*

Skin popping: injecting drugs under the skin

Skinning: injecting drugs subcutaneously*

Skuffle: PCP

Skunk: marijuana; heroin

Slab: crack

Slam: to inject a drug

Slammin'/Slamming: amphetamine

Slanging: selling drugs

Sleeper: heroin; depressant

Sleepers: barbiturates*

Sleepwalker: heroin addict*

Sleet: crack

Sleigh ride: cocaine

Slick superspeed: methcathinone

Slime: heroin

Smack: heroin

Smears: LSD

Smoke: heroin and crack; crack; marijuana

Smoke a bowl: marijuana

Smoke Canada: marijuana

Smoke-out: under the influence of drugs

Smoking: PCP

Smoking gun: heroin and cocaine

Smurf: cigar dipped in embalming fluid

Snap: amphetamine

Snappers: amyl nitrite*; isobutyl nitrite

Sniff: to inhale cocaine; inhalant; methcathinone

Sniffer bags: $5 bag of heroin intended for inhalation

Snop: marijuana

Snort: to inhale cocaine; use inhalant

Snorts: PCP

Snot: residue produced from smoking amphetamine

Snot balls: rubber cement rolled into balls and burned

Snow: cocaine; heroin; amphetamine

Snow bird: cocaine

Snow lights: visual hallucinations after cocaine use, image of flashing bright lights*

Snow pallets: amphetamine

Snow seals: cocaine and amphetamine

Snow soke: crack

Snow white: cocaine

Snowball: cocaine and heroin

Snowcaps: cocaine sprinkled over marijuana bong hits*

Snowcones: cocaine

Soaper: Sopor (methaqualone)*

Society high: cocaine

Soda: injectable cocaine used in Hispanic communities

Softballs: depressant

Soles: hashish

Soma: PCP

Somatomax: GHB (gamma hydroxy butyric acid)*

Sopors: Sopor (methaqualone)*

Source: drug supplier or drug supply*

Space base: crack dipped in PCP; hollowed out cigar refilled with PCP and crack

Space blasting: smoking cocaine and PCP together*

Space cadet: crack dipped in PCP

Space dust: crack dipped in PCP

Space ship: glass pipe used to smoke crack

Spaceball: PCP used with crack

Spaced: intoxicated by psychedelic drug*

Spark it up: to smoke marijuana

Sparkle plenty: amphetamine

Sparklers: amphetamine

Special "K": ketamine

Special la coke: ketamine

Speckled birds: amphetamines*

Speckled eggs: amphetamines*

Specks: LSD*

Speed: methamphetamine; amphetamine; crack

Speed boat: marijuana, PCP, crack

Speed for lovers: MDMA

Speed freak: habitual user of methamphetamine

Speedball: heroin and cocaine; amphetamine; methylphenidate (Ritalin) mixed with heroin

Speedball artist: one who injects heroin and cocaine mixture*

Speedballs-nose-style: the practice of snorting cocaine

Spider blue: heroin

Spike: to inject a drug; needle

Spivias: amphetamine

Splash: amphetamine

Spliff: marijuana cigarette

Splim: marijuana

Split: half and half or to leave

Splitting: rolling marijuana and cocaine

Splivins: amphetamine

Spoon: 1/16 ounce of heroin; paraphernalia used to prepare heroin for injection

Spores: PCP

Sporting: to inhale cocaine

Spray: inhalant

Spring: giving a marijuana cigarette to another*

Sprung: person just starting to use drugs

Square mackerel: marijuana, term from Florida

Square time Bob: crack

Squirrel: smoking cocaine, marijuana and PCP; LSD

Stack: marijuana

Stacking: taking steroids without a prescription

Stanley's stuff: LSD*

Star: LSD blotter acid with star-shaped design*; methcathinone; cocaine; amphetamine

Stardust: cocaine; PCP

Star-spangled powder: cocaine

Stash: place to hide drugs

Stash areas: drug storage and distribution areas

Stat: methcathinone

Steamboat: inhaling marijuana smoke trapped in toilet paper roll or similar device used to burn last embers of the butt*

Steerer: person who directs customers to spots for buying crack

Stem: cylinder used to smoke crack

Stems: marijuana

Step on: dilute drugs

Stick: marijuana; PCP

Sticks: marijuana stems and waste*

Sting: police trap set for unwitting criminals*

Stink weed: marijuana

Stoned: under the influence of drugs

Stones: crack

Stoney weed: marijuana

Stool: police informant; to cooperate with police*

Stoppers: depressant

Stove top: crystal methamphetamine

STP: PCP

Straight: not using drugs*

Straw: marijuana cigarette

Strawberries: depressant

Strawberry: female who trades sex for crack or money to buy crack

Strawberry fields: LSD

Strawberry shortcake: amphetamine

Street, on the: using drugs; out looking for drugs*

Street, the: where addicts congregate and exchange drugs*

Strung out: addicted to drugs with severe symptoms*

Studio fuel: cocaine

Stuff: any drug, especially narcotics*

Stumbler: depressant

Stumblers: barbiturates*

Sugar block: crack

Sugar cubes: LSD

Sugar lumps: LSD

Sugar weed: marijuana

Sugar: cocaine; crack cocaine; LSD; heroin

Sunrise: yellow LSD*

Sunshine: LSD

Super: PCP

Super acid: ketamine

Super C: ketamine

Super cools: PCP laced cigarettes*

Super flu: heroin withdrawal symptoms*

Super grass: marijuana with PCP*

Super ice: smokable methamphetamine

Super joint: PCP

Super kools: PCP

Super pot: marijuana

Super Sopors: Parest (methaqualone)*

Super weed: marijuana with PCP*; PCP

Supergrass: marijuana

Superman: LSD

Supers: methaqualone*

Supper: Sopor (methaqualone)*

Surfer: PCP

Sweet dreams: heroin

Sweet Jesus: heroin

Sweet Lucy: marijuana

Sweet Morpheus: morphine

Sweet stuff: heroin; cocaine

Sweeties: amphetamine

Sweets: amphetamine

Swell up: crack

Swingman: drug pusher*

Swishers: cigars in which tobacco is replaced with marijuana

Synthetic cocaine: PCP

Synthetic THT: PCP

Syrup and beans: Doriden (glutethimide) and codeine*

T

T: cocaine; marijuana

T.N.T. : heroin; fentanyl

Tabs: LSD; tablets of any drug*

TAC/Tac: PCP

Tail lights: LSD

Taima: marijuana

Take off: to get intoxicated; to inject narcotics; to rob*

Take off artists: heroin addicts who rob other addicts to get drugs*

Taking a cruise: PCP

Taking care of business: heroin addicts life and actions on the street*

Taking on a number: smoking marijuana*

Takkouri: marijuana

Talco: cocaine

Tall: intoxicated (from "high"); Talwin (pentazocine)*

Tango & Cash: fentanyl

Tapping the bags: when dealers remove small amounts of heroin from a bag before selling it, thus short weighting the buyer*

Tar: opium; heroin

Tardust: cocaine

Taste: heroin; small sample of drugs

Taxing: price paid to enter a crackhouse; charging more per vial depending on race of customer or if not a regular customer

T-birds: Tuinal (amobarbital/ secobarbital combo)*

T-buzz: PCP

Tea: marijuana; PCP

Tea head: habitual marijuana user*

Tea party: to smoke marijuana

Teardrops: dosage units of crack packaged in the cut-off corners of plastic bags

Tease and bees: Talwin (pentazocine) and PBZ (pyribenzamine) used as a heroin substitute*

Tease and blues: Talwin (pentazocine) and PBZ (pyribenzamine) used as a heroin substitute*

Tease and pies: Talwin (pentazocine) and PBZ (pyribenzamine) used as a heroin substitute*

Tecata: heroin

Tecatos: Hispanic heroin addicts

Teddies and bettys: Talwin (pentazocine) and PBZ (pyribenzamine) used as a heroin substitute*

Teenager: cocaine

Teeth: cocaine; crack

Temple balls: hashish*

Ten cent pistol: heroin dose laced with poison*

Ten Pack: 1,000 dosage units of LSD

Tens: 10mg amphetamine tablets*

Tension: crack

Texas pot: marijuana

Texas tea: marijuana

Tex-mex: marijuana

Thai sticks: bundles of marijuana soaked in hashish oil; marijuana buds bound on short sections of bamboo

THC: tetrahydrocannabinol; PCP (erroneously used)*

Therobolin: injectable steroid

Thing: heroin; cocaine; main drug interest at the moment

Third eye: introspective vision from psychedelic use*

Thirst monsters: heavy crack smokers

Thirteen: marijuana

Thoroughbred: drug dealer who sells pure narcotics

Three hundreds: Quaaludes (methaqualone)*

Threes: Tylenol with Codeine No. 3,*

Thrust: isobutyl nitrite

Thrusters: amphetamine

Thumb: marijuana

Thunder: heroin

Tic: PCP in powder form

Tic tac: PCP

Ticket: LSD

Ticket to ride: LSD*

Tie: belt of tourniquet used to inject drugs*; to inject a drug

Tie off: tighten tourniquet to facilitate injection*

Tie up: tighten tourniquet to facilitate injection*

Tighten up: provide drugs*

Tigre: heroin

Tigre de Blanco: heroin

Tigre de Norte: heroin
Tijuana: marijuana*
Tin: container for marijuana
Tish: PCP
Tissue: crack
Titch: PCP
TJ: marijuana (from Tijuana)*
Toak: to inhale smoke, especially marijuana*
Toasted: intoxicated*
Toilet water: inhalant
Toke: to inhale cocaine; to smoke marijuana
Toke pipes: small pipes in which marijuana is smoked*
Toke up: to smoke marijuana
Toncho: octane booster which is inhaled
Tongs: heroin
Tooey: Tuinal (amobarbital/secobarbital combo)*
Tooles: depressant
Tools: equipment used for injecting drugs
Tooly: toluene*
Toot: cocaine; to inhale cocaine
Tooties: depressant
Tootsie roll: heroin
Top gun: crack
Topi: peyote cactus (contains mescaline)*
Topo: crack
Tops: peyote
Tops and bottoms: Talwin (pentazocine) and PBZ (pyribenzamine) used as a heroin substitute*
Torch: marijuana
Torch cooking: smoking cocaine base by using a propane or butane torch as a source of flame

Torch up: to smoke marijuana
Torn up: intoxicated*
Tornado: crack cocaine
Torpedo: choral hydrate in an alcoholic beverage*; crack and marijuana
Toss up: female who trades sex for crack or money to buy crack
Totally spent: MDMA hangover
Toucher: user of crack who wants affection before, during, or after smoking crack
Tout: person who introduces buyers to sellers
Toxy: opium
Toys: hypodermic syringe and injection paraphernalia*; opium
TR-6s: amphetamine
Track: to inject a drug
Tracks: row of needle marks on a person
Tragic magic: crack dipped in PCP
Trails: LSD induced perception that moving objects leave multiple images or trails behind them; cocaine
Trank: PCP
Tranq: depressant
Trap: hiding place for drugs
Travel agent: LSD supplier
Trays: bunches of vials
Tricycles and bicycles: Talwin (pentazocine) and PBZ (pyribenzamine) used as a heroin substitute*
Trip: a psychedelic drug use experience; to be intoxicated on psychedelic drugs*; LSD; alpha-ethyltyptamine
Tripped: intoxicated*

Trippers: LSD*

Tripping: intoxicated on psychedelic drugs, especially LSD*

Troop: crack

Trophobolene: injectable steroid

Truck drivers: amphetamine

Trupence bag: marijuana

T's and blues: Talwin (pentazocine) and PBZ
(pyribenzamine) used as a
heroin substitute*

T's and B's: Talwin (pentazocine)
and PBZ (pyribenzamine)
used as a heroin substitute*

TT 1: PCP

TT 2: PCP

TT 3: PCP

Tuie: Tuinal (amobarbital/
secobarbital combo)*

Turbo: crack and marijuana

Turf: place where drugs are sold

Turkey: cocaine; amphetamine

Turnarounds: amphetamines,
especially Biphetamine (am-
phetamine/dextroamphetamine
combo)*

Turned on: introduced to drugs;
under the influence

Turp: elixir of terpin hydrate
and codeine*

Tustin: marijuana

Tutti-frutti: flavored cocaine

Tweak mission: on a mission to
find crack

Tweaker: crack user looking for
rocks on the floor after a police raid

Tweaking: drug-induced paranoia; peaking on speed

Tweaks: crack cocaine

Tweek: methamphetamine-like
substance

Tweeker: methcathinone

Twenty rock: crack cocaine

Twenty: $20 rock of crack

Twenty-five: LSD

Twist: marijuana cigarette

Twists: small plastic bags of
heroin secured with a twist
tie

Twistum: marijuana cigarette

Two for nine: two $5 vials or
bags of crack for $9

Twoies: Tuinal (amobarbital/
secobarbital combo)*

U

U.C.: undercover officer*

U.S.P.: amphetamine

Ultimate: crack

Uncle: Federal agents

Uncle Miltie/Milty: Miltown
(meprobamate)*

Unkie: morphine

Unotque: marijuana

Up: state of intoxication*;
stimulant drug*

Up against the stem: addicted to
smoking marijuana

Up and down the lines: collapsed veins due to repeated
injections*

Uppers: amphetamine

Uppies: amphetamine

Ups and downs: depressant

Using: taking drugs*

Utopiates: hallucinogens

Uzi: crack; crack pipe

V

V: Valium

Valo: nasal inhalant

Vega: a cigar wrapping refilled with marijuana

Video head cleaner: butyl nitrite*

Vidrio: heroin

Vipe: marijuana*

Viper: marijuana smoker*

Viper's weed: marijuana

Vitamin Q: Quaalude (methaqualone)*

Vitamin R: Ritalin (methylphenidate)*

Vodka acid: LSD

W

Wac: PCP on marijuana

Wack: PCP

Wacky dust: cocaine*

Wacky terbacky: marijuana*

Wacky weed: marijuana

Wafer: LSD*

Wake and Bake: marijuana

Wake ups: amphetamine

Wallbangers: methaqualone (Quaalude or Mandrax)*

Wasted: under the influence of drugs; murdered

Water: methamphetamine; PCP; a mixture of marijuana and other substances within a cigar

Wave: crack

Weasel dust: cocaine*

Wedding bells: LSD

Wedge: LSD

Weed: marijuana

Weed tea: marijuana

Weekend habit: irregular narcotics use*

Weekend warrior: irregular drug user*

Weightless: high on crack

West coast: methlylphenidate (Ritalin)

West Coast turnaround: amphetamines, especially Biphetamine (amphetamine/dextroamphetamine combo)*

Wet: blunts mixed with marijuana and PCP; methamphetamine

Whack: crack cocaine

Whackatabacky: marijuana

Wheat: marijuana

Wheels: amphetamine

When-shee: opium

Whiffenpoppers: amyl nitrite*

Whiffle dust: amphetamine

Whippets: nitrous oxide

White: amphetamine; heroin

White ball: crack

White boy: heroin

White cloud: crack smoke

White cross: methamphetamine; amphetamine

White dust: LSD

White ghost: crack

White girl: cocaine; heroin

White horizon: PCP

White horse: cocaine

White junk: heroin

White lady: cocaine; heroin

White lightning: LSD

White mosquito: cocaine

White nurse: heroin

White Owsley's: LSD

White powder: cocaine; PCP

White stuff: heroin

White sugar: crack

White tornado: crack

White-haired lady: marijuana

Whiteout: isobutyl nitrite

Whites: amphetamine

Whiz bang: cocaine and heroin

Whore pills: Quaalude (methaqualone)*

Wicked: a potent brand of heroin

Wild cat: methcathinone and cocaine

Window glass: LSD

Window pane: LSD

Wings: heroin; cocaine

Winstrol: oral steroid

Winstrol V: veterinary steroid

Wired: intoxicated on amphetamines; addicted to heroin*

Witch: heroin; cocaine

Witch hazel: heroin

Wobble weed: PCP

Wolf: PCP

Wollie: rocks of crack rolled into a marijuana cigarette

Wolminic nasal spray: methamphetamine

Wonder star: methcathinone

Woolah: a hollowed out cigar refilled with marijuana and crack

Woolas: cigarette laced with cocaine; marijuana cigarette sprinkled with crack

Woolies: marijuana amd crack or PCP

Wooly blunts: Marijuana and crack or PCP

Working: selling crack

Working half: crack rock weighing half gram or more

Working man's cocaine: methamphetamine

Works: equipment for injecting drugs

Worm: PCP

Wrecking crew: crack

X

X: marijuana; MDMA; amphetamine

X-ing: MDMA

XTC: MDMA

Y

Yahoo/yeaho: crack

Yale: crack

Yayoo: crack cocaine

Yeah-O: crack cocaine

Yeh: marijuana

Yellow: LSD; depressant

Yellow bam: methamphetamine

Yellow bullets: depressant

Yellow dimples: LSD

Yellow fever: PCP

Yellow jackets: depressant

Yellow jackets: Nembutal (pentobarbital)*

Yellow powder: methamphetamine

Yellow submarine: marijuana

Yellow submarines: Nembutal (pentobarbital) (a yellow downer capsule)*

Yellow sunshine: LSD

Yen pop: marijuana

Yen Shee Suey: opium wine

Yen sleep: restless, drowsy state after LSD use

Yeo: crack cocaine

Yerba mala: PCP and marijuana

Yerba: marijuana

Yerhia: marijuana

Yesca: marijuana

Yesco: marijuana

Yeyo: cocaine, Spanish term

Yimyom: crack

Ying Yang: LSD
Yuppie psychedelic: MDMA*

Z

Z: 1 ounce of heroin
Zacatecas purple: marijuana
from Mexico
Zambi: marijuana
Zay: a mixture of marijuana and
other substances within a cigar
Zen: LSD
Zero: opium
Zig Zag man: LSD; marijuana;
marijuana rolling papers

Zip: cocaine
Zol: marijuana cigarette
Zombie weed: marijuana with
PCP*; PCP
Zombie: PCP; heavy user of
drugs
Zonked: intoxicated*
Zooie: holds butt of marijuana
cigarette
Zoom: PCP; marijuana laced
with PCP
Zoomers: individuals who sell
fake crack and then flee
Zoquete: heroin
Zulu: bogus crack

Chapter 64

Resource Guide for Parents

A large body of research findings shows that the family contributes both risk and protective factors to the lives of adolescents; it affects both vulnerability and resilience to drug abuse.

The parent's attitude and parental permissiveness toward the youth's use is a key factor in teenage drug use, as much as or more so than peer pressure. One 1993 study conducted by the Johnson Institute in Minneapolis found that when school-age youth are allowed to drink at home, they not only are more likely to use alcohol and other drugs outside the home, but also are more likely to develop serious behavioral and health problems related to substance use. The survey indicated that most parents allow for "supervised" underage drinking, which is a bigger factor in use and abuse than peer pressure.

Several studies have examined the comparative value of communication from parents and perceived pressure from peers to use alcohol and other drugs. One study confirms that parental support and communication from parents does appear to play a role in adolescent behavior, and openness in communication may be considered a protective measure against possible use. Communication, family management, and monitoring are important predictors of adolescent drinking,

Information in this chapter was compiled from *Growing Up Drug-Free,* U.S. Department of Education, 1998; and *Parenting Is Prevention: Resource Guide*, Substance Abuse and Mental Health Services Administration, 1998; all contact information was verified and updated April 2000.

515

delinquency, and related problem behaviors, even after taking into account critical demographic and family factors, including socioeconomic indicators, age, gender, race of the youth, family structure, and family history of abuse.

The issue of lack of monitoring has received considerable attention in recent years. One study found that latchkey youth who were home alone two or more days per week were four times more likely to have gotten drunk in the past month than those youth who had parental supervision five or more times a week. Another study found that children who had the least monitoring initiated drug use at earlier ages. The contrast in risk of initiating alcohol, tobacco, or other drug use across levels of parent monitoring was greatest when children were under 11 years old. At older ages there was no difference in risk for these drugs. However, for marijuana, cocaine, and inhalant drugs, there was a sustained risk of starting to use these drugs for youth who received low levels of monitoring in middle childhood.

Some authors have emphasized the importance of the parent's influence on the youth's choice of friends. Adolescents whose friends use drugs are very likely to use drugs themselves. And family variables may influence the choice of friends and thereby influence the risk of drug use. Adolescents who come from families where alcohol and other drugs are used are much more likely to use drugs themselves and choose friends who use drugs. And when parental monitoring is high, adolescents are much less likely to choose friends who use drugs. Thus, parents have powerful influence on their adolescents by their influence on their choice of friends and their monitoring of the peer selection process.

The likelihood of youths' associating with drug-using friends is reduced by a close relationship with their parents and by knowing that their friends disapprove of drug use. Students do not use drugs if they are unwilling to jeopardize their relationship with their parents and nonusing friends. They are also less likely to use drugs if they think their parents and friends disapprove of drug use and if their friends do not use drugs themselves.

Working at least 20 hours a week during the school year is a risk; it brings the adverse consequences of fatigue as well as excessive leisure income. It may also lessen the parent's ability to monitor the youth's time, choice of friends, and use of money. It is associated with higher levels of emotional distress, substance use, and earlier age of sexual debut.

Information on Drug Prevention and Treatment

African American Family Services (AAFS)
2616 Nicollet Ave., South
Minneapolis, MN 55408
Toll Free: (800) 557-2180
Phone: (612) 871-7878
Web site: http://www.aafs-mn.org

A comprehensive resource center with a specific focus on substance abuse within the African-American community. Through AAFS, individuals and organizations may purchase culturally sensitive on-site training packages, books, pamphlets, videos, and pre-assembled journal article packets related to chemical dependency and African-American client populations. Adult and adolescent outpatient treatment services.

American Cancer Society
1599 Clifton Rd. NE
Atlanta, GA 30329
Toll Free: (800) 227-2345
Web site: http://www.cancer.org

Offers literature on smoking and referrals to local chapters.

American Council for Drug Education
164 W. 74th St.
New York, NY 10023
Toll Free: (800) 488-DRUG
E-Mail: acde@phoenixhouse.org
Web site: www.acde.org

Provides information on the effects of drug usage and offers treatment referrals through its hotline. Referrals: (800) DRUG-HEL(P) and www.drughelp.org. For immediate specific assistance or referral: (800) COC-AINE; (888) MAR-IJUA(NA); (800) HEL-P111; (800) 9HE-ROIN; (800) REL-APSE; (800) CRI-SIS9.

Center for Substance Abuse Prevention (CSAP)
5600 Fishers Lane, Rockwall II Building, Suite 900
Rockville, Maryland 20857
Phone: (301) 443-0365
E-Mail: nnadal@samshsa.gov
Web site: http://www.samhsa.gov/csap

Center for Substance Abuse Prevention (CSAP)
(continued)

A division of the U.S. Dept. of Health and Human Services that provides a wide variety of resources and information on science-based prevention strategies and programs.

Center for Substance Abuse Treatment (CSAT)
Rockville, MD 20847-2345
Phone: (301) 443-5700
Web site: http://www.samhsa.gov/csat

A division of the U.S Dept. of Health and Human Services whose hotline provides counseling referrals and treatment options in your state.

Hazelden Foundation
P.O. Box 11
Center City, MN 5511
Toll Free: (800) 257-7810
E-Mail: info@hazelden.org
Web site: http://www.hazelden.com

A foundation that distributes educational materials and self-help literature on quitting alcohol, tobacco, and drugs.

Join Together
441 Stuart St., 7th Fl.
Boston, MA 02116
Phone: (617) 437-1500
Fax: (617) 437-9394
E-Mail: info@jointogether.org
Web site: http://www.jointogether.org

A national resource that provides publications, information, and linkages between groups and individuals working to prevent, reduce, and treat substance abuse and gun violence in their communities.

National Clearinghouse for Alcohol and Drug Information (NCADI)
P.O. Box 2345
Rockville, MD 20847-2345
Toll Free: (800) SAY-NOTO
Web site: http://www.health.org

A resource that provides a wide variety of federal government agency publications dealing with alcohol and other drug abuse.

National Council on Alcoholism and Drug Dependence, Inc.
12 W. 21st St., 7th Fl.
New York, NY 10010
Toll Free: (800) NCA-CALL
Phone: (212) 206-6770
Fax: (212) 645-1690
E-Mail: national@ncadd.org
Web site: http://www.ncadd.org

An organization that provides information, including literature and referrals on how to overcome alcohol and drug addiction.

National Crime Prevention Council
1000 Connecticut Avenue, N.W.
13th Floor
Washington, D.C. 20036
Toll Free: (800) 627-2911
Web site: http://www.ncpc.org

An organization that works to prevent crime and drug use by providing parents and children with audio-visual materials, reproducible brochures, and other publications.

National Institute on Drug Abuse
6001 Executive Blvd.
Bethesda, Maryland 20892-9561
Phone: (301) 443-1124
Web site: http://www.nida.nih.gov

NIDA supports more than 85% of the world's research on the health aspects of drug abuse and addiction.

Parents and Adolescents Recovering Together Successfully (PARTS)
7825 Engineer Road, Suite 202
San Diego, CA 92111
Phone: (619) 293-0650
Fax: (858) 560-5445
Web site: http://www.teendrughelp.org

A self-help group that supports families in recovery.

Parent to Parent
3805 Presidential Parkway, Suite 207
Atlanta, GA 30341
Toll Free: (800) 229-2038
Phone: (770) 451-5484
Fax: (770) 458-4091
E-Mail: info@parenttoparentofga.org
Web site: www.parenttoparentofga.org

An organization that empowers parents to counter influences of drug culture in their children's lives.

Partnership for a Drug-Free America
405 Lexington Ave., 16th Floor
New York, NY 10174
Phone: (212) 922-1560
Web site: http://www.drugfreeamerica.org

An organization that works with the advertising industry to develop anti-drug public service messages and operates a comprehensive web site for parents.

PTA Drug and Alcohol Abuse Prevention Project
330 North Wabash Ave., Suite 2100
Chicago, IL 60611-3690
Toll Free: (800) 307-4782
Phone: (312) 670-6782
Fax: (312) 670-6783
Web site: http://www.pta.org (for PTA members only)

With the GTE Corporation, creators of "Common Sense: Strategies for Raising Alcohol and Drug-Free Children," a new area of the National PTA's Children First Web site. Focuses on learning the facts about alcohol and other drugs, setting clear limits for children, providing positive role models, and building strong bonds within the family and school. Program offers effective, easy-to-use ideas and materials, enjoyable games and activities.

Safe and Drug-Free Schools Program
U.S. Department of Education
400 Maryland Ave. SW
Washington, D.C. 20202-6123
Toll Free: (877) 433-7827 for publications
Phone:(202) 260-3954

E-Mail: safeschl@ed.gov

Web site: http://www.ed.gov/offices/OESE/SDFS

The federal government's primary vehicle for preventing drug use and violence among youth. Provides funding and technical support for school-based education and prevention activities.

SafeHomes

c/o Erie County Council for the Prevention of Alcohol and Substance Abuse

4255 Harlem Rd.

Amherst, NY 14226

Phone: (716) 839-1157

Fax: (716) 839-1159

E-Mail: sally@eccpasa.org

Web site: www.eccpasa.org

A national organization that encourages parents to sign a contract stipulating that when parties are held in one another's homes they will adhere to a strict no-alcohol/no-drug-use policy.

Youth Power

2000 Franklin St., Suite 400

Oakland, CA 94612

E-Mail: youth@youthpower.org

Web site: http://www.youthpower.org

Formerly "Just Say No" International, a program that now emphasizes youth empowerment, self-esteem and a sense of community through volunteering, tutoring peers, cleaning up the environment, and helping senior citizens.

Profiles of Selected Parenting Programs

AVANCE, Inc.
301 S. Frio, Suite 310
San Antonio, TX 78207
Phone: (210) 270-4630
Fax: (210) 270-4612

Main Purpose: To stabilize and strengthen parent-child relationships, stimulate success in school, and strengthen the parental role as an advocate for the child.

Target Group: At-risk parents with children under age 4, especially Hispanic parents.

Description: AVANCE consists of 27 lessons taught over a month-long period covering the role of parents in children's development: cognitive, physical, social, and emotional. The program includes an emphasis on language development and effective discipline. In one class, parents are taught to make toys that teach their pre-schoolers skills and concepts through play. A community resources class teaches parents how to access needed services. Services that support participation include home visits, transportation, and child care while parents attend classes. Classes are held for fathers in the evenings. Parents can take ESOL classes, GED, and college-level classes. The program is located in three Texas communities serving over 6,000 parents and children annually.

Effective Black Parenting Program (EBPP)
Center for the Improvement of Child Caring
11331 Ventura Boulevard, Suite 103
Studio City, CA 91604-3147
Phone: (818) 980-0903
Fax: (818) 753-1054
Web site: www.ciccparenting.org

Purpose: Foster family communication and combat juvenile delinquency, substance abuse, and other negative outcomes.

Target: African American parents of children ages 2 through 12.

Description: EBPP is a cognitive-behavioral program specifically created for African American parents that seeks to foster effective family communication, healthy identity, extended family values, child growth and development, and self-esteem. The program facilitates efforts to combat child abuse, substance abuse, juvenile delinquency, gang violence, learning disorders, behavior problems, and emotional disturbances.

EBPP is based on a prosocial achievement orientation to African American parenting that recognizes the special pressures in inner-city communities that make it difficult for parents to maintain this orientation.

Its basic ideas are derived from the writings of African American parenting scholars, from research with African American parents, and from adaptations of parenting skills that have been found helpful in raising children of all ethnic and socioeconomic backgrounds.

The program has two possible formats: a class with 15 3-hour training sessions that emphasize role playing and home behavior projects, and a 1-day seminar for large groups. Black educators and mental health professionals teach basic child management skills using culturally appropriate methods. Each of the parenting strategies and skills is taught by making reference to African proverbs such as "Children are the reward of life," and "A shepherd does not strike his sheep." Systematic use of these proverbs helps to ground the program in the wisdom of African ancestors, and is one of the many ways that the program promotes cultural pride. Interactive groups address topics including appropriate and inappropriate behavior, discipline, pride, coping with racism, African-origin family values, preventing drug abuse, and single parenting. Two companion programs for the general population of parents and for Latino parents are available.

Evaluation: EBPP was field tested on two cohorts of parents and their first- and second-grade children. Pre-post changes were compared in a quasi-experimental design with 109 treatment and 64 control families. Significant reduction of parental rejection was observed, along with improvements in the quality of family relationships and child behaviors. At 1-year follow-up, reductions in rejection and problem behaviors were maintained. Both the long and short versions have been well received in African American communities nationwide, and 1,500 instructors have been trained and are delivering the programs.

Families and Schools Together (FAST)
Wisconsin Center for Education Research
University of Wisconsin-Madison
3200 Monroe
Madison, WI 53711
Phone: (608) 663-3882
Fax: (608) 663-2382
Web site: www.wcer.wisc.edu/fast

Families and Schools Together (FAST) *(continued)*

Main Purpose: To prevent school failure, enhance family functioning, prevent familial substance abuse, and reduce stress.

Target Group: Parents of children who are at risk for substance abuse and other problems.

Description: FAST is a collaborative program that attempts to reduce causal factors related to the above-mentioned problems by starting with young children and using a family-based model. Children (ages 4 through 9) who display behavior problems (at school or at home), poor self-esteem, short attention span, and hyperactivity are targeted by teachers for this multifamily program. National replication of two new adaptations for early childhood and middle school children began in 1997. The multilevel prevention curriculum applies decades of research funded and published by the National Institute of Mental Health (NIMH) from psychology, psychiatry, family therapy, family stress, social support, and community organizing.

The core of the program involves eight weekly multifamily meetings usually held in schools, during which positive experiences in family interaction are facilitated by a collaborative leadership team. The team has at least four members: a parent partner, a school partner, a community-based mental health partner, and a community-based substance abuse prevention partner. Each session features the following key elements: a shared family meal, communication games played at a family table, time for couples, a self-help parent group, one-to-one quality play, and a fixed door prize that each family wins once. The program attempts to strengthen bonds within families, among families, and between family and community.

At the end of 8 weeks, families graduate from the program and participate in monthly follow-up meetings, FASTWORKS, for 2 years. The program develops a support network that empowers the parents to be the primary prevention agents for their own children. FAST collaborates with schools, parents, and not-for-profit human service agencies to strengthen the family's internal bonds as well as its bonds with the school and the community. The follow-up meetings are run by parent graduate volunteers, with backup support from the collaborative leadership team.

Evaluation: Evaluation results after 8 weeks show statistically significant improvements in the child's classroom and home behaviors and self-esteem, in family closeness, and in parent involvement in school. Social isolation is reduced. Follow-up data suggest that children continue to improve and some parents self-refer for counseling and substance abuse treatment, get jobs, go back to school, and attend community events. Long-term evaluation indicates that these gains are maintained and that the program facilitates the families' development of connections with the community. FAST is now active in 25 states; Washington, DC; and Canada.

Families Can Make A Difference: A Substance Abuse Prevention Program
Child Development and Family Studies
Purdue University
West Lafayette, IN 47907-1269
Phone: (765) 494-2937
Fax: (765) 494-0503

Main Purpose: To prevent substance abuse.

Target Group: Parents of pre-teens (8 through 12 years).

Description: Designed to help parents develop a better understanding of how they can help children avoid or stop substance abuse, the program is based on research indicating the effectiveness of strategies such as building effective communication, setting limits, and close family bonding. The main components of the program are a videotape, follow-up discussion, and related exercises. The detailed facilitator's guide contains three presentation formats: Two are intended for delivery to parent groups, and one is for community groups. The program was developed at Purdue University in 1992 by V. L. Spurlock and colleagues including Dena Targ.

Evaluation: Pre- and post-evaluation questionnaires are available from Dena Targ at the address above.

Focus on Families
Social Development Research Group
9725 Third Avenue NE, Suite 401
Seattle, WA 98115
Phone: (206) 685-1997
Fax: (206) 543-4507
Web site: http://staff.washington.edu/sdrg

Main Purpose: Reduce parents' risk for relapse, cope with relapse incidents, reduce drug use episodes. Increase family management skills. Reduce child risk factors and increase protective factors; decrease incidence of substance abuse among children.

Focus on Families *(continued)*

Target Group: Addicted parents of children ages 3 through 14.

Description: Most appropriate for parents enrolled in methadone treatment, and who have had at least 90 days of treatment prior to beginning the program. Families participate in a 5-hour family retreat to learn about the curriculum, identify goals, and participate in trust-building activities. This is followed by 32 sessions of 90 minutes each, held twice weekly for 16 weeks. Sessions are held in the mornings for parents, with practice sessions in the evening for parents and children together. Topics covered include family goal setting, relapse prevention, communication skills, management skills, family expectations about substance use, teaching skills to children, and helping kids succeed at school. Sessions and follow-up home care are provided by master's-level therapists.

Evaluation: Parent outcomes: The experimental group had higher scores than controls on all skill measures (for example, problem solving, self-efficacy, social support). The experimental group had fewer deviant peers than the control group. They reported a 65 percent reduction in heroin use frequency compared to controls and were six times less likely to use cocaine in the last month than the control group. Child outcomes showed no significant differences between experimental and control children in drug use or delinquency.

Los Niños Bien Educados
Center for the Improvement of Child Caring
11331 Ventura Boulevard, Suite 103
Studio City, CA 91604-0903
Phone: (818) 980-0903
Fax: (818) 753-1054
Web site: www.ciccparenting.org

Main Purpose: To enable parents to assist their children with the challenges of growing up in the U.S.

Target Group: Latino parents.

Description: Written by Drs. Lupita Montoya Tannatt and Kerby T. Alvy, the program is based on child-rearing research with Latino families and recommendations of nationally respected Latino educators and mental health specialists. Los Niños presents a wide range of basic child-rearing skills, along with "dichos" or Latino proverbs, used to make the learning and use of skills compatible with Latino cultural traditions. Parents learn how to praise effectively, to confront, to use family conversations, and to employ "time out" procedures. The program is widely used in schools, mental health and social service agencies, churches, and hospitals. It addresses school dropout prevention and drug and child abuse. The program is taught as a 12-session class for groups of parents, with the last session serving as a graduation celebration. In addition to basic program materials, an audiocasette presentation is available for instructors.

Evaluation: The initial field testing of the program in the 1980s was with newly immigrated Latino families, and it was found to be highly successful. Participating parents perceived their relationships with their kindergarten children as being either better or much better, whereas parents who did not attend the classes saw their relationships with their children as being the same or getting worse over a comparable time period. Children's behavior improvements were reported by parents and confirmed by teachers' reports. Los Niños Bien Educados is now being used nationwide with a variety of Latino Americans. It has become the centerpiece of parent involvement programs in numerous school districts, as well as serving as part of dropout prevention projects. The program is also being used by a variety of communities as part of their efforts to combat poor outcomes for youth.

MELD

123 North Third Street, Suite 507
Minneapolis, MN 55401
Phone: (612) 332-7563
Fax: (612) 344-1959
E-Mail: meldctrl@aol.com
Web site: http://www.meld.org

Main Purpose: To strengthen families by improving the quality of parenting in the U.S.

Target Group: Parents of newborns to 3-year-olds.

Description: The program uses peer support groups to help strengthen families by reducing the social isolation that can lead to child abuse and neglect. Various program activities are undertaken to increase parents' knowledge of child development; to increase parents' ability to solve problems, make decisions, and manage family life; and to nurture parents' personal growth.

Support peer groups meet weekly or twice a month for a period of 2 years. Groups are facilitated by community volunteers who are carefully

recruited, trained, and supervised by a local certified MELD professional. The curriculum encompasses health, child development, child
guidance, family management, home and community safety, balancing work and family, and accessing community resources.

The basic program has been adapted for adolescent mothers and
fathers, African American young mothers, Hispanic and Southeast
Asian parents, deaf and hard-of-hearing parents, first-time adult
parents, and parents of children with special needs. The curriculum
and activities can be used by low-literacy audiences and address the
concerns of low-income parents.

Evaluation: A MELD Young Moms program was studied at seven
sites and found to have resulted in a positive and significant shift in
attitudes and beliefs about parenting and nurturing children. Some
outcomes included more appropriate expectations in line with the
child's abilities; increased awareness of the child's needs and better
response to those needs; and reduced belief in the value of corporal
punishment.

The Parent Project

Northern Illinois Council on Alcoholism and Substance Abuse
(NICASA)
31979 N. Fish Lake Road
Round Lake, IL 60073
Phone: (847) 546-6450
Fax: (847) 546-6760

Main Purpose: Establish networks for working parents, improve
parent/child relationships; help balance work and family life; improve
corporate climate for workers; improve parents' skills in preventing
substance abuse and other problems that occur in teen years.

Target Group: Working parents of children ages birth through
18.

Description: The program is presented at worksites during lunch
hour. It addresses common issues such as balancing work and family, communication, discipline, learning styles, sibling relationships,
sex role conditioning, substance abuse, and other issues. It also focuses on specific developmental issues: child care, tantrums, sleeping and eating patterns, communicating with school personnel, peer
pressure, and establishing family policies regarding substance use.
School performance, male/female relationships, and increasing levels of responsibilities as children grow older are also addressed.

Evaluation: A longitudinal study of 191 parents, using a quasi-experimental design, showed that parents in a high-dosage group reported significant and lasting changes in their child's behavior, and rated children's behavior more positively. Their parenting practices changed positively and punitiveness declined. Parental stress and depression were reduced. Increases in substance abuse knowledge and negative attitudes toward drug use were noted.

Parenting Wisely (PW): An Interactive CD-ROM Program
Family Works, Inc.
Technology and Enterprise Building
20 East Circle Drive, Suite 190
Athens, OH 45701
Phone: (740) 593-9505
Fax: (740) 593-0186
E-Mail: familyworks@familyworksinc.com
Web site: www.familyworksinc.com

Main Purpose: Enhance family relationships and decrease conflict; enhance child adjustment and reduce problem behaviors including substance abuse.

Target Group: Parents, especially low-literacy parents of at-risk children, ages 6 through 18.

Description: Video programs that overcome illiteracy barriers are suitable for families who don't usually attend or finish parenting education classes. The interactive video format was chosen based on research showing its superiority to other forms including lecture, group discussion, and self-paced reading.

PW is based on social learning theory, family systems theory, and cognitive theory. The effective parenting skills selected for focus in this program were chosen because of their general acceptance among experts as critical both to the formation of well adjusted children and adolescents and to the amelioration of the problems common to today's children and adolescents.

The program covers communication and problem-solving skills, respect, discipline and reinforcement, chore and homework responsibilities, supervising kids whose peers are a bad influence, step family problems, single-parent issues, violence, and other problems experienced by today's families. It can be delivered in one to two sessions lasting about 3 hours.

Parents view videotaped scenes of nine common family problems. For each problem, parents choose a solution. Some solutions result in a worsening of the situation, while others improve the situation. After the solution is played out, it is critiqued. The critiques are the meat of the program, for they point out errors parents made in that scene and explain why these errors led to more problems. The critiques also explain why the effective parenting solution is best, and each parent has an option to have the computer read the material aloud.

The program was developed to be used by parents totally unfamiliar with computers, as well as by more experienced audiences.

Evaluation: The efficacy of the PW program is being thoroughly evaluated by feedback from parents, teens, courts, and social service agencies. User satisfaction is very high, as rated in five separate evaluation studies. Parents find the program easy to use, realistic and relevant to their concerns, helpful in dealing with children's problem behaviors, and helpful in building their confidence. Parents with preteens and teens (many of whom are delinquents) showing significant behavior problems were evaluated before and after (1 week, 1 month, 3 months, 6 months) using the program. They showed increased knowledge of parenting principles and skills, increased use of the specific skills taught in the program, and reductions in problem behaviors of their children. Reductions in child problem behaviors were clinically significant in half of the children, and the children scored in the normal range of behavior a month after parents used the program. Most parents reported at least moderate improvement in children's behavior. Using matched and randomly assigned control groups, evaluators found no improvement or a worsening of behavior among children of the higher-risk families. These treatment effects are very robust and comparable to interventions taking at least five times longer and requiring trained professionals to deliver.

Parent to Parent
3805 Presidential Parkway, Suite 207
Atlanta, GA 30340
Toll Free: (800) 229-2038
Phone: (770) 451-5484
Fax: (770) 458-4091
E-Mail: info@parenttoparentofga.org
Web site: www.parenttoparentofga.org

Purpose: Empower parents to counter influences of drug culture in the children's lives.

Target: Parents of children of all ages.

Description: Parent to Parent offers a unique approach in helping parents deal with the difficult issues of the 1990s. It is not a program that attempts to preach to parents about how to raise their children, nor does it attempt to impose its own standards or values upon parents. Instead, it is an interesting and dynamic video-based workshop designed to bring parents together for the purpose of helping their children through the challenging passage into adulthood. The content of Parent to Parent is contained in eight video sessions:

- The Me Within
- Put Yourself In The Way
- Awareness Is Your Best Friend
- Remember The Difference
- Expect and Inspect
- Never Cry Alone
- Take Time For Yourself
- When All Else Fails

Parent to Parent is designed to challenge the thinking of the participants. Each session of the program is conducted by a local facilitator who uses the video modules to convey information regarding issues such as alcohol and drug use, character development, communication skills, and more. The real power of Parent to Parent occurs when the facilitator has turned off the video module and leads the group in exercises and discussions. It is here that parents begin to internalize the information and develop a plan of action that fits the needs of their individual families. Groups engage in discussions regarding a wide range of topics including:

- Establishing and communicating a family belief system
- Developing a trustworthy child
- Understanding the difference between consequences and punishment
- Recognizing the signs of alcohol or drug use
- Setting realistic expectations

Evaluation: Communities conduct their own evaluations. Evaluations have been completed in Montgomery County, Maryland;

Syracuse, New York; Cobb County, Georgia; and Spartanburg, South Carolina, among others. Results in Spartanburg show that after training, parents were significantly more aware of the harmful effects of drugs on youngsters, made more use of good parenting skills, became more aware of the presence of drugs in their children's environment, and observed positive changes in children's attitudes.

Preparing for the Drug-Free Years (PDFY)

130 Nickerson Street, Suite 107
Seattle, WA 98109
Toll Free: (800) 736-2630
Fax: (206) 286-1462
Web site: www.drp.org

Main Purpose: Reducing risks of drug abuse and other behavioral problems.

Target Group: Parents of children in grades 4 through 9.

Description: PDFY is designed for use before children begin experimenting with drugs. Its focus is on family relations, family management practices, and family conflict resolution. Parents acquire the skills to reduce children's risk factors for drug abuse. They also learn the principles of social development strategy to strengthen family bonding.

PDFY features two volunteer workshop leaders, one of whom is a parent, who deliver the program in five 2-hour sessions or ten 1-hour sessions. Parents learn to increase children's opportunities for family involvement, teach needed skills, and provide reinforcement and consequences for behavior. Discussion topics include: the nature of the problem, reducing risks by strengthening family bonds, conduct of family meetings, fostering of communication, establishing a family position on drugs, reinforcing refusal skills, anger management, and creating a parent support network. PDFY is based on the research of Hawkins, Catalano, and colleagues on risk and protective factors for adolescent substance abuse.

Evaluation: An evaluation in rural Iowa, employing an experimental, longitudinal design, showed improvement in parenting behavior, general child management, and parent-child affective quality for parents in the intervention group. Some results are available from an experimental study with follow-up assessments, also in rural Iowa.

Strengthening Families Program (SFP)
University of Utah
250 South
1850 East, Room 215
Salt Lake City, UT 84112-0920
Phone: (801) 581-8498
Fax: (801) 581-5872
Web site: www.strengtheningfamilies.org

Main Purpose: To reduce risk factors for substance abuse and other problem behaviors.

Target Group: High-risk children of substance abusers; families with children ages 6 through 10.

Description: SFP builds on protective factors by improving family relationships, parenting skills, and improving the youth's social and life skills. Modifications of the original program have been made for various target groups. Originally developed for children of high-risk substance abusers, the program is also widely used for general audiences. SFP provides 14 weekly meetings of 2 to 3 hours in length. Three separate courses are offered: Parent Training, Children's Skills Training, and Family Life Skills Training. Parents learn how to gain the child's attention and reinforce positive behavior; they also acquire skill in communication, substance use education, problem solving, limit setting, and maintenance. Kids learn communication, understanding feelings, social skills, problem solving, resisting peer pressure, substance use issues, and rule compliance. Families jointly practice therapeutic child play and conduct weekly meetings to address issues and plan activities. Incentives to participation include transportation, child care, and family meals.

Evaluation: Numerous evaluations have been done. Results based on pre-post and 6-month follow-up show that the three-component design is powerful. SFP improved risk status in 1) children's problem behaviors, emotional status, and prosocial skills; 2) parents' parenting skills; and 3) family environment and functioning. Positive results were noted in family relationships and organization, increased family cohesion, and reduced conflict. Better sibling relationships, family-oriented activities, and clarity of rules were seen, and less social isolation of parents was found. Also, parents reported decreases in drug use, depression, and use of corporal punishment, and increased parental efficacy. Children were less impulsive, behaved more appropriately at home and school, and reported less intent to use drugs.

Strengthening Multi-Ethnic Families and Communities
1220 S. Sierra Bonita Avenue
Los Angeles, CA 90019-2552
Phone: (323) 936-0343
Fax: (323) 936-7130
E-Mail: dr_mls@earthlink.net

Main Purpose: To reduce drug/alcohol use, teen suicide, juvenile delinquency, gang involvement, child abuse, and domestic violence.

Target Group: Ethnic and culturally diverse parents of children ages 3 through 18.

Description: This program integrates various proven prevention/ intervention strategies that reduce violence against self, the family, and the community. Its short-term objectives are to increase the parents' sense of competence; the positive interactions and relationships among the family, the parents, and the children; the child's self-esteem, self-discipline, and social competency; and the involvement of parents in community activities. Parent training classes are held in churches, schools, community agencies, and other locations. The program includes 12 3-hour sessions taught in consecutive weeks. Five major components are cultural/spiritual values, rites of passage, positive discipline, enhancing relationships, and family/community violence and community involvement. Materials are available in English, Spanish, Vietnamese, and Korean. A Russian translation is in progress.

Evaluation: A pre-post evaluation design is available. Evaluation data from 22 parent groups show significant improvement in parents' sense of competence, family/parent/child interaction, and child competence and behavior. Program participation helped increase parent involvement in community and school activities. Other reports offer evidence that the program helps parents meet child-rearing challenges, promotes family and community bonding, promotes pride in cultural heritage, and reduces life-threatening risks for children.

Internet Resources on Parenting

Administration on Children, Youth and Families (ACYF)
Web site: www.acf.dhhs.gov/programs/acyf

Adolescence Directory On-Line
Web site: http://education.indiana.edu/cas

Children Youth and Families at Risk (CYFAR)
Web site: www.reeusda.gov/4h/cyfar

Early Childhood Educators' and Family Web Corner
Web site: http://users.sgi.net/~cokids/

National Child Care Information Center (NCCIC)
Web site: http://ericps.ed.uiuc.edu/nccic/abtnccic.html

National Clearinghouse on Alcohol and Drug Information (NCADI)
Web site: www.health.org

National Clearinghouse for Families and Youth (NCFY)
Web site: www.acf.dhhs.gov

National Criminal Justice Reference Service (NCJRS)
Web site: http://www.ncjrs.org/homepage.htm

National Network for Family Resiliency (NNFR)
Web site: www.hec.ohio-state.edu/famlife/family/fammain.htm

National Parent Information Network
Web site: http://npin.org

The National Parenting Center (TNPC)
Web site: http://www.tnpc.com

Parents Place
Web site: http://www.parentsplace.com

Partnership for a Drug-Free America
Web site: http://www.drugfreeamerica.org

Strengthening America's Families
Web site: www.ciccparenting.org

White House Office of National Drug Control Policy
Web site: http://www.projectknow.com

National Family Organizations for Substance Abuse Prevention

America Cares, Inc.
P.O. Box 60865
Washington, DC 20039
Phone: (301) 681-7861
Web site: http://www.americacares.org/main.htm

African American Parents for Drug Prevention
311 Martin Luther King Drive, Suite C-203
Cincinnati, OH 45219
Phone: (513) 475-5359
Fax: (513) 281-1645
Web site: http://www.emory.edu/NFIA/CONNECTIONS/AAPDP

Community Anti-Drug Coalitions of America (CADCA)
901 North Pitt St., Suite 300
Alexandria, VA 22314
Toll Free: (800) 54-CADCA
Phone: (703) 706-0560
Fax: (703) 706-0565
E-Mail: info@cadca.org
Web site: www.cadca.org

Mothers Against Drunk Driving
511 East John Carpenter Freeway, Suite 700
Irving, TX 75062
Toll Free: (800) GET-MADD
Phone: (214) 714-6233
Fax: (792) 869-2206
Web site: http://www.madd.org

National Asian Pacific American Families Against Substance Abuse, Inc.
340 East Second Street, Suige B-409
Los Angeles, CA 90012
Phone: (213) 625-5795
Fax: (213) 625-5796
Web site: http://www.napafasa.org

National Association for Native American Children of Alcoholics
1000 Union Street
Seattle, WA 98101
Toll Free: (800) 322-5601
Phone: (206) 903-6574
E-Mail: nanaco@nanco.org

National Families in Action
2957 Clairmont Road, N.E., Suite 150
Atlanta, GA 30329
Phone: (404) 248-9676
Fax: (404) 248-1312
Web site: http://www.nationalfamilies.org

National Family Partnership
2490 Coral Way, Suite 501
Miami, FL 33145-3444
Toll Free: (800) 856-4173
Phone: (305) 856-4173
Fax: (305) 856-4176
Web site: http://www.nfp.org

National Hispano/Latino Community Prevention Network
P.O. Box 2215
Espanola, NM 87532
Phone: (505) 747-1889
Fax: (505) 747-1623

Parents Resource Institute for Drug Education, Inc.
Web site: http://www.prideusa.org

Chapter 65

Mutual Self-Help Groups

Mutual self-help groups have a long history of helping people experiencing problems related to their own or others alcohol and other drug use. Often they are included as part of formal treatment programs, but participation in formal treatment services is not required. Many participate in mutual self-help groups to support lifelong recovery from alcohol and other drug problems. Groups are located in most communities, and are usually free of charge, relying on donations alone to offset expenses, such as meeting room space.

Mutual self-help groups are based on the premise that sharing with others who have similar problems can be emotionally healing for people with alcohol, tobacco, and other drug problems, including family members and friends. Also, people who have experienced similar problems can be among the best sources for referrals, advice, and moral support. The following are some of the major self-help groups, many of which are available in most communities:

Adult Children of Alcoholics (ACOA)
P.O. Box 3216
Torrance, CA 90510
Phone: (310) 534-1815
E-Mail: info@adultchildren.org
Website: http://www.adultchildren.org

Excerpted from *Prevention Primer: An Encyclopedia of Alcohol, Tobacco, and Other Drug Prevention Terms,* National Clearinghouse for Alcohol and Drug Information, 1993. Contact information updated and verified in April 2000.

Adult Children of Alcoholics (ACOA) *(continued)*

ACOA groups are for adults whose parents and/or grandparents had or currently have alcohol problems. For a printed meeting guide, send a legal size self-addressed stamped envelop. Information is also available through Al-Anon Family Groups (see below). Children of alcoholics may also be interested in the activities of the National Association for Children of Alcoholics (NACoA; see below).

Al-Anon Family Groups
1600 Corporate Landing Parkway
Virginia Beach, VA 23454-5617
(757) 563-1600
(800) 4AL-ANON
Web site: http://www.al-anon.org

Al-Anon Family Groups include Al-Anon for adult family members and friends of alcoholics, Al-Anon Adult Children Groups for adult children of alcoholics, and Alateen for youthful family members of alcoholics. Local groups are listed in most telephone directories.

Alcoholics Anonymous
P.O. Box 459, Grand Central Station
New York, NY 10163
(212) 870-3400
Web site: http://www.alcoholics-anonymous.org

Alcoholics Anonymous (AA) is for alcoholics who want to stop drinking and regain sobriety. AA has more than one million members in 114 countries. Through AA's 12 Steps of recovery and participation in a group, members uphold that:

1. they are willing to accept help,

2. self-examination is critical,

3. the admission of personal shortcomings to another individual is necessary, and

4. helping peers through this process helps their personal growth and recovery.

Local groups are listed in most telephone directories under "alcohol" or "alcoholism" in the yellow pages.

Families Anonymous

P.O. Box 3475
Culver City, California 90231
Toll Free: (800) 736-9805
Phone: (310) 815-8010
Fax: (310) 815-9682
Web site: http://familiesanonymous.org

Families Anonymous, Inc. (FA) is for families facing alcohol and other drug problems. FA is a group of concerned relatives and friends "who have faced up to the reality that the problems of someone close to us are seriously affecting our lives and our ability to function normally." Based on the 12 Steps of Alcoholics Anonymous, the organization was formed primarily for persons concerned about alcohol and other drug problems of a family member, especially children. Over the years, it has expanded to include concern about related behavioral problems, including hostility, truancy, and running away.

National Association for Children of Alcoholics

11426 Rockville Pike
Suite 100
Rockville, MD 20852
Toll Free: (888) 554-2627
Phone: (301) 468-0985
Web site: http://www.health.org/nacoa

National Association for Children of Alcoholics (NACoA) is a national nonprofit organization that is a resource for children of alcoholics of all ages.

Nar-Anon World Service Office

P.O. Box 2562
Palos Verdes Peninsula, CA 90274
Phone: (213) 547-5800
Web site: http://naranon.com

This group is a companion, but separate, program to Narcotics Anonymous. It is for family members of those with drug problems. They learn to view addiction as a disease, reduce family tension, and encourage the drug user to seek help.

Narcotics Anonymous

P.O. Box 9999
Van Nuys, CA 91409
Phone: (818) 773-9999
Fax: (818) 700-0700
Web site: http://www.na.org

Narcotics Anonymous (NA) is a mutual self-help program based on the 12 Steps of Alcoholics Anonymous. NA members are "men and women for whom drugs had become a major problem." It is a program of complete abstinence from all mind-altering drugs. If a local group is not listed in your telephone directory, the World Service Office can provide information.

Rational Recovery

P.O. Box 800
Lotus, CA 95651-0800
(530) 621-4374
E-Mail: icc@rational.org
Web site: http://www.rational.org

Rational Recovery is a mutual self-help group for alcohol and other drug problems that uses a mental health approach based on rational emotive therapy. Most people attend meetings for a year and, unlike AA, don't identify themselves as powerless over alcohol. Following the principles described in *The Small Book* by Jack Trimpey, members learn mental health tools to change their thinking. Nationwide, groups are now available in about 500 cities. Groups are also available in Canada, Australia, Japan, Panama, and the U.S. Virgin Islands.

Women for Sobriety, Inc.

P.O. Box 618
Quakertown, PA 18951
(215) 536-8026
Web site: http://www.womenforsobriety.org

Women for Sobriety, Inc. (WFS) is a national organization with local units that address the specific needs of women with alcohol-related problems. The program can be used in combination with other alcohol treatment programs or as an alternative to other mutual-help groups.

Chapter 66

Federal Agencies

The complex system that makes up the Federal Government includes many agencies that deal with primary, secondary, or tertiary prevention with varying levels of involvement.

This chapter includes addresses for these agency and a brief description of their involvement with alcohol, tobacco, and other drug problem prevention activities.

Administration for Children and Families
Department of Health and Human Services HHS
370 L 'Enfant Promenade SW
Washington, DC 20047
Phone: (202) 401-9215
Web site: http://www.acf.dhhs.gov

The Administration for Children and Families promotes services and programs to support the well-being of children and families.

Administration for Native Americans
200 Independence Avenue, SW
Room 344-F, Hubert Humphrey Building
Washington, DC 20201
(continued on next page)

Excerpted from *Prevention Primer: An Encyclopedia of Alcohol, Tobacco, and Other Drug Prevention Terms,* National Clearinghouse for Alcohol and Drug Information, 1993. Contact information updated and verified in April 2000.

Phone: (202) 690-7776
E-Mail: ana@acf.dhhs.gov
Web site: http://www.acf.dhhs.gov/programs/ana

The Administration for Native Americans (ANA) promotes the economic and social self-sufficiency of American Indians, Native Alaskans, and Native Hawaiians through the provision of grants, training, and technical assistance. Its efforts include prevention efforts targeting this population.

Bureau of Indian Affairs
Office of Public Affairs
MS-4542 MIB
1849 C Street, N.W.
Washington, DC 20240-0001
Phone: (202) 208-3711
Fax: (202) 501-1516
Web site: http://www.doi.gov/bureau-indian-affairs.html

The Bureau of Indian Affairs (BIA), under the Assistant Secretary for Indian Affairs, establishes the priorities, policies, planning, and evaluation requirements for prevention activities that target BIA employees, tribal governing bodies, and reservation/village constituents in 32 States. Acting through the Deputy to the Assistant Secretary for Indian Affairs, the Office serves as the senior advisor to the Assistant Secretary on aspects of prevention initiatives.

Centers for Disease Control and Prevention
1600 Clifton Road
Atlanta, GA 30333
Toll Free: (800) 311-3435
Phone: (404) 639-3534
Web site: http://www.cdc.gov

The Centers for Disease Control and Prevention (CDC) is the Federal agency charged with protecting the public health of the Nation. Through its Planned Approach to Community Health (PATCH) program, the CDC works with State and local health departments and community members to organize local intervention programs. The CDC provides materials and technical assistance and communities invest time and resources to make the programs work. PATCH programs have focused on such areas as smoking cessation and alcohol problems.

Center for Substance Abuse Prevention (CSAP)
Substance Abuse and Mental Health Services Administration
(SAMHSA)
5600 Fishers Lane
Rockwall II Building, Suite 900
Rockville, MD 20857
(301) 443-0365
Web site: http://www.samhsa.gov/csap

Established in 1986 to lead the Federal Government's efforts toward the prevention and intervention of alcohol, tobacco, and other drug problems, the Center for Substance Abuse Prevention (CSAP) administers two major prevention programs, the "Community Partnership" and "High-Risk Youth" grant programs, as well as other prevention programs and activities, including the National Clearinghouse for Alcohol and Drug Information.

Center for Substance Abuse Treatment (CSAT)
Substance Abuse and Mental Health Services Administration
(SAMHSA)
5600 Fishers Lane
Rockwall II Building, Tenth Floor
Rockville, MD 20857
(301) 443-5700
E-Mail: info@treatment.org
Web site: http://www.samhsa.gov/csat

The Center for Substance Abuse Treatment (CSAT) funds residential and non-residential treatment programs serving pregnant and postpartum women and their children, grants to States for additional alcohol and other drug services, counselor training programs, alcohol and other drug recovery services in State and local criminal justice systems, demonstration programs of national significance, as well as the State block grant program.

Coast Guard
Public Affairs Staff
2100 Second Street, SW
Washington, DC 20593
Phone: (202) 267-2229
Web site: http://www.uscg.mil
(continued on next page)

The United States Coast Guard (USCG) is a branch of the Armed Forces and an agency of the Department of Transportation. Stopping drug smuggling into the United States is a high priority, and the Coast Guard is expanding its educational programs in this area. It also develops and directs a national boating safety program, encouraging recreational boaters to avoid alcohol and other drugs.

Department of Defense
Health Affairs
1200 Defense Pentagon
Washington, DC 20301-1200
Phone: (703) 697-2111
Web site: http://www.defenselink.mil

Through the Department of Defense (DoD), prevention and education efforts are implemented worldwide through education, training, public service announcements on Armed Forces radio and television, posters, and pamphlets.

U.S. Department of Education
Drug Abuse Prevention Oversight Staff
Office of the Secretary
400 Maryland Avenue, SW
Washington, DC 20202-0120
Toll Free: (800) USA-LEARN
TTY: (800) 437-0833
Phone: (202) 401-3030
Fax: (202) 401-0689
E-Mail: CustomerService@inet.ed.gov
Web site: http://www.ed.gov/index.html

The Department of Education (DoEd) administers the largest block of Federal funds devoted to the prevention of alcohol and other drug problems. Its Division of Drug-Free Schools and Communities has two branches. The first, the State and Local Programs Branch, provides formula funding through State education agencies and governors' offices. It also oversees DoEd's five Regional Centers for Drug-Free Schools and Communities that supply technical assistance to schools and communities. The second branch of the Division of Drug-Free Schools and Communities is the Discretionary Programs Branch, which oversees grant competitions for State and local education agencies in five discretionary grant programs, including programs for school personnel training and school-based community programs in alcohol and other drug prevention education.

DoEd's Fund for the Improvement of Postsecondary Education (FIPSE) addresses the problem of alcohol and other drugs on campuses by providing funds for prevention initiatives.

DoEd has also developed a wide range of prevention materials that are available through the Center for Substance Abuse Prevention's National Clearinghouse for Alcohol and Drug Information.

Department of Housing and Urban Development
Drug Information and Strategy Clearinghouse
P.O. Box 8577
Silver Spring, MD 20907
Toll Free: (800) 955-2232
Web site: http://www.hud.gov

The Department of Housing and Urban Development (HUD) operates the HUD Drug Information and Strategy Clearinghouse that deals specifically with alcohol and other drug problems in public housing projects.

Department of Justice
Office of Justice Programs
810 Seventh Streeet
Washington, DC 20531
Phone: (202) 307-0703
Fax: (202) 514-5958
http://www.ojp.usdoj.gov

The Department of Justice (DoJ) forms partnerships with State and local governments to help policymakers, practitioners, and citizens understand what crime costs in terms of public safety and the social and economic health of communities. It awards formula grants to States and to specific crime prevention programs.

DoJ operates the National Criminal Justice Reference Service (NCJRS), which provides comprehensive information on criminal justice issues on the national and international level, and the Drugs & Crime Data Center & Clearinghouse (DCDCC), which specializes in the collection of data on drugs and crime.

Among the primary prevention programs sponsored by the DoJ is the National Citizens Crime Prevention Campaign, which is operated through the National Crime Prevention Council. Through this effort, numerous print and video materials on prevention have been developed.

Department of Labor
Washington, DC 20210
Substance Abuse Information Database
Phone: (202) 219-6197
Web site: http://www.notes.dol.gov/SAID.nsf

Through the Substance Abuse Information Database (SAID), the U.S. Department of Labor provides employers, and those organizations that work with employers, with information that will assist them in developing workplace substance abuse programs. It describes prevention materials and where they can be obtained. It provides information related to Federal and State legislation, as well as information on studies and surveys on how drugs and alcohol affect the workplace.

Department of Veterans Affairs
810 Vermont Avenue, NW
Washington, DC 20420
Toll Free: (800) 827-1000
Web site: http://www.va.gov

Formerly the Veterans Administration, the Department of Veterans Affairs (VA) became a Cabinet-level department in March 1984. The primary mission of the VA with regard to alcohol and other drug problems is to provide treatment services to eligible veterans with dependence disorders. Because of the VA's treatment focus, prevention activities concentrate on secondary and tertiary prevention. Most treatment programs, through academic affiliations and community outreach activities, are also involved in primary prevention.

Drug Enforcement Administration
Washington, DC 20537
Phone: (202) 307-7936
Web site: http://www.usdoj.gov/dea

The Drug Enforcement Administration (DEA) is responsible for the enforcement of Federal drug laws and regulations. It has conducted prevention programs in conjunction with numerous national organizations, including the National High School Athletic Coaches Association, the Ladies Professional Golf Association, the National Youth Sports Coaches Association, and the Boy Scouts of America. DEA also develops and distributes a variety of publications and videos on prevention.

Federal Bureau of Investigation
Community Outreach Program
935 Pennsylvania Avenue, NW
Suite 4944
Washington, DC 20535
Phone: (202) 324-2080
Web site: http://www.fbi.gov

The Federal Bureau of Investigation (FBI) is the lead Federal investigative agency within the Department of Justice. Among other prevention activities, the FBI disseminates drug demand reduction materials to appropriate organizations, makes public presentations on drug awareness, and works closely with demand reduction specialists of other organizations. The FBI headquarters and field offices work with citizens from across the country who are actively involved in drug prevention and education efforts.

Indian Health Service
Alcoholism and Substance Abuse Program Branch
Room 6A-53
5600 Fishers Lane
Rockville, MD 20857
Phone: (301) 443-4297
E-Mail: Feedback@ihs.gov
Web site: http://www.ihs.gov/medicalprograms/alcohol

The Alcoholism and Substance Abuse Program Branch of the Indian Health Service (IHS) has initiated a number of programs that provide prevention services to members of American Indian and Native Alaskan communities.

National Highway Traffic Safety Administration
Traffic Safety Programs (NTS-21)
400 Seventh Street, SW
Washington, DC 20590
Toll Free: (888) 327-4236
Web site: http://www.nhtsa.dot.gov

A major focus of the National Highway Traffic Safety Administration (NHTSA) is the prevention of impaired driving. NHTSA provides resources to State and community law enforcement agencies, as well as impaired driving programs, and has developed a range of prevention publications.

549

National Institute on Alcohol Abuse and Alcoholism

National Institutes of Health
6000 Executive Boulevard
Willco Building
Bethesda, Maryland 20892
Phone: (301) 443-3885
Web site: http://www.niaaa.nih.gov

The National Institute on Alcohol Abuse and Alcoholism (NIAAA) is a research organization that focuses on alcohol-related problems. In addition to providing leadership to the research community, NIAAA supports scientific information dissemination and public education activities to inform the public of the risks and consequences associated with alcohol abuse and alcohol dependence.

National Institute on Drug Abuse

National Institutes of Health
6001 Executive Blvd.
Bethesda, MD 20892
Phone: (301) 662-1124
Web site: http://www.nida.nih.gov

The National Institute on Drug Abuse (NIDA) is the lead Federal agency for drug abuse research. NIDA disseminates its research findings to the public through various means—such as the press, community education programs, NIDA's Drug Abuse Hotline, and publications distributed by CSAP's National Clearinghouse for Alcohol and Drug Information.

Office of Juvenile Justice and Delinquency Prevention

810 Seventh Street
Washington, DC 20531
Phone: (202) 307-5911
Fax: (202) 307-2093
Juvenile Justice Clearinghouse: (800) 638-8736
Web site: http://ojjdp.ncjrs.org

Part of the Department of Justice, the Office of Juvenile Justice and Delinquency Prevention (OJJDP) provides national leadership and resources to help States and local jurisdictions improve their juvenile justice systems. Program priorities are prevention and control of illegal drug use by juveniles, prevention and control of serious juvenile crime, and missing and exploited children.

Office of National Drug Control Policy
Executive Office of the President
Washington, DC 20503
Phone: (202) 395-6700
Web site: http://www.whitehousedrugpolicy.gov

The Office of National Drug Control Policy (ONDCP) is headed by the Director of National Drug Control Policy, a Presidential appointee, commonly referred to as the "drug czar." ONDCP is charged with explaining the nature of the illicit drug problem in America and presenting a policy that includes roles for the Federal, State, and local governments, and the private sector. It also produces documents addressing national alcohol- and drug-related priorities in areas such as criminal justice, drug treatment, education, community action, the workplace, international, interdiction, and research. Copies of these publications are available from CSAP's National Clearinghouse for Alcohol and Drug Information.

Office of Personnel Management
1900 E Street, NW
Washington, DC 20415
Phone: (202) 606-1800
Web site: http://www.opm.gov

The Office of Personnel Management (OPM) is an independent agency in the executive branch that oversees and regulates matters pertaining to civil service personnel management. OPM's primary function related to alcohol and other drug problem prevention focuses on workplace employee assistance programs. OPM provides regulatory and policy guidance in the Code of Federal Regulations; the Federal Personnel Manual; and through publications, conferences, and seminars regarding EAPs for Federal civilian employees. Additionally, OPM is required to report annually to Congress on programs to prevent problems for Federal civilian employees.

Substance Abuse and Mental Health Services Administration
5600 Fishers Lane
Rockville, MD 20857
Phone: (301) 443-4980
E-Mail: info@samhsa.gov
Web site: http://www.samhsa.gov

The Substance Abuse and Mental Health Services Administration (SAMHSA) administers alcohol and other drug and mental health service-related programs. SAMHSA's focus is on prevention, intervention, and treatment services and its primary role is to coordinate the delivery of these services to health professionals and the general public. SAMHSA is made up of three agencies: the Center for Substance Abuse Prevention (CSAP), the Center for Substance Abuse Treatment (CSAT), and the Center for Mental Health Services (CMHS).

Chapter 67

Federal Drug Data Sources

In an effort to allocate resources and formulate drug policy, a variety of information sources are utilized to quantify America's drug problem. The information in this chapter identifies 25 Federal sources of drug data, while highlighting the frequency of data sets, the sponsoring agencies, target populations and areas of coverage. The sources are either produced or sponsored by 16 different agencies within the Federal Government. This information will provide an understanding of the research and statistical information available to guide the laws, regulations, and practices that are critical to public policy.

Prevalence of Use

National Household Survey on Drug Abuse (NHSDA)

Sponsoring Agency: Substance Abuse and Mental Health Services Administration

Information Available: Presents prevalence for drug and alcohol by age, sex, and region

Population: Household population age 12 and older

Geographic area: National

Frequency/Year started: Annually; started 1976

"Federal Drug Data Sources," from http://whitehousedrugpolicy.gov/drugfact/sources.html; last updated May 1999.

Monitoring the Future (MTF)

Sponsoring Agency: National Institute on Drug Abuse

Information Available: Reports estimates of drug, alcohol, and tobacco use, and attitudes toward drugs of abuse among American youths

Population: 6th, 8th, 10th, and 12th graders, and young adults age 19

Geographic area: National

Frequency/Year started: Annually; started 1972

Worldwide Survey of Substance Abuse and Health Behaviors among Military Personnel

Sponsoring Agency: U.S. Department of Defense

Information Available: Measures substance use and health behaviors among military personnel

Population: Active-duty military personnel in the Army, Navy, Marines, and Air Force

Geographic area: U.S. military bases world-wide

Frequency/Year started: Every two to four years; started 1980

Hispanic Health and Nutrition Examination Survey III (HHANES)

Sponsoring Agency: National Center for Health Statistics

Information Available: Assesses health status and drug and alcohol use of Hispanic Americans

Population: Hispanic household members age 12 to 74

Geographic area: National

Frequency/Year started: 1988 to 1994; last survey was in 1994; started 1988

National Longitudinal Survey of Youth

Sponsoring Agency: U.S. Department of Labor

Information Available: Tracks employment, vocational achievement, family composition, and alcohol and drug use

Population: Individuals age 14 to 22

Geographic area: National

Frequency/Year started: Annually; started 1979

National Youth Survey

Sponsoring Agency: National Institute of Mental Health and the National Institute on Drug Abuse

Information Available: Assesses family, peer, and other influences on delinquent behaviors and substance abuse

Population: Youths and one parent

Geographic area: National

Frequency/Year started: Annually; started 1976

Community Epidemiology Work Group (CEWG)

Sponsoring Agency: National Institute on Drug Abuse

Information Available: Provides early warning and epidemiology of drug use patterns, trends, and consequences, including risk factors and stages of use

Population: Data gathered from public health agencies, medical and treatment facilities, criminal justice and correctional offices, law enforcement agencies, and other sources unique to local areas

Geographic area: Local; multi-jurisdictional

Frequency/Year started: Semi-annual; started 1976

Arrestee Drug Abuse Monitoring Program (ADAM) (Formerly Drug Use Forecasting (DUF)

Sponsoring Agency: National Institute of Justice

Information Available: Monitors the extent of drug use among arrestees by demographic characteristics, charge at arrest, treatment history, and socioeconomic characteristics

Population: Adult arrestees and juvenile detainees

Geographic area: Local, multi-jurisdictional

Frequency/Year started: Annually; started 1997 (DUF 1986 to 1996)

Consequences of Drug Use

The Economic Costs of Alcohol and Drug Abuse in the United States

Sponsoring Agency: National Institute on Drug Abuse and the National Institute on Alcohol Abuse and Alcoholism

Information Available: Estimates costs for health care, lost productivity, and criminal justice costs due to drug and alcohol abuse

Population: Not applicable

Geographic area: National

Frequency/Year started: Initial study; started 1992

National Maternal and Infant Health Survey

Sponsoring Agency: Centers for Disease Control and Prevention and National Center for Health Statistics

Information Available: Monitors maternal nutrition and substance abuse as well as infant health

Population: Mothers and their infants

Geographic area: National

Frequency/Year started: 1988 and 1991; started 1988; follow up survey 1991

Youth Risk Behavior Surveillance System

Sponsoring Agency: Centers for Disease Control and Prevention

Information Available: Monitors priority health-risk behaviors which contribute to the leading causes of mortality and morbidity among youths and adults

Population: School aged youth grades 9 through 12

Geographic area: National

Frequency/Year started: Every two years; started 1990

Drug Abuse Warning Network (DAWN)

Sponsoring Agency: Substance Abuse and Mental Health Services Administration

Information Available: Monitors drug abuse patterns and trends and assesses the health hazards associated with drug abuse by involvement of drugs in deaths and emergency department episodes

Population: Drug related deaths and emergency department episodes

Geographic area: Multi-jurisdictional

Frequency/Year started: Annually; started 1972

Substance Abuse Treatment and Prevention

National Drug and Alcoholism Treatment Unit Survey (NDATUS)

Sponsoring Agency: National Institute on Drug Abuse and the National Institute on Alcohol Abuse and Alcoholism

Information Available: Identifies and describes drug abuse and alcoholism treatment facilities, characteristics of programs, and funding

Population: Alcohol and/or drug treatment programs and facilities

Geographic area: National

Frequency/Year started: Annually from 1980 to 1993; started 1980; last survey was in 1993

Census of State and Federal Correctional Facilities

Sponsoring Agency: Bureau of Justice Statistics

Information Available: Describes state-operated confinement and community-based facilities including the number of inmates or residents in counseling for drug dependency

Population: State correctional facility inmates

Geographic area: National

Frequency/Year started: Every five to seven years; started 1974

Services Research Outcomes Study (SROS)

Sponsoring Agency: Substance Abuse and Mental Health Services Administration and the Department of Health and Human Services

Information Available: Presents treatment outcomes of persons completing substance abuse treatment programs

Population: Drug abusers discharged from drug abuse treatment facilities

Geographic area: National

Frequency/Year started: One time study; started 1995

Source and Volume of Illegal Drugs

International Narcotics Control Strategy Report (INCSR)

Sponsoring Agency: U.S. Department of State

Information Available: Provides production estimates for a variety of illicit drugs by source country

Population: Not applicable

Geographic area: International

Frequency/Year started: Annually; information available for 1997 and 1998

National Narcotics Intelligence Consumers Committee (NNICC)

Sponsoring Agency: Drug Enforcement Administration and multiple federal agencies

Information Available: Collects, analyzes, and disseminates strategic national/international intelligence on the availability of drugs

Population: Not applicable

Geographic area: International

Frequency/Year started: Annually; started 1978

Pulse Check

Sponsoring Agency: Office of National Drug Control Policy

Information Available: Describes current trends in illicit drug use and drug markets based on nationwide interviews conducted with ethnographers and epidemiologists, law enforcement officials, and drug treatment providers

Population: Ethnographers, epidemiologists, law enforcement officials, and drug treatment providers

Geographic area: Multi-jurisdictional

Frequency/Year started: Quarterly until 1996; currently bi-annually; started 1992

Law Enforcement

Uniform Crime Reports: Crime in the United States (UCR)

Sponsoring Agency: Federal Bureau of Investigation

Information Available: Presents data on the number of offenses, including drug related offenses known to the police, arrests, and clearances

Population: 98% of the total population

Geographic area: Local, state, national

Frequency/Year started: Monthly; started 1930

System to Retrieve Information from Drug Evidence (STRIDE)

Sponsoring Agency: Drug Enforcement Administration

Information Available: Analyzes drugs bought or seized by DEA and several states and local agencies

Population: Substances seized or bought by DEA

Geographic area: National

Frequency/Year started: Ongoing; started 1971

Law Enforcement Management and Administrative Statistics (LEMAS)

Sponsoring Agency: Bureau of Justice Statistics

Information Available: Provides national data on the management and administration of law enforcement agencies including the existence of laboratory testing facilities, drug enforcement units, and drug education units

Population: Law enforcement agencies

Geographic area: National

Frequency/Year started: Periodically; started 1987

Processing Drug Offenders

National Corrections Reporting Program (NCRP)

Sponsoring Agency: Bureau of Justice Statistics

Information Available: Tracks prisoners entering and leaving custody or supervision whose most serious offense was drug trafficking or possession

Population: Prison and parole admissions and releases

Geographic area: Multi-jurisdictional, Federal and State

Frequency/Year started: Annually; started 1983

Juvenile Court Statistics

Sponsoring Agency: Office of Juvenile Justice and Delinquency Prevention

Information Available: Describes the cases and juveniles processed for drug related delinquency by the juvenile courts in the United States

Population: Cases disposed of by juvenile courts

Geographic area: National

Frequency/Year started: Annually; started 1929

Institutionalized Offenders and Drugs

Survey of Inmates in Local Jails

Sponsoring Agency: Bureau of Justice Statistics

Information Available: Describes the characteristics of inmates in local jails by drug and alcohol use, criminal history, current offense, health care, and socioeconomic status

Population: Jail inmates

Geographic area: National

Frequency/Year started: Every five to six years; started 1972

Survey of Inmates in State Correctional Facilities

Sponsoring Agency: Bureau of Justice Statistics

Information Available: Describes the characteristics of inmates in state correctional facilities by drug and alcohol use, criminal history, current offense, health care, and socioeconomic status

Population: State prison inmates

Geographic area: National

Frequency/Year started: Every five to seven years; started 1974

Juveniles Taken into Custody

Sponsoring Agency: Office of Juvenile Justice and Delinquency
Prevention

Information Available: Monitors juvenile custody facilities and
residents with drug related offenses

Population: Private and public juvenile custody facilities

Geographic area: National

Frequency/Year started: Annually; started 1988

Chapter 68

Drug Enforcement Administration Division Offices

National Office

U. S. Drug Enforcement Administration (DEA)
Information Services Section
700 Army Navy Drive
Arlington, VA 22202
DEA Website: http://www.usdoj.gov/dea

DEA Division Offices

Aviation Operations Center
2300 Horizon Road
Ft. Worth, TX 76177-5300
Phone: (817) 837-2000
Fax: (817) 837-2252

DEA Atlanta Division
75 Spring Street, S.W.
Room 740
Atlanta, GA 30303
Phone: (404) 331-4401
Fax: (404) 331-0166

Excerpted from *Drugs of Abuse*, U.S. Department of Justice, Drug Enforcement Administration (DEA); contact information updated and verified in April 2000.

DEA New England Division
15 New Sudbury
Room E400
Boston, MA 022203
Phone: (617) 557-2100
Fax: (617) 557-2135

DEA Caribbean Division
2432 Loiza Street
Santurce, PR 00913
Phone: (809) 253-4200

DEA Chicago Division
230 S. Dearborn Street
Suite 1200
Chicago, IL 60604
Phone: (312) 353-7875

DEA Dallas Division
1880 Regal Row
Dallas, TX 75235
Phone: (214) 640-0801
Fax: (214) 640-0889

DEA Detroit Division
431 Howard Street
Detroit, MI 48226
Phone: (313) 234-4000
Fax: (313) 234-4141

EPIC (El Paso Intelligence Center)
11339 SSG Sims Street
El Paso, TX 79908-8098
Phone: (915) 760-2000

DEA Houston Division
1433 West Loop South
Suite 600
Houston, TX 77027
Phone: (713) 693-3000
Fax: (713) 693-3067

DEA Los Angeles Division
255 East Temple Street, 20th Floor
Los Angeles, CA 90012
Phone: (213) 894-2650
Fax: (213) 894-4244

DEA Miami Division
8400 N.W. 53rd Street
Miami, FL 33166
Phone: (305) 590-4870
Fax: (305) 590-4500

DEA New Orleans Division
3 Lakeway Center, Suite 1800
3838 N. Causeway Blvd, Suite 1800
Metairie, LA 70002
Phone: (504) 840-1100
Fax: (504) 840-1322

DEA New York Division
99 Tenth Avenue
New York, NY 10011
Phone: (212) 337-3900
Fax: (212) 337-2799

DEA Newark Division
970 Broad Street, Room 806
Newark, NJ 07102
Phone: (973) 273-5000

DEA Philadelphia Division
600 Arch Street, Room 10224
Philadelphia, PA 19106
Phone: (215) 861-3474
Fax: (215) 861-3281

DEA Phoenix Division
3010 North 2nd Street, Suite 301
Phoenix, AZ 85012
Phone: (602) 664-5600
Fax: (602) 664-5611

DEA Denver Field Division
115 Inverness Drive East
Englewood, CO 80112-5116
Phone: (303) 705-7300

DEA San Diego Division
4560 View Ridge Avenue
San Diego, CA 92123
Phone: (858) 616-4100
Fax: (858) 616-4084

DEA San Francisco Division
450 Golden Gate Ave.
San Francisco, CA 94102
(415) 436-7900

DEA Seattle Division
400 2nd Avenue West
Seattle, WA 98119
Phone: (206) 553-5443
Fax: (206) 553-1576

DEA St. Louis Division
7911 Forsythe Boulevard
Suite 500
St. Louis, MO 63105
Phone: (314) 5384600
Fax: (314) 538-4798

DEA Washington, D. C. Division
801 I St. N.W.
Washington, DC 20001
Phone: (202) 305-8500
Fax: (202) 616-5797

Chapter 69

State Resources

Alabama

Department of Mental Health/Retardation
Substance Abuse Division
P.O. Box 301410
Montgomery, AL 36130-1410
Phone: (334) 242-3961
Fax: (334) 242-3759
Web site: http://www.mh.state.al.us

Alaska

Department of Health and Social Services
Division of Alcoholism and Drug Abuse
P.O. Box 110607
Juneau, AK 99811-0607
Toll Free: (800) 478-2072 (in-state)
Phone: (907) 465-2071
Fax: (907) 465-2185
Web site: http://health.hss.state.ak.us

Excerpted from *Enforcing the Underage Drinking Laws Program: A Compendium of Resources*, U.S. Department of Justice, Office of Juvenile Justice and Delinquency Prevention, May 1999.

Arizona

Department of Health Services
Bureau of Substance Abuse and Mental Health
2122 East Highland Street
Phoenix, AZ 85016
Phone: (602) 381-8999
Fax: (602) 553-9142
E-mail: alelatr@hs.state.az.us
Web site: http://www.hs.state.az.us

Arkansas

Department of Health
Bureau of Alcohol and Drug Abuse Prevention
Freeway Medical Center
5800 West 10th Street
Suite 907
Little Rock, AR 72204
Phone: (501) 280-4511
Fax: (501) 280-4532
Web site: http://health.state.ar.us

California

Department of Drug and Alcohol Abuse
1700 K Street
Sacramento, CA 95814
Phone: (916) 445-1943
Fax: (916) 323-5873
E-mail: sjantz@adp.cahwnet.gov
Web site: http://www.adp.cahwnet.gov

Colorado

Department of Human Services
Alcohol and Drug Abuse Division
4055 S. Lowell Blvd.
Denver, CO 80236
Phone: (303) 866-7480
Fax: (303) 866-7481
Web site: http://www.cdhs.state.co.us

Connecticut

Division of Community Based Regulations
P.O. Box 340308
410 Capitol Avenue
Hartford, CT 06134-0308
Phone: (860) 509-8045
Fax: (860) 509-7541
Web site: http://www.state.ct.us

Delaware

Division of Alcoholism, Drug Abuse, and Mental Health
Department of Health and Social Services
1901 North DuPont Highway
New Castle, DE 19720
Phone: (302) 577-4461
Fax: (302) 577-4486
Web site: http://www.state.de.us/dhss

District of Columbia

Department of Human Services
Addiction Prevention and Recovery Administration
1300 First Street NE, Third Floor
Washington, DC 20002
Phone: (202) 727-9393
Fax: (202) 727-0092
Web site: http://www.dchealth.com/apra

Florida

Department of Children and Families
Alcohol, Drug Abuse and Mental Health Program Office
1317 Winewood Boulevard
Building 6, Third Floor
Tallahassee, FL 32399-0700
Phone: (850) 487-2920
Fax: (850) 487-2239
Web site: http://www.state.fl.us/cf_web/adm

Georgia

Substance Abuse Services
Division of Mental Health, Mental Retardation and Substance Abuse
2 Peachtree Street NW, 22nd Floor
Atlanta, GA 30303
Phone: (404) 657-2252
Fax: (404) 657-2160
E-mail: blhoopes@dhr.state.ga.us
Web site: http://www2.state.ga.us/Departments/DHR/mhmrsa.html

Hawaii

Department of Health
Alcohol and Drug Abuse Division
601 Kamokila Blvd.
Kapolei, HI 96707
Phone: (808) 692-7506
Web site: http://www.hawaii.gov/doh

Idaho

Department of Health and Welfare
Division of Family and Community Services
P.O. Box 83720
Boise, ID 83720-0036
Phone: (208) 334-5700
Fax: (208) 334-6699
Web site: http://www2.state.id.us/dhw

Illinois

Office of Alcoholism and Sugstance Abuse
Department of Human Services
100 North Ninth Street
Springfield, IL 62701
Phone: (217) 785-7769
Fax: (217) 785-0954
Web site: http://www.state.il.us/agency/dhs

Indiana

Bureau of Chemical Addictions
Division of Mental Health
Family and Social Services Administration
402 West Washington Street, Room W353
Indianapolis, IN 46204-2739
Phone: (317) 232-7800
Fax: (317) 233-3472
Web site: http://www.state.in.us

Iowa

Division of Substance Abuse and Health Promotion
Lucas State Office Building, Fourth Floor
321 East 12th Street
Des Moines, IA 50319
Phone: (515) 281-4417
Fax: (515) 281-4535
Web site: http://idph.state.ia.us/sa.htm

Kansas

Department of Social and Rehabilitative Services
Alcohol and Drug Abuse Services
Biddle Building
300 Southwest Oakley
Topeka, KS 66606
Phone: (913) 296-3925
Fax: (913) 296-0494
Web site: http://www.state.ks.us/public/srs/

Kentucky

Department of Mental Health/Mental Retardation Services
Division of Substance Abuse
100 Fair Oaks Lane, Fourth Floor
Frankfort, KY 40621
Phone: (502) 564-3487
Fax: (502) 564-6533
Web site: http://dmhmrs.chr.state.ky.us

Louisiana

Department of Health and Hospitals
Office for Addictive Disorders
P.O. Box 2790-BIN #18
Baton Rouge, LA 70821
Phone: (225) 342-6717
Fax: (225) 342-3875
Web site: http://www.dhh.state.la.us

Maine

Office of Substance Abuse
AMHI Complex
Marquardt Building
#159 State House Station
Augusta, ME 04333-0159
Phone: (207) 287-2595
TTY: (207) 287-4475
Fax: (207) 287-4334
Web site: http://www.state.me.us/dmhmrsa/osa

Maryland

Alcohol and Drug Abuse Administration
201 West Preston Street, Fourth Floor
Baltimore, MD 21201-2399
Phone: (410) 767-6910
Fax: (410) 333-7206
TTY: (410) 767-6921
Toll Free: (877) 4MD-DHMH [877-463-3464]
Web site: http://www.maryland_adaa.org

Massachusetts

Department of Public Health
Bureau of Substance Abuse Services
250 Washington Street
Boston, MA 02108
Phone: (617) 624-5111
TTY: (617) 536-5872
Fax: (617) 624-5185
Web site: http://www.state.ma.us/dph

Michigan

Department of Community Health
Center for Substance Abuse Services
3423 North Martin Luther King Boulevard
P.O. Box 30195
Lansing, MI 48909
Phone: (517) 335-8810
Fax: (517) 335-8837
Web site: http://www.mdmh.state.mi.us

Minnesota

Department of Human Services
Chemical Dependency Program Division
444 Lafayette Road
St. Paul, MN 55155-3823
Phone: (651) 296-3933
Fax: (612) 297-1862
Web site: http://www.dhs.state.mn.us

Mississippi

Department of Mental Health
Division of Alcohol and Drug Abuse
1101 Robert E. Lee Building
Jackson, MS 39201
Phone: (601) 359-1288
Fax: (601) 359-6295
Web site: http://www.dmh.state.ms.us

Missouri

Department of Mental Health
Division of Alcohol and Drug Abuse
1706 East Elm Street
P.O. Box 687
Jefferson City, MO 65102
Phone: (573) 751-4942
Fax: (573) 751-7814
E-mail: mailto:dmhmail@maildmh.state.mo.us
Web site: http://www.modmh.state.mo.us

Montana

Addictive and Mental Disorders Division
P.O. Box 202951
1400 Broadway
Helena, MT 59620-2951
Phone: (406) 444-3964
Fax: (406) 444-4435
E-mail: rmena@mt.gov
Web site: http://www.dphhs.mt.us

Nebraska

Mental Health, Substance Abuse and Addiction Services
P.O. Box 94728
Lincoln, NE 68509-4728
Phone: (402) 479-5578
Fax: (402) 479-5162
E-mail: hhsinfo@hhs.state.ne.us
Web site: http://www.hhs.state.ne.us/sua/suaindex.htm

Nevada

Bureau of Alcohol and Drug Abuse
505 East King Street, Room 500
Carson City, NV 89713
Phone: (775) 684-4190
Fax: (775) 684-4185
Web site: http://www.state.nv.us/hr

New Hampshire

Department of Health and Human Services
Office of Alcohol and Drug Abuse Prevention
State Office Park South
105 Pleasant Street
Concord, NH 03301
Phone: (603) 271-6104
Fax: (603) 271-6116
Web site: http://www.dhhs.state.nh.us

New Jersey

Department of Health
Division of Addiction Services
120 South Stockton Street
Trenton, NJ 08625-0362
Phone: (609) 292-5760
Fax: (609) 292-3816
Web site: http://www.state.nj.us/health/as/admin.htm

New Mexico

Department of Health
Division of Substance Abuse
1190 St. Francis Drive
P.O. Box 26110
Santa Fe, NM 87502-6110
Phone: (505) 827-2601
Fax: (505) 827-0097
Web site: http://www.health.state.nm.us

New York

Office of Alcoholism and Substance Abuse Services
1450 Western Avenue
Albany, NY 12203-8200
Phone: (518) 473-3460
Web site: http://www.oasas.state.ny.us

North Carolina

Department of Human Resources
Division of Mental Health, Developmental Disabilities, and Substance
Abuse Services
3001 Mail Service Center
Raleigh, NC 27699-3001
Phone: (919) 733-7011
Web site: http://www.dhhs.state.nc.us

North Dakota

Department of Human Services
Division of Mental Health, Alcohol and Drug Abuse
600 South Second Street
Suite 1E
Bismarck, ND 58504-5729
Phone: (701) 328-8920
Fax: (701) 328-8969
E-mail: soerhk@state.nd.us
Web site: http://lnotes.state.nd.us/dhs/dhsweb.nsf

Ohio

Department of Alcohol and Drug Addiction Services
280 North High Street
12th Floor
Columbus, OH 43215-2537
Phone: (614) 466-3445
Fax: (614) 752-8645
Web site: http://www.state.oh.us/ada/odada.htm

Oklahoma

Department of Mental Health and Substance Abuse Services
P.O. Box 53277
Oklahoma City, OK 73152-3277
Phone: (405) 522-3908
Fax: (405) 522-3650
Web site: http://www.odmhsas.org

Oregon

Office of Alcohol and Drug Abuse Programs
500 Summer Street NE
Third Floor
Salem, OR 97310-1016
Phone: (503) 945-5763
TTY: (503) 945-5893
Fax: (503) 378-8467
E-mail: oadap.info@state.or.us
Web site: http://www.oadap.hr.state.or.us

Pennsylvania

Office of Drug and Alcohol Programs
P.O. Box 90
Health and Welfare Building
Harrisburg, PA 17108
Phone: (717) 783-8200
Fax: (717) 787-6285
Web site: http://www.health.state.pa.us

Rhode Island

Rhode Island Department of Health
Canon Building
31Capitol Hill, Room 401
Providence, RI 02908-5097
Phone: (401) 222-2231
TTY: (800) 745-5555
Fax: (401) 222-6548
Web site: http://www.health.ri.org

South Carolina

Department of Alcohol and Other Drug Abuse Services
3700 Forest Drive
Suite 300
Columbia, SC 29204
Phone: (803) 734-9553
Fax: (803) 734-9663
Web site: http://www.daodas.state.sc.us

South Dakota

Department of Human Services
Division of Alcohol and Drug Abuse
Hillsview Plaza, East Highway 34
500 East Capitol Avenue
Pierre, SD 57501-5070
Phone: (605) 773-3123
Fax: (605) 773-7076
E-mail: info@dada
Web site: http://www.state.sd.us/dhs/dhs

Tennessee

Department of Health
Alcohol and Drug Abuse Services
Cordell Hall Building
425 Fifth Avenue North, Third Floor
Nashville, TN 37247-0101
Phone: (615) 741-1921
Fax: (615) 532-2419
E-mail: Ddenton@mail.state.tn.us
Web site: http://www.state.tn.us/hh.html

Texas

Commission on Alcohol and Drug Abuse
9001 North IH 35
Suite 105
Austin, TX 78753-5233
Phone: (512) 349-6600
Fax: (512) 837-0998
Web site: http://www.texas.gov/agency/517.html

Utah

Department of Human Services
Division of Substance Abuse
120 North 200 West, Room 201
Salt Lake City, UT 84103
Phone: (801) 538-3939
Toll Free Hotline: (888) 918-8500
Fax: (801) 538-4696
Web site: http://www.hsdsa.state.ut.us/

Vermont

Agency of Human Services
Office of Alcohol and Drug Abuse Programs
108 Cherry Street
Burlington, VT 05402-0070
Phone: (802) 651-1560
Fax: (802) 651-1573
E-mail: mlaplan@vdh.state.vt.us
Web site: http://www.state.vt.us/adap/

Virginia

Office of Substance Abuse Services
Department of Mental Health, Mental Retardation, and Substance Abuse Services
P.O. Box 1797
Richmond, VA 23218
Phone: (804) 786-3906
Fax: (804) 371-0091
Web site: http://www.dmhmrsas.state.va.us

Washington

Department of Social and Health Services
Division of Alcohol and Substance Abuse
P.O. Box 45330
Olympia, WA 98504-5330
Phone: (360) 438-8200
Fax: (360) 438-8078
Web site: http://www.wa.gov/dshs

West Virginia

Department of Health and Human Resources
Office of Behavioral Health Services
Division of Alcoholism and Drug Abuse
350 Capital St., Rm. 350
Charleston, WV 25301-3702
Phone: (304) 558-0627
Fax: (304) 558-1008
E-mail: obhs@wvdhhr.org
Web site: http://www.wvdhhr.org

Wisconsin

Department of Health and Family Services
Division of Community Services
Bureau of Substance Abuse Services
P.O. Box 7851
1 West Wilson Street
Madison, WI 53707-7851
Phone: (608) 267-7164
Fax: (608) 266-1533

Wisconsin (continued)
E-mail: langejb@dhfs.state.wi.us
Web site: http://www.dhfs.state.wi.us/substabuse/index.htm

Wyoming

Department of Health
Division of Behavioral Health
Substance Abuse Program
6101 Yellowstone Road, 259-B
Cheyenne, WY 82002-0480
Phone: (307) 777-7094
Fax: (307) 777-5580
Web site: http://wdbh.state.wy.us

American Samoa

Department of Human Resources
Government of American Samoa
Pago Pago, AS 96799
Phone: 011-684-633/4606
Web site: http://www.government.as/medical.htm

Guam

Department of Mental Health and Substance Abuse
790 Governor Carlos G. Gamacho Road
Tamuning, GU 96911
Phone: (671) 647-5330
Fax: (671) 649-6948
Web site: http://ns.gov.gu/government.html

Puerto Rico

Department of Health
Mental Health and Anti-Addiction Services Administration
P.O. Box 70184
San Juan, PR 00936-0184
Phone: (787) 274-7676

Virgin Islands

Department of Human Services
Knud Hansen Complex, Building A 1303
Hospital Ground
St. Thomas, US VI 00802
Phone: (340) 774-0930
Fax: (340) 774-3466
E-mail: humanservice@usvi.org
Web site: http://www.usvi.org/humanservices/index.html

Index

Index

Page numbers followed by 'n' indicate a note. Page numbers in *italics* indicate a table or illustration.

A

AA *see* Alcoholics Anonymous
AAFS *see* African American Family Services
abstinence facilitation, defined 457
acetaminophen 128
ACOA *see* Adult Children of Alcoholics
acquired immune deficiency syndrome (AIDS) 295
  cocaine use 160–61
  marijuana use 82
  opiods use 13
  women 358–59
Acri, Jane 340
ACS *see* American Cancer Society
ACTH *see* adrenocorticotropin
acupuncture, detoxification 281
acute abstinence syndrome, defined 457
acute psychosis, defined 457
ACYF *see* Administration on Children, Youth, and Families

ADAM see *Arrestee Drug Abuse Monitoring*
ADAW see *Alcoholism & Drug Abuse Week*
addiction 91–121
  children 385–86
  cocaine 8
  defined 457
  questions and answers 91–102
  research 99–100
  treatment 111, 305–9, 349–52
    opiates 311–25
Addiction Research Foundation (Toronto) 339
Addiction Severity Index (ASI) 346, 351
ADHD *see* attention deficin hyperactivity disorder
AdipexP (phentermine) 142
Administration for Children and Families (DHHS), contact information 543
Administration for Native Americans (ANA), contact information 543–44
Administration on Children, Youth, and Families (ACYF), web site 535
Adolescence, "Polydrug-using adolescent mothers and their infants receiving early intervention" (Field, et al.) 237

585

Adolescence Directory On-Line, web site 535
adolescents
  alcoholism 5
  depression 265–67
  drug abuse prevention 382–83
    research 433–36
  drug use statistics 33–37
  family therapy 369–70
  hallucinogens 13
  inhalant abuse 15, 391
  marijuana use 25, 190
  methadone 278
Adopt-A-School 449
adrenocorticotropin (ACTH) 114, 116
Adult Behavior Checklist (ABC) 345
Adult Children of Alcoholics (ACOA), contact information 539–40
aerosols 14, 175–76
AET *see* alpha-ethyltryptamine
African American Family Services (AAFS), contact information 517
African American Parents for Drug Prevention, contact information 536
African Americans
  drug abuse prevention 437–40
  substance abuse prevention 446–49
age factor
  alcoholism 4
  cocaine abuse 157
  marijuana experimentation 7
Agency for Health Care Policy and Research (AHCPR) 121
agonists
  defined 458
  opioids 120, 317–18
AHCPR *see* Agency for Health Care Policy and Research
AIDS *see* acquired immune deficiency syndrome
Alabama Department of Mental Health/Retardation, Substance Abuse Division, contact information 567
Al-Anon Family Groups, contact information 540
Alaska Department of Health and Social Services, Division of Alcoholism and Drug Abuse, contact information 567

alcohol abuse statistics 4, 40–41
alcohol and other drug (AOD), described 275
Alcoholics Anonymous (AA)
  abstinence approach 101
  contact information 540
  long-term support 6
  recovery program 11
alcoholism 4
  benzodiazepine withdrawal 284
  diagnosis 5–6
  statistics 3
Alcoholism & Drug Abuse Week (ADAW), relapse prevention strategy 353n, 354, 355
Alcohol Misuse Prevention Project, drug abuse prevention curricula 426
alcohol use
  dopamine 106
  overview 4–6
  pregnancy 43
  students 442–44
Alfenta (fentanyl) 132
alfentanil 132
aliphatic nitrites 176
Allen, Walter, III 30
alpha-ethyltryptamine (AET) 144
  street terms 466, 481, 493, 509
alprazolam 136
  withdrawal 283
Alurate (aprobarbital) 135
alveolar macrophages 249, 254–55
Alvy, Kerby T. 526
AMA *see* American Medical Association
amanita muscaria mushrooms 482
America Cares, Inc., contact information 536
American Academy of Child and Adolescent Psychiatry, contact information 19
American Academy of Psychiatrists in Alcoholism and Addictions, contact information 19
American Cancer Society (ACS), contact information 517
American Council for Drug Education, contact information 517

American Council on Drug Education, contact information 20
American Health Foundation, Know Your Body
contact information 421
drug abuse prevention curricula 426–27
American Indians
peyote 143
substance abuse prevention 452–53
violence 60–63
American Journal of Orthopsychiatry, "Prenatal cocaine exposure and childhood psychopathology..." (Scherling, et al.) 237
American Journal of Psychiatry
"Disproportionate suicidiality in patients with comorbid major depression...(Cornelius, et al.) 271
"Tryptophan depletion and attenuation of cue-induced craving for cocaine" (Satal, et al.) 343
The American Journal on Addictions, "Craving for cocaine in addicted users: Role of serotonergic mechanisms" (Buydens-Branchey, et al.) 343
The American Journal on the Addictions, serotonin agonist 341
American Management Association
drug testing in the workplace 404
drug testing trends 402
American Medical Association (AMA)
medical treatment for opiate addiction 312
trends in prescription drug abuse 29–30
American Psychiatric Association
depression and substance use 267
substance abuse facts 3n
web site 21
American Psychiatric Press, Inc., contact information 19
American Samoa Department of Human Resources, contact information 580
American School Health Association, drug abuse prevention curricula 415n

American Society of Addiction Medicine, contact information 20
amobarbital 16, 135
street terms 475, 478, 485
amobarbital/secobarbital 501, 508, 509, 510
amotivational syndrome 7
amphetamines 4, 139–40, 151–54
detoxification 286–87
dopamine 106
jail inmates 66–68
street terms 465–513
amphetamine sulfate, street terms 468, 502
amyl nitrite 14, 176, 177
street terms 466, 471, 498, 500, 504, 505, 511
Amytal (amobarbital) 16, 135
Amytal (amobarbital sodium) 466, 470
ANA *see* Administration for Native Americans
anabolic steroids 49, 148–50, 219–22
defined 148
Anadrol (oxymetholone) 149
analgesia, defined 458
analog, defined 458
Anavar (oxandrolone) 149
androgenic anabolic steroids, described 219
anesthetics 14
cocaine 138
defined 458
anhedonia, defined 458
animal studies
BChE 337
cocaine 158, 232
dopamine 106, 107–9
hallucinogens 142–43
marijuana 251
marijuana use 189
Ritalin 212
Annals of Internal Medicine, "Medicinal applications of delta-9... (Voth, et al.) 86
anorectic drugs 141–42
anorexia, defined 458
Antabuse (disulfiram) 6

antagonists
  defined 458
  opioids 120, 317–18
antidepressants
  cocaine use 11
  defined 458
Anti-Drug Abuse Act (1986) 51
Anti-Drug Abuse Act (1988)
  drug control strategy 71
  user accountability 55, 56
appetite enhancement 82
appetite suppressants 3
aprobarbital 135
Aqua Net hair spray 497
Archives of General Psychiatry
  "Adult outcome of hyperactive boys:
    educational achievement..."
    (Mannuzza, et al.) 346
  "Long-term therapeutic use of ben-
    zodiazepines..." (Rickels, et al.)
    284
Arizona Department of Health Services, Bureau of Substance Abuse
  and Mental Health, contact information 568
Arkansas Department of Health,
  Bureau of Alcohol and Drug Abuse
  Prevention, contact information
  568
Arrestee Drug Abuse Monitoring
  (ADAM) 64
  emerging drug problems 70
  federal drug data sources 555
  methamphetamine use 204
arthralgia, defined 458
Asian American community, substance abuse prevention 451–52
Aspergillus 83
aspirin 128
Association for Medical Education
  and Research in Substance Abuse,
  contact information 20
ataxia, defined 458
Ativan (lorazepam) 136
attention deficin hyperactivity disorder (ADHD) 139, 211, 345–47
authorizing order, defined 458
Automated Reports and Consolidated
  Orders System (ARCOS) 53

AVANCE, Inc., contact information
  522
Aymara Indians, cocaine before birth
  235

B

Bailey, William J. 200
Bakalar, J. 86
Baker, Gail Amato 390
barbiturates 16, 49, 134–35
  detoxification 288
  jail inmates 66–68
  street terms 467, 470, 483, 489,
    504, 507
basuco 467
Baxter, Lewis 101
BChE *see* butyrylcholinesterase
"Behavioral Change through Treatment" 305n
Behavioral Health Management
  "The Addicted Brain: An Era of Sci-
    entific Breakthroughs" (Peck)
    99n
  "The Changing Face of Addictions
    Treatment: With Society's
    Help..." (Washousky, et al.) 349n
behavioral therapy
  cocaine abuse 162–63
  drug addiction 305–9, 349
  heroin abuse 173–74
Behnke, Mary Lou 237
Benzedrine (amphetamine sulfate)
  139, 468, 498, 502
benzene 176
benzocaine, street terms 475, 476,
  482, 500
benzodiazepines 26, 133–34
  detoxification 282–86
  listed 16, 136–37
benzphetamine 141
Best Foundation, Project Alert 422–23
  contact information 424
  drug abuse prevention curricula
    426–27
Beveridge, R. A. 86
BIA *see* Bureau of Indian Affairs
binge drinking 5

binges
cocaine use 9
hallucinogens 14
Biphetamine, street terms 469, 492, 510
BJS *see* Bureau of Justice Statistics
blood-borne medications 333–38
Blum, Terry 402, 403, 404
boldenone 149
Bolla, Karen I. 245, 246
Bonagura, N. 346
Bontril (phendimetrazine) 142
Boy Scouts of America, prevention programs 548
brain
addiction 91–102
addiction pathway, described 99
cocaine 157–58
nucleus accumbens 106
Branchey, Marc 343
Brevital (methohexital) 134
Brook, Judith 437, 438
Brown, Jesse 446
The Brown University Child and Adolescent Behavior Letter, depression and substance use 265n
The Brown University Digest of Addiction Theory and Application
methylphenidate (Ritalin) 346
"Methylphenidate reduces drug cravings..." (Levin, et al.) 345n
serotonin agonist 341n
substance abuse and violent death 269n
Bukoski, W. J. 436n
Buprenex (buprenorphine) 131
buprenorphine 120, 129, 131, 279, 329–32
defined 458
Bureau of Indian Affairs (BIA), contact information 544
Bureau of Justice Statistics (BJS)
drugs and crime facts 59
federal drug data sources 557, 559–61
web site 59n
"Bureau of Justice Statistics (BJS)"
drugs and crime facts 59
Profile of Jail Inmates 63

"Bureau of Justice Statistics (BJS)", continued
Substance Abuse and Treatment, State and Federal Prisoners 60, 63
Substance Abuse and Treatment of Adults on Probation 63, 66
Violence by Intimates 64
Bureau of Labor Statistics (BLS)
drug testing trends 402
Survey of Employer Anti-Drug Programs 403, 405
butabarbital 135
butalbital 135
Butisol (butabarbital) 135
Butts, Calvin O. 446
butyl nitrite 14, 176, 511
butyrylcholinesterase (BChE) 335, 336
Buydens-Branchey, Laure 341, 343

C

CADCA *see* Community Anti-Drug Coalitions of America
Cadet, Jean Lud 242, 246
caffeine 152
California
Department of Drug and Alcohol Abuse, contact information 568
supreme court decisions, *Tarasoff v. Regents of the Univ. of Cal* 298
California State University, prevention strategies 444
cannabis 146–47
street terms 489, 502, 503
see also marijuan
Cannabis sativa 79, 146, 185
Cantab Pharmaceuticals, cocaine molecule immunization 334
Capaldina, Lisa 79n, 86
carisoprodol 129
Carmona, Gilberto 335
Caron, Marc 109
Case, W. G. 284
Catapres (clonidine) 277–78
cathine 141
cathinone 140, 141, 198

Cathula edulis 141, 198, 491, 500
CDC *see* Centers for Disease Control and Prevention
cellulitis, defined 458
CENAPS Corp., relapse prevention strategy 353, 354, 355
Census of State and Federal Correctional Facilities, federal drug data sources 557
Center for Substance Abuse Prevention (CSAP)
  contact information 517–18, 545
  drug use and HIV transmission 228
  effects of marijuana 249n
  Hispanic/Latino population 449
  prevention strategies 446
  trends in workplace substance abuse 39n
  Youth Substance Abuse Prevention Initiative 72
Center for Substance Abuse Treatment (CSAT)
  contact information 518
  detoxification 275n
  drug use and HIV transmission 228
  legal and ethical issues 289n
  Replicating Effective Treatment for Methamphetamine Dependence study 72
  Targeting Treatment Capacity Expansion Program 72
Center for the Improvement of Child Caring
  Effective Black Parenting Program (EBPP), contact information 522–23
  Los Niños Bien Educados, contact information 526–27
Centers for Disease Control and Prevention (CDC)
  block grant program 75, 76
  drug use and HIV transmission 225n, 228, 229
  federal drug data sources 556
  mandatory reporting 295
  nonsmoking behavior 18
  Planned Approach to Community Health (PATCH)
    contact information 544

Centers for Disease Control and Prevention (CDC), continued
  treatment methods for women 359
  Youth Risk and Behavioral Survey System 222n
central nervous system (CNS)
  benzodiazepines 136
  depressants 133
  marijuana 79
  methamphetamine 201
  toluene 176
Centrax (prazepam) 136
CEWG *see* Community Epidemiology Work Group
chemical dependencies
  employees 40
  treatment 306–7
children
  anabolic steroid use 220–22
  detoxification programs 290
  drug abuse prevention 373–90
    programs, listed 415–32
    research 433–36
  HIV transmission 225
  inhalant abuse 15
Children Youth and Families at Risk (CYFAR), web site 535
chloral hydrate 16, 134
  street terms 489, 490, 491, 495, 499, 509
chlordiazepoxide 16, 136
  withdrawal 283
chloroform 176
chronic benign pain, defined 462
chronic obstructive pulmonary disease (COPD)
  defined 458
  marijuana use 250, 252–53
cigarette smoking *see* nicotine
cleaning fluids 14
clomipramine 101
clonazepam 26, 136
clonidine 277–78, 318
clorazepate 16, 136
clouded sensorium, defined 458
CNS *see* central nervous system
Coast Guard, contact information 545–46

coca
 defined 458
 see also *Erythroxylon coca*
cocaethylene, defined 458
cocaine 49, 138–39, 155–64, 239–44
 detoxification 286–87, 341–43
 dopamine 106–7
 drug abuse trends 23–24
 jail inmates 65, 66–68
 overview 8–11
 pregnancy 43
 street terms 8, 156, 466–513
 stress systems 115
 treatment 162–63
 see also crack cocaine
"Cocaine Abuse and Addiction"
 (NIDA) 457n
Cocaine Anonymous
 recovery program 11
 treatment methods and medications
  307
cocaine hydrochloride 138, 474
cocaine paste 467, 468
cocaine psychosis, described 9–10
codeine 49, 50, 128–29
 street terms 475, 498, 508
Code of Federal Regulations, regulatory and policy guidance 551
coffee 3
 see also caffeine
cognitive therapy
 addiction 110, 349
 heroin abuse 173
"cold turkey," defined 459
Colorado Department of Human Services, Alcohol and Drug Abuse Division, contact information 568
"Common Sense: Strategies for Raising Alcohol and Drug-Free Children" 520
*Communicating About Alcohol and
 Other Drugs: Strategies for Reaching Populations at Risk* 446, 449
Community Anti-Drug Coalitions of
 America (CADCA), contact information 536
Community Epidemiology Work
 Group (CEWG)
 emerging drug problems 70

Community Epidemiology Work
 Group (CEWG), continued
 "Epidemiologic Trends in Drug
  Abuse" 27
 epidemiology of drug abuse 191n
 marijuana use 189, 190
 MDMA (ecstasy) 194, 195, 196n
 methylphenidate (Ritalin) research
  212n
 trends in drug abuse 23
Community Epidemiology Work
 Group (CEWG) 555
Comprehensive Crime Control Act
 (1984) 50
Comprehensive Drug Abuse Prevention and Control Act (1970) 45, 201
Comprehensive Methamphetamine
 Control Act (1996) 202
Conlon, Michael 237
Connecticut Division of Community
 Based Regulations, contact information 569
controlled substance analogues, described 51
Controlled Substances Act (CSA) 45–57
 amphetamines 151
 anabolic steroid abuse 148
 anorectic drugs 142
 barbiturate substitutes 135
 benzodiazepines 136
 cannabis distribution 147
 drug types 125, 128, 129
 inhalants 150
 methamphetamine 201
 methcathinone 140, 199
 penalties provision 55
 stimulants 137
Convention on Psychotropic Substances (1971) 51
COPD *see* chronic obstructive pulmonary disease
Core Alcohol and Drug Survey 443
Cornelius, J. R. 271
Cornell University Medical, Life
 Skills Training
 contact information 421–22
 drug abuse prevention curricula
  426–28
corticosteroids 81

corticotropin releasing factor (CRF)
114, 116, 339–40
cortisol 116
*Cost Effectiveness and Cost Benefit
Research of Drug Abuse Prevention*
(Bukoski) 436n
"Costs, benefits, and cost effectiveness of comprehensive drug abuse
prevention" (Pentz) 436n
Council of State and Territorial Epidemiologists, block grant program
75–76
crack cocaine 138
adolescent usage 35
described 8, 156
detoxification 286–87
street terms 465–513
withdrawal symptoms 93
see also cocaine
craving, defined 459
CRF *see* corticotropin releasing factor
CSAP *see* Center for Substance Abuse
Prevention
CSAT *see* Center for Substance Abuse
Treatment
Culbreth, Henry 355
cyclohexyl nitrite 176
CYFAR *see* Children Youth and Families at Risk

D

Dalmane (flurazepam) 136
street terms 477
Damasio, Antonio 108
DARE America
contact information 420
drug abuse prevention curricula
426, 427
Darvon (dextropropoxyphene) 49, 131
DAWN *see* Drug Abuse Warning Network
DEA *see* Drug Enforcement Adminis-
tration
Deca-Durabolon (nandrolone) 149
decisional capacity, defined 459
Delaware Division of Alcoholism,
Drug Abuse, and Mental Health,
contact information 569

Delaware Model 307
delirium, defined 459
delirium tremens (DT)
alcoholism 5
defined 459
delta-9-tetrahydrocannabinol (THC)
79, 146–48, 185–86
delusions, defined 459
dementia, alcoholism 5
Demerol (meperidine) 120, 131
street terms 499
denial, drug abuse 10, 11
depressants 132–37
drug abuse trends 26
street terms 467–513
depression
adolescents 265–67
alcoholism 5
dopamine 95
designer drugs, defined 459
Desoxyn (methamphetamine) 471, 497
DET *see* diethyltryptamine
detoxification 275–88
cocaine use 11
defined 459
heroin 172–74
opiate addiction 13
pregnancy 44
see also withdrawal symptoms
*Detoxification from Alcohol and Other
Drugs* 275n, 289n, 457n
detoxification programs 289–304
DeVille, Kenneth A. 237
dexamethasone 81
Dexamyl (dextroamphetamine/
amobarbital) 475, 478, 485
Dexedrine (dextroamphetamine) 139
street terms 472, 478
dextroamphetamine 139
street terms 472, 475, 478, 485, 510
dextropropoxyphene 132, 279–80
DHHS *see* US Department of Health
and Human Services
*Diagnostic and Statistical Manual of
Mental Disorders, Fourth Edition
(DSM-IV)*
addictions treatment 351
methylphenidate (Ritalin) 345
Dianabol (methandrostenolone) 149

diaphoresis, defined 459
diazepam 16, 136
  street terms 495
  withdrawal 283
Didrex (benzphetamine) 141
diethylproprion 141
diethyltryptamine (DET) 143
Dilaudid (hydromophone) 30
  street terms 478, 482, 488
dimethyltryptamine (DMT) 143–44
  street terms 465, 466, 472, 478,
    479, 481
Diphetamine, street terms 482
District of Columbia, Department of
  Human Services, contact information 569
disulfiram 6, 162
Djahed, B. 86
DMT *see* dimethyltryptamine
DOB *see* 4-bromo-2,5-
  dimethoxyamphetamine
DoJ *see* US Department of Justice
Dolophine (methadone) 131, 479
DOM *see* 4-Methyl-2,5-
  dimethoxyamphetamine
dopamine 94–95, 100, 103–7
  defined 459
Doral (quazepam) 136
Doriden (glutethimide) 129, 135
  street terms 475, 479, 493, 507
Dretchen, Kenneth 336
dronabinol 79–81, 146
  versus marijuana 82–84
drub abuse *see* substance abuse
"Drug Abuse: Research Shows Treatment is Effective, but Benefits May
  be Overstated" 361n
Drug Abuse Information and Treatment Referral Line, contact information 20
Drug Abuse Warning Network
  (DAWN)
  emerging drug problems 69, 70
  federal drug data sources 556
  heroin use in the United States 168
  methamphetamine abuse 203
  scope of cocaine use 157
  trends in drug abuse 23–24, 27
  trends in prescription drug abuse 29

Drug and Alcohol Dependency, "Craving: Consensus of status and
  agenda for future research"
  (Pickens, et al.) 343
Drug Enforcement Administration
  (DEA)
  buprenorphine update 331
  contact information 548
  controlled substances 50, 52
  Controlled Substances Act (CSA)
    45, 46
  amendment 51
  dextropropoxyphene (Darvon) 279
  distribution records 53
  division offices 563–66
  Drug and Chemical Evaluation Sec-
    tion 180
  drugs and crime facts 59
  federal drug data sources 558, 559
  ketamine use 179n
  LAAM reclassification 278
  LSD (Lysergic Acid Diethylamide) 181
  marijuana 79
  methamphetamine clandestine
    laboratories 207
  methamphetamine law enforcement
    statistics 206
  methamphetamine use 205
  methcathinone laboratories 198
  methylphenidate 212
  production quotas 54
  rohypnol dependence 217
  trends in prescription drug abuse
    29, 30
  types of drugs 125n
Drug-Induced Rape Prevention and
  Punishment Act (1996) 166
Drug Information and Strategy Clearinghouse, contact information 547
Drug Policy Information Clearinghouse, contact information 201n
drug receptors, defined 459
Drugs and Crime Facts 59n
"Drug Slang Dictionary" (IPRC) 465n
Drugs of Abuse
  Controlled Substances Act (CSA) 45n
  Drug Enforcement Administration
    (DEA) 563n
  types of drugs 125n

drug testing 399–400, 401–14
drug tolerance, defined 459
drug use
  detection 69–77
  overview 6–18
Drug Use Forecasting (DUF) see *Arrestee Drug Abuse Monitoring*
DT *see* delirium tremens
dual diagnosis, defined 460
Durabolin (nandrolone) 149
Dusenbury, Linda 415n
duty to warn, defined 460
dysphoria, defined 460

E

Early Childhood Educators' and Family Web Corner, web site 535
"The Economic Costs of Alcohol and Drug Abuse in the United States" 555–56
ecstasy (drug) *see* methylenedioxymethamphetamine
ecstasy liquid *see* gamma hydroxy butyric acid
Educational Development Center, Teenage Health Teaching Modules
  contact information 424–25
  drug abuse prevention curricula 426–27
Effective Black Parenting Program (EBPP), Center for the Improvement of Child Caring 522–23
Effective Medical Treatment of Opiate Addiction 311n
electrolytes
  defined 460
  inhalant abuse 15
electrostimulation, detoxification 281–82
embalming fluid 25
"Emerging Drug Problems: Despite Changes in Detection and Response Capability, Concerns Remain" 69n
Emperin compound with codeine 482
employee assistance programs (EAP)
  drug testing 405
  illicit drug use 40

employee assistance programs (EAP), continued
  substance abuse prevention 396, 398–99
employees, substance abuse statistics 39–41
encephalopathy, defined 460
ephedrine 26, 152
"Epidemiologic Trends in Drug Abuse" 191n
  MDMA (Ecstasy) 196n
  methylphenidate (Ritalin) 212n
  trends in drug abuse 27
Equanil (meprobamate) 49, 135
  withdrawal 283
Equipoise (boldenone) 149
Erie County Council for the Prevention of Alcohol and Substance, SafeHomes, contact information 521
Erythroxylon coca 138, 155
  see *also* cocaine
etazolam 136
ethchlorvynol 16
ether 176
ethical issues, detoxification programs 289–304
ethnic factors
  cocaine abuse 156
  drug abuse prevention 437–40
  drug use, pregnancy 44
  HIV transmission 226
ethylestrenol 149
Evans, S. M. 345n, 347
Eyler, Fonda Davis 237

F

FA *see* Families Anonymous
Falco, Mathea 415n
Families and Schools Together (FAST) 523–25
  contact information 523
Families Anonymous (FA)
  contact information 541
  support group 11
family action plans 10–11
family issues
  cocaine use 10

family issues, continued
   drug abuse prevention 373–90
   research 435–36
FAST *see* Families and Schools Together
Fastin (phentermine) 470
FBI *see* Federal Bureau of Investigation
FDA *see* US Food and Drug Administration
Federal Bureau of Investigation (FBI)
   Community Outreach Program contact information 549
   federal drug data sources 559
   The Uniform Crime Reporting Program (UCR) 60
"Federal Drug Data Sources," web site 553n
The Federal Justice Statistics Program 59
The Federal Personnel Manual 551
Federal Register
   controlled substances 50
   scheduling of a substance 51
fenfluramine 142
fentanyl 120, 132, 174
   street terms 466, 474, 477, 482, 484, 485, 487, 489, 491, 496, 499, 507
Fergeson, Paul 343
Field, Tiffany M. 237
Finajet (trenbolone) 149
financial considerations
   addiction treatments 350–52
   drug abuse prevention 97
   marijuana 84
Fioricet (butalbital) 135
Fiorinal (butalbital) 135
flashbacks 142
Florida Department of Children and Families, contact information 569
flunitrazepam 26, 136, 217
fluoxymesterone 149
flurazepam 136
Focus on Families, Social Development Research Group 525–26
   contact information 525
formaldehyde, street terms 466, 493

4-bromo-2,5-dimethoxyamphetamine (DOB) 145
4-bromo-2,5-dimethoxyphenethylamone (2C-B; NEXUS) 145
4-Methyl-2,5-dimethoxyamphetamine (DOM; STP) 144–45
   street terms 497, 503
Fowler, Joanna 107, 110
Fox, Barbara 334, 335
The Fraternity Insurance Purchasing Group (FIPG) 444
freebase 8, 155–56
French, Michael T. 414
freon 482
Fullilove, M. T. 281
Fullilove, R. E. 281
Fusarium 83

G

gamma hydroxy butyrate (GHB) 26, 165–66
   street terms 166, 483, 494
gamma hydroxy butyric acid (GHB) 485, 493, 503, 505
GAO *see* General Accounting Office
gases 175–76
gender factor
   adolescent drug abuse statistics 35
   alcoholism 4
   cigarette smoking statistics 17
   cocaine abuse 156
   marijuana experimentation 7
General Accounting Office (GAO)
   drug abuse prevention curricula 415
   effective treatment 361n
   emerging drug problems 69n
General Motors 40
genetic factors
   addiction 92, 109–10
   marijuana use 254
   see also heredity
Georgia Substance Abuse Services, contact information 570
GHB *see* gamma hydroxy butyric acid
Gieringer, D. 86

glossary
  drug street terms 465–513
  substance abuse terms 457–63
glue 150
glutethimide 129, 135
  street terms 475, 479, 493, 498, 507
Gorelick, David 333
Gorski, Terence T. 353, 354
grand mal seizures, defined 460
granisetron HCl 81
Greenblatt, D. J. 284
Grinspoon, L. 86
Growing Healthy, National Center for
  Health Education
  contact information 421
  drug abuse prevention curricula
    426–27
*Growing Up Drug-Free: How to
  Teach Your Child About Drugs*
  373n, 515n
GTE Corporation 520
Guam Department of Mental Health
  and Substance Abuse, contact infor-
  mation 580

H

hair sprays 14
halazepam 136
Halcion (triazolam) 136
  withdrawal 283
hallucinations, cocaine use 10
hallucinogens 142–46
  adolescent usage 35
  detoxification 287
  drug abuse trends 26–27
  jail inmates 66–68
  overview 13–14
  see also lysergic acid diethylamide
    (LSD); mescaline; peyote
Halotestin (fluoxymesterone) 149
halothane 14, 176
Harrison Narcotic Act (1914)
  opiate addiction treatment 312
  semi-synthetic narcotics 129
Hartwell, Tyler D. 401n, 414
Harvard Mental Health Letter, cocaine before birth 231n

Harvard University, marijuana study 92
hashish 148
  described 83
  street terms 469, 481, 486, 495,
    497, 499, 501, 508
hash oil 148
Hatzidimitriou, George 248
Hawaii Department of Health, contact information 570
Hazelden Foundation, contact information 518
hemp plants 83
  see also marijuana
hepatitis
  cocaine use 161
  heroin use 171
  opiate users 312
  opiods use 13
heredity
  alcoholism 5, 377
  marijuana use 185
  see also genetic factors
Herning, Ronald 242, 243
heroin 129–30
  addiction treatment 13
  adolescent usage 34
  dopamine 106
  drug abuse trends 24
  jail inmates 66–68
  street terms 465–513
  stress hormones 115
"Heroin Abuse and Addiction" (NIDA)
  457n
heroin substitute *see* methadone
hexane 176
HHANES *see* Hispanic Health and
  Nutrition Examination Survey III
  (HHANES)
HHS *see* US Department of Health
  and Human Services
Hispanic Health and Nutrition Examination Survey III (HHANES)
  554
Hispanics, substance abuse prevention 449–51
  see also Puerto Ricans
histoplasmosis 83
HIV *see* human immunodeficiency
  virus

HIV Prevention Community Planning, drug use and HIV transmission 229
Hoffman, Albert 144
homicide statistics *61*, 270
homosexual community, substance abuse 444–46
hormones, stress 114
hospital emergency departments
cocaine abuse 157
drug abuse 29
heroin abuse 168
Household Drug Survey, cocaine use 139
HUD *see* US Department of Housing and Urban Development
Hudson, Jeffrey 343
human immunodeficiency virus (HIV) 295
cocaine use 160–61
drug use 225–29
heroin use 167, 171–72
opiate users 312
women 358–59
hydrocodone 49, 129, 130
hydromophone, street terms 478, 482
hyperpyrexia, defined 460
hyperreflexia, defined 460
hypertension, defined 460
hypnotics 15–17
detoxification 282–86

I

Idaho Department of Health and Welfare, contact information 570
IDU *see* injection drug users
IHS *see* Indian Health Service
Illinois Department of Human Services, contact information 570
immigrants, drug abuse prevention 437–40
ImmuLogic Pharmaceutical Corporation 334
immune system
drug interceptions 334–35
marijuana 257–58
INCSR *see* International Narcotics Control Strategy Report

Indiana Bureau of Chemical Addictions, contact information 571
Indiana Prevention Resource Center
amphetamines 151n
methcathinone 197n
Indian Health Service (IHS), contact information 549
infants
cocaine exposure 231–37
maternal opiods use 13
inhalants 14–15, 150, 175–78
abuse prevention 391–94
adolescent usage 35
detoxification 288
jail inmates 67
street terms 466, 467, 499, 503
injection drug users (IDU) 225, 227–29
"Inmates in local Jails" 63
inositol 138
Institute for Prevention Research, STAR
contact information 424
drug abuse prevention curricula 427–28
Institute of Medicine
effective treatment 363, 366
medical efficacy of marijuana 84
insurance coverage, detoxification 293–94
International Journal of Addiction, "Alcohol and crimes of violence: Present issues (Murdoch, et al.) 271
International Narcotics Control Strategy Report (INCSR) 558
international treaties, illicit drugs 51
interventions 10–11
psychosocial 110
intravenous drugs, jail inmates 68
involuntary commitment, defined 460
Ionamin (phentermine) 142
Iowa Division of Substance Abuse and Health Promotion, contact information 571
Isaacson, J. H. 347
isobutyl nitrite, street terms 471, 475, 486, 487, 491, 493, 500–502, 505, 508, 511
isoquinolines 128

J

jail inmates, drug use 63, 66–68
JB (226-N-Methyl-3-Piperidyl benzitate hydrochloride) 492
Johanson, C. E. 343
Johns Hopkins University
  MDMA and brain injury 247
  School of Medicine, detrimental effects of heavy cocaine use 245
Johnson Institute, parent resource guide 515
Johnston, Lloyd 34
joint, described 83
Join Together, contact information 518
Journal of Clinical Psychiatry
  "The dual diagnosis of attention-deficit/hyperactivity disorder..." (Schubiner, et al.) 347
  methylphenidate (Ritalin) 345
  "Methylphenidate treatment for cocaine abusers with adult..." (Levin, et al.) 347
The Journal of Neuropsychiatry and Clinical Neurosciences, detrimental effects of heavy cocaine use 245
The Journal of Neuroscience, MDMA (Ecstasy) and brain injury 247
Journal of School Health, "A review of the Evaluation of 47 Drug Abuse Prevention Curricula Available Nationally" (Dusenbury, et al.) 415n
Journal of Substance Abuse Treatment, "Acupuncture heroin detoxification: a single-blind clinical trial" (Washburn, et al.) 281
Journal of the American Medical Association
  "Alcohol and illicit drug abuse and the risk of violent death in the home (Rivara, et al.) 271
  cocaine before birth 231
  methadone treatment 327
  substance abuse and violent death 269
"Juvenile Court Statistics" 560
"Juveniles Taken into Custody" 561

K

Kansas Department of Social and Rehabilitative Services, contact information 571
Kaposi's sarcoma (KS) 177
Kaufman, Marc 240, 241, 242
Kellermann, Arthur L. 271
Kentucky Department of Mental Health/Mental Retardation Services, contact information 571
ketamine 26, 179–80
  street terms 473, 485, 487, 489, 491, 500, 505, 507
khat 141, 198
King, Paul K. 30
Kleber, H. D. 345n, 347
Klein, R. G. 346
Klonopin (clonazepam) 26, 136
Know Your Body, American Health Foundation
  contact information 421
  drug abuse prevention curricula 426–27
Kopelman, Loretta M. 237
Kreek, Mary Jeanne 113, 114, 115, 116
Krystal, J. H. 343

L

LAAM *see* levo-alpha-acetyl-methadol
lactose 138
LAC - USC Medical Center, trends in prescription drug abuse 30
Ladies Professional Golf Association, prevention programs 548
Lake, Antonia 415n
Landry, Donald 336, 337
La Roche Pharmaceuticals 217
laughing gas *see* nitrous oxide
Law Enforcement Management and Administrative Statistics (LEMAS) program
  drugs and crime facts 59
  federal drug data sources 559
legal issues, detoxification programs 289–304

legislation
   amphetamine control 140
   prescription medications 53–54
   see also Anti-Drug Abuse Act; Com-
      prehensive Crime Control Act;
      Comprehensive Drug Abuse Pre-
      vention and Control Act; Con-
      trolled Substances Act; Drug-In-
      duced Rape Prevention and Pun-
      ishment Act
LEMAS *see* Law Enforcement Management and Administrative Statistics
Leshner, Alan I. 34, 91–98, 99–102,
   111, 245, 247, 327
"Let's Talk Facts about Teen Suicide"
   267
Levin, Frances R. 345, 346, 347
Levin, Jonathan 240, 242
levo-alpha-acetyl-methadol (LAAM)
   131, 173, 277, 278–79, 306–8, 313,
   318, 320, 331
   defined 460
Lewin Group, effective treatment 362
Lewis, David 111
Librium (chlordiazepoxide) 16, 136,
   492
   withdrawal 283
lidocaine 138, 470
Liggett Group, addiction 104
liver disorders
   cirrhosis 5
   inhalant abuse 15
   opiods use 13
Lockridge, Oksana 336
Lophophora williamsii 143
lorazepam 81, 136
Los Angeles Times, "Prescription
   Fraud: Abusing the System"
   (Weikel) 29
Los Niños Bien Educados, contact in-
   formation 526–27
Lotusate (talbutal) 135
Louisiana Department of Health and
   Hospitals, contact information 572
LSD *see* lysergic acid diethylamide
Luminal (phenobarbital) 135
lung cancer, marijuana 7–8, 250,
   255–57

lysergic acid diethylamide (LSD) 13,
   144, 181–84
   street terms 465–513

M

MADD *see* Mothers Against Drunk
   Driving
Maine Office of Substance Abuse,
   contact information 572
*Making the Grade: A Guide to School
   Drug Prevention Programs* 417
Mandrax (methaqualone) 511
Manisses Communications Group Inc.
   depression and substance use 265n
   methylphenidate (Ritalin) 345n
   relapse prevention strategy 353n
   serotonin agonist 341n
   substance abuse and violent death
      269n
mannitol 138
Mannuzza, S. 346
MAO B 107, 110
marijuana 147–48, 185–91
   adolescent usage 34
   detoxification 287
   drug abuse trends 24–25
   jail inmates 64, 66–68
   lung disorders 249–63
   medicinal use 79–87
   overview 6–8
   pregnancy 43
   street terms 25, 185, 465–513
   see also cannabi
Marijuana, the Forbidden Medicine
   (Grinspoon, et al.) 86
"Marijuana as an antiemetic drug:
   How useful is it today?" (Schwartz,
   et al.) 86
*Marijuana Medical Handbook: A
   Guide to therapeutic use* (Rosenthal,
   et al.) 86
"Marijuana to prevent nausea and
   vomiting in cancer patients"
   (Schwartz, et al.) 86
Marinol (dronabinol) 146
Maryland Alcohol and Drug Abuse Ad-
   ministration, contact information 572

Massachusetts Department of Public Health, contact information 572
Massachusetts Institute of Technology, dopamine releasing neurons 107
Maxibolin (ethylestrenol) 149
Mazanor (mazindol) 142
mazindol 142
MBD *see* minimum brain dysfunction
McCann, Una 248
McDowell, D. M. 345n, 347
McKernin, Craig 343
MDA *see* 3,4-methylenedioxyamphetamine
MDMA *see* methylenedioxy-methamphetamine
Mebaral (mephobarbital) 135
mebrobamate, street terms 495
Medicaid
    addictions treatment 350
    legal and ethical issues 303
medical comorbidity, defined 461
Medical Economics Publishing, "Does Marijuana Have a Place in Medicine?" (Capaldina, et al.) 79n
medical emergency, defined 461
medically debilitated, defined 461
Medicare, legal and ethical issues 303
medication discontinuation, defined 461
Medquest Communications, Inc.
    addicted brain publication 99n
    addictions treatment 349n
MELD 527–28
    contact information 527
memory, dopamine 107–9
Mendoza, Carmen T. 271
mental deficits, cocaine use 239–44
meperidine 131, 174
    defined 461
    street terms 499
mephobarbital 135
meprobamate 16, 135, 510
    withdrawal 283
mescaline 13, 143
    street terms 468, 470, 472–74, 489, 493–95, 499, 509
mesolimbic pathway, described 100
meta-chlorophenylpiperzine 341

methadone 49, 116, 120, 131–32, 172, 278, 305–8
    defined 461
    dopamine 110
    safety factors 327–28
    street terms 466, 479
methadone maintenance treatment (MMT) 313, 314, 315–16, 319–25, 368
    described 13
methamphetamine 49, 139, 201–9
    detoxification 286–87
    drug abuse trends 25
    jail inmates 66–68
    street terms 152–53, 468, 471, 474, 476–78, 481–86, 488, 491, 492, 494, 497, 501, 504–7, 510–12
    withdrawal symptoms 93
"Methamphetamine" 201n
methamphetamine hydrochloride 140
methandriol 149
methandrostenolone 149
methaqualone 16, 26, 133, 135
    street terms 478, 479, 491–93, 500, 501, 505, 507, 511, 512
    withdrawal 283
methcathinone 26, 140–41, 197–200
    street terms 197, 468, 473, 476, 480, 483, 484, 489, 500, 504–6, 510, 512
Methedrine (methamphetamine) 139
methohexital 134
methylene chloride 177
methylenedioxy-methamphetamine (MDMA) 26, 145, 193–96
    long term brain injury 247–48
    street terms 193, 475, 477, 478, 479, 481, 488, 491, 493, 502, 503, 505, 509, 512, 513
methylphenidate 26, 141, 211–12, 212n, 345, 346
    ADHD 345–47
    street terms 505, 511
methylprednisolone acetate 81
methyltestosterone 149
metyrapone 116
Michigan Department of Community Health, contact information 573
midazolam 136

Mikuriya, T. 86
Miltown (meprobamate) 16, 135, 510
  withdrawal 283
minimum brain dysfunction (MBD)
  139
MiniThin 492
Minnesota Department off Human
  Services,
  contact information 573
Minnesota Model 306
Mississippi Department of Mental
  Health, contact information 573
Missouri Department of Mental
  Health, contact information 573
MMT *see* methadone maintenance
  treatment
Monitoring the Future study (NIDA)
  33–37
  annual survey on drug use 178n
  cocaine use 157
  emerging drug problems 69, 70
  federal drug data sources 554
  inhalants use 177
  LSD 182, 184n
  marijuana use 189
  MDMA 195, 196n
  methamphetamine use 203
  PCP 214
  steroids 220
  Youth Risk and Behavioral Survey
    System 222n
Montague, P. Read 107, 108
Montana Addictive and Mental Disorders Division, contact information
  574
Monthly Labor Review, "Prevalence of
  Drug Testing in the Workplace"
  (Hartwell, et al.) 401n
morning glory seeds, street terms
  482
morphine 49, 128
  addiction 119–21
  street terms 476, 477, 480, 481,
    484, 495, 496
  stress hormones 115
Mothers Against Drunk Driving
  (MADD), contact information 536
MS-Contin (morphine) 128
MSIR (morphine) 128

MTF *see* Monitoring the Future
Mueller, Beth A. 271
Murdoch, D. 271
mushrooms, aminata muscaria 482
  see also psilocybin; psilocyn
myalgia, defined 461

N

NA *see* Narcotics Anonymous
nalbuphine 120, 129
naloxone 120, 129, 173
naltrexone 129, 173, 308
nandrolone 149
NAPAFASA *see* National Asian Pacific American Families Against
  Substance Abuse, Inc.
naptha 503
Nar-Anon World Service Office
  contact information 541
  support group 11
narcolepsy 139, 151, 211
narcotic-dependent, defined 461
narcotics 125–32
  treatment programs, defined 461
  see also opiate
Narcotics Anonymous (NA)
  contact information 542
  recovery program 11
  treatment methods and medications
    307
NASADAD *see* National Association
  of State Alcohol and Drug Abuse Directors
Nash, J. Madeleine 103n, 111
National Asian Pacific American
  Families Against Substance Abuse,
  Inc. (NAPAFASA) 452
  contact information 536
National Association for Children of
  Alcoholics, contact information 541
National Association for Native
  American Children of Alcoholics,
  contact information 537
National Association of State Alcohol
  and Drug Abuse Directors
  (NASADAD) 203
  contact information 20

National Center for Health Education, Growing Healthy
contact information 421
drug abuse prevention curricula 426–27
National Center for Health Statistics, federal drug data sources 554, 556
National Center for HIV, STD, and TB Prevention 225n
National Child Care Information Center (NCCIC), web site 535
National Clearinghouse for Alcohol and Drug Information (NCADI)
annual survey 360n
cocaine addiction 163–64
cocaine publication 155n
contact information 20, 174, 394, 518
drug abuse prevention
publications 547
research publication 436
strategies 441n
terms 539n, 543n
emerging drug problems publications 72
epidemiology of drug abuse 191n
heroin abuse and addiction 174
heroin use in US 167n
inhalant abuse fact sheet 391n
LSD 184n
marijuana use 190n
MDMA 196n
Monitoring the Future study 178n
"National Household Survey on Drug Abuse" 27
National Pregnancy and Health Survey 44n
web site 535
Youth Risk and Behavioral Survey System 222n
National Clearinghouse on Families and Youth (NCFY), web site 535
National Corrections Reporting Program (NCRP) 560
National Council on Alcoholism and Drug Dependence, Inc., contact information 20, 519
National Crime Prevention Council, contact information 519

"The National Crime Victimization Survey (NCVS)"
drugs and crime facts 59
offenders under the influence 60
National Criminal Justice Reference Service (NCJRS) 547
web site 535
National Drug and Alcoholism Treatment Unit Survey (NDATUS) 557
National Drug and Alcohol Treatment Referral Service, contact information 394
National Drug Strategy Network 29n
National Families in Action, contact information 537
National Family Partnership, contact information 21, 537
National High School Athletic Coaches Association, prevention programs 548
National Highway Traffic Safety Administration (NHTSA), contact information 549
National Hispano/Latino Community Prevention Network, contact information 537
National Household Survey on Drug Abuse (NHSDA)
cocaine use 156
emerging drug problems 69, 70
federal drug data sources 553
heroin use in US 167
inhalants use 178
LSD 183, 184n
marijuana use 190, 191n
MDMA 195, 196n
PCP 215
treatment methods for women 360
trends in drug abuse 23, 27
National Inhalant Prevention Coalition, contact information 394
National Institute of Justice (NIJ)
Arrestee Drug Abuse Monitoring (ADAM) 64–65
methamphetamine abuse 204
Drug Use Forecasting (DUF)
trends in drug abuse 25
federal drug data sources 555

National Institute of Mental Health
(NIMH)
Drug Abuse Reporting Program
(DARP) 367
federal drug data sources 555
MDMA (Ecstasy) and brain injury
247
methylphenidate (Ritalin) 211
parent resource guide 524
serotonin agonist 342
web site 212
National Institute on Alcohol Abuse
and Alcoholism (NIAAA)
contact information 21, 550
federal drug data sources 555–56,
557
National Institute on Drug Abuse
(NIDA)
addicted brain 99
antistress medications 339n
block grant program 75
buprenorphine update 329, 331
Center for Substance Abuse Treatment 309
Clinical Inpatient Research Unit
246
cocaine abuse 162, 239n, 240, 241,
243
cocaine addiction 162
cocaine publication 155n
Community Epidemiology Work
Group
marijuana use 190n
methylphenidate 211
patterns in drug use 168
trends in drug abuse 23
contact information 164, 519
detrimental effects of heavy cocaine
use 245
drug abuse research 73
Drug Abuse Treatment Outcome
Study 366, 367, 369
drug prevention and treatment publications 71
drug use and HIV transmission 228
effective treatment 363
emerging drug problems 69, 76
enzymes 335
ethnic identification 437, 439

National Institute on Drug Abuse
(NIDA), continued
federal drug data sources 554, 555–
56, 557
government-produced cigarettes 83
heroin addiction 12
heroin addicts at special risk 171
heroin use in US 167n
hotline 11
illegal drug use survey 6
Infofax
contact information 36, 121, 164
Monitoring the Future study 36–37
inhalants 175n
use in schools 177–78
LSD 181n, 183, 184n
marijuana use 185n, 189
MDMA 193n, 196n
brain injury 247n
Medications Development Division
333n, 340
methadone maintenance treatment
324, 327
methamphetamine 201, 202
methylphenidate research 212n
Monitoring the Future study 33, 35
National Pregnancy and Health
Survey 43, 44n
pain medications and addiction 119,
120
parent's guide 385
PCP 213n, 214
prevention
inhalant abuse 391
research 433, 436n
treatment services 71
steroids 219n, 220
stress 113n
study of buprenorphine 173
treatment methods
medications 305n, 308
women 357n
Treatment Outcome Prospective
Study 366, 367–68
trends in prescription drug abuse
29
web site 37, 97
Youth Risk and Behavioral Survey
System 222n

National Institutes of Health (NIH)
drug abuse research 73
drug use and HIV transmission 228
effective treatment 369
medical efficacy of marijuana 84
methadone treatment 327
National Institute on Alcohol Abuse
and Alcoholism (NIAAA) 21, 550
National Institute on Drug Abuse
(NIDA) 21, 550
web site 97, 212
National Longitudinal Survey of
Youth 554
National Maternal and Infant Health
Survey 556
National Narcotics Intelligence Con-
sumers Committee (NNICC) 558
National Network for Family Resiliency (NNFR), web site 535
National Parent Information Net-
work, web site 535
The National Parenting Center
(TNPC), web site 535
National Self-Help Clearinghouse,
contact information 21
National Youth Sports Coaches Asso-
ciation, prevention programs 548
National Youth Survey 555
Native Alaskan community, sub-
stance abuse prevention 452–53
Nature
activation of the dopamine system 94
brain-imaging technology 104
dopamine rush 107
nausea, treatment 80–81
NCADI *see* National Clearinghouse
for Alcohol and Drug Information
NCCIC *see* National Child Care Infor-
mation Center
NCFY *see* National Clearinghouse on
Families and Youth
NCJRS *see* National Criminal Justice
Reference Service
NDATUS *see* National Drug and Alco-
holism Treatment Unit Survey
(NDATUS)
Nebraska Mental Health, Substance
Abuse and Addiction Services, con-
tact information 574

Neighborhood Watch, anti-drug policy
389
Nembutal (pentobarbital) 16, 135
street terms 469, 496, 512
withdrawal 283
Nemoto, Tooru 439, 440
nervous system, inhalant abuse 15
Nestler, Eric 104, 110
neuroadaptation, defined 461
Neurology, memory impairment 246
neurons
addiction 106
defined 462
neurotransmitters 104, 106, 114–17
Nevada Bureau of Alcohol and Drug
Abuse, contact information 574
New England Journal of Medicine,
"Effect of cocaine use on the fetus"
(Volpe) 237
New Hampshire Department of
Health and Human Services, con-
tact information 574
New Jersey Department of Health,
contact information 575
New Mexico Department of Health,
contact information 575
News Briefs, "Prescription Drug
Abuse Rivals Illicit Drug Abuse,
Some see Double..." 29n
New York Office of Alcoholism and
Substance Abuse Services, contact
information 575
New York State Psychiatric Institute
(NYSPI) 345
NEXUS *see* 4-bromo-2,5-
dimethoxyphenethylamone
NHSDA *see* National Household Sur-
vey on Drug Abuse (NHSDA)
NHTSA *see* National Highway Traffic
Safety Administration
NIAAA *see* National Institute on Al-
cohol Abuse and Alcoholism
NICASA *see* Northern Illinois Council
on Alcoholism and Substance Abuse
nicotine 17–18
detoxification 287
dopamine 106–7, 110
NIDA *see* National Institute on Drug
Abuse

NIDA Notes
antistress medications 339n
"Blood-Borne Medications Could Intercept Drugs before They Reach the Brain" (Zickler) 333n
"Cocaine Abuse May Lead to Strokes and Mental Deficits" (Stocker) 239n
"Drug Use among America's Teenagers Shows Slight Downward Trend" 33n
"Ethnic Identification and Cultural Ties May Help Prevent Drug Use" (Zickler) 437n
"High School and Youth Trends" 33n
NIDA Research Report
"Cocaine Abuse and Addiction" 155n
"Heroin Abuse and Addiction" 167n
NIH *see* National Institutes of Health
NIH Consensus Program Information Center, contact information 311n, 324
NIJ *see* National Institute of Justice
NIMH *see* National Institute of Mental Health
nitrites 176–77
see also amyl nitrite; butyl nitrite; cyclohexyl nitrite; isobutyl nitrite
nitrous oxide 14, 176
street terms 483, 485, 496, 504, 511
NNFR *see* National Network for Family Resiliency
Noctec (chloral hydrate) 16
nonmalignant pain, defined 462
North Carolina Department of Human Resources 575
North Dakota Department of Human Services, contact information 576
Northern Illinois Council on Alcoholism and Substance Abuse (NICASA) 528–29
NTP *see* narcotics: treatment programs
nucleus accumbens 106, 158
NYSPI *see* New York State Psychiatric Institute
nystagmus, defined 462

O

obsessive compulsive disorder 110–11
Obstetrics and Gynecology Clinics of North America
Cocaine in pregnancy: Recent data on maternal and fetal risks (Plessinger, et al.) 237
"Moral and social issues regarding pregnant women..."(DeVille, et al.) 237
Office for Minority Health, prevention strategies 453
Office of Juvenile Justice and Delinquency Prevention (OJJDP)
contact information 550
federal drug data sources 560–61
Office of National Drug Control Policy (ONDCP) 311
block grant program 75
contact information 551
drug control strategy 77
Drug-free Communities Support Program 71
drug use and HIV transmission 228
federal drug data sources 558
methadone maintenance treatment (MMT) 324
methamphetamine 201n
"Pulse Check" 70
scope of cocaine use 156
Subcommittee on Data, Evaluation, and Interagency Coordination 76
Office of Personnel Management (OPM), contact information 551
Ohio Department of Alcohol and Drug Addiction Services, contact information 576
OJJDP *see* Office of Juvenile Justice and Delinquency Prevention
Oklahoma Department of Mental Health and Substance Abuse Services
contact information 576
ondansetron HC1 dihydrate 81, 84
ONDCP *see* Office of National Drug Control Policy
opiate abstinence syndromes 277

opiates
  detoxification 277–82, 288, 311–25
  jail inmates 66–68
  overview 11–13
  stress hormones 115
  see also narcotics
opioid analogs 174
opioid peptides 114, 115, 120
opioids 4, 461
  addiction 119–21
opiophobia, described 120
opium 119, 125, 128
  street terms 466, 468, 469, 474,
    479, 480, 484–86, 495–99, 507,
    509
OPM *see* Office of Personnel Management
opportunistic infections 82
Oregon Office of Alcohol and Drug
  Abuse Programs, contact information 576
ORLAAM *see* levo-alpha-acetyl-methadol
orthostatic hypotension, defined 462
overdose
  heroin 169
  sedatives 16
oxandrolone 149
oxazepam 136
  withdrawal 283
oxycodone 129, 130
  street terms 498, 499
oxymetholone 149
oxymorphone 129

P

pain medications, addiction 119–21
paint thinner 150
pancreatitis, defined 462
Papaver somniferum 127
paregoric, street terms 483, 497
*Parenting Is Prevention: Resource
  Guide* 515n
Parenting Wisely (PW): An Interactive CD-ROM Program 529–30
The Parent Project, contact information 528–29

Parents and Adolescents Recovering
  Together Successfully (PARTS), contact information 519
"A Parent's Guide to Preventing Inhalant Abuse" 391n
Parents Place, web site 535
Parents Resource Institute for Drug
  Education, Inc., web site 537
Parent Teacher Association (PTA),
  anti-drug policy 387
Parent to Parent, contact information
  520, 530–32
Parest (methaqualone) 507
paresthesia, defined 462
Park, Alice 111
Parke Davis & Company,
  methcathinone studies 198
Parkinson's disease
  dopamine 95, 106
  meperidine 131
Partnership for a Drug-Free
  America
  contact information 520
  web site 520, 535
PARTS *see* Parents and Adolescents
  Recovering Together Successfully
PATCH *see* Planned Approach to
  Community Health
Patient Care, "Does Marijuana Have
  a Place in Medicine" (Capaldina, et
  al.) 79n
patient rights, detoxification programs 292
Paxipam (halazepam) 136
PBZ *see* pyribenzamine
PCP *see* phencyclidine
PDFY *see* Preparing for the Drug-Free Years
Peck, Richard L. 99–102
Pediatrics, "Birth outcome from a
  prospective, matched study of prenatal crack/cocaine use" (Eyler, et
  al.) 237
Pennsylvania Office of Drug and Alcohol Programs, contact information 577
pentazocine 132
  street terms 491, 504, 507–10

pentobarbital 16, 135
  street terms 469, 496, 512
  withdrawal 283
pentobarbital challenge, defined 462
Pentothal (thiopental) 134
Pentz, M. A. 436n
Percodan (oxycodone) 498, 499
peyote 13, 143
  street terms 467, 471, 473, 482,
    486–88, 496, 503, 509
phenanthrenes 128
phencyclidine (PCP) 13–14, 26–27,
  49, 145–46, 213–15
  detoxification 287
  street terms 14, 26–27, 465–513
phendimetrazine 142
phenmetrazine hydrochloride, street
  terms 500
phenobarbital 135
  street terms 481, 499
  withdrawal 283, 286
phentermine 142, 470
phenylpropanolamine 152
  street terms 500
Phil, R. O. 271
physical dependence, defined 462
Pickens, Jeffrey 237
Pickens, R. W. 343
Placidyl (ethchlorvynol) 16
Planned Approach to Community
  Health (PATCH), contact information 544
Plegine (phendimetrazine) 142
Plessinger, Mark A. 237
poly-drug users
  defined 462
  treatment 349
Pondimin (fenfluramine) 142
poppies 127–28
*Practice Guideline for the Treatment
  of Patients with Nicotine Dependence* 19
*Practice Guideline for the Treatment
  of Patients with Substance Use Disorders: Alcohol, Cocaine, Opioids* 19
prazepam 136
pregnancy
  cocaine use 10, 161, 231–37
  drug use trends 43–44

pregnancy, continued
  heroin use 171
  marijuana 8
  marijuana use 187–89
  opiate addiction 13, 317
  sedatives 16–17
Prelu-2 (phendimetrazine) 142
Preludin (phenmetrazine hydrochloride) 30
  street terms 500
Preparing for the Drug-Free Years
  (PDFY), contact information 532
President and Fellows of Harvard
  College, cocaine before birth 231n
*Preventing Drug Use Among Children
  and Adolescents: A Research-Based
  Guide* 97, 436
*Prevention Primer: An Encyclopedia
  of Alcohol, Tobacco, and Other Drug
  Prevention Terms* 441n, 539n, 543n
prisoners, drug use 63, 66–68
prochlorperazine maleate 81
Project Alert, Best Foundation 422–
  23
  contact information 423
  drug abuse prevention curricula
    427
ProSom (etazolam) 136
protracted abstinence syndrome, defined 462
Prozac 104
psilocybin 143
  street terms 471, 473, 482, 484,
    487, 492, 493, 495, 496, 502–4
psilocyn 143
  street terms 471, 473, 484, 493,
    495, 496, 504
psychiatric concerns, marijuana 7
psychotherapists, alcoholism 6
PTA *see* Parent Teacher Association
PTA Drug and Alcohol Abuse Prevention Project, contact information
  520
Public Law 101-226, prevention strategies 443
Puerto Ricans 437–39
  see also Hispanics
Puerto Rico Department of Health,
  contact information 580

"Pulmonary hazards of smoking marijuana as compared with tobacco" (Wu, et al.) 86
"Pulse Check"
drug control strategy 71
federal drug data sources 558
Purdue University, Families Can Make A Difference: A Substance Abuse Prevention Program 525
PW *see* Parenting Wisely: An Interactive CD-ROM Program
pyramiding, described 149
pyribenzamine (PBZ) 504, 508–10

Q

Quaalude (methaqualone) 16, 26, 135
jail inmates 66–68
street terms 478, 479, 491–93, 500, 501, 508, 511, 512
quazepam 136
Quechua Indians, cocaine before birth 235
Quick American Archives, marijuana publication 86

R

racial factor
drug use, pregnancy 44
HIV transmission 226
Rational Recovery, contact information 542
raves
described 145
GHB use at 166
ketamine use at 180
receptor system, drugs 93–94
Reckitt & Colman Pharmaceuticals, Inc., buprenorphine update 329
Recovery Attitude Treatment Evaluator (RATE) 351
recrudescence, defined 462
relapse prevention 353–55
antistress medications 339–40
defined 463
stress 113

Relapse Prevention Counseling for African-Americans: A Culturally Specific Model (Williams) 354, 355
Renalso, Vicki J. 30
reproductive capability, marijuana 8
Research Triangle Institute, drug use costs report 3
Restoril (temazepam) 136
Rhode Island Department of Health, contact information 577
Ricaurte, George 248
Rickels, K. 284
Rios, Rafael 105, 108, 111
Ritalin (methylphenidate) 26, 141, 211–12, 212n, 345, 346
street terms 491, 499, 505, 511
Rivara, Frederick P. 269, 271
Rivotril (benzodiazepine) 26
RJR Nabisco 104
Rodman, Nathaniel F. 401n, 414
Rohypnol (flunitrazepam) 26, 136, 166, 217–18
street terms 217, 482, 483, 493, 495, 499, 502
Rosenthal, E. 86
Ross, D. 271
Roxanol (morphine) 128
rush, defined 463
Rushforth, Norman B. 271

S

Safe and Drug-Free Schools Program, contact information 520–21
A Safe Haven (Chicago) 106
SafeHomes 521
Sager, Alka 31
SAID *see* Substance Abuse Information Database
Salk Institute 107
Salloum, I. M. 271
SAMHSA *see* Substance Abuse and Mental Health Services Administration
Sanorex (mazindol) 142
Satel, S. L. 343
Scafidi, Frank 237
Scherling, Donald 237
schizophrenia, dopamine 95, 106

Schubiner, H. 347
Schuster, Charles 107
Schwartz, R. H. 86
Schweizer, E. 284
secobarbital 16, 135
   street terms 470, 493, 499, 501, 503
   withdrawal 283
Seconal (secobarbital) 16, 135
   street terms 470, 493, 499, 501, 503
   withdrawal 283
Secretary's Youth Substance Abuse
   Prevention Initiative: Resource Pa-
   pers 249n
sedatives 15–17
   detoxification 282–86
seizures
   cocaine use 9
   grand mal, defined 460
   treatment 136
selegeline 162
Self, David 110
septicemia, street terms 476
Serax (oxazepam) 136
   withdrawal 283
serotonin 104
   agonists 341–43
   antagonists 80, 81
Services Research Outcomes Study
   (SROS) 557
SFP *see* Strengthening Families Program
Shaffer, David 265
Shaham, Yavin 339
Shalala, Donna E. 33, 34
Sheridan, M. J. 86
side effects
   amphetamines 153–54
   anabolic steroid use 219–20
   cocaine use 9–10, 158–60
     impaired function 245–46
     mental deficits 239–44
   heroin use 169–71
   inhalant use 15, 150, 177, 392
   LSD 144
   marijuana use 7–8, 186–87
   MDMA 193–94
   methamphetamine use 202
   methcathinone use 199–200
   narcotics 125–26
   opiate use 12

side effects, continued
   PCP 145–46
   PCP use 213–14
   sedative-hypnotics 16
   stimulants 137–38
Siemianowski, Daniel G. 30
signs, defined 463
Simmons, Steve 30
Simpson, Don 30, 31
Single Convention on Narcotic Drugs
   (1961) 51
sleeping pills *see* sedatives
The Small Book (Trimpey) 542
smoking cessation programs 18
Social Development Research Group,
   Focus on Families 525–26
   contact information 525
solvents 175
   detoxification 288
Soma (carisoprodol) 129
Somes, Grant 271
somnolence, defined 463
Sopor (methaqualone) 16, 135
   street terms 505, 507
The Sourcebook of Criminal Justice
   Statistics 59
South Carolina Department of Alcohol and Other Drug Abuse Services,
   contact information 577
South Dakota Department of Human
   Services, contact information 577
Sparenborg, Steven 333, 334
spray paints 14
Spurlock, V. L. 525
SROS *see* Services Research Outcomes Study
stanozolol 149
STAR Institute for Prevention Research
   contact information 424
   drug abuse prevention curricula
     427–28
State of Wisconsin, trends in workplace substance abuse 40
Steele, Paul D. 401n, 414
steroids
   street terms 466, 471, 478, 480,
     494, 500, 501, 506, 510, 512
   see also anabolic steroids

Stewart, Jane 339, 340
Stilkind, Jerry 91n, 98
stimulants 137–42
  adolescent usage 34
  detoxification 286–87
  drug abuse trends 25–26
  jail inmates 66–68
Stocker, Steven 113n, 239n, 244
STP *see* 4-Methyl-2,5-
  dimethoxyamphetamine
Strain, Eric C. 327
*Street Terms: Drugs and The Drug
  Trade* (ONDCP) 465n
Strengthening America's Families,
  web site 535
Strengthening Families Program,
  contact information 533
Strengthening Multi-Ethnic Families
  and Communities, contact information 534
stress
  drug addiction 113–17
  treatment 339–40
Strickland, Tony 241, 243
STRIDE *see* System to Retrieve Information from Drug Evidence
stroke, cocaine use 9, 239–44
strychnine 167
  street terms 467, 482
"Studies Link Stress and Drug Addiction" (Stocker) 113n
Sublimaze (fentanyl) 132
substance abuse
  crime statistics 59–68
  overview 3–22
  prevention 96–97, 415–32
    programs, listed 415–32
  research 73
  statistics 3
    nationwide 23–27
    prescription medications 29–31
  types, described 125–50
  workplace 401–14
  see also alcohol abuse; *individual drugs*
"Substance Abuse Among Women in
  the United States" 44n
Substance Abuse and Mental Health
  Services Administration (SAMHSA)
  annual survey 360n

Substance Abuse and Mental Health
  Services Administration
  (SAMHSA), continued
  block grant program 75
  Center for Substance Abuse Preven-
    tion 545
  contact information 21, 551–52
  detoxification 275n
  drug use and HIV transmission 228
  emerging drug problems 76
  epidemiology of drug abuse 191n
  federal drug data sources 553, 556,
    557
  Knowledge Development and Appli-
    cation program 72
  legal and ethical issues 289n
  LSD 184n
  MDMA 196n
  methamphetamine use 203
  "National Household Survey on
    Drug Abuse" 27, 178n
  National Treatment Improvement
    Evaluation Study 366, 367
  parent resource guide 515n
  prevention and treatment services 71
  "Substance Abuse Among Women in
    the United States" 44n
  Substance Abuse Prevention and
    Treatment 72
  trends in workplace substance
    abuse 39n
  "Violence Data Exchange Teams" 70
*Substance Abuse and Treatment,
  State and Federal Prisoners*
  "Bureau of Justice Statistics (BJS)"
    60
Substance Abuse Information Data-
  base (SAID) 548
substance dependence *versus* sub-
  stance abuse 4
Substance Disorder Diagnostic
  Schedule (SUDDS) 351
Sufenta (fentanyl) 132
sufentanil 132
Superman syndrome, described 154
Surital (thiamylal) 134
Survey of Inmates in Local Jails 560
Survey of Inmates in State and Fed-
  eral Correctional Facilities 63, 66

Survey of Inmates in State Correctional Facilities 63, 560–61
symptom rebound, defined 463
symptoms, defined 463
System to Retrieve Information from Drug Evidence (STRIDE) 559

T

tachycardia, defined 463
Talarico, Lori D. 79n, 87
talbutal 135
Talwin (pentazocine) 49, 132
  street terms 491, 504, 507–10
Tannatt, Lupita Montoya 526
Targ, Dena 525
Targeted Attention Deficit Disorder Symptoms Scale (TADDS) 345–46
Tashkin, Donald P. 79n, 86, 263
tea 3
  see also caffeine
TEDS see *Treatment Episode Data Set (TEDS)*
Teenage Health Teaching Modules, Educational Development Center 424–25
  contact information 424
  drug abuse prevention curricula 427
teenagers *see* adolescents
temazepam 136
Tennessee Department of Health, contact information 578
The Tennessee Statewide Clearinghouse
  contact information 166, 218
  GHB (Gamma-Hydroxybutyrate) distribution 165n
  rohypnol 217n
Tenuate (diethylproprion) 141
Tepanil (diethylproprion) 141
terpin hydrate with codeine 483, 510
testosterone 149, 219
tetanus, opiate use 13
tetrahydrocannabinol (THC) 251, 508
Texas Commission on Alcohol and Drug Abuse, contact information 578

THC *see* delta-9-tetrahydrocannabinol; tetrahydrocannabinol
thebaine 129
therapeutic dosage, defined 463
thiamylal 134
thiopental 134
Thomas, George A. 349n, 352
3,4-methylenedioxyamphetamine (MDA) 145, 194
Time, "Addicted: Why Do People Get Hooked?" (Nash) 103n
Time Life Syndication, addiction publication 103n
Tinsley-Williams, Alberta 446
TNPC *see* The National Parenting Center
tobacco use
  marijuana experimentation 7
  pregnancy 43
  pulmonary damage 250
  see also nicotine
tolerance, defined 463
toluene 150, 176, 509
tranquilizers
  jail inmates 66–68
  see also sedatives
Tranxene (clorazepate) 16, 136
treatment
  addictions 111, 305–9, 349–52, 361–70
    opiates 311–25
    women 357–60
  chemical dependencies 306–7
  cocaine 162–63
  financial considerations 350–52
  heroin addiction 13
  Medicaid 350
  nausea 80–81
  poly-drug users 349
  seizures 136
  stress 339–40
Treatment Episode Data Set (TEDS) 70
"Treatment Medications" 305n
"Treatment Methods" 305n
trenbolone 149
triage, defined 463
triazolam 136
  withdrawal 283

trichloroethylene 150
Trimpey, Jack 542
The Trustees of Indiana University
  amphetamines 151n
  methcathinone 197n
tuberculosis, opiate users 312
Tucker, Eric C. 30
Tuinal (amobarbital/secobarbital)
  501, 508, 509, 510
2C-B *see* 4-bromo-2,5-
  dimethoxyphenethylamone
Tylenol (acetaminophen) 49
  with codeine 128
  street terms 479, 482, 508
Tzelepis, A. 347

U

UCR *see* "Uniform Crime Reports:
  Crime in the United States"
"Uniform Crime Reports: Crime in
  the United States" (UCR)
  federal drug data sources 559
The United States Coast Guard
  (USCG), contact information 545–46
University of Illinois at Chicago, So-
  cial Competence Promotion Pro-
  gram 423–24
  contact information 424
  drug abuse prevention curricula
    426–27
University of Michigan
  Institute for Social Research
    contact information 420
  LSD 184n
  marijuana use 190n
  MDMA 196n
  Monitoring the Future study
    (MTF) 33, 35, 178n
  web site 37
  Youth Risk and Behavioral Survey
    System 222n
  methamphetamine use 203
University of Minnesota, Project
  Northland
  contact information 423
  drug abuse prevention curricula
    427–28

up-regulation, defined 463
US Bureau Census
  drug and alcohol testing in the
    workplace 408
  prevention strategies 450
US Consumer Product Safety Com-
  mission (CPSC), inhalant abuse fact
  sheet 391n
US Court of Appeals, controlled sub-
  stances challenge 50
US Department of Defense 554
  Health Affairs, contact information
    546
US Department of Education 546–47
  contact information 373n
  Drug Abuse Prevention Oversight,
    contact information 546
  Fund for the Improvement of
    Postsecondary Education
    (FIPSE) 444
  Network of Colleges and Universities
    Committed to the Elimination of
    Drug and Alcohol Abuse 444
  parent resource guide 515n
  Safe and Drug-Free Schools Pro-
    gram 520–21
US Department of Health, Education,
  and Welfare 250
US Department of Health and Hu-
  man Services (DHHS)
  Administration for Children and
    Families, contact information 543
  buprenorphine update 332
  Center for Substance Abuse Treat-
    ment, contact information 386
  Controlled Substances Act (CSA)
    45, 46
  drug use problems 76
  federal drug data sources 557
  mandatory reporting 296
  methadone maintenance treatment
    (MMT) 322
  Youth Substance Abuse Prevention
    Initiative 72
US Department of Housing and Urban Development (HUD)
  Drug Information and Strategy
    Clearinghouse, contact informa-
    tion 547

US Department of Justice (DoJ)
Bureau of Justice Statistics, web
site 59n
Controlled Substances Act (CSA)
45n
ketamine use 179n
medical treatment for opiate addiction 311
methadone maintenance treatment
(MMT) 324
National Criminal Justice Reference Service (NCJRS)
Office of Justice Programs, contact information 547
Office of Juvenile Justice and
Delinqency Prevention, contact
information 550
web site 535
see also Drug Enforcement Administration
US Department of Labor
drug testing in the workplace 401n
federal drug data sources 554
Substance Abuse Information Database (SAID), contact information 548
workplace substance abuse program
395n
US Department of State, federal drug
data sources 558
US Department of Transportation
(DOT)
drug and alcohol testing in the
workplace 409
drug testing in the workplace 404
US Drug-Free Schools and Communities Act Amendments (1989) 443
user accountability, described 55–56
US Food and Drug Administration
(FDA)
approval of LAAM 173, 277
buprenorphine
approval 279
update 329, 330, 331
clonidine for opiate withdrawal
278
Controlled Substances Act 46
dispensing records 54
GHB distribution 165

US Food and Drug Administration
(FDA), continued
methadone maintenance treatment
321, 322
methylphenidate 212
tobacco regulation 104
treatment methods and medications
308
USIA Electronic Journal, "Addiction
is a Brain Disease" (Stilkind) 91n
Utah Department of Human Services,
contact information 578
Utah Power & Light 40

V

Valium (diazepam) 16, 49, 136
street terms 495, 510
withdrawal 283
Vermont Agency of Human Services,
contact information 578
Versed (midazolam) 136
vertigo, defined 463
Veterans Administration, contact in-
formation 548
Vilensky, William 79n, 87
violence, substance abuse 60–63,
269–71
Virginia Office of Substance Abuse
Services, contact information 579
Virgin Islands Department of Human
Services, contact information 581
Volkow, Nora 104, 105, 107, 108, 241
Volpe, Joseph J. 237
Voth, E. A. 86

W

Washburn, A. M. 281
Washington Department of Social
and Health Services, contact infor-
mation 579
Washousky, Richard C. 349n, 352
water pipes 82
Wayne State University 107
Weikel, Dan 29
Wender Utah Rating Scale (WURS)
345

West Virginia Department of Health and Human Resources, contact information 579
WFS *see* Women for Sobriety, Inc.
White House Office of National Drug Control Policy, web site 535
Williams, Roland 353, 354, 355
Winstrol (stanozolol) 149
Wisconsin Department of Health and Family Services, contact information 579–80
Wise, Roy 106
withdrawal, defined 463
withdrawal symptoms 4, 5
  addiction 93
  depressants 134
  narcotics 126–27
  opiates 12
  see also detoxification
women, addiction treatment 357–60
Women for Sobriety, Inc. (WFS), contact information 542
Woods, James R., Jr. 237
workplace
  drug testing 399–400, 401–14
  substance abuse prevention 395–400
  substance abuse statistics 39–42

Worldwide Survey of Substance Abuse and Health Behaviors among Military Personnel 554
Wu, T-C 86
Wyoming Department of Health, contact information 580

X

Xanax (alprazolam) 49, 136
  withdrawal 283

Y

Yale University Press, marijuana publication 86
Yokel, Robert 106
Youth Power, contact information 521
"Youth Risk Behavior Surveillance System" 556

Z

Zickler, Patrick 35, 333n, 437n
zidovudine 317

Health Reference Series
COMPLETE CATALOG

AIDS Sourcebook,
1st Edition

Basic Information about AIDS and HIV Infection, Featuring Historical and Statistical Data, Current Research, Prevention, and Other Special Topics of Interest for Persons Living with AIDS

Along with Source Listings for Further Assistance

Edited by Karen Bellenir and Peter D. Dresser. 831 pages. 1995. 0-7808-0031-1. $78.

"One strength of this book is its practical emphasis. The intended audience is the lay reader . . . useful as an educational tool for health care providers who work with AIDS patients. Recommended for public libraries as well as hospital or academic libraries that collect consumer materials."
— Bulletin of the Medical Library Association, Jan '96

"This is the most comprehensive volume of its kind on an important medical topic. Highly recommended for all libraries." — Reference Book Review, '96

"Very useful reference for all libraries."
— Choice, Association of College and Research Libraries, Oct '95

"There is a wealth of information here that can provide much educational assistance. It is a must book for all libraries and should be on the desk of each and every congressional leader. Highly recommended."
— AIDS Book Review Journal, Aug '95

"Recommended for most collections."
— Library Journal, Jul '95

AIDS Sourcebook, 2nd Edition

Basic Consumer Health Information about Acquired Immune Deficiency Syndrome (AIDS) and Human Immunodeficiency Virus (HIV) Infection, Featuring Updated Statistical Data, Reports on Recent Research and Prevention Initiatives, and Other Special Topics of Interest for Persons Living with AIDS, Including New Antiretroviral Treatment Options, Strategies for Combating Opportunistic Infections, Information about Clinical Trials, and More

Along with a Glossary of Important Terms and Resource Listings for Further Help and Information

Edited by Karen Bellenir. 751 pages. 1999. 0-7808-0225-X. $78.

"Highly recommended."
— American Reference Books Annual, 2000

"Excellent sourcebook. This continues to be a highly recommended book. There is no other book that provides as much information as this book provides."
— AIDS Book Review Journal, Dec-Jan 2000

"Recommended reference source."
— Booklist, American Library Association, Dec '99

"A solid text for college-level health libraries."
— The Bookwatch, Aug '99

Cited in Reference Sources for Small and Medium-Sized Libraries, American Library Association, 1999

Alcoholism Sourcebook

Basic Consumer Health Information about the Physical and Mental Consequences of Alcohol Abuse, Including Liver Disease, Pancreatitis, Wernicke-Korsakoff Syndrome (Alcoholic Dementia), Fetal Alcohol Syndrome, Heart Disease, Kidney Disorders, Gastrointestinal Problems, and Immune System Compromise and Featuring Facts about Addiction, Detoxification, Alcohol Withdrawal, Recovery, and the Maintenance of Sobriety

Along with a Glossary and Directories of Resources for Further Help and Information

Edited by Karen Bellenir. 635 pages. 2000. 0-7808-0325-6. $78.

SEE ALSO Drug Abuse Sourcebook, Substance Abuse Sourcebook

Allergies Sourcebook

Basic Information about Major Forms and Mechanisms of Common Allergic Reactions, Sensitivities, and Intolerances, Including Anaphylaxis, Asthma, Hives and Other Dermatologic Symptoms, Rhinitis, and Sinusitis

Along with Their Usual Triggers Like Animal Fur, Chemicals, Drugs, Dust, Foods, Insects, Latex, Pollen, and Poison Ivy, Oak, and Sumac; Plus Information on Prevention, Identification, and Treatment

Edited by Allan R. Cook. 611 pages. 1997. 0-7808-0036-2. $78.

Alternative Medicine Sourcebook

Basic Consumer Health Information about Alternatives to Conventional Medicine, Including Acupressure, Acupuncture, Aromatherapy, Ayurveda, Bioelectromagnetics, Environmental Medicine, Essence Therapy, Food and Nutrition Therapy, Herbal Therapy, Homeopathy, Imaging, Massage, Naturopathy, Reflexology, Relaxation and Meditation, Sound Therapy, Vitamin and Mineral Therapy, and Yoga, and More

Edited by Allan R. Cook. 737 pages. 1999. 0-7808-0200-4. $78.

"Recommended reference source."
— Booklist, American Library Association, Feb '00

Alzheimer's, Stroke & 29 Other Neurological Disorders Sourcebook, 1st Edition

Basic Information for the Layperson on 31 Diseases or Disorders Affecting the Brain and Nervous System, First Describing the Illness, Then Listing Symptoms, Diagnostic Methods, and Treatment Options, and Including Statistics on Incidences and Causes

Edited by Frank E. Bair. 579 pages. 1993. 1-55888-748-2. $78.

SEE ALSO Brain Disorders Sourcebook

Alzheimer's Disease Sourcebook, 2nd Edition

Basic Consumer Health Information about Alzheimer's Disease, Related Disorders, and Other Dementias, Including Multi-Infarct Dementia, AIDS-Related Dementia, Alcoholic Dementia, Huntington's Disease, Delirium, and Confusional States

Along with Reports Detailing Current Research Efforts in Prevention and Treatment, Long-Term Care Issues, and Listings of Sources for Additional Help and Information

Edited by Karen Bellenir. 524 pages. 1999. 0-7808-0223-3. $78.

Arthritis Sourcebook

Basic Consumer Health Information about Specific Forms of Arthritis and Related Disorders, Including Rheumatoid Arthritis, Osteoarthritis, Gout, Polymyalgia Rheumatica, Psoriatic Arthritis, Spondyloarthropathies, Juvenile Rheumatoid Arthritis, and Juvenile Ankylosing Spondylitis

Along with Information about Medical, Surgical, and Alternative Treatment Options, and Including Strategies for Coping with Pain, Fatigue, and Stress

Edited by Allan R. Cook. 550 pages. 1998. 0-7808-0201-2. $78.

Asthma Sourcebook

Basic Consumer Health Information about Asthma, Including Symptoms, Traditional and Nontraditional Remedies, Treatment Advances, Quality-of-Life Aids, Medical Research Updates, and the Role of Allergies, Exercise, Age, the Environment, and Genetics in the Development of Asthma

Along with Statistical Data, a Glossary, and Directories of Support Groups and Other Resources for Further Information

Edited by Annemarie S. Muth. 650 pages. 2000. 0-7808-0381-7. $78.

Back & Neck Disorders Sourcebook

Basic Information about Disorders and Injuries of the Spinal Cord and Vertebrae, Including Facts on Chiropractic Treatment, Surgical Interventions, Paralysis, and Rehabilitation

Along with Advice for Preventing Back Trouble

Edited by Karen Bellenir. 548 pages. 1997. 0-7808-0202-0. $78.

Blood & Circulatory Disorders Sourcebook

Basic Information about Blood and Its Components, Anemias, Leukemias, Bleeding Disorders, and Circulatory Disorders, Including Aplastic Anemia, Thalassemia, Sickle-Cell Disease, Hemochromatosis, Hemophilia, Von Willebrand Disease, and Vascular Diseases

Along with a Special Section on Blood Transfusions and Blood Supply Safety, a Glossary, and Source Listings for Further Help and Information

Edited by Karen Bellenir and Linda M. Shin. 554 pages. 1998. 0-7808-0203-9. $78.

Brain Disorders Sourcebook

Basic Consumer Health Information about Strokes, Epilepsy, Amyotrophic Lateral Sclerosis (ALS/Lou Gehrig's Disease), Parkinson's Disease, Brain Tumors, Cerebral Palsy, Headache, Tourette Syndrome, and More

Along with Statistical Data, Treatment and Rehabilitation Options, Coping Strategies, Reports on Current Research Initiatives, a Glossary, and Resource Listings for Additional Help and Information

Edited by Karen Bellenir. 481 pages. 1999. 0-7808-0229-2. $78.

SEE ALSO Alzheimer's, Stroke & 29 Other Neurological Disorders Sourcebook, 1st Edition

Breast Cancer Sourcebook

Basic Consumer Health Information about Breast Cancer, Including Diagnostic Methods, Treatment Options, Alternative Therapies, Help and Self-Help Information, Related Health Concerns, Statistical and Demographic Data, and Facts for Men with Breast Cancer

Along with Reports on Current Research Initiatives, a Glossary of Related Medical Terms, and a Directory of Sources for Further Help and Information

Edited by Edward J. Prucha. 600 pages. 2000. 0-7808-0244-6. $78.

SEE ALSO Cancer Sourcebook for Women, 1st and 2nd Editions, Women's Health Concerns Sourcebook

Burns Sourcebook

Basic Consumer Health Information about Various Types of Burns and Scalds, Including Flame, Heat, Cold, Electrical, Chemical, and Sun Burns

Along with Information on Short-Term and Long-Term Treatments, Tissue Reconstruction, Plastic Surgery, Prevention Suggestions, and First Aid

Edited by Allan R. Cook. 604 pages. 1999. 0-7808-0204-7. $78.

SEE ALSO Skin Disorders Sourcebook

Cancer Sourcebook, 1st Edition

Basic Information on Cancer Types, Symptoms, Diagnostic Methods, and Treatments, Including Statistics on Cancer Occurrences Worldwide and the Risks Associated with Known Carcinogens and Activities

Edited by Frank E. Bair. 932 pages. 1990. 1-55888-888-8. $78.

Cited in Reference Sources for Small and Medium-Sized Libraries, American Library Association, 1999

New Cancer Sourcebook, 2nd Edition

Basic Information about Major Forms and Stages of Cancer, Featuring Facts about Primary and Secondary Tumors of the Respiratory, Nervous, Lymphatic, Circulatory, Skeletal, and Gastrointestinal Systems, and Specific Organs; Statistical and Demographic Data; Treatment Options; and Strategies for Coping

Edited by Allan R. Cook. 1,313 pages. 1996. 0-7808-0041-9. $78.

"The amount of factual and useful information is extensive. The writing is very clear, geared to general readers. Recommended for all levels."
—*Choice, Association of College and Research Libraries, Jan '97*

Cancer Sourcebook, 3rd Edition

Basic Consumer Health Information about Major Forms and Stages of Cancer, Featuring Facts about Primary and Secondary Tumors of the Respiratory, Nervous, Lymphatic, Circulatory, Skeletal, and Gastrointestinal Systems, and Specific Organs

Along with Statistical and Demographic Data, Treatment Options, Strategies for Coping, a Glossary, and a Directory of Sources for Additional Help and Information

Edited by Edward J. Prucha. 1,069 pages. 2000. 0-7808-0227-6. $78.

Cancer Sourcebook for Women, 1st Edition

Basic Information about Specific Forms of Cancer That Affect Women, Featuring Facts about Breast Cancer, Cervical Cancer, Ovarian Cancer, Cancer of the Uterus and Uterine Sarcoma, Cancer of the Vagina, and Cancer of the Vulva; Statistical and Demographic Data; Treatments, Self-Help Management Suggestions, and Current Research Initiatives

Edited by Allan R. Cook and Peter D. Dresser. 524 pages. 1996. 0-7808-0076-1. $78.

". . . written in easily understandable, non-technical language. Recommended for public libraries or hospital and academic libraries that collect patient education or consumer health materials."
—*Medical Reference Services Quarterly, Spring '97*

"Would be of value in a consumer health library. . . . written with the health care consumer in mind. Medical jargon is at a minimum, and medical terms are explained in clear, understandable sentences."
—*Bulletin of the Medical Library Association, Oct '96*

"The availability under one cover of all these pertinent publications, grouped under cohesive headings, makes this certainly a most useful sourcebook."
—*Choice, Association of College and Research Libraries, Jun '96*

"Presents a comprehensive knowledge base for general readers. Men and women both benefit from the gold mine of information nestled between the two covers of this book. Recommended."
—*Academic Library Book Review, Summer '96*

"This timely book is highly recommended for consumer health and patient education collections in all libraries." —*Library Journal, Apr '96*

SEE ALSO *Breast Cancer Sourcebook, Women's Health Concerns Sourcebook*

Cancer Sourcebook for Women, 2nd Edition

Basic Consumer Health Information about Specific Forms of Cancer That Affect Women, Including Cervical Cancer, Ovarian Cancer, Endometrial Cancer, Uterine Sarcoma, Vaginal Cancer, Vulvar Cancer, and Gestational Trophoblastic Tumor; and Featuring Statistical Information, Facts about Tests and Treatments, a Glossary of Cancer Terms, and an Extensive List of Additional Resources

Edited by Edward J. Prucha. 600 pages. 2000. 0-7808-0226-8. $78.

SEE ALSO *Breast Cancer Sourcebook, Women's Health Concerns Sourcebook*

Cardiovascular Diseases & Disorders Sourcebook, 1st Edition

Basic Information about Cardiovascular Diseases and Disorders, Featuring Facts about the Cardiovascular System, Demographic and Statistical Data, Descriptions of Pharmacological and Surgical Interventions, Lifestyle Modifications, and a Special Section Focusing on Heart Disorders in Children

Edited by Karen Bellenir and Peter D. Dresser. 683 pages. 1995. 0-7808-0032-X. $78.

". . . comprehensive format provides an extensive overview on this subject."
—*Choice, Association of College and Research Libraries, Jun '96*

". . . an easily understood, complete, up-to-date resource. This well executed public health tool will make valuable information available to those that need it most, patients and their families. The typeface, sturdy non-reflective paper, and library binding add a feel of quality found wanting in other publications. Highly recommended for academic and general libraries. "
—*Academic Library Book Review, Summer '96*

SEE ALSO *Healthy Heart Sourcebook for Women, Heart Diseases & Disorders Sourcebook, 2nd Edition*

Communication Disorders Sourcebook

Basic Information about Deafness and Hearing Loss, Speech and Language Disorders, Voice Disorders, Balance and Vestibular Disorders, and Disorders of Smell, Taste, and Touch

Edited by Linda M. Ross. 533 pages. 1996. 0-7808-0077-X. $78.

"This is skillfully edited and is a welcome resource for the layperson. It should be found in every public and medical library." —*Booklist Health Sciences Supplement, American Library Association, Oct '97*

Congenital Disorders Sourcebook

Basic Information about Disorders Acquired during Gestation, Including Spina Bifida, Hydrocephalus, Cerebral Palsy, Heart Defects, Craniofacial Abnormalities, Fetal Alcohol Syndrome, and More

Along with Current Treatment Options and Statistical Data

Edited by Karen Bellenir. 607 pages. 1997. 0-7808-0205-5. $78.

"Recommended reference source."
— *Booklist, American Library Association, Oct '97*

SEE ALSO Pregnancy & Birth Sourcebook

■

Consumer Issues in Health Care Sourcebook

Basic Information about Health Care Fundamentals and Related Consumer Issues, Including Exams and Screening Tests, Physician Specialties, Choosing a Doctor, Using Prescription and Over-the-Counter Medications Safely, Avoiding Health Scams, Managing Common Health Risks in the Home, Care Options for Chronically or Terminally Ill Patients, and a List of Resources for Obtaining Help and Further Information

Edited by Karen Bellenir. 618 pages. 1998. 0-7808-0221-7. $78.

"Both public and academic libraries will want to have a copy in their collection for readers who are interested in self-education on health issues."
— *American Reference Books Annual, 2000*

"The editor has researched the literature from government agencies and others, saving readers the time and effort of having to do the research themselves. Recommended for public libraries."
— *Reference and User Services Quarterly, American Library Association, Spring '99*

"Recommended reference source."
— *Booklist, American Library Association, Dec '98*

■

Contagious & Non-Contagious Infectious Diseases Sourcebook

Basic Information about Contagious Diseases like Measles, Polio, Hepatitis B, and Infectious Mononucleosis, and Non-Contagious Infectious Diseases like Tetanus and Toxic Shock Syndrome, and Diseases Occurring as Secondary Infections Such as Shingles and Reye Syndrome

Along with Vaccination, Prevention, and Treatment Information, and a Section Describing Emerging Infectious Disease Threats

Edited by Karen Bellenir and Peter D. Dresser. 566 pages. 1996. 0-7808-0075-3. $78.

Death & Dying Sourcebook

Basic Consumer Health Information for the Layperson about End-of-Life Care and Related Ethical and Legal Issues, Including Chief Causes of Death, Autopsies, Pain Management for the Terminally Ill, Life Support Systems, Insurance, Euthanasia, Assisted Suicide, Hospice Programs, Living Wills, Funeral Planning, Counseling, Mourning, Organ Donation, and Physician Training

Along with Statistical Data, a Glossary, and Listings of Sources for Further Help and Information

Edited by Annemarie S. Muth. 641 pages. 1999. 0-7808-0230-6. $78.

"This book is a definite must for all those involved in end-of-life care." — *Doody's Review Service, 2000*

■

Diabetes Sourcebook, 1st Edition

Basic Information about Insulin-Dependent and Noninsulin-Dependent Diabetes Mellitus, Gestational Diabetes, and Diabetic Complications, Symptoms, Treatment, and Research Results, Including Statistics on Prevalence, Morbidity, and Mortality

Along with Source Listings for Further Help and Information

Edited by Karen Bellenir and Peter D. Dresser. 827 pages. 1994. 1-55888-751-2. $78.

". . . very informative and understandable for the layperson without being simplistic. It provides a comprehensive overview for laypersons who want a general understanding of the disease or who want to focus on various aspects of the disease."
— *Bulletin of the Medical Library Association, Jan '96*

■

Diabetes Sourcebook, 2nd Edition

Basic Consumer Health Information about Type 1 Diabetes (Insulin-Dependent or Juvenile-Onset Diabetes), Type 2 (Noninsulin-Dependent or Adult-Onset Diabetes), Gestational Diabetes, and Related Disorders, Including Diabetes Prevalence Data, Management Issues, the Role of Diet and Exercise in Controlling Diabetes, Insulin and Other Diabetes Medicines, and Complications of Diabetes Such as Eye Diseases, Periodontal Disease, Amputation, and End-Stage Renal Disease

Along with Reports on Current Research Initiatives, a Glossary, and Resource Listings for Further Help and Information

Edited by Karen Bellenir. 688 pages. 1998. 0-7808-0224-1. $78.

"This comprehensive book is an excellent addition for high school, academic, medical, and public libraries. This volume is highly recommended."
— *American Reference Books Annual, 2000*

"An invaluable reference." — *Library Journal, May '00*

Selected as one of the 250 "Best Health Sciences Books of 1999." — *Doody's Rating Service, Mar-Apr 2000*

"Recommended reference source."
— *Booklist, American Library Association, Feb '99*

". . . provides reliable mainstream medical information . . . belongs on the shelves of any library with a consumer health collection." — *E-Streams, Sep '99*

"Provides useful information for the general public."
— *Healthlines, University of Michigan Health Management Research Center, Sep/Oct '99*

■

Diet & Nutrition Sourcebook, 1st Edition

Basic Information about Nutrition, Including the Dietary Guidelines for Americans, the Food Guide Pyramid, and Their Applications in Daily Diet, Nutritional Advice for Specific Age Groups, Current Nutritional Issues and Controversies, the New Food Label and How to Use It to Promote Healthy Eating, and Recent Developments in Nutritional Research

Edited by Dan R. Harris. 662 pages. 1996. 0-7808-0084-2. $78.

"Useful reference as a food and nutrition sourcebook for the general consumer." — *Booklist Health Sciences Supplement, American Library Association, Oct '97*

"Recommended for public libraries and medical libraries that receive general information requests on nutrition. It is readable and will appeal to those interested in learning more about healthy dietary practices."
— *Medical Reference Services Quarterly, Fall '97*

"An abundance of medical and social statistics is translated into readable information geared toward the general reader." — *Bookwatch, Mar '97*

"With dozens of questionable diet books on the market, it is so refreshing to find a reliable and factual reference book. Recommended to aspiring professionals, librarians, and others seeking and giving reliable dietary advice. An excellent compilation." — *Choice, Association of College and Research Libraries, Feb '97*

SEE ALSO Digestive Diseases & Disorders Sourcebook, Gastrointestinal Diseases & Disorders Sourcebook

■

Diet & Nutrition Sourcebook, 2nd Edition

Basic Consumer Health Information about Dietary Guidelines, Recommended Daily Intake Values, Vitamins, Minerals, Fiber, Fat, Weight Control, Dietary Supplements, and Food Additives

Along with Special Sections on Nutrition Needs throughout Life and Nutrition for People with Such Specific Medical Concerns as Allergies, High Blood Cholesterol, Hypertension, Diabetes, Celiac Disease, Seizure Disorders, Phenylketonuria (PKU), Cancer, and Eating Disorders, and Including Reports on Current Nutrition Research and Source Listings for Additional Help and Information

Edited by Karen Bellenir. 650 pages. 1999. 0-7808-0228-4. $78.

"This reference document should be in any public library, but it would be a very good guide for beginning students in the health sciences. If the other books in this publisher's series are as good as this, they should all be in the health sciences collections."
— *American Reference Books Annual, 2000*

"Recommended reference source."
— *Booklist, American Library Association, Dec '99*

SEE ALSO Digestive Diseases & Disorders Sourcebook, Gastrointestinal Diseases & Disorders Sourcebook

■

Digestive Diseases & Disorders Sourcebook

Basic Consumer Health Information about Diseases and Disorders that Impact the Upper and Lower Digestive System, Including Celiac Disease, Constipation, Crohn's Disease, Cyclic Vomiting Syndrome, Diarrhea, Diverticulosis and Diverticulitis, Gallstones, Heartburn, Hemorrhoids, Hernias, Indigestion (Dyspepsia), Irritable Bowel Syndrome, Lactose Intolerance, Ulcers, and More

Along with Information about Medications and Other Treatments, Tips for Maintaining a Healthy Digestive Tract, a Glossary, and Directory of Digestive Diseases Organizations

Edited by Karen Bellenir. 335 pages. 1999. 0-7808-0327-2. $48.

"Recommended reference source."
— *Booklist, American Library Association, May '00*

SEE ALSO Diet & Nutrition Sourcebook, 1st and 2nd Editions, Gastrointestinal Diseases & Disorders Sourcebook

■

Disabilities Sourcebook

Basic Consumer Health Information about Physical and Psychiatric Disabilities, Including Descriptions of Major Causes of Disability, Assistive and Adaptive Aids, Workplace Issues, and Accessibility Concerns

Along with Information about the Americans with Disabilities Act, a Glossary, and Resources for Additional Help and Information

Edited by Dawn D. Matthews. 616 pages. 2000. 0-7808-0389-2. $78.

"Recommended reference source."
— *Booklist, American Library Association, Jul '00*

"An involving, invaluable handbook."
— *The Bookwatch, May '00*

Domestic Violence & Child Abuse Sourcebook

Basic Information about Spousal/ Partner, Child, and Elder Physical, Emotional, and Sexual Abuse, Teen Dating Violence, and Stalking, Including Information about Hotlines, Safe Houses, Safety Plans, and Other Resources for Support and Assistance, Community Initiatives, and Reports on Current Directions in Research and Treatment

Along with a Glossary, Sources for Further Reading, and Governmental and Non-Governmental Organizations Contact Information

Edited by Helene Henderson. 600 pages. 2000. 0-7808-0235-7. $78.

Drug Abuse Sourcebook

Basic Consumer Health Information about Illicit Substances of Abuse and the Diversion of Prescription Medications, Including Depressants, Hallucinogens, Inhalants, Marijuana, Narcotics, Stimulants, and Anabolic Steroids

Along with Facts about Related Health Risks, Treatment Issues, and Substance Abuse Prevention Programs, a Glossary of Terms, Statistical Data, and Directories of Hotline Services, Self-Help Groups, and Organizations Able to Provide Further Information

Edited by Karen Bellenir. 629 pages. 2000. 0-7808-0242-X. $78.

SEE ALSO Alcoholism Sourcebook, Substance Abuse Sourcebook

Ear, Nose & Throat Disorders Sourcebook

Basic Information about Disorders of the Ears, Nose, Sinus Cavities, Pharynx, and Larynx, Including Ear Infections, Tinnitus, Vestibular Disorders, Allergic and Non-Allergic Rhinitis, Sore Throats, Tonsillitis, and Cancers That Affect the Ears, Nose, Sinuses, and Throat

Along with Reports on Current Research Initiatives, a Glossary of Related Medical Terms, and a Directory of Sources for Further Help and Information

Edited by Karen Bellenir and Linda M. Shin. 576 pages. 1998. 0-7808-0206-3. $78.

"Overall, this sourcebook is helpful for the consumer seeking information on ENT issues. It is recommended for public libraries."
—*American Reference Books Annual, 1999*

"Recommended reference source."
—*Booklist, American Library Association, Dec '98*

Endocrine & Metabolic Disorders Sourcebook

Basic Information for the Layperson about Pancreatic and Insulin-Related Disorders Such as Pancreatitis, Diabetes, and Hypoglycemia; Adrenal Gland Disorders Such as Cushing's Syndrome, Addison's Disease, and Congenital Adrenal Hyperplasia; Pituitary Gland Disorders Such as Growth Hormone Deficiency, Acromegaly, and Pituitary Tumors; Thyroid Disorders Such as Hypothyroidism, Graves' Disease, Hashimoto's Disease, and Goiter; Hyperparathyroidism; and Other Diseases and Syndromes of Hormone Imbalance or Metabolic Dysfunction

Along with Reports on Current Research Initiatives

Edited by Linda M. Shin. 574 pages. 1998. 0-7808-0207-1. $78.

"Omnigraphics has produced another needed resource for health information consumers."
—*American Reference Books Annual, 2000*

"Recommended reference source."
—*Booklist, American Library Association, Dec '98*

Environmentally Induced Disorders Sourcebook

Basic Information about Diseases and Syndromes Linked to Exposure to Pollutants and Other Substances in Outdoor and Indoor Environments Such as Lead, Asbestos, Formaldehyde, Mercury, Emissions, Noise, and More

Edited by Allan R. Cook. 620 pages. 1997. 0-7808-0083-4. $78.

"Recommended reference source."
—*Booklist, American Library Association, Sep '98*

"This book will be a useful addition to anyone's library." —*Choice Health Sciences Supplement, Association of College and Research Libraries, May '98*

". . . a good survey of numerous environmentally induced physical disorders . . . a useful addition to anyone's library."
—*Doody's Health Sciences Book Reviews, Jan '98*

". . . provide[s] introductory information from the best authorities around. Since this volume covers topics that potentially affect everyone, it will surely be one of the most frequently consulted volumes in the Health Reference Series." —*Rettig on Reference, Nov '97*

Family Planning Sourcebook

Basic Consumer Health Information about Planning for Pregnancy and Contraception, Including Traditional Methods, Barrier Methods, Permanent Methods, Future Methods, Emergency Contraception, and Birth Control Choices for Women at Each Stage of Life

Along with Statistics, Glossary, and Sources of Additional Information

Edited by Amy Marcaccio Keyzer. 600 pages. 2000. 0-7808-0379-5. $78.

SEE ALSO Pregnancy & Birth Sourcebook

Fitness & Exercise Sourcebook

Basic Information on Fitness and Exercise, Including Fitness Activities for Specific Age Groups, Exercise for People with Specific Medical Conditions, How to Begin a Fitness Program in Running, Walking, Swimming, Cycling, and Other Athletic Activities, and Recent Research in Fitness and Exercise

Edited by Dan R. Harris. 663 pages. 1996. 0-7808-0186-5. $78.

"A good resource for general readers."
— *Choice, Association of College and Research Libraries, Nov '97*

"The perennial popularity of the topic . . . make this an appealing selection for public libraries."
— *Rettig on Reference, Jun/Jul '97*

Food & Animal Borne Diseases Sourcebook

Basic Information about Diseases That Can Be Spread to Humans through the Ingestion of Contaminated Food or Water or by Contact with Infected Animals and Insects, Such as Botulism, E. Coli, Hepatitis A, Trichinosis, Lyme Disease, and Rabies

Along with Information Regarding Prevention and Treatment Methods, and Including a Special Section for International Travelers Describing Diseases Such as Cholera, Malaria, Travelers' Diarrhea, and Yellow Fever, and Offering Recommendations for Avoiding Illness

Edited by Karen Bellenir and Peter D. Dresser. 535 pages. 1995. 0-7808-0033-8. $78.

"Targeting general readers and providing them with a single, comprehensive source of information on selected topics, this book continues, with the excellent caliber of its predecessors, to catalog topical information on health matters of general interest. Readable and thorough, this valuable resource is highly recommended for all libraries."
— *Academic Library Book Review, Summer '96*

"A comprehensive collection of authoritative information." — *Emergency Medical Services, Oct '95*

Food Safety Sourcebook

Basic Consumer Health Information about the Safe Handling of Meat, Poultry, Seafood, Eggs, Fruit Juices, and Other Food Items, and Facts about Pesticides, Drinking Water, Food Safety Overseas, and the Onset, Duration, and Symptoms of Foodborne Illnesses, Including Types of Pathogenic Bacteria, Parasitic Protozoa, Worms, Viruses, and Natural Toxins

Along with the Role of the Consumer, the Food Handler, and the Government in Food Safety; a Glossary, and Resources for Additional Help and Information

Edited by Dawn D. Matthews. 339 pages. 1999. 0-7808-0326-4. $48.

"This book takes the complex issues of food safety and foodborne pathogens and presents them in an easily understood manner. [It does] an excellent job of covering a large and often confusing topic."
— *American Reference Books Annual, 2000*

"Recommended reference source."
— *Booklist, American Library Association, May '00*

Forensic Medicine Sourcebook

Basic Consumer Information for the Layperson about Forensic Medicine, Including Crime Scene Investigation, Evidence Collection and Analysis, Expert Testimony, Computer-Aided Criminal Identification, Digital Imaging in the Courtroom, DNA Profiling, Accident Reconstruction, Autopsies, Ballistics, Drugs and Explosives Detection, Latent Fingerprints, Product Tampering, and Questioned Document Examination

Along with Statistical Data, a Glossary of Forensics Terminology, and Listings of Sources for Further Help and Information

Edited by Annemarie S. Muth. 574 pages. 1999. 0-7808-0232-2. $78.

"There are several items that make this book attractive to consumers who are seeking certain forensic data. . . . This is a useful current source for those seeking general forensic medical answers."
— *American Reference Books Annual, 2000*

"Recommended for public libraries."
— *Reference & User Services Quarterly, American Library Association, Spring 2000*

"Recommended reference source."
— *Booklist, American Library Association, Feb '00*

"A wealth of information, useful statistics, references are up-to-date and extremely complete. This wonderful collection of data will help students who are interested in a career in any type of forensic field. It is a great resource for attorneys who need information about types of expert witnesses needed in a particular case. It also offers useful information for fiction and nonfiction writers whose work involves a crime. A fascinating compilation. All levels."
— *Choice, Association of College and Research Libraries, Jan 2000*

Gastrointestinal Diseases & Disorders Sourcebook

Basic Information about Gastroesophageal Reflux Disease (Heartburn), Ulcers, Diverticulosis, Irritable Bowel Syndrome, Crohn's Disease, Ulcerative Colitis, Diarrhea, Constipation, Lactose Intolerance, Hemorrhoids, Hepatitis, Cirrhosis, and Other Digestive Problems, Featuring Statistics, Descriptions of Symptoms, and Current Treatment Methods of Interest for Persons Living with Upper and Lower Gastrointestinal Maladies

Edited by Linda M. Ross. 413 pages. 1996. 0-7808-0078-8. $78.

". . . very readable form. The successful editorial work that brought this material together into a useful and understandable reference makes accessible to all readers information that can help them more effectively understand and obtain help for digestive tract problems."
— *Choice, Association of College and Research Libraries, Feb '97*

SEE ALSO *Diet & Nutrition Sourcebook, 1st and 2nd Editions, Digestive Diseases & Disorders Sourcebook*

Genetic Disorders Sourcebook, 1st Edition

Basic Information about Heritable Diseases and Disorders Such as Down Syndrome, PKU, Hemophilia, Von Willebrand Disease, Gaucher Disease, Tay-Sachs Disease, and Sickle-Cell Disease, Along with Information about Genetic Screening, Gene Therapy, Home Care, and Including Source Listings for Further Help and Information on More Than 300 Disorders

Edited by Karen Bellenir. 642 pages. 1996. 0-7808-0034-6. $78.

"Recommended for undergraduate libraries or libraries that serve the public."
— *Science & Technology Libraries, Vol. 18, No. 1, '99*

"Provides essential medical information to both the general public and those diagnosed with a serious or fatal genetic disease or disorder."
— *Choice, Association of College and Research Libraries, Jan '97*

"Geared toward the lay public. It would be well placed in all public libraries and in those hospital and medical libraries in which access to genetic references is limited." — *Doody's Health Sciences Book Review, Oct '96*

Genetic Disorders Sourcebook, 2nd Edition

Basic Consumer Information about Hereditary Diseases and Disorders, Including Cystic Fibrosis, Down Syndrome, Hemophilia, Huntington's Disease, Sickle Cell Anemia, and More

Along with Facts about Genes, Gene Therapy, Genetic Screening, Ethics of Gene Testing, Genetic Counseling, a Glossary of Genetic Terminology, and a Resource List for Help, Support, and Further Information

Edited by Kathy Massimini. 650 pages. 2000. 0-7808-0241-1. $78.

Head Trauma Sourcebook

Basic Information for the Layperson about Open-Head and Closed-Head Injuries, Treatment Advances, Recovery, and Rehabilitation

Along with Reports on Current Research Initiatives

Edited by Karen Bellenir. 414 pages. 1997. 0-7808-0208-X. $78.

Health Insurance Sourcebook

Basic Information about Managed Care Organizations, Traditional Fee-for-Service Insurance, Insurance Portability and Pre-Existing Conditions Clauses, Medicare, Medicaid, Social Security, and Military Health Care

Along with Information about Insurance Fraud

Edited by Wendy Wilcox. 530 pages. 1997. 0-7808-0222-5. $78.

"Particularly useful because it brings much of this information together in one volume. This book will be a handy reference source in the health sciences library, hospital library, college and university library, and medium to large public library."
— *Medical Reference Services Quarterly, Fall '98*

Awarded "Books of the Year Award"
— *American Journal of Nursing, 1997*

"The layout of the book is particularly helpful as it provides easy access to reference material. A most useful addition to the vast amount of information about health insurance. The use of data from U.S. government agencies is most commendable. Useful in a library or learning center for healthcare professional students."
— *Doody's Health Sciences Book Reviews, Nov '97*

Health Resources Sourcebook

Basic Consumer Health Information about Sources of Medical Assistance, Featuring an Annotated Directory of Private and Public Consumer Health Organizations and Listings of Other Resources, Including Hospitals, Hospices, and State Medical Associations

Along with Guidelines for Locating and Evaluating Health Information

Edited by Dawn D. Matthews. 500 pages. 2000. 0-7808-0328-0. $78.

Healthy Aging Sourcebook

Basic Consumer Health Information about Maintaining Health through the Aging Process, Including Advice on Nutrition, Exercise, and Sleep, Help in Making Decisions about Midlife Issues and Retirement, and Guidance Concerning Practical and Informed Choices in Health Consumerism

Along with Data Concerning the Theories of Aging, Different Experiences in Aging by Minority Groups, and Facts about Aging Now and Aging in the Future; and Featuring a Glossary, a Guide to Consumer Help, Additional Suggested Reading, and Practical Resource Directory

Edited by Jenifer Swanson. 536 pages. 1999. 0-7808-0390-6. $78.

"Recommended reference source."
— *Booklist, American Library Association, Feb '00*

SEE ALSO *Physical & Mental Issues in Aging Sourcebook*

Healthy Heart Sourcebook for Women

Basic Consumer Health Information about Cardiac Issues Specific to Women, Including Facts about Major Risk Factors and Prevention, Treatment and Control Strategies, and Important Dietary Issues

Along with a Special Section Regarding the Pros and Cons of Hormone Replacement Therapy and Its Impact on Heart Health, and Additional Help, Including Recipes, a Glossary, and a Directory of Resources

Edited by Dawn D. Matthews. 336 pages. 2000. 0-7808-0329-9. $48.

SEE ALSO *Cardiovascular Diseases & Disorders Sourcebook, 1st Edition, Heart Diseases & Disorders Sourcebook, 2nd Edition, Women's Health Concerns Sourcebook*

Heart Diseases & Disorders Sourcebook, 2nd Edition

Basic Consumer Health Information about Heart Attacks, Angina, Rhythm Disorders, Heart Failure, Valve Disease, Congenital Heart Disorders, and More, Including Descriptions of Surgical Procedures and Other Interventions, Medications, Cardiac Rehabilitation, Risk Identification, and Prevention Tips

Along with Statistical Data, Reports on Current Research Initiatives, a Glossary of Cardiovascular Terms, and Resource Directory

Edited by Karen Bellenir. 612 pages. 2000. 0-7808-0238-1. $78.

SEE ALSO *Cardiovascular Diseases & Disorders Sourcebook, 1st Edition, Healthy Heart Sourcebook for Women*

Immune System Disorders Sourcebook

Basic Information about Lupus, Multiple Sclerosis, Guillain-Barré Syndrome, Chronic Granulomatous Disease, and More

Along with Statistical and Demographic Data and Reports on Current Research Initiatives

Edited by Allan R. Cook. 608 pages. 1997. 0-7808-0209-8. $78.

Infant & Toddler Health Sourcebook

Basic Consumer Health Information about the Physical and Mental Development of Newborns, Infants, and Toddlers, Including Neonatal Concerns, Nutrition Recommendations, Immunization Schedules, Common Pediatric Disorders, Assessments and Milestones, Safety Tips, and Advice for Parents and Other Caregivers

Along with a Glossary of Terms and Resource Listings for Additional Help

Edited by Jenifer Swanson. 585 pages. 2000. 0-7808-0246-2. $78.

Kidney & Urinary Tract Diseases & Disorders Sourcebook

Basic Information about Kidney Stones, Urinary Incontinence, Bladder Disease, End Stage Renal Disease, Dialysis, and More

Along with Statistical and Demographic Data and Reports on Current Research Initiatives

Edited by Linda M. Ross. 602 pages. 1997. 0-7808-0079-6. $78.

Learning Disabilities Sourcebook

Basic Information about Disorders Such as Dyslexia, Visual and Auditory Processing Deficits, Attention Deficit/Hyperactivity Disorder, and Autism

Along with Statistical and Demographic Data, Reports on Current Research Initiatives, an Explanation of the Assessment Process, and a Special Section for Adults with Learning Disabilities

Edited by Linda M. Shin. 579 pages. 1998. 0-7808-0210-1. $78.

Named "Oustanding Reference Book of 1999."
— *New York Public Library, Feb 2000*

"An excellent candidate for inclusion in a public library reference section. It's a great source of information. Teachers will also find the book useful. Definitely worth reading."
— *Journal of Adolescent & Adult Literacy, Feb 2000*

"Readable . . . provides a solid base of information regarding successful techniques used with individuals who have learning disabilities, as well as practical suggestions for educators and family members. Clear language, concise descriptions, and pertinent information for contacting multiple resources add to the strength of this book as a useful tool."
— *Choice, Association of College and Research Libraries, Feb '99*

"Recommended reference source."
— *Booklist, American Library Association, Sep '98*

"This is a useful resource for libraries and for those who don't have the time to identify and locate the individual publications."
— *Disability Resources Monthly, Sep '98*

Liver Disorders Sourcebook

Basic Consumer Health Information about the Liver and How It Works; Liver Diseases, Including Cancer, Cirrhosis, Hepatitis, and Toxic and Drug Related Diseases; Tips for Maintaining a Healthy Liver; Laboratory Tests, Radiology Tests, and Facts about Liver Transplantation

Along with a Section on Support Groups, a Glossary, and Resource Listings

Edited by Joyce Brennfleck Shannon. 591 pages. 2000. 0-7808-0383-3. $78.

"Recommended reference source."
— *Booklist, American Library Association, Jun '00*

Medical Tests Sourcebook

Basic Consumer Health Information about Medical Tests, Including Periodic Health Exams, General Screening Tests, Tests You Can Do at Home, Findings of the U.S. Preventive Services Task Force, X-ray and Radiology Tests, Electrical Tests, Tests of Blood and Other Body Fluids and Tissues, Scope Tests, Lung Tests, Genetic Tests, Pregnancy Tests, Newborn Screening Tests, Sexually Transmitted Disease Tests, and Computer Aided Diagnoses

Along with a Section on Paying for Medical Tests, a Glossary, and Resource Listings

Edited by Joyce Brennfleck Shannon. 691 pages. 1999. 0-7808-0243-8. $78.

"A valuable reference guide."
— *American Reference Books Annual, 2000*

"Recommended for hospital and health sciences libraries with consumer health collections."
— *E-Streams, Mar '00*

"This is an overall excellent reference with a wealth of general knowledge that may aid those who are reluctant to get vital tests performed."
— *Today's Librarian, Jan 2000*

Men's Health Concerns Sourcebook

Basic Information about Health Issues That Affect Men, Featuring Facts about the Top Causes of Death in Men, Including Heart Disease, Stroke, Cancers, Prostate Disorders, Chronic Obstructive Pulmonary Disease, Pneumonia and Influenza, Human Immunodeficiency Virus and Acquired Immune Deficiency Syndrome, Diabetes Mellitus, Stress, Suicide, Accidents and Homicides; and Facts about Common Concerns for Men, Including Impotence, Contraception, Circumcision, Sleep Disorders, Snoring, Hair Loss, Diet, Nutrition, Exercise, Kidney and Urological Disorders, and Backaches

Edited by Allan R. Cook. 738 pages. 1998. 0-7808-0212-8. $78.

"This comprehensive resource and the series are highly recommended."
— *American Reference Books Annual, 2000*

"Recommended reference source."
— *Booklist, American Library Association, Dec '98*

Mental Health Disorders Sourcebook, 1st Edition

Basic Information about Schizophrenia, Depression, Bipolar Disorder, Panic Disorder, Obsessive-Compulsive Disorder, Phobias and Other Anxiety Disorders, Paranoia and Other Personality Disorders, Eating Disorders, and Sleep Disorders

Along with Information about Treatment and Therapies

Edited by Karen Bellenir. 548 pages. 1995. 0-7808-0040-0. $78.

"This is an excellent new book . . . written in easy-to-understand language." — *Booklist Health Sciences Supplement, American Library Association, Oct '97*

". . . useful for public and academic libraries and consumer health collections."
— *Medical Reference Services Quarterly, Spring '97*

"The great strengths of the book are its readability and its inclusion of places to find more information. Especially recommended." — *Reference Quarterly, American Library Association, Winter '96*

". . . a good resource for a consumer health library."
— *Bulletin of the Medical Library Association, Oct '96*

"The information is data-based and couched in brief, concise language that avoids jargon. . . . a useful reference source." — *Readings, Sep '96*

"The text is well organized and adequately written for its target audience." — *Choice, Association of College and Research Libraries, Jun '96*

". . . provides information on a wide range of mental disorders, presented in nontechnical language."
— *Exceptional Child Education Resources, Spring '96*

"Recommended for public and academic libraries."
— *Reference Book Review, 1996*

Mental Health Disorders Sourcebook, 2nd Edition

Basic Consumer Health Information about Anxiety Disorders, Depression and Other Mood Disorders, Eating Disorders, Personality Disorders, Schizophrenia, and More, Including Disease Descriptions, Treatment Options, and Reports on Current Research Initiatives

Along with Statistical Data, Tips for Maintaining Mental Health, a Glossary, and Directory of Sources for Additional Help and Information

Edited by Karen Bellenir. 605 pages. 2000. 0-7808-0240-3. $78.

Mental Retardation Sourcebook

Basic Consumer Health Information about Mental Retardation and Its Causes, Including Down Syndrome, Fetal Alcohol Syndrome, Fragile X Syndrome, Genetic Conditions, Injury, and Environmental Sources

Along with Preventive Strategies, Parenting Issues, Educational Implications, Health Care Needs, Employment and Economic Matters, Legal Issues, a Glossary, and a Resource Listing for Additional Help and Information

Edited by Joyce Brennfleck Shannon. 642 pages. 2000. 0-7808-0377-9. $78.

"From preventing retardation to parenting and family challenges, this covers health, social and legal issues and will prove an invaluable overview."
— *Reviewer's Bookwatch, Jul '00*

■

Obesity Sourcebook

Basic Consumer Health Information about Diseases and Other Problems Associated with Obesity, and Including Facts about Risk Factors, Prevention Issues, and Management Approaches

Along with Statistical and Demographic Data, Information about Special Populations, Research Updates, a Glossary, and Source Listings for Further Help and Information

Edited by Wilma Caldwell. 400 pages. 2000. 0-7808-0333-7. $48.

■

Ophthalmic Disorders Sourcebook

Basic Information about Glaucoma, Cataracts, Macular Degeneration, Strabismus, Refractive Disorders, and More

Along with Statistical and Demographic Data and Reports on Current Research Initiatives

Edited by Linda M. Ross. 631 pages. 1996. 0-7808-0081-8. $78.

■

Oral Health Sourcebook

Basic Information about Diseases and Conditions Affecting Oral Health, Including Cavities, Gum Disease, Dry Mouth, Oral Cancers, Fever Blisters, Canker Sores, Oral Thrush, Bad Breath, Temporomandibular Disorders, and other Craniofacial Syndromes

Along with Statistical Data on the Oral Health of Americans, Oral Hygiene, Emergency First Aid, Information on Treatment Procedures and Methods of Replacing Lost Teeth

Edited by Allan R. Cook. 558 pages. 1997. 0-7808-0082-6. $78.

"Unique source which will fill a gap in dental sources for patients and the lay public. A valuable reference tool even in a library with thousands of books on dentistry. Comprehensive, clear, inexpensive, and easy to read and use. It fills an enormous gap in the health care literature." — *Reference and User Services Quarterly, American Library Association, Summer '98*

"Recommended reference source."
— *Booklist, American Library Association, Dec '97*

Osteoporosis Sourcebook

Basic Consumer Health Information about Primary and Secondary Osteoporosis, Juvenile Osteoporosis, Related Conditions, and Other Such Bone Disorders as Fibrous Dysplasia, Myeloma, Osteogenesis Imperfecta, Osteopetrosis, and Paget's Disease

Along with Information about Risk Factors, Treatments, Traditional and Non-Traditional Pain Management, and Including a Glossary and Resource Directory

Edited by Allan R. Cook. 600 pages. 2000. 0-7808-0239-X. $78.

SEE ALSO *Women's Health Concerns Sourcebook*

■

Pain Sourcebook

Basic Information about Specific Forms of Acute and Chronic Pain, Including Headaches, Back Pain, Muscular Pain, Neuralgia, Surgical Pain, and Cancer Pain

Along with Pain Relief Options Such as Analgesics, Narcotics, Nerve Blocks, Transcutaneous Nerve Stimulation, and Alternative Forms of Pain Control, Including Biofeedback, Imaging, Behavior Modification, and Relaxation Techniques

Edited by Allan R. Cook. 667 pages. 1997. 0-7808-0213-6. $78.

"The text is readable, easily understood, and well indexed. This excellent volume belongs in all patient education libraries, consumer health sections of public libraries, and many personal collections."
— *American Reference Books Annual, 1999*

"A beneficial reference." — *Booklist Health Sciences Supplement, American Library Association, Oct '98*

"The information is basic in terms of scholarship and is appropriate for general readers. Written in journalistic style . . . intended for non-professionals. Quite thorough in its coverage of different pain conditions and summarizes the latest clinical information regarding pain treatment."
— *Choice, Association of College and Research Libraries, Jun '98*

"Recommended reference source."
— *Booklist, American Library Association, Mar '98*

■

Pediatric Cancer Sourcebook

Basic Consumer Health Information about Leukemias, Brain Tumors, Sarcomas, Lymphomas, and Other Cancers in Infants, Children, and Adolescents, Including Descriptions of Cancers, Treatments, and Coping Strategies

Along with Suggestions for Parents, Caregivers, and Concerned Relatives, a Glossary of Cancer Terms, and Resource Listings

Edited by Edward J. Prucha. 587 pages. 1999. 0-7808-0245-4. $78.

"A valuable addition to all libraries specializing in health services and many public libraries."
— *American Reference Books Annual, 2000*

Physical & Mental Issues in Aging Sourcebook

Basic Consumer Health Information on Physical and Mental Disorders Associated with the Aging Process, Including Concerns about Cardiovascular Disease, Pulmonary Disease, Oral Health, Digestive Disorders, Musculoskeletal and Skin Disorders, Metabolic Changes, Sexual and Reproductive Issues, and Changes in Vision, Hearing, and Other Senses

Along with Data about Longevity and Causes of Death, Information on Acute and Chronic Pain, Descriptions of Mental Concerns, a Glossary of Terms, and Resource Listings for Additional Help

Edited by Jenifer Swanson. 660 pages. 1999. 0-7808-0233-0. $78.

SEE ALSO Healthy Aging Sourcebook

Plastic Surgery Sourcebook

Basic Consumer Health Information on Cosmetic and Reconstructive Plastic Surgery, Including Statistical Information about Different Surgical Procedures, Things to Consider Prior to Surgery, Plastic Surgery Techniques and Tools, Emotional and Psychological Considerations, and Procedure-Specific Information

Along with a Glossary of Terms and a Listing of Resources for Additional Help and Information

Edited by M. Lisa Weatherford. 400 pages. 2000. 0-7808-0214-4. $48.

Podiatry Sourcebook

Basic Consumer Health Information about Foot Conditions, Diseases, and Injuries, Including Bunions, Corns, Calluses, Athlete's Foot, Plantar Warts, Hammertoes and Clawtoes, Club Foot, Heel Pain, Gout, and More

Along with Facts about Foot Care, Disease Prevention, Foot Safety, Choosing a Foot Care Specialist, a Glossary of Terms, and Resource Listings for Additional Information

Edited by M. Lisa Weatherford. 600 pages. 2000. 0-7808-0215-2. $78.

Pregnancy & Birth Sourcebook

Basic Information about Planning for Pregnancy, Maternal Health, Fetal Growth and Development, Labor and Delivery, Postpartum and Perinatal Care, Pregnancy in Mothers with Special Concerns, and Disorders of Pregnancy, Including Genetic Counseling, Nutrition and Exercise, Obstetrical Tests, Pregnancy Discomfort, Multiple Births, Cesarean Sections, Medical Testing of Newborns, Breastfeeding, Gestational Diabetes, and Ectopic Pregnancy

Edited by Heather E. Aldred. 737 pages. 1997. 0-7808-0216-0. $78.

SEE ALSO Congenital Disorders Sourcebook, Family Planning Sourcebook

Public Health Sourcebook

Basic Information about Government Health Agencies, Including National Health Statistics and Trends, Healthy People 2000 Program Goals and Objectives, the Centers for Disease Control and Prevention, the Food and Drug Administration, and the National Institutes of Health

Along with Full Contact Information for Each Agency

Edited by Wendy Wilcox. 698 pages. 1998. 0-7808-0220-9. $78.

Rehabilitation Sourcebook

Basic Consumer Health Information about Rehabilitation for People Recovering from Heart Surgery, Spinal Cord Injury, Stroke, Orthopedic Impairments, Amputation, Pulmonary Impairments, Traumatic Injury, and More, Including Physical Therapy, Occupational Therapy, Speech/Language Therapy, Massage Therapy, Dance Therapy, Art Therapy, and Recreational Therapy

Along with Information on Assistive and Adaptive Devices, a Glossary, and Resources for Additional Help and Information

Edited by Dawn D. Matthews. 531 pages. 1999. 0-7808-0236-5. $78.

Respiratory Diseases & Disorders Sourcebook

Basic Information about Respiratory Diseases and Disorders, Including Asthma, Cystic Fibrosis, Pneumonia, the Common Cold, Influenza, and Others, Featuring Facts about the Respiratory System, Statistical and Demographic Data, Treatments, Self-Help Management Suggestions, and Current Research Initiatives

Edited by Allan R. Cook and Peter D. Dresser. 771 pages. 1995. 0-7808-0037-0. $78.

"Designed for the layperson and for patients and their families coping with respiratory illness. . . . an extensive array of information on diagnosis, treatment, management, and prevention of respiratory illnesses for the general reader." — *Choice, Association of College and Research Libraries, Jun '96*

"A highly recommended text for all collections. It is a comforting reminder of the power of knowledge that good books carry between their covers." — *Academic Library Book Review, Spring '96*

"A comprehensive collection of authoritative information presented in a nontechnical, humanitarian style for patients, families, and caregivers." — *Association of Operating Room Nurses, Sep/Oct '95*

■

Sexually Transmitted Diseases Sourcebook

Basic Information about Herpes, Chlamydia, Gonorrhea, Hepatitis, Nongonoccocal Urethritis, Pelvic Inflammatory Disease, Syphilis, AIDS, and More

Along with Current Data on Treatments and Preventions

Edited by Linda M. Ross. 550 pages. 1997. 0-7808-0217-9. $78.

■

Skin Disorders Sourcebook

Basic Information about Common Skin and Scalp Conditions Caused by Aging, Allergies, Immune Reactions, Sun Exposure, Infectious Organisms, Parasites, Cosmetics, and Skin Traumas, Including Abrasions, Cuts, and Pressure Sores

Along with Information on Prevention and Treatment

Edited by Allan R. Cook. 647 pages. 1997. 0-7808-0080-X. $78.

". . . comprehensive, easily read reference book." — *Doody's Health Sciences Book Reviews, Oct '97*

SEE ALSO *Burns Sourcebook*

Sleep Disorders Sourcebook

Basic Consumer Health Information about Sleep and Its Disorders, Including Insomnia, Sleepwalking, Sleep Apnea, Restless Leg Syndrome, and Narcolepsy

Along with Data about Shiftwork and Its Effects, Information on the Societal Costs of Sleep Deprivation, Descriptions of Treatment Options, a Glossary of Terms, and Resource Listings for Additional Help

Edited by Jenifer Swanson. 439 pages. 1998. 0-7808-0234-9. $78.

"This text will complement any home or medical library. It is user-friendly and ideal for the adult reader." — *American Reference Books Annual, 2000*

"Recommended reference source." — *Booklist, American Library Association, Feb '99*

"A useful resource that provides accurate, relevant, and accessible information on sleep to the general public. Health care providers who deal with sleep disorders patients may also find it helpful in being prepared to answer some of the questions patients ask." — *Respiratory Care, Jul '99*

■

Sports Injuries Sourcebook

Basic Consumer Health Information about Common Sports Injuries, Prevention of Injury in Specific Sports, Tips for Training, and Rehabilitation from Injury

Along with Information about Special Concerns for Children, Young Girls in Athletic Training Programs, Senior Athletes, and Women Athletes, and a Directory of Resources for Further Help and Information

Edited by Heather E. Aldred. 624 pages. 1999. 0-7808-0218-7. $78.

"Public libraries and undergraduate academic libraries will find this book useful for its nontechnical language." — *American Reference Books Annual, 2000*

"While this easy-to-read book is recommended for all libraries, it should prove to be especially useful for public, high school, and academic libraries; certainly it should be on the bookshelf of every school gymnasium." — *E-Streams, Mar '00*

■

Substance Abuse Sourcebook

Basic Health-Related Information about the Abuse of Legal and Illegal Substances Such as Alcohol, Tobacco, Prescription Drugs, Marijuana, Cocaine, and Heroin; and Including Facts about Substance Abuse Prevention Strategies, Intervention Methods, Treatment and Recovery Programs, and a Section Addressing the Special Problems Related to Substance Abuse during Pregnancy

Edited by Karen Bellenir. 573 pages. 1996. 0-7808-0038-9. $78.

"A valuable addition to any health reference section. Highly recommended." — *The Book Report, Mar/Apr '97*

"... a comprehensive collection of substance abuse information that's both highly readable and compact. Families and caregivers of substance abusers will find the information enlightening and helpful, while teachers, social workers and journalists should benefit from the concise format. Recommended."
— *Drug Abuse Update, Winter '96/'97*

SEE ALSO Alcoholism Sourcebook, Drug Abuse Sourcebook

Traveler's Health Sourcebook

Basic Consumer Health Information for Travelers, Including Physical and Medical Preparations, Transportation Health and Safety, Essential Information about Food and Water, Sun Exposure, Insect and Snake Bites, Camping and Wilderness Medicine, and Travel with Physical or Medical Disabilities

Along with International Travel Tips, Vaccination Recommendations, Geographical Health Issues, Disease Risks, a Glossary, and a Listing of Additional Resources

Edited by Joyce Brennfleck Shannon. 613 pages. 2000. 0-7808-0384-1. $78.

Women's Health Concerns Sourcebook

Basic Information about Health Issues That Affect Women, Featuring Facts about Menstruation and Other Gynecological Concerns, Including Endometriosis, Fibroids, Menopause, and Vaginitis; Reproductive Concerns, Including Birth Control, Infertility, and Abortion; and Facts about Additional Physical, Emotional, and Mental Health Concerns Prevalent among Women Such as Osteoporosis, Urinary Tract Disorders, Eating Disorders, and Depression

Along with Tips for Maintaining a Healthy Lifestyle

Edited by Heather E. Aldred. 567 pages. 1997. 0-7808-0219-5. $78.

"Handy compilation. There is an impressive range of diseases, devices, disorders, procedures, and other physical and emotional issues covered . . . well organized, illustrated, and indexed."
— *Choice, Association of College and Research Libraries, Jan '98*

SEE ALSO Breast Cancer Sourcebook, Cancer Sourcebook for Women, 1st and 2nd Editions, Healthy Heart Sourcebook for Women, Osteoporosis Sourcebook

Workplace Health & Safety Sourcebook

Basic Information about Musculoskeletal Injuries, Cumulative Trauma Disorders, Occupational Carcinogens and Other Toxic Materials, Child Labor, Workplace Violence, Histoplasmosis, Transmission of HIV and Hepatitis-B Viruses, and Occupational Hazards Associated with Various Industries, Including Mining, Confined Spaces, Agriculture, Construction, Electrical

Work, and the Medical Professions, with Information on Mortality and Other Statistical Data, Preventative Measures, Reproductive Risks, Reducing Stress for Shiftworkers, Noise Hazards, Industrial Back Belts, Reducing Contamination at Home, Preventing Allergic Reactions to Rubber Latex, and More

Along with Public and Private Programs and Initiatives, a Glossary, and Sources for Additional Help and Information

Edited by Chad Kimball. 600 pages. 2000. 0-7808-0231-4. $78.

Worldwide Health Sourcebook

Basic Information about Global Health Issues, Including Nutrition, Reproductive Health, Disease Dispersion and Prevention, Emerging Diseases, Health Risks, and the Leading Causes of Death

Along with Global Health Concerns for Children, Women, and the Elderly, Mental Health Issues, Research and Technology Advancements, and Economic, Environmental, and Political Health Implications, a Glossary, and a Resource Listing for Additional Help and Information

Edited by Joyce Brennfleck Shannon. 500 pages. 2000. 0-7808-0330-2. $78.

Health Reference Series Cumulative Index 1999

A Comprehensive Index to the Individual Volumes of the Health Reference Series, Including a Subject Index, Name Index, Organization Index, and Publication Index;

Along with a Master List of Acronyms and Abbreviations

Edited by Edward J. Prucha, Anne Holmes, and Robert Rudnick. 990 pages. 2000. 0-7808-0382-5. $78.